Better Homes & Gardens

SEWING BOOK

PRINTED IN THE UNITED STATES OF AMERICA.

10

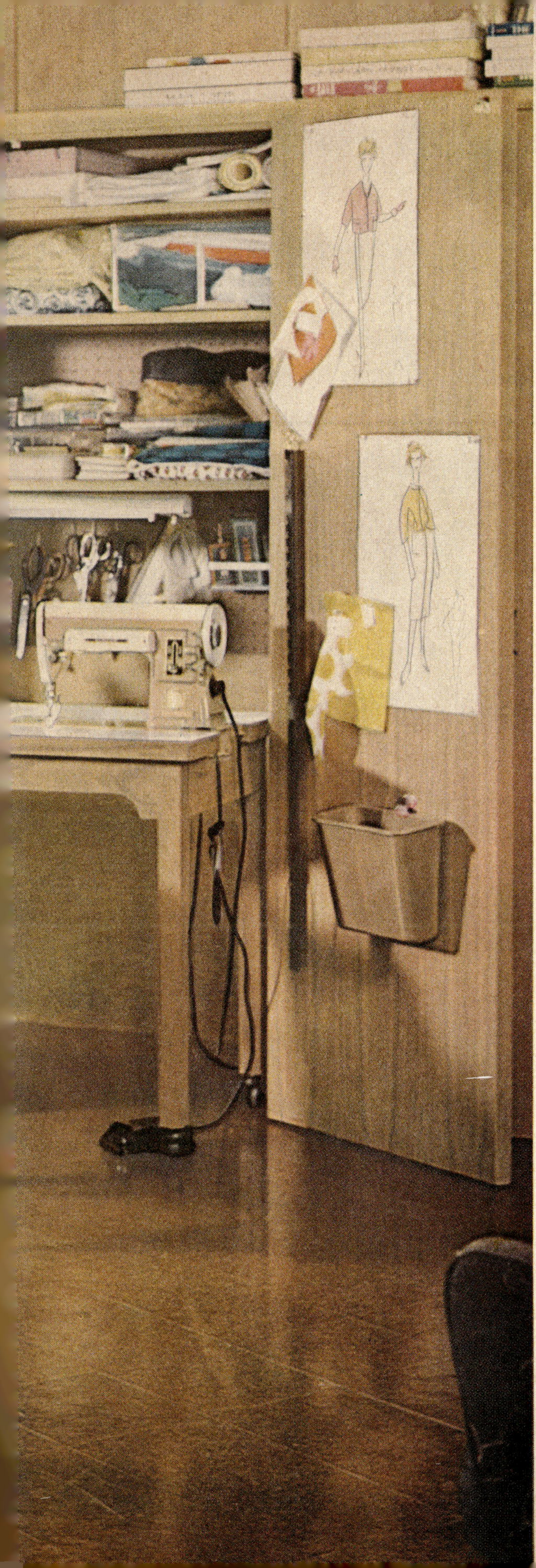

Better Homes & Gardens

SEWING BOOK

Quick, easy professional ways
to simplify home sewing

← *Create fashions with a custom-made look in your own home sewing center*

Contents

Glamorous new fashions for yourself—attractive, long-wearing clothes for the children—beautiful new slip covers and draperies for your home—are all yours for the making!

Sewing can be relaxing and fun, and it's easy to learn. The old-fashioned, laborious methods of sewing have been replaced by new techniques and equipment. Now, the well-dressed woman can have more clothes by making them herself. The fabrics will be better, and the workmanship more expert.

In preparing this new book, we had the good fortune to work with Miss Lucille Rivers, a commercial dressmaker in New York.

To help women learn the easy, professional methods of sewing she describes in the book, Miss Rivers has drawn upon her long experience in working with pattern-makers, fabric manufacturers, and department stores. These sewing ideas are based on common sense—practical ideas and professional tricks that show the easy way to give clothes and home furnishings a custom-made look.

Miss Rivers is known as the nation's "sewing lady" of radio, television, and the lecture circuit. Recently, she expanded her American lecture tours to include Australia and New Zealand.

In this book our primary objective is to encourage women to sew, and experience the rewards of this creative hobby.

The Editors

Better Homes & Gardens

Chapter 1

Basic sewing equipment

When starting a new hobby most people are inclined to invest in expensive equipment which may end up gathering dust in a closet. Sewing is one hobby where this is not necessary.

Most of the equipment you'll need you probably have in your home already. Of course, there are innumerable gadgets available which are supposed to make sewing easier and more fun. Some are real timesavers. Others will appeal only to the gadgeteer. As you start to sew, you can decide which of this equipment you want to buy. In any event, visit the notions department of your store and have the fun of looking around. You'll find new and amazing gadgets that will prove helpful in many ways.

For the novice, the list of equipment which follows is more than adequate. Additional equipment for more advanced sewing, such as tailoring and designing, is also included.

Equipment

Scissors

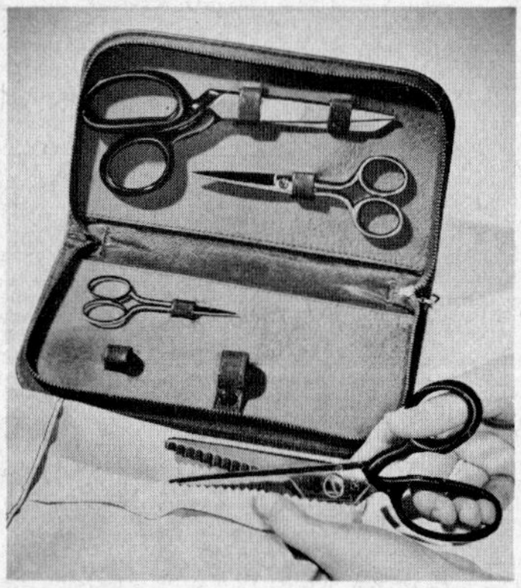

Shears

Cutting shears eight to ten inches long with a bent handle are best. The bent handle makes it possible to cut faster and easier while the fabric remains flat on the table. Keep your shears sharp. *Never* use them for anything but cutting fabrics.

Scissors

Scissors about six inches long with good sharp points are preferable. Always have them convenient to your machine, since you will use them for clipping, slashing, trimming, and other cutting operations.

Embroidery scissors

These scissors are not necessary equipment, but they are extremely useful for ripping, cutting threads, clipping, and for fine or delicate detail.

Pinking shears

Get a size of pinking shears that is comfortable for you to use. Try them out for weight. Use them only for pinking seams, or decorative edges on felt. Shears are also made that cut scallops. They are too heavy to use for cutting out an entire garment, and this much cutting would quickly dull them. Also, pinking shears will not give you an accurate edge at armholes, necklines, or any shaped pattern piece.

Pins

Insist on good steel pins, and buy them by the box. They are less expensive when purchased this way and are easier to use. Most of us can take pins from a box more easily than from a pin cushion. Since you will learn to sew with no basting, the convenience of your pins is important. Keep a box at the machine, the table, and the ironing board.

Six- or eight-inch ruler

There is one sold by a notions company that is particularly good. It is made of metal and has a slide for marking hems. The width of the ruler is convenient for marking buttonholes. (Later you will use your ruler as you learn the easy way to make corded bound buttonholes used by professionals.) Keep the ruler at your sewing machine so that you can measure and check as you sew.

Ironing board

Undoubtedly, you have an ironing board at home, but if you use it for ironing the family laundry, the board will be too hard for pressing. Get an extra-thick pad and cover to use over the board. When you sew, your iron and ironing board are most important. The professional dressmaker actually does a good deal of "sewing" at the ironing board. Be sure it is set up when you start to sew. As you learn these short, easy methods, you will realize how important "press as you sew" can be.

Sleeve board

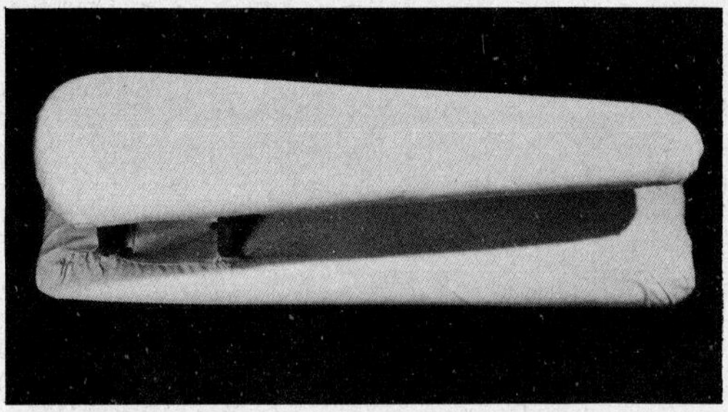

You'll find that you are going to use this sleeve board for many more things than pressing a sleeve. The stationary rather than folding board is more satisfactory, but if storage space is a problem, the collapsible board can be used successfully. Make your board do double duty by padding and covering the base as well as the top. You can use the covered base for pressing short seams as you assemble your garment, and for doing many of the short-cut professional tricks worked at the ironing board that make sewing easier.

Steam iron

The instant steam or dry iron is preferable. It is impossible to do really professional sewing without one. You probably have one for pressing and caring for your clothes, but if not, do get one. It is a tremendous timesaver for professional work.

Tailor's chalk

Be sure you get chalk, not wax. It comes in many colors, but white will usually be enough. Chalk has replaced marking with the old-fashioned, time-consuming tailor's tacks. It is faster and more accurate.

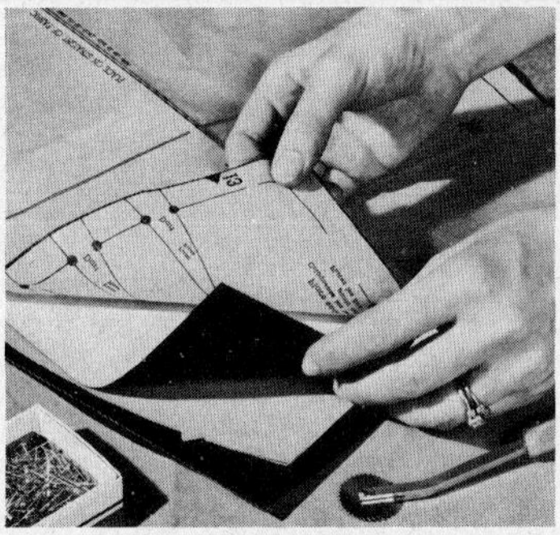

Tracing wheel and carbon paper

The *tracing wheel* is not a necessity; all marking can be done with tailor's chalk. However, there are many instances when the tracing wheel is faster. Some people prefer to do all marking this way. You can wait and decide when you read Chapter 5 on marking and assembling your garment. *Dressmaker's carbon paper* is not the blue carbon used in typing. It is a special carbon to be used with the tracing wheel. It comes in several colors, but white and yellow are probably all you will need.

Tape measure

Get a good strong tape measure, either plastic or plastic-coated, so that it won't stretch. Be sure it is numbered from either end. You'll probably end up wearing it around your neck, tailor-fashion, so that it is instantly convenient as you sew. You'll use it in countless sewing operations.

Yardstick

You'll use it for checking lines and hems. If you decide to try your hand at altering a pattern, this is necessary equipment.

Press cloth

A press cloth is not a necessity if you use a steam iron. You can make your own press cloth of muslin, or buy a chemically treated one. Tailors buy a heavy muslin, rub beeswax in it and keep pressing the cloth until it is permanently set. When they use this cloth, they put it over the garment and wet it with a sponge. Pressing over the wet cloth creates heavy steam. (Just good for coats and suits.) The chemically treated cloths give directions for use.

The steam iron, however, can be used directly on most fabrics, with no shine. Test a small piece of fabric first. If it shines on the right side, try it on the reverse side. If it still shines, you'll need the press cloth with the steam iron to press it correctly.

As you become more proficient, there is additional equipment you will want. Some you can make yourself. Other items may be more costly and can be purchased only if needed.

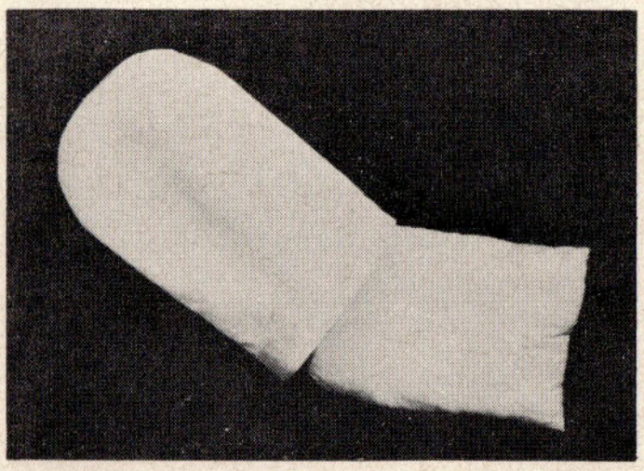

Tailor's mitt

This is called many things—dressmaker's cushion, pressing cushion. Buy one if you like, but the one you make will be more satisfactory.

Here's how to make it:

A. Cut two rectangles from a heavyweight muslin—6½ by 9 inches. Round the corners at one end.

B. Sew all around, leaving the straight end open for stuffing.

C. Turn right side out. Stuff with wool scraps, cotton wadding, or sawdust. Sew up open end.

D. Cut two more rectangles of the same muslin, 7½ by 11 inches. Round the corners at one end.

E. Sew together, leaving one end open (like a pillowcase). Hem the open end of the case.

F. Slip the cushion into the case and your mitt is ready to use. The case can easily be removed for washing. The mitt is used for pressing shaped parts of your garment.

Follow these easy steps

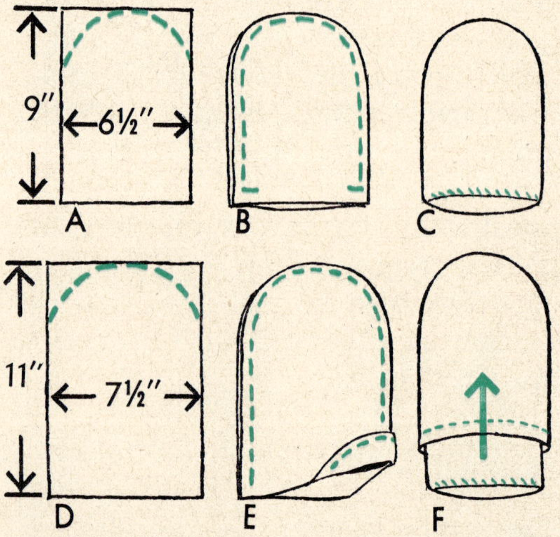

Skirt marker

Many types are available. Look them over in the notions department. You can mark your own hems accurately with the chalk squirting type. This is something to be considered if you live alone. The pin marker is equally accurate, but you will need someone (maybe a willing husband) to do the pinning for you.

Tailor's ham

When you reach the suit-making stage, you will need this pressing and tailoring aid, known picturesquely as a "tailor's ham." You'll find it useful in many ways, especially for tailoring. The hams are not available in stores so you must make your own. You'll need ¾ yard of very heavy muslin or drill.

Make a pattern of heavy paper from which to cut the "ham."

A. Draw a line 18 inches long (1-4), divide and mark the line in thirds.

Draw a line 13 inches long across the first line, on one of these marks (2).

Draw a line 11 inches long across on the remaining mark (3).

The shape of the cushion is formed by drawing from points 1-2-3-4 and back to 1.

B. Fold on the long line and cut around the shaping line to form a ham-shaped piece.

Mark the pattern on the drill. Allow seam allowances, and cut out except at the wide end where the fabric is left on.

Sew around the shape, but leave the end open where the fabric is left on. Baste the shape of the wide end on the drill. Baste-stitch a wide hem in the open ends of the fabric and turn the shape right side out.

The ham can be stuffed with wool scraps or sawdust. Wool scraps are preferable. Be sure they are colorfast. Cut up old wool blankets, wool clothes, or wool scraps. You'll need lots. Dump the wool scrap in a tub of water and let it soak.

C. Slide curtain rods through the ends of the "ham" and hang it up over the sink or a pan. Stuff it with wet wool scrap. When you think you have filled it, you are only beginning! Pack it down tight and keep putting in more scrap. Shape it as you go. When you have it full, mold it to a finished line at the open end and baste the two layers together along this line to hold the shaping. Hang it up to dry in a warm, dry place. Let it hang until it is completely dry—sometimes it takes several days.

D. When it is dry, trim off the excess fabric.

E. Leave seam allowances and turn them under.

F. Sew up the open end with fine stitches so the seam is smooth.

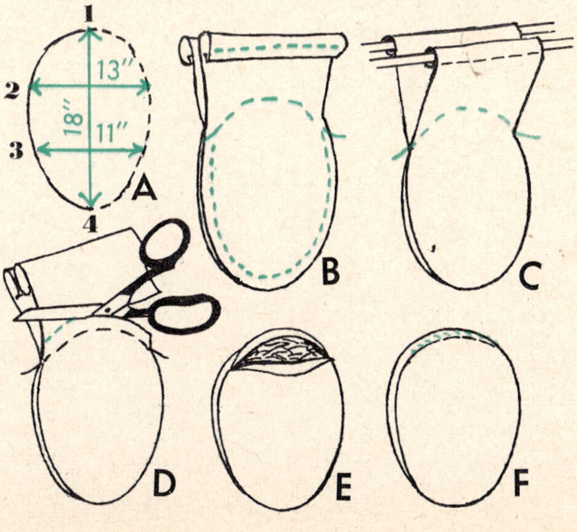

Velvet or needle board

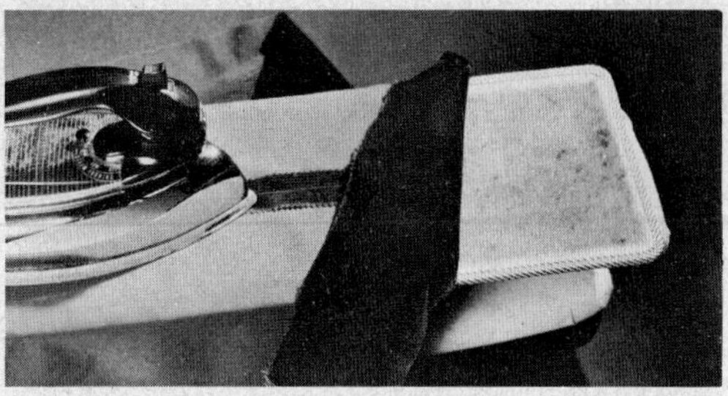

This is not often part of home equipment because it is rather expensive. It is made of a heavy canvas-type board with fine wires all along one side. When pressing nap fabrics such as velvet or corduroy, the fabric is put face down on the wire. The nap fits between the wires and can be pressed with no fear of crushing or marking. It can also be used for soft woolens, such as doeskin or duvetyn. It is particularly practical if you do much sewing on these fabrics. These boards come in different sizes; one practical for home use costs about $12.00. Ask your notions department buyer about securing one, or go to a tailor supply shop.

Dress form

Unless it is an actual duplication of your own figure, the dress form is not a great help in fitting. However, collars, shoulder lines and other details can be checked on a standard form.

There are dress forms which can be made to conform to your body. These are rather lightweight and not too practical if also used for designing.

The adjustable form can be used very satisfactorily in conjunction with the fitting of the muslin you will learn to make in Chapter 3. A standard form, a size smaller than yourself, can also be used with the muslin. These forms are sturdy, and will hold up if you decide to style or design your own clothes, in which case, a dress form will be a necessity.

In Chapter 3 you will learn to fit a basic muslin to your own figure. Adjustments can be permanently sewed into the muslin, and the muslin used later over the dress form so that it is an actual duplication of your figure. This is the only kind of form to fit over. The reason for using an adjustable form, or the standard form a size smaller, is that the muslin is put on this smaller figure and then padded to duplicate your own body size as closely as possible for fitting.

Sewing machine

No matter how beautifully you sew, you don't want to make a whole dress by hand. It is unnecessarily time-consuming. If you don't have a sewing machine, you can rent one by the month for very little cost. If you are considering buying a machine, it might be a good idea to rent a different brand each month until you find the one you like best. Also, it will give you time to decide how serious you are about sewing. If you plan to do a lot of sewing, you may decide to buy one of the wonderful new machines that does practically everything. This is a lifetime investment, so be sure it's what you want.

You'll get instructions for the use and care of the machine when you purchase it. If you have an old machine you've been using, have your machine company service it for you and show you how to care for it properly to keep it in good condition.

Chapter 2

A look at the commercial pattern

A commercial pattern is a vital part of sewing equipment. Unless a woman knows how to make her own pattern, it is the only guide she has for style and size of a garment.

Pattern manufacturers provide a wealth of sewing information for you. It is worth-while to read thoroughly your pattern envelope and the sewing instruction guide enclosed. The more you learn about your pattern, the greater help it will be to you.

In this book, you will learn how to eliminate *complicated fittings*. This sewing and fitting technique is based on correct use of the commercial pattern. Generally, a pattern is chosen according to the bust measurement. The bodice is the most difficult to alter, so buy the size that gives you the best fit in the bust. Later, exceptions to this rule will be explained.

The waist and hipline are easiest to take in or let out, so don't be concerned if these pattern measurements are not the same as yours.

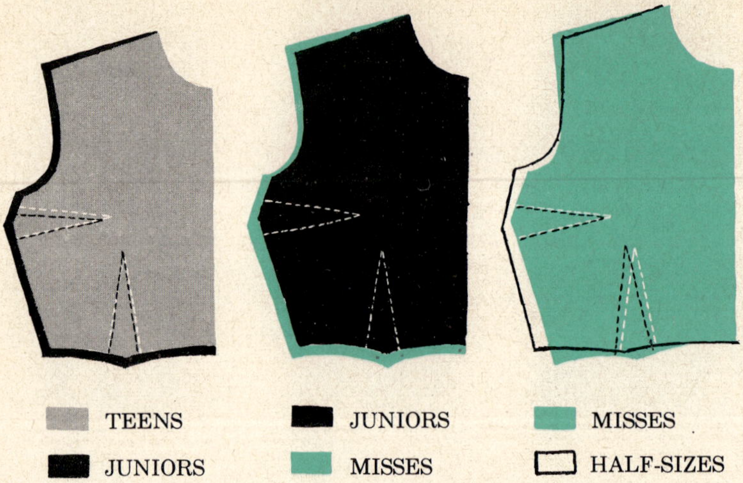

Commercial patterns are available in a range of figure types as well as sizes.

Facts about patterns

All pattern companies use the same standard body measurements. These have been established by the National Bureau of Standards. A size 14 from one company has the same proportions and body ease as all others in size 14.

If you wear a size 14 pattern in a dress, you take the same size in a suit, coat, or blouse. The pattern allows all the ease necessary for proper fit and for the lining. It also allows enough ease so the suit jacket may be worn over a blouse, and so a coat may be worn over another garment.

Never buy a pattern by your ready-to-wear size. Each manufacturer sets his own sizing. Expensive clothes are usually cut large, which is why some women can wear a size 10 in one ready-made dress, and a 12 or 14 in others. There is no uniformity of size in ready-to-wear clothing. Patterns are made to fit various figure types. You can buy patterns for misses', women's, half-size, junior, teen-age, sub-teen, and girls' figure types. You'll see the importance of buying your pattern in the correct figure type when you read Chapter 3 on the alteration pattern.

Compare your measurements with the measurement charts on the next page to learn which figure type and size pattern will most nearly fit you.

You will find references throughout this book to the commercial pattern and its use. Study this chapter carefully and become familiar with the sewing information included with every commercial pattern.

Check your measurements

Junior

SIZE	9	11	13	15	17
Bust	30½	31½	33	35	37
Waist	23½	24½	25½	27	28½
Hip	32½	33½	35	37	39
Back	15	15¼	15½	15¾	16

Girls'

SIZE	7	8	10	12	14
Chest	25	26	28	30	32
Waist	22½	23	24	25	26
Hip	27	28	30	32½	35
Back waist length	11	11½	12¼	13	13¾

Misses'

SIZE	10	12	14	16	18	20
Bust	31	32	34	36	38	40
Waist	24	25	26	28	30	32
Hip	33	34	36	38	40	42
Back	15¾	16	16¼	16½	16¾	17

Sub-teen

SIZE	8s	10s	12s	14s
Bust	28	29	31	33
Waist	23	24	25	26
Hip	31	32	34	36
Back waist length	13½	13¾	14	14¼

Half-sizes

SIZE	12½	14½	16½	18½	20½	22½	24½
Bust	33	35	37	39	41	43	45
Waist	27	29	31	33	35	37½	40
Hip	37	39	41	43	45	47	49
Back	15¼	15½	15¾	16	16¼	16½	16¾

Teen

SIZE	8	10	12	14	16
Bust	29	30	32	34	36
Waist	23	24	25	26	28
Hip	31	32	34	36	38
Back waist length	14½	14¾	15	15¼	15½

Women's

SIZE	40	42	44	46	48	50
Bust	42	44	46	48	50	52
Waist	34	36	38½	41	43½	46
Hip	44	46	48	50	52	54
Back	17⅛	17¼	17⅜	17½	17⅝	17¾

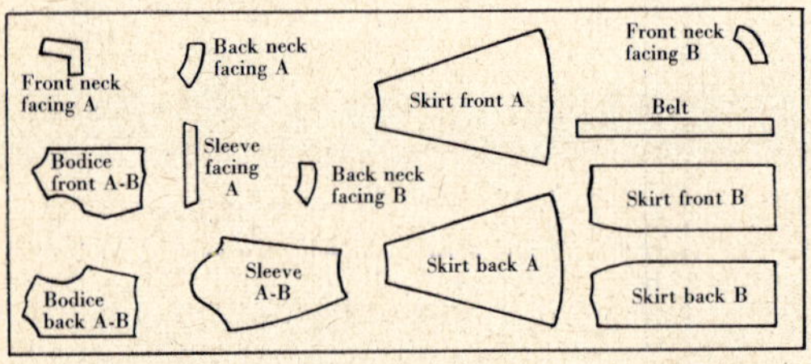

FABRIC REQUIRED	Sizes	10	12	14	16	18
VIEW A						
35″ Without Nap	Yds.	4⅞	4⅞	4⅞	5	5⅛
39″ Without Nap	Yds.	4½	4½	4½	4⅞	4⅞
45″ Without Nap	Yds.	3⅞	4	4	4¼	4¼
Skirt Lining (Optional) 39″ Fabric	Yds.	1¾	1¾	1¾	1¾	1¾
VIEW B						
35″ Without Nap	Yds.	3¼	3⅜	3⅜	3⅞	3⅞
45″ Without Nap	Yds.	2½	2⅝	2⅞	3	3
52″ Without Nap	Yds.	2⅛	2¼	2¼	2⅜	2⅜

BODY MEASUREMENTS		10	12	14	16	18
Bust	Ins.	31	32	34	36	38
Waist	Ins.	24	25	26	28	30
Hip	Ins.	33	34	36	38	40
Back waist length	Ins.	15¾	16	16¼	16½	16¾
Finished A or B length from back of regular neckline (2-inch hem)	Ins.	44½	45	45½	45¾	46

SUGGESTED FABRICS: Linen, printed silk or cotton, synthetic mixtures, tweed, lightweight wool, jersey, crepe.
NOTE: Not suitable for diagonal prints or diagonal weaves.

NOTIONS: Thread, 12″ or 14″ dress placket zipper, wide belt; View A—ribbon seam binding; View B—Opt. ribbon binding.

Pattern envelopes

Study your pattern envelope carefully. It contains the following valuable information:

1 Several views or styles that can be made from the pattern are shown. Examine each view and decide which style you want to make. Fabric requirements are based on these views.

2 A diagram of the number and shape of pattern pieces is shown on the back of the envelope.

3 The back gives a fabric requirement chart, showing the amount needed for each view. Fabrics come in 35-36, 39, 42-44 and 50-52 inch widths. The pattern companies choose the fabric widths they consider most suitable to the style of the dress. Standard widths are: Cottons and linens, 35-36; silks, 39 (and sometimes 45); blended fabrics, 42-45; wools and some blends, 50-52.

4 A body measurement chart shows comparative sizes at a glance.

5 Suggested fabrics for the style are listed, as well as those not suitable.

6 Notions needed are listed.

7 If the style is shown in check, stripe, or plaid, it has been especially designed for them, and will be easier to cut and make in one of them.

8 There is also a guide for cutting and assembling your dress.

Chapter 3

The alteration pattern

Years ago, women were taught to take their measurements, compare them to the pattern, then adjust the pattern to these measurements before they cut their garments. In this way they were able to eliminate unnecessary fitting before the garment was even cut. It worked in theory, or when an expert took their measurements. But when a woman did her own measuring, there was too much margin for error; another method had to be devised to eliminate unnecessary fitting.

A look at the professional fields of ready-to-wear and pattern design seemed to provide the answer.

Ready-to-wear designers help in making the first pattern for a dress. It is made to fit the proportions of a tall, willowy, professional model who wears the dress in the showroom. Once the dress is accepted into the line, it is sent to the factory where it is re-cut to the manufacturer's standard size or body line.

Each manufacturer has his own master pattern or "sloper" based on his body line or standard size.

This is the reason why women who buy ready-made clothes usually look for a particular brand name or designer. They maintain that a size 14 in a certain brand fits them perfectly. Actually, they have been fortunate enough to find a manufacturer whose clothes are cut in a body line that fits them. All of the size 14s in this brand would fit equally well, regardless of style, because they are made from the master pattern for the same proportioned figure.

This is also true with pattern companies. All patterns in one size are made to fit the same proportioned figure, regardless of style. The empire or basque-type bodice may allow only three inches of ease, while the shirt style may allow as much as five inches, but both are still made for the same figure. The style determines the difference in amount of ease allowed.

To keep this uniformity of size, all the pattern companies work from a

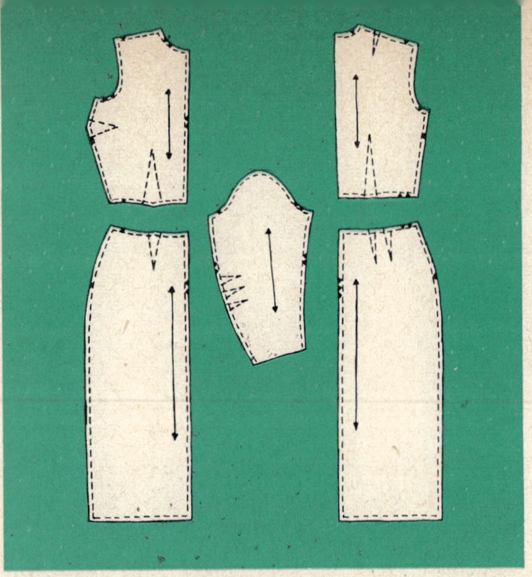

master pattern or "sloper." The sloper consists of a front and back bodice, a front and back skirt, and sleeve. If you were able to buy this sloper in your correct size in a commercial pattern, you could eliminate the need ever to fit yourself again.

Some pattern companies have brought out basic patterns, but whether or not these are actually based on their master patterns is questionable. Unless they are, the patterns will not work in the following method for eliminating fitting.

You can easily make your own master pattern or sloper from a regular style pattern. Sometimes, one pattern gives you all the pieces; otherwise,

you may have to buy three patterns—one for the bodice, one for the skirt, and one for the sleeve. It is well worth the investment if it saves future fitting time for you.

Once you learn to use this pattern, you will find that fitting has been almost entirely eliminated. With this basic pattern to work from, your fitting will simply consist of the try-on of an almost completed dress, requiring only minor adjustments, if any at all are needed.

When you buy your basic pattern, you will need only three measurements: (1) Bust (2) waist and (3) hips. Bust and hip measurements should be taken over the fullest part. Hold the tape tight, with fingers between the tape measure and body.

If you are an in-between size—for example, if a size 16 is too large, but a size 14 measures too small, you must also consider the amount of ease allowed in the pattern. All patterns are cut to allow from 3 to 5 inches of ease, depending on dress style.

This amount is generally enough to take care of the slightly larger measurements of the small-boned, softer figure. In this case, the smaller size pattern will probably be best.

A large-boned, firm-fleshed or muscular figure usually needs all the ease provided in clothes. The larger pattern will probably give the better fit for this figure.

Patterns are available in a range of sizes in several figure types—subteen, teen, girls, junior, misses, women's, and half sizes. If you have found a type that fits you best, buy your basic pattern in the same category. Adjustments cannot be transferred from one figure type pattern to another, because each one is cut for a completely different body line.

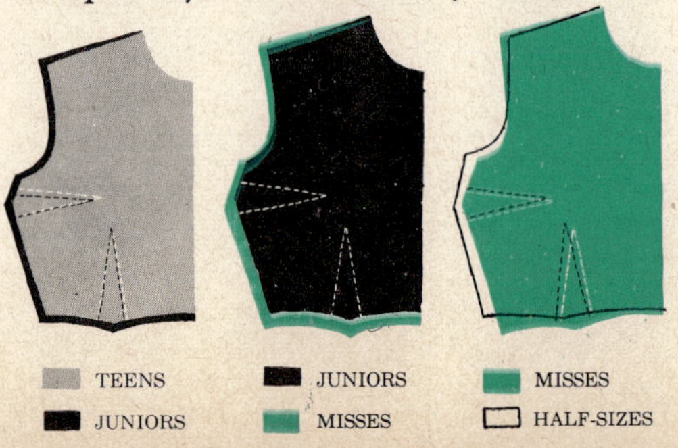

How to make the basic pattern

Cut out your basic pattern in muslin, exactly like the pattern. Sew up the darts and seams, assembling the bodice and sleeves first. Later, when the size is correct, assemble the skirt.

Make no alterations in stitching on this basic muslin. It must be identical to the pattern. Baste it together, or sew with a large stitch on the sewing machine. The bodice should always be left open down the front, since it is easier to put on and fit this way. Be sure to mark the center front line. Slip the bodice on inside out and pin down the center front line. Check how your body compares with the body line of your pattern.

There is still another factor to check in determining size. Some figures have a very broad back or full bust, but are otherwise small. A pattern bought by bust measurement would probably fit around this figure, but be very large everywhere else. To determine the correct size for these figures, check the armhole on the muslin. It should be well up under the arm. This is important because the high armhole gives greater comfort and freedom of movement. Never alter the armhole. It is important to buy a size which gives you a correct fit at the armhole. This sometimes means taking a pattern several sizes smaller than you measure. It is much easier to alter for a broad back or full bust, and keep the better proportion at the armhole and neckline.

If you decide your muslin is too big, re-cut it to a smaller size, sew it up and put it on, ready to fit. If it is too tight across the bust, pin it as best you can, ignoring the center front line. You will have a perfect fit when you are finished.

Cut your muslin exactly like the pattern. Sew up darts and seams, assembling the bodice and sleeves first (A). Leave bodice open down the front. Put it on and pin center front line (B).

Take care of all the standard adjustments first, such as lengthening or shortening the waist. When adjusting for waist length, always check at the side seam first. This is the only place where you can determine whether it is actually the waist length of the muslin that needs altering.

If the side back waist is too long, shorten across the entire back the same amount shortened at the side. This is vitally important—sometimes the center back will still seem too long, even after the alteration has been made. This indicates that a posture fault is causing the extra drop in the waist. The rest of the adjustment must be made across the shoulders, rather than any additional shortening in the waist itself.

How to make straight adjustments

Too-long waistline

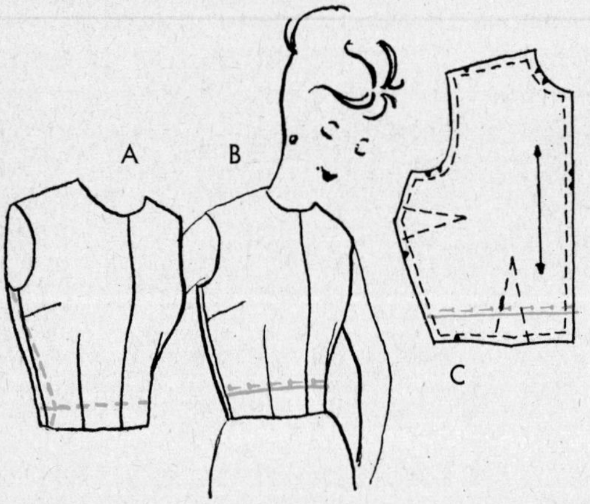

If the waistline is too long at the front and back as well as at the sides, the entire waistline must be shortened (A). Pin a tuck across both back and front between bust and waistline. Your pattern usually indicates where this line should be. The depth of the tuck, in this case, would be the same front and back (B). Make all adjustments in the pattern at the same points (C).

(Illustrations show the fault, correction and pattern adjustments.)

Too-short waistline

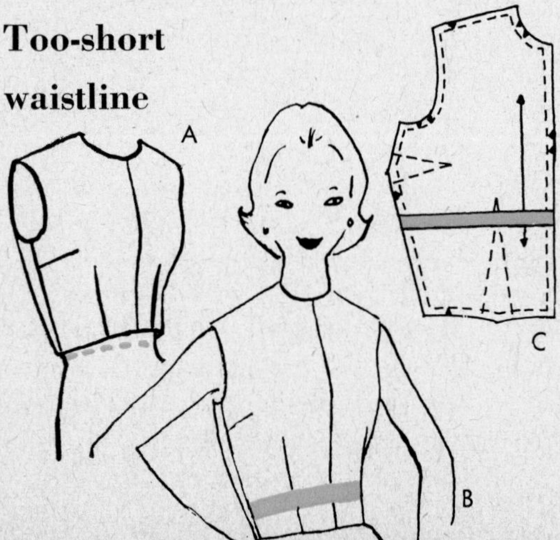

If your muslin is too short in the waist (A), lengthen it by cutting along the alteration line and inserting fabric (B). Make the pattern adjustment by cutting at the same point. Insert tissue to lengthen the pattern (C).

Too-wide shoulders

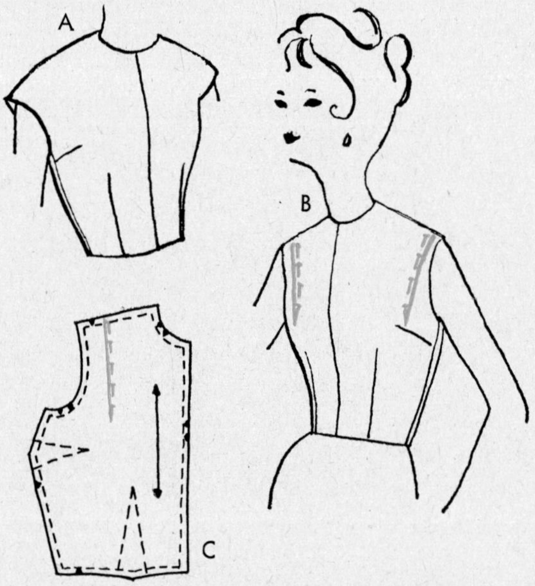

If the shoulders are too wide (A), fold a tuck from the top of the shoulder along the side of the armhole, tapering to nothing toward the bust. The tuck should be the same width from the shoulder to the armhole notch, tapering to nothing below that point (B). Mark and fold into the pattern the same way (C).

Before you adjust your pattern for figure faults, read the following carefully. (You may cheat a little when telling your age, but be honest when analyzing your figure problems!)

Adjustments for figure types

Full-busted figure

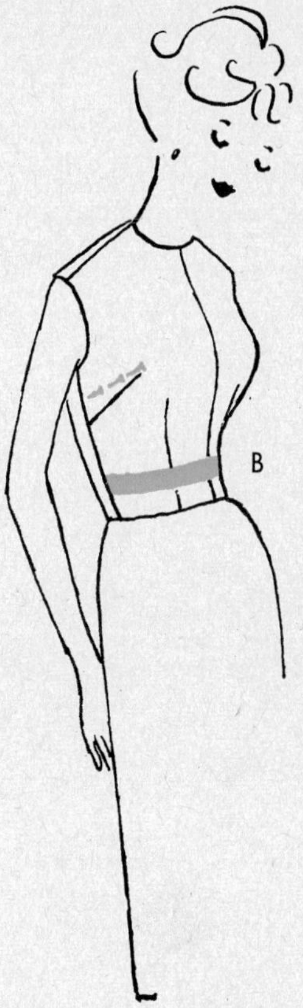

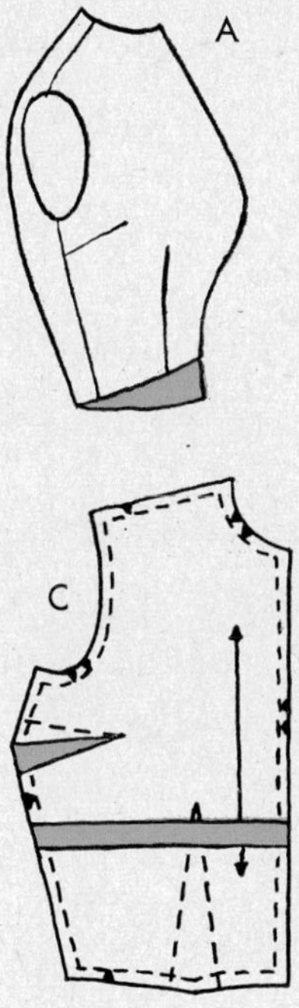

If the waistline is the right length at the back and sides but short in front directly under the bust, the figure needs more cupping for the bust than the pattern allows (A).

Cut along the alteration line and lengthen the front waist the necessary amount. Pin a piece of fabric there. At the bust dart, take in the amount added to the front length, making the dart deeper (B). This will give more cupping for the full bust, and since nothing has been done to the back and sides, the seams will be even. The side seam dart should run directly toward the point of the bust, and should be no less than an inch from the bust (C).

Make the entire dart higher or lower, if needed. Always be sure that the bust darts run upward to give a younger and more youthful lift to the bustline for the full-busted figure.

Flat-chested figure

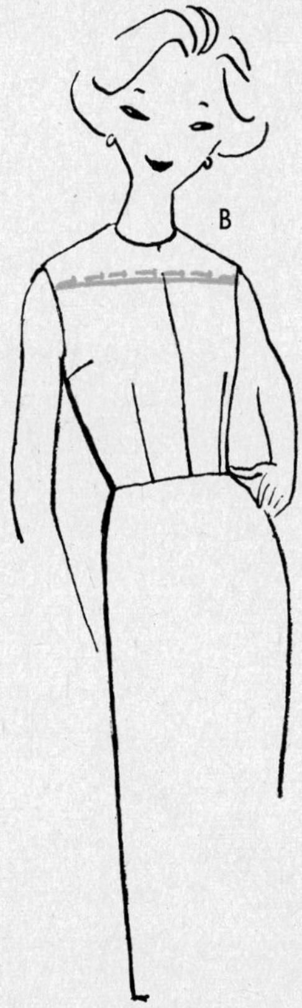

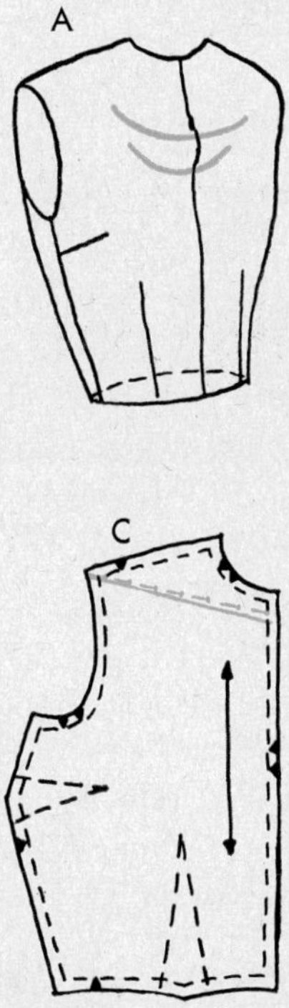

Usually with this figure fault, the back length is correct, but the front waistline is too long and droops at the center front (A). Eliminate the extra length by taking a dart from under the neckline, tapering to nothing toward the armhole (B). Make the same adjustment in the pattern (C).

Small-busted figure

For this figure the amount of fullness over the bustline is more than is needed (A). If the shoulders are narrow as well, take a tuck from the top of the shoulder straight down toward the waistline, eliminating the extra fullness (B). If the shoulders are normal, and only the bustline has to be made smaller, a dart can be fitted from the waistline up to the notch at the front armhole of your basic muslin. Transfer these same alterations to your pattern (C).

Small-busted, flat-chested figure

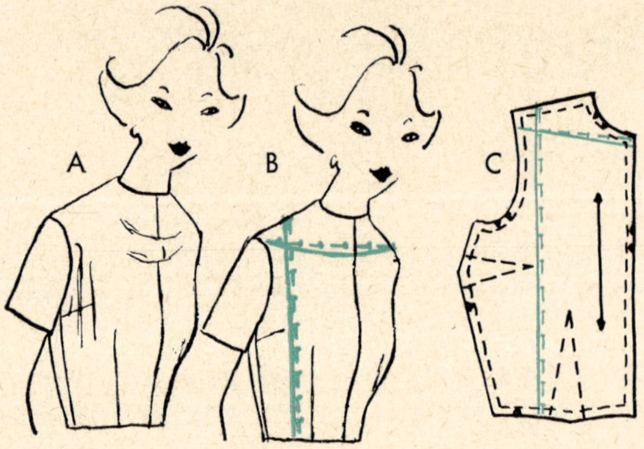

This figure requires a combination of alterations (A). Fit the same dart used to adjust for the flat-chested figure to eliminate the extra length at the front waistline. Follow the instructions at left to correct for the small bust (B). Make the same corrections in the pattern (C).

Full-busted, flat-chested figure

As the full-busted figure becomes round-shouldered, the chest becomes flat (A). Follow instructions for the full-busted figure, lengthening the front and taking up the dart. Then alter as for the flat-chested figure (B). Transfer the alterations to the pattern at the same points (C).

Round back

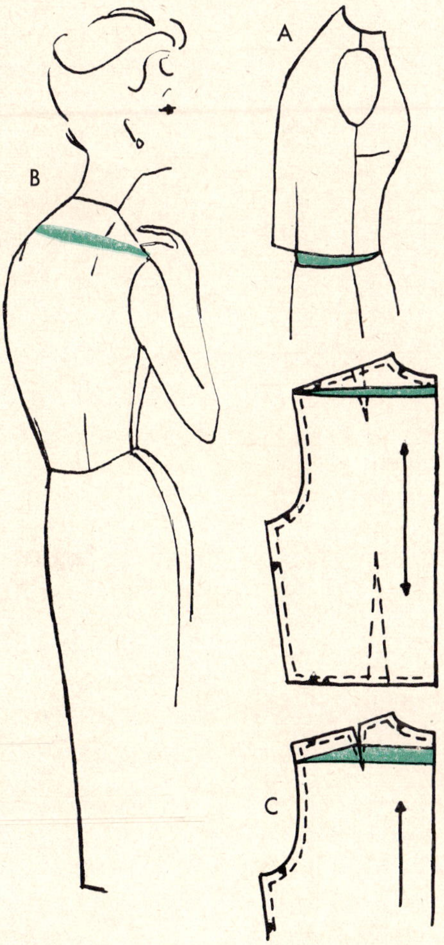

The back waistline will seem too short at the center back (A). Slash the back from under the back neck across toward each armhole. Open the necessary amount, insert a piece of fabric, and pin into place (B). When more than one-half inch is needed, the figure is generally very round-shouldered and needs more fitting.

Slash as before. Then slash through the center of the shoulder dart and spread as shown (C). This makes the back longer, and gives a deeper dart which shapes the shoulders to take care of a more rounded back.

Too-erect figure

The back waistline is too long at the center back (A). To eliminate this length, pin a dart under the back neckline tapering to nothing toward the armholes (B). Make the same adjustment in the pattern (C).

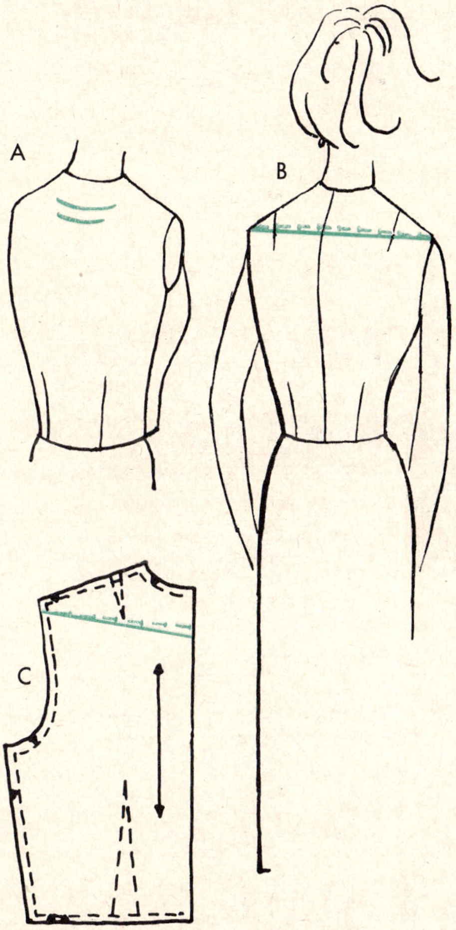

NOTE:
Altering the basic pattern at points below the neck and toward the armhole is also necessary for many other types of figure faults. For instance: Sloping shoulders, square shoulders, or round shoulders all require variations of this same adjustment. It is not

difficult to figure them out if you analyze your type carefully. Here's a good tip: Clothes should hang from the shoulders. When you put on a garment, the slope of the shoulder should be the same as your own.

Square shoulders

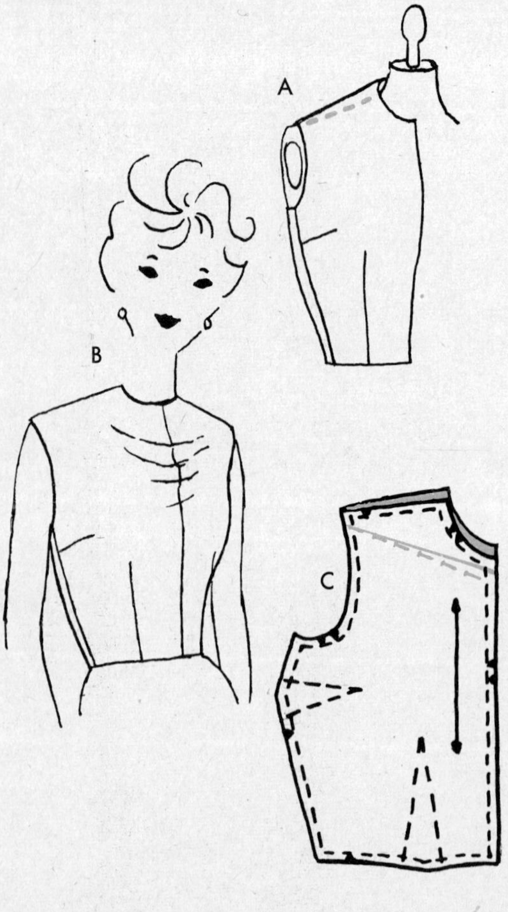

If your shoulders are more square than the pattern allows, you will find that when you put on your muslin, the top of the armhole will hit your shoulder first and the neck will be too high (A). This extra fabric will droop and the front of the dress will seem to sag (B). The dart used across the front will change the slope of the shoulders to fit yours, and the dress will hang correctly (C). If a fold forms under the back neckline, use the same adjustment there.

Sloping shoulders

If the shoulder of your garment fits at the neck, but not at the top of the arm (A); if the fabric droops, causing folds to form under the arm and along the armhole seams (B), slash from under the neck toward the armhole to correct this (C). Notice that all adjustments are done within the basic pattern to insure keeping the correct armhole and neckline.

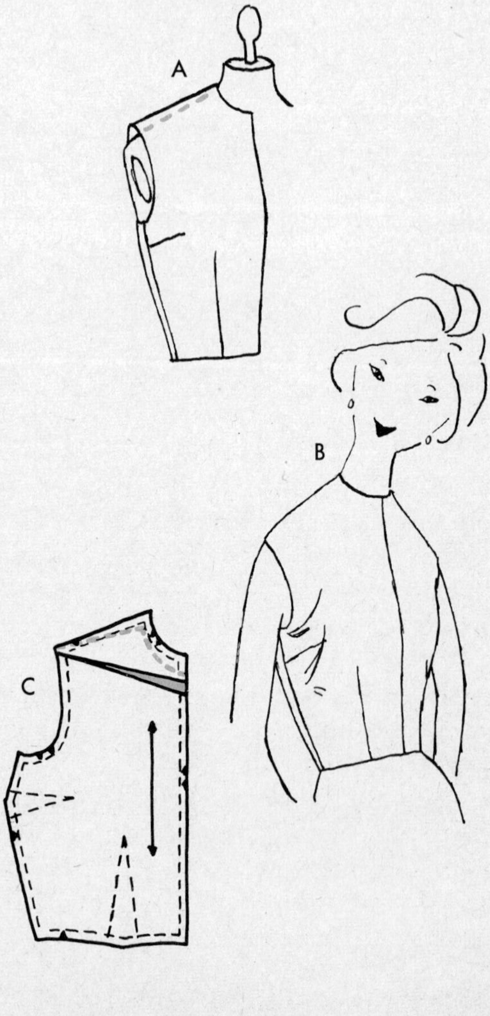

Adjustments for pattern size

Very full bust

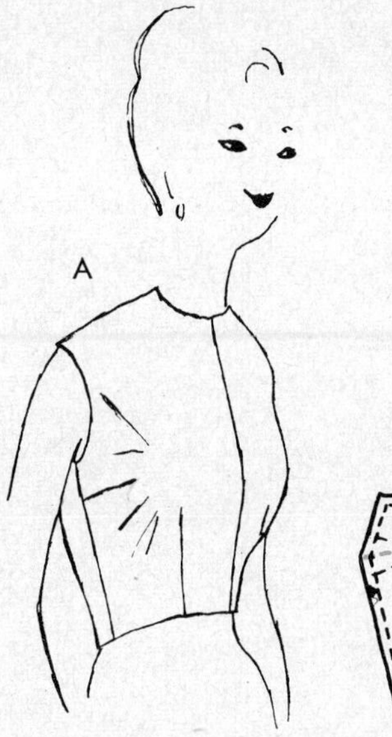

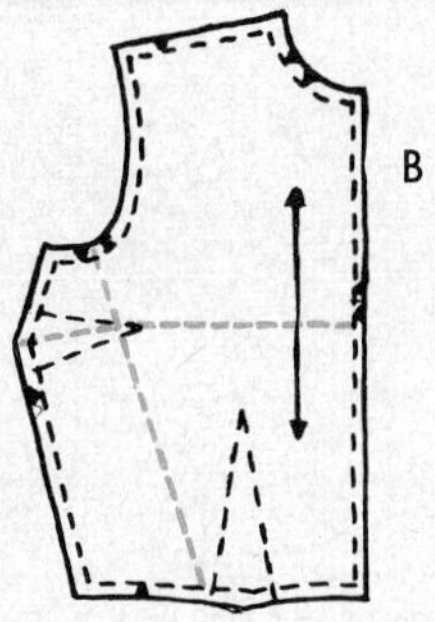

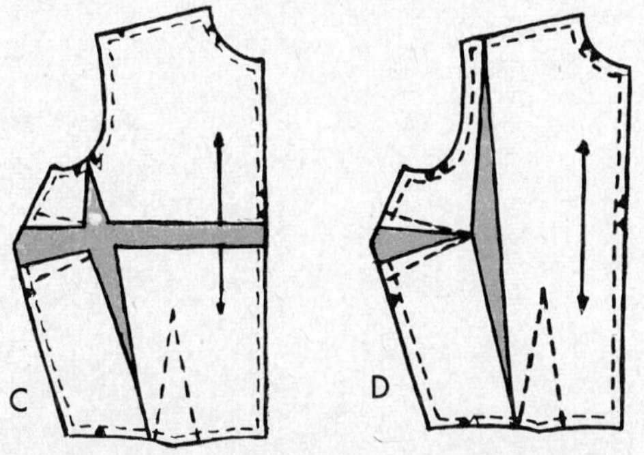

Usually, you buy your basic pattern according to bust measurement, but when bust fullness is extreme, a pattern bought by this measurement would be much too large at the neck and armhole. Buy the size that gives the best fit at the armholes, regardless of bust measurement. This smaller pattern will probably fit well except across the bust, where it will be too tight for your figure (A).

Make the bust size larger by slashing the pattern from waistline to armhole, and from the center of the bust dart toward the point (B). By spreading the pattern here you get more fullness for the larger bust. The dart becomes larger and deeper, which gives more cupping.

If the waistline also needs to be lengthened, as is often the case, continue cutting from the point of dart straight across the front of the pattern and lengthen as needed. Shape the dart to fit correctly (C). If the waist needs enlarging, spread the pattern at the waistline slash.

For the extremely full-busted figure, slash the pattern to the shoulder and spread. Usually, with this adjustment, the shoulders have to be narrowed with a tuck from the center shoulder toward the bust (D).

Full back

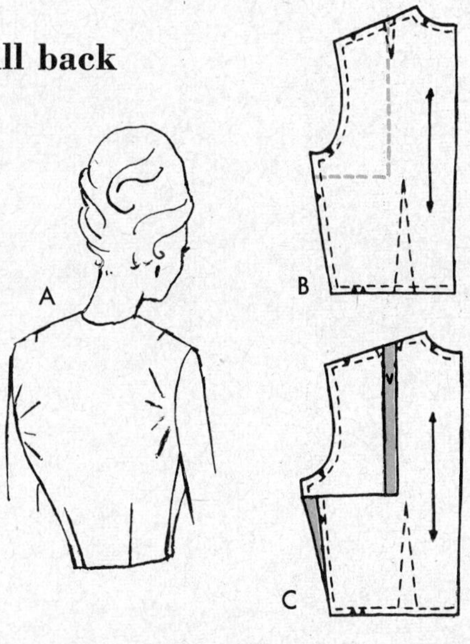

Often, what should be your correct pattern size seems too small because the back is tight, although the rest of the pattern fits properly (A). You need only to broaden the shoulders for a comfortable fit.

To make an adjustment, slash across

under the armhole and up through the shoulder, moving this piece out on the shoulder to give the necessary fullness across the back (B). The back shoulder must be made broader because the figure is round-shouldered. Extra fullness is needed across the shoulder blades but not at the top of the shoulder. To make back and front shoulders fit, it is usually necessary to make a dart at the back shoulder. This takes up the extra fabric so front and back shoulder seams are even (C) and gives a better fit to the rounded back.

If the entire back is too broad, the pattern can be slashed from waistline to shoulder and spread.

Combination of both types

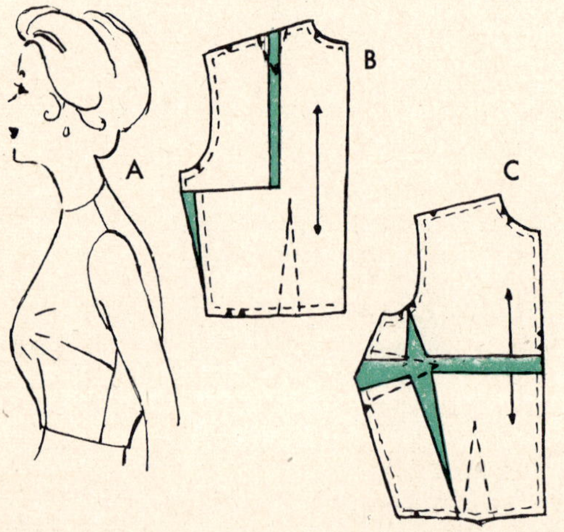

The overweight or matronly figure may have a combination of these figure problems. The bust may be too low and full, although the shoulders are narrow. The back may be fleshy and rounded through the shoulders (A). Choose a pattern that provides a high armhole and alter for the broad back (B) and low full bust (C). For the low bust, lower the side darts. Mark these darts before you slash your pattern to alter for the full bust.

Decreasing the waistline

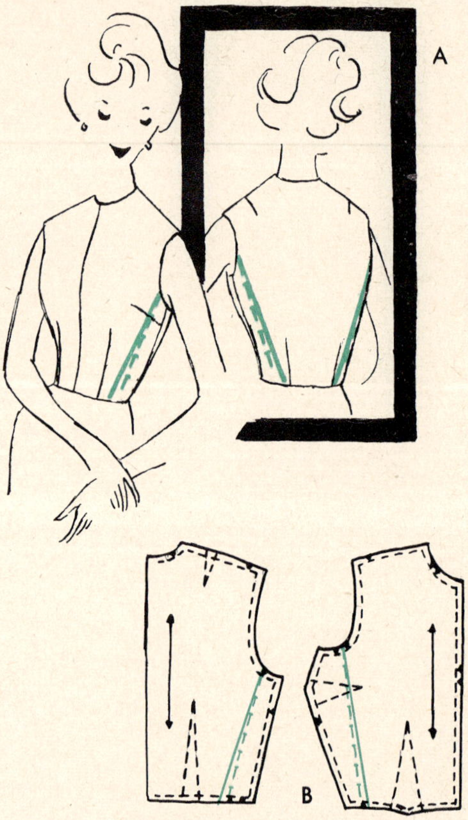

Before adjusting the waistline for size on your muslin, check the underarm seamline. It should be straight up and down, pulling neither to front nor back. If the waistline is too big, take a dart on both the back and front bodice from waistline toward armhole, to give a snug fit (A). Pin the dart in back and front bodice pieces at the same points. The dart shapes toward the armhole but does not alter the armhole size (B).

Increasing the waistline

To increase the waistline, add to the outside of the pattern at the waist. Since you have two front seam edges and two back seam edges, divide the amount you need to increase the waistline by four and add it at the side seams of the back and front waist (A). Add this amount at the waistline of the skirt as well. There are additional waistline adjustments that have to be made, depending upon your particular figure faults.

For instance, if the underarm seam of the bodice pulls toward the front, it means that the front of the figure protrudes and the increase in size should be made only on the front waist.

To make this alteration, slash your basic pattern from the waistline to the armhole, and insert the amount needed at the front to correct the underarm seam (B).

If the back is more full, the seam will pull toward the back. Adjust this the same way (C). If the waistline is to be increased more than two inches, it is advisable to slash the back and front pieces to make the adjustments within the basic pattern, rather than on the outside seams (D).

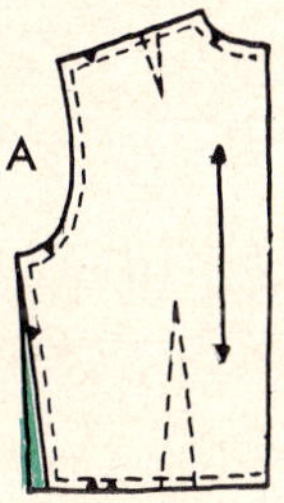

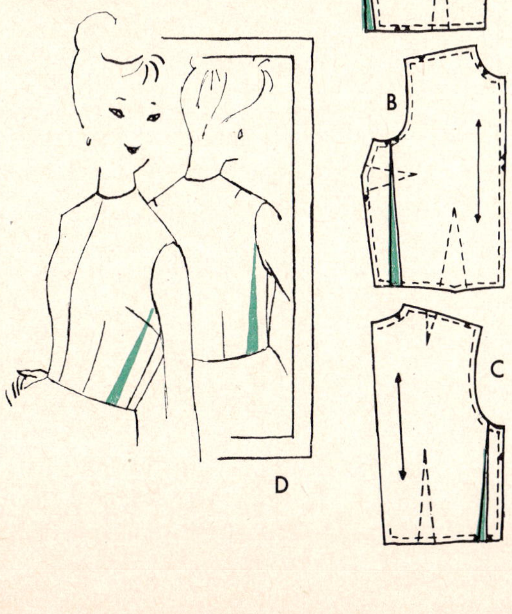

Full bust, small waistline

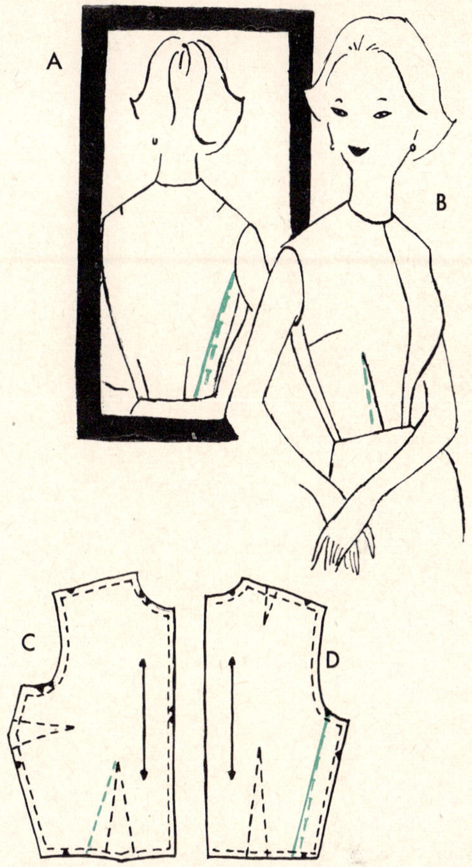

With the small waistline and full bust, the waist adjustment can also be used to give a better bust fit. The back waistline is made smaller by taking a dart at the side of the waist, from the waistline toward the armhole (A). Make the front waistline smaller by taking a deeper waistline dart. Fit the dart on the outside edge of the dart line (B). On the pattern, mark the front dart deeper only on the outside line of the dart, so that the bodice and skirt darts will line up (C). Alter the back like the muslin (D). Never take back darts in deeper; the back bodice will appear to bulge, the figure will look round-shouldered.

Fitting the skirt

Baste the skirt to the fitted bodice and begin to fit. This may mean some "putting on and taking off" which can be a little trying, but remember that you will have to do it only once. Then, no more fitting!

If you decided the smaller size muslin bodice was better for you, then, regardless of how the skirt fits, use the same size skirt pattern. It is less confusing to work with the same size pattern for the entire garment. The bodice will give a better fit, and the skirt is easy to adjust.

Matching bodice and skirt darts

The darts toward the center on the front and back bodice should always form a continuous line. This is why the darts should be taken in or let out only on the outside line.

Fitting for the small hip

When the waist and hip are both smaller than the pattern, a tuck can be taken the whole length of the muslin, and folded into the pattern at the same point (A and B).

When only the hips are smaller and need adjusting, fit out the excess fullness at the side seam of the muslin. You can fold this same amount off the pattern before it is cut, or you can fit it out and leave it in the seam of the finished garment.

If the front or back of the skirt has a puff below the darts that can't be fitted out, the darts are too deep, giving more shaping than is needed (C). Refit the darts, making them smaller by letting out on the outside line of the dart. Remove the excess from the waist and hip size by taking a tuck the length of the muslin. Correct the pattern in the same way (D).

Generally, this adjustment is needed only in the back, except when the stomach is also flat. In that case, further adjustment will be necessary.

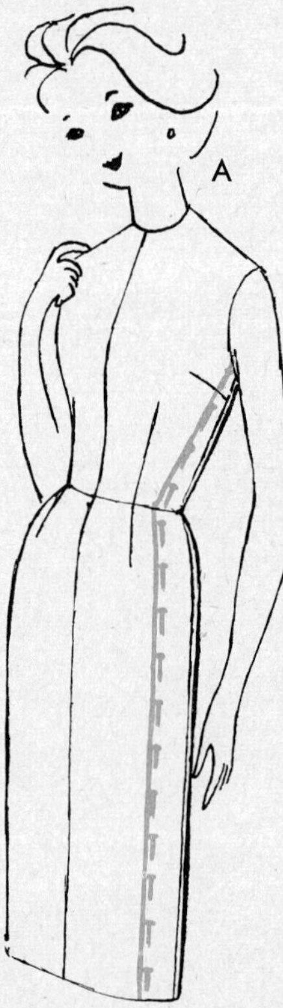

A

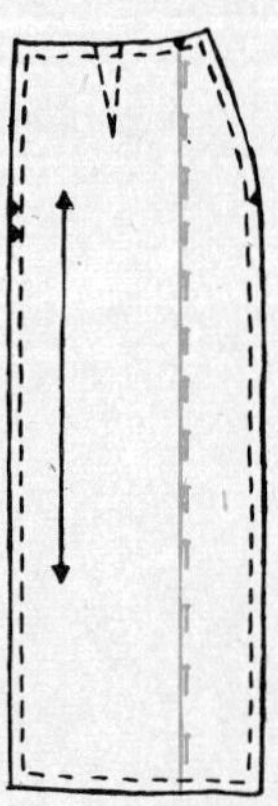

B

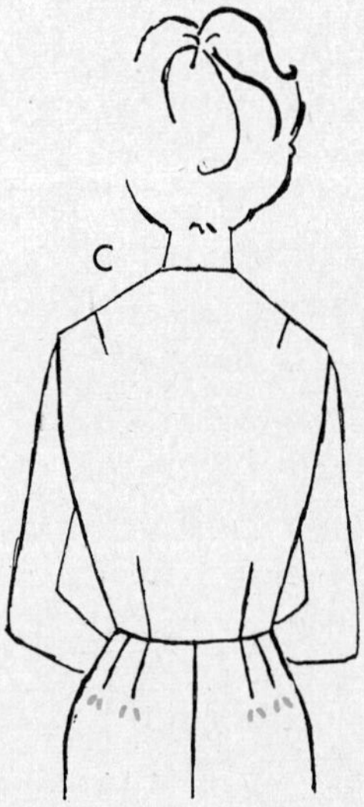

C

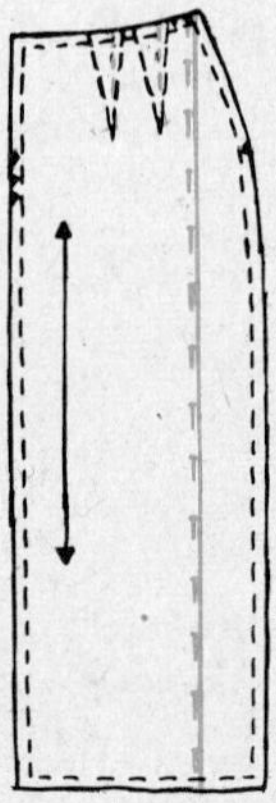

D

Fitting for the full hip

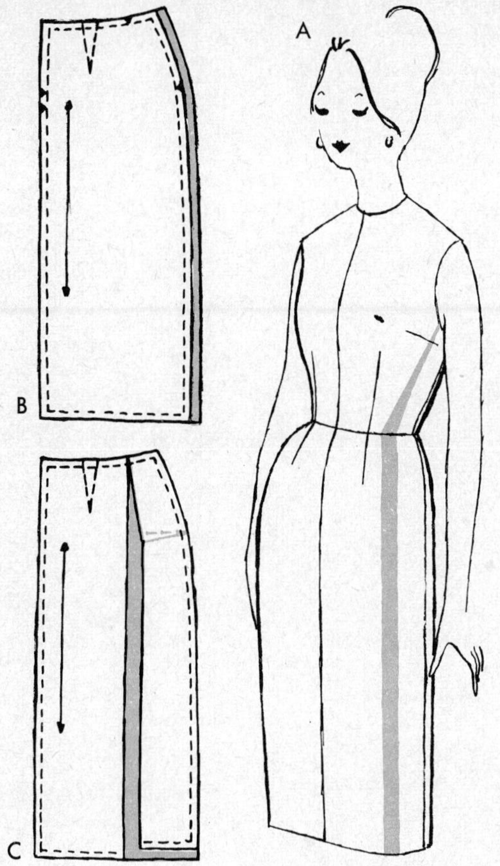

When the hips are wider than the pattern size, let out the seams of your muslin and, when cutting your dress, add the necessary amount at the same places. If a large amount has to be added at the hip and not at the waist, the muslin can be slashed from the hem to the waist about 4 inches in from the side seam. Spread the muslin the amount needed for the correct hip size and pin a piece of fabric here to hold (A).

To adjust the pattern, add the same amount at the side seam (B). The amount spread at the fullest part of the hip should be the same as at the hem line.

To remove the extra flare, pin a dart across the side skirt at the fullest part of the hip. Taper the dart from nothing at the side seam toward the slash to shape the skirt.

Make the same adjustment in the pattern (C) as on the muslin.

Increasing the skirt waistline

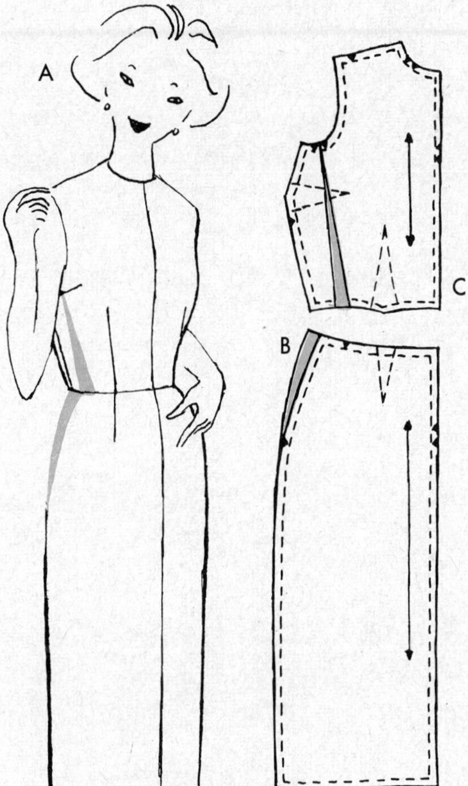

The skirt waist size is increased by adding at the side seam of the muslin or pattern (A and B). The skirt is never slashed to adjust the waist size as is sometimes done to alter the bodice waistline (C).

Increase the skirt waist size by the same amount and at the same point as the bodice waistline was increased; that is, on the front skirt piece only, on the back skirt piece only, or on both front and back pieces.

Decreasing the skirt waistline

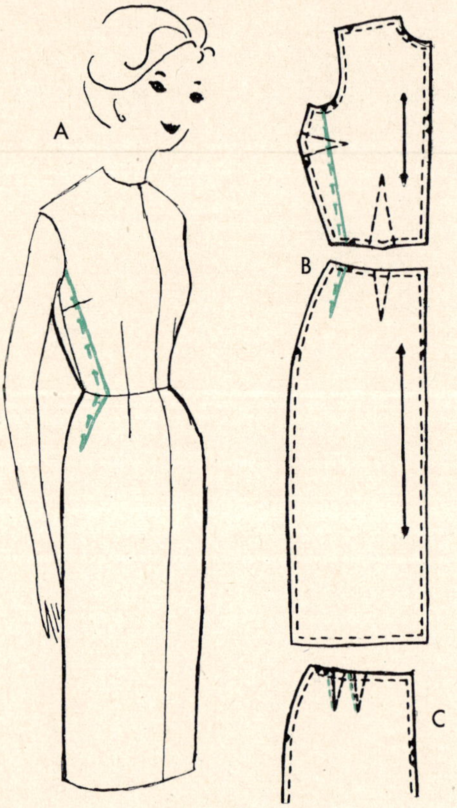

To decrease waist size, fold a dart from the waistline toward the hip. Alter the skirt the same amount as the bodice (A and B). If the waist is very small in proportion to the hips, alter the skirt back waist by making fitting darts slightly deeper. Adjust the darts only on the side toward the side seam, never on the side toward the center back (C). Do not make the skirt front fitting darts deeper, except when fitting for large pelvic bones. Altering bodice darts is exactly the reverse. The front darts of the bodice can be made deeper to give a better fit to the bust when making the waistline smaller, but back darts are never made deeper, as this makes the figure appear to be round-shouldered.

Sway-back

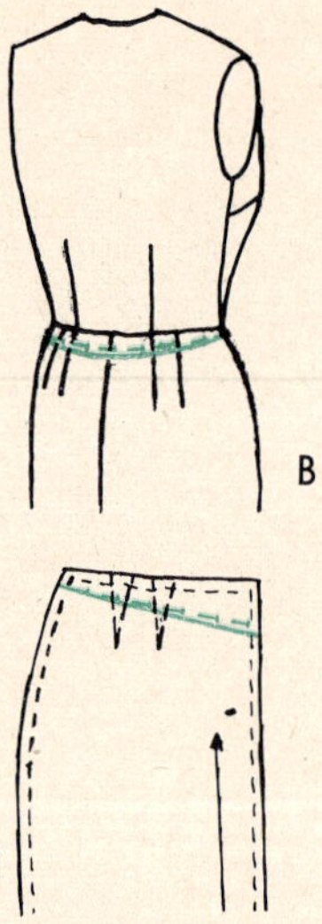

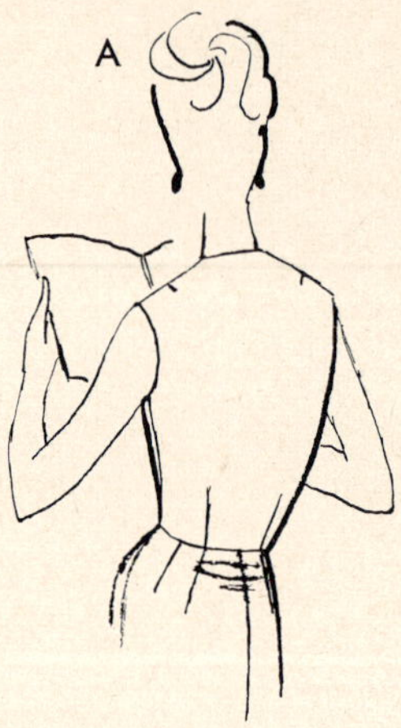

Usually with this figure fault, folds appear across the top of the skirt just below the waistline (A). Pin the fold across the top of the skirt, tapering it to nothing at either side so that it fits correctly (B). Check the grain line, making sure it runs evenly around the fullest part of the hips. Make the adjustment in your pattern at the same point (C).

High abdomen

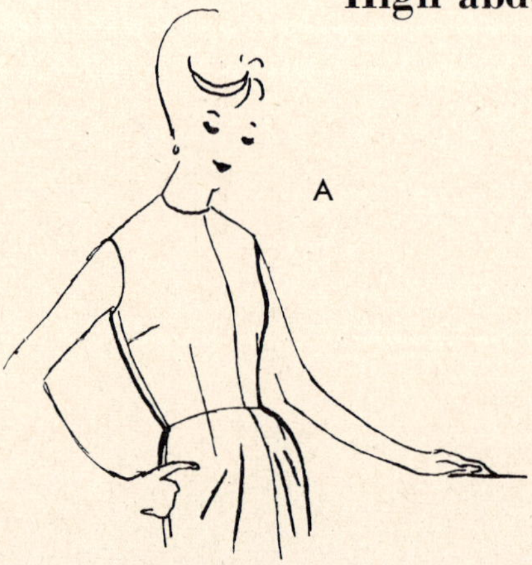

With this fault, the skirt rides up at center front (A). To correct, open the skirt at the center-front waistline

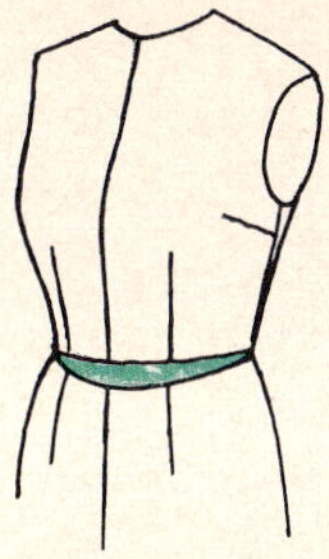

B

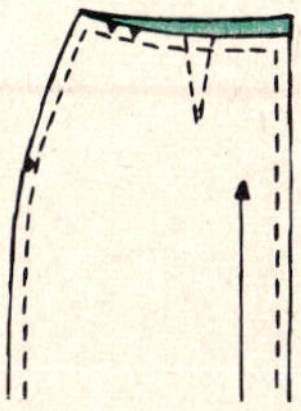

C

and drop it until it hangs smoothly (B). It may be necessary to add fabric here to give even more length at the waistline seam. Make the adjustment by adding this amount to the top of the skirt pattern to correct for this figure fault, giving a good fit at the waist (C).

Flat derriere

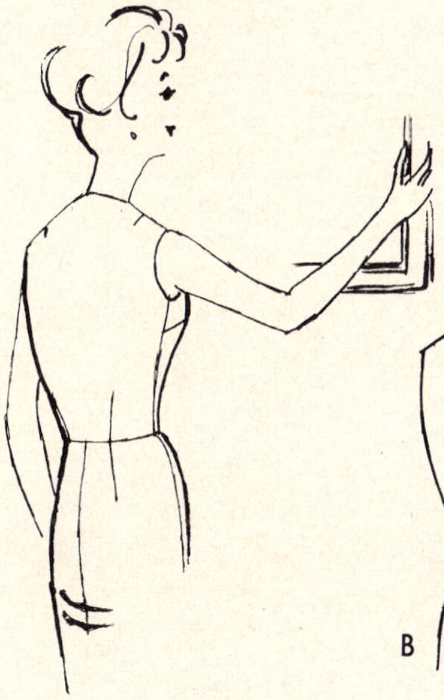

A

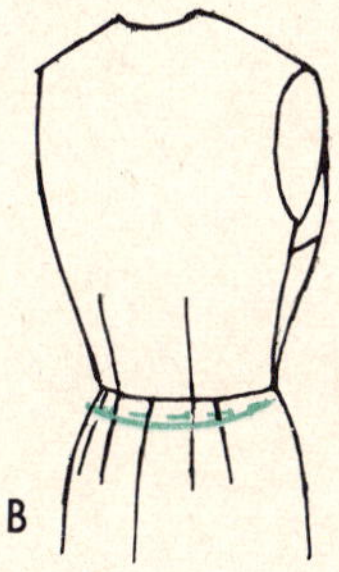

B

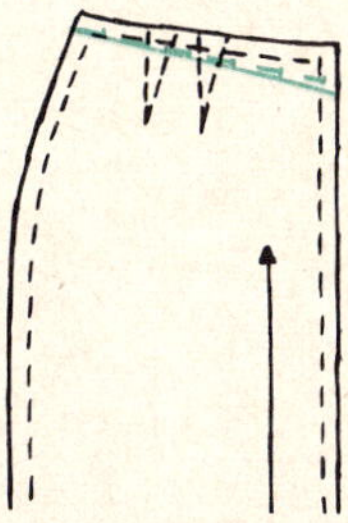

C

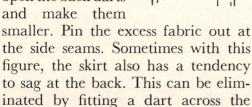

When the figure is flat in back, the amount of shaping for the full derriere is not needed (A). To eliminate this, open the back darts and make them smaller. Pin the excess fabric out at the side seams. Sometimes with this figure, the skirt also has a tendency to sag at the back. This can be eliminated by fitting a dart across the top of the skirt under the waistline, as for the sway-back figure (B). To adjust the pattern, re-mark the back darts making them smaller on the outside line only. Fold the dart across the pattern under the waistline as you did for the sway-back figure (C). To remove the excess fullness across the skirt, pin a tuck the length of the skirt close to the side seam.

Large pelvic bone

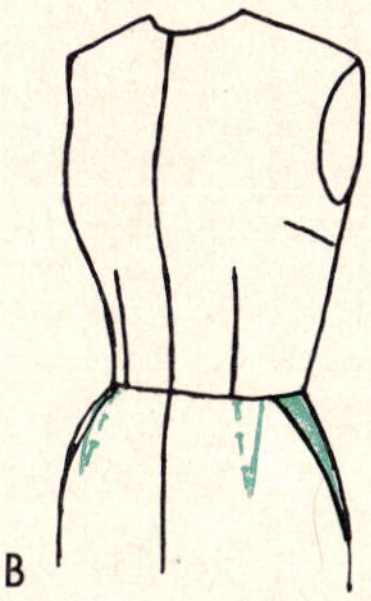

B

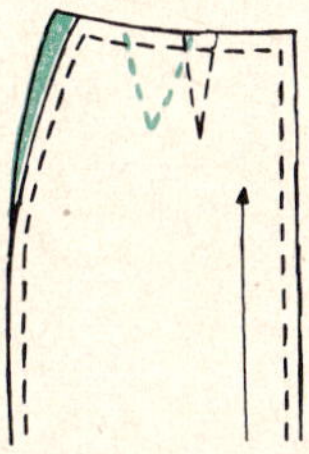

C

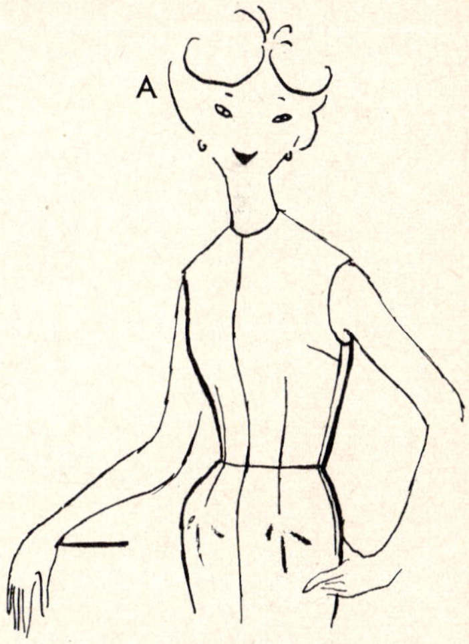

A

This is almost exclusively a fault of the junior figure. The hipbone protrudes, causing a bad fit at the side seam and waistline of the skirt (A). Take a dart from the waistline toward the hipbone. If the front skirt has a dart, move it nearer the side seam so that it fits over the hipbone. Then make it deeper so the fit is smooth. This may mean enlarging the front waistline, which is done by adding extra fabric at the waist seams (B). To adjust the pattern, re-mark the waistline darts at the correct point. If the waist size has to be increased, add the extra amount onto the outside waist seams (C).

Sleeves

Now you are ready to baste the sleeves into the bodice and check the fit. If there are three darts in the sleeve, the center dart should come at the point of the elbow when the arm is bent. If there is just a single dart, as in the three-quarter sleeve, the point of the dart should be toward the point of the elbow.

If a dart is too high on the arm, slash across the upper sleeve and lengthen it so that the darts are at the correct point on the arm. The sleeve forearm can then be lengthened or shortened according to the length of the arm.

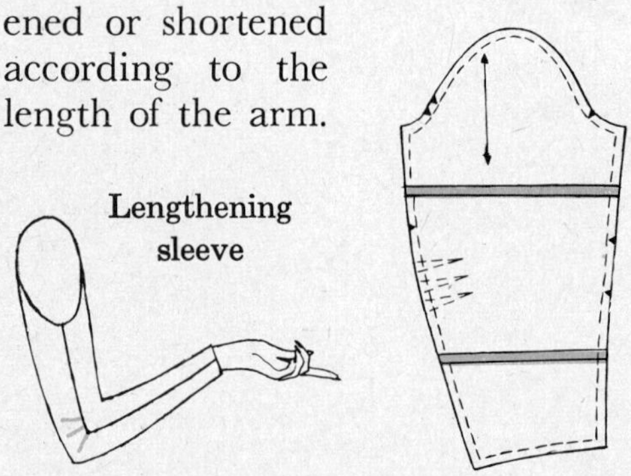

If the darts are below the elbow, take a tuck across the upper part of the sleeve to shorten. Lengthen or shorten the sleeve forearm to the arm length.

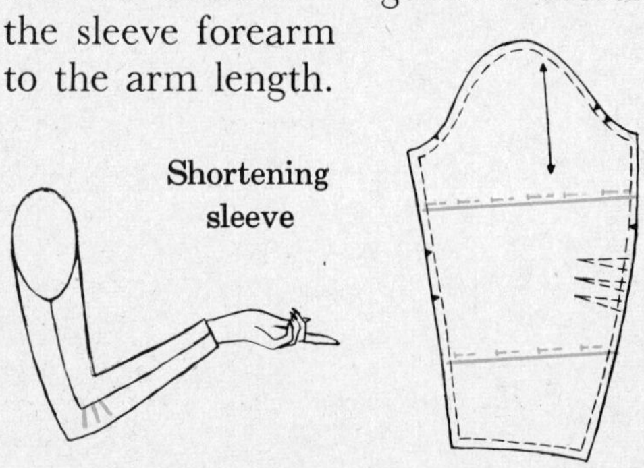

If the elbows are exceptionally pointed, even though the darts are in the right place, the sleeve may feel too tight and pull from the shoulder. More elbow room is needed. To check, pin each dart a little deeper and test by bending the elbow. When it feels comfortable, measure the amount added to the dart. When adjusting the sleeve pattern, slash through the center of the darts toward the inside sleeve seam and spread each dart the necessary amount. The darts are deeper when sewed and give more cupping at the elbow for a more comfortable sleeve. If the sleeve was lengthened or shortened, adjust the pattern at the same points as on the muslin.

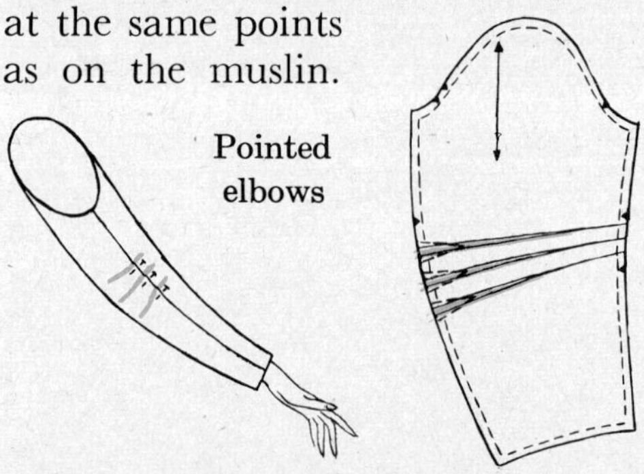

The figure with a full upper arm usually needs more fullness at the top of the sleeve, but not a larger armhole. To increase sleeve size without increasing armhole size, slash the length of the sleeve through the center, and spread the required amount. When adjusting the pattern, slash the length of the sleeve and spread. Take darts from the slash toward the cap of the sleeve to make it lie flat. The darts taper to nothing at the armhole and do not affect armhole size.

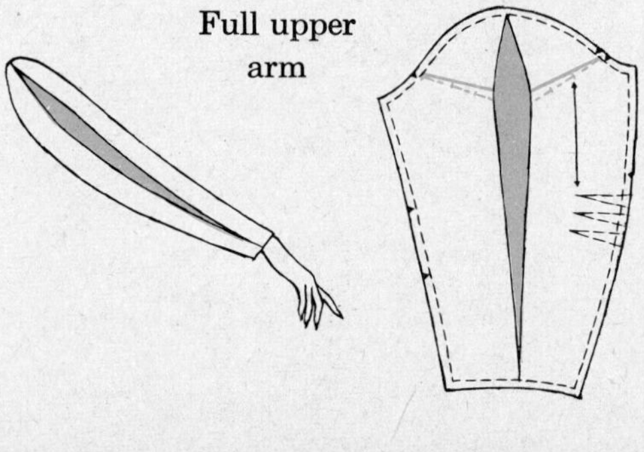

Adjustments for special types

Kimono sleeve

The same alteration used for adjusting the shoulder of a set-in sleeve can be used to narrow or widen the shoulder of the kimono sleeve. The sketches show adjustments needed.

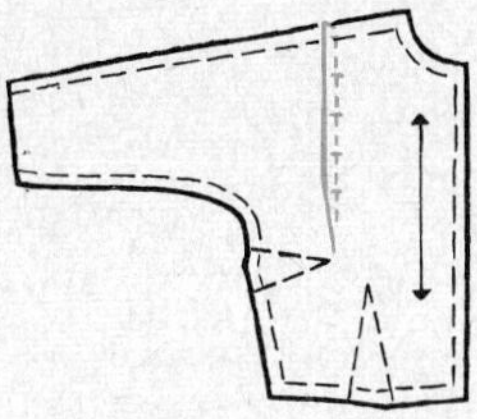

Narrow shoulders

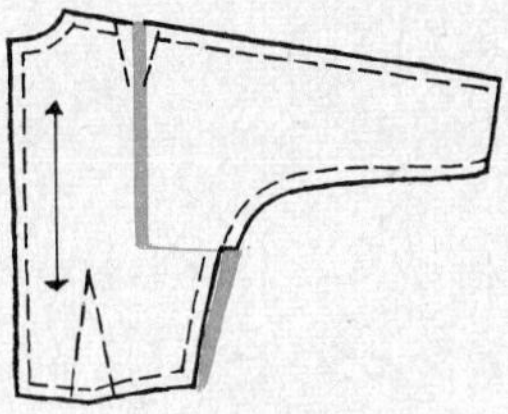

Wide shoulders

Lengthen or shorten the waistline in the same way as on the basic muslin.

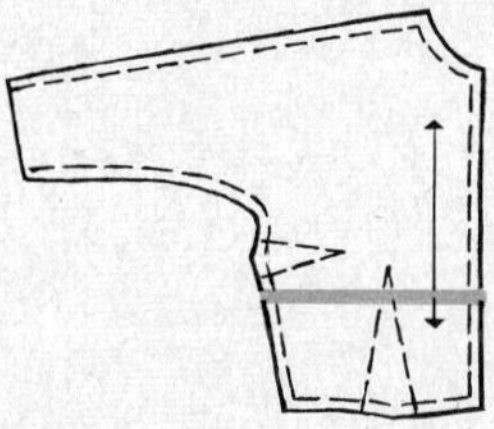

Long waistline

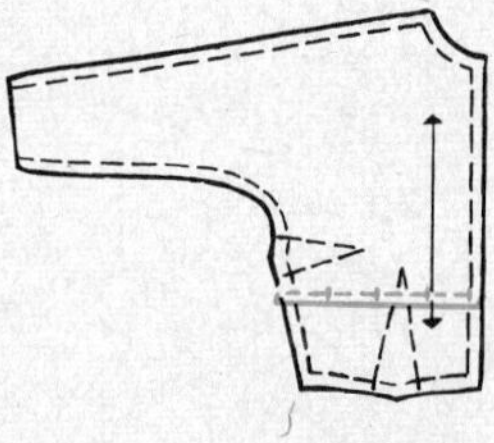

Short waistline

Eliminate the bust fullness in the same way as on the basic muslin, with a tuck running the length of the bodice. To increase for a larger bust, follow instructions given for increasing for a full bust on the basic pattern.

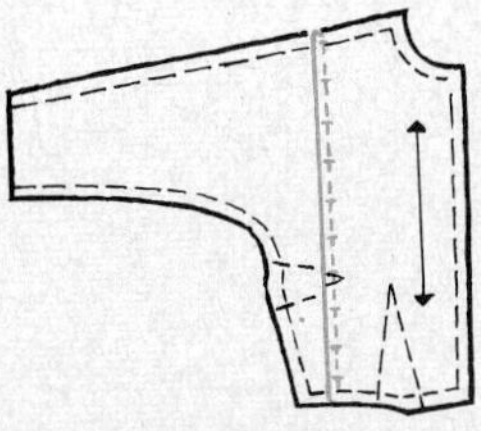

Small bust

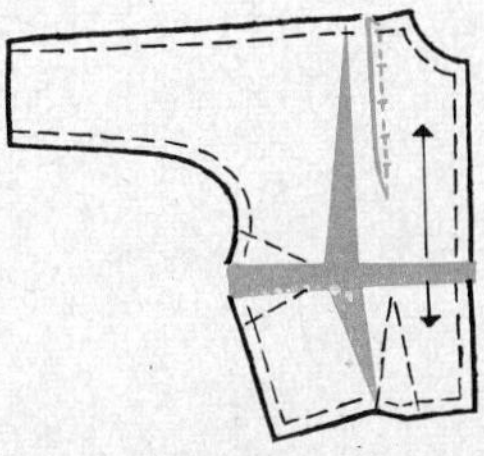

Full bust

On the shoulder line of the kimono sleeve, mark the finished width of your shoulder. Take this measurement from your basic pattern. If you need to adjust your pattern for square shoulders, fold the dart from under the neck toward this mark.

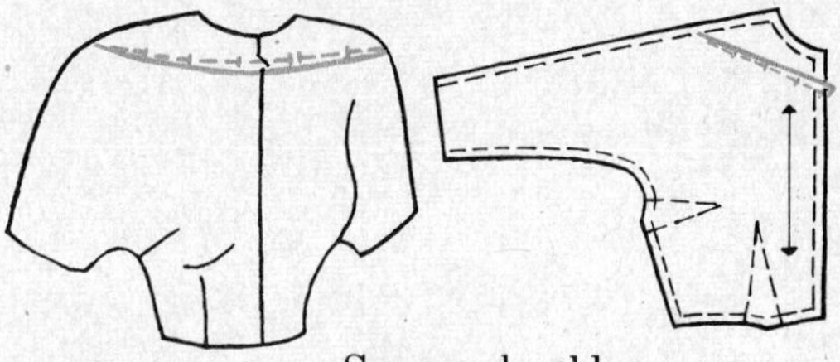

Square shoulders

If you are adjusting the pattern for a sloping shoulder, slash from under the neck toward this mark.

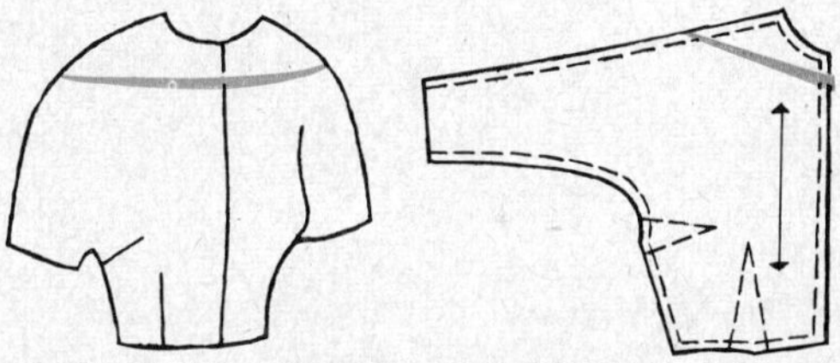

Sloping shoulders

To increase the pattern for the broad back, follow the instructions given on the basic pattern. If the front shoulder needs to be narrowed, but not the back, increase the size of the back dart to fit the front. This adjustment will give a more comfortable fit.

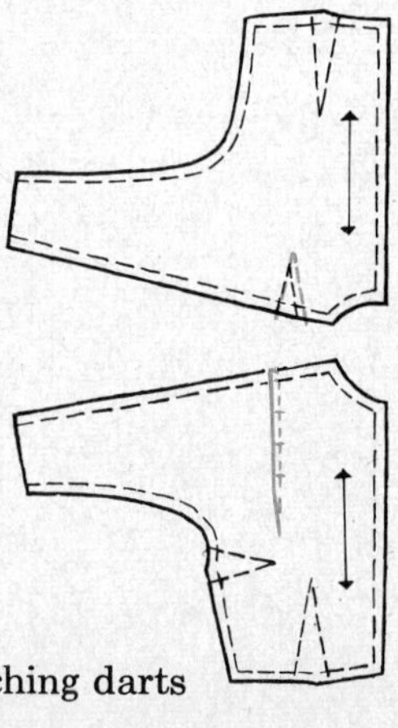

Matching darts

Raglan sleeve

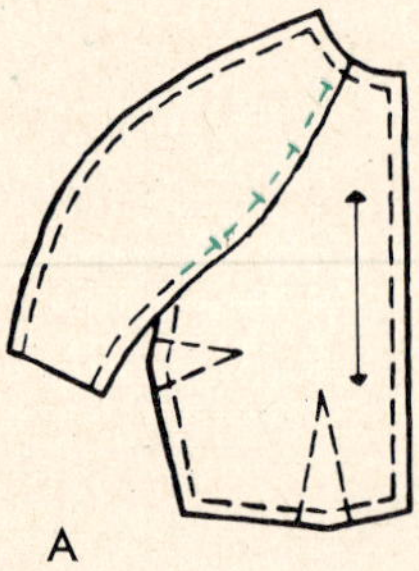

Pin the sleeve to the bodice, matching seam lines, and the pattern will be the same as the kimono sleeve (A). Make all adjustments just as for the kimono sleeve pattern, then unpin the pattern pieces and the adjustments will remain in the corrected pieces (B and C).

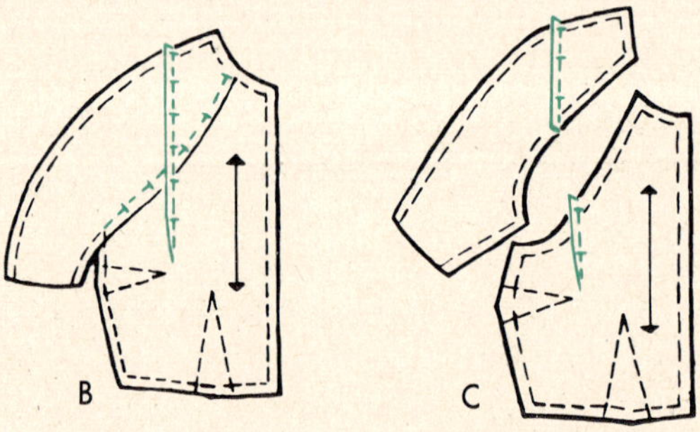

On a pattern in which the one-piece sleeve forms the back and front shoulder of the bodice, the adjustment for the narrow front shoulder and normal back is handled a little differently than on the regular sleeve. Narrow the front shoulder on the front part of the sleeve pattern; fold out a dart in the back shoulder section of the sleeve to fit it to the front (D).

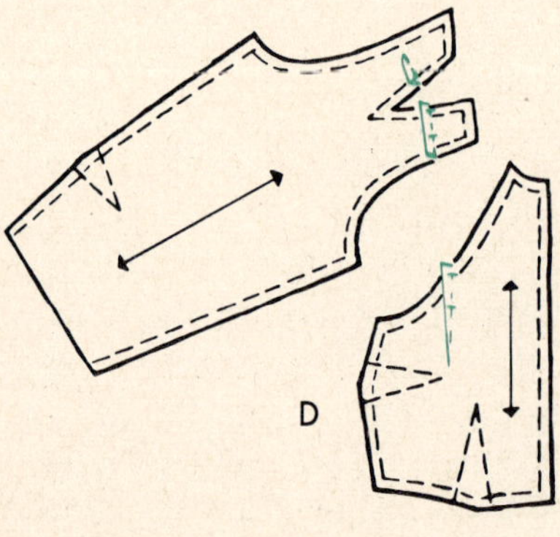

Princess line

Lengthening and shortening waistline

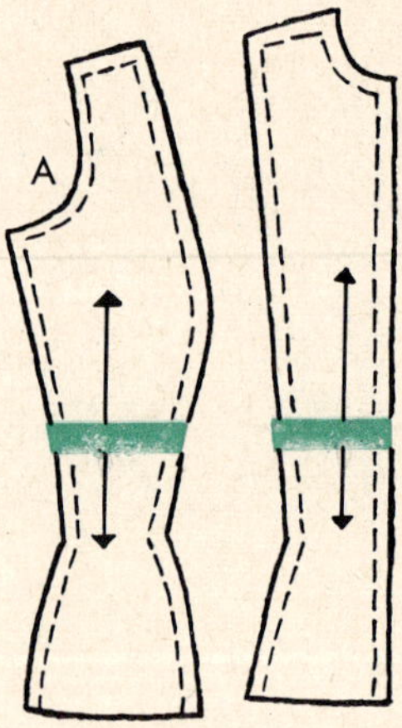

Lengthen (A) or shorten the waist between waistline and bustline on the princess style—the same as you do for any other style.

Correcting the shoulder slope

When correcting the shoulder slope, pin pattern pieces together; then fold in and pin the dart across the back or front (A). Leave alteration pinned in place, but unpin pattern pieces (B).

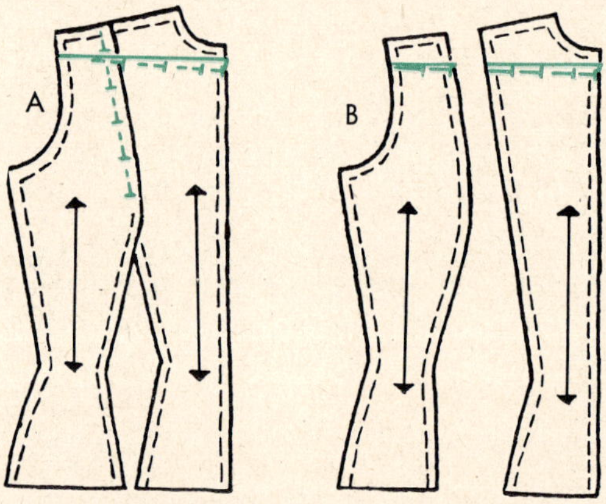

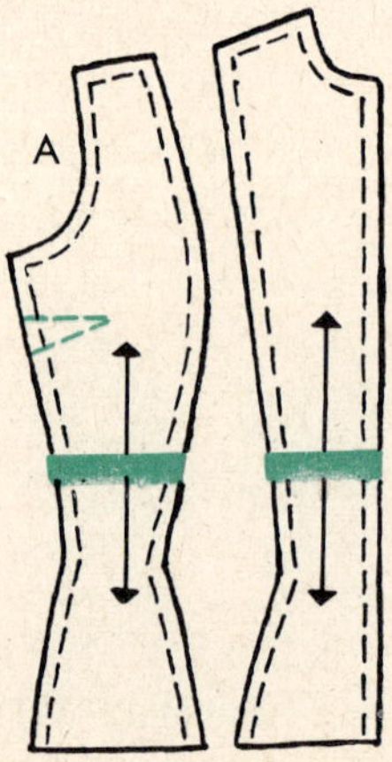

Adjustments for the full bust

Adjustment for the fuller bust can be made in two ways: lengthen the waistline; then sew in a bust dart (A). Or,

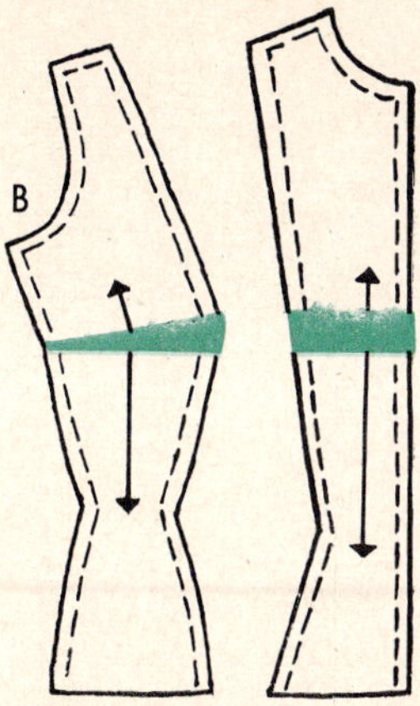

lengthen the front waist the necessary amount; then slash the side gore at the bustline to the side seam. Spread the slash at the front seam the amount the waist has been lengthened. This has the same effect as a dart. It gives a deeper slope at the side gore toward the shoulder, more cupping for bust.

Increasing the waistline

To increase the waistline, additions can be made at the outside seam for a small amount (A). If a larger amount is to be added, slash in on the waistline mark, then slash toward the armhole and swing open the needed amount (B). The same amount can be added toward the hipline. Waistline can be decreased in the same way (C).

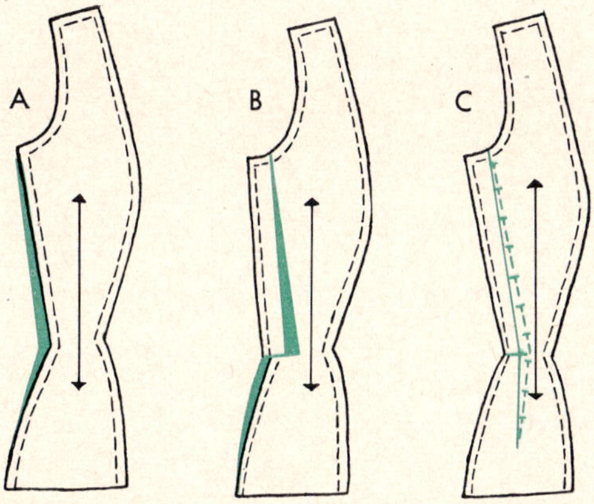

Alterations on suits and coats will be illustrated in detail in Chapters 11 and 12 on tailoring.

This method of sewing not only eliminates the need for future fitting, but also prevents over-fitting, a big fault of home dressmaking.

Determine your type

There are many combinations of figure problems. The basic principles of all fitting and adjustments, however, have been discussed. Only you can determine which ones apply to you.

As an example, the small-busted figure also often has a narrow front shoulder, and needs a pattern adjustment for both figure problems. The same figure could also be flat-chested and round-shouldered which would require additional adjustments.

Once you have fitted your basic muslin, you can make adjustments on all patterns of the same size. Make them exactly like those on your fitted basic and eliminate the need for fitting. Also remember that if you made your original basic in a size 12 misses pattern and you now want to use a teen pattern, you must make a new basic pattern to fit the teen body line. Adjustments cannot be transferred from one body line to another.

Do not fit patterns over the basic muslin. You only need a record of your adjustments. Apply the same adjustments to any dress, regardless of style. In this way, you insure keeping the dress line and style intended by the designer. Apply the same adjustments to suits or coats. You will not need your basic pattern again unless you gain or lose weight. It has served its purpose —to show you how your body compares in size with the one used for a standard commercial pattern.

Now that you know the adjustments needed, take the pattern pieces and adjust them to your correct size before cutting the fabric. Pin or baste tissue paper under the pattern at points where it has to be increased.

Fitting a muslin to the small figure

Each figure has its own fitting problems. This woman has difficulty getting a pattern small enough without buying a teen size. Although her bust measures 34, she used a size 10 pattern for her basic muslin.

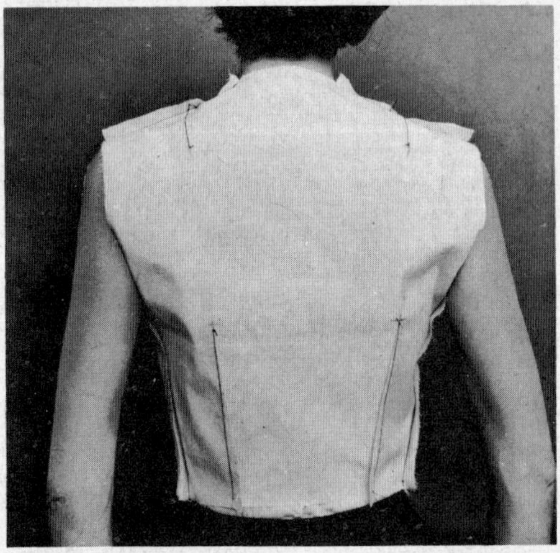

1 First, she checked the back of the muslin. The waistline was much too short, and the shoulders seemed too narrow for this broad-shouldered figure.

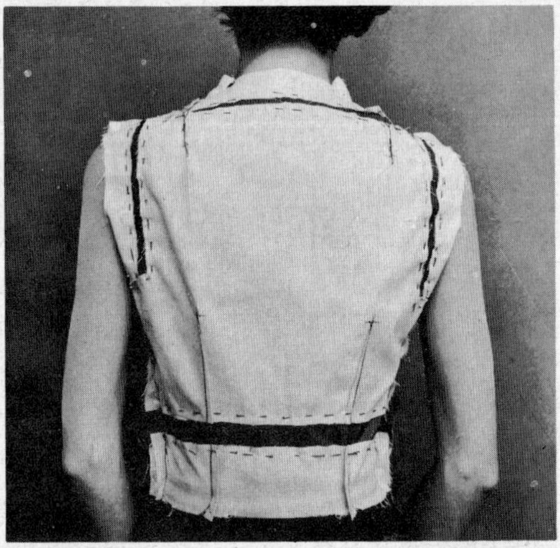

2 She lengthened the back waistline of her basic muslin by slashing the muslin and inserting additional fabric.

3 Fitting was needed for round shoulders as well as for broad shoulders.

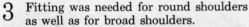

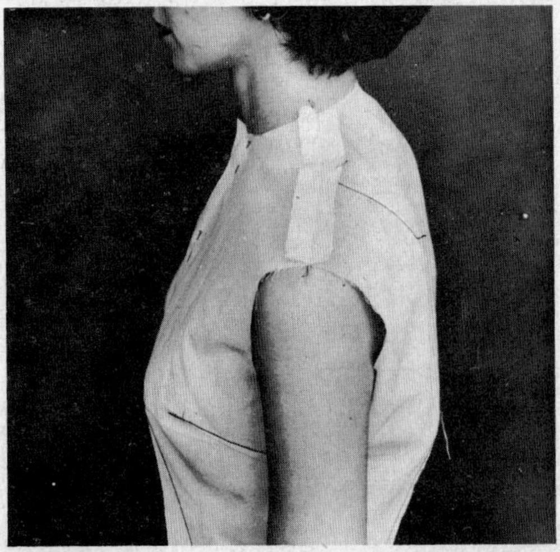

4 To broaden back shoulder, she slashed across under the arm, up to the shoulder. The back shoulder dart was taken deeper, giving a better fit for round shoulders, bringing back armhole close to the shoulder.

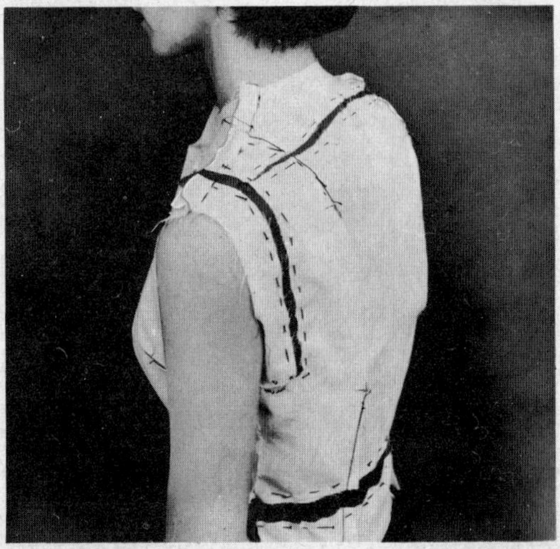

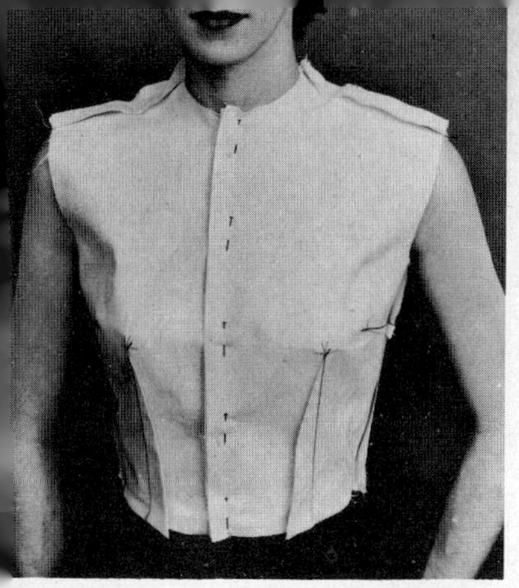

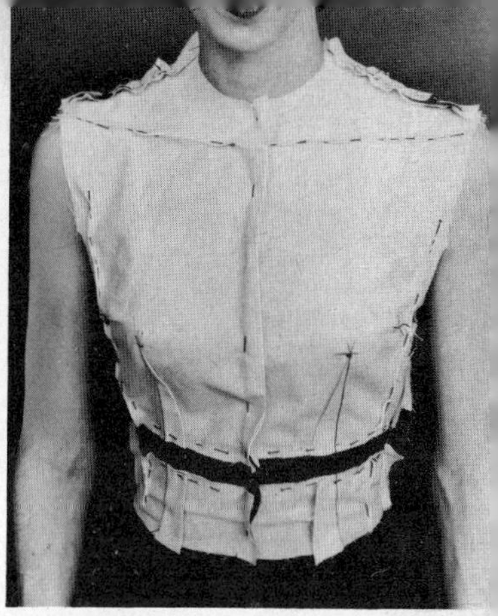

←

5 The front muslin was too short across the waistline, but dipped in the front. The shoulder width seemed correct.

→

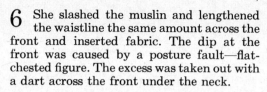

6 She slashed the muslin and lengthened the waistline the same amount across the front and inserted fabric. The dip at the front was caused by a posture fault—flat-chested figure. The excess was taken out with a dart across the front under the neck.

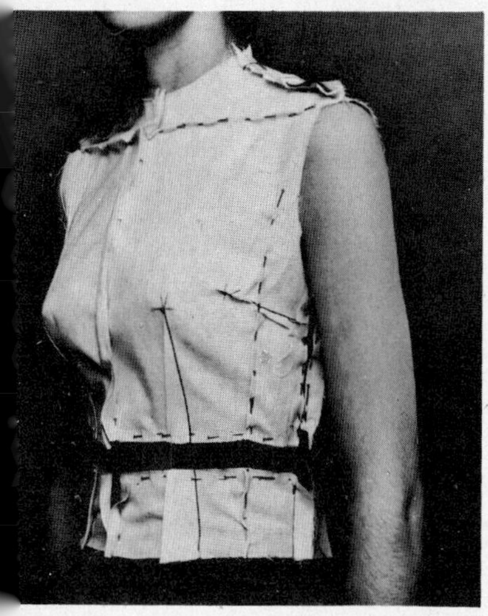

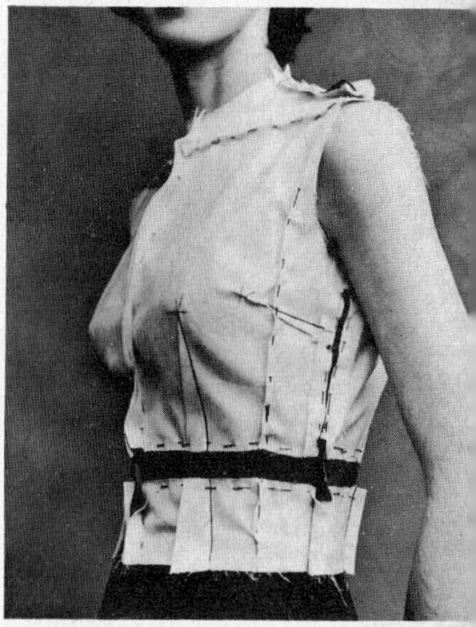

←

7 The front shoulder was the correct width so no fitting was needed there. When the back shoulders were broadened, the upper back also became broader, giving more fullness in the whole top of the muslin.

→

8 For this small-busted figure the excess fullness had to be removed from the front without making the front shoulders narrower. To do this, she took a dart from the side of the armhole to the waist; it also decreased the front waistline which was too large.

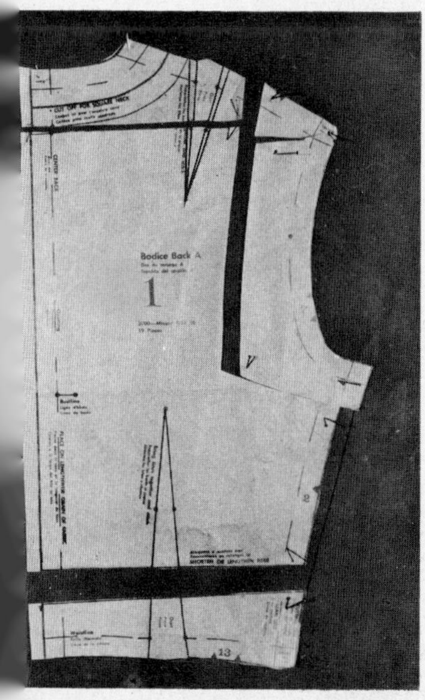

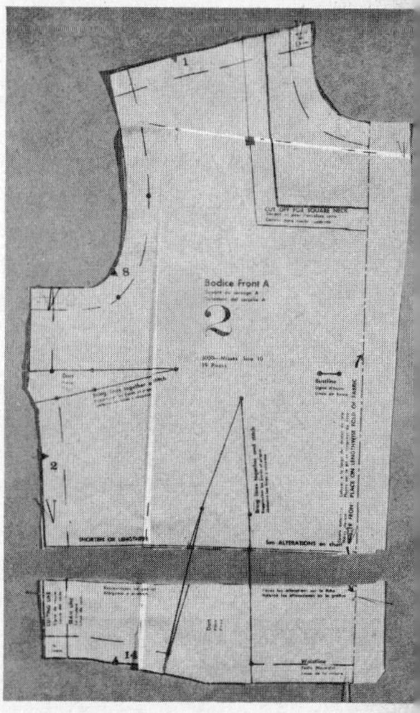

← 9 The back pattern piece was altered like the fitted muslin. It was slashed under the neck and opened for the round shoulders. She broadened the shoulders only by slashing from under the arm up to the shoulder and spread this whole section. The back shoulder dart was made wider. The pattern was cut from the jog at the underarm, tapering to nothing at the waist. She lengthened the waistline by cutting across the pattern and spreading it the necessary amount.

→

10 The front pattern was also altered like the fitted muslin. A dart was fitted out under the front neck for the flat-chested figure. She fitted a dart from the waistline to the side of the armhole to narrow for the small bust and waistline in front. The pattern was then slashed across the front to give added length at the waist.

How to fit the half-size figure type

This woman measures 40 in bust size, but is short and stocky, and needs a half-size pattern. She made her muslin in size 16½ which has a 37-inch bust. The smaller size fit better at the armhole, and was easily adjusted.

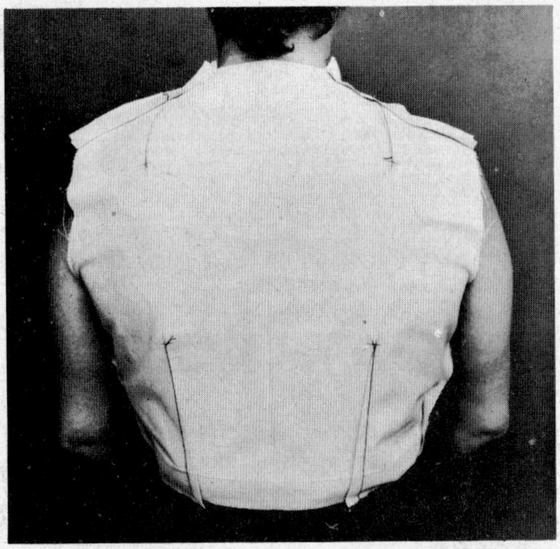

1 The back of the muslin was too narrow through the shoulders. The waist length, however, was right for this half-size figure.

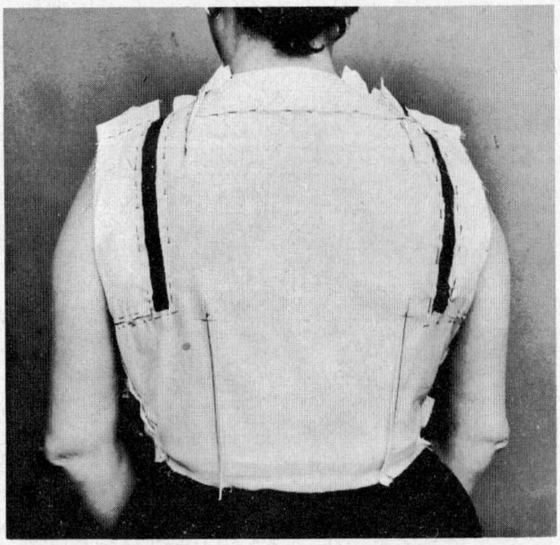

2 She widened the back shoulders by slashing under the arm and up to the shoulder. She spread the pattern enough to give a good fit when she pulled her arms forward.

3 The shoulder dart was made deeper to fit round shoulders, and to narrow the shoulders at the top of the muslin.

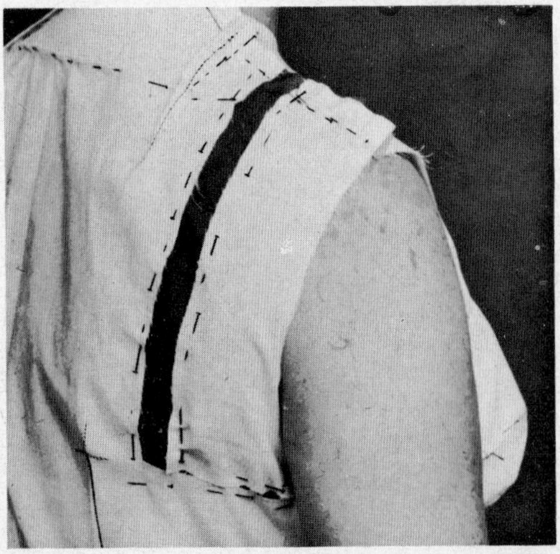

4 The front muslin was too broad through the shoulders and too short in the waist length. The bust needed more cupping for a good fit, and to eliminate folds under arms.

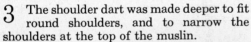

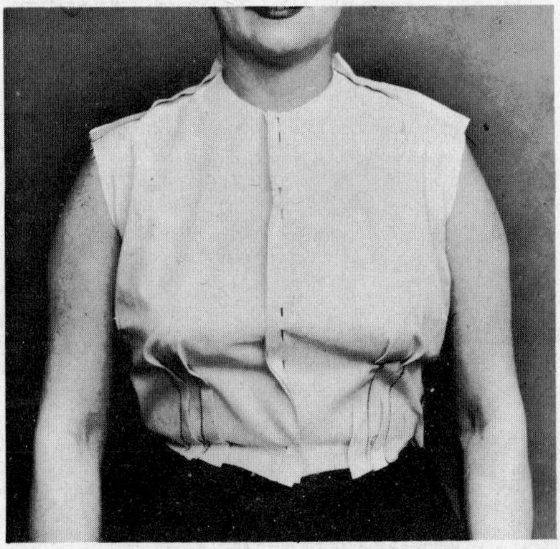

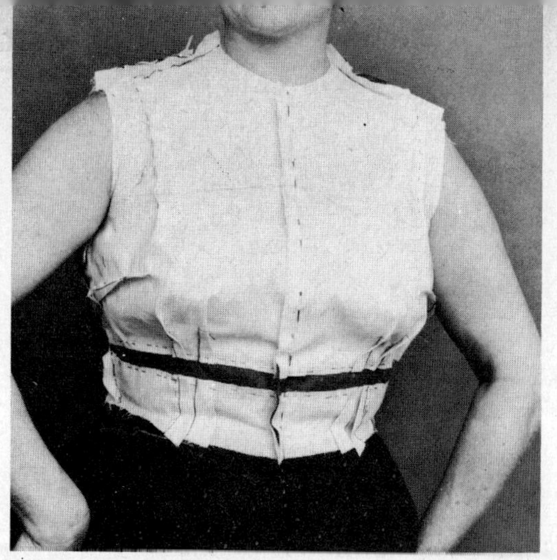

5 She narrowed the front with a dart from the shoulder toward the bustline, and fitted a deeper dart under the arm. The waistline was lengthened only in the front.

6 The profile view of the muslin shows a poor fit, although muslin did fit around the figure and the armhole size was good.

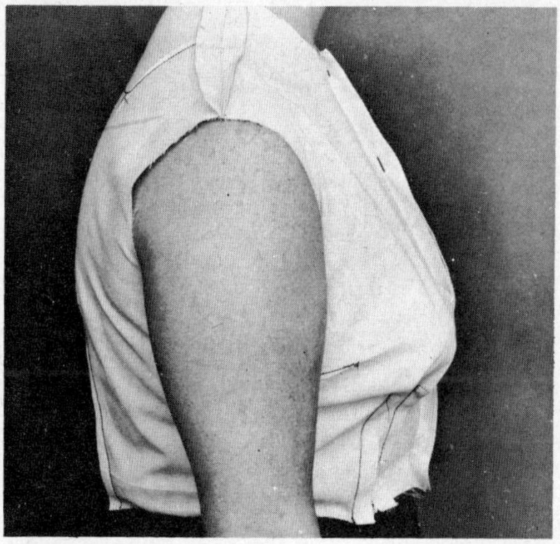

7 This profile view shows how a dress molds the figure when properly fitted, and it makes this type of figure look much taller, slimmer and more youthful.

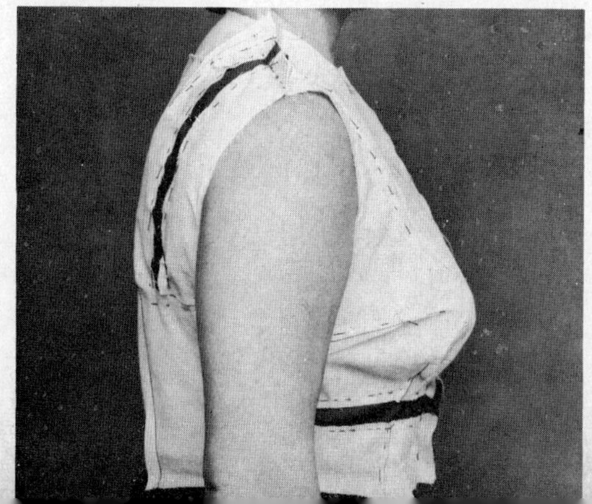

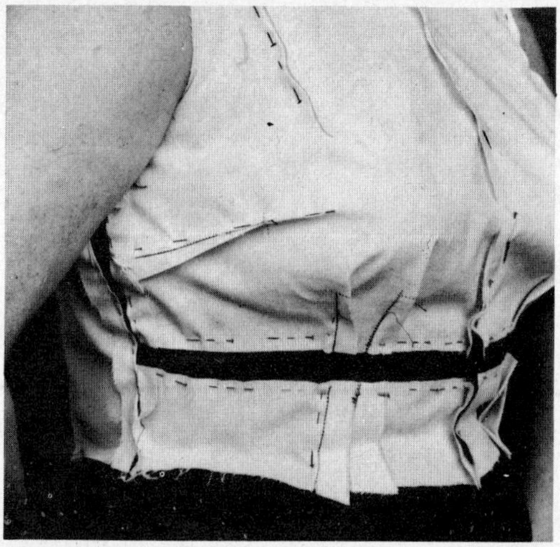

8 Broadening the back shoulders results in an increase in the size of the upper back, and also extends the underarm seam in the back muslin pattern. This gives more fullness to the bust, as shown above, and maintains the proper underarm fit.

9 *The back pattern* (right) needed few alterations because the half-size pattern was well proportioned for this figure. The back shoulders were made broader by slashing the pattern from the underarm up through the shoulder. The shoulder was spread the same amount as on the muslin. The back shoulder dart was only marked deeper, ready to be sewed. *The front pattern* (left) needed narrowing through the shoulder. This was done by folding a tuck the same depth from shoulder to armhole, and then smoothing it to nothing toward the bust. She marked the bust dart deeper as pinned on the muslin. The front waist was lengthened by slashing through the pattern and opening the same amount as on the muslin. The waistline darts were high, so were marked to be stitched lower. These released darts are more flattering for the low-busted type of figure.

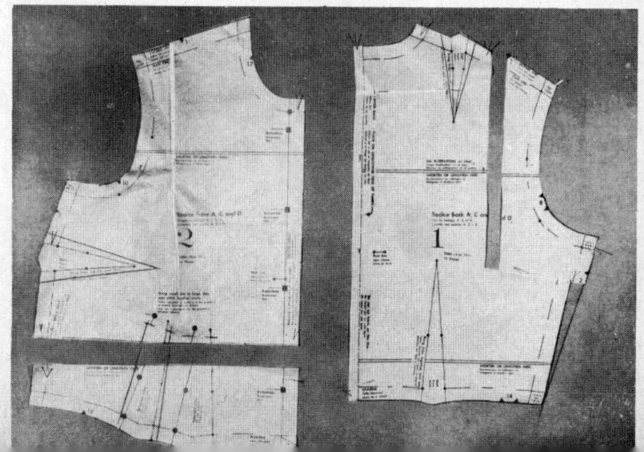

Adjusting a muslin for the large bust

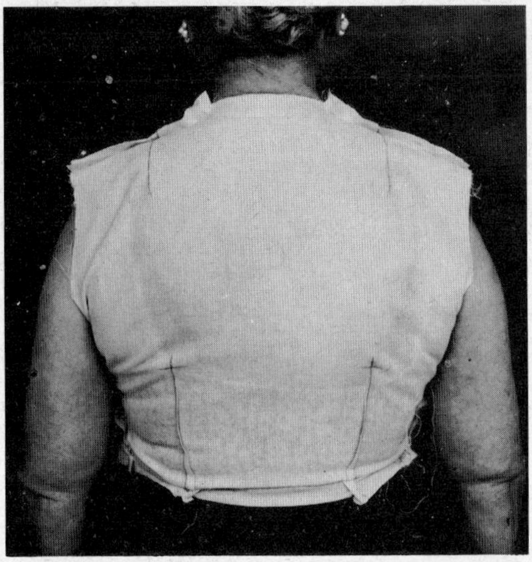

1 She checked the back first. The waist was too long, the top shoulder was too wide, but the rest of the back was too narrow.

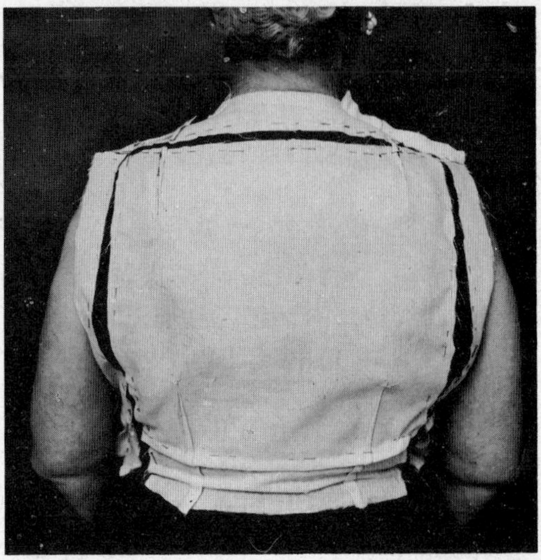

2 She shortened the waistline an even amount across the back. This shortened the center back waist which showed an adjustment was needed for round shoulders. She slashed the muslin from waist to shoulder to increase the waist size and add width across shoulder blades where it was needed.

3 A deeper shoulder dart narrowed the top of the shoulder and gave a better fit to the round shoulders. This also made the back armhole fit snugly. By slashing and opening the upper back under the neck, she made the center back waist longer and added to the fit of the back shoulders.

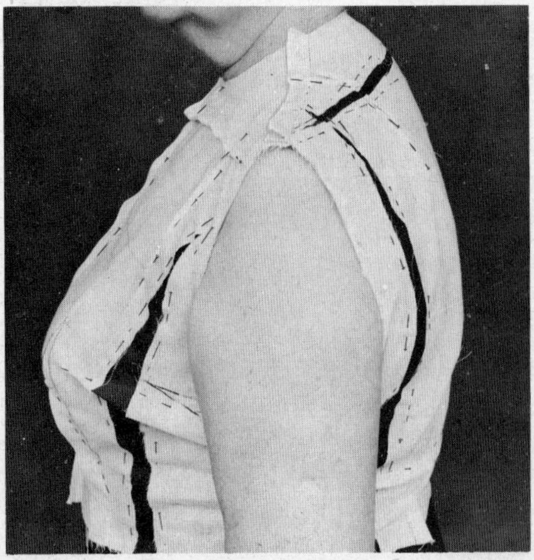

4 The adjustments were made in the pattern at the same points and for the same amount. The waistline was shortened with a tuck. The pattern was slashed from waist to shoulder to increase waist size, and across under the neck to add length at center back. Shoulder dart was marked to be sewed deeper.

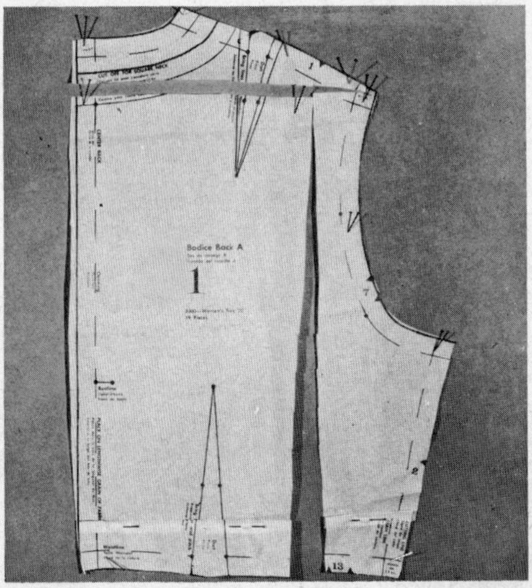

Although this figure measured three inches larger in the bust, she made her basic muslin in a size 40 which gave a better fitting armhole.

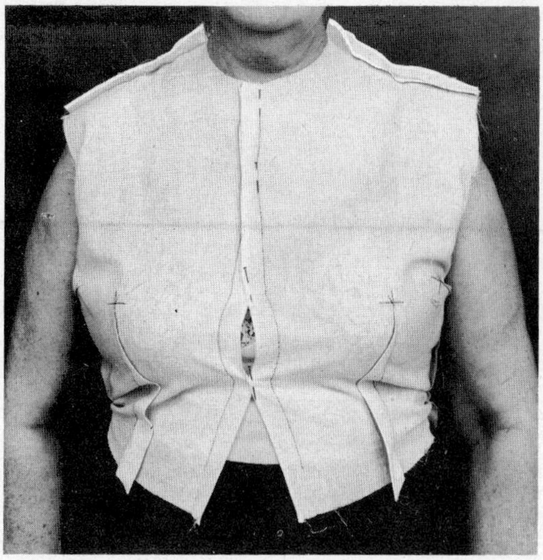

5 Next, she checked the front of the muslin. The waistline was too long, and the shoulders were also too broad. The front of the muslin did not meet, indicating that the waistline needed to be enlarged to correctly fit this figure type.

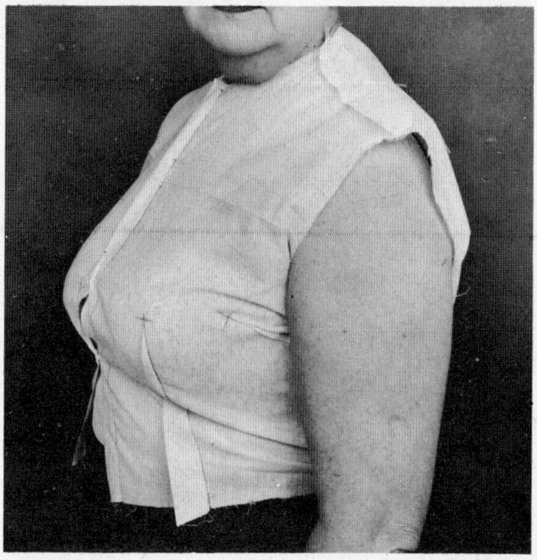

6 Checking the side front of the muslin showed that the side dart was too high and not deep enough to give proper cupping to the bust. The waist darts were too long, and extended up over the bust, making the bustline of the muslin appear too tight.

7 The bust dart was ripped out, and pinned lower and deeper. The waist dart was ripped out and made shorter, giving needed fullness at the bust. The waistline needed enlarging in the front, so the muslin was slashed to the armhole and spread.

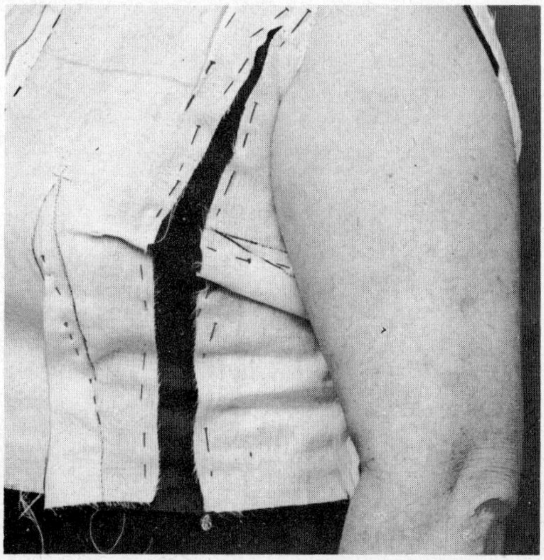

8 The deeper side dart eliminated most of the waist length, and the rest was taken up in a dart across the pattern under the neck. She made the shoulders narrower with a tuck taken from the top of the shoulder down toward the bustline.

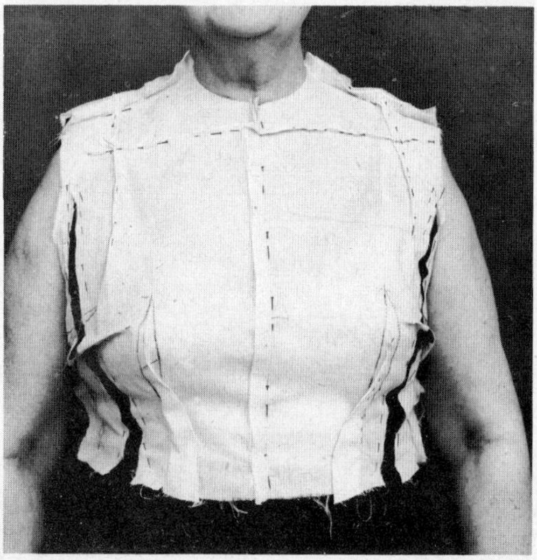

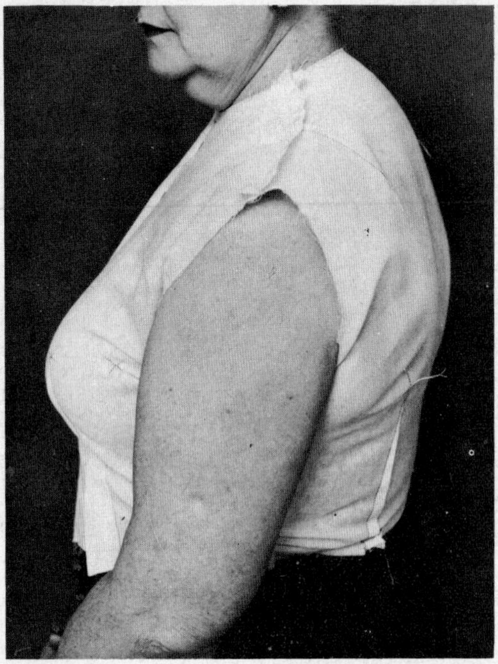

9 This profile of the unfitted muslin shows how bust seemed to sag, figure slump.

10 Notice how the correctly fitted muslin seems to take off years and pounds.

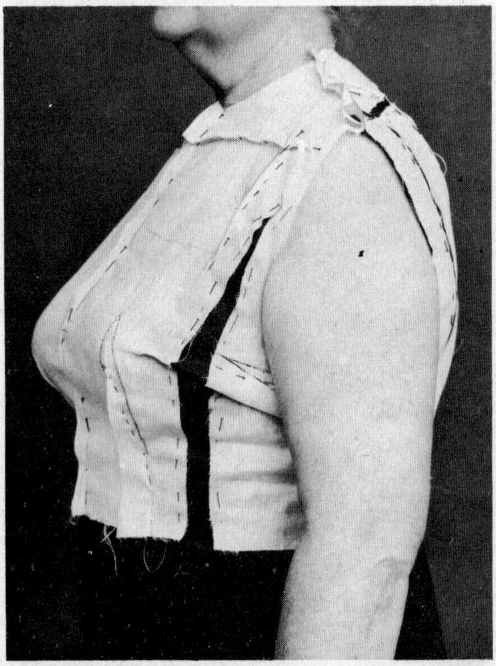

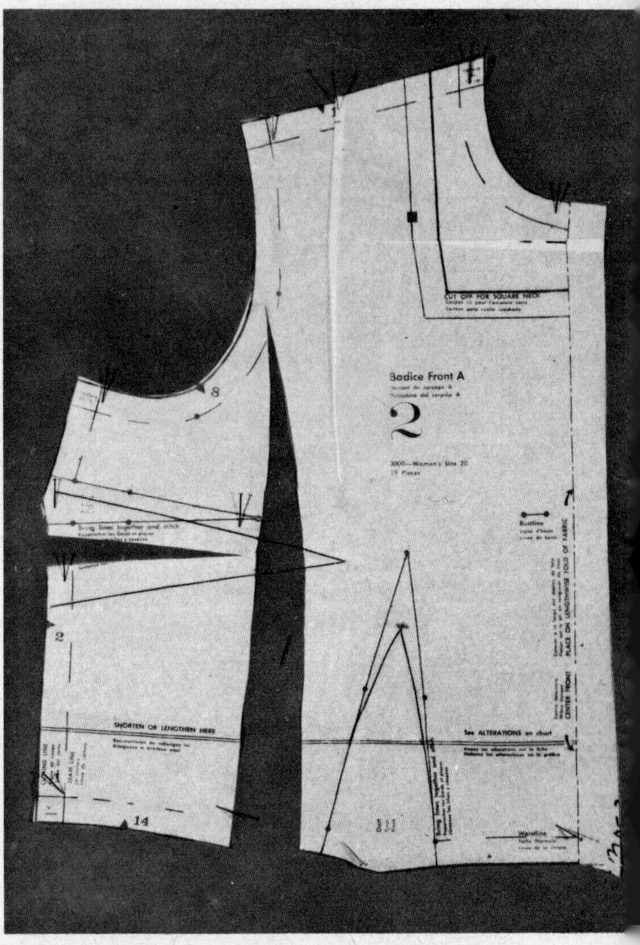

11 The front pattern was easily adjusted in spite of what might appear to be rather complicated fittings.

She narrowed the shoulder from the top toward the bust with a tuck the same depth down to the armhole notch, where it tapers to nothing toward the bust.

She then re-marked the waist dart and made it lower to give a better fit.

The bust dart was made lower and deeper and marked on the pattern.

Next, she shortened the center waist length the same amount and in the same place as she did on the muslin.

The waist size was increased as on the muslin by slashing the pattern toward the armhole and spreading it the necessary amount to make it fit correctly.

Chapter 4

Cutting your dress

During a question-and-answer period at a sewing clinic, a woman in the audience asked this question:

"I can sew beautifully; my fitting is excellent; the finished dress looks as good as that of any professional—but how do I get up enough courage to cut the fabric!"

If this is the reaction of a fairly experienced sewer, it isn't hard to imagine how a beginner must feel when she is ready to cut her dress. Once there may have been a real reason for this fear—when a sewer couldn't be sure whether her dress was really going to fit, and was afraid of ruining several yards of fabric.

With today's professional ways of altering a pattern and fitting the dress before it is even cut out, there is no reason to be concerned about the fit of the finished dress.

Before you begin cutting, here are some things you'll want to know.

First, buy your pattern in the same size as your alteration muslin.

Choose the style or view you are going to make and check the amount of yardage you will need. The amount will depend on the width of the fabric, the view, and whether the fabric you have selected has a nap.

Remove from the pattern envelope only the pattern pieces you will need for the style you are going to make. Put all others back in the envelope to avoid cutting unnecessary pieces.

With a new pattern, you can smooth out the wrinkles by hand. Pattern pieces only need to be pressed when you are re-using an old pattern that has been carelessly folded. Fold pattern pieces carefully as you put them away. Practice neat sewing habits as you go, and you'll find you save work.

Next, check your fitted muslin against the pattern pieces, and make the pattern alterations. Fit your dress before a piece is cut or sewed.

Don't fit pattern pieces over the muslin. Measure and transfer the muslin alterations to the dress pattern.

Know these pattern markings

All commercial patterns are now printed, which makes them easy to use. Take time to read thoroughly all the information printed on the pattern piece itself and you can't go far wrong in making up the dress.

If this is your first experience with a printed pattern, here are some of the pattern markings you'll want to become familiar with.

Margins

First, you'll notice that all patterns have an extra margin that extends beyond the actual cutting line of the pattern itself. This is a safety margin to insure that you always get the correct size. When patterns are printed, they are piled up many ply deep and cut with a knife around each piece. If the patterns were trimmed along the actual cutting line, you could never be sure of an accurate size. There is a natural shifting of the thin paper, no matter how carefully it is cut, and some of the actual pattern could be cut away. By cutting well outside the actual cutting line, the cutters leave a margin of safety on the pattern.

Cutting line

It isn't necessary to cut off this margin before you cut your dress. When you lay out your pattern pieces, lap the margin so that the cutting lines come together. When you cut your dress, cut along the actual cutting line and the margin will drop away. This extra margin is an advantage, because the fabric will shift less when it is cut through the paper.

Many alterations can be marked on the pattern margin in red pencil. This saves time and also gives you a permanent record of adjustments made.

Seam allowance line

Inside the cutting line, there is a broken line printed all around the pattern. This is the seam allowance line which shows you where to sew the pieces together. There is a 5/8-inch seam on all patterns unless a design detail calls for a wider or narrower seam, in which case the pattern will be marked. Follow the correct seam line. Professionals adhere to this line exactly. You will see how important this is when you learn professional short cuts in sewing.

Fold line

Some pattern pieces may show a lighter line, or a single line on one side. Printed along this line will be directions such as "Center front or back, place on fold," or just "Place on fold." This means that it is just half a piece and is to be cut all in one—like a back or front waist. Usually the piece is cut on the lengthwise fold of goods or parallel to the selvage, unless the pattern specifies otherwise.

Grain line

Every pattern piece has an arrow or a heavy line to indicate the grain line. Place the arrow so that it is on the straight thread of the fabric. It is important to follow the grain line because many times it is used to give a special hang to a skirt or some other

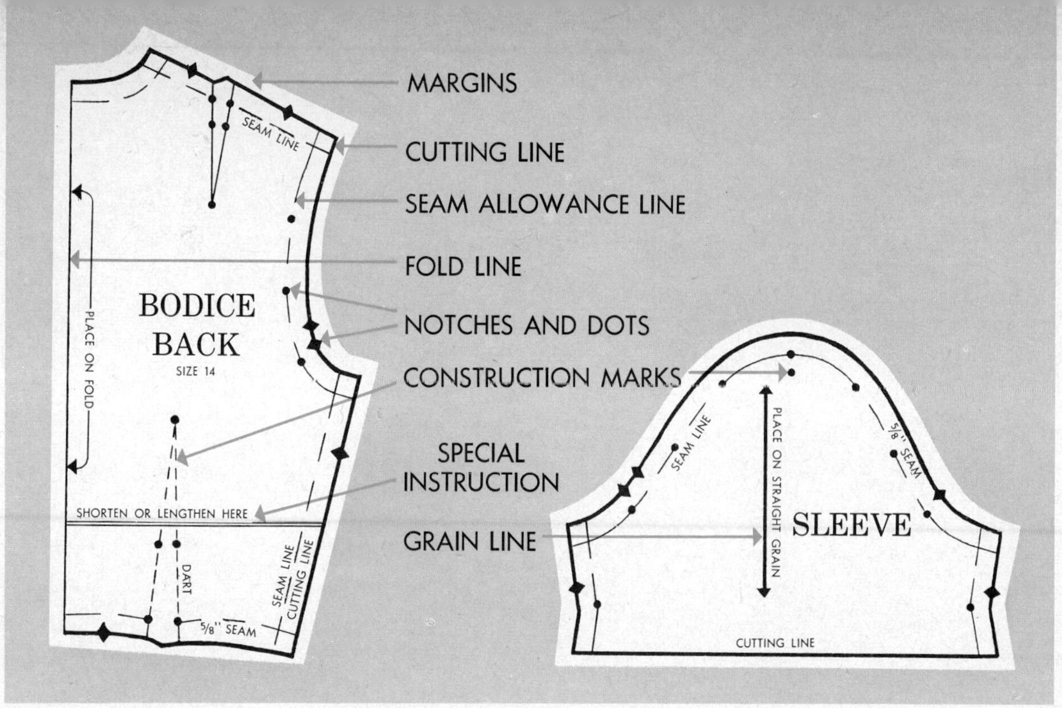

part of a garment. The entire style or hang of the garment can be spoiled if the grain line is ignored. Along this mark you'll find printed "Cut on lengthwise of goods"—the up-and-down grain, or parallel to the selvage.

If the piece can be cut on the cross-grain as well without spoiling the style of the dress, the pattern instructions will say "Cut on lengthwise or crosswise of goods."

Collars, cuffs, yokes, pockets and other trimming details can usually be cut on either grain unless the pattern instructs otherwise. This is especially true with striped fabrics, since the use of the stripe on the cross-grain can serve as a trimming on the garment.

On fabrics like satin, or napped fabrics, a difference in shade occurs if the pieces are cut on a different grain. On fabrics such as these, cut all pieces on the same grain, regardless of your pattern instruction.

Construction marks

Tucks, darts, pleats, buttonholes, center front or back lines, placement for pockets or trimming details are all printed on your pattern.

Notches and dots

Also carefully note the notches—triangular markings along the seam-line edge of your pattern. They are numbered to help you correctly match and assemble the pattern.

Dot markings on a pattern indicate special points where a seam is matched to another to give proper ease. For example, at the top of the sleeve there is a dot to indicate where it joins the shoulder seam of the garment.

Special instructions

Any additional marks will be explained by special instructions on your pattern. You'll find lines which will show you where shirring is to be used, or where alterations should be made. Any special sewing instructions you'll need are also included.

After you have adjusted the pattern and become familiar with the pattern markings, you are ready to concentrate on the fabric for your garment.

Follow the grain line carefully as you lay out your pattern.

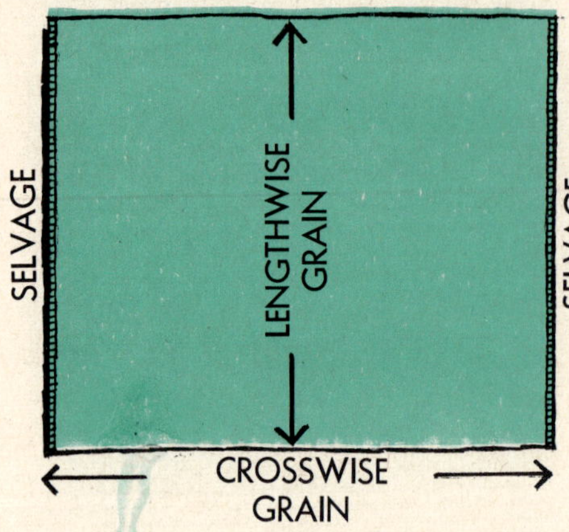

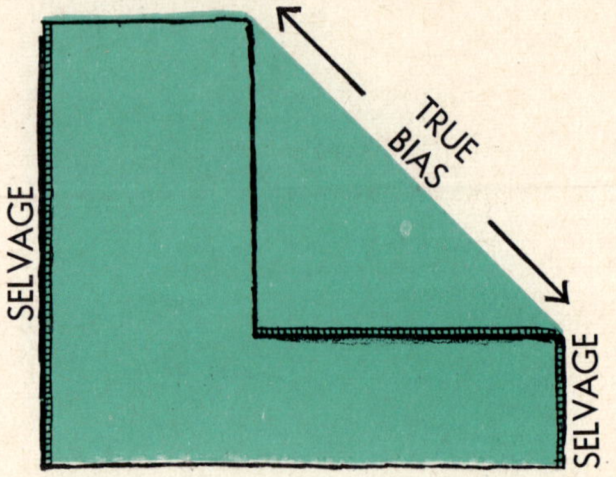

"Grain" refers to the lengthwise and crosswise threads in your fabric; lengthwise grain runs parallel to the selvage, and crosswise grain runs from selvage to selvage. Follow the grain line in cutting your fabric because it affects the hang of the garment.

You can find the true bias of your fabric by folding back a corner, with a crosswise thread parallel to the selvage or a lengthwise thread. The diagonal line formed is the true bias. A bias edge has the greatest stretch, ravels less than any other cut edge.

Selecting your fabric

If you are going to make your own clothes, buy good fabrics. Much work goes into each garment, so make it worthwhile by using quality fabrics. And it's much easier to sew on good material. You won't have to learn to control the fabric at the same time you are learning to master the steps in sewing. You'll also have an added incentive to do a good job, when you have a little more money invested in your fabric.

The fabric industry has seen drastic advances and changes in the last ten years. The development of the man-made fibers alone has been so rapid that it is almost impossible to keep up with new types on the market. Many of them are a blending of several fibers to create a new type of fabric. Some of the new synthetics are blended with natural fibers to give new characteristics to these old favorites. New finishes also have been developed that give special properties to both man-made and natural fibers. There are finishes that make fabrics faster-drying, increase washability, make them crease-resistant, soil- and stain-resistant, and generally make fabrics easier to care for and more long-wearing.

The important thing is that the advancement in fabric development has also brought a change in home sewing techniques. The old methods of preparing fabrics for cutting can be discarded! Modern fabrics are easier to use and give better wear.

Preparing fabrics for cutting

Woolens

In the past all woolens had to be sponged or shrunk before they could be cut. Now this is almost never necessary. Many woolen manufacturers have a special department to handle the production of "over-the-counter" fabrics—those made especially for the home sewing trade.

Better woolens are all preshrunk before they are sold. Most manufacturers print either on the wrong side or along the selvage that the fabric is sponged, ready to cut.

Be sure to check carefully, however, when you buy fabric on sale. Although these sale fabrics may be from top fabric manufacturers, in many cases they are left over from the ready-to-wear trade. Fabrics sold for ready-to-wear manufacture are not sponged by the fabric-makers as they are for the home sewing trade. Therefore, it's a good idea to check with a salesperson in the store, or test a piece of the fabric yourself at home to make sure it is preshrunk.

If you should get a piece that hasn't been sponged, it is easy to have it done. Many stores offer this service to their piece goods customers for a few cents extra per yard. Or, take the fabric to your dry cleaner who will put it through the press for a small fee.

Wool crepe should never be sponged. Some manufacturers guarantee their fabrics against shrinkage, and label them accordingly. If a woman should then treat the fabric in any way before cutting, the guarantee is void.

Before you cut your fabric, be sure it is on-grain. To get the straight grain, clip the selvage at the end and tear across the fabric. If it won't tear, pull a thread and cut along this line. Remember that the proper preparation of the fabric is vital in sewing.

Cut or tear fabric to check grain.

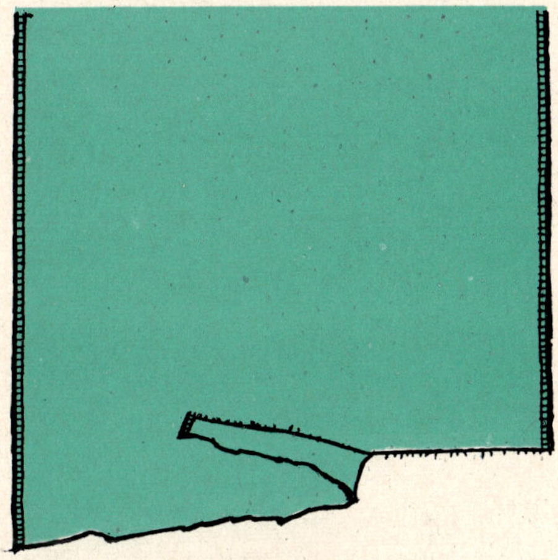

Tearing

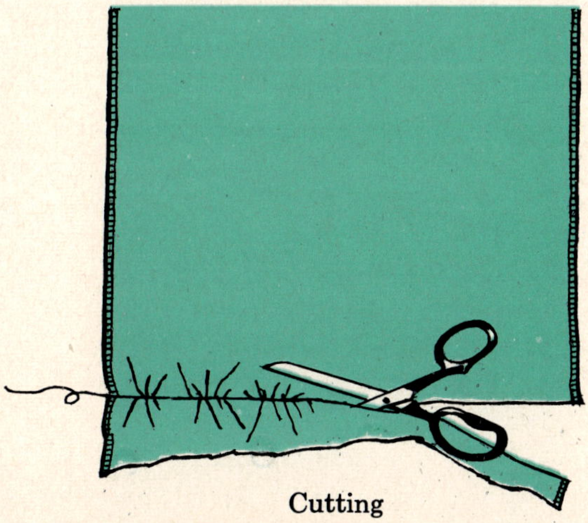

Cutting

Now lay it flat on the table and see if the ends are even. If one end looks shorter than the other, it has been stretched off-grain in finishing.

Be sure fabric is on-grain.

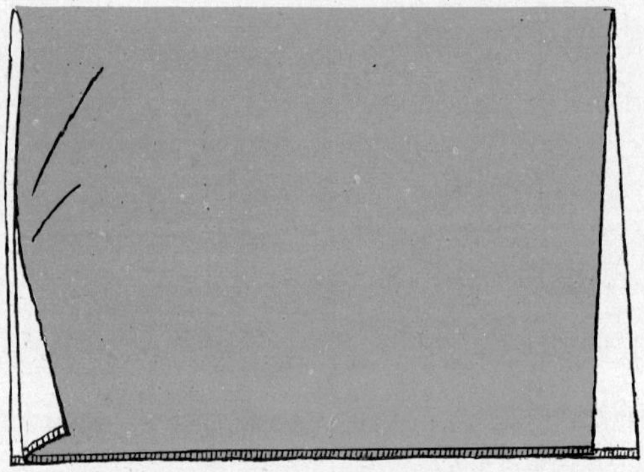

Point this out to your dry cleaner and he can stretch the fabric back in shape as he steams it.

If you prefer to do it yourself, the fabric can only be straightened when damp. A steam iron will straighten it if it is only slightly off-grain. If it must be straightened quite a lot, however, you will have to treat it as was formerly done to shrink wool.

Wet a sheet and wring it out. Put half the sheet lengthwise on a flat surface, and place half the lengthwise fold of wool on this. Fold the other half of the sheet over the wool and fold the remainder of the wool on top of the sheet. Roll it carefully with the sheet on the outside.

Let it stand for several hours, or until the moisture has penetrated the fabric. Unfold, smooth and stretch the fabric into shape or on-grain.

Let it dry, press lightly with the steam iron, and it is ready to cut.

Treat woolens as for shrinking to straighten the grain.

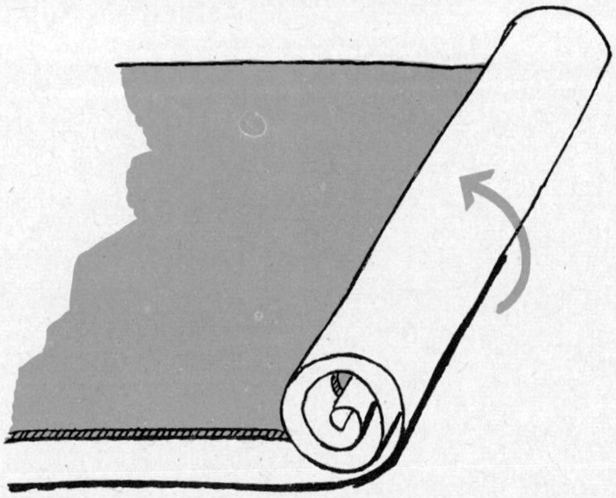

Smooth fabric and stretch lightly to straighten the grain.

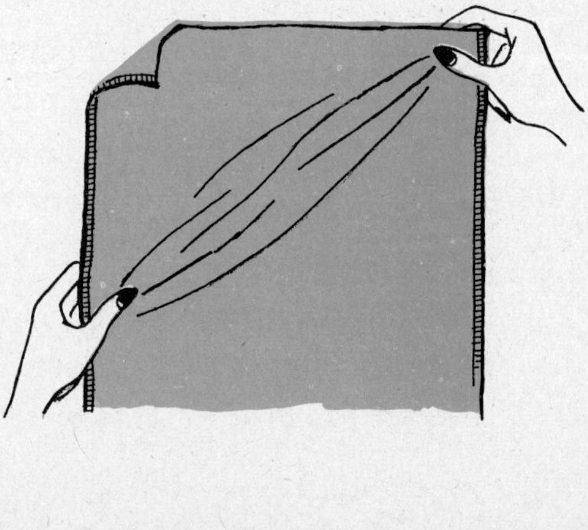

Linen

Although linens are often treated for crease-resistance, this finish does not necessarily control shrinking. It is always better to shrink linen before you cut it. This can be done by using a steam iron, or by pressing with a damp cloth.

To be sure the grain is straight, pull a thread across the end and cut on this line. *Linens can't be torn.* Linens never have to be stretched into shape after cutting. The texture is such that they can be straightened by smoothing the fabric with your hands.

Cotton

All cottons once had to be shrunk before they could be cut. Now, although there are countless different finishes used on cottons, no matter what the finish, shrinking is no longer necessary before making a garment.

As with woolens, most cottons you buy are processed especially for the home sewer, so there is no need to worry about shrinkage in quality cottons. The only exceptions are inexpensive fabrics, or special sale goods.

Before cutting cotton, it is important to check the grain line. Tear across the end of the fabric to see if it is straight. It is better, of course, to cut on-grain, but if you like a certain print, and find that it has been stretched off-grain in the finishing, it is still possible for you to use it. Most cottons have what is called a resin finish, which won't wash out or dry clean away. It would be useless to dampen these fabrics and try to stretch them into shape. As long as the print is not distorted by being off-grain, it is perfectly safe to cut your garment and sew it up without worry.

In the past when a dress was cut off-grain, it would lose its shape when it was washed or dry cleaned. When fabrics are treated with resin finishes, however, this cannot happen.

Shrinking cotton

If you should buy an inexpensive cotton or a special sale cotton, it is a good idea to check it to see if it has been preshrunk. These fabrics are often leftovers from a group of designer fabrics. They are not likely to be preshrunk, since they probably came from a ready-to-wear manufacturer and were not intended for over-the-counter sale. Also, many imported cottons are not preshrunk.

To test a cotton fabric to see if it is preshrunk, tear across the ends of the cotton to get the straight grain. Leave the cotton folded as it comes off the bolt. Roll it up, forming loose, easy folds. Fill a basin or tub with lukewarm water. Let the cotton soak until it is wet through. Don't wring it out; squeeze gently to remove as much water as possible.

Hang it over a shower bar or clothesline to dry. Smooth it with your hands as it is hanging.

If the fabric was off-grain, stretch it into shape when it is almost dry. If it is off-grain, it will show at the ends where the fabric is torn.

Iron it while it is still slightly damp. The ironing can be done while the fabric is still folded on the lengthwise fold. Iron first on one side and then on the other to give the fabric a smooth finish. Your cotton fabric is now ready for you to cut and sew up.

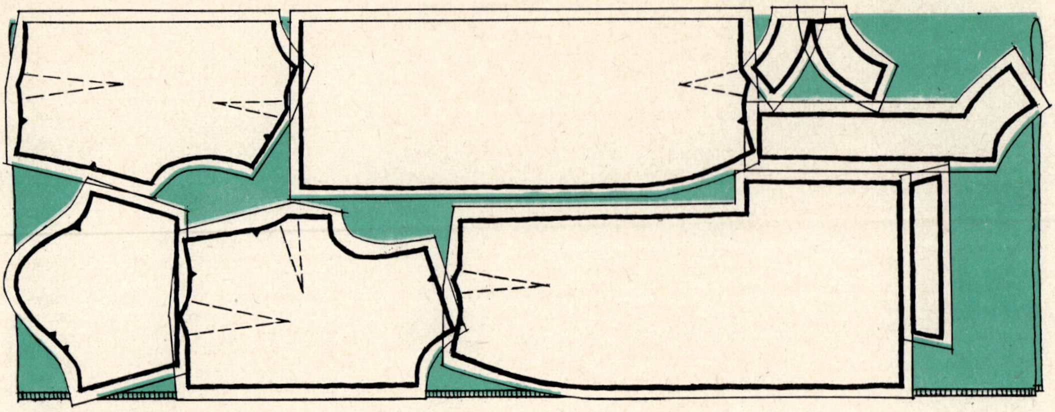

Lay out all your pattern pieces and pin them to the fabric before your start to cut.

Cutting

After you have altered the pattern according to your muslin, and the fabric has been straightened, you are ready to cut your dress.

In the pattern envelope, you'll find an instruction sheet covering all phases of cutting and sewing the dress. There is a layout guide for cutting the garment. It is planned by experts, according to the size of the pattern, the various styles that can be made, and the different widths of fabric that can be used. Check the layout that applies to your particular dress and fabric, and draw a circle around it.

Follow this layout carefully and you can't go wrong. Lay out all the pieces before you cut. If you have no table large enough to lay out all your fabric at once, pin as many pieces as possible. Then fold the material over and slide more fabric onto the table until all the pieces have been pinned. As you start to cut out your pattern, unroll the folded material as you work.

If you have been sewing for a long time, you have probably given up following the "cutting guide" and have developed a system of your own. There is no rule against this, so long as you are sure to lay out all the pattern pieces to make certain there is enough fabric before you cut.

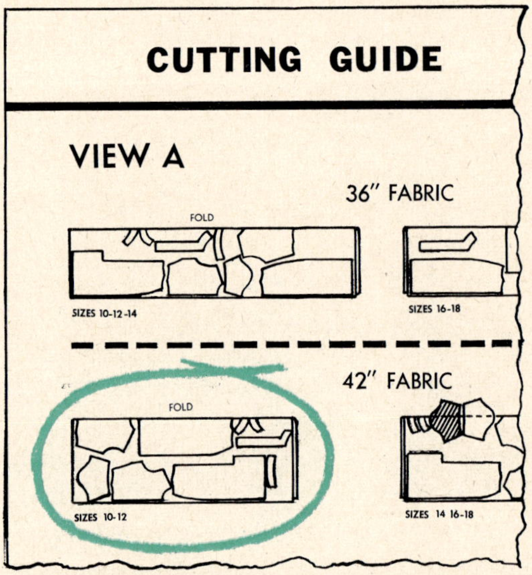

The pattern sheet has a layout guide for the view and width of fabric you are using.

Grain line

As you pin the pattern to the material, be sure all your pieces are on the straight of the goods. Do this by checking the line or arrow on the pattern that indicates the grain line.

This line should always run parallel to the selvage. To make sure it does, measure with a ruler from the selvage to each end of the line, making sure the pattern pieces are straight and correctly placed on your material.

Fold line

Remember that a single line along the edge of a pattern piece indicates that it is to go on the fold of goods. Place the single line on the fold, not on the margin edge.

Margins

The extra margins outside the cutting lines can be overlapped so that the cutting lines of the different pattern pieces almost meet. The cutting line is an accurate guide, so follow it exactly as shown.

Cutting shears

Use the long shears with the bent handle for cutting, and be sure to use long, even strokes. Never use your pinking shears to cut out a garment. They are hard to manipulate and are not accurate for shaping around darts, armholes, necklines, or other intricate details. Besides, this much cutting would soon make pinking shears dull and difficult to use.

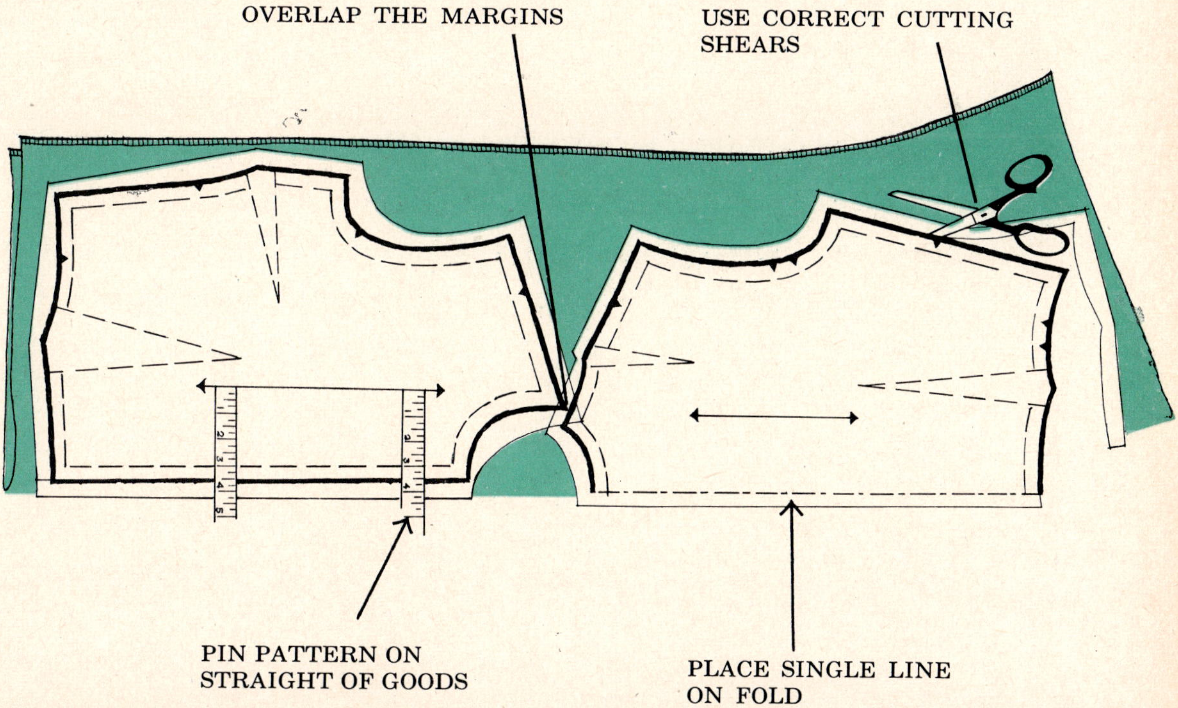
OVERLAP THE MARGINS
USE CORRECT CUTTING SHEARS
PIN PATTERN ON STRAIGHT OF GOODS
PLACE SINGLE LINE ON FOLD

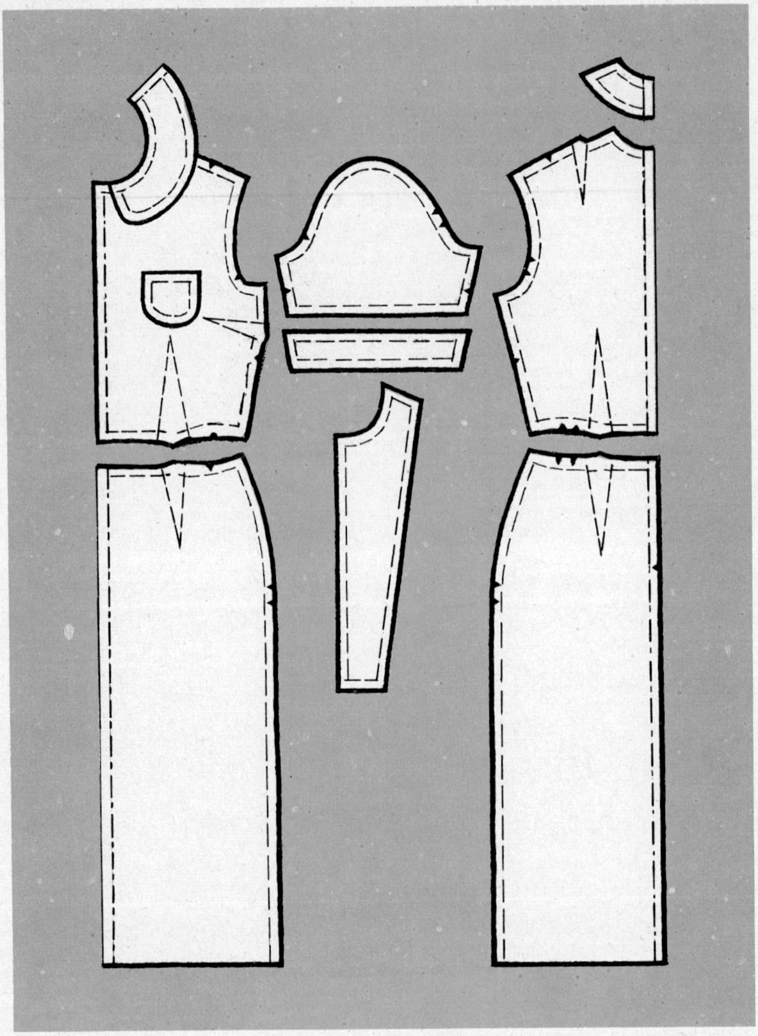

Lay out your dress for assembly

Lay out the cut-out pieces of your dress on the table so that you have a visual picture of how the assembled garment will look.

Now that you have finished cutting your garment, you may be wondering how to proceed. Here is a definite system to follow that will help you now and in all future sewing.

First, mentally picture the various parts of the garment you are making. Lay out all the pattern pieces as they will be sewed together. Start with the bodice. Lay the front and back on the table as they will be joined. If there is a collar piece, put it at the neck as it will be sewed. Next, find the facing pieces. Check to see where and how these will be used. If there is a pocket detail, place it where it will be sewed on the dress. Proceed the same way as you lay out the skirt pieces of your dress.

You will find that you have eliminated the confusion of unrelated pattern pieces and that you have a clear, visual picture of how the entire garment goes together.

Handling special fabrics

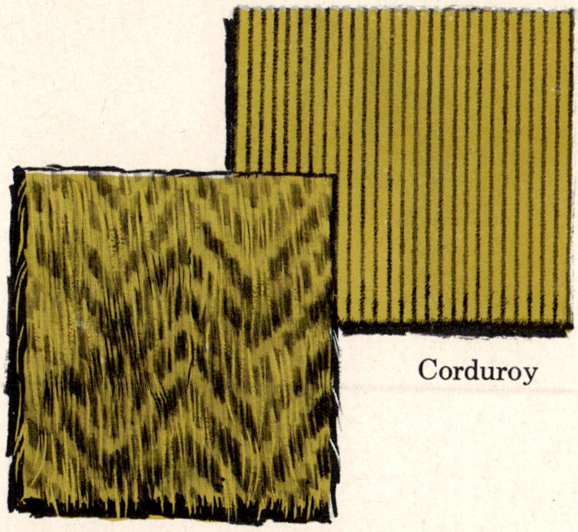

Wool Fleece

Corduroy

Some fabrics require special care in cutting. You are not likely to choose one of these for your first sewing attempt, but as you continue to sew, you may want to use one of them. It is a good idea to learn about these fabrics so you will have no fear of trying them. It is more fun to be able to make any style and use any fabric you want for greater variety in the finished results of your sewing efforts.

Nap fabrics

These fabrics have a definite surface texture, and must be cut in one direction to avoid shading.

Velvets, corduroys, and velveteens have a raised nap and must be cut with the nap running up toward the top of the dress. To find which way the nap runs, rub your hand along the surface of the material. If it ruffles up like an animal's fur, the nap runs up in that direction, and all pattern pieces must be cut that way.

If you make the mistake of cutting your pieces in both directions, the garment will appear to have been cut from different colors. When all pieces are cut with the nap running up, you get the full benefit of the rich color; it is called "looking into the nap."

Other nap fabrics such as panne velvet, wool broadcloth (or face-cloth as it is sometimes called), fleeces, textured woolens, camel's hair—in fact, all other types of nap or surface fabrics—are cut with the nap running down. Again, all pieces must be cut one way to avoid shading. These fabrics are cut with the nap running down so that the fabric will wear better, and will never look roughed up from sitting or moving.

Fabrics with a definite surface texture must be laid out and cut in one direction to avoid shading and to get the full benefit of the color.

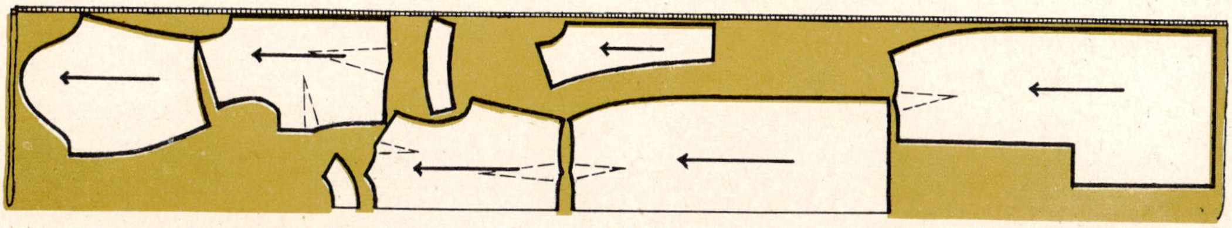

Cutting prints

One-directional prints

Some prints, plaids, stripes, and checks must be cut one way, just as a nap fabric is cut.

Always examine your print fabric to see how the motif is repeated. If there is a definite pattern, such as a sprig of flowers with the flower design all pointing the same way, then it is a one-directional print and must be cut like a nap fabric.

When purchasing any of these printed fabrics, consult your pattern guide for yardage and buy the amount required for nap fabric. You'll learn the correct way to cut plaids and stripes later in this chapter.

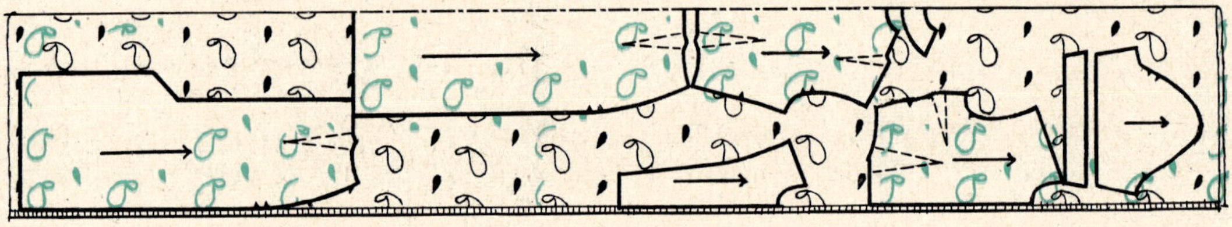

Allover prints

When the print you select has an allover effect with no definite design or direction, it can be cut and handled like a plain fabric.

Or, a print may have a definite design, but if it has been printed with the motif repeated in either direction, it can also be cut like a plain fabric.

Large scattered prints

It is no longer necessary to cut these prints so that the same large motif is in a corresponding place on the dress. Care must still be used in order not to get all the design on one side of the garment and none on the other. The preferred method of cutting these prints is called "spotting the print." This means that areas of color or motif balance each other on the dress, but are not matched exactly. This eliminates the waste of material which occurs when you try to match large prints on a garment.

Place the design so that it gives a pleasing effect of balance and color. Be careful not to place flowers in embarrassing places. This can happen easily and looks ludicrous.

For instance, cut a flowered pattern so there is a large flower at the shoulder on one side, and one just under the bust on the other side.

Also, watch the placement of design on a skirt. Try to avoid having the pattern all run around the skirt at the same level. On the side panels, place the design at hip level, but on the front panel move it down toward the hem. Use good judgment and taste in placing and cutting prints.

WRONG RIGHT

Use a method called "spotting the print" to balance color and motif as you cut prints.

Cutting stripes

There are four different types of stripes—length stripes, cross stripes and diagonal stripes; the fourth is the one-directional version of any of the other three types.

The direction of a stripe is determined by the varying widths or colors which are used in it, and by the sequence in which these stripes are arranged on the fabric.

Length stripes

The peppermint or candy stripe can be cut in either direction and with very little difficulty.

This stripe runs the length of the goods. When cutting a garment from this stripe, decide on the stripe to be used in the center skirt front and follow this stripe in cutting the waist and skirt pieces.

Aside from centering, there is little matching to be done.

If the skirt is gored, the seams must chevron. In other words, where the seams join, the stripes must come together to form a point.

To be sure that the seams chevron, check the notches where the skirt seams join. Make sure that the seams fall on the corresponding notches. When cutting to chevron, the point can be up or down.

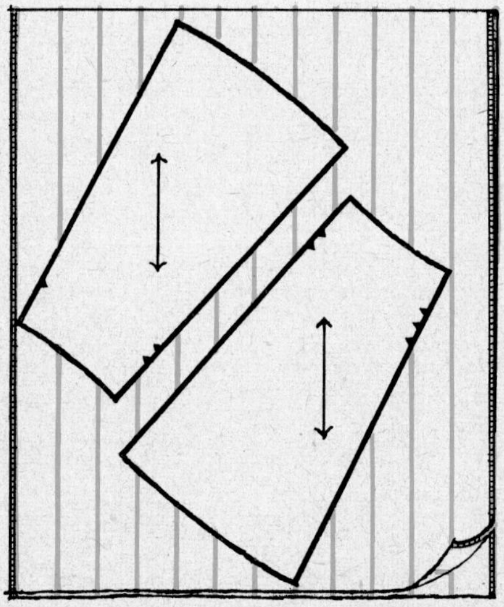

Length stripe　　Cross stripe　　Diagonal stripe　　One-directional

Cross stripes

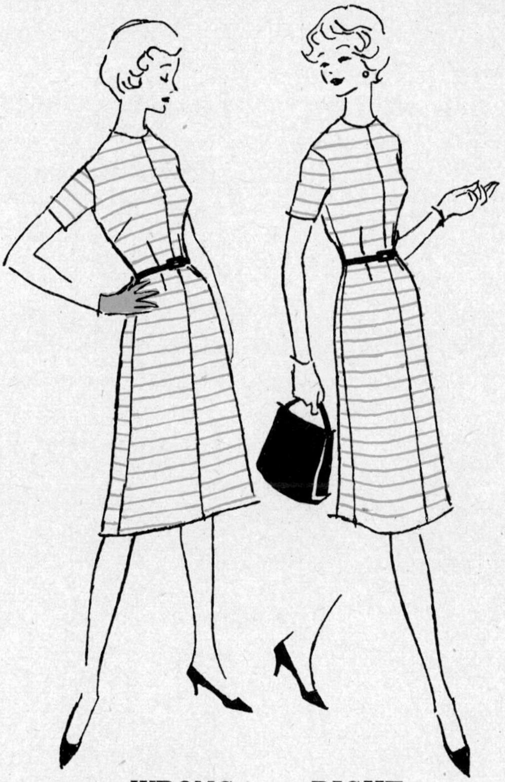

WRONG　　RIGHT

The places to watch when matching cross stripes are at the side seams, gores in the skirt, and armholes. The stripe must appear as one continuous line around the figure.

To match the side seam of the front and back waist, be sure that the notches are placed on a corresponding stripe of the fabric.

Also put the sleeve and armhole notches of the front and back waist pieces on a matching stripe when cutting. Lay skirt pieces so that matching notches are also on the same stripe.

In cutting a cross-grain stripe, pattern pieces can be cut in either direction and interlocked to save on the amount of fabric needed.

It is only when the cross stripe is one-directional that all of your pattern pieces should be cut in one direction to assure a matched look.

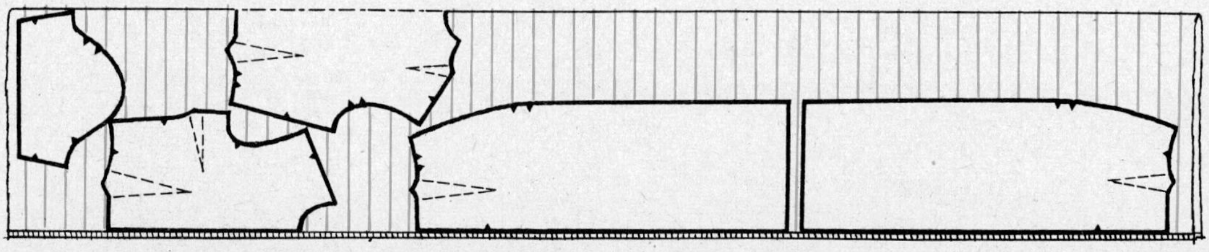

Diagonal stripes

Here's a stripe cut to chevron.

Diagonal stripes cannot be cut to give a chevron effect unless the fabric is reversible, or is cut with the cross-grain against the up-and-down grain.

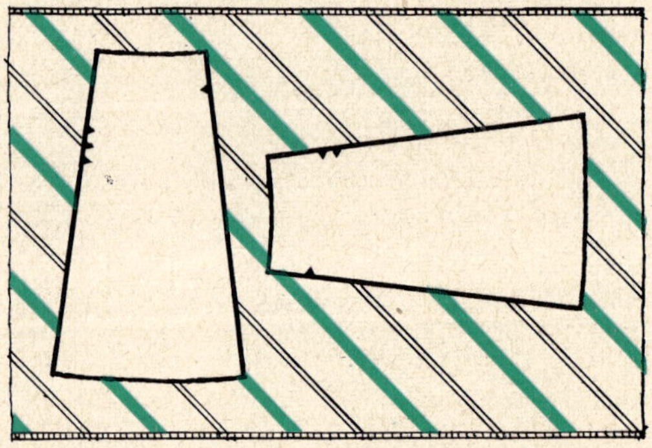

Cut pattern on diagonal stripe.

The diagonal stripe is always printed on the fabric. These stripes are not often made by manufacturers.

Usually a dress featuring a diagonal stripe is cut so the entire garment is on the diagonal, with no attempt made to chevron the stripes in it.

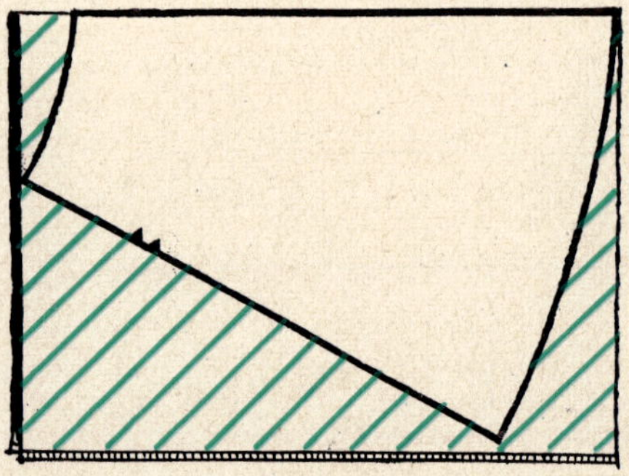

One-directional stripes

As explained in Chapter 2, a pattern manufacturer usually illustrates a pattern in a stripe or plaid if the design has been planned for this type of fabric. This means that the sweep of the skirt is the same on all pieces so that it can be chevroned. The style of the dress is simple and uncluttered so that matching is not difficult.

When working with a one-directional stripe, it is better to select a style of dress with a seam down the center back and front, or one that can be cut with such seams without spoiling the style of the dress.

It is sometimes difficult to tell whether a stripe is one-directional when the fabric has graduated widths of stripes and several colors in one piece of material.

An easy test is to fold the fabric lengthwise, and then turn back one side of the fabric across the end. If it is a balanced stripe, all the stripes on the upper fold will match the stripes on the under side. If they do not match, it is a one-directional stripe.

Balanced stripe

One-directional stripe

To match, such stripes must be folded on the cross-grain. The pieces cannot be cut on a lengthwise fold; thus the need for a pattern with seams in front and back or one that can be cut with such seams.

Choose pattern with front and back seams for these stripes.

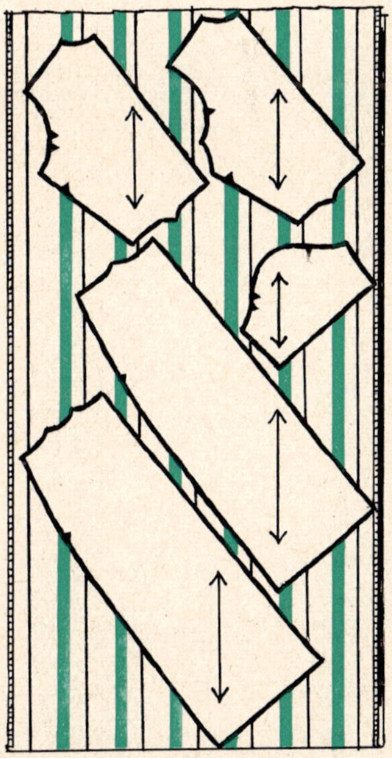

Cutting plaids

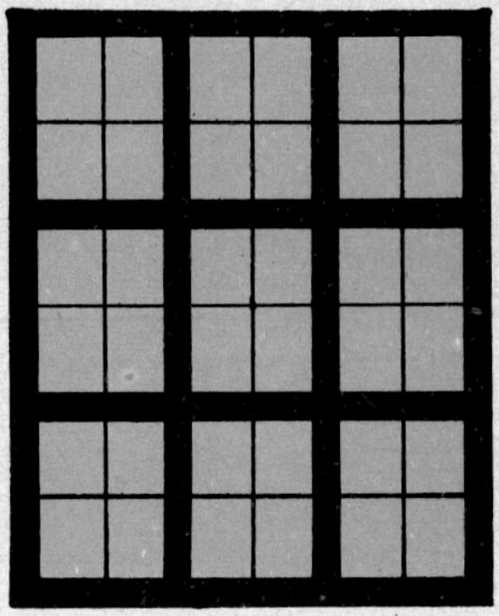

Balanced plaid

Balanced plaids

Even or balanced plaids are easiest to cut. They match on the crosswise or up-and-down plaid. It is sometimes hard to recognize a balanced plaid. To test, fold lengthwise and then turn back one side of the fabric at the end, as you do to test stripe. If identical plaids fall one on top of the other, the plaid is a balanced one on the cross-grain. Now fold the fabric on the cross-grain and turn back the top layer along the selvage. If the upper and under plaids match, it is a balanced plaid that can be cut in either direction.

WRONG

Chevroning a skirt

Cut skirt pieces so the center of the back and front are on the same plaid as the bodice pieces. If the skirt is flared, the seams should match around the skirt as well as up and down, to form a chevron. To match the seams, be sure the skirt notches are on the stripe around the skirt and on the same plaid running up and down.

RIGHT

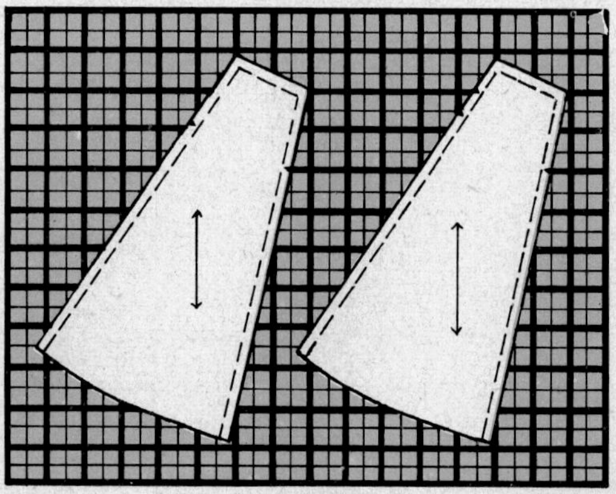

Cutting a dress

WRONG

RIGHT

When laying out your pattern on a plaid, *always start* with the front bodice. This is the focal point of your dress, so matching must begin here. Always place the center front line of the dress on the center of a plaid stripe. If you do not, the dress will look off-balance, and the plaid will look uneven, poorly matched.

Cut the center back on the same plaid, and the shoulder seams will also usually match. Match the side seams of the front and back bodice pieces by placing matching notches on the same plaid stripe.

Match the sleeves by lining up the front and back bodice notches and the front and back sleeve notches on matching plaid stripes.

If the front bodice has an underarm fitting dart, it is sometimes impossible to have the underarm seam match below this dart. It is far more important to match the top of the bodice so the sleeves can also be matched. Poor matching here is far more distracting to the eye than it is at the underarm seam of the dress.

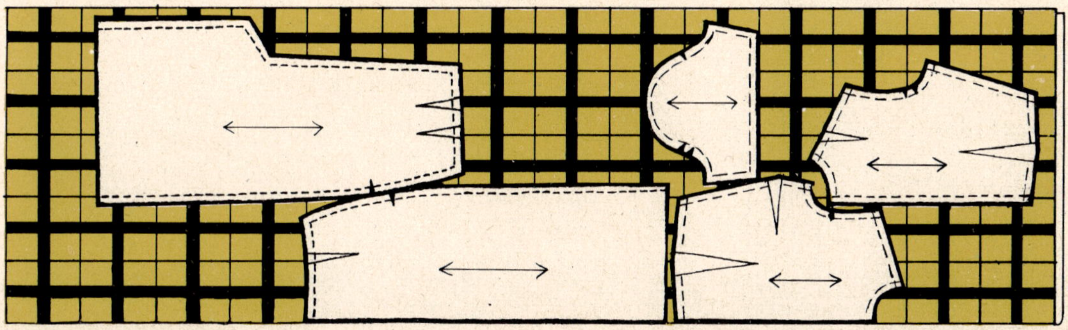

One-way, one-directional plaids

This term is not meant to confuse. A one-way, one-directional plaid is one that balances across, but not up and down. Or, it may balance up and down, but not across.

If it is one-directional across, but not up and down, fold the fabric on the cross-grain and cut all the pieces on the double to match them.

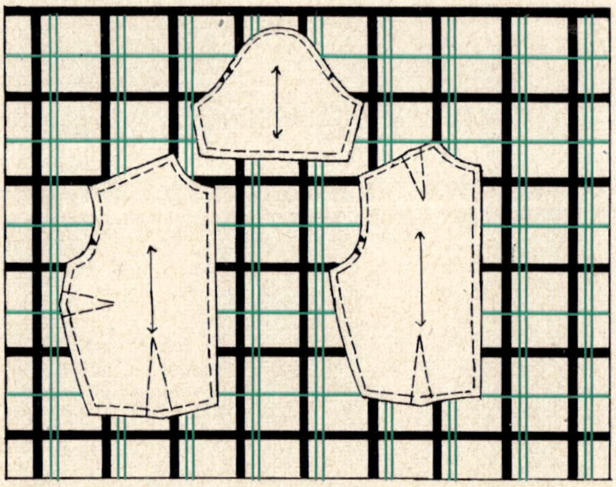

Choose a style that either opens, or has a seam, down the front or back. The bodice should be in two pieces if the plaid is to balance.

If the plaid is balanced across, but not up and down, cut all the pieces on the fold, but with all of them going in one direction, as you would when cutting a one-directional print.

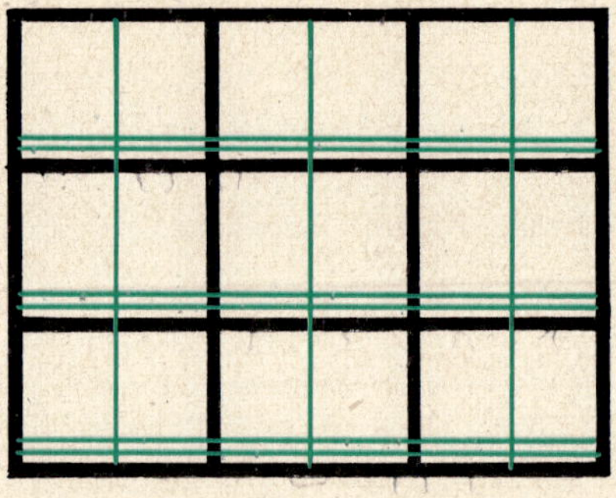

Tips on matching sleeves

Sleeveless dress

On a sleeveless or drop shoulder dress, it is better to match at the underarm seam, since there is no sleeve set in.

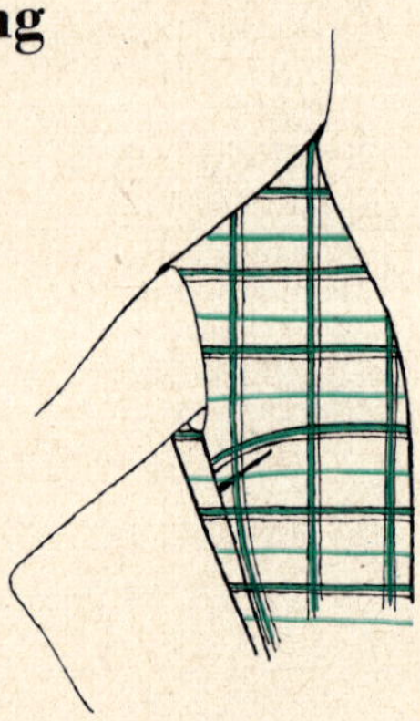

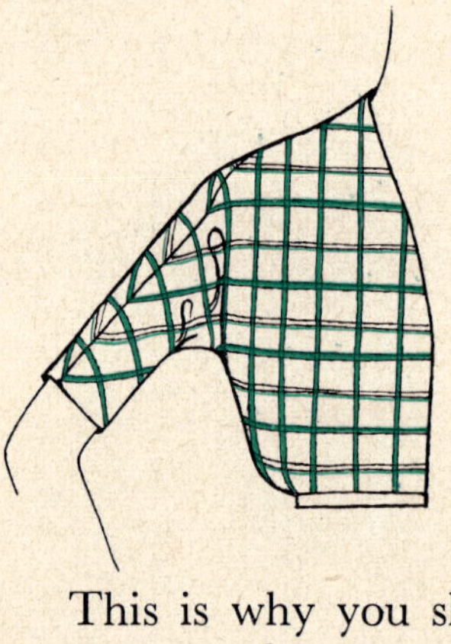

Kimono sleeve

When a dress has a long kimono sleeve, it is important that the shoulder seam chevron along top.

This is why you should check the pattern to be sure it is suitable to cut in plaid. Generally, the front shoulder in a pattern is cut on a greater angle than the back shoulder. In a plaid, this would mean that the shoulder seams would not match at any point. When a pattern is planned for plaid, however, the slope of the back and front shoulder are the same to assure that the seams will chevron.

One-directional, two-way plaids

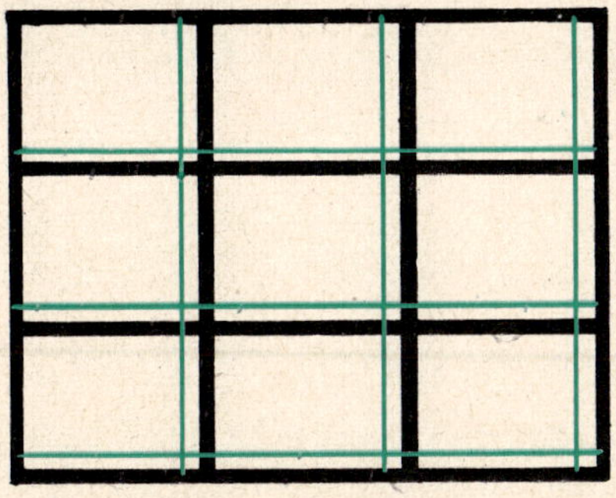

These plaids, admittedly, are complicated to cut unless the fabric can be cut on either side. Again, it is better to pick a style where none of the pieces are cut on a fold. It is best to cut out individually all the pieces that make up half of the dress. Then, reverse the fabric and cut the other half by matching to the original.

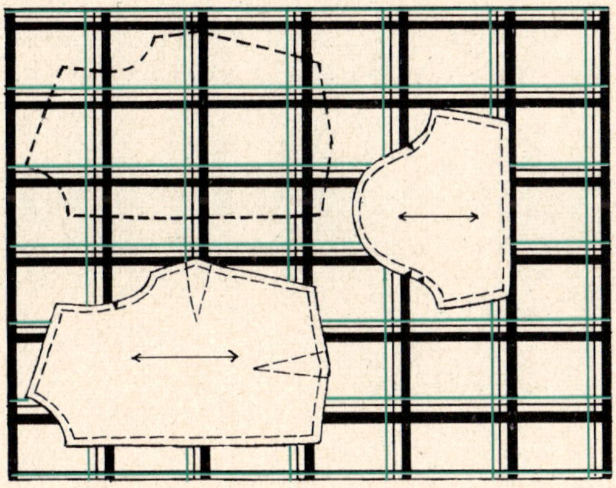

Bodice without center seam.

Follow all the rules for matching plaids. This type of plaid can also be cut so the plaid is continuous across the front of the garment in the same sequence as across the fabric design. However, it can only be done on the most simple type of dress where there is little piecing necessary.

Bodice with center seam.

Tricks in sewing plaids

There are many techniques in sewing and fitting that can make plaids look like what they're not.

Here is a trick for making up a plaid dress: Suppose you have a piece of black-and-blue plaid, and you want your dress to look predominantly dark. Cut the dress with the black stripe running down the center front and the dress will look primarily black, even though the fabric has equal amounts of black and blue.

If you want the dress to look predominantly blue, make the blue plaid stripe the center of your dress.

Blue stripe centered.

Black stripe centered.

Cutting tips

Plaids

Never cut a dress in plaid or check if the pattern specifically warns against it. Some styles should be avoided at all costs because they will not match. Princess-line dresses, as a rule, are too cut up to match. In fact, any style with too much detail is usually a bad choice for a plaid fabric. Yokes, pockets, collars and other trimming details can sometimes be cut on the bias, which eliminates the need to match and also gives a nice trimming effect.

No yardage is given on a pattern for cutting plaids, since it is impossible to know how large the "plaid repeat" will be. The safest rule is to allow the amount given for nap fabrics, plus two "repeats of plaid."

Checks

Any check that is ¼ inch or less in size does not have to be matched in cutting. On larger checks, follow the rules for cutting plaids.

Checks can also be one-directional. Watch carefully; a one-directional check is usually determined by the placement of color.

Jersey

Wool jersey comes in a tubular piece that is economical to cut since both sides are fold edges. It does not need to be sponged or shrunk before cutting, and it is treated to prevent stretching of the length so it is easy to work with and sew.

The fold edge of jersey is often stretched or twisted slightly in the finishing process. This is hard to straighten or press out. If used down the front or back of a dress, this line would be very conspicuous. When you have pieces to cut on the fold, be sure to refold the jersey so you are always cutting on a fresh fold of the cloth.

Some new jerseys have a nap, or are textured. To be safe, always cut jersey with all pieces going in one direction. Tricks in sewing jersey will be discussed in Chapter 8.

Heavy wools

Here's a tip that will help you cut heavy wools or fleeces. No matter how carefully you smooth out a wool fabric, there is a tendency for the pieces to stick together.

After you have finished cutting all your pattern pieces, unpin the pattern and shake out the cut pieces. Put them together again as they were and repin the pattern.

You will find, in many cases, that the under piece will be slightly larger than the upper piece. Recut them so that they are even, and you will be ready to sew up your dress.

Trimming details cut on the bias

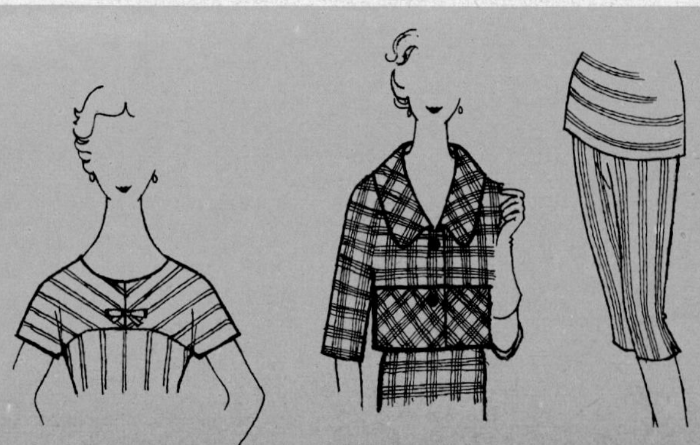

Chapter 5

Assembling the dress

Now the fun of sewing really begins as you start to put your dress together. Today you can learn to sew the fast, easy, professional way, but still retain the quality associated with custom dressmaking. New equipment, quality fabrics and accurate printed patterns all help to make sewing easier and more enjoyable. And your basic muslin almost eliminates fitting problems.

After you have arranged the pattern pieces, and have visualized how the garment goes together, it's time to mark and sew the cutout pieces. It is no longer necessary to tailor-tack or baste before sewing. If you are a beginner, and don't know what a "tailor-tack" is, simply forget the term. It was one of the most time-consuming of all the old methods, and was not particularly accurate.

Marking notches

Now you are going to learn to put your garment together so quickly that you won't need markings that must last for a long time. The new way to mark notches, for instance, is simply to slash from the center of the notch toward the point for about ¼ inch. This is enough of a mark to work from, and is fast to do. If you prefer to cut out on the notch as the pattern shows, do so, though it takes unnecessary time and material. Be sure to mark every notch. They are printed on the pattern to help you match pieces and join them correctly.

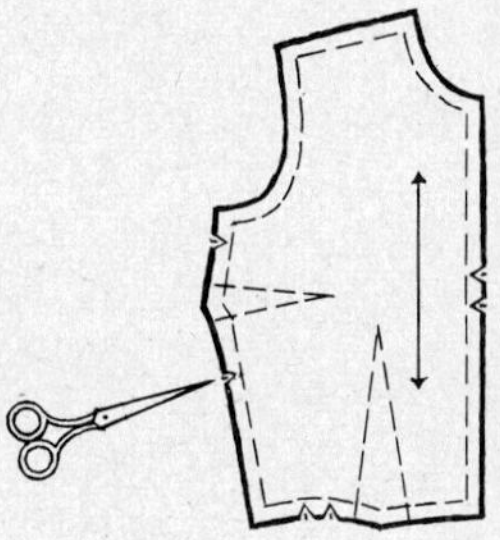

For example, a princess-line dress has notches above and below the bustline on the front and side front gores. The notches are important because the side gore has a different shape than the front gore, and has fullness to be eased at a certain point. By matching notches, bust fullness will be correct.

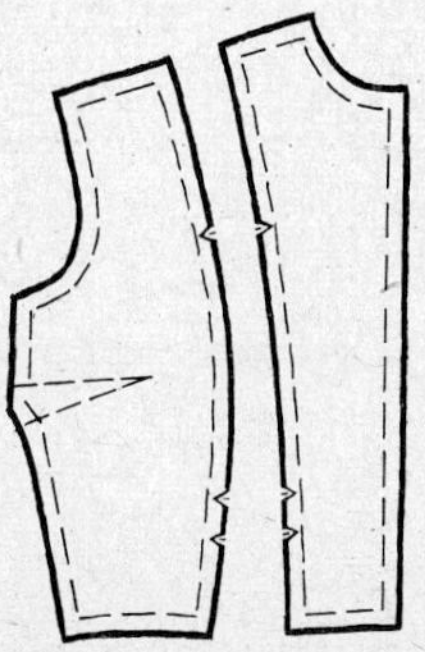

Marking darts and tucks

You will find darts clearly marked on your pattern. In fact, all construction details, such as tucks, shirring, and pleats, are also printed on the pattern, and should be marked on the fabric before the pattern is removed from the cut-out pieces.

First, mark the darts. There are two new methods that have replaced the old tailor-tacks. Both methods are much faster and more accurate.

Pin and chalk method

There is the pin and chalk method. Mark the dart by a pin at the point of the dart, and on either side at about two-inch intervals. In pinning, put the pin in and out only once with the head close to the pattern. At the end of the dart where it finishes in the seam, clip in for about ¼ inch.

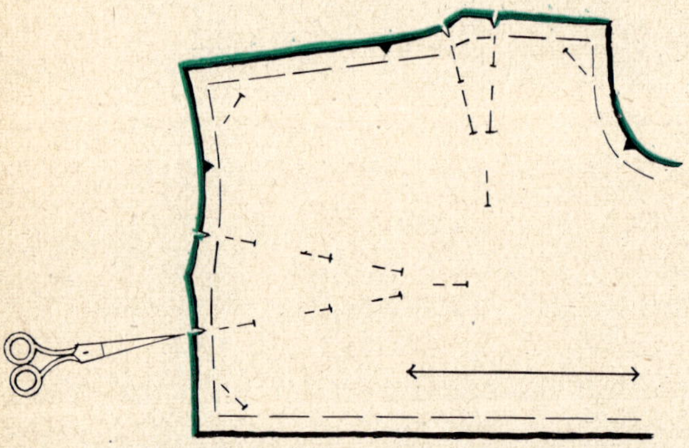

Do this for all darts. Now remove the pattern from the material by pushing the head of the pin through the tissue and sliding the pattern off the point of the pin and the fabric.

The pins remain in the cut-out material, and you are ready to mark the darts for sewing. It doesn't matter which side of the material is on the outside when you mark it. If the right sides of the material are together, take tailor's chalk and mark along the pins on the wrong side of the cut-out pieces; and then remove the pins.

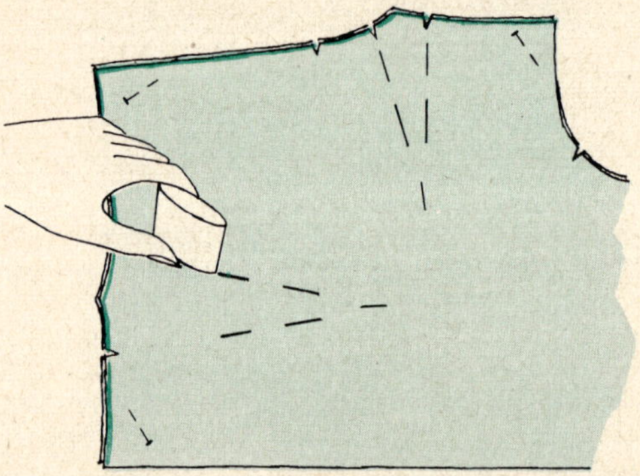

If the wrong sides are together, without removing the pins, fold back one piece and mark with chalk at the points where the pins still hold the fabric. Once the material is marked, remove the pins and the darts are ready to be sewed. The chalk mark is clearly visible on the fabric and indicates the proper shaping of the dart.

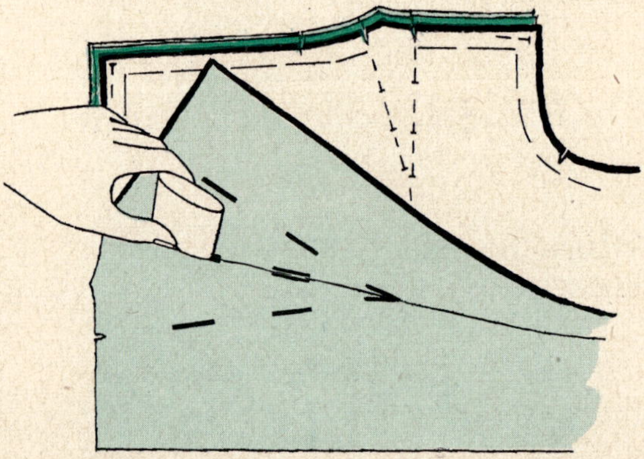

Tracing wheel method

The other method of marking darts is with a tracing wheel and carbon. When you mark double layers of fabric with the wrong sides folded together, fold the carbon paper with the carbon sides out. Slip it between the two layers of fabric and, with a tracing wheel, mark the shape of the dart.

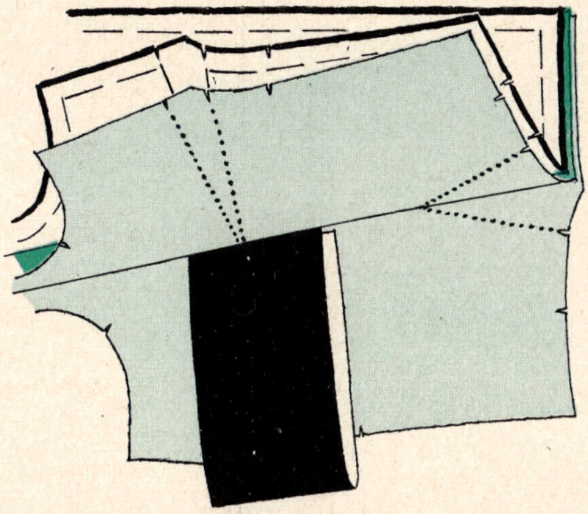

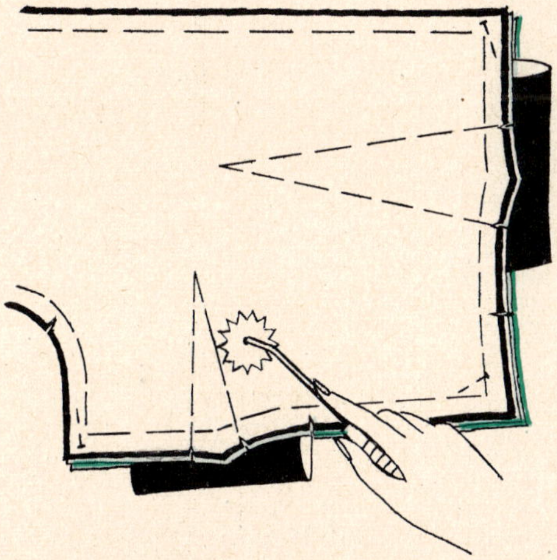

When the wrong sides of the fabric are on the outside, slip one sheet of carbon paper under the fabric and another on top of the fabric, under the pattern piece. The carbon sides of the paper should be against the fabric. Again, use the tracing wheel to mark the darts on your fabric.

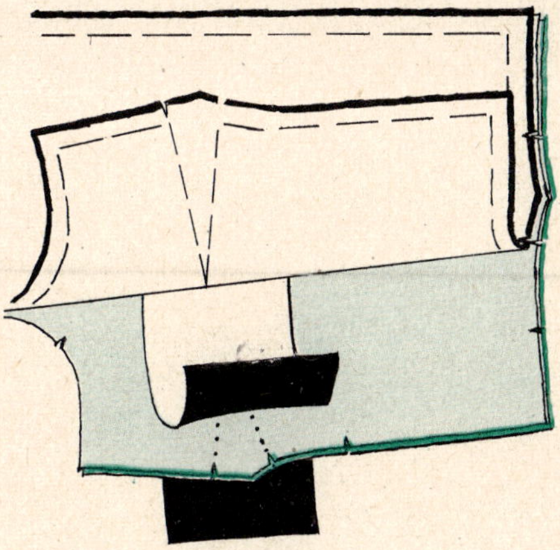

Functions of the dart

The dart has a vital function in dressmaking. It is more than just a means of fitting. It also helps create the contour and line of the fashion silhouette.

First, consider the importance of the dart in fitting. Here are some tips that will help you make your garment better fitting.

When sewing in a shaped dart, one that finishes in a point, be sure to taper it gradually toward the point.

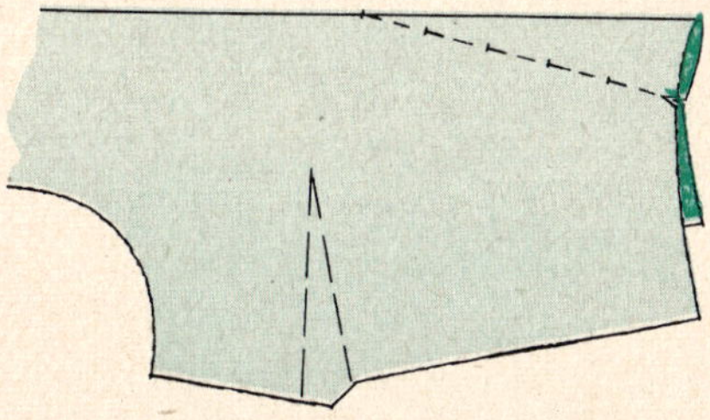

You may have found sometimes that when you finished sewing the dart it would not press smooth and flat. Instead it puffed out at the end.

This is because you shaped the dart too quickly toward the point. If you find it hard to sew the dart so that it tapers to a point, draw a straight line with your tailor's chalk from the wide part of the dart to the point, and follow this line as you sew.

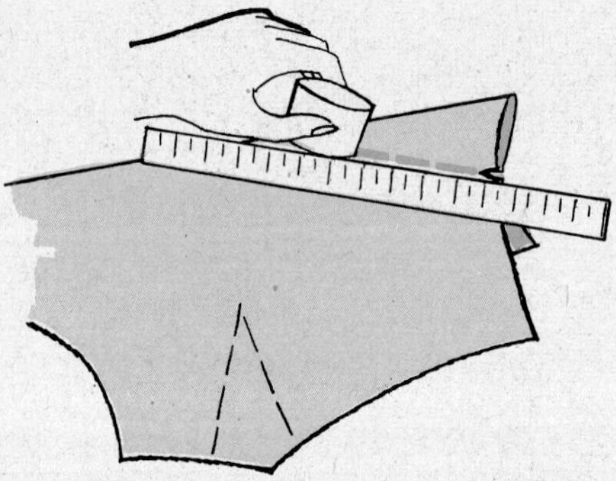

For darts used to create a style silhouette, you must be exceedingly careful in marking the actual printed dart line on the pattern.

Sometimes the dart is planned to give a concave line to a dress, at other times to give a convex line. Mark these darts with the tracing wheel, rather than tailor's chalk and pins, to be sure of getting the proper shaping. A rounded hipline can be created by using a convex dart.

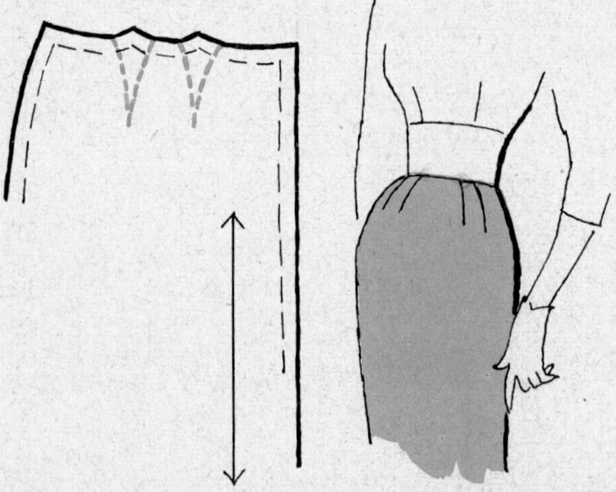

A flat diaphragm look is created with a concave shaping of the darts.

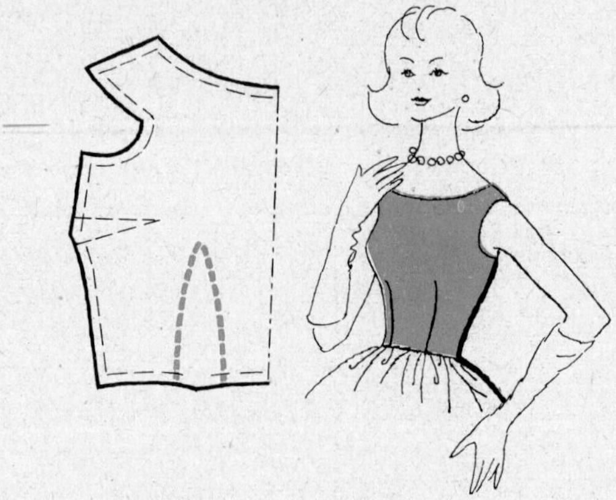

In the curve and shaping of a sheath dress, the convex and concave darts are both used. After the darts have been stitched on a sheath or a dress with no waistline seam, they must be clipped at the waistline point to help keep the garment from wrinkling around the waistline.

One rule of professional dressmaking is always to press all seams and darts as you sew them. You'll find a special section on "Pressing Tips" at the end of this chapter.

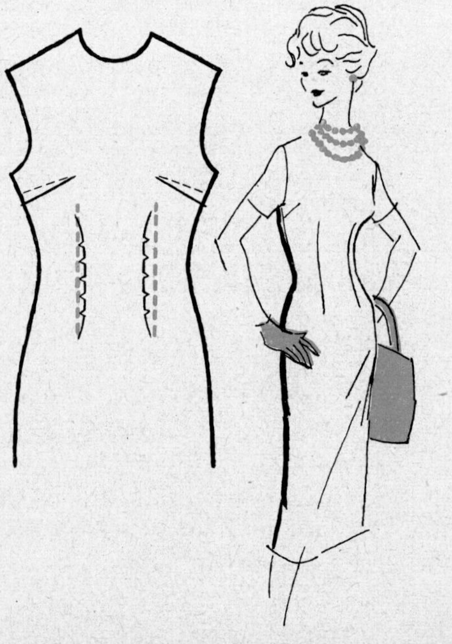

Shirring and gathering

When shirring is to be used, your pattern will be marked with two lines showing exactly where it goes. Mark for shirring as you do for notches; that is, slash the seam for about 1/4 inch at either end of the gather lines.

The easy way to shirr is by machine. Simply enlarge the stitch on the machine, loosen the upper tension, and sew two rows of stitching about 1/4 inch apart. Make the first row on the seam allowance line. As you begin your shirring, sew between the slashes on the right side of the fabric.

Another tip: Usually, dressmakers suggest the largest stitch on the machine for gathering. However, on soft, sheer fabrics, such as chiffon, the gathers will be finer if you use a smaller machine stitch. Try to gauge the size of the stitch by the weight and texture of the fabric you are using.

Sometimes the style of the pattern requires additional rows of gathers. You can sew as many rows as you like by machine. When gathering, the trick is to ease all the rows on the bobbin threads at once.

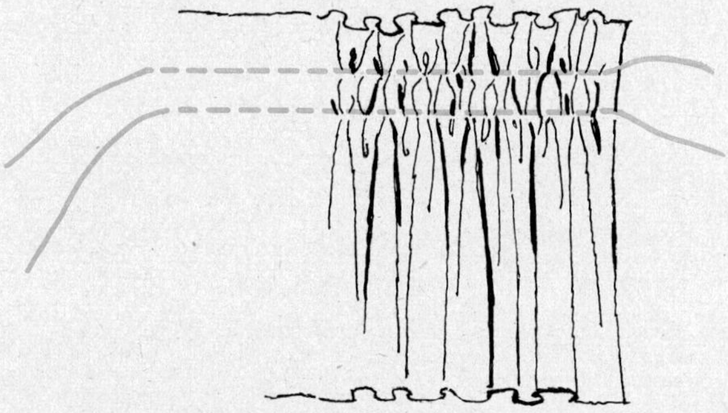

Sew two rows of stitching about 1/4 inch apart.

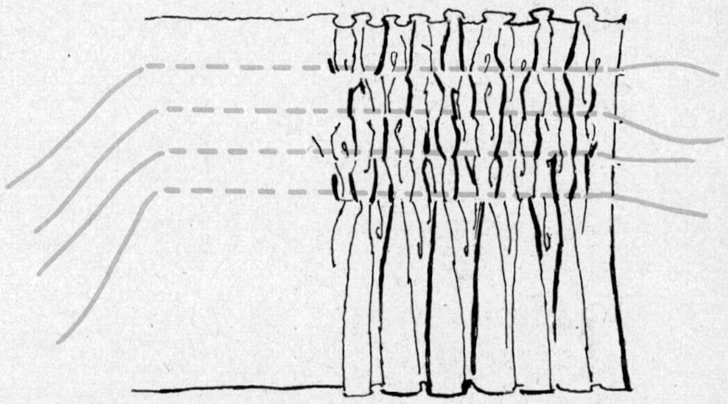

Ease all added rows on bobbin threads at once.

Shirr by easing the fabric along on the bobbin thread. If the shirring is very full, with a lot of fabric to be eased in, use nylon thread in the bobbin because it is stronger and less likely to break as you shirr.

Use at least two rows of stitching when you gather, so your fabric will not roll and will be easier to handle. The advantage of gathering by machine is that it can be done rapidly, and you can always be sure that the gathers will be even.

The pattern also indicates the placement of pockets and other trimming details. Mark them on the dress fabric with tailor's chalk.

The only detail you do not mark now is for bound buttonholes. When you learn the professional way to make them, you'll also learn how to mark them a fast and accurate way.

Chapter 6 will explain professional tricks in finishing a dress that eliminate the "loving hands at home" look and make sewing much easier.

Sew your dress in sections

Now you are ready to assemble your dress in sections. Earlier in this chapter you learned to sort the pieces to get a visual idea of how the dress will be put together. Now follow this same system as you actually assemble the cut-out pieces of your dress.

Make the skirt first, since it is the easiest to sew. Take the skirt, a piece at a time, and mark all notches, darts, tucks or shirring before you remove the pattern. Start with either the front or back piece, but *only remove the pattern as you are ready to sew.*

After you have sewed the detail on each skirt piece, you are ready to sew up the seams. The reason you are able to assemble this much of the skirt is because you fitted your basic muslin first and are sure of the size. You can sew all tucks, darts, gathers, or other detail while the garment is in pieces and easy to handle and sew.

Pinning is far faster and much easier than the old method of basting all seams. Mark and match all notches on the skirt seams. Pin them together, with the pins parallel to the seam and the pin heads toward you. Be sure to keep the top and bottom edges of the skirt pieces even. When the pieces shift so the front edge hangs below the back edge, the side seam of the skirt will bubble, because more fullness has been sewed in the back seam. This cannot be pressed out. Smooth out the seam by ripping it out and restitching it with both of the seams even.

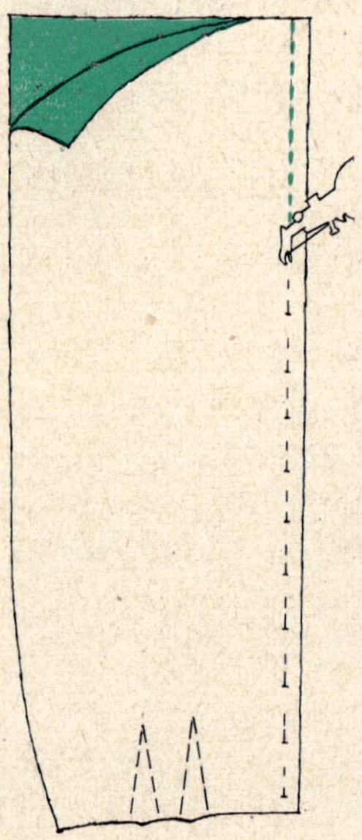

Let the skirt hang while you put the bodice together.

Mark and sew all tucks, notches, shirring, or other details. If the dress opens down the front, mark the center front with a basting line so it is clearly defined at the try-on.

Pockets and other trimmings are also made at this point and pinned in place on the dress for the try-on.

It is a good idea to check these trimming details before they are permanently sewed to be sure they are becoming, and are in the most flattering places for your figure.

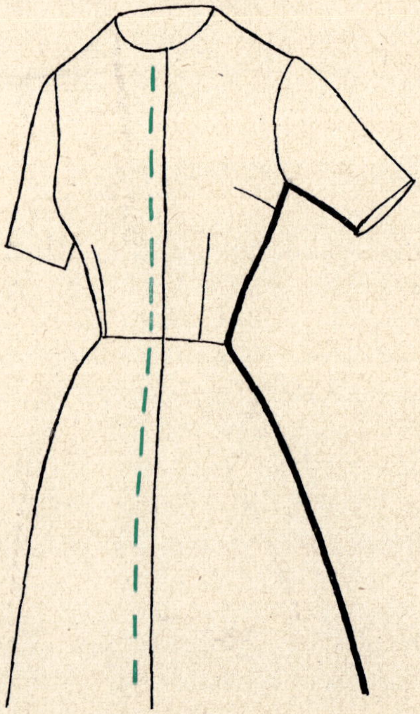

You can also sew up the sleeves. Mark the darts at the elbow for a three-quarter or long sleeve. You can safely sew in the darts because the sleeve length and the placement of the darts was checked when you first fitted your basic muslin.

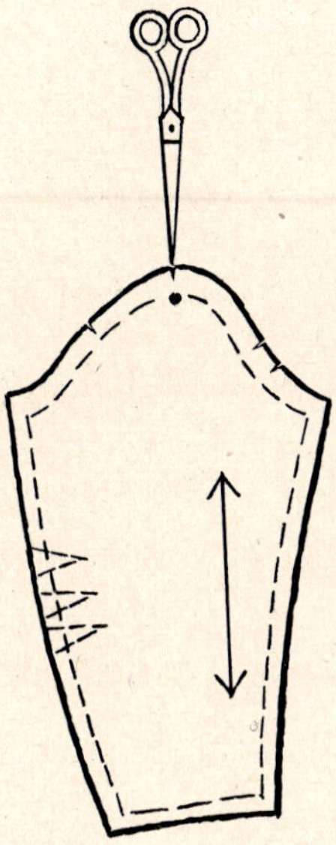

Next, mark the circle at the top of the sleeve. Mark it with a slash of the scissors as you do for a notch. This indicates where the top of the sleeve matches the shoulder seam. Also sew underarm seam.

If you are uncertain about how to put some of the pattern pieces together because of a style detail, turn to the instruction sheet in your pattern envelope. It will give you explicit directions for making and assembling every detail of the dress.

Each section you have sewed together is now ready to be pinked and pressed. Pink the seam and then press it open. After you have sewed across the end of a seam, it is hard to pink it neatly because the seam edges are caught in a cross seam.

If you don't have pinking shears, it is a good idea to invest in a pair. They are timesaving, give a neat finish to seams, and will help to keep the fabric from raveling.

There are several other ways that seams can be finished, depending on the weave and weight of the fabric.

Here are a few types of seam finishes you can use for different fabrics.

Seam finishes

Pinked seams

Pinked seams are used most often. Pinking is faster and provides an adequate finish on a firm fabric. It prevents fraying and gives a neater appearance. Pinking shears can also be used for decorative effects. Special pinking shears are made that cut a scalloped edge. Pinking shears can also be used for cutting decorative edges, as well as for finishing.

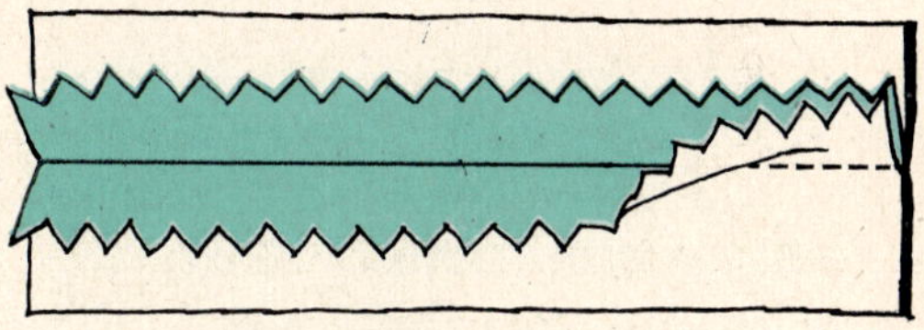

Pinked

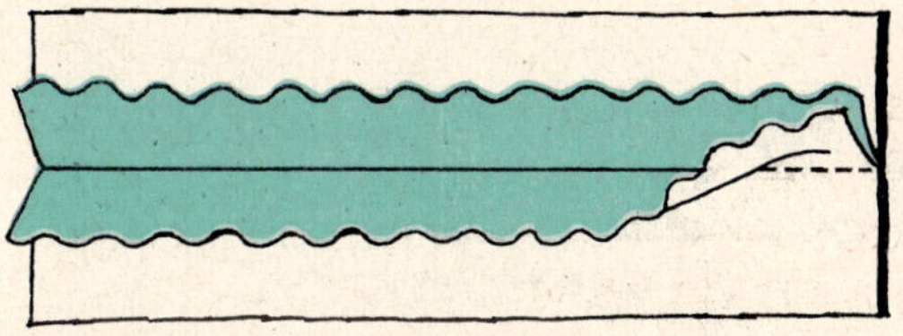

Scalloped

Stitched-edge seams

If the fabric has a slight tendency to ravel, it is a good idea to stitch along the edge of the seam after it has been pinked. The stitched-edge seam looks neat, and the extra stitching will help to prevent the fabric from raveling.

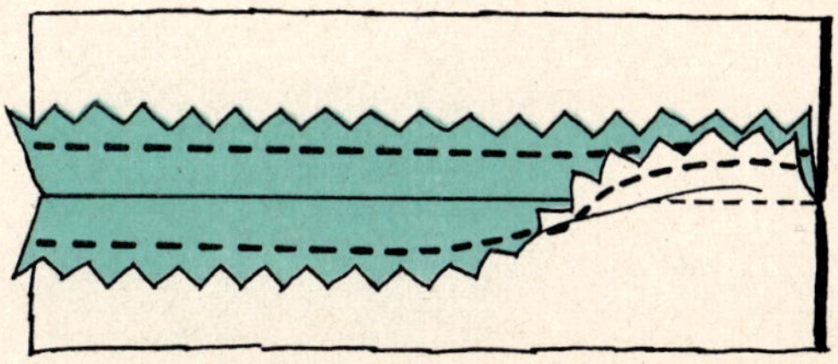

The pinked edges can also be stitched on a zigzag sewing machine if you have that type. Or, the seams can simply be finished with a zigzag stitch, a quick, easy finishing method.

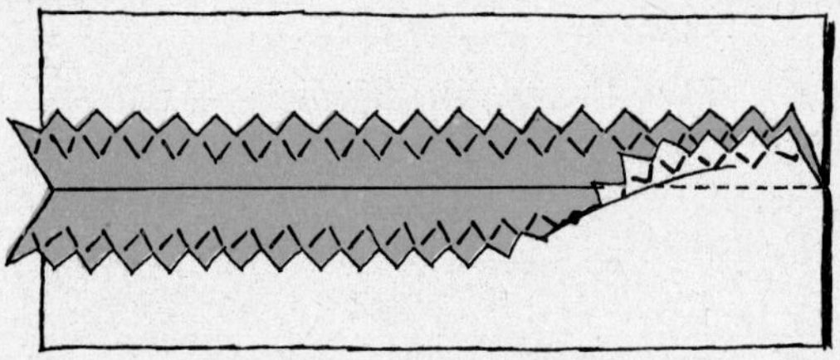

On lightweight fabrics that ravel excessively, turn the raw edge under about 1/4 inch, and stitch close to the turned edge for a neat seam.

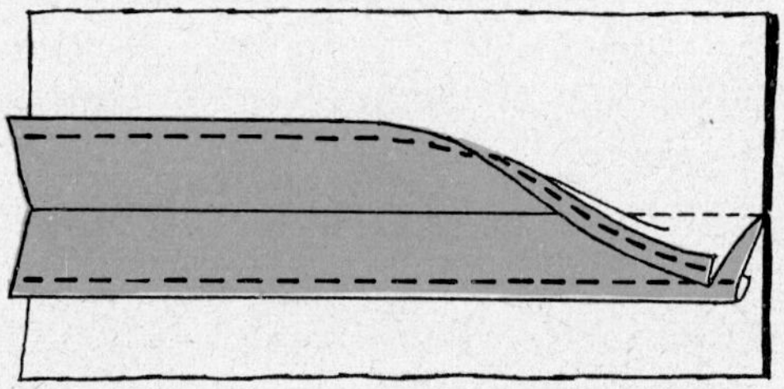

Bound edges

It is better to bind the edges on heavy fabrics that have a tendency to ravel. Use a seam binding or silk bias binding. Crease the binding in the center, then place it over the seam edge and stitch. This type of seam is also used in unlined jackets. You'll find detailed instructions for making them discussed in Chapter 12 on tailoring.

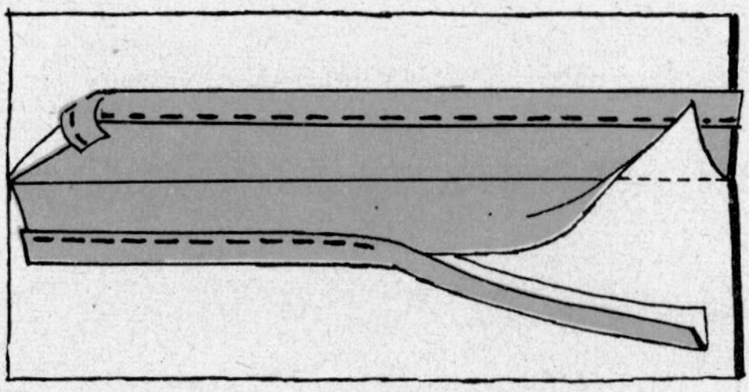

Hand-finished seams

On very sheer fabrics, turn the seam edge under and overcast by hand to prevent the fabric from raveling.

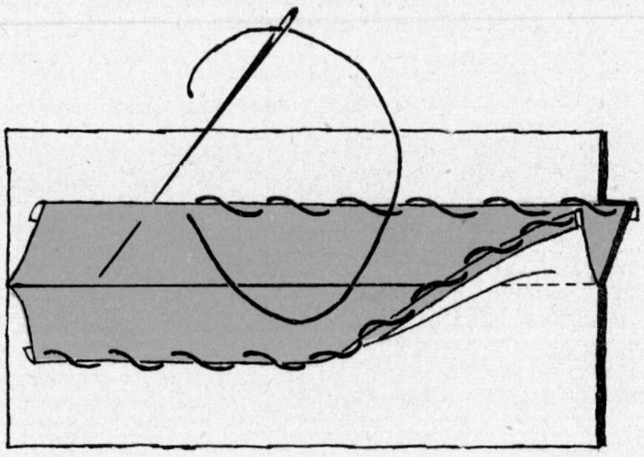

On firmer fabrics, the raw edge can be overcast along the raw seam, or can be pinked and then overcast.

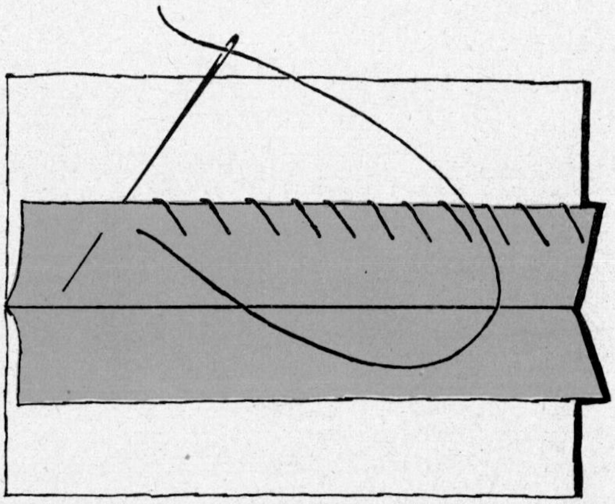

If the seams are to be pressed to one side, then overcast both edges together for a neat finish.

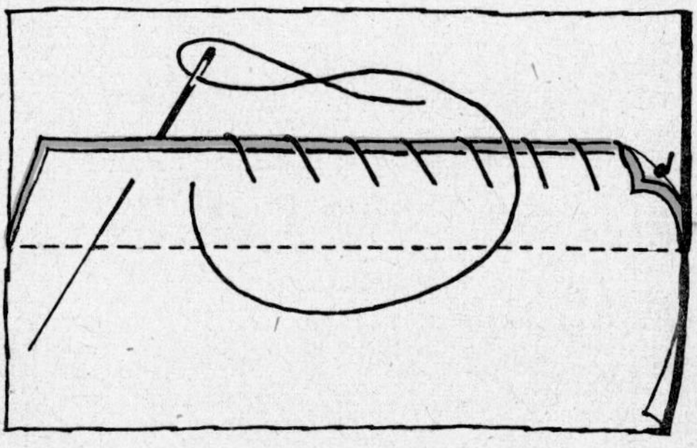

Pressing tips

Here's a good rule to follow for really professional-looking clothes—press as you sew. As each section of your dress is sewed, it should be pressed. Here are some definite rules to follow in pressing all details on your dress. They'll improve the appearance and make sewing it easier.

Darts

Darts are used to mold, shape, or fit. It is important for a dart to keep the contour you have sewed into it, so never press a dart on a flat board. Slide the tailor's mitt onto the end of your sleeve board with the cushion part on top of the board.

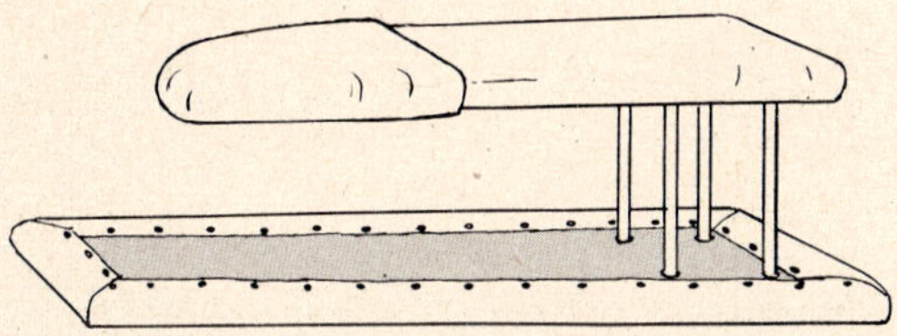

When you press darts, mold them over the cushion. For best results always have the point of the dart toward the round end of the cushion.

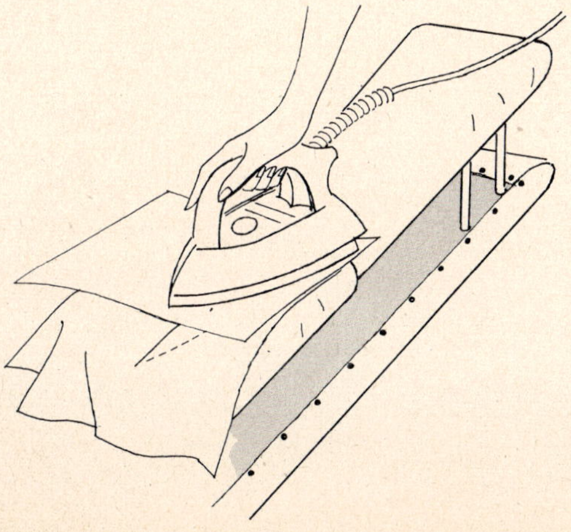

How to press

Skirt darts are always pressed toward the center of the skirt.

Press waist darts toward the center of the bodice.

Bust darts are pressed down. (Always stitch the dart so that it shapes up toward the point of the bust.)

Shoulder darts on a dress are pressed toward the center, and elbow darts are always pressed down.

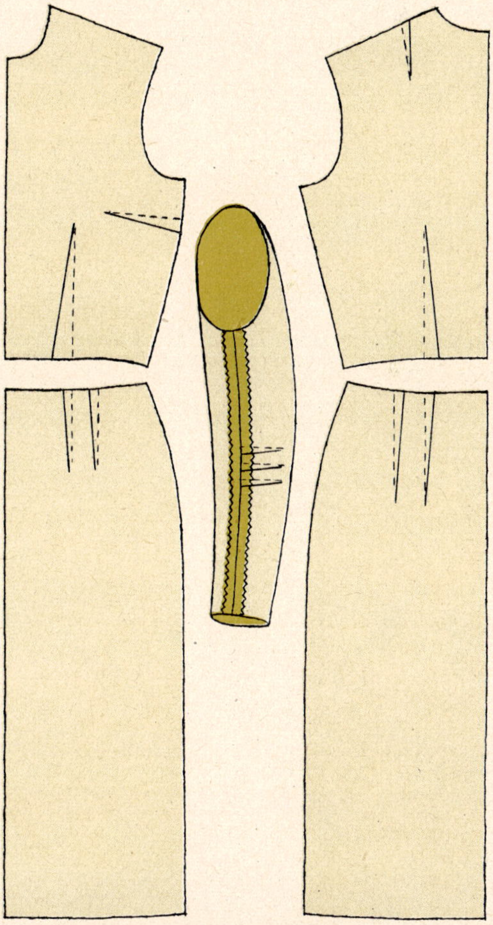

Pressing shirring

Never press over shirring; it spoils the soft, puffy effect. Press seams with shirring away from the shirring. For instance, when a dress has a dirndl skirt, press the seam up into the waist. At the shoulder, if there is front shirring, the seam is always pressed toward the back of the garment.

Never press a shirred seam open.

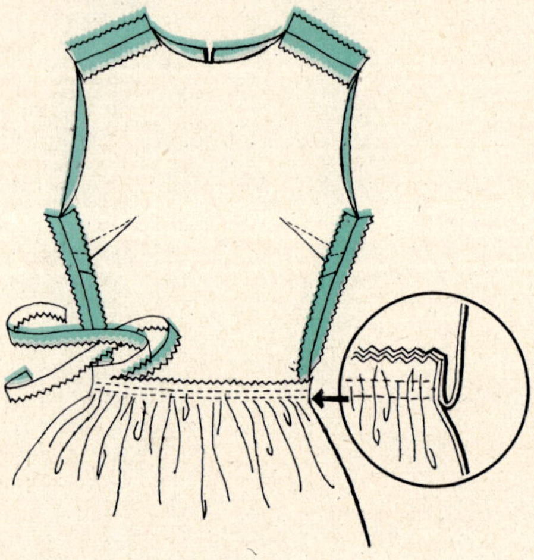

Pressing seams

Generally, all straight seams are pressed open unless the pattern indicates otherwise. (Sometimes, a design detail will call for special handling.) Press both edges of the seam together along the stitching line; then open and press flat. This makes the seam easier to press and gives a smoother seam. Press hip seams or other shaped seams over the tailor's mitt or on the tailor's ham. This technique will be illustrated in Chapter 11 on tailoring.

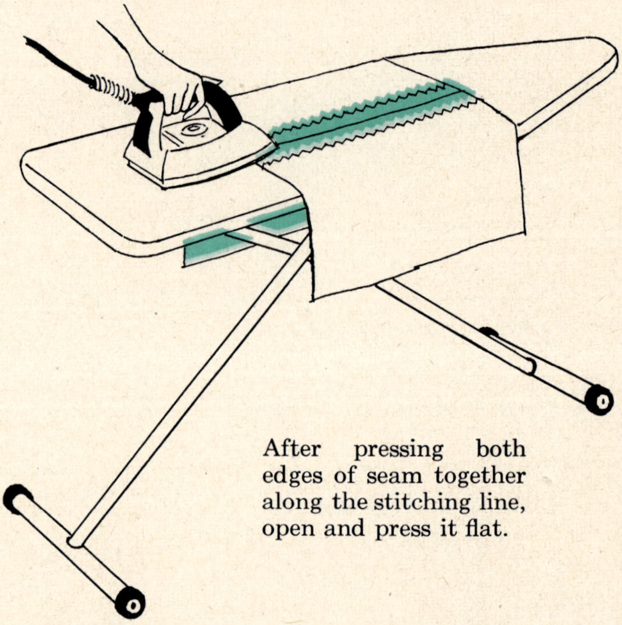

After pressing both edges of seam together along the stitching line, open and press it flat.

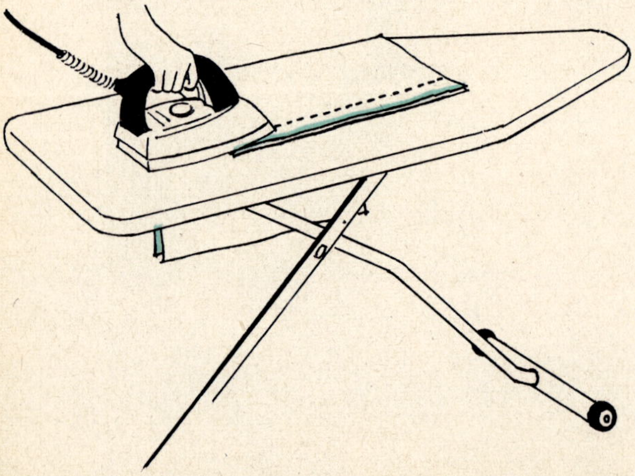

When the seam is curved (such as a waistline seam), it must be clipped and molded over the tailor's mitt to give it shape. Place the tailor's mitt over the end of your sleeve board and press the seam carefully.

Clip and mold seam over a tailor's mitt to give it shape.

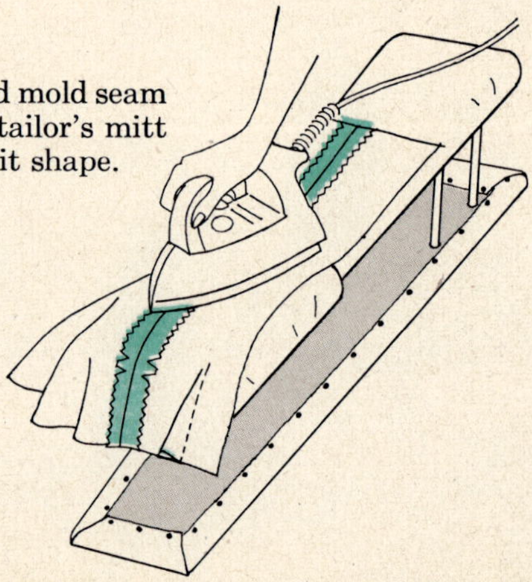

Interfacings, interlinings, linings

Years ago, clothes were constructed over a framework of boning, stays, and crinolines to achieve a special effect. It took a professional dressmaker to make a dress.

Today, we are fortunate in having new fabrics to help us achieve the line or style we want (no matter how elaborate) with a minimum of trouble. New under fabrics, now being used for interfacings and interlinings, have been the means of giving far greater scope to the use of all other fabrics. Before these new fabrics were created, no one had ever heard of making a suit of lace, or a beautifully tailored coat of a soft silk crepe.

Designers of ready-to-wear have taken full advantage of these new developments. They use outer fabrics in new and unique ways, depending on the under fabrics for the framework or construction detail. You can also take advantage of them to make sewing easier, and achieve that coveted ready-to-wear look in your clothes.

Let's understand the difference between interfacing and interlining. An *interfacing* is used to reinforce finishing details such as facings, collars, cuffs, pockets, buttonholes, and to prevent stretching and raveling of the fabric.

Interlinings are used to help create style details. Sometimes, if a fabric lacks body, the whole garment is bolstered up by the interlining, which gives body and texture. Crispness or contour can also be built in, no matter what the texture of the outer fabric. Interlinings can also be used to help retain the correct size of garments. They lend body to garments made of soft, stretchy fabrics or knits.

Often, the same under fabric serves as both interfacing and interlining.

Linings are usually of much finer fabrics than are the under fabrics. They are soft and firm, and are used to finish the inside of clothes. They also help to give body and texture, and add quality to the garment.

Interlining and interfacing fabric

It is important for you to become acquainted with the variety of fabrics that can be used for interfacing and interlining, and to learn when and how to use them.

A number of commercial interfacing fabrics are available, in two major types—woven and non-woven.

The non-woven type is made by fusing fibers together. There is no grain line, so it can be cut in any direction, will not ravel, and never loses its shape. One of the non-woven fabrics is made with a bias stretch. Actually, there is no grain in this fabric either, but it is not as static as the others, and can be stretched on the diagonal, which makes it more pliable and soft. It also retains its shape, and never ravels.

The other type of commercial interfacing is a woven fabric, preshrunk, with a very smooth texture. It is finished in different weights and degrees of crispness. This type is particularly good in making suits.

Before these commercial products were available, there were basic fabrics used to interface and interline garments, and these are still used for many specific purposes.

Some of these fabrics are organdy, organza, net, taffeta, lawn, percale, cambric, muslin, linen, and any other fabric which serves the purpose.

Where to use interlinings

The style of dress you are making and the type of fabric chosen will determine the best interlining to use. The weight and texture of the outer fabric is an important consideration. The interfacing should never impose itself on the outer fabric.

If you were using a soft silk print, for instance, you would never use a heavy, non-woven interfacing. It would make the silk look harsh, and the skirt would move and bend as the under fabric does. Instead, use a lightweight, bias, non-woven fabric that gives the garment body, yet blends with silk. Taffeta, or one of the commercial, woven interfacings with a soft finish could also be used.

It is hard to set rules, with so many different fabrics available. A good test is to try the outer fabric over different weights of interfacings until you find one that gives the texture you want.

The style of the dress is the other determining factor. Once, when you wanted to make a tailored dress, you had to pick a firm fabric suitable for tailoring. Now, you can choose a silk surah or any other soft fabric and, with the proper interfacing, you can make it into a tailored suit. This is why sewing is such fun. You can use real selectivity and imagination in choosing fabrics for your sewing needs.

Take a look at ready-to-wear and see how the designers have adapted fabrics. Lace bathing suits, chiffon suits, brocade shirt dresses, velvet slacks—there is no limit to the clothes you can make when you learn to use these under fabrics correctly.

Analyzing the style

Let's imagine, for example, that you have picked a pattern with a very full skirt. The pattern clearly indicates a bouffant look. The skirt should puff out sharply from the waist, but your fabric is too soft to give the right effect. You could put a petticoat under it, but the effect would not be quite right at the waistline.

The answer is an interlining. It can be of lightweight, non-woven interfacing, taffeta, organza (if it is a very sheer upper fabric), or a crisp, woven interfacing. The trick is in the way you make your skirt. If you want it to puff out at the waist, make up the outer skirt first. Cut the underskirt from the same pattern and sew it up. Put the wrong side of the lining skirt against the wrong side of the upper skirt. Shirr or pleat the top of the skirt (whichever the pattern shows), keep-

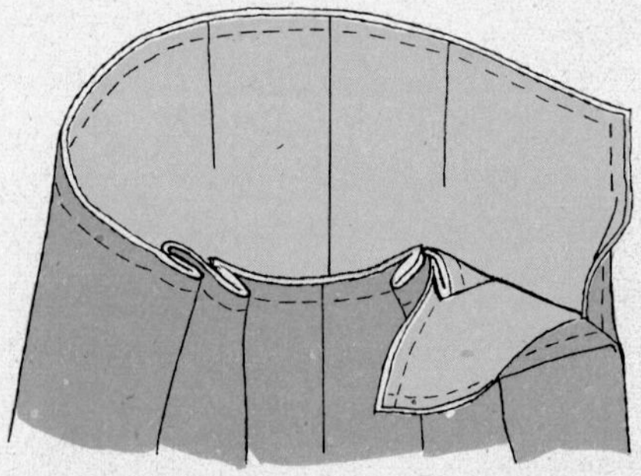

ing the lining and skirt together. This

will give the effect you want. Handle the two layers of fabric as if you were working on just a single skirt layer.

The lining is put in with lining seams against the seams of the skirt so the inside of the dress looks smoother and more finished. The lined look of the dress will give you a wonderfully luxurious feeling.

Mounting a skirt

If your skirt is to have a bell shape, or is darted to fit the waist, but be very full to the bottom of the hem, it must be made to retain this shape. To do this, you will "mount the skirt." After you have cut your dress, take the pattern pieces of the skirt and cut the entire skirt of a non-woven interfacing, (pick the weight suitable for your upper fabric). Lay out the pattern pieces on the interfacing, regardless of grain. Since it is non-woven, it can be cut in any direction.

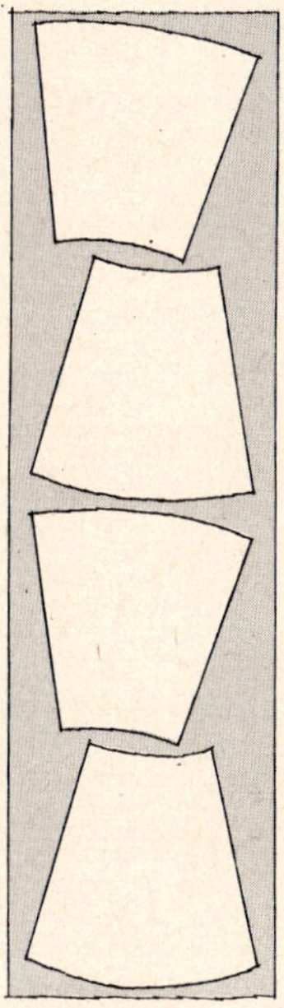

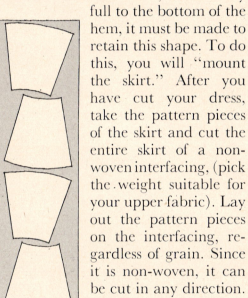

Lay each skirt piece over the matching interfacing piece with the right sides up. Pin them together carefully; then sew all around the outside edge, except at the hem. It is usually better to sew on the interfacing side to prevent shifting of the fabric.

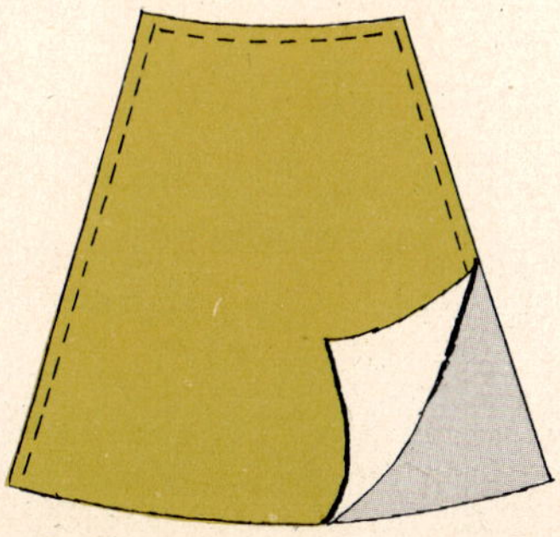

Once the interfacing is applied, sew up both the interfacing and skirt fabric as if working with a single layer of fabric.

If there are any darts in the waistline of the skirt, sew through the center of the dart to hold the two layers of fabric together. Then sew the darts. Mounting a skirt in this way assures that it will retain its shape.

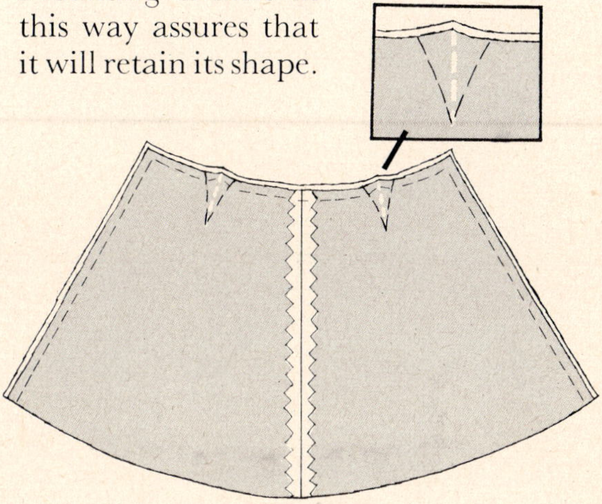

Interlining the peg-top skirt

This is a slim, straight skirt with trouser pleats or soft folds at either side of the waistline. To look as the skirt should, these pleats must stay sharp and remain in place.

After the skirt front is cut, use the same pattern piece and cut the upper front in taffeta or a commercial interfacing. Cut a piece about 12 inches deep, or long enough to fall well below the hipline, so that a mark won't show around the hip at the point where the skirt lining ends.

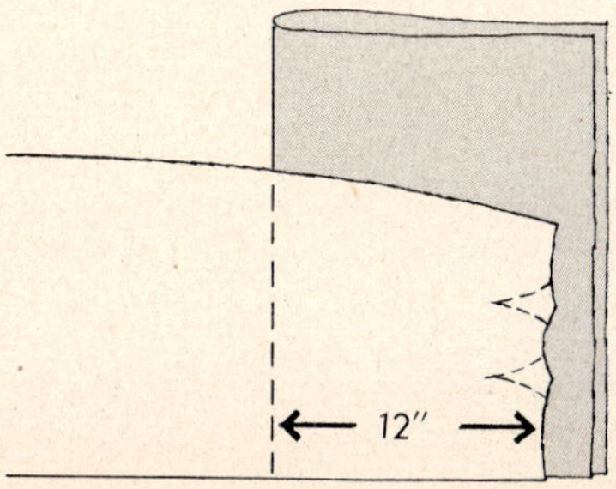

Remove the pattern and fit the interlining against the inside of the front skirt. Stitch around side seams and across top to hold the two pieces of fabric together. Now fold in the pleats and sew them into place.

Interlining the sheath

Don't confuse this with *lining* which will also be discussed in this chapter. When a sheath dress is made of a soft stretchy fabric, or a knit such as a jersey, the dress has to be mounted to prevent stretching and to keep the style lines. Use a very soft under fabric so that it will blend with the upper fabric but also have a firm texture. For jersey, a China silk would work well. For linen, an organdy or voile would serve, while you might use taffeta under a bulkier fabric. A soft, commercial, woven fabric could also be used for the interlining.

Cut the sheath dress from the upper fabric and then cut the pieces again from the interlining. Mark the darts, tucks, or other markings on the interlining. After the pattern is removed, place the pieces of the cut-out dress over the interlining and pin into place, with the wrong side of the dress on the unmarked side of the interlining. Pin the two layers of fabric together all around (except the hem) just outside the seam allowance.

Here is a trick professionals use. When the two pieces have been put together, press completely before pinning, just in case there should be a little shrinkage in one or the other of the fabrics. Also, the heat of the iron causes the layers of fabric to adhere so that they are easier to pin and sew together.

Another trick is to sew through the center of the dart, holding the fabrics together; then sew in the darts. Otherwise, the outer fabric may slip, forming a bubble on the right side.

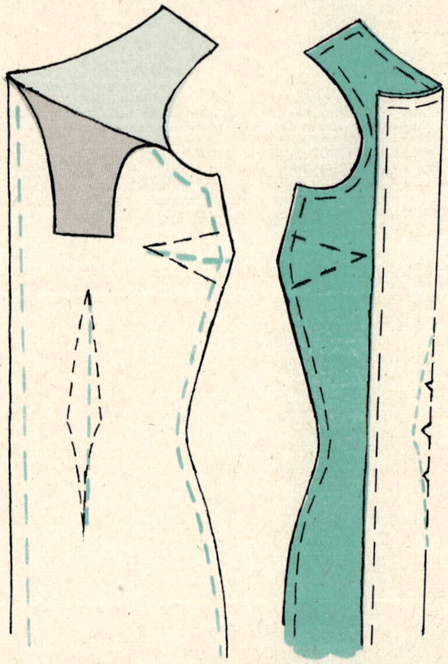

Hemming the interlined dress

After the skirt is made, it is customary to let it hang for at least 24 hours. This lets the fabric of the skirt stretch, if it is going to, before the hem is put in. It eliminates redoing the hem after the dress has been worn a few times. Some fabrics and styles of skirts have a tremendous amount of stretch, while a firmer fabric, or a fairly straight skirt has practically none at all. It is good insurance, however, to let all skirts hang out before hemming. The skirt is usually made first so it can be hanging out while you are making the bodice and the sleeves.

When you mount a full skirt on a non-woven interfacing, it is not necessary to hang the skirt, no matter what the upper fabric may be. Since there is no grain line, there is no stretch in the interfacing. The hems can be marked and sewed at once.

Measure and mark the hemline all around; then turn back the hem on the marks and press. Measure from the fold edge for the depth of hem desired and cut off the excess. If you want the skirt to stand out sharply,

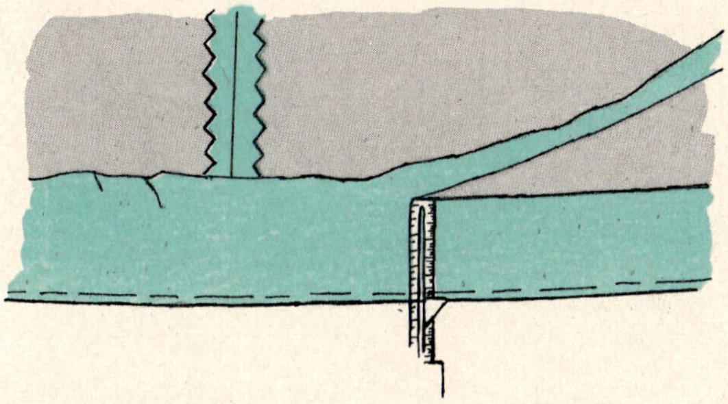

leave the interfacing in the hem. It will give extra body and crispness at this point. Otherwise, cut it away at the crease line and just turn the fabric back, over the interfacing. If the skirt is a straight dirndl type, finish the hem by sewing a binding along the edge of the hem and then sewing it by hand to the interlining. The hem will not show on the right side of the finished garment.

If the skirt is circular or fairly full, and the hem has to be eased in, run a shirring thread around the edge of the hem and ease in the fullness to fit inside the hem. Be sure the seams of the hem line up with the seams of the skirt. Sew a seam binding on the eased-in edge and tack the hem to the interfacing. Both of these methods insure flat, smooth hems.

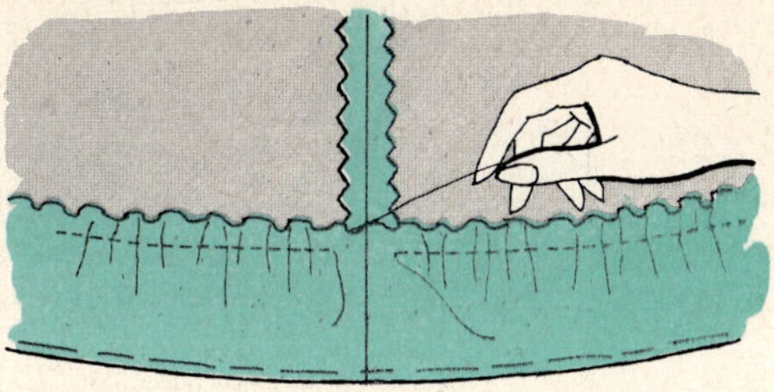

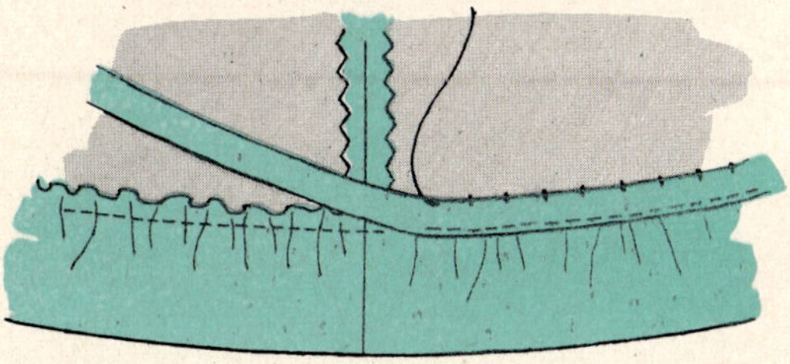

Hemming the interlined sheath

Again, mark for the length you want, turn back the hem and press. Measure the depth of hem you wish to have and cut off the excess. (Hems in the straight skirt should be about 3 inches, no more.) Since the interlining is sewed into the seams for the whole length of the dress, it is turned into the hem and trimmed along with the upper fabric. Sew a seam binding to the edge of the hem, holding both layers together. Turn and finish the dress as if it were one piece of fabric.

On a stretchy fabric, it is better

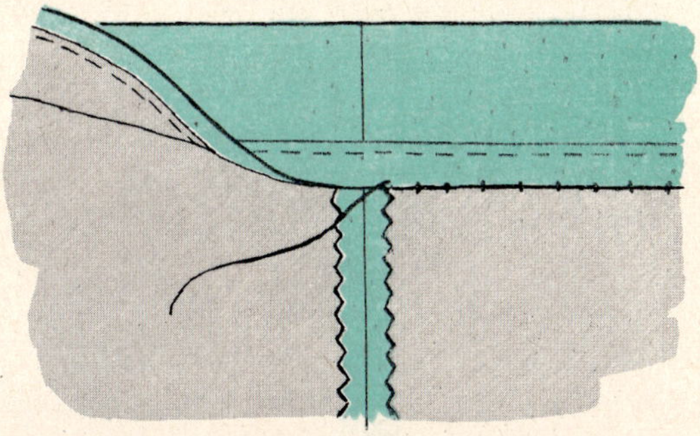

to finish the hem in a different way. The reason for this is that the upper fabric may stretch a little, and the lining may not, causing the upper fabric to bubble at the hem. To prevent this, sew the lining to the side seam for about *5 inches below the hip.* At this point, clip the lining seam allowance in to the seamline.

When sewing up the side seam of the sheath, sew all four thicknesses of fabric to this clip mark. From this clip mark on, sew just the upper fabric thicknesses together.

Sew the lining seam separately from this point so that it hangs freely inside the skirt. Mark separate hems in the dress and lining. Make the lining of the skirt approximately ½ to 1 inch shorter than the skirt.

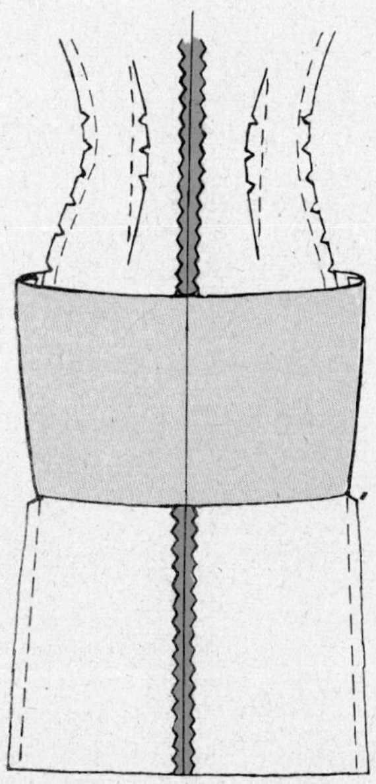

Interfacings

There are specific places where interfacings are used in a dress. Interfacings are discussed with professional sewing tricks in Chapter 6.

Linings

Linings are used to finish off the inside of a garment, and also to give body and quality to it. With the exception of some cottons, skirts are nearly always lined, no matter what the fabric.

Cut the lining from the same pattern that you used for the skirt. Make the lining up separately. Before you finish the top of the skirt, drop the lining into it, and pin the skirt and lining together all around the waistline. Carefully place the inside of the lining against the inside of the skirt.

If there are any pleats or tucks at the skirt waistline, fold these into both layers of fabric at once.

Only darts are sewed into each piece separately. Now sew the bodice to the

skirt as if there were only one thickness of fabric in the skirt.

If you are making a two-piece dress, apply the waistband at this point. When the skirt is lined, the inside of the skirt has a clean, smooth line. It will give your morale a boost to see how luxurious and professionally-made the inside of your skirt looks.

Make the hems separately in the skirt and lining, as you do for the sheath dress. The hem on the outer skirt is turned to the inside; the lining hem of the skirt will be turned to the side that shows the raw seams.

Lining the back of a skirt

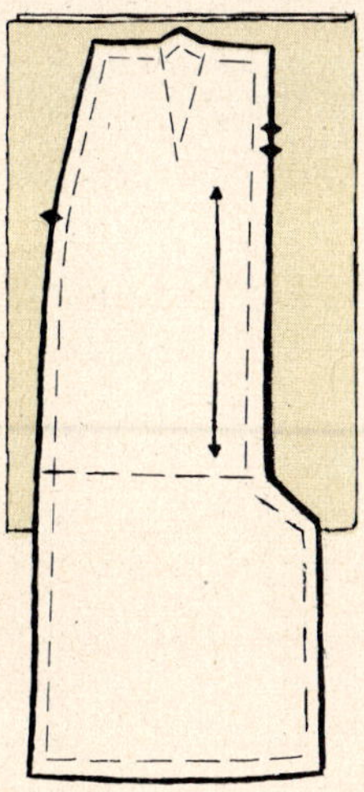

On very soft, spongy fabrics such as tweed, the back of the skirt has a tendency to sit out or bag. This can be overcome by cutting the back skirt pattern again in taffeta, China silk or any other firm fabric. Cut it long enough to come well below the hips. Put the cut piece against the wrong side of the back skirt before you sew it up. Fit the lining smoothly and make it just a little tighter than the upper skirt fabric. Sew the two pieces together as you do when mounting a skirt. Now make up your skirt,

building the lining right in. This will help prevent a baggy seat in the skirt and will preserve its shape longer. Correct fitting of the back skirt will help even more to preserve the skirt fit.

Try the dress

To review: Assemble skirt pieces and press. While the skirt hangs, sew bodice pieces together and press. Make sleeves and trimming details—pockets, collars, and cuffs.

Join skirt and waist. Sew together on the inside with a long machine-stitch. Machine-baste the sleeves.

Now try the dress for a fitting. There may be a few additional alterations necessary, but they will be minor ones. Sometimes, style points on the dress will be more flattering to you with a little nipping in.

Have the belt, buttons, or other accessory ideas handy to try. The dress is so nearly completed, you can get a clear idea of how the finished garment is going to look.

As you try the dress and pin it up, carefully check these fitting points.

If the waist is too long, pin a tuck around the waist, shortening it as you did on the muslin.

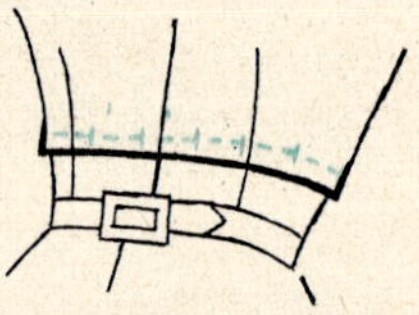

If the shoulders are still a little wide, pin a tuck from the shoulder next to the armhole seam until the sleeve sets correctly. This is done at the same point as on the muslin.

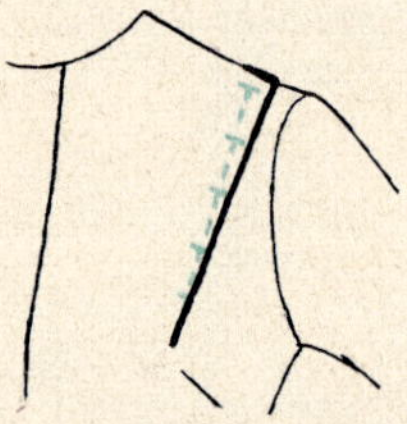

If the dress drops at the front waistline, pin a dart across the front under the neck.

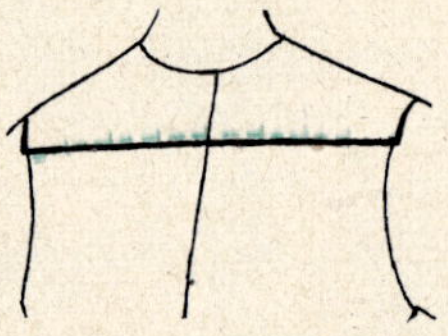

If the waist dart needs a little more shaping, pin it so it fits correctly. Check again for minor adjustments at all the points where you originally fitted yourself. Pin collar and cuffs in place to get the finished effect. Any trimmings can be changed or modified now if needed.

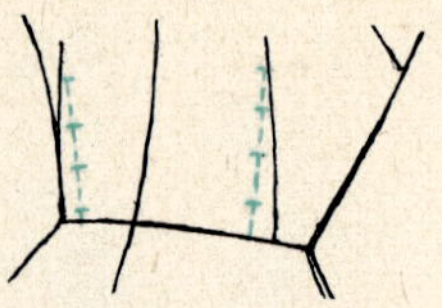

Mark the hem now or leave it until last. Remove the dress, and separate skirt, waist, and sleeves. Now finish up the dress, a section at a time.

First, make any needed adjustments in the skirt, and then finish as much of it as you can.

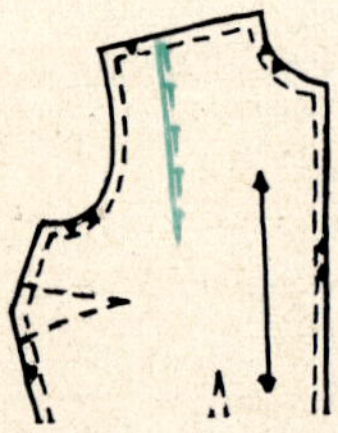

On the bodice, narrow the shoulders by the same tuck used on the muslin.

Find the pattern piece with the original shoulder adjustment and take in the additional amount. Rip open the shoulder and underarm seams, and re-cut to the corrected pattern. Since you are cutting from a pattern, you can be sure the shape of the armhole is still correct.

If the dart under the neckline in front or back was taken deeper, make the adjustment in the corresponding pattern piece. Lay the corrected pattern over the dress and re-cut to the corrected pattern.

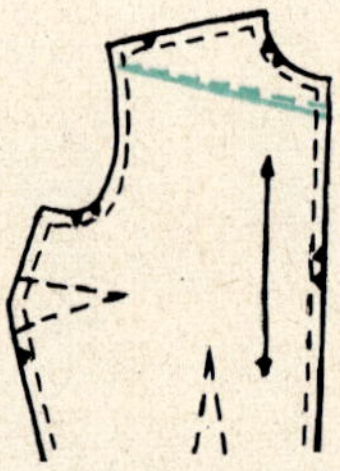

Make any other bodice adjustments. Then see Chapter 6 for finishing details. Finish the sleeves, and you will have a completed skirt, bodice, and pair of sleeves all ready to be assembled into a finished dress.

Chapter 6

Professional sewing tricks

There are "tricks to every trade," and the sewing trade is certainly no exception! Shortcuts and newer methods are constantly being developed to speed up and improve workmanship.

These same methods can be a help to home sewers. Too often, it is the finishing touches on a dress that make it look homemade.

A poorly made buttonhole, a badly rolled collar, square corners that aren't quite square—all detract from the quality appearance of your clothes and give them that "loving hands at home" look. Professionally made clothes have a quality look because the detail is so beautifully finished. Strangely enough, these professional tricks are easier and faster to do than many of those learned at home.

In this chapter you'll learn how to use professional methods for making cord-bound buttonholes, and collars that roll as beautifully as those on expensive ready-to-wear. There are tips on sewing curved insets, making sharp angle corners, and using facings and interfacings. You'll also learn how to make bias bindings.

The bound buttonhole is an example of these easier, faster methods. A dozen ways of making it are taught in home sewing. None of these methods are too accurate and all of them require long practice.

In the sewing trade only one type of bound buttonhole is used—the cord-bound buttonhole. It is easy and foolproof to make. The cord-bound buttonhole can be used on all fabrics except sheers (where this type of buttonhole is never used).

It is easy to do the finishing details before you assemble your dress. If the dress opens down the front, you will want to make the buttonholes before you join the waistline or finish the neck. In the future you can make the buttonholes before the dress is even assembled for a try-on.

Cord-bound buttonhole

Before you start your buttonhole, have on hand the actual button you are going to use. With the following method of marking, choose any size button and use as many as you like.

If you want more buttons than indicated by your pattern, it is no trick to mark and place them.

Measure buttons accurately to make sure buttonholes are the correct size.

Flat buttons: Measure across the top, making your buttonhole the diameter of the button, plus ⅛ inch.

Thick, chunky buttons: Measure by cutting a slash in a scrap of fabric. Slide button through slash. When button goes through easily, measure the slash for the size of your buttonhole.

Now you are ready to start your cord-bound buttonhole.

Making the cording

To make the cording for your buttonholes, cut a strip of true bias 1¼ inches wide from your dress fabric. (If you are short of fabric, use small pieces of fabric 1 inch longer than your buttonholes. Be sure these pieces are on the true bias.)

Fold this bias piece over cable cord ⅛ inch in diameter, or over a No. 9 cord, and stitch by machine close to the cord. Use the cording foot on your sewing machine and stretch the bias slightly as you sew. It is important to do this carefully, because this covered cord forms the lip of your cord-bound buttonhole.

Always use the same size cording. If the fabric is heavy, the cording will automatically be heavier after it is covered. It adjusts itself to whatever weight fabric you use.

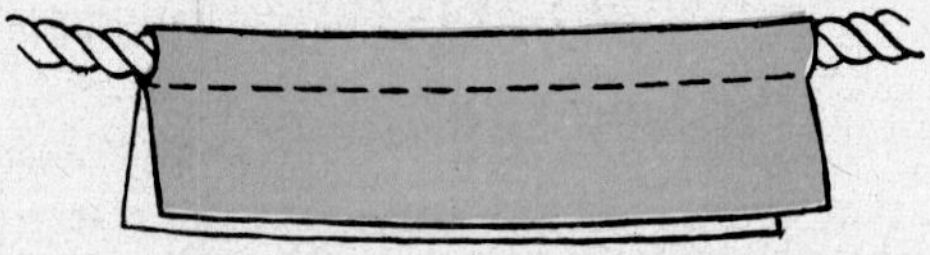

Here's a trick that's helpful. If you're sewing on a dark fabric where self-colored stitching would be hard to see, sew the cording with a bright-colored thread. It won't show on the finished buttonhole, and will be easy to see against the fabric when you sew the pieces of cord to the garment.

Measure for placement of buttonholes

Take the pattern piece marked for the buttonholes, and make a tissue paper tracing of it. The finished tracing will look like a facing piece.

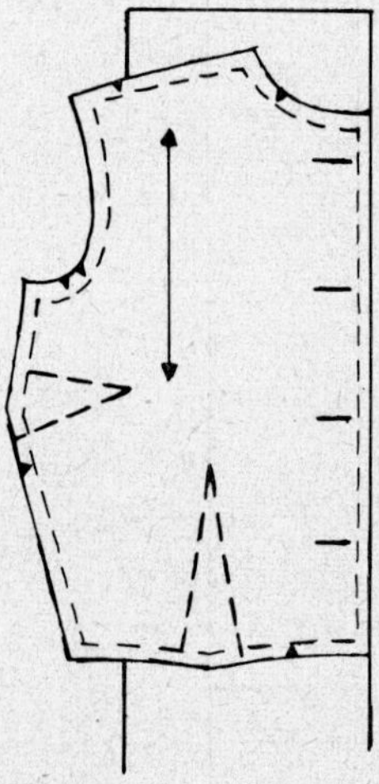

Next, check the pattern for the center front line—or the line where the buttons start.

Use a ruler to draw a vertical line on the tracing at this point.

Measure in from this line the exact width of button

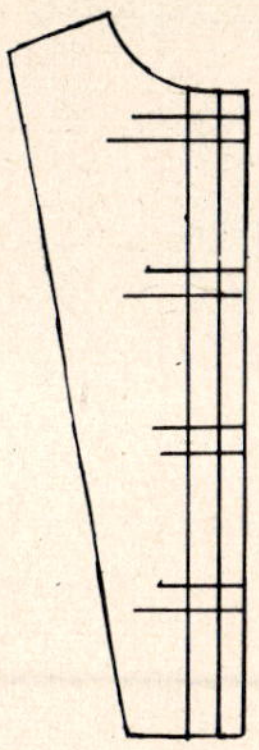

holes, and draw another vertical line at this point.

You'll now have two vertical lines running parallel to each other.

Across these vertical lines, draw two horizontal lines to show exact placement of each buttonhole. Distance between the two lines should be equal to four thicknesses of the covered cording.

Fold the cord as illustrated and measure. The weight of the fabric will effect the width of this space.

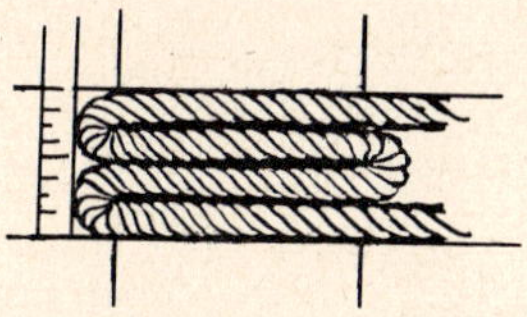

Four thicknesses of cord divide two horizontal lines.

If the dress has an attached facing, carefully press it back on the fold line.

Now your tissue pattern is ready. Pin it firmly in position on the front of the *right side* of your dress.

You'll stitch through the tissue, but not through the facing, when you sew the cording in place. Pin the tissue tracing from the fold line.

To prevent raveling, use an interfacing under the buttonholes. A lightweight, non-woven interfacing is best; taffeta or organdy can also be used. Pin the interfacing to the wrong side of dress under buttonhole markings.

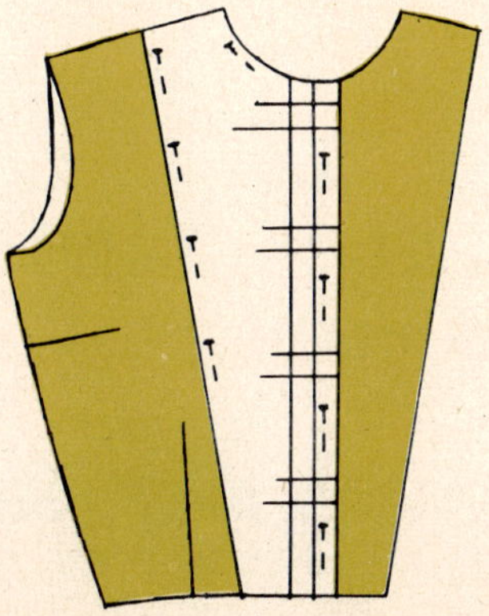

Put the regular sewing foot back on the machine, and you're ready to sew the cording in place where indicated.

Sew cording in place

First, cut the cording into lengths 1 inch longer than the buttonholes. Sew the first strip of cording with the fold edge along the upper line of the buttonhole, and the seam allowance toward the center. Sew from one vertical line to the other. The cording should extend $\frac{1}{2}$ inch on either side of the buttonhole. If your sewing machine sews backward, sew back and forth a few stitches at either end of the cording to make it secure.

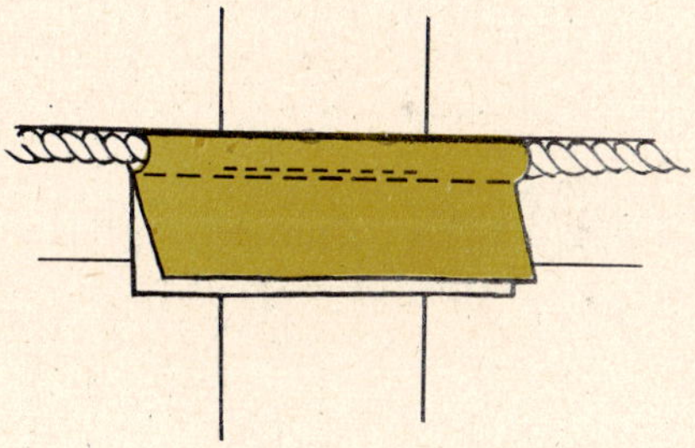

Sew the second strip of cord along the lower line of the buttonhole, with seam allowance toward the center. *Don't cut off the seam allowance.* It makes the buttonhole easier to work, and can be trimmed away later. When sewing on the cording, sew inside the stitching line. The buttonhole will be finer and the stitching won't show. Contrasting thread used to stitch the bias on the cord will help you stitch the cord correctly in place.

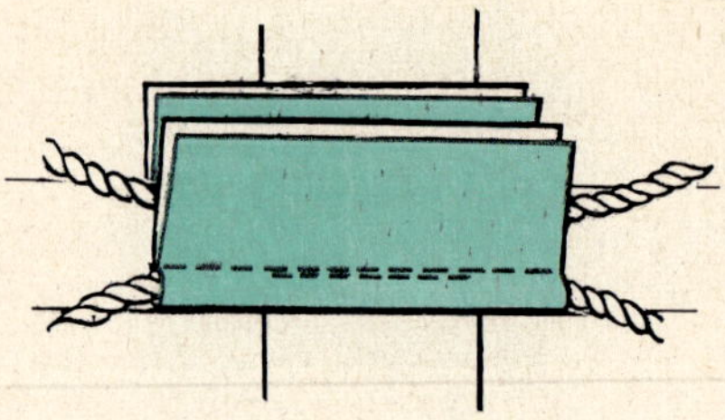

Stitch cording to all the buttonhole marks at once. Turn the dress to the wrong side and check stitching lines of buttonholes. Make sure all stitching lines are the same length and are spaced the same width apart.

If the lengths aren't equal, it's easy to rip out a few stitches to correct them. If the stitching lines aren't the same distance apart, however, rip out the incorrect cording and correctly restitch it in place.

Stitching even. **Rip out uneven stitches.**

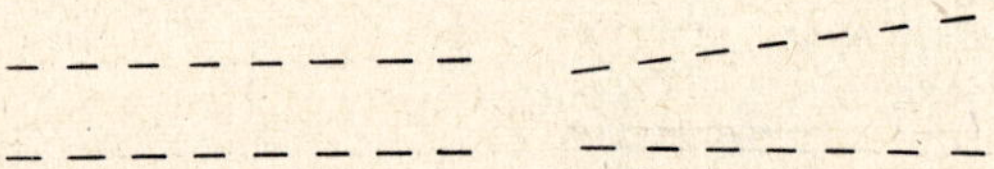

When all your buttonhole lines are stitched correctly, tear off the tissue diagram. Then, on the wrong side, slash through the center of each buttonhole to about ¼ inch from each end. Then slash diagonally into the corner of each buttonhole.

This is a vital place in the buttonhole. These ends are used in finishing the buttonhole, so be sure to cut them carefully. Then turn the cording to the inside of the garment, and the cords will automatically form the buttonhole lip.

Slashed center.

Diagonal slashes.

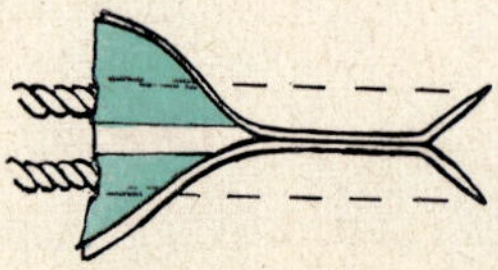

Finishing the buttonhole

Fold the dress out of the way and stitch the small extended point, formed when you cut into the corners of each buttonhole, to the cording (A). Keep the cords close together when sewing this point. Sew back and forth a few times to make the point secure and to square the corners (B).

As you sew across the points, make sure the interfacing is caught in.

To finish the back of the buttonhole, sew as you would for any bound buttonhole (C). See the section on finishing the cord-bound buttonhole in Chapter 7.

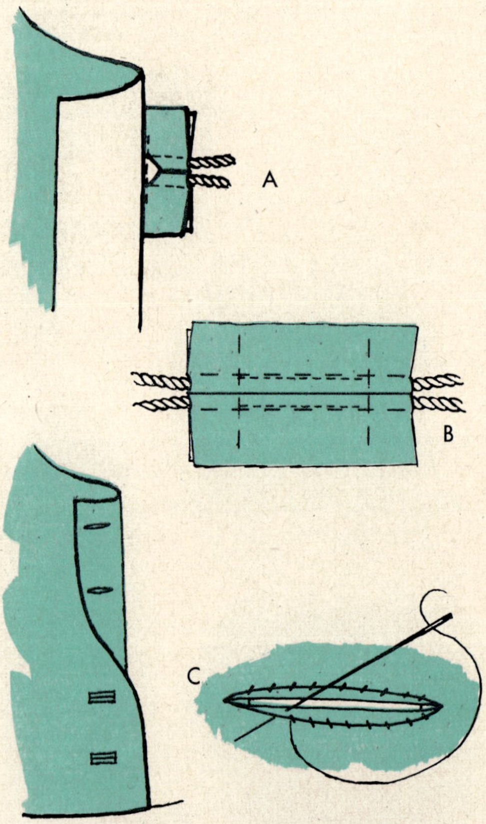

Finished buttonhole.

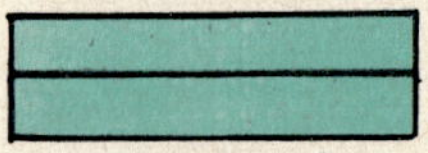

Peter Pan collar

The collar of a garment is quite prominent, and there's nothing worse than the curling edges of a "dog-eared" collar. Here's a professional trick that prevents curling.

Roll and shape the collar before it is sewed to the dress.

This type of collar is usually interfaced. Choose the interfacing to suit the dress fabric used. On cottons, you might use organdy, batiste, lawn, or a commercial woven or non-woven type of interfacing.

There are slight differences in the way the non-woven and woven interfacings are used for collars.

Non-woven interfacing

Cut the upper and under collar and the interfacing from the pattern piece. Trim away the seam allowance on the

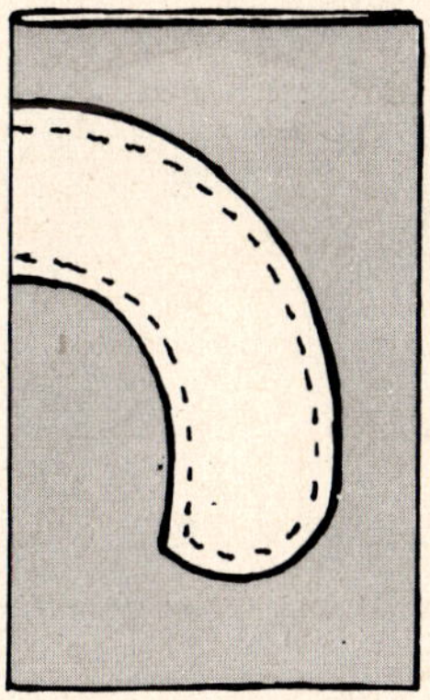

outside edges of the interfacing except at the neckline. This is done on the non-woven interfacing because these fabrics are crease-resistant and, if sewed into the seam, could not be pressed to give a fine, sharp edge around the collar. Place the non-woven interfacing against the wrong side of the under collar and stitch it carefully into position.

The stitching should be very close

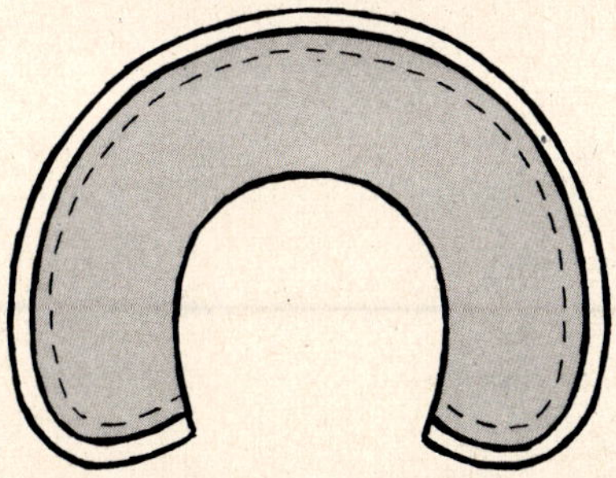

to the edge of the non-woven interfacing. Since this is firm and won't ravel, the edge will act as a guideline, as well as permanently insuring a uniform shape to this collar.

To make the collar roll correctly, always make the upper collar a little larger than the under collar. On suits,

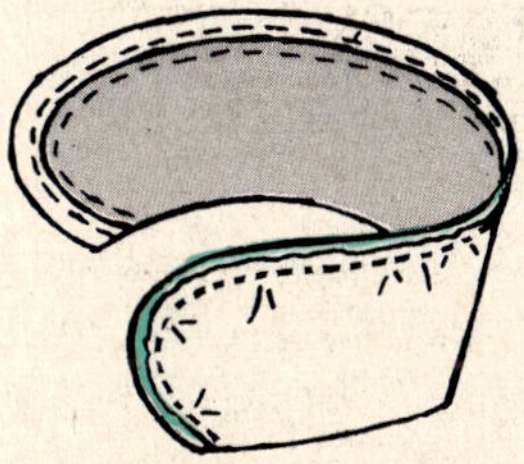

the pattern usually makes this allowance. On dresses, the collars are cut from the same pattern piece, so it is necessary for you to make the proper allowance on the upper collar.

The amount of difference in size depends on the weight of the fabric. If you bring the upper collar in 1/8 inch from the edge of the under collar, it should provide enough ease for the collar to roll correctly in an average weight fabric. On a heavier fabric, it may be necessary to allow slightly more ease in the collar.

As you pin the collars together,

ease the upper collar slightly all around. This ease provides enough space for the upper collar to roll over the under collar and interfacing.

If you are sure of the amount to trim, you can cut the under collar smaller before sewing the collars together. The ease will be allowed in the upper collar before pinning the two collars together.

Here's another professional trick. When you trim your seam allowance, graduate the seam widths. This means that the upper collar seam allowance

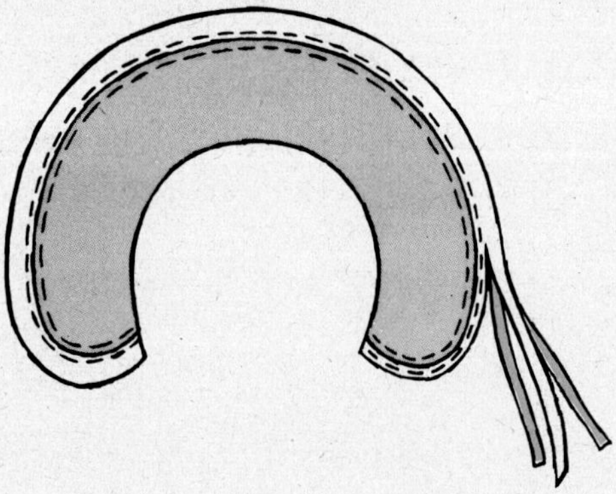

will be trimmed about ¼ inch and the under collar seam allowance will be trimmed only half that amount. This makes the edge of the collar more flat. Clip the seam every ¼ inch all around the curve of the collar before you turn the collar to the right side. This will

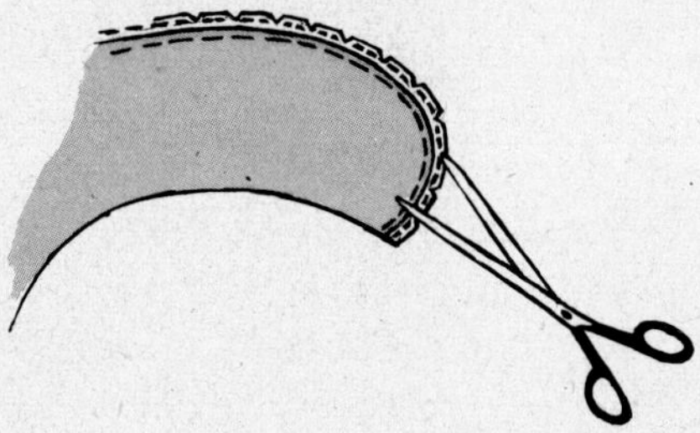

make the outside edge of the collar lie smooth and even.

When you've used a non-woven interfacing, you can usually press around the collar without basting. Otherwise, baste all around before pressing.

Always bring the seamline back slightly on the underside so a fold edge is along the outside edge of the collar. The collar edge will then press flat and smooth.

Now for another professional trick. Place the right side of the collar face down on a table. Roll it back over

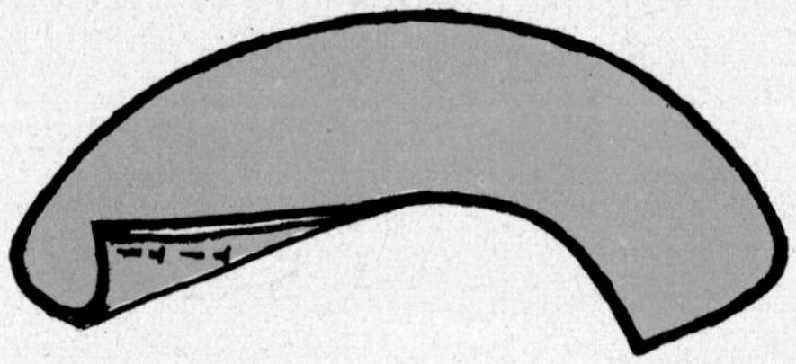

your hand at the neckline and pin the edges together. The upper collar seam allowance will usually be a little short at the neck edge.

If the collar rolls right, however, this is not important. Just stitch the three thicknesses together at the seamline, regardless of where the upper collar edge comes.

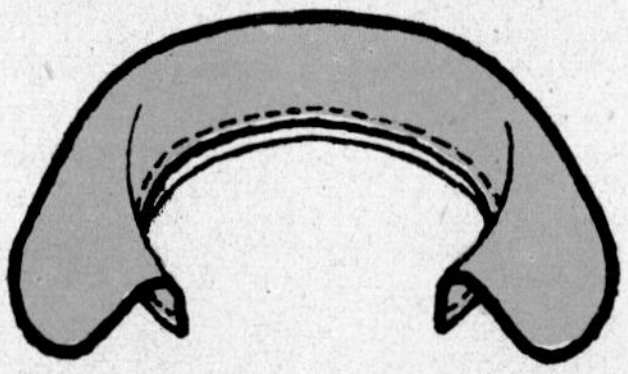

Woven interfacing

When you use a woven interfacing, it is not necessary to cut away the seam allowance before it is sewed to the under collar. Otherwise, follow the same instructions for making the shaped collar.

Cuffs are made and permanently rolled in the same way before they are sewed to the sleeves.

Applying the collar

Even though you've made a collar that rolls correctly, be careful as you

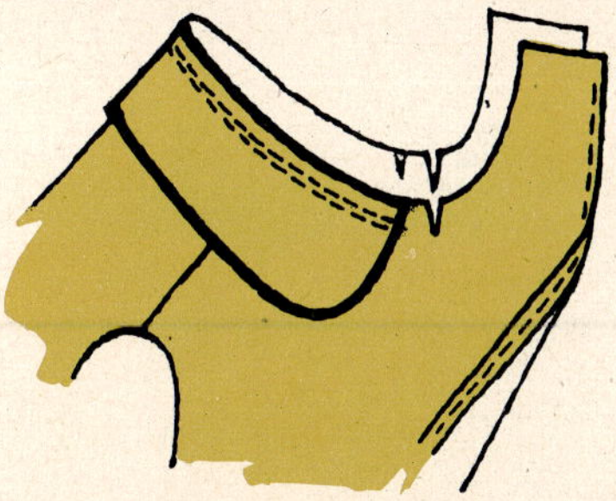

sew it to the neckline. A professional tip will help you correctly sew the collar in place.

First, mark the center back of the collar and neckline with a short clip mark, as you do for notches. Starting at the center front, pin the collar in place all around the neck. Match the neckline notches and the center back marks. After the collar is pinned, sew it in place.

It's easier to pin and sew only the collar itself first; the facings can be pinned and sewed afterward. Don't try to pin the collar and facing pieces at the same time.

At this point the professional sewer checks the collar again. When the collar is pinned on, it is eased slightly all around the neck.

You usually sew on a collar from the left side of the neck around to

WRONG RIGHT

the right side, and there is a tendency for the ease to shift slightly as you sew. Unless you are careful, you may find all the ease has shifted to the right side of the collar. This will make the left side look shorter.

To prevent this, sew from the center toward the right side. Then start at the center again and sew toward the left side. This will keep the ease from shifting to one side.

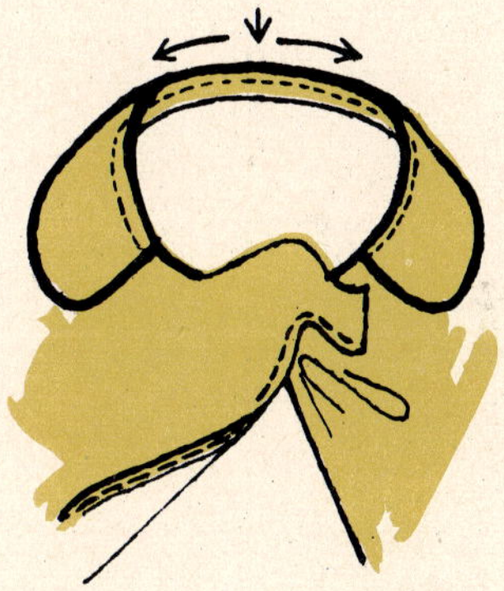

All shaped collars can be made in the same general way as the Peter Pan collar. The same technique is used, no matter what size the collar may be.

There are, however, various ways the collar may be applied. This depends on the dress style.

When the Peter Pan collar is used on the *one-piece front*, it is important the collar meet in front and the ends be the same length. Bring the front edges of the collar together.

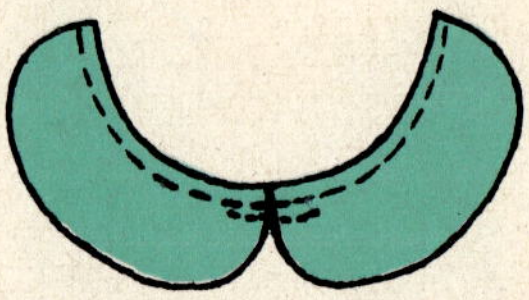

Stitch about an inch on either side of the front edges on the seam allowance line. This holds the fronts in place before sewing the collar to the dress.

On some styles, the collar extends to the very edge of the front opening.

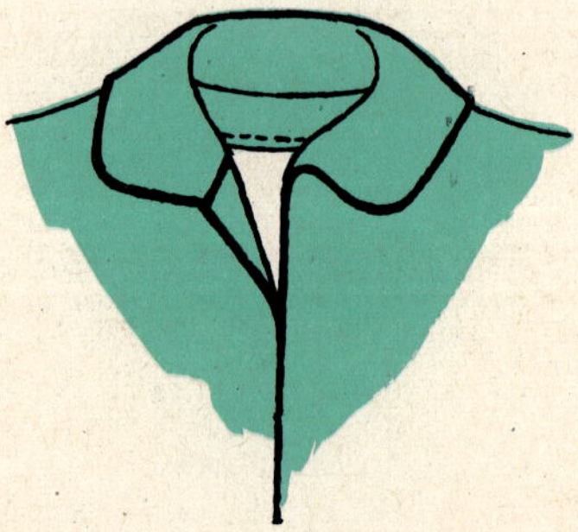

It's hard to make this collar line up with the front edge of the dress unless you use a simple trick. If an attached facing that folds back is used, slash down on the fold edge of the facing to the seam allowance line. As you pin the collar to the neck, the front corner

of the collar seam allowance will extend through this slash. This brings the seam allowance lines of both the collar and neckline together at the point where they should be sewed to form a smooth front line from the collar to the neck opening.

When a stitched-on facing is used, the neckline seam is left open to the seam allowance line so the collar can be applied in the same way.

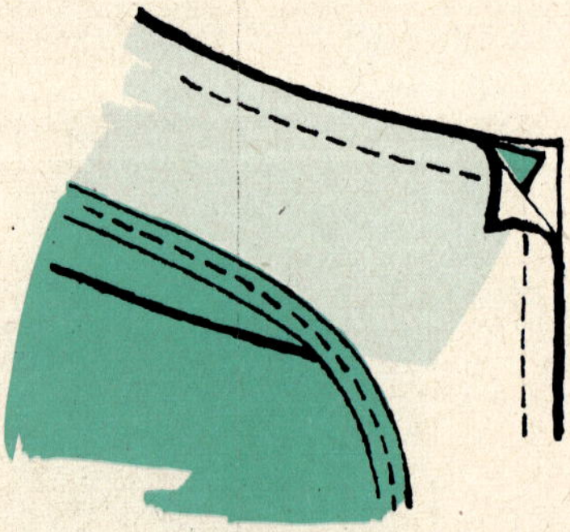

V neck with a collar

This is another type of collar that is difficult to apply. An example of this is the sailor collar. The front edges of this collar should come together at the exact center of the front point.

To accomplish this, measure and mark the seam allowance at the front V of the neck. Stitch on this line

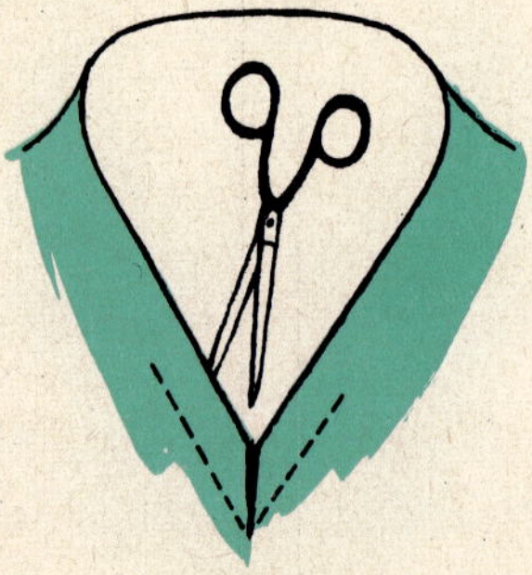

for 2 inches on either side of the point. The stitching can be done in contrasting thread. Slash down to the stitching line at this point. When you pin the collar in place, the front edges of the collar will slide through this

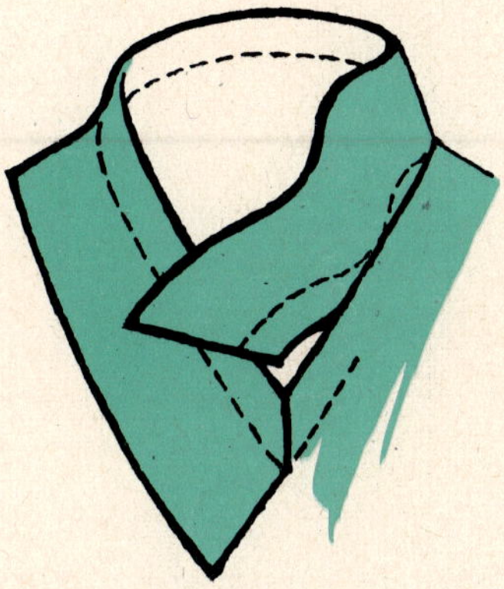

slash, and the seam allowance line of the collar will be pinned at the end point of the slash.

Stitch the edges to the front of the dress to hold them before the facing is applied. Pin the facing so the collar

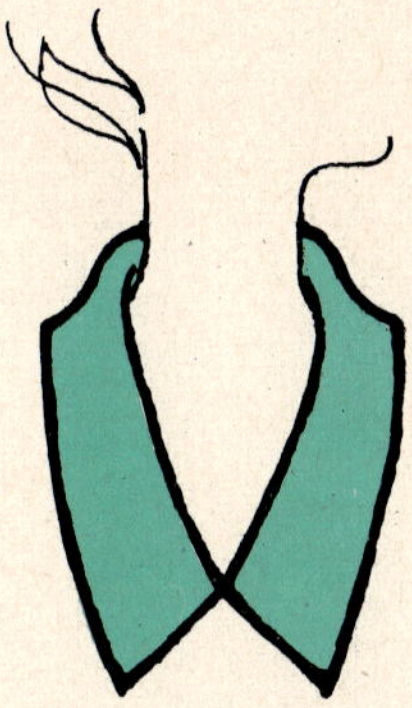

is between the facing and the front. Sew them together from the bodice side. At the point, sew just outside of the original stitching line which holds the collar. Clip the facing to the depth of the V in front before turning it to the inside. Trim and clip the seam.

Curved insets

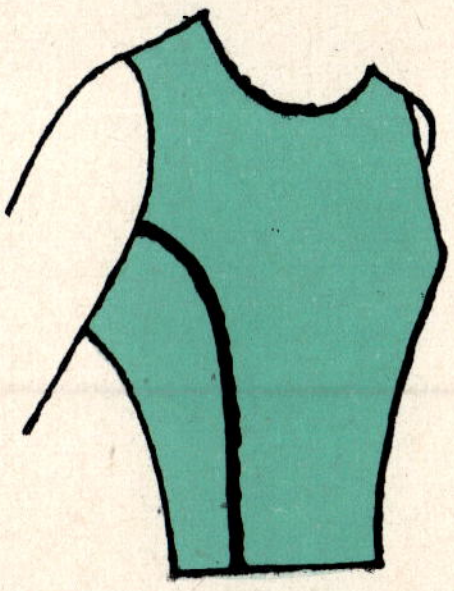

This curved detail should always have a clean, clearly defined outline.

Again, it's a professional trick that's easy to do which assures this.

After you clip all the notches for matching, remove the pattern from the pieces to be joined. Before sewing the curved seams together, run a machine-stitch along the seam allowance line of the individual pieces. On the inside curved seam, clip into this stitching line every ½ inch. Pin the seam together with the clipped seam on the top. Keep the edges of both seams even. Stitch just inside the original stitching line when sewing the seams together, and you'll have a firm, perfectly shaped seam. There is a tendency for this type of seam to stretch and ripple unless it is first sewed on the inside. Patterns often suggest outside stitching on the yoke or curved seam edges as a trim. Always sew the seam first on the inside. Do the trimming stitch after you have pressed the seam.

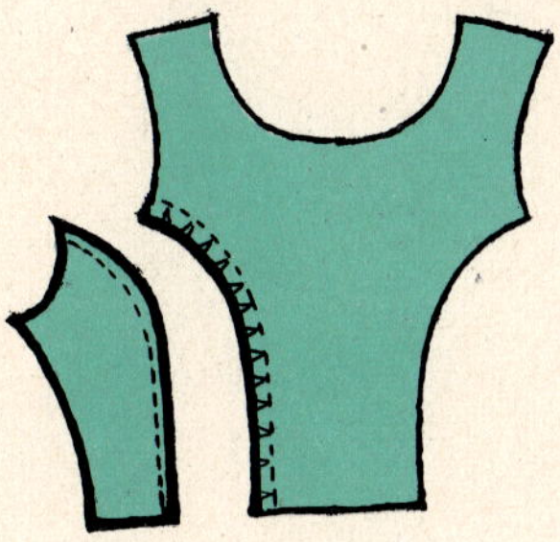

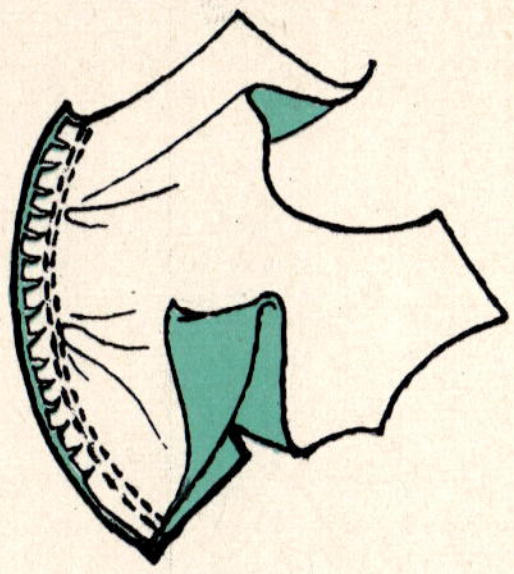

Angle corners

Many construction details—corners and angle joinings, for example—require the same general sewing method. Learn to make these correctly and use the same method for many styles. Sketches show similar constructions.

Angle corner is formed by underarm piecing.

Yoke seam meets underarm seam, forming an angle corner.

Inset gusset has angle corners at every point where it joins.

Dropped shoulder line forms angle seam where it meets armhole line.

Pocket and trimming detail form double angle corners.

Side panel forms angle corner with underarm seam.

For some reason, sewing two pieces of fabric together to form a corner seems to cause trouble for the average sewer. Corners are not sharp and clear, or they start to fray before they are even sewed. If you follow the pattern seam allowance very carefully, the corners will be sharp, won't fray.

Usually, it's the seam allowance at a corner which is confusing because of the degree of the angle. Here's a professional method that solves all the problems. Measure and mark the seam allowances on the pieces to be joined for 2 inches from either side of the corner. To measure correctly, use a ruler.

At a right angle to the seam, measure in the amount of the seam allowance (this is ⅝ inch, unless the pattern specifies otherwise).

Using the ruler, draw a chalk line on this mark, parallel to the seam edge. Now measure and mark the

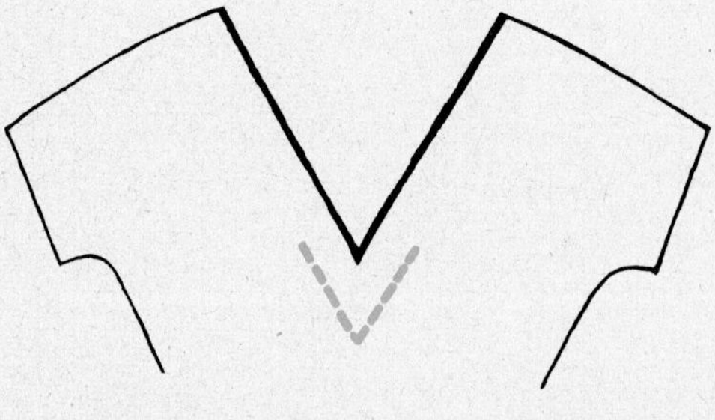

other angle of the corner. Stitch along these lines for 2 inches on either side of the corner. Use thread in a contrasting color. Now clip into the corner as close to the stitching as possible without cutting through the stitches. The slash will be much deeper than the seam allowance because you've cut at an angle. Sometimes it is as much as 1 inch in depth. A common mistake is to slash into the corner only 5⁄8 inch, instead of

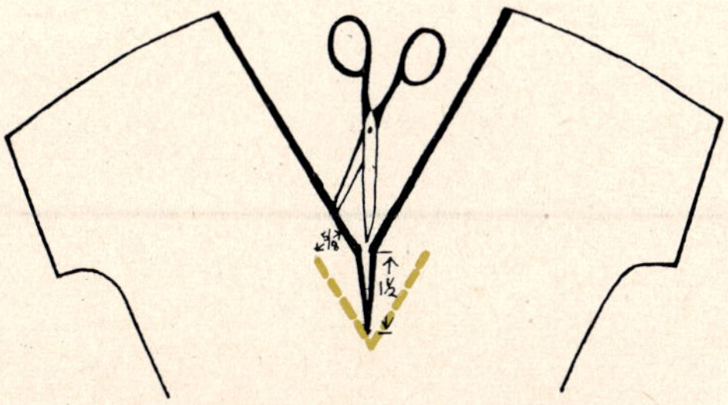

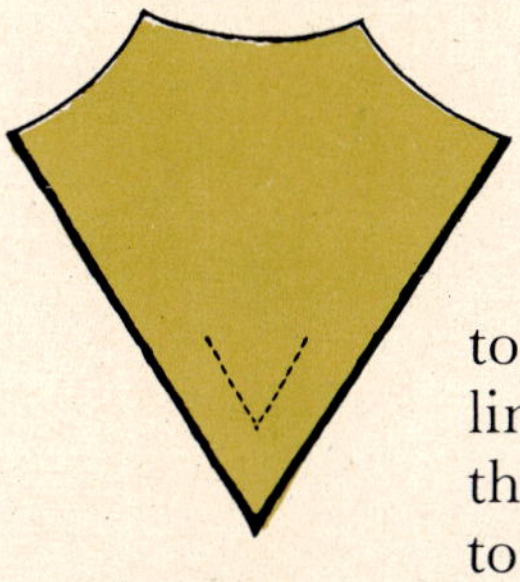

to the actual seamline. On the point that is to be joined to this corner, measure the seam allowance and mark it with chalk. Stitch on this line for 2 inches at either side of the point —again in thread of a contrasting color so it will show against the fabric.

The base of the slash should be at the point of the stitched seam allowance line on the piece to be inserted. Pin the rest of the seam at one side of the slash mark. Always pin and sew

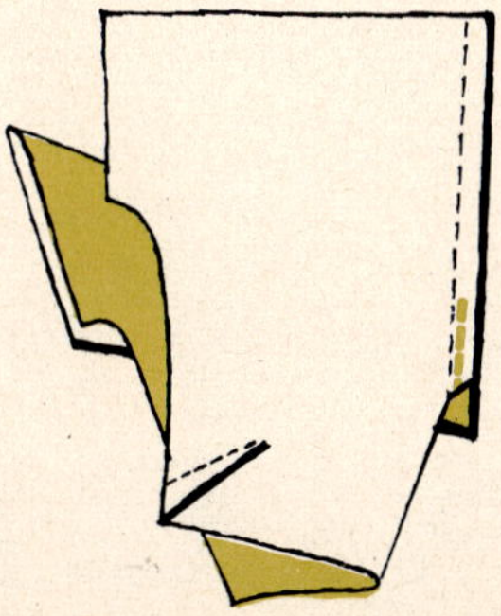

the seams with slash side turned up.

Now swing the slash open and pin the seams together

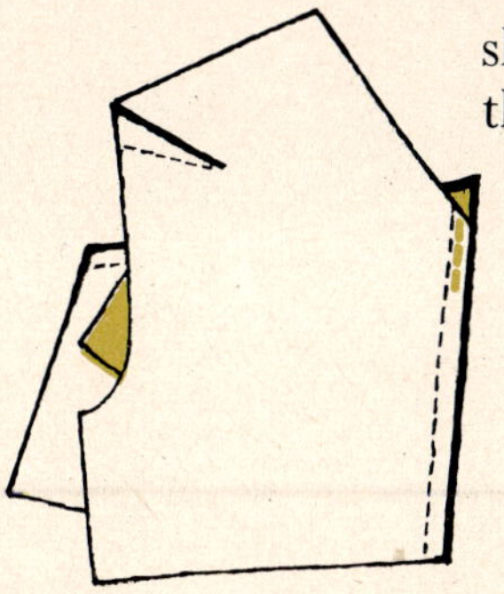

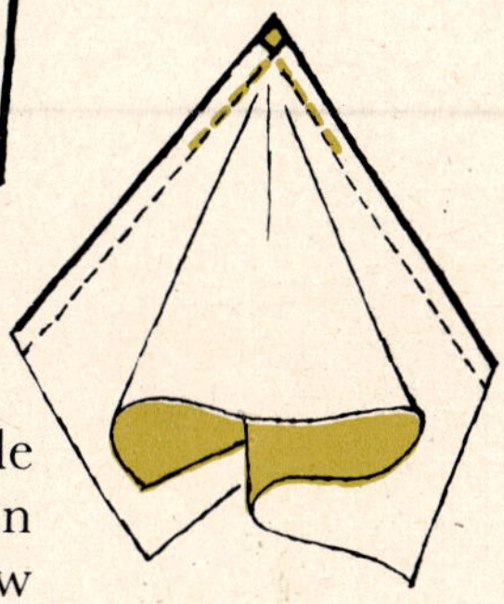

at the other side of the angle. When you start to sew the pieces together, stitch just inside the original stitching line on both pieces for a perfect corner.

If the fabric is soft or loosely woven, it is a good idea to reinforce the corner with an interfacing to prevent raveling. China silk, taffeta, lawn, or organdy can be used. Cut a small piece and sew it in the corner as you do the stitching for the seamline. Keep the interfacing flat along the inside of

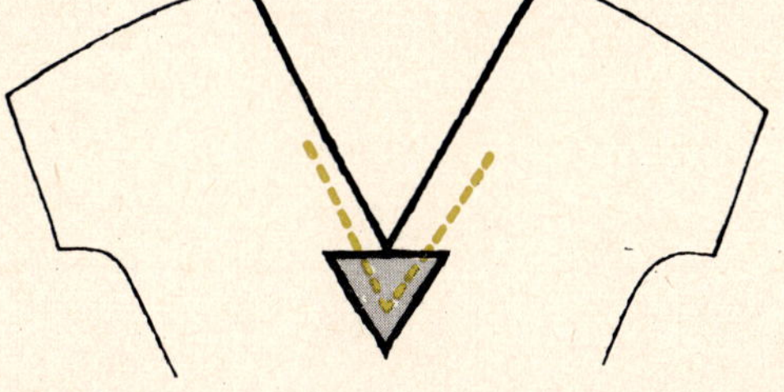

the dress as you do your stitching.

When you join for the point, sew it in with the regular seam.

Many other places on your clothes will also have to be marked and sewed like this. The shawl collar, for instance, is done exactly the same way.

Shawl collar

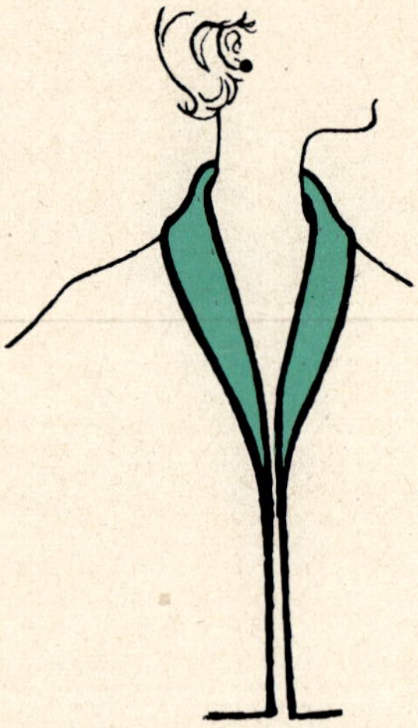

Mark and stitch the seam allowance 2 inches in each direction from the point where the neck and shoulder seams meet on the bodice back. Do the

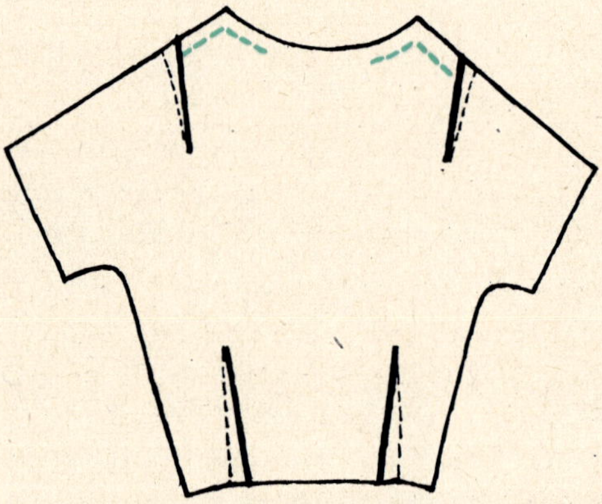

same on the corner of collar and facing. This can be done with thread of a contrasting color which is easier to see and will not show on the finished side. After the

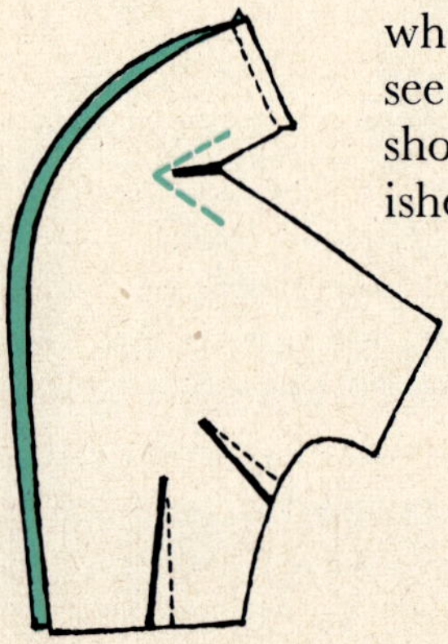

corner has been stitched, clip in at an angle to this stitching line.

Pin the front and back shoulder

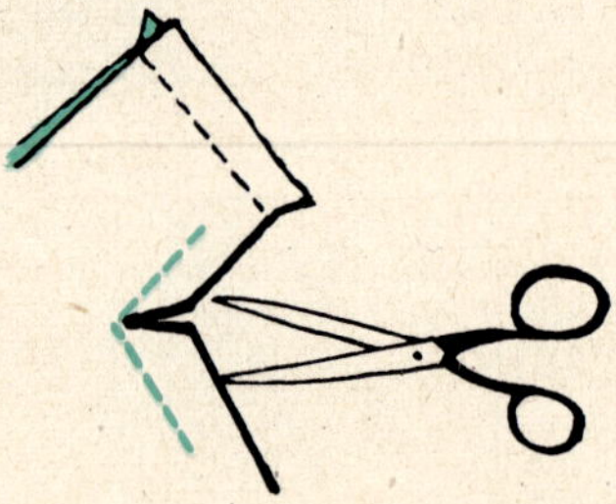

seams together. The base of the slash on the front shoulder should meet the point on the back shoulder and neck.

The slash spreads open as the collar is pinned to the back neckline. Stitch within the original stitching line when

joining the back and front bodice at this corner. Check both sides of the seam to be sure they're even.

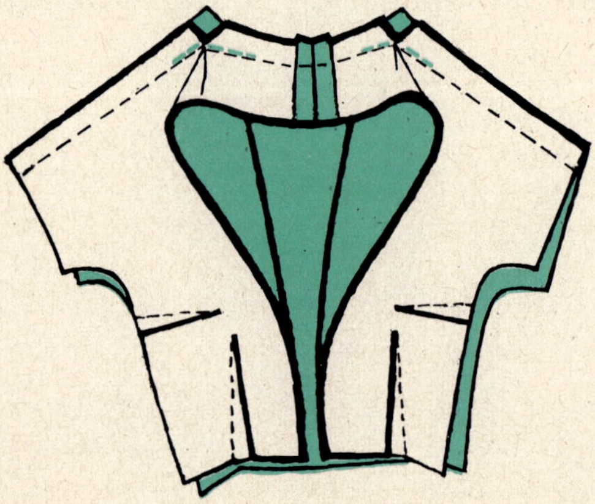

Gussets

Here's another construction detail based on the same principle. Treat the slash end of the gusset in the same way as you treated a corner.

Mark the slash line very carefully from your pattern. Cut a piece of fabric $1\frac{1}{2}$ by 3 inches. Use any lightweight, firm interfacing.

Place this piece of fabric on the underside of your garment at the end of the slash line. Catch this piece in place as you sew the line of stitching that reinforces the corner.

When sewing, carefully follow the lines marked from the pattern. The angle of these lines is important. As you come to the end of the slash line, take one extra stitch across the end before sewing the other side of the

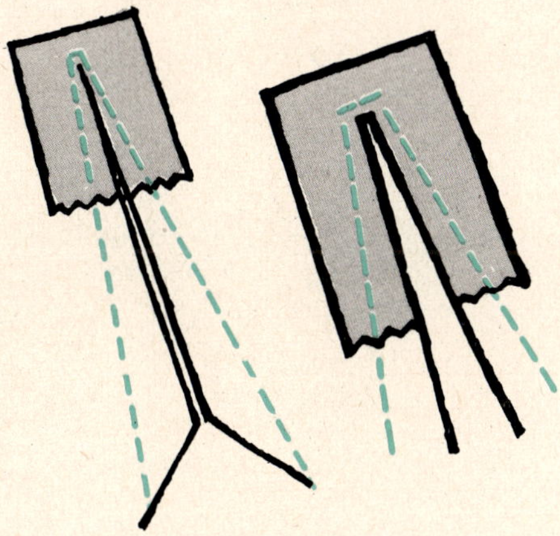

slash. Mark the seam allowance at the points of the gusset pieces and stitch for 1 inch on either side.

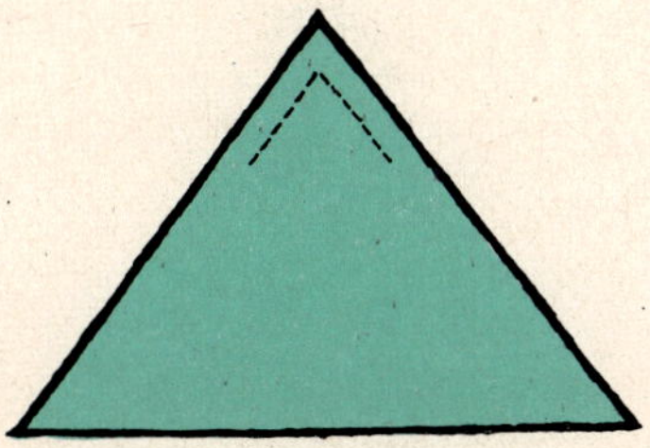

Now with the right sides together, pin the gusset into the slash. Start at the end of the slash and pin it to the point of the gusset.

The stitching lines of contrasting colored thread on each of these pieces will serve as guide lines.

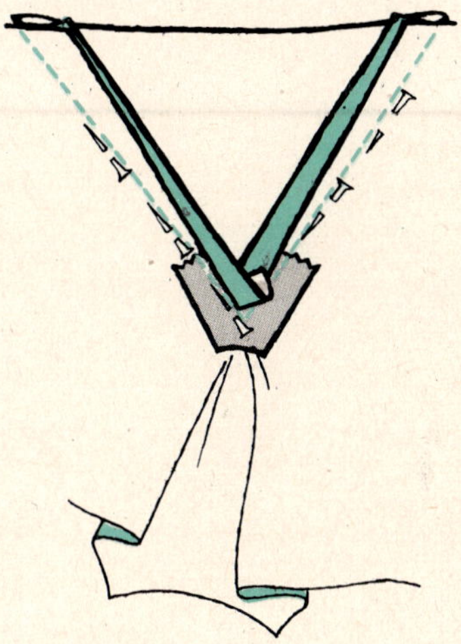

Pin one side of the slash to one side of the gusset piece; spread the other side of the slash open and pin it to the other side of the gusset.

Take a full $\frac{5}{8}$-inch seam on the gusset as you sew the pieces together. On the slash, the seam allowance is $\frac{5}{8}$ inch at the opening of the slash, but slopes to nothing at the end of the slash. This is why the stitching is needed as a guide line and for reinforcement at this delicate corner.

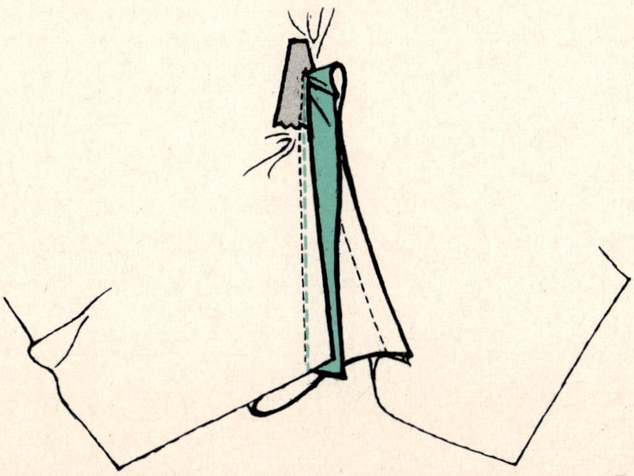

Facings

When the dress opens down the front it is advisable to interface it. On the buttonhole side, the interfacing is cut like the facing and put to the wrong side of the front so the buttonholes can be made right through it.

If it is a fold-back facing, the interfacing is only cut to the fold line. Blind-tack the edges of the interfacing to the dress with a catch-stitch. If it

is a convertible neckline that may be opened, then interface the left side of the neck in the same way.

If the fronts close up to the neckline, the interfacings on the left side can be stitched to the facings by machine, then turned to the inside.

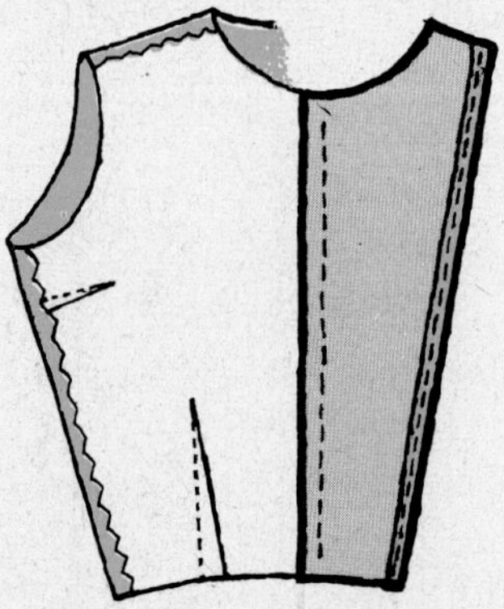

If the facings are sewed to the front, the interfacings can be sewed into the seam with the exception of the non-woven type of interfacing.

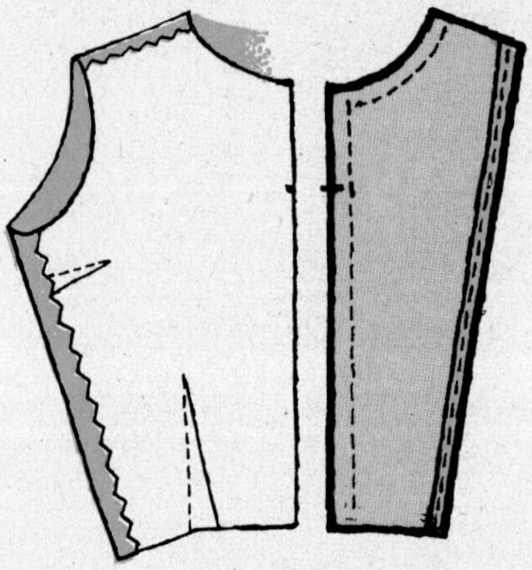

Children's clothes can be finished with bias at the neck, but in women's clothes, a shaped facing is a finer finish. If your pattern doesn't include a shaped facing for the back (or front) of the neck, you can easily cut it from the pattern of the back and front bodice. The back and front facings should be sewed together. Turn the edges back ¼ inch and sew.

Facings used with a collar

You have already sewed the collar to the neck of your garment. It is only necessary to pin the right side of the facing over the right side of the dress on the seam allowance line and sew. The collar is between the two fabric layers and will not slip, since it's already firmly sewed in place.

It isn't necessary to interface the back neck facing when a collar is used. Trim the seam allowance and then clip around the neck about every ¼ inch.

Facings for other types of necklines

Round neck

Choose the interfacing to suit your dress fabric. Cut the facings and interfacings from the same pattern pieces.

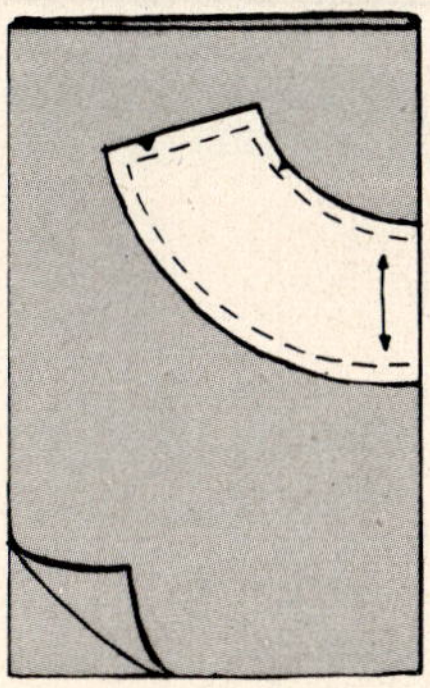

If the non-woven type of interfacing is used, cut away the neck seam allowance on the interfacing.

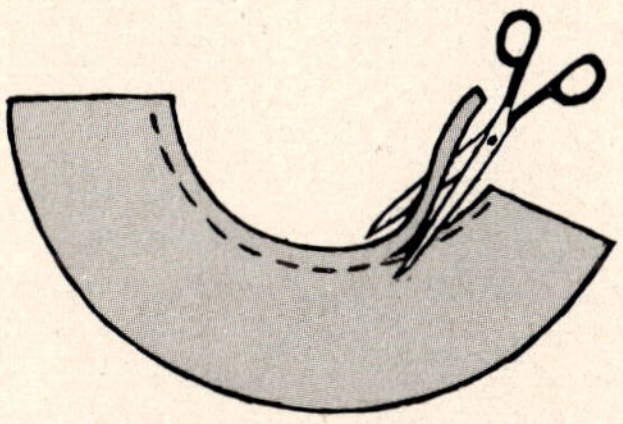

The shoulder seams of the facings and interfacings are sewed separately. Place the interfacing against the wrong side of the facing. The neckline seam allowance will extend all around. Stitch the interfacing into place.

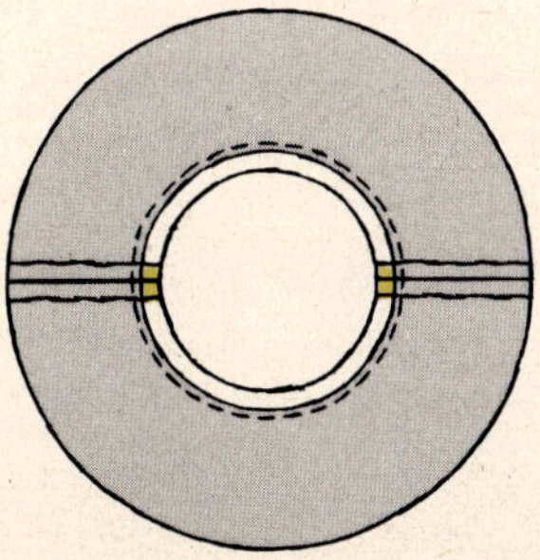

If the fabric ravels, cut ¼ inch of the interfacing at the outside edge, turn upper fabric back and sew.

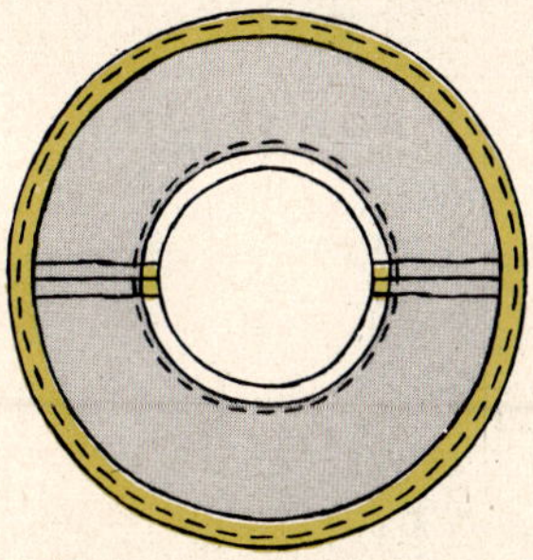

On a firm or heavy fabric, stitch the outside edges together and pink.

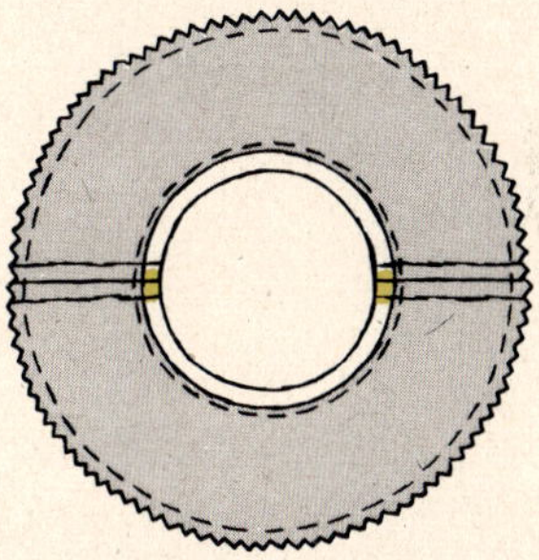

Put the right side of the facing to the right side of the neck and stitch. The trick is to stitch along the edge of the interfacing, not through it. Trim the neckline seam away in graduated widths. Then carefully clip around the neckline about ½ inch to the stitching line.

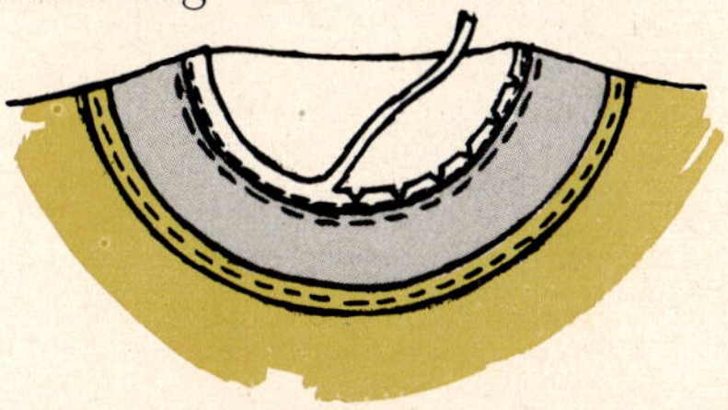

When using any woven fabric as interfacing, it isn't necessary to cut away the seam allowance at the neckline. Sew the facings and interfacings together before stitching the facings to the dress. Follow the same method in sewing all other details.

Square neckline

Cut interfacing and facing from the same pattern piece. Choose the interfacing to suit the upper fabric. On a non-woven interfacing, cut away the seam allowance at the neckline. Be careful to make a square corner.

To be sure the corners are correct, it's a good idea to mark the seam allowance at each corner with tailor's chalk. Sew with contrasting thread.

Follow the instructions given for the round neck when applying the interfacing to facings. As you sew the

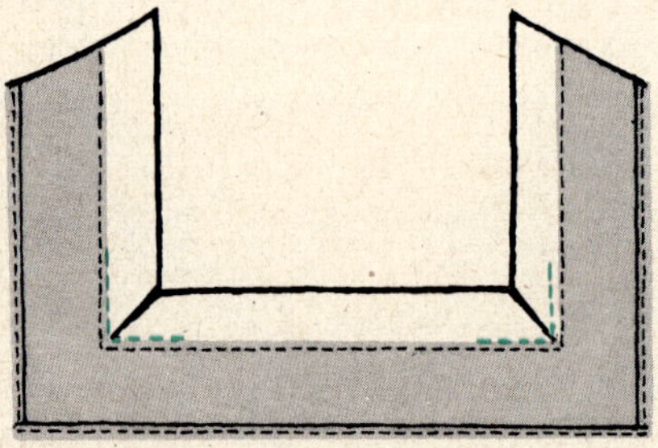

facings to the neck, be sure to follow the stitching marks at each corner for really sharp corners.

Again, graduate the neckline seams as you trim them. It is only necessary to clip around the neck at the back where it is curved. The most important thing is to slash well into the corners, all the way to the stitching, for a really professional look.

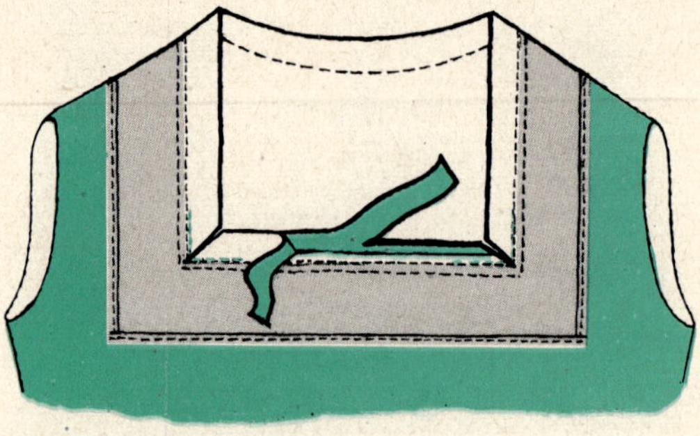

Shaped neckline

For this neckline, use a non-woven interfacing only. This helps to achieve and retain the shape of the neckline.

Cut the interfacing and facing from the same pattern piece. On the interfacing cut away the neckline seam and the design detail to the finished line. Sew it to the facing along the edge. The non-woven interfacing will not ravel and acts as a guide line so the detail will be perfectly matched. Follow the instructions given for facing the round neck of your garment.

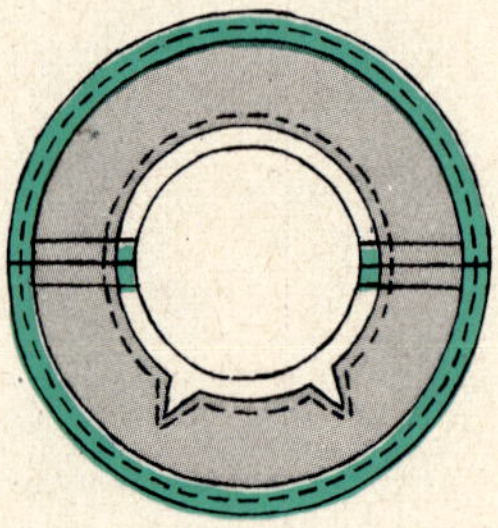

Facing the sleeveless dress

The sleeveless dress has become popular for dress-up clothes as well as for playtime fashions. Sometimes this dress top is completely lined.

In many patterns, the neck and armholes are faced all in one piece. It is a better finish when made this way. The professional way can be done entirely by machine, and is very fast.

Facing the top of a dress

Sew all of the bodice together except the shoulder seams. Sew facings together, except for the shoulders.

Now put the right side of the facing against the right side of the dress and stitch to 2 inches from the end of the shoulder seam on both the neckline and the armhole. Trim away half of the seam allowance where the neckline and armholes have been faced, and clip the seam all around. Then turn the garment to the right side and press.

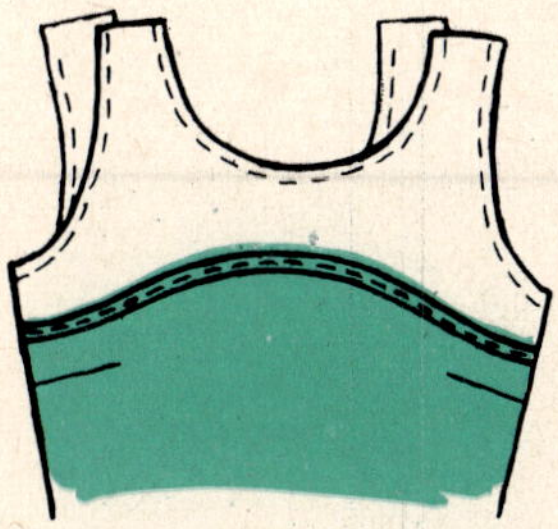

Now, here's the professional trick.

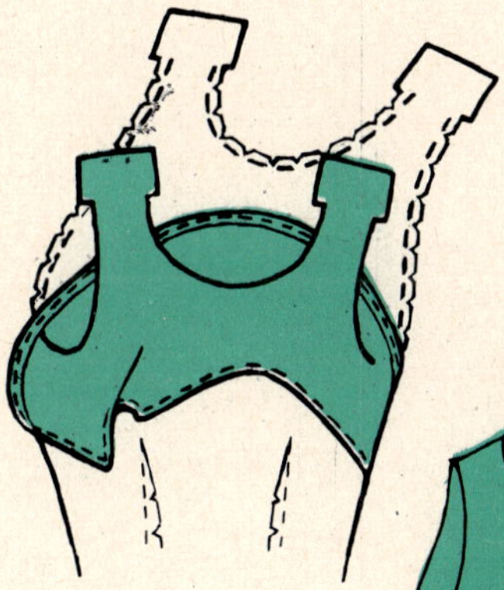

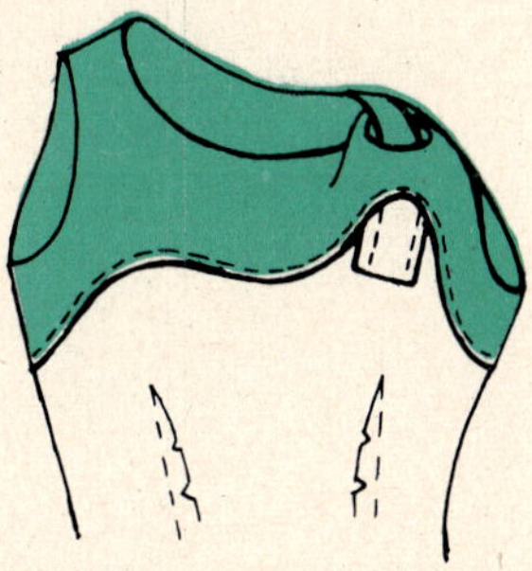

Turn the back shoulder strap inside out. Slide the front shoulder strap into the back strap. The right side of the front will be against the right side of the back. Pin the front and back shoulder seams together and sew.

The front and back facing will also come together. Pin them and sew.

Now pull the front even farther into back strap so openings at the side of the shoulder straps are clear. Press open the shoulder seams. Stitch the openings on either side, and trim the seam. Pull the front strap into position. This will automatically turn the back shoulders right side out. The whole top of the dress will be faced, with only minor tacking to be done to finish the dress. If the top of the dress is to be completely lined in self-fabric, it is done in the same way.

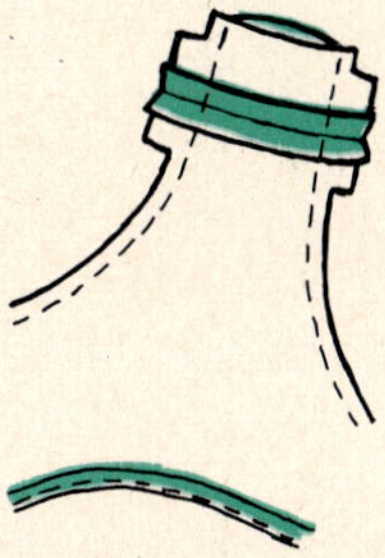

When the top is to be lined in a China silk or other type of lining, however, the dress and lining are sewed together—wrong side of lining against wrong side of dress, as was done when lining the sheath.

The facing pieces are cut of self-fabric and are handled as though the dress were not lined. This is because soft or contrasting linings have a tendency to roll out and show at the neck edges.

If the dress is lined with a more crisp fabric, like taffeta, the fabric has enough body to serve as a facing. In that case, apply the lining to the dress as if it were a facing.

Bias

Bias is made by cutting the material on the diagonal grain. This creates greater elasticity, which means that the material can be used in many more ways than a straight piece of fabric.

It must be cut on the true bias, however, or it will twist and pull and be difficult to use. Many home sewers have difficulty with a bias they make themselves, but can use commercial bias with no trouble. The trick is to make from self-fabric a binding as easy to use as the commercial binding. Here's how it's done.

Bias binding

To get a true bias, fold your material so the crosswise thread runs parallel to the lengthwise thread or selvage. Mark the width you want with chalk and cut. Cut the bias strip twice the width it will be when finished, plus ½ inch seam allowance.

Join all the bias pieces on the length of the goods. Fold the bias on the

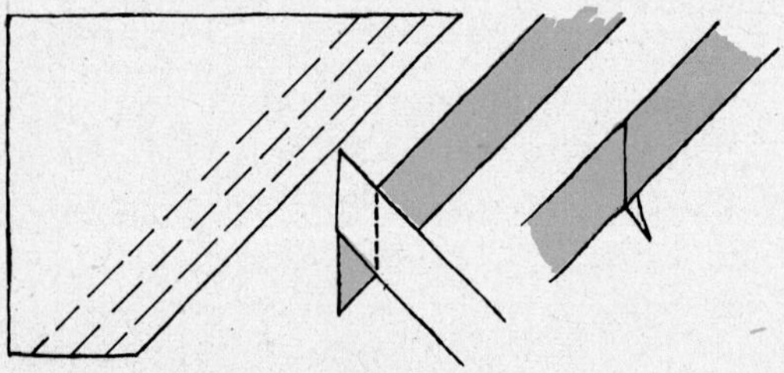

CUTTING JOINING

length and press. Trim the edges so the entire length of the bias is even. Bias piece is now pressed and ready to use. It will be as easy to work with as any of the commercial bindings you've used in the past.

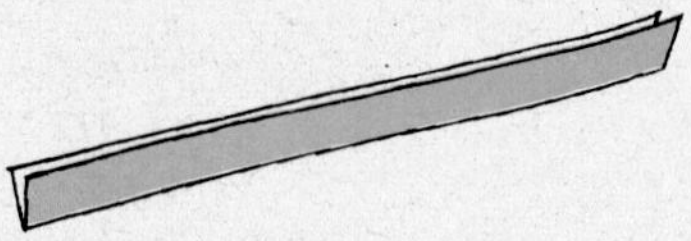

Roll binding (French piping)

This is used on sheer fabrics or as a trim. Take the pressed binding and sew the raw edges to the edges of the garment, right sides together.

Trim the seam to half the width of the binding and roll the fold edge over it. Tack in place just under the stitching line. Stretch the binding as you sew it so it will finish smooth and flat against the neck.

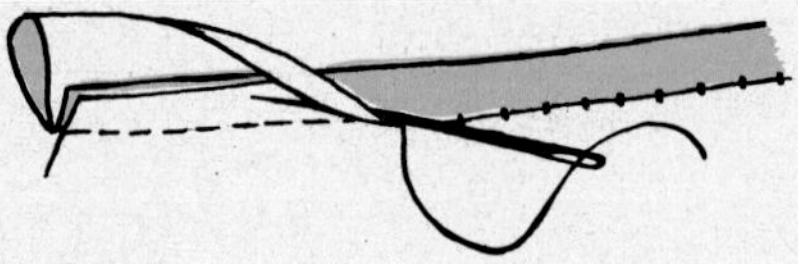

Bias facing

For a smooth, flat bias facing, trim one side of the bias off between the fold edge and the raw edge.

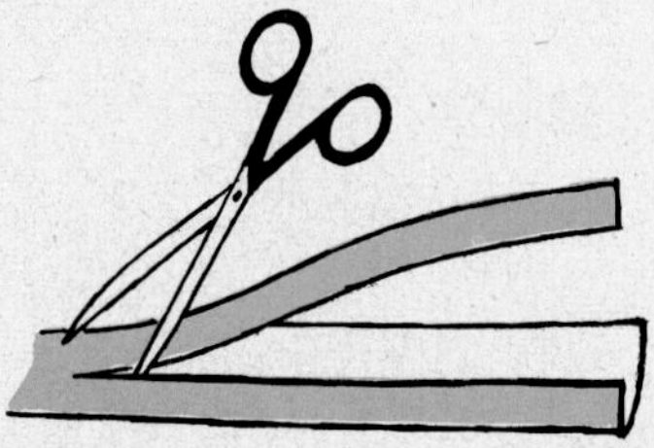

If the bias is to be used on a curve (around a neck, for example), curve the bias to the shape of the neck with an iron before applying it.

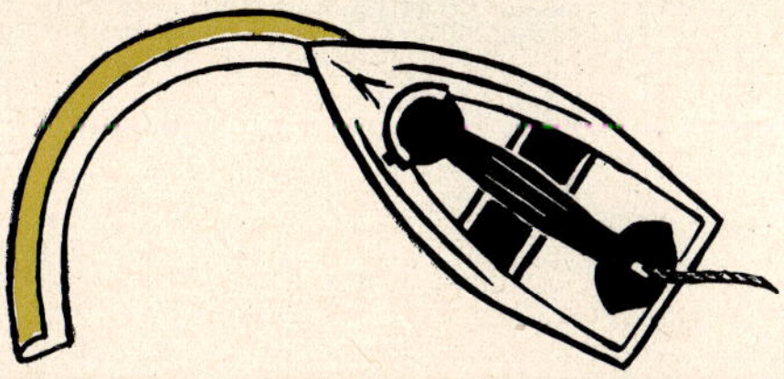

Sew the raw edge to the neckline. The fold edge should be held flat along the neck where it will be tacked. Clip in every ½ inch on the neckline seam to the stitching. Then turn bias to inside and slip-stitch into place.

This method of making bias binding is quick and easy. It makes an even bias with the outer edge folded and ready to be finished.

Bias cording—piping

Formerly, bias bindings were only used on children's clothes and aprons. Fashions are now featuring self-bindings and cording on necklines, pockets, and jacket edges. Jackets, in particular, use self-fabric bindings and cording, as well as braids, quite extensively. Here is a professional trick for handling self-cording.

Cording

This is a decorative trim used in seams and around collars. Cut the bias and cover the cording as you did for the cord buttonhole. The same ⅛-inch cording is generally used, so the bias should be 1¼ inches.

On rare occasions, a heavier cording is used for a trim. The bias should then be cut wider. There should always be a ½ inch seam allowance.

If the cording is to be used in the edge of a collar, sew the cord to the right side, with seam edges of collar and cording even. Clip cording seam.

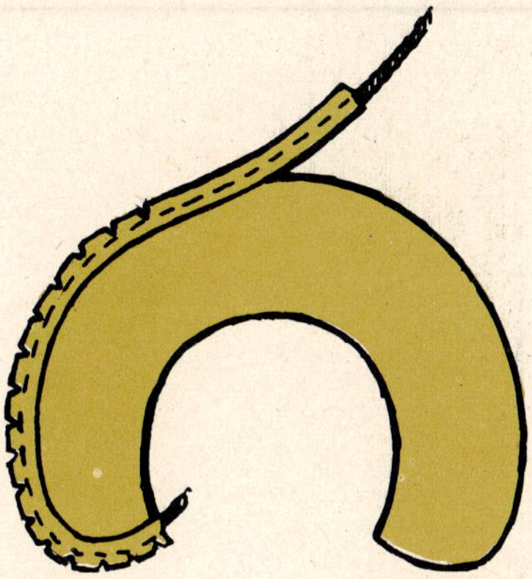

Pin the facing to the collar with the stitching line of the cording showing.

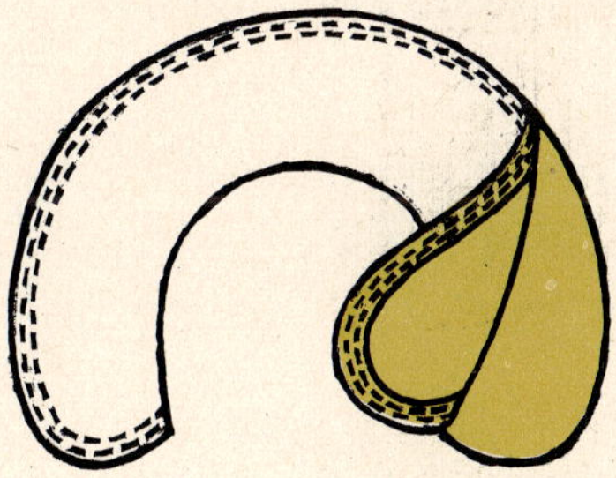

Sew the upper and under collars together along this stitching line. Trim seam, turn collar to right side, and the cording will be perfect.

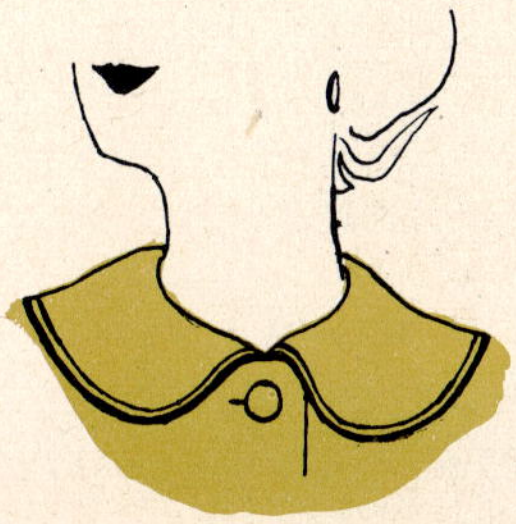

The same method is used for cording the seam of your garment. Sew the cording to the right side first so you can see it is accurate. Then permanently join the cording by stitching along the original cord stitching line on the wrong side.

Corded piping and facing

When a cording is used around the neck, armhole, or sleeve, you can use the bias of the cording as the finish rather than a separate facing.

Cut the bias about 3 inches wide. Press this bias strip in half on the length. Then cut away one side of it as you did for bias facing. Leave a ½-inch turn-back. Fold the other edge over the cording and sew the cording in place where indicated.

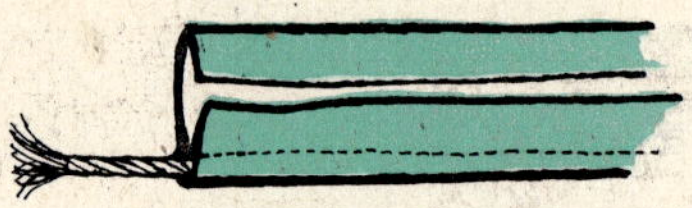

Put this side face down on the right side of the dress and sew. The bias will extend well beyond the seam edge of the dress. If the binding is used on

a curved seam such as the neck, this seam will have to be clipped all around as you do on any curve.

Turn the bias to the inside and

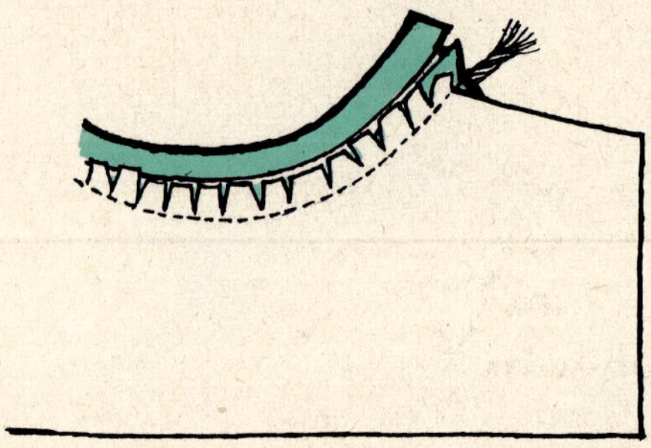

press, and you'll have a corded edge on the garment with a deep bias facing ready to be tacked in place.

If the cording is to be used on a

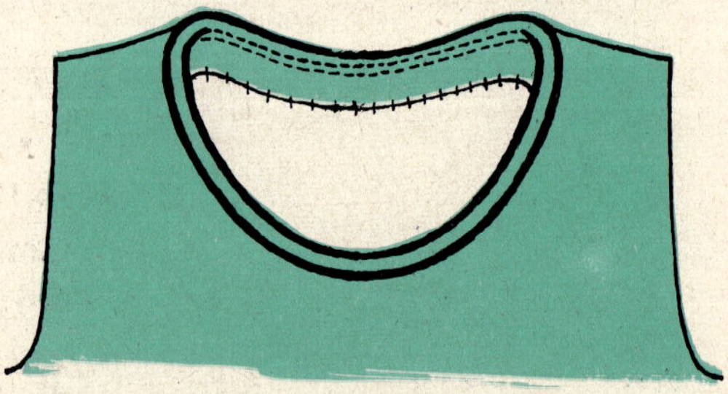

curved seam such as a neckline, ease the bias piece enough so it will follow the curve of the neck. Steam press it so any fullness will be smoothed. When the bias is sewed and turned to the inside of the garment, it will make a smooth, flat facing.

Tubing (or "spaghetti")

Tubing or spaghetti is used for frogs, loops, belts, and many other decorative trimmings. There are several types of decorative tubing that you can make for different uses.

Plain tubing is soft and pliable, used for spaghetti trim. It can be any thickness. It is made over cable cord, so get the weight cord that will give you the thickness you want for your design detail. Cut the bias the length you want, making sure it is wide

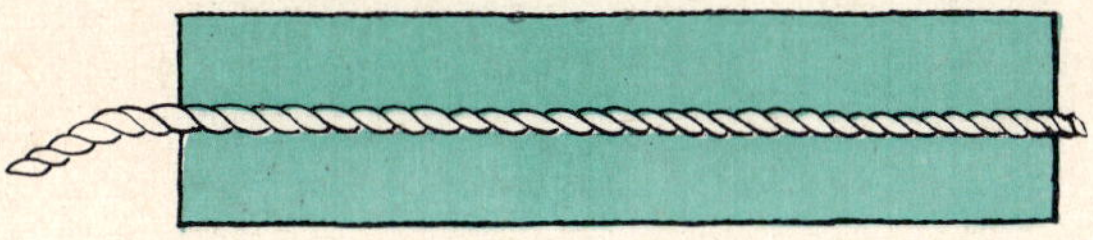

enough to cover the cable cord. Cut a piece of cable cord the same length. Fold the bias over the cording and stitch with the cording foot. Stretch the bias as much as possible. At the end of the cording, sew the bias to

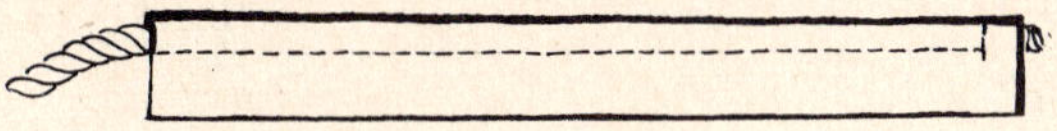

the cord. If you want the tubing to be soft, cut away the seam allowance close to the seamline.

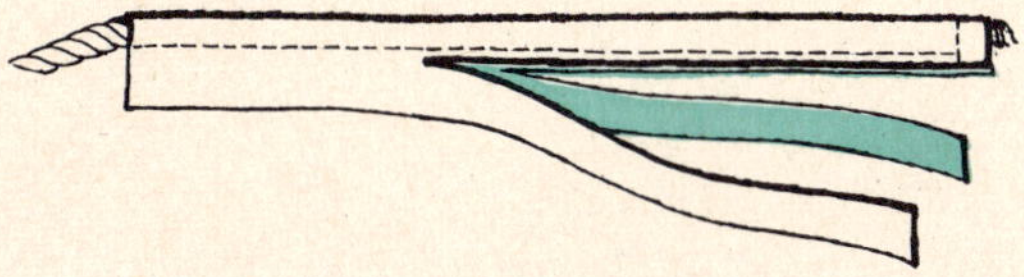

Holding the cord at the open end, slide the bias down over the cord until it turns inside out on itself.

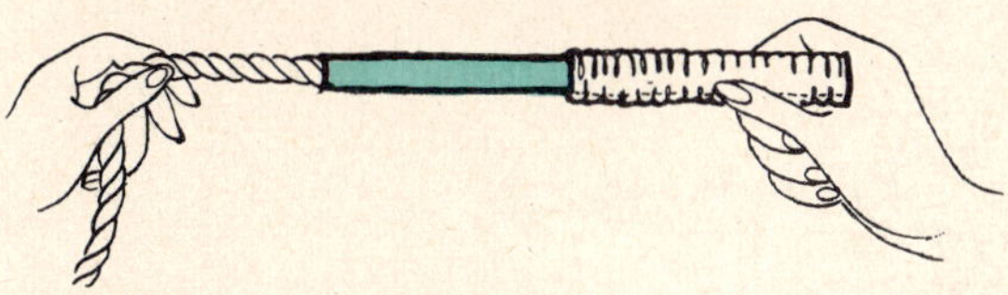

The cording is free and can be cut off. The tubing will be even for the whole length since the cording helped to shape it. However, the tubing will be soft since it has no filler.

For a firmer tubing, work the same way but leave the seam allowances untacked. As the tubing turns inside out, the seam allowance rolls up inside, forming a filler and making it much more firm. The weight of the fabric and the width of the seam will determine the firmness of the tubing.

Corded tubing

Choose the cording thickness you want, and cut the cable cord twice the length of the bias. Fold the bias

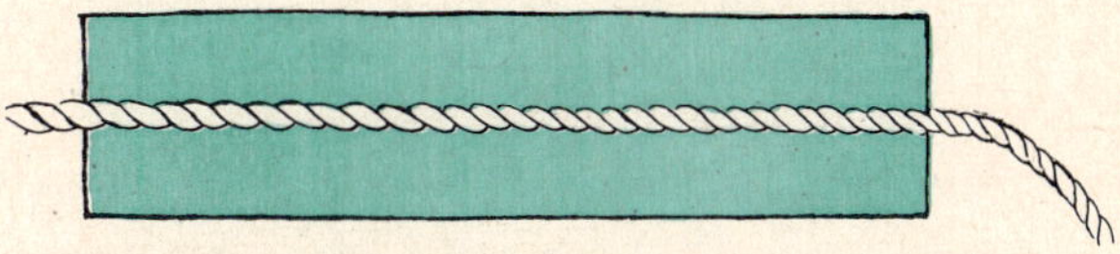

over one end of the cord and sew with a cording foot. Be sure to stretch the bias, as you sew. At the end of the bias, sew the bias to the cord. This will leave about half the cord un-

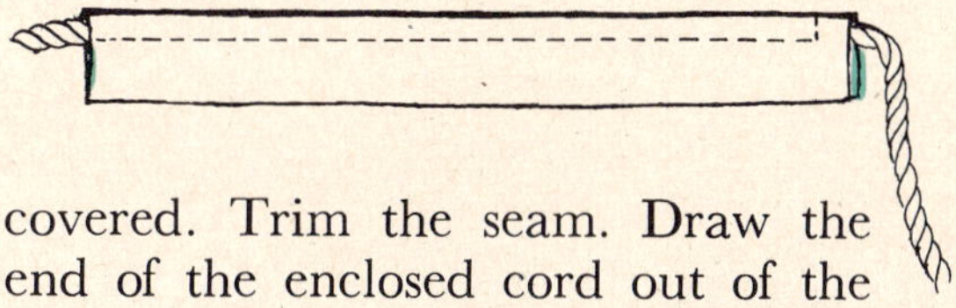

covered. Trim the seam. Draw the end of the enclosed cord out of the

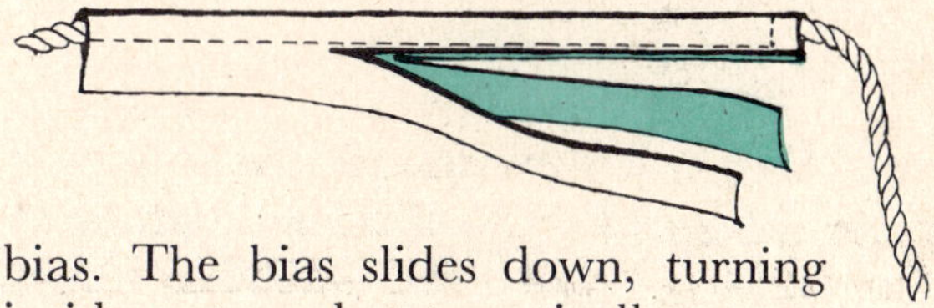

bias. The bias slides down, turning inside out, and automatically covering the other end of the cord.

The exposed end can then be cut

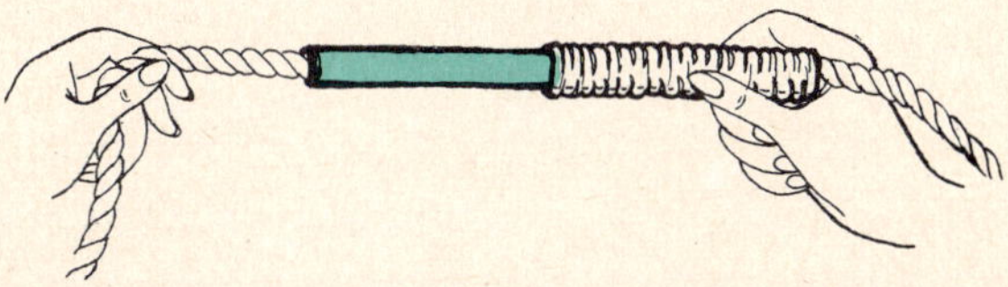

away, and you will have a firm corded bias tubing. (See sketch below.)

Pockets

Some pockets are utilitarian while others have a decorative effect. It's a good idea to learn to make both kinds so that you can use each style as needed to finish your dress.

Side seam pockets

These pockets, set in the side seam, are very practical. You may want to add them to your dress whether the pattern shows them or not.

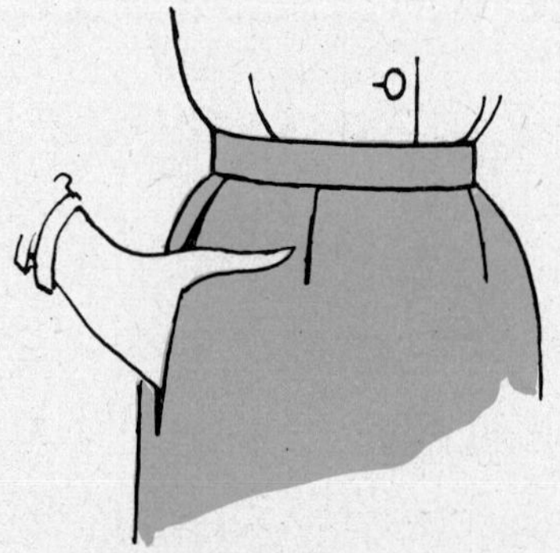

Before the side seams of your skirt have been joined, place the right side of the pocket against the right side of the skirt and sew to about 3 inches from the bottom of the pocket or to where it's marked on the pattern.

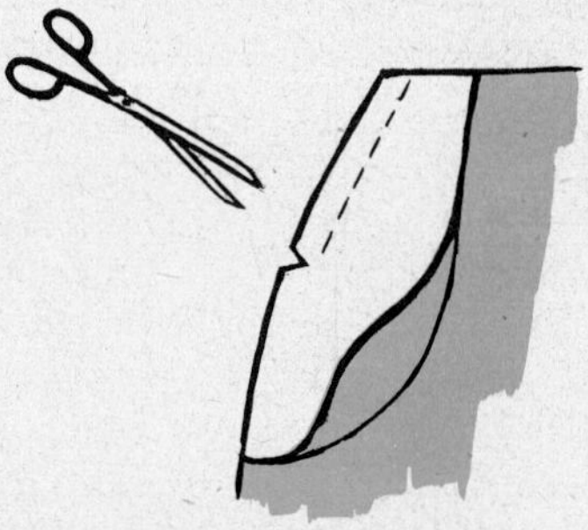

Clip into the stitching line at the base of the stitching. Trim the seam. Turn the pocket to the inside.

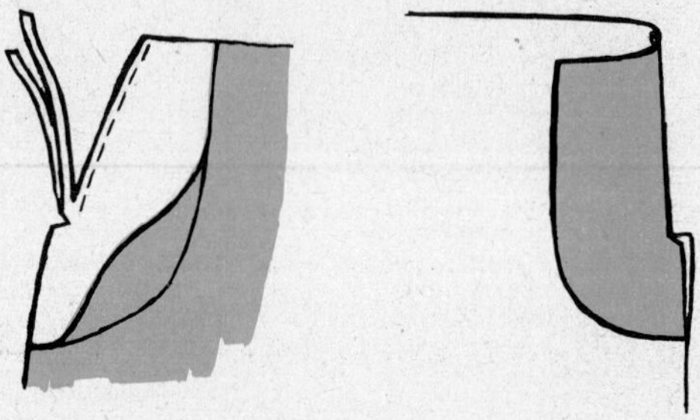

Next, put the right side of the second pocket piece against the front pocket piece and stitch all around.

Stitch the pocket pieces to the front skirt at the base of the pocket on the seam allowance line.

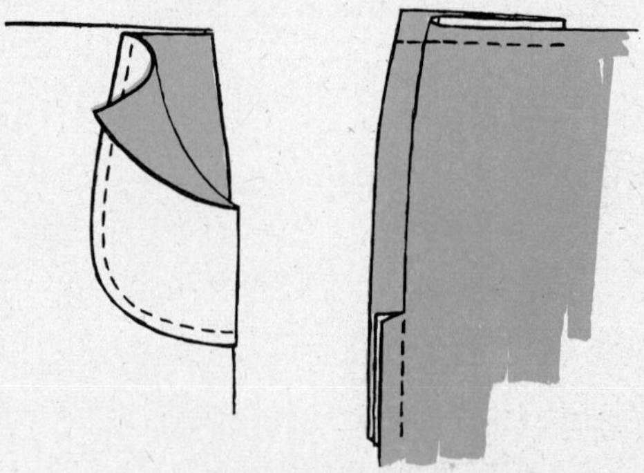

Put the right side of the back and front skirts together and stitch them up the side seam. Stitch on the front side of the skirt, just inside the line of stitching that holds the pocket pieces in place. Making a side seam pocket is as easy as sewing a seam.

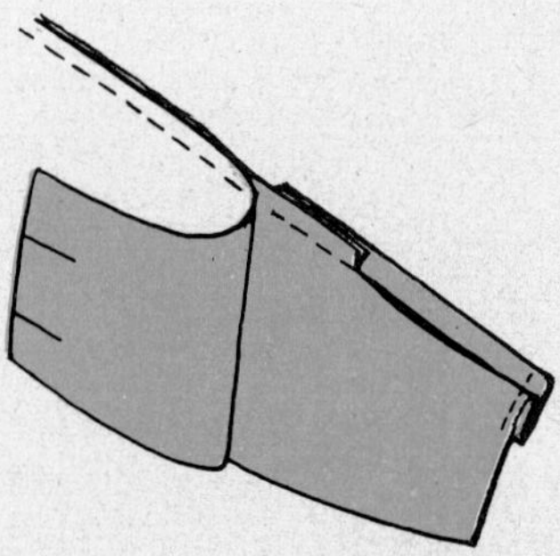

Slash pocket

This pocket is made with two pieces of fabric much like the cord buttonhole. (In fact, the corded buttonhole makes a beautiful pocket.)

For the slash pocket, cut two pieces of fabric 1 inch wide and the length of your pocket, plus the seam allowance. Fold the pieces in half on the length and press. Stitch through the

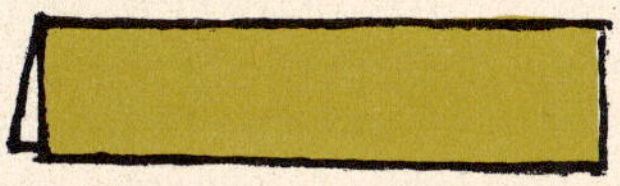

center of each piece. Be sure to have a ¼ inch space on the fold side.

Mark with a basting thread for the placement of the pocket on the dress.

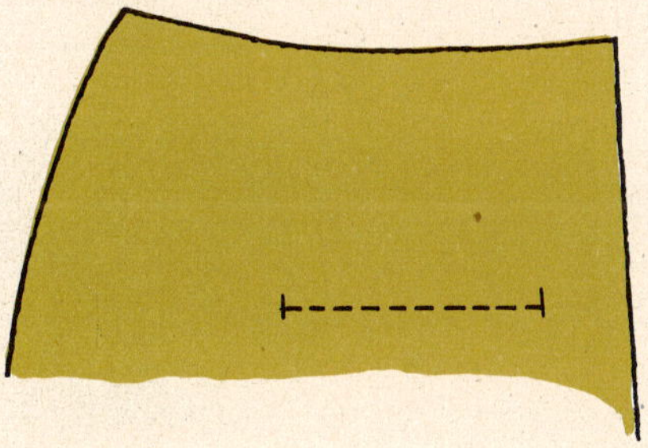

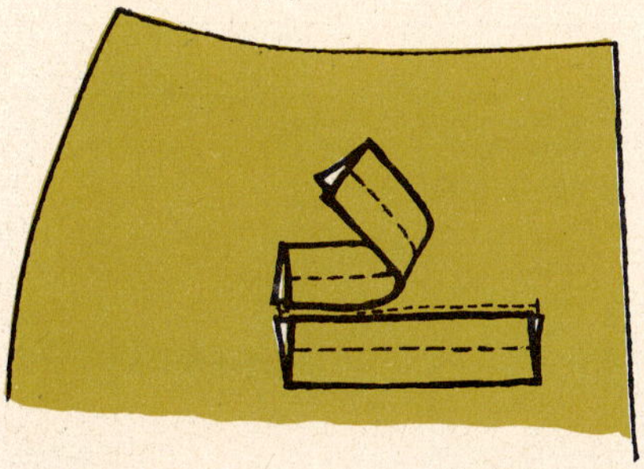

Stitch the raw edges of the pocket pieces to either side of the basting line to ½ inch from either end. If your dress fabric is soft or ravels easily, reinforce it with an interfacing as you did for the buttonholes.

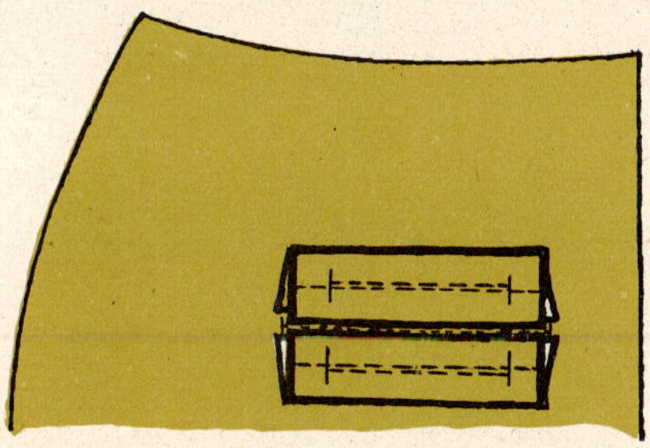

Turn the garment to the wrong side and check the stitching lines. They should be the same length and should be ½ inch apart. If they are uneven, rip the piece and resew it before anything is cut. When the stitching lines are even, slash through the center to ½ inch from either end, then slash diagonally into the corners.

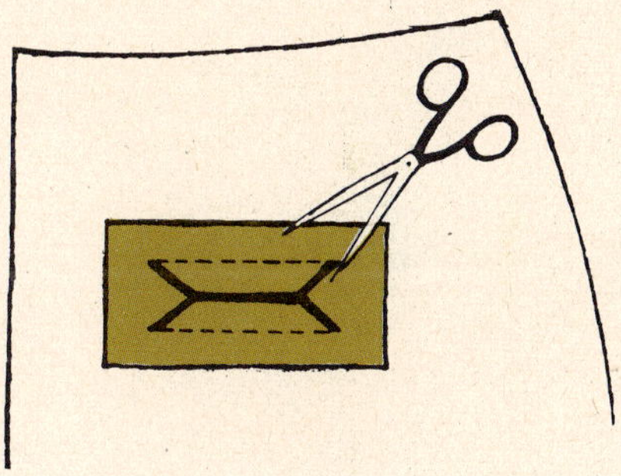

Turn the welt pieces to the inside to form the pocket. Fold back the dress and stitch the V at each end of the pocket to the welt pieces to

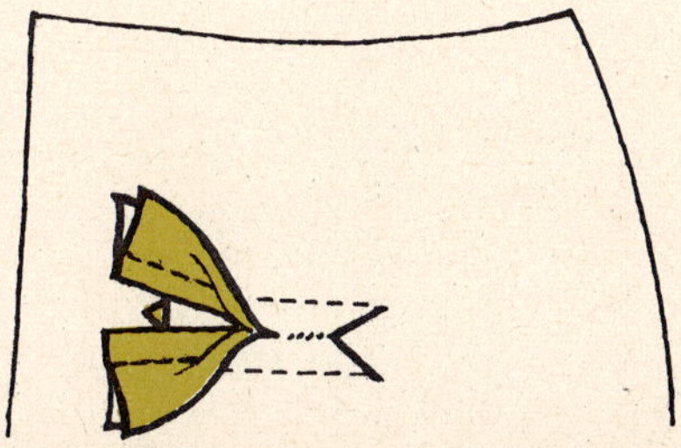

finish the opening to the pocket.

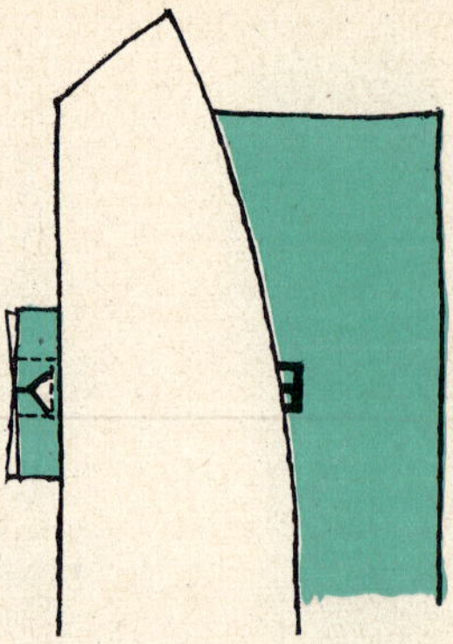

Now cut out 2 pocket pieces, the same width as welts. Decide on depth of your pocket and make under-pocket ½ inch less than upper pocket. Sew the deeper pocket piece to the upper edge of the welt seam. Be sure to sew it along the original stitching line of the welt, or the upper welt will appear to pucker. The under-pocket piece is stitched to the lower welt. The edge of the pocket piece is along the edge of the lower

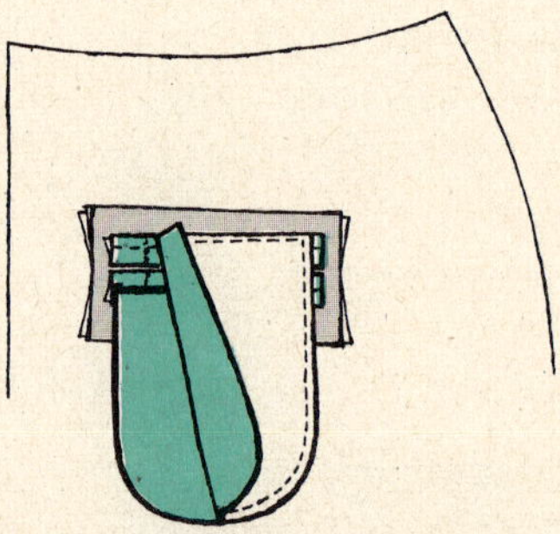

welt, but it is stitched along the original stitching line of the welt.

Finish the pocket by stitching its outer edges. Be sure to catch the triangles at either end of the welt into the seam. The finished pocket will look like a giant buttonhole.

Patch pocket

Before removing the pattern, clip on either side for the depth of the hem. Turn under the seam allowance on the upper edge of the pocket and stitch (A). Turn the hem to the right side of the pocket and stitch along the pocket on the seam allowance line (B).

Clip the seam allowance around the curve of the pocket (C). Turn the hem to the wrong side of the pocket and baste back the seam allowance all around (D). Press the hem, pin the pocket to the dress and top-stitch the edges (E). The pocket can be edge-stitched or sewed about ¼ inch in from the edge for trimming detail.

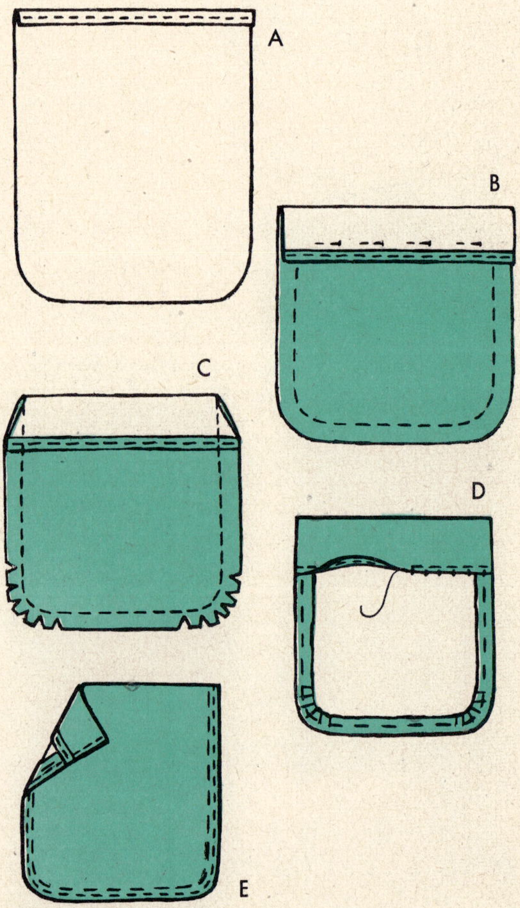

Chapter 7

Finishing details

A dress is not finished until the last stitch is taken. Just the way a button is sewed on can sometimes spoil it. If the facings are not tacked correctly, a smart dress can look dowdy. All of these finishing details, however, can be easily learned.

There is another phase of finishing not so easily learned—how to know when and where to use the right detail. For instance, what type of button is most suitable? What is the correct width of hem for the style of dress and the type of fabric you are using? How should certain points on the dress be pressed? Will a self-belt or a ready-made belt be more suitable? The answers to these questions depend on your knowledge of sewing and your own good judgment. This book will help to give you the skill and knowledge; the judgment will come as you gain more sewing experience.

The big mistake most women make is in overdoing hand finishing. They try to "nail down" everything so tightly that it ruins the appearance of the finished garment. Professionals say that clothes should look "pasted together." In other words, the finishing should be so inconspicuous that it hardly seems to exist. If you can sew a fine seam, save it for embroidery or baby garments. Used on your own clothes, it can ruin a dress.

Up to this point your dress is still in pieces. The bodice should have all the machine details, such as buttonholes, collars, facings, and pockets done. It should be ready for the hand finishing. Some women like to put the entire dress together and do the hand work last, but it is easier to do while the dress is still in sections.

Hand-stitching needed for finishing

Too often, a great deal of time is used to teach many different types of hand stitches—most of which are seldom, if ever, used. In this chapter, the following stitches will be used for the different types of finishings that are shown.

Running stitch

This is the most basic stitch in sewing. It is often used for gathering, mending, tucking. Pass the needle through the fabric, taking several stitches at a time. Draw the thread through the fabric and repeat.

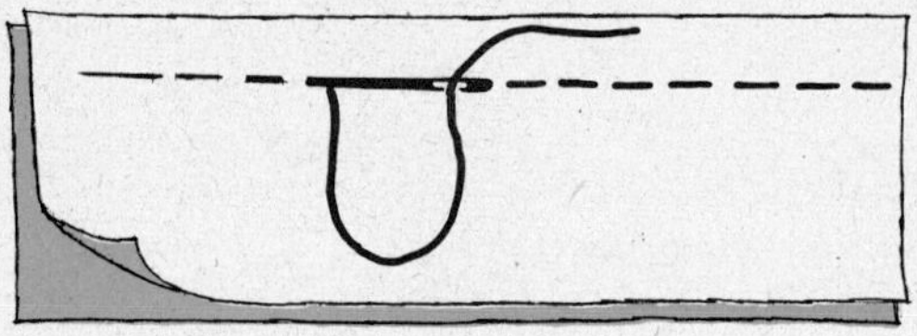

Backstitch

This is used where a stitch as firm as machine-stitching is needed. Take a small stitch, in and out of the fabric and pull the thread through. Go back, putting the needle in at the end of the preceding stitch. Bring it out a stitch ahead. Continue forward, back under, and forward again.

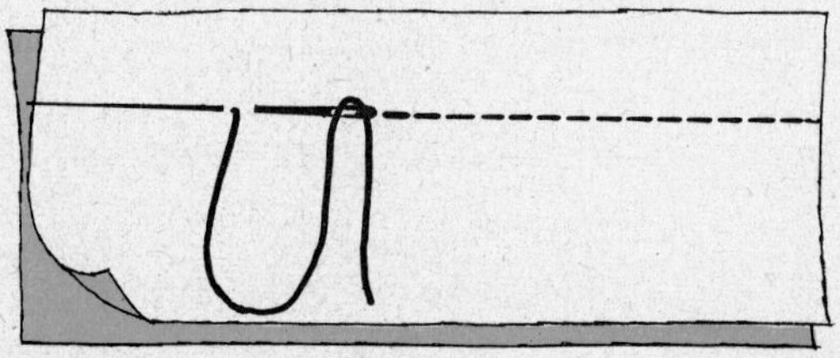

Even basting

Make this stitch the length needed, depending on where it is used. For basting before pressing, the stitch can be about ½ inch long, since there is no strain on it.

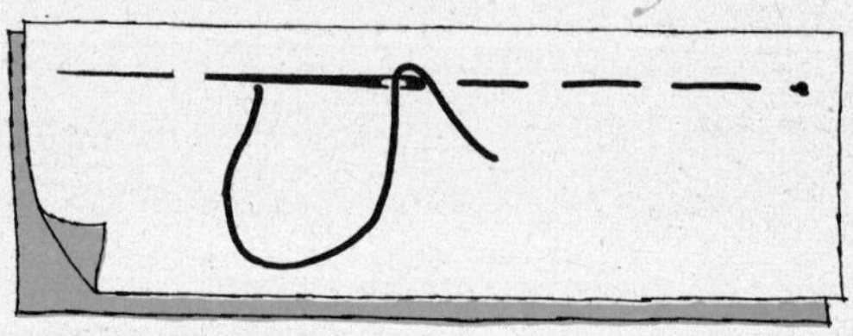

Overcasting

Use this stitch to finish a seam or an edge. The stitch goes through the fabric, over the edge, and through the fabric again in the same direction.

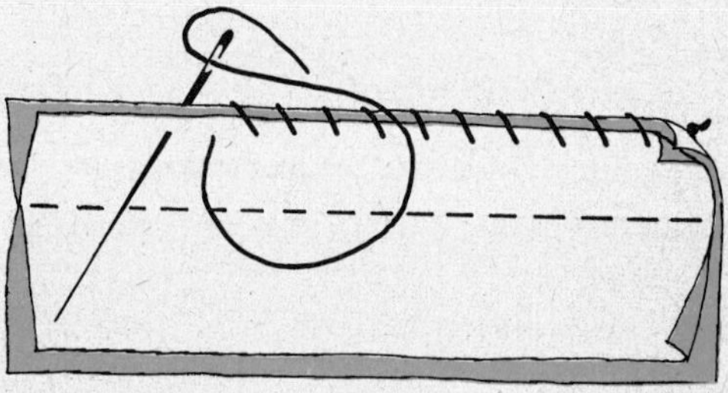

Slip-stitch

This is used to make the finish on hems and facings almost invisible. Knot the thread and slip the needle in the fold. Bring the needle out of the fold and take up a thread of the fabric at the same point. Slip the needle through the fold for about ½ inch. Continue this stitch. Keep it loose. Every few inches you can make a backstitch to hold. On hems, the stitch can be as long as ¾ inch. On facings, it is sometimes made even longer. This stitch should be used where there is no strain on it.

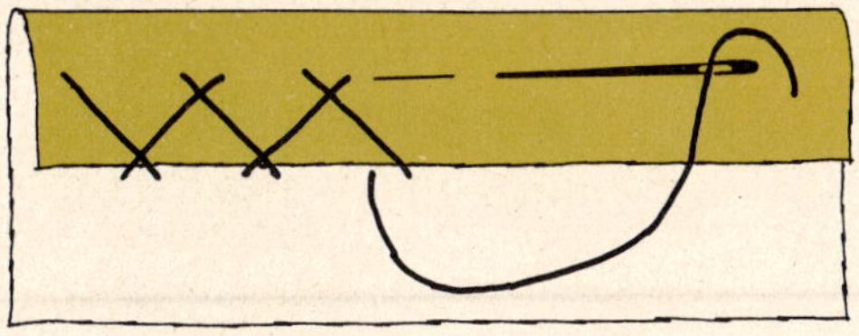

Catch-stitch

This stitch is used to finish hems on fabrics that don't fray, and to tack facings so the stitch won't hold too tightly and show on the right side. Work from left to right, taking a tiny stitch first on the hem or facing, then on the garment. Bring the needle toward you and then back. Keep the stitches even and loose.

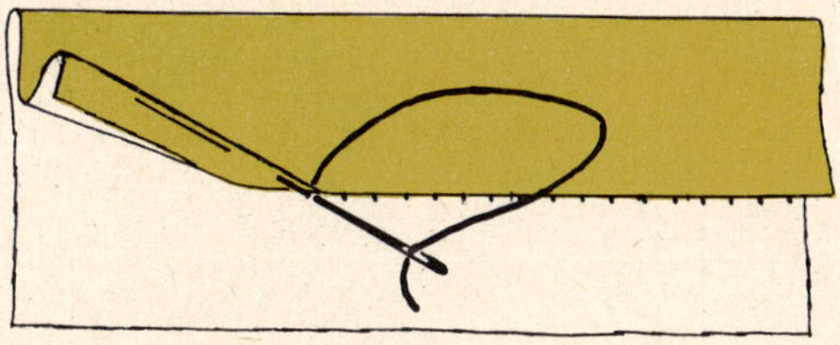

Hemming stitch

Bring the needle through the edge of the hem and take up one or two threads of the fabric underneath. These stitches are small, but do not show on the right side. This stitch is seldom used in hemming skirts.

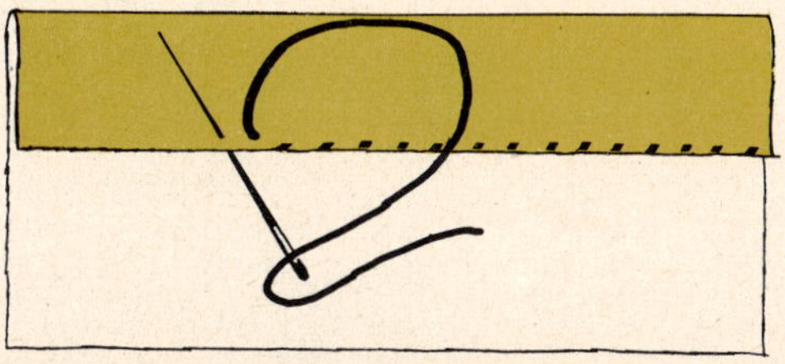

Facings

There are many types of facings used on the bodice. No matter what type of interfacing or finish you may have used on the square, V, boat, or round neck, the facings are only tacked to the neck at a few strategic places.

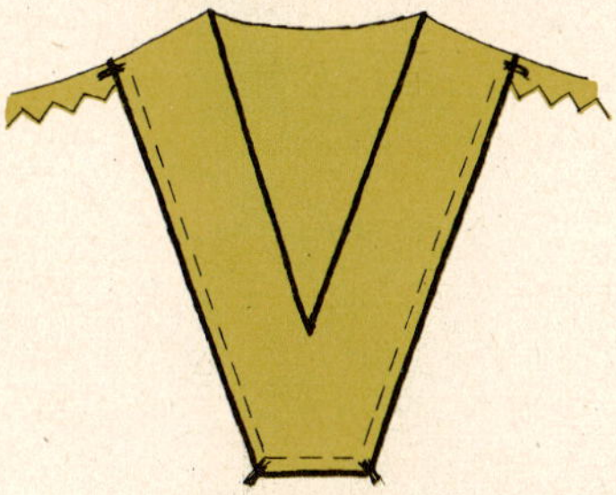

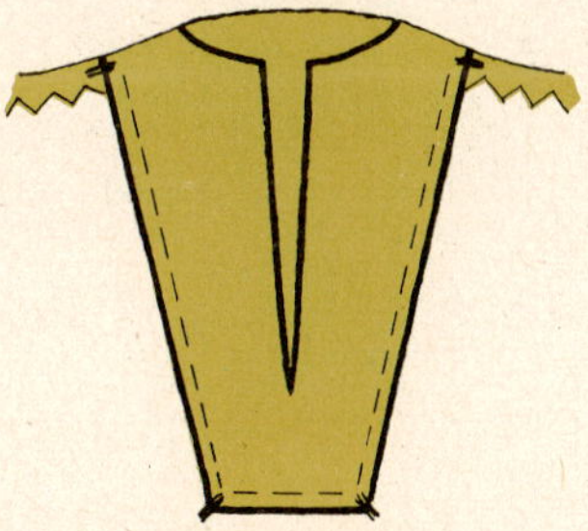

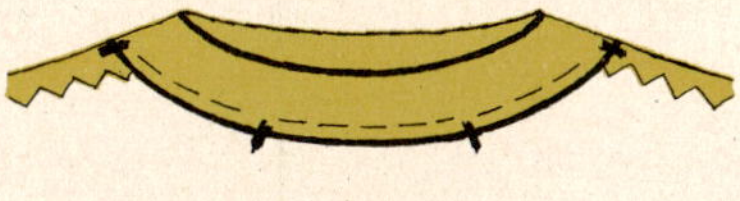

Button-down-the-front dress

The button-down-the-front dress, with or without a collar, also needs very little finishing. In fact, tacking the facings to the dress down the front is a sign of a real beginner! The only reason for finishing the facings is to hold them to the inside of the dress.

When you finish the buttonholes on the inside of one side of the dress and sew the buttons to the other side, the facings on the button-front dress are automatically held in place. You need only to tack the shoulder seams and a few points at the back of the neck for a neat finish.

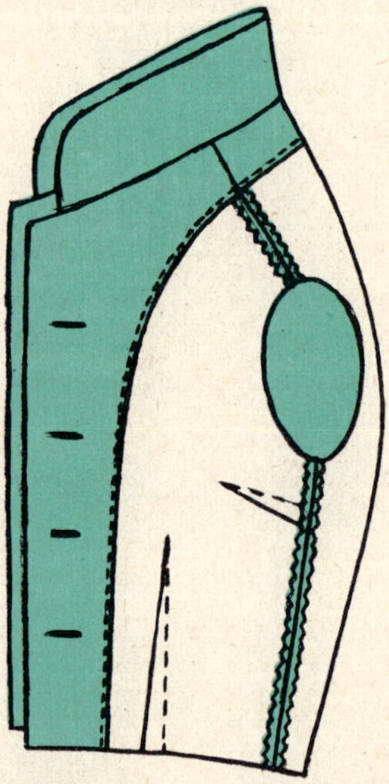

Shawl collar

The facings are usually cut the same as the front of the dress with the back collar attached. This type of neck needs no back facing. The back collar finishes the back neck and also holds the facing in place.

Before the facing is applied to the dress, turn back the inside edge $\frac{1}{4}$ inch and stitch. Do not turn back the

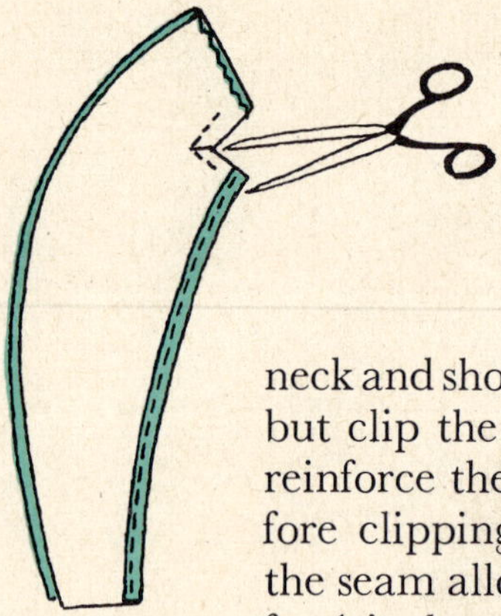

neck and shoulder seam, but clip the corner. To reinforce the corner before clipping, stitch on the seam allowance line for 1 inch on either side of the corner. Clip in to this stitching line. Sew the facing (A) to the dress. Trim the seam, then turn and press. The only finishing needed on this facing is at the shoulder and neck seams (B) which are turned under and tacked into place, finishing the collar and back neck (C). It is not necessary to finish the facing at any other points,

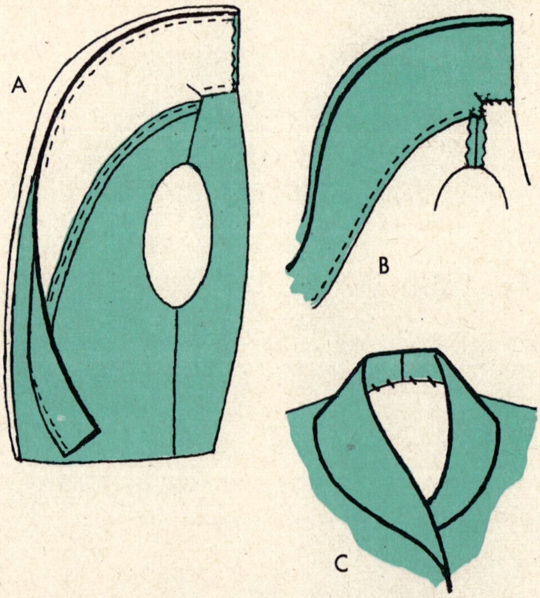

except if buttons are used. Then, of course, the buttonholes and buttons securely hold the facings in place down the front of the dress.

Buttonholes and buttons

Finishing buttonholes

Although this is discussed in Chapter 6, it is a good idea to review it here. The cord-bound buttonhole is easy to make but still must be carefully finished by hand to avoid puckering the front of the dress.

Fold the facing back to the inside and baste it all around the finished buttonhole, holding facing and dress front together. Spread the buttonhole from the right side, and slash the facing the length of the buttonhole.

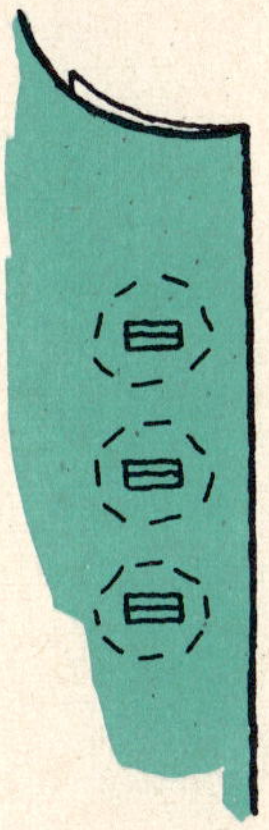

Turn it to the wrong side. Then slash the facing about 1/8 inch longer than the stitching which is at each end of buttonhole.

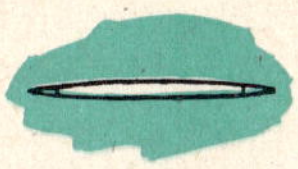

Turn under the slash edge. Hem it to the underside of the buttonhole. This forms an elliptical shape.

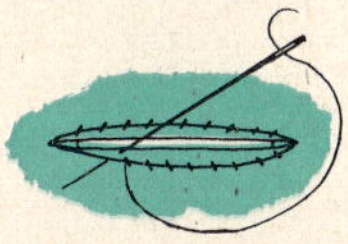

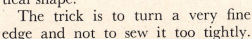

The trick is to turn a very fine edge and not to sew it too tightly. Otherwise, the facing will look shrunken, causing the front of the dress to indent along each buttonhole, and the right front will be slightly shorter than the left dress front.

WRONG

RIGHT

Sewing on a button

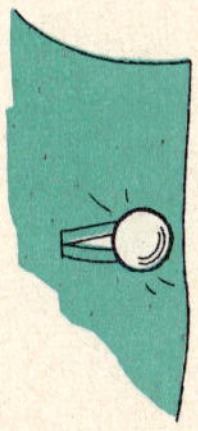

The whole appearance of a dress can be spoiled by the way a button is sewed on. If the button is sewed too tightly to the dress, the buttonhole can't close snugly under it and so the buttonhole spreads, causing the front of the dress to pucker and the buttons to look as though they are misplaced. To sew the button correctly, mark the correct position for it. Remember that the button does not stay in the center of the buttonhole. It slides to the left corner, which is why the left end of the buttonhole starts at the center front line. Lap the closing and pin it in position. Put a pin through the buttonhole at the left or outer end to mark for placing the button.

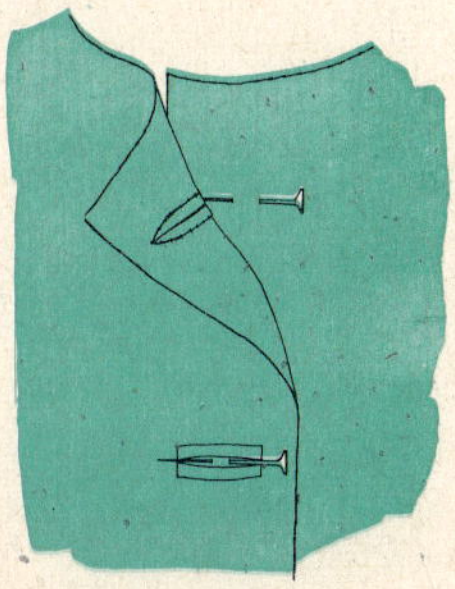

Use a double thread, a heavy duty, or buttonhole twist to sew the buttons. Take a stitch where the button is to be sewed and then roll the fabric over the index finger (A). With the thumb, hold the button against the fabric, but well away from the button mark. Sew on the button (B). A long stitch will form between the button and the mark on the fabric. After the button has been sewed, hold it to the end of the long stitch while you wind the thread under it, forming the stem (C). The advantage of this method is that the stem can be made any length

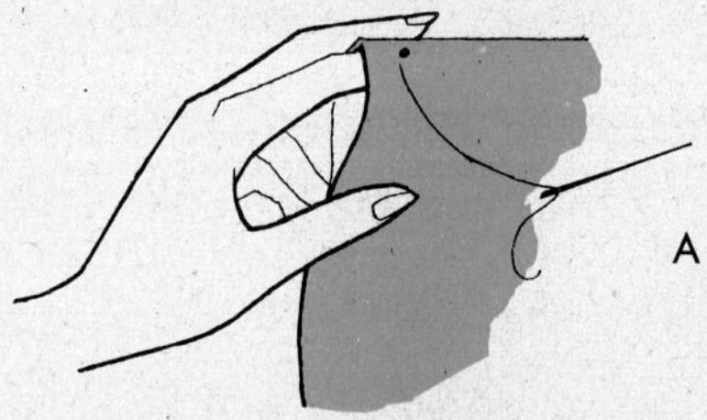

A

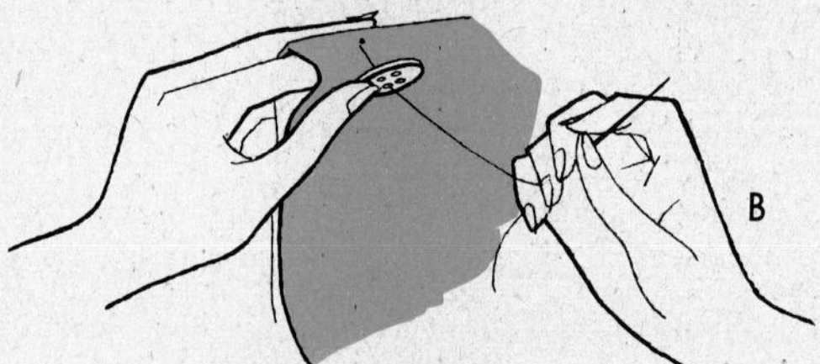

B

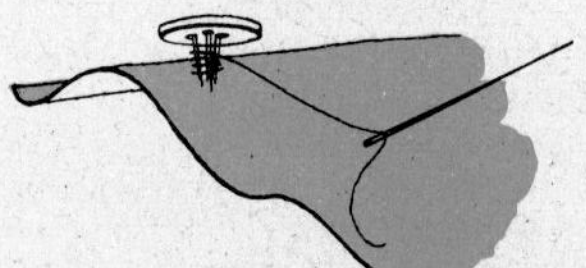

C

needed, depending on the thickness of the buttonhole that fits around it.

Another method is to take a stitch in the fabric where a button goes. Place a match or toothpick across the top of the button, and sew through the

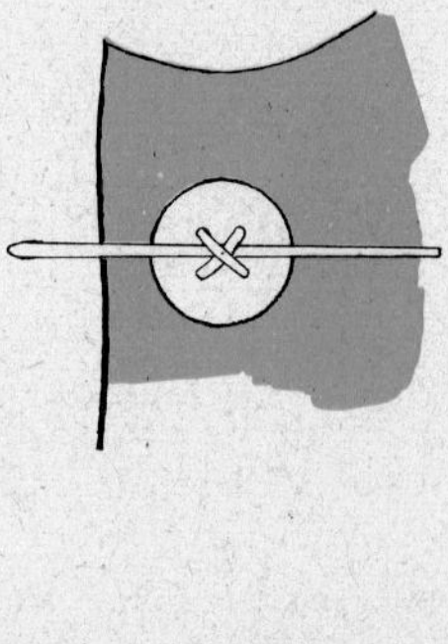

holes of the button, joining it to the fabric. After the button has been sewed, remove the matchstick and wind the thread around the threads under the button, forming a stem or shank.

The buttonhole will close tightly around this stem, and the button will ride on top of the buttonhole, which prevents the front from puckering and makes a neat closing.

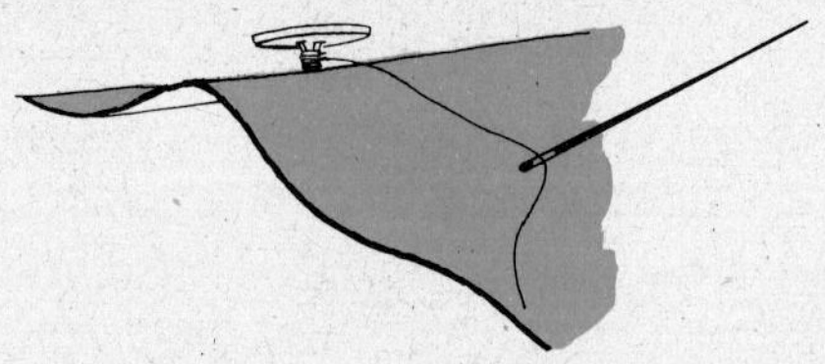

The shank button, whether metal or self-shank, should also be sewed with a stem. Sew the button very loosely, then wind the thread underneath the button to form the stem. It does not need to be as high as the other type of stem, since the shank itself raises the button.

When a heavy button is used, or a regular button is sewed on one thickness of fabric, it is advisable to use a stay underneath. The stay can be a small button or a piece of fabric. Sew it to the wrong side of the garment as you sew on the button.

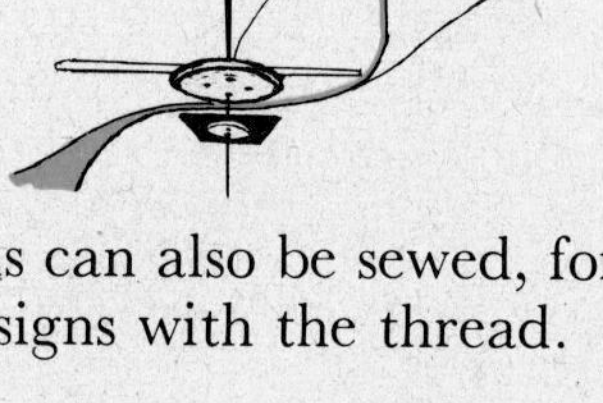

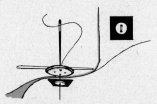

Buttons can also be sewed, forming many designs with the thread.

Snaps, hooks and eyes

Sewing on snaps

To sew the snap, mark carefully so that the socket and ball of the snap are directly opposite from each other when the joining is correctly lapped.

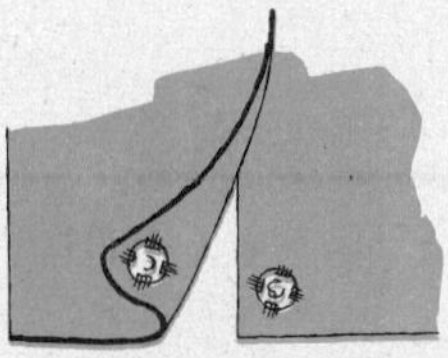

Place the socket side of the snap on the overlap of the garment, the ball part on the underlap. Sew through each hole several times, going under the snap as you sew from hole to hole. Be sure that the stitches do not show on the right side of the garment. Fasten the thread securely when the snap is sewed. Be sure the snap is close to the edge you want held in place.

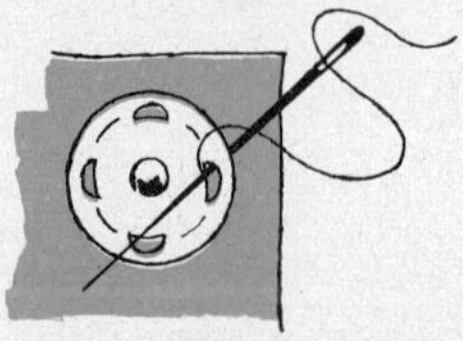

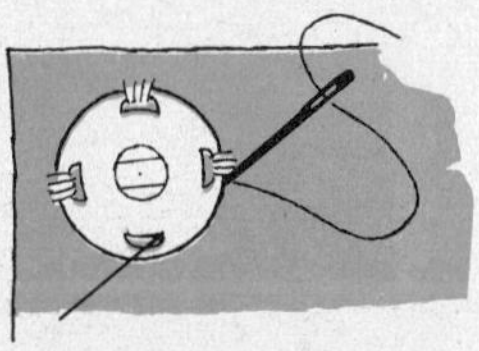

Snaps are useful in many places, but *never* use them down the front of a dress instead of buttonholes.

Learn when to use a snap and when to use a hook and eye. Use the snap when there is no tension; for instance, at a buttoned neckline to hold the corner in place under the collar (A). Or use them between widely spaced buttons to keep the front of the garment from bulging (B). Put a snap at the sleeve placket to hold it closed (C). Use it to hold detachable collars and cuffs (D), or to hold the left side of a double-breasted dress in place (E). They are also effective as lingerie strap holders. These are only a few of the places where the snap is preferred, all points where there is no strain.

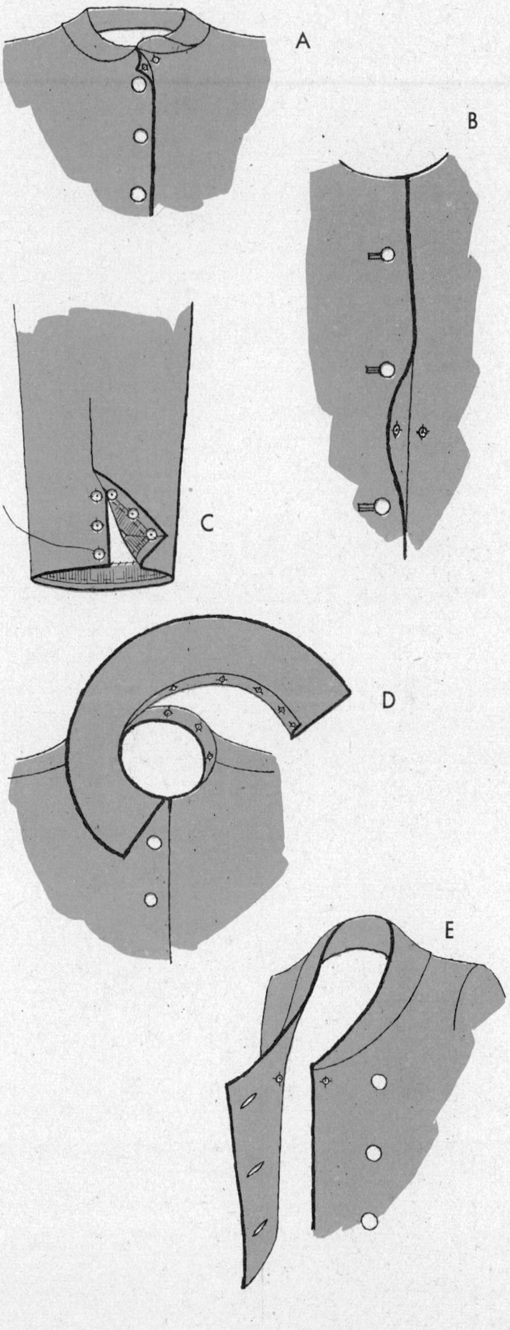

Sewing hooks and eyes

Use hooks and eyes where there is strain or tension, or to close some part of a garment inconspicuously. There are two types of eyes. Use the straight, or bar type when the edges of the garment overlap. Use the round or loop eye when the edges come together. Use the same hook with both.

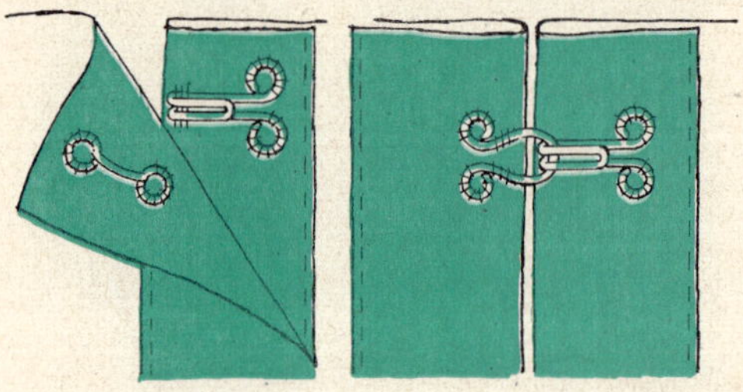

Mark the position for the hook and eye on the garment. The hook is used on the overlap or right-hand side of the closure. Sew the hook about ⅛ inch from the edge of the garment, using an overcast stitch to sew the loops of the hook. Then sew a few stitches to hold the hook firm. Make sure the stitches do not show on the right side of the garment. Sew the loops of the eye in the same way. The bar should come just under the bend of the hook when the garment is lapped correctly. When using the round eye, sew it with the loop extending slightly beyond the edge of the garment.

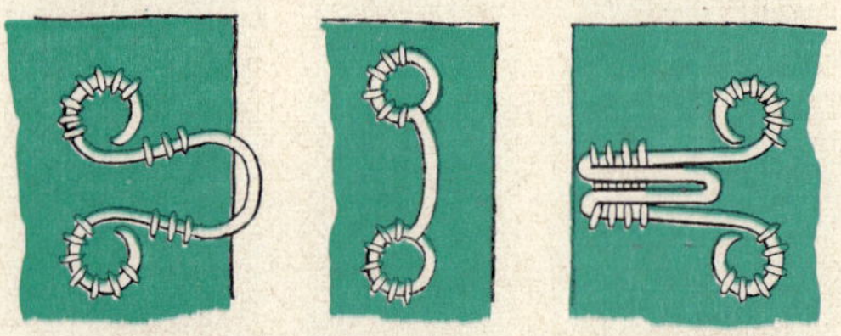

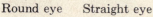

Round eye **Straight eye** **Hook**

Sometimes a hook and eye is needed on a garment that may be worn open, as a jacket. Since the eye will show, make it by hand, using the same color thread as for the garment.

Sew two strands of thread on the underlap where the eye is to go. Cover the strands with a blanket stitch, made by bringing the needle under the strands and through the loop formed.

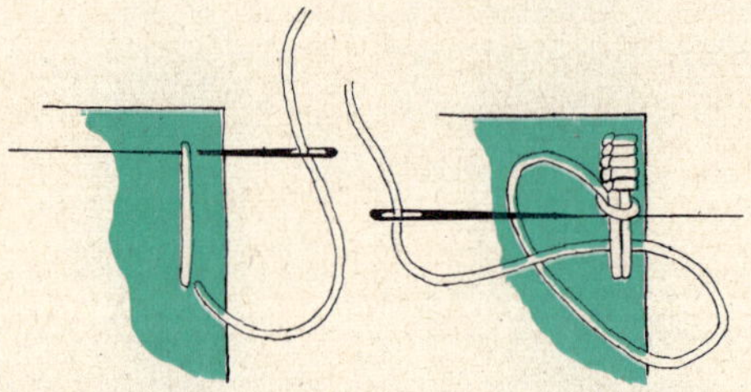

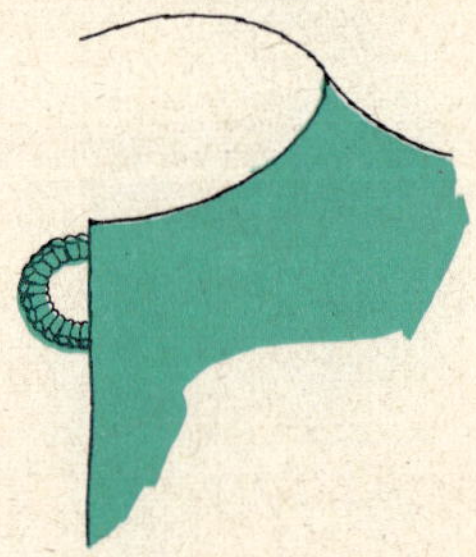

This type of eye can also be used at the top of a back neck opening. Use straight eye in the following places: at the waistband of a skirt (A), the waistline of a coat dress (B), and on the inside waistband of a dress (C).

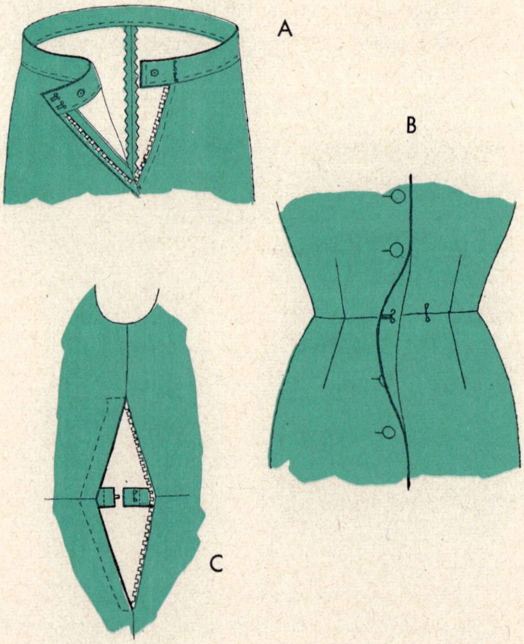

Sleeves

Before setting the sleeves into the finished bodice, it is a good idea to finish them completely. There are as many types of sleeves as there are styles of dresses, but the sewing tricks presented in this chapter may be applied, in one way or another, to any sleeve you make.

Sleeves may be raglan, kimono, or set-in, but all come in just three lengths—short, three-quarter, and long. Each type of sleeve requires different finishing details.

Finishing the short sleeve

When the short sleeve is cut with allowance for the hem, there are two ways it can be finished. First, sew up the underarm seam and press. Then turn under the hem and press.

On cotton or other washable fabrics, turn under ¼ inch on the hem edge and stitch. Carefully slip-stitch the hem to the sleeve.

For other fabrics, sew a seam binding to the edge of the hem and slip-stitch to the sleeve. (The hem can also be made in the same way on the three-quarter sleeve.)

Facings

Often, the short sleeve is shaped so that it has to be faced. Usually, a shaped facing is included in the pattern, although sometimes a bias facing is recommended.

When a shaped facing is used, sew up the underarm seam of the sleeve and the facing. Press the seams open. Pin the right side of the facing to the right side of the sleeve. Here is the trick: To fit correctly and be smooth, the facing should be slightly smaller than the sleeve. Take the facing in, if necessary, and then ease the sleeve, as you sew the facing and sleeve together. Turn the facing to the inside, bring back the facing a small amount, and baste around the edge. Press. Turn under the edge of the facing ¼ inch and stitch. If the fabric is heavy, sew a seam binding to the facing edge to finish.

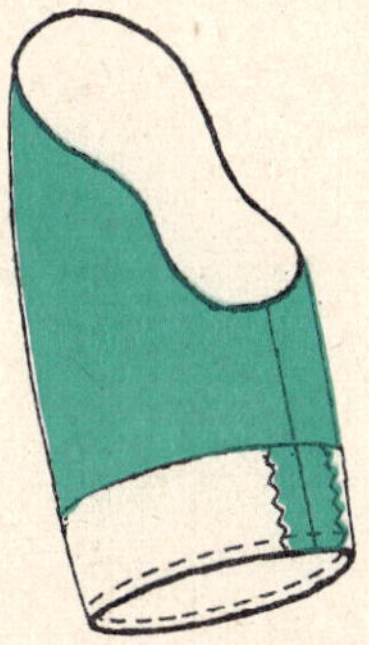

Turn, baste facing edge.

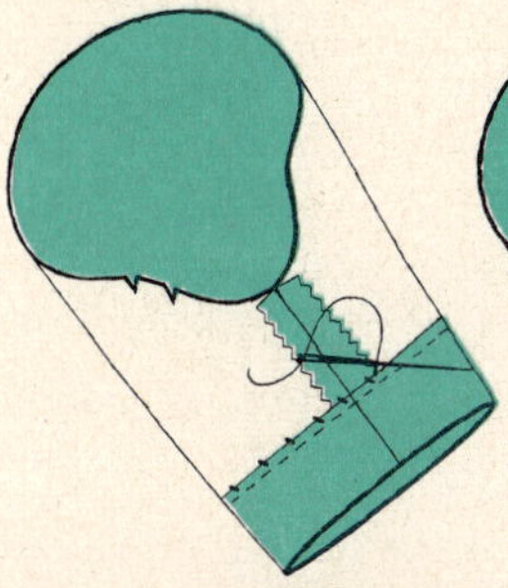

Slip-stitched hem.

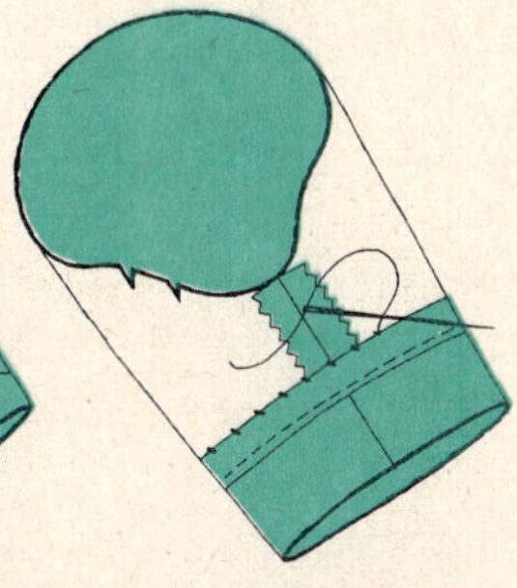

Sew seam binding.

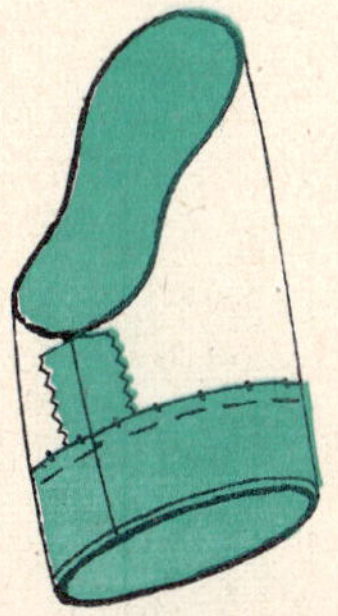

Slip-stitch facing.

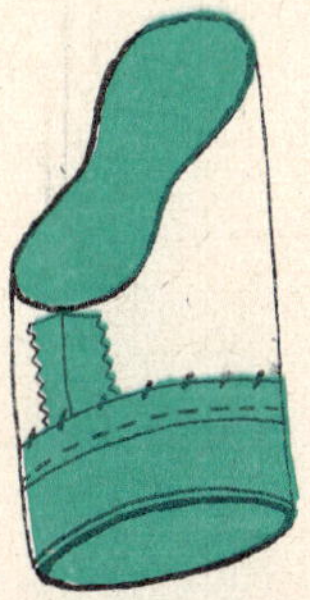

Seam binding on facing.

Bias facing

Cut the bias facing about 2 inches wide, and shape it slightly with the iron. Starting at the underarm seam of the sleeve, pin the bias to the sleeve edge. Cut the bias the size of the sleeve, plus seam allowances. Join the bias on the straight grain. Sew the bias to the sleeve edge, turn to the inside, press. Turn under and stitch a ¼-inch seam at the edge of the bias and slip-stitch to the sleeve.

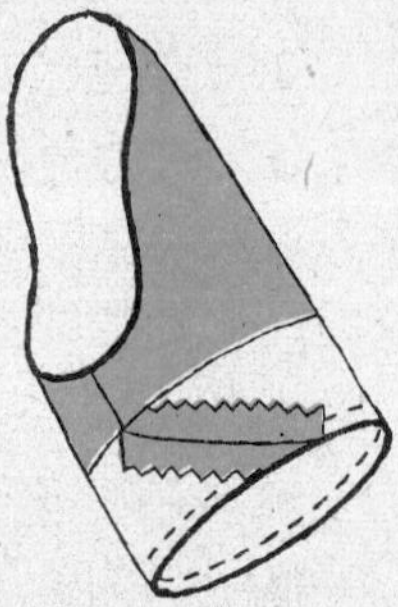

Sew bias to sleeve.

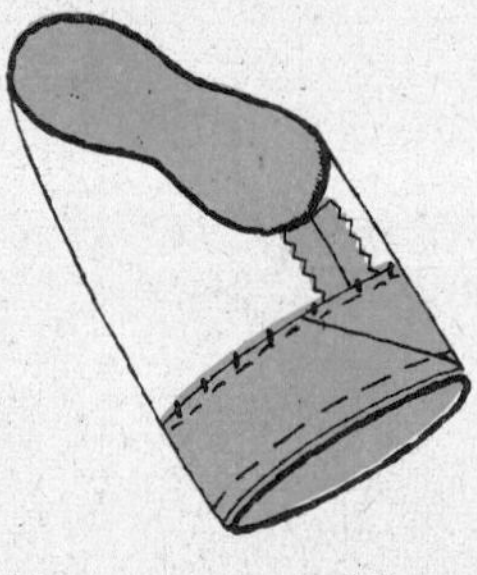

Turn, press and hem.

On a heavy fabric, the facings can be cut from a different fabric so the finish will not be bulky. Taffeta is excellent. On soft or stretchy fabrics, interface the shaped sleeve facings like the neckline. The same type of interfacing is generally used. See Chapter 5 for more information on interfacings. (The same facings can be used on the three-quarter sleeve.)

Applying cuffs

For the short sleeve, the cuffs are usually made separately and are then applied to the sleeve. They are applied with either a shaped facing, a bias facing, or with a self-finish.

Making the two-piece cuff

Cut the upper and under cuff pieces. Then, from the same pattern, cut the interfacing. If a non-woven type is used, cut off the seam allowance on the outside edge. Sew the underarm

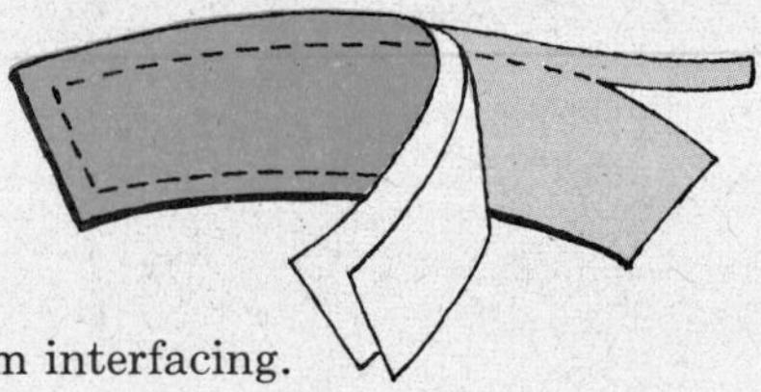

Trim interfacing.

seams of each cuff piece, making the upper cuff slightly larger, and press open. Lap the interfacing seam, stitch and trim. Pin the interfacing to the under cuff and stitch. The lower edges will be even. The upper edge of the interfacing will be at the seam allowance line. Pin the right sides of the cuff pieces together, with the upper cuff on the outside. Sew on the under-cuff side along the edge of the inter-

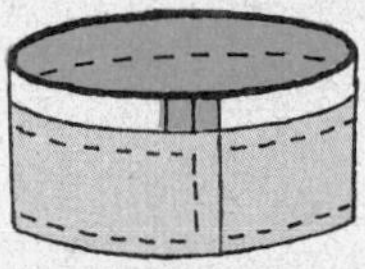

Lap interfacing seam.

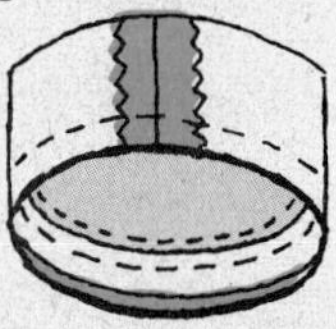

Sew under cuff side.

facing. (Non-woven interfacing is not sewed into the seam.)

Trim the seam allowance to graduated widths. Turn the cuff to the right side. Baste, bringing the under cuff

Trim seams in graduated widths.

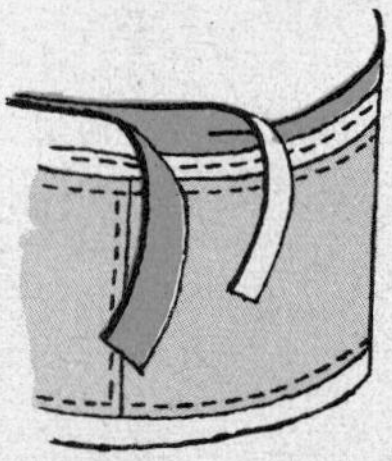

in slightly from the edge, and press.

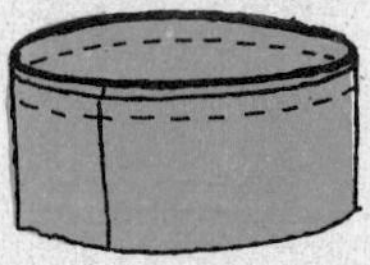

Roll the cuff back with the upper cuff on the outside as it will be applied.

Since the upper cuff has to roll over the interfacing and under cuff, the seam edge may be slightly shorter. Pin and sew it this way. The cuff has now been correctly rolled and stitched and can be applied to the sleeve. When a woven interfacing is used, it is better to cut it on the bias. There is no need to cut away the upper seam allowance. The woven interfacing can be sewed right in with the regular seam, because it will press flat and give a sharp crease at the edge of the cuff.

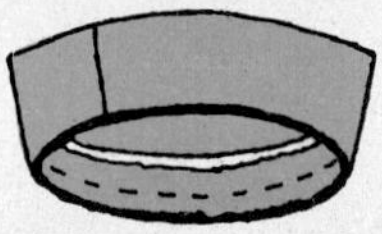

Making the one-piece cuff

Cut the upper and under cuff in one piece. Fold through the center and press. Cut the interfacing half the

width of the cuff, or to the fold line. Cut away the underarm seam allowance on the interfacing. Press the cuff on the length. Pin the interfacing from the lower edge to the fold line and stitch. This stitched side becomes the under cuff.

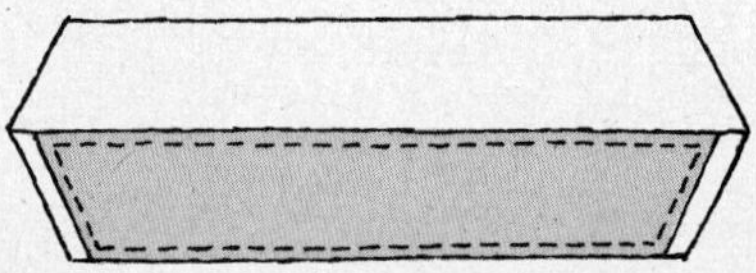

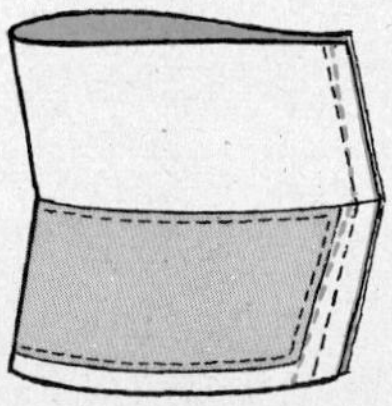

Sew up the underarm seam of the cuff. Make the upper cuff a little larger by taking a smaller seam at the upper section.

Press open the under seam. Fold the cuff on the original fold line and press again. Roll the cuff back with the upper cuff on the outside. Pin the open edges together—the upper edge will be a little short. Sew it this way and the roll of the cuff will be correct before it is sewed to the sleeve. (Both woven and non-woven interfacings are applied in the same manner for this type of cuff.)

Sewing cuff to sleeve

Both the one-piece and the two-piece cuffs are first sewed to the sleeve edge; then the facing is applied. The same method used for facing a sleeve can also be used for the sleeve with a cuff. Instructions for either the shaped or bias facing are given at the beginning of this chapter.

When the cuff is self-finished, the lower edges are *not* sewed together before the cuff is applied.

On a washable dress, the cuff can be applied entirely by machine. Pin the right side of the upper cuff to the wrong side of the sleeve and stitch.

Turn under the free edge of the under cuff and pin along the stitching line. Turn the cuff up over the sleeve to be sure it rolls right. Leave the outside cuff slightly longer for a better roll on the finished sleeve.

Machine-stitch the pinned edge of the cuff to the sleeve.

On non-washable fabric, self-finish the cuff by hand. Pin the free edge of the under cuff to the right side of the sleeve and stitch. Press the seam into the cuff. Turn the sleeve right side out, then carefully roll the cuff back over the sleeve.

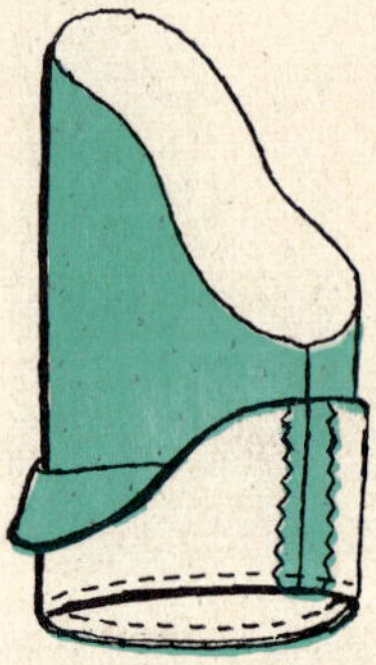
Turn right side out.

Roll the cuff back.

Turn, slip-stitch.
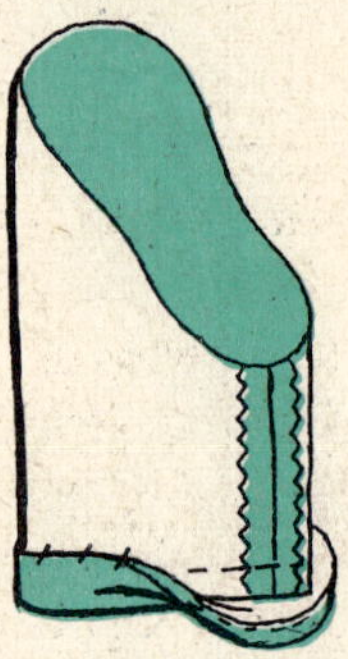

Pin the cuff to the sleeve as it will roll. Then turn the sleeve inside out. Turn under free edge of the outside cuff and slip-stitch along the stitching line, and the sleeve is finished. Turning the cuff back before sewing it insures that the cuff is rolling correctly.

Apply the separate cuff to the three-quarter sleeve in the same way as described above.

Finishing three-quarter sleeve

Generally, the finishing on the short and three-quarter sleeve is similar, and the same technique is used. However, there is one cuff treatment that is almost exclusively used with the three-quarter sleeve. This is the cuff cut all in one piece with the sleeve, and finished with a separate facing.

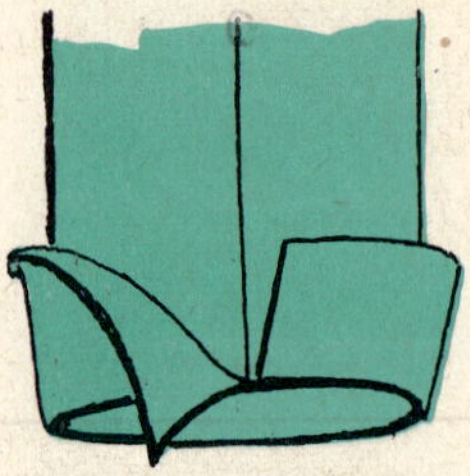
All-in-one cuff facing.

Sometimes it is a simple turned-up cuff, or a faced cuff with a side opening, which is more difficult.

Sleeve and cuff in one

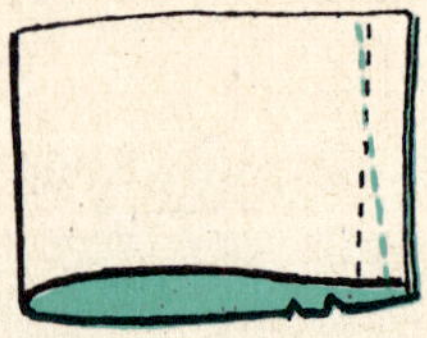

The sleeve seam is sewed and pressed open. Before you sew the facing, remember the facing is always made smaller so it will fit smoothly inside the sleeve. The outer cuff is always made a little larger so it will roll correctly. This facing combines the two. It is outer cuff and inside facing in one. Here is a trick to use when sewing the seam. On the part that forms the cuff, take a more shallow seam to make the cuff a little larger, and as you sew it to the facing part, take a deeper seam to make the facing smaller.

Cut the interfacing from the facing pattern. Cut it on the bias if it is a woven fabric. Join the interfacing seam and press open.

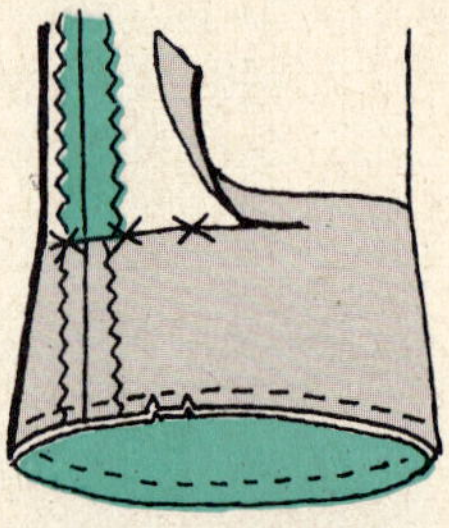
Catch-stitch edge.

Pin the interfacing to the wrong side of the sleeve. Sew it to the edge of the sleeve by machine. Trim off ⅝ inch from the loose edge of the interfacing. Then catch-stitch interfacing to the sleeve. Now pin and stitch the facing to the lower edge of the sleeve, with the right sides together. The facing forms the outer cuff and, since it was made a little larger, it will have to be eased in.

Trim the seam allowance to graduated widths. Turn the facing to the inside and baste the edge, bringing the sleeve edge in slightly. Now lightly press the sleeve.

Turn the sleeve right side out and

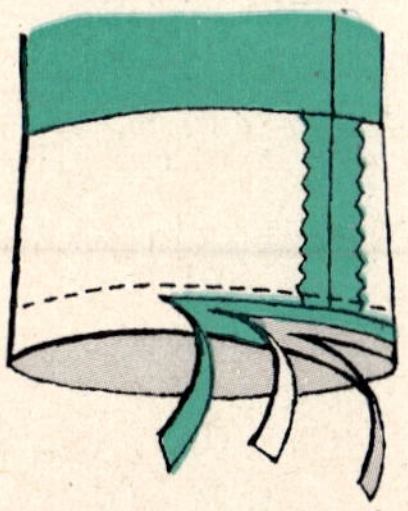

Trim seam allowance.

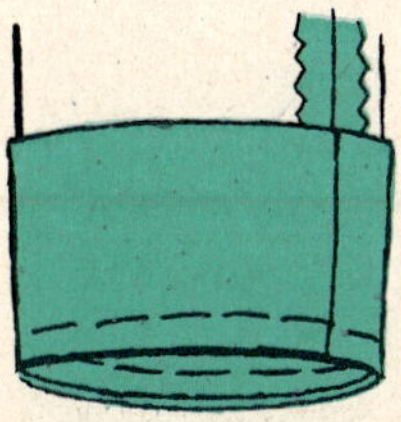

Turn facing inside.

roll the cuff back on the sleeve. Pin to hold it in the correct position. Turn the sleeve wrong side out. Turn under the facing edge and stitch. Slip-stitch it to the sleeve. The cuff is sure to roll correctly when it is sewed in place on the dress.

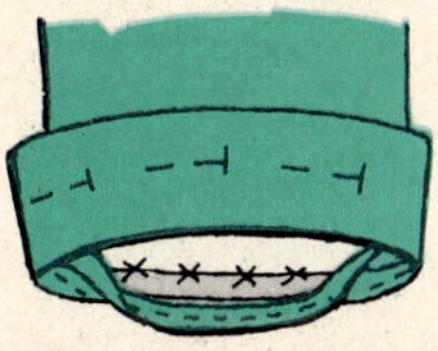

Pin to hold in position.

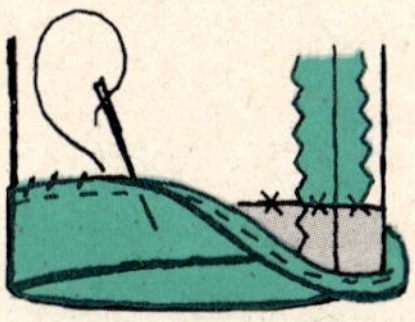

Slip-stitch facing.

Sleeve and open cuff in one

When the sleeve is only slashed to create an open cuff, it is relatively simple to make. If the opening of the cuff is formed by the continuation of a dart or seam, it may be more complicated. A simple technique that is used by professionals will make this type of sleeve easy to do.

Slash-type opening

Follow the same procedure as you did for the cuff and facing in one. Sew up the sleeve and facing the same way. Cut the interfacing and sew it to the sleeve in the same way. After you have applied the interfacing to the sleeve, mark where the slash is to be. Run a line of machine-stitching along the marked seamline of the slash. Slash between these lines to the point.

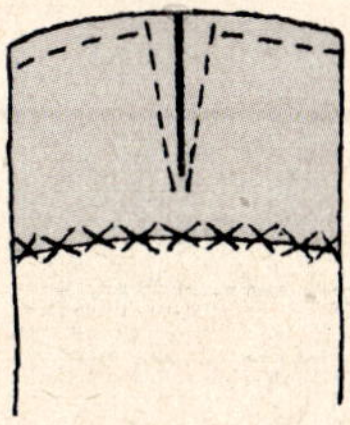

Stitch along slash.

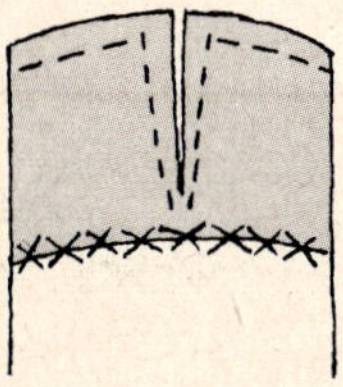

Slash between lines.

Pin the right side of the facing to the right side of the sleeve and stitch on the sleeve side. Ease the facing in slightly as you pin it. Along the slash, sew just outside the stitched line.

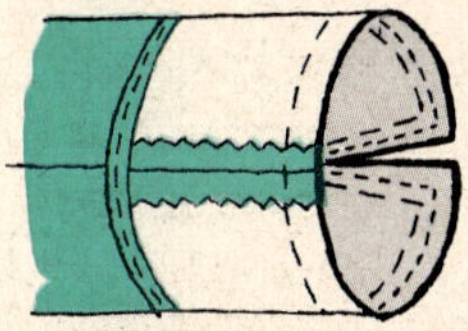

Sew outside slash line.

Slash the facing after it is sewed. Trim the seam allowance to graduated widths. Turn the facing to the inside, and baste close to the edge, bringing the sleeve back slightly. Baste around the slash the same way and press lightly. Roll the cuff back to the right side and pin into place. Slip-stitch the facing in place as on the other faced cuff.

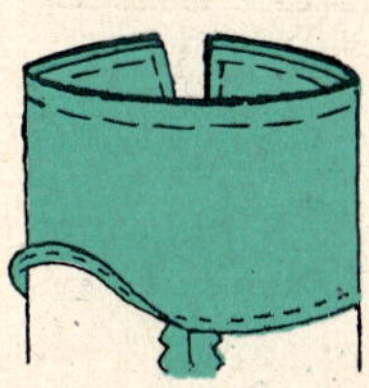

Slip-stitch the facing.

Baste close to edge.

Cuff opening at seam

Whether the opening for the cuff

comes on a seam or a dart, be sure to check your pattern and carefully mark the point to which you sew. Mark it on both the sleeve and facing.

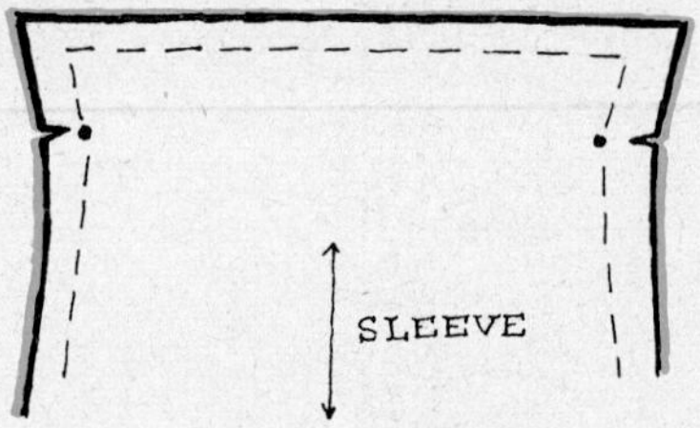

Mark the pattern . . .

for sleeve and facing.

Sew up the sleeve and facing seams and press. At the point where the cuff is to open, clip into the stitching line on both the sleeve and facing.

Again, make the facing a little larger than the sleeve at the open edge, but a little smaller where it is to finish inside the sleeve.

Cut and apply the interfacing on the sleeve as you did for the cuff in one. There is no need to sew the seam on the interfacing, since it will be trimmed away, and the seam edges lapped to the sleeve seam and tacked.

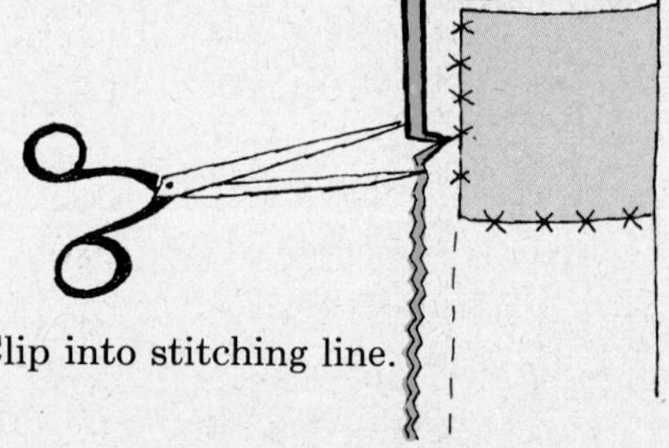

Clip into stitching line.

Pin the right side of the facing to the right side of the sleeve. Be sure to ease the facing as you pin. For the cuff opening, carefully match the clipped seam on the sleeve with the clipped seam on the facing. Sew the two pieces together from this point. Finish it as you did the cuff with the slash opening described on page 121.

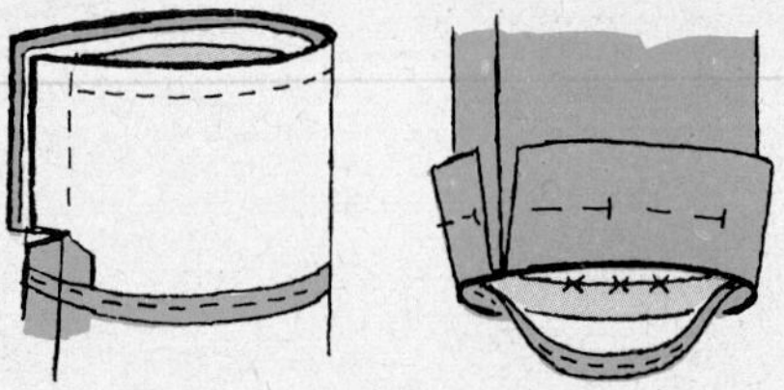

Match clipped seams. Sew together, finish.

French cuffs, shirt sleeves, and gathered sleeves will be illustrated in Chapter 9 on play clothes.

Long sleeve

The same detail used on the three-quarter sleeve can also be used on the long sleeve. There is one finish, however, that is needed only on the long sleeve. That is the placket opening at the wrist on the tight-fitting sleeve described below.

Placket

On the long sleeve, the lower end of the sleeve is left open for about 4 inches so that the hand can pass through easily. Use seam binding for a flat and easy-to-apply finish.

Sew the seam binding to the back sleeve opening, $\frac{1}{8}$ inch from the edge of the seam. Continue sewing around the bottom edge of the sleeve on the $\frac{5}{8}$ inch seamline, and up the front opening just outside of the regular $\frac{5}{8}$ inch seamline.

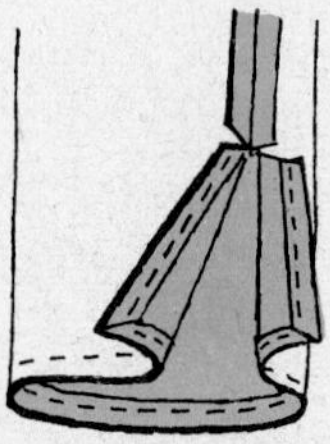

Stitch around opening.

Turn the binding to the inside and

hem to the inside of the sleeve. Miter the corners, turn under the ends and finish. Press. Then lap the top of the back seam over the front and stitch by hand into position. Sew snaps at the sleeve opening.

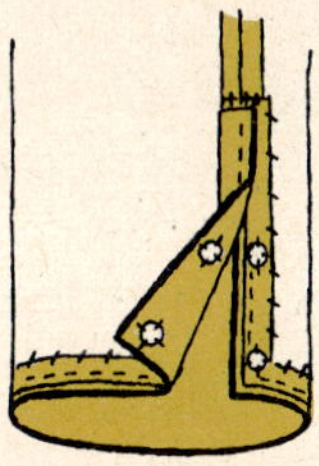

Sew snaps at opening.

Setting in the sleeve

Now you can set the sleeves into the finished bodice. Many women believe they have trouble setting the sleeve because the patterns are cut too big. The sleeve is purposely cut larger than the armhole, so that the sleeve can be molded and shaped to fit the top of the shoulder. Remember that the armhole seam is well in on the shoulder for a correct fit. The sleeve must be capped to fit out smoothly over the top of your arm.

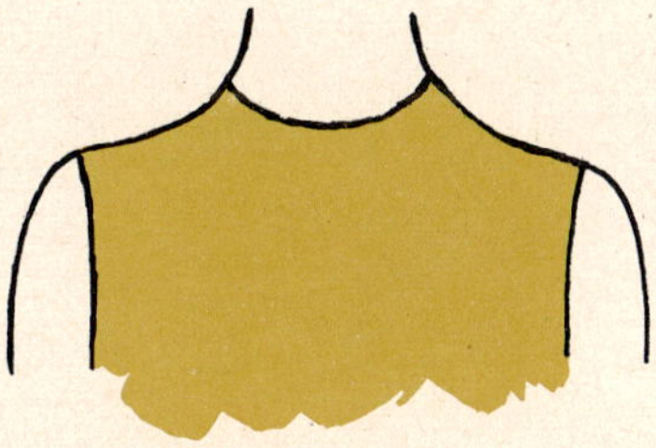

The capping is easy if you use a professional trick. Using the largest stitch on your machine, run two rows of shirring along the sleeve top from notch to notch. Put one row on the seam allowance line; run second ¼ inch closer to the edge.

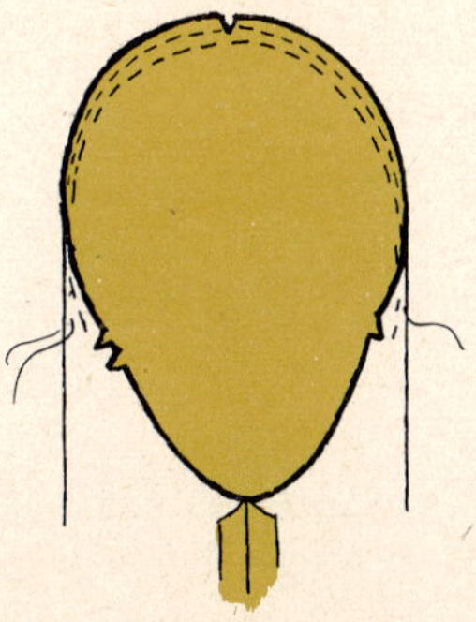

Sew on the right side of the sleeve so that the bobbin thread is on the inside. Hold both the bobbin threads. Ease the top of the sleeve along the thread so a cap, or cupping, forms.

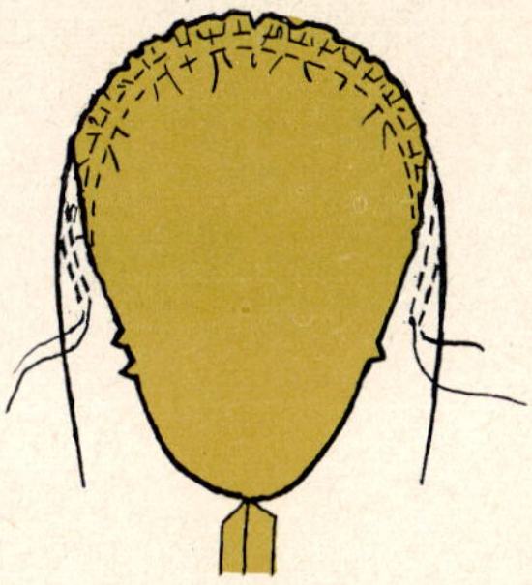

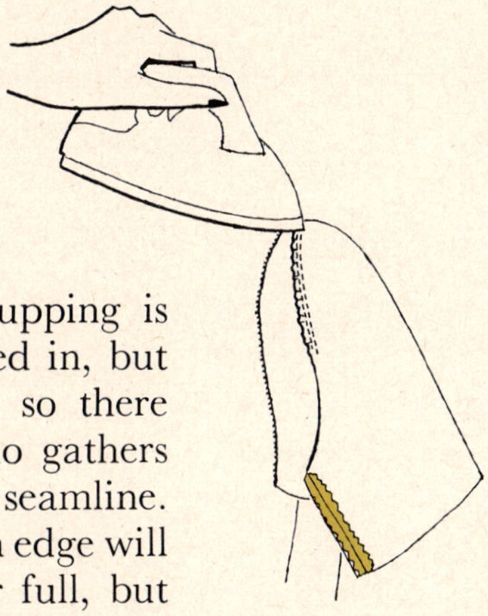

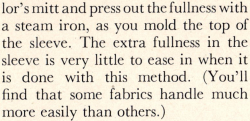

This cupping is not shirred in, but eased in, so there will be no gathers along the seamline. The seam edge will be rather full, but it can be steamed flat. Place the seam edge over your tailor's mitt and press out the fullness with a steam iron, as you mold the top of the sleeve. The extra fullness in the sleeve is very little to ease in when it is done with this method. (You'll find that some fabrics handle much more easily than others.)

Another trick to get the sleeve in the correct armhole is to turn the sleeve and bodice right side out. Check the notches. Put your hand into the neck and out through the armhole of the bodice. Hold the correct sleeve for that armhole by the underarm seam and bring it to the underarm of the armhole. Hold the two together while you turn the bodice inside out.

Sleeve is now in the correct armhole, ready to be pinned. It can be pinned and sewed easily and accurately—much better than by basting. Pin the

underarm of the sleeve and bodice together. The pins should be parallel to the seam and on the seam allowance line. Next, match the sleeve front and back notches to the bodice and pin in the same way. At top of the sleeve, match slash mark (made when you originally marked the sleeve) to the shoulder seam and pin. The key points are now pinned.

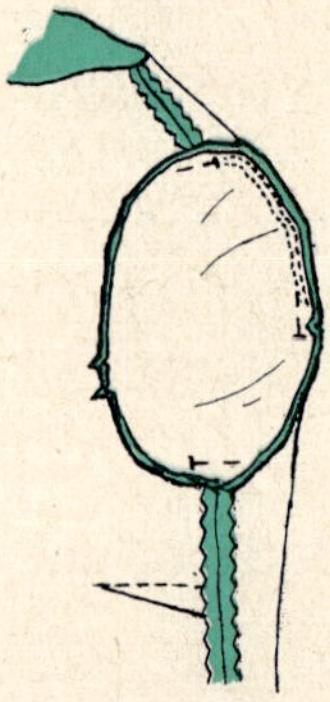

The rest of the sleeve eases into the armhole, with the pins placed parallel to the seams. Pin so closely that the head of one pin is actually touching the point of the other. The sleeve should fit perfectly if it has been eased enough. If there is still too much fullness, you can ease it a little more.

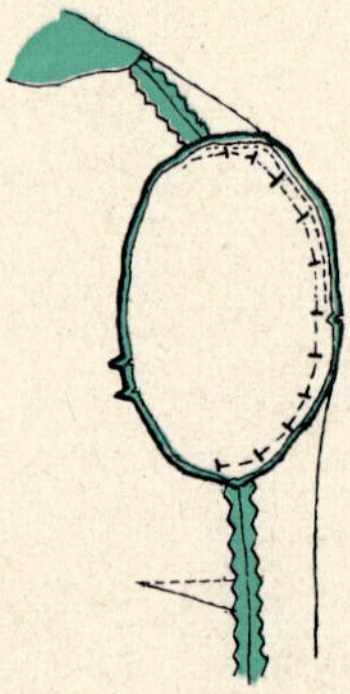

To sew, start at the underarm seam on the sleeve side. Sew from pin to pin. The heads of the pins will be toward you, and you can easily remove them as you sew.

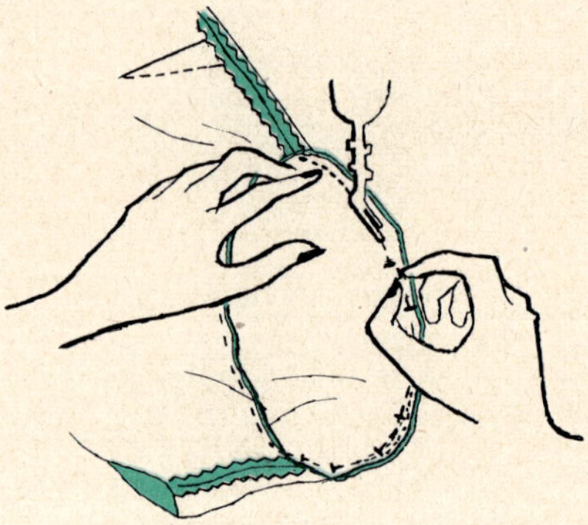

Pink or finish the seam allowance, then press lightly along the seam on the sleeve side to smooth fullness.

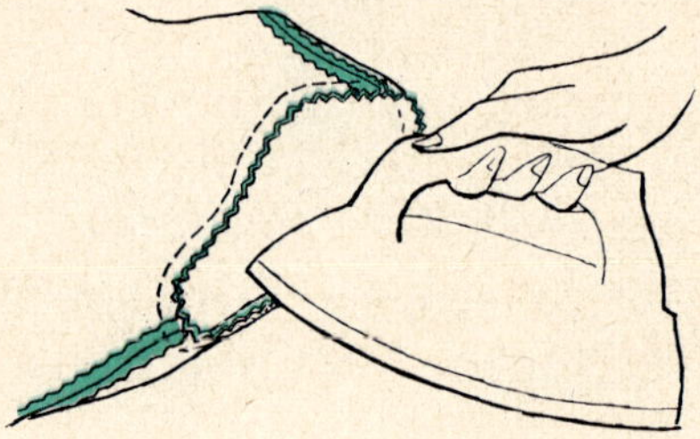

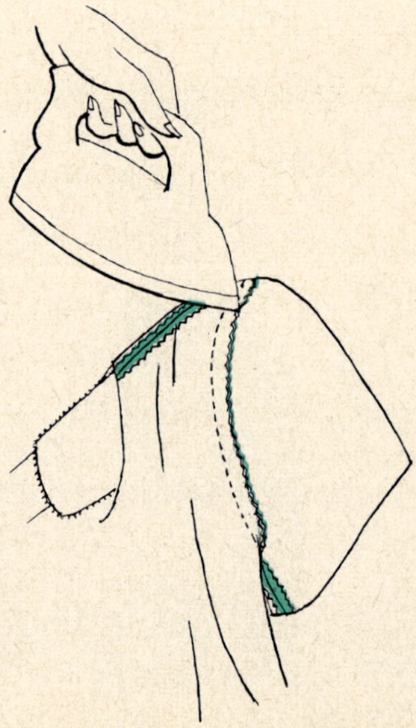

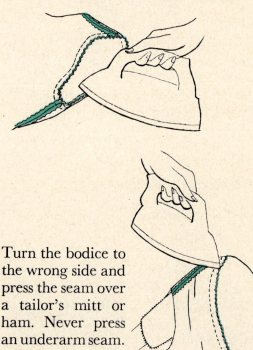

Turn the bodice to the wrong side and press the seam over a tailor's mitt or ham. Never press an underarm seam.

The rest of the armhole seam is generally pressed toward the sleeve.

Kimono sleeve

The underarm seam of the kimono sleeve is always reinforced, since no gusset is used. Reinforcement is necessary because, to make the underarm seam smooth, it must be clipped around the curve and could easily tear. The reinforcement can be done by machine or hand, depending on the quality of the dress and the type of fabric. Here are several ways to reinforce a sleeve. Choose the most suitable method.

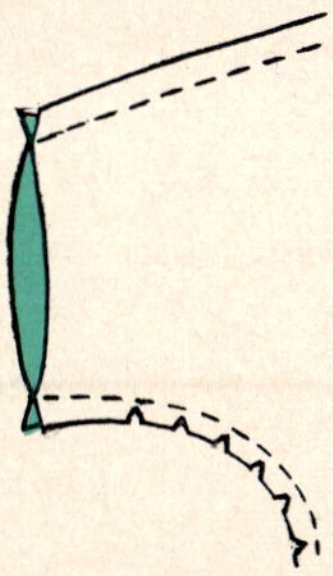

By machine

Fold a piece of seam binding in half on the length and press. As you sew the underarm seam, catch the binding at the same time. Make it long enough to cover the whole curve of the seam where it will be clipped. Clip the seam and press it open.

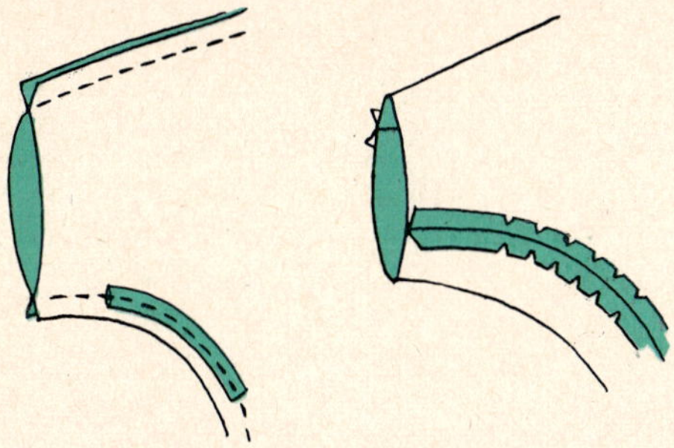

Another method is to sew the seam, clip it and press it open. Fold the seam binding on the length and press. Baste the binding along the center of the seam on the wrong side. Turn the garment right side out and stitch $\frac{1}{8}$ inch on either side of the seam.

You can also do this with a fine zigzag stitch if you have this type of machine or an attachment.

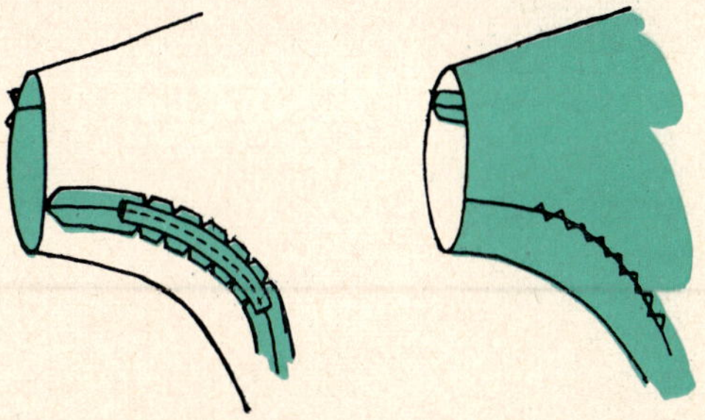

By hand

Sew the side seam by machine. Clip, press open the seam. Press seam binding in half on the length. (You can use seam binding or a $\frac{1}{4}$-inch satin or taffeta ribbon.) Place the binding or ribbon in the center of the seam on the inside of the dress. Take a fine running stitch by hand down the center, catching it to the center seam. Do a fine hemming stitch all around.

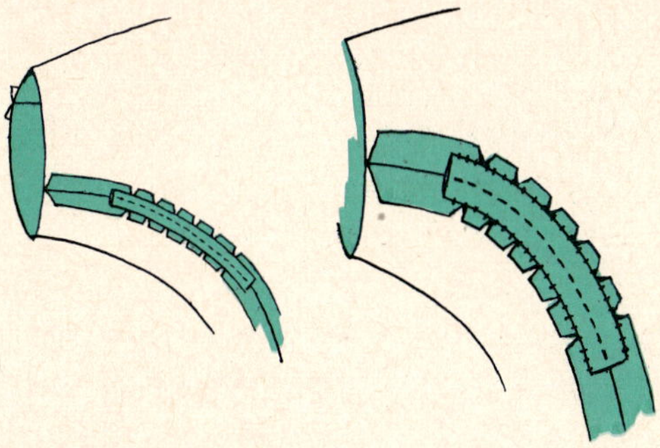

Raglan sleeve

This sleeve is handled in a slightly different manner from most of the other sleeves. First, sew up the shoulder dart or seam and press.

Next, join the sleeve to the back

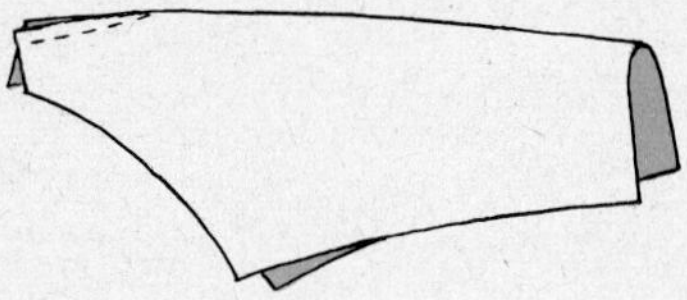

and front bodice pieces before sewing the underarm seam. Be sure to clip the seam at the underarm curve, then press it open. Stitch the underarm bodice and sleeve seams all in one.

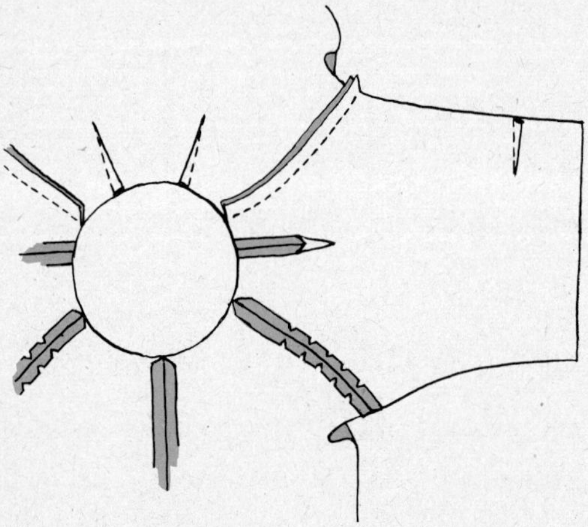

Press the underarm seam open. It may be necessary to clip at the underarm seam to make it lie flat.

After you have finished and joined the bodice and sleeves, you are ready

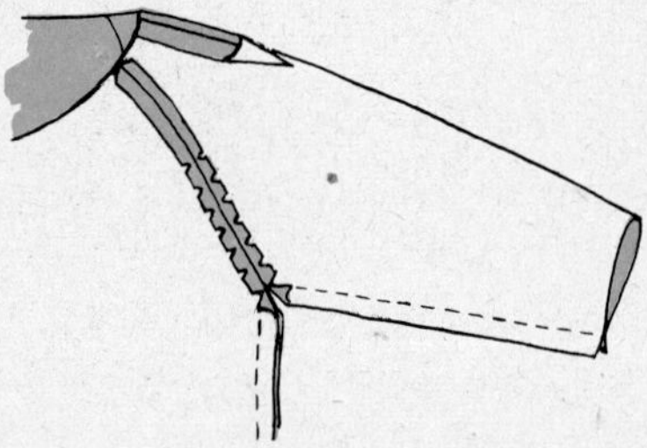

to work on the skirt. The skirt can be finished completely before it is joined to the bodice. It is easier to handle a section of the garment at a time. The work will be neater and more professional-looking when the whole garment is finally assembled.

Skirts

The only major finishing needed on the skirt is the hem, and of course, pressing. There are many types of hems. Analyze the style of the skirt and the fabric in order to decide on the correct hem to use.

Circular hem

On the full circular skirt, never make more than a $2\frac{1}{2}$-inch hem. Otherwise, it will look bulky and will have too much ease. Press back the hem on the hemline mark. Measure in for the depth of hem and cut off the excess.

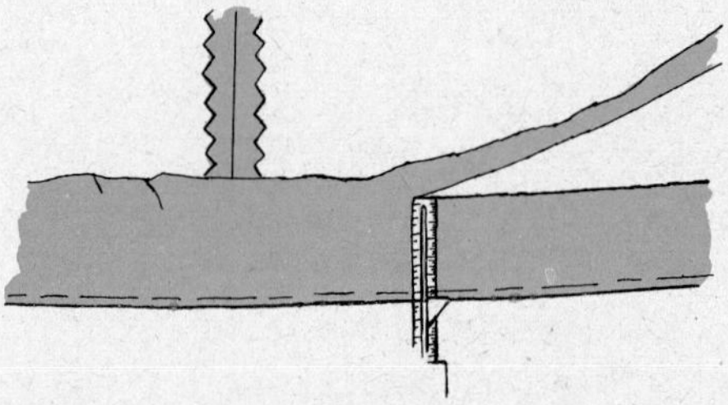

Sew around the edge of the hem by machine on the right side close to the edge. Use a large stitch on the machine. If the skirt has gores, stitch from one seam to the other, starting new stitching at each gore. This lets you ease in the fullness on only one gore at a time. If the skirt has more than six gores, run the shirring to take in two gores at a time.

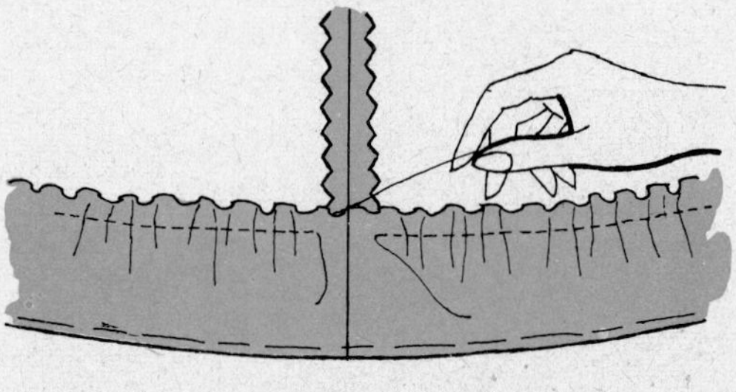

Ease in all the hem fullness so it is smooth and flat to the inside of the skirt. On the gored skirt, be sure that the seams line up correctly, one on top of the other.

Sew a seam binding on the edge of the hem and slip-stitch into place.

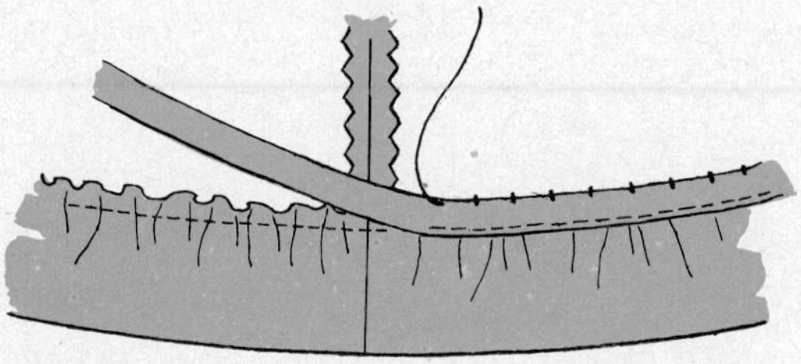

Circular hem on a sheer

Mark the hem in the same way on the sheer, turn, press, and trim. Instead of using a seam binding on the edge, turn under ¼ inch on the hem and sew all around by machine with a large stitch. Ease in the hem fullness so the hem is flat and smooth inside the skirt. Be sure the seams are placed one over the other. Pin into place. Slip-stitch the fold edge of the hem to the skirt.

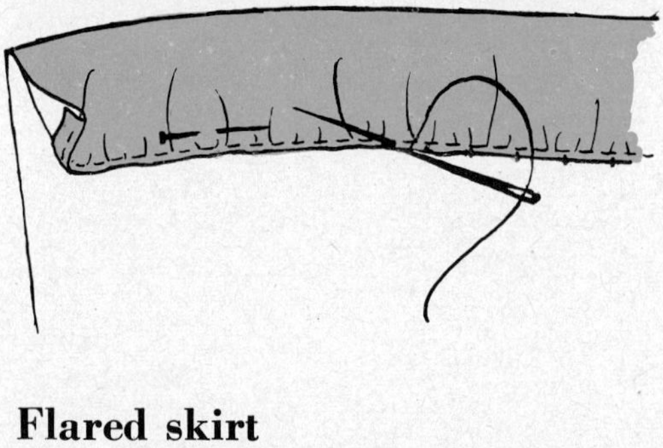

Flared skirt

Never use more than a 3-inch hem on a slightly flared skirt. Turn, press, and trim the hem to the desired depth. If the hem is slightly flared, you can apply the seam binding without first easing the hem. Hold the binding slightly taut as you stitch it to the hem, which will usually ease it enough. Slip-stitch to the skirt, making sure all seamlines match.

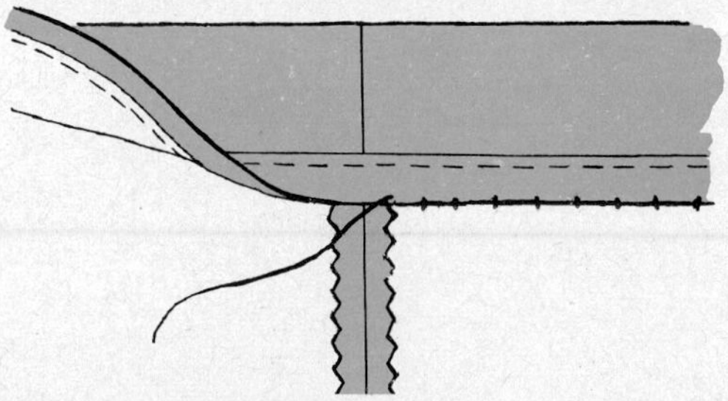

If the skirt has more flare, it may be difficult to ease. Follow the same method used on the circular skirt. Ease on a shirring thread before you sew on the seam binding.

Dirndl or gathered skirt

Depending on the fabric, you can use a deep hem on this type of skirt.

Sheer

A sheer dress looks more fashionable if the hem is from 6 to 12 inches deep. It must be carefully done to keep the quality look which the deep hem gives a dress. Measure, turn, and trim the hem. Press at the hemline.

Turn the edge of the hem under ¼ inch and press. Pin the hem carefully in place so all the seams match. Sew the hem with a long slip-stitch.

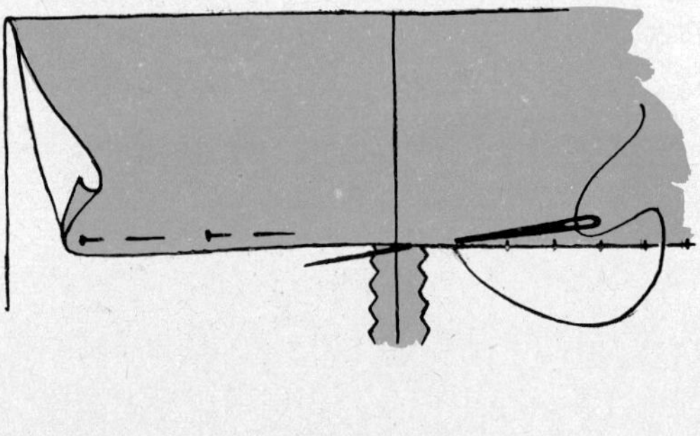

Cotton

On a cotton dress, press back, mark and trim the hem. Then turn under ¼ inch on the edge of the hem and stitch. Pin the hem into place and slip-stitch to the dress.

Remember the seams of the skirt must match when the hem is pinned.

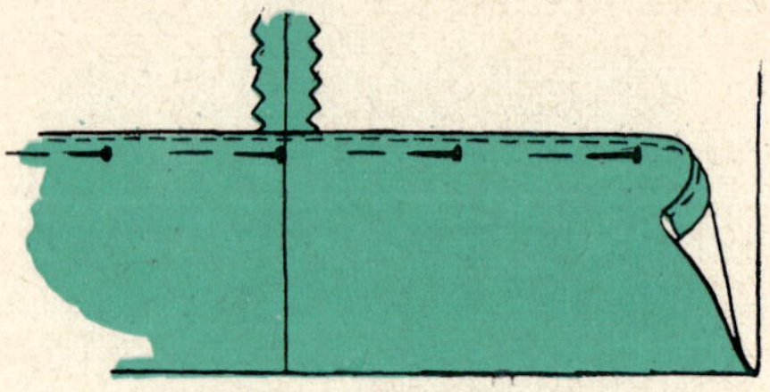

Other fabrics

Turn, press, and trim the hem in the same way as for cotton. Then sew a seam binding to the edge of the hem before sewing it to the dress.

Pleat at the hem

This hem should be flat but should stay in pleat. Before turning the hem, press open the pleat seam to twice the depth of the hem. Slip-stitch the hem to the skirt. Then clip to the stitching line at the top of the hem on the pleat seam to release the seam so the hem and pleat can be correctly pressed in a sharp line.

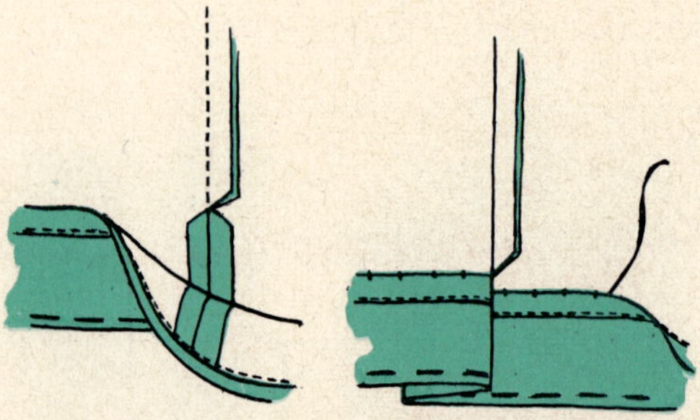

Hems with facings or slits

The facing must finish back over the hem on the open-front dress. Turn up the hem and finish it according to the style of skirt and type of fabric. Slip-stitch the hem to the skirt to the point where the facing laps.

Fold the facing back over the hem and finish to the hem.

The facing and hem are cut away under the facing on heavy fabric.

Finish the slit skirt with the hems of the slits turned back. They are sewed to the hem after the hem has been turned and pressed.

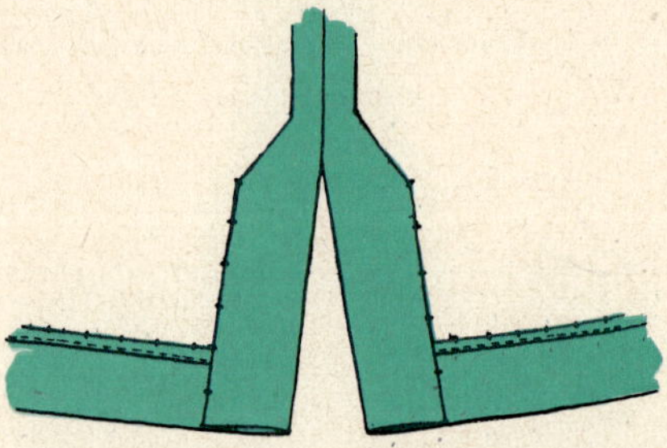

Depending on the weight of your fabric, use seam binding on the edge of the slit facings, or just turn the facings back by machine.

Joining bodice and skirt

Now you are ready to join the bodice and skirt. Turn the skirt wrong side out, and the bodice right side out. Drop the bodice inside the skirt and pin them together. Match the side seams, darts, center back and front seams, and any other parts of the skirt and bodice that should match. Sew together on the bodice side.

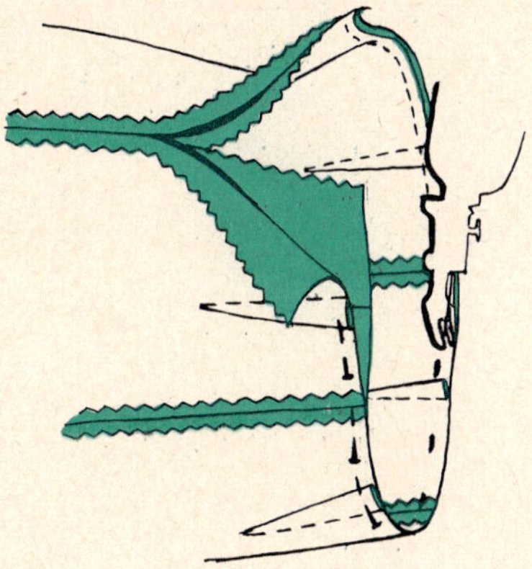

After the waistline is stitched, sew a seam binding just under the original waist seam on the bodice side. Be sure the seam binding which you select has been pre-shrunk before it is sewed, so the waistline will be firm and remain the same size.

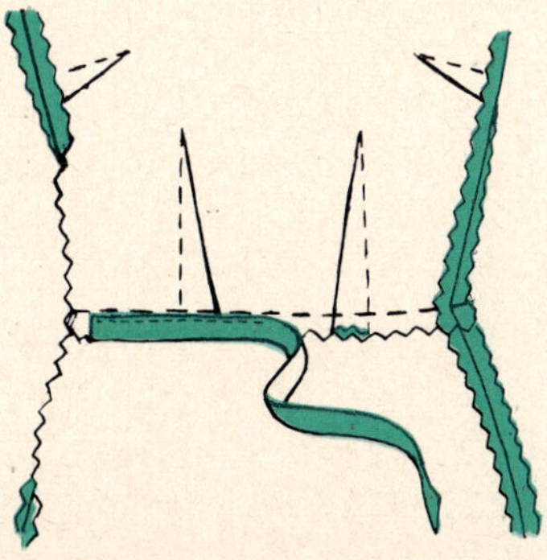

Press the waistline seam down into the skirt in all cases except on a shirred or pleated skirt. Because of the bulk of the fabric, press these skirts with the seam toward the bodice.

Open-front dress

On the coat-type dress, the joining at the waistline also takes care of the facing. Pin and sew the right side of the bodice to the right side of the skirt, starting from the center front line. Press the bodice facing back and pin in with the bodice front.

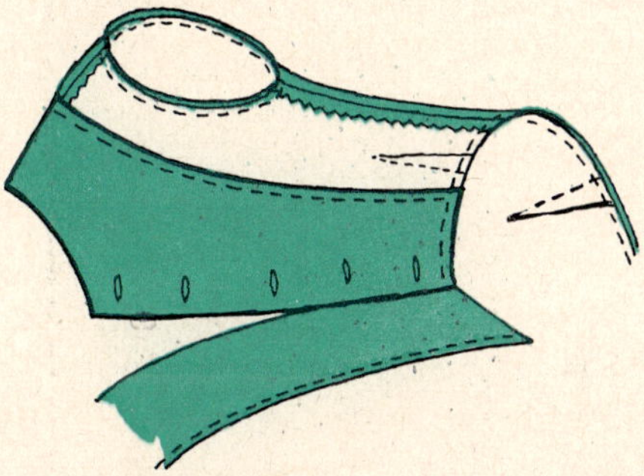

Stitch the skirt and bodice together on the bodice side. After stitching, fold the skirt facing back so the bodice is between the facing and the skirt, and stitch. The facings will

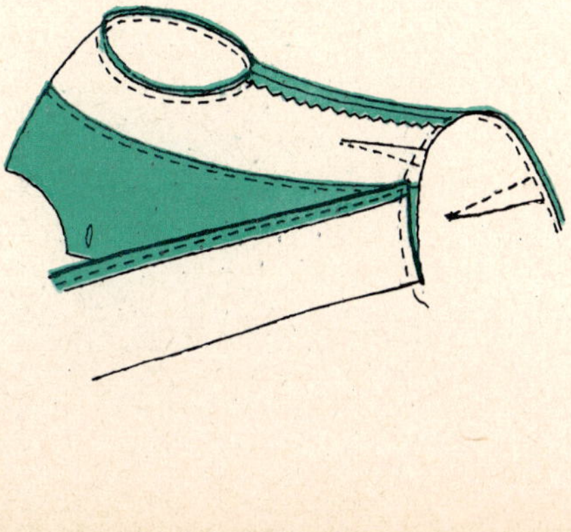

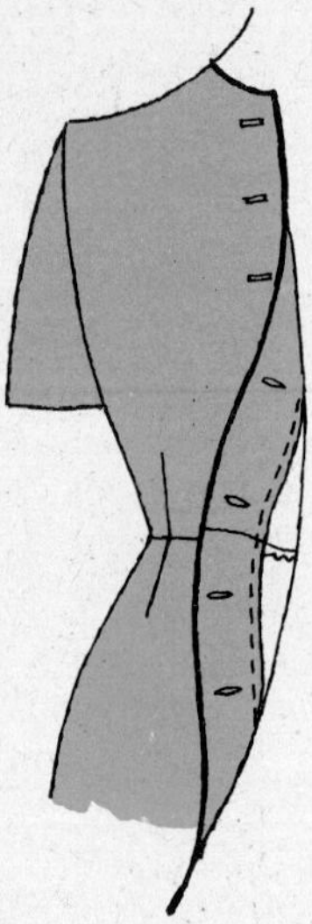

be securely held in place and they will not need to be hand stitched.

Ribbon waistline

The best finish to use in the waistline is grosgrain ribbon. It keeps the waistline in place and also prevents stretching. Measure the grosgrain around the waist and cut it 3 inches longer. Turn back one end of the ribbon for ½ inch, and then fold under another ½ inch, and hem. Sew a hook on this end of the ribbon.

On the other end, turn under ½ inch and then fold under 1 inch. Hem this end, and sew the eye ½ inch in from the edge. Tack the center of the ribbon to the inside waistline so that the hook and eye come at the opening of the dress.

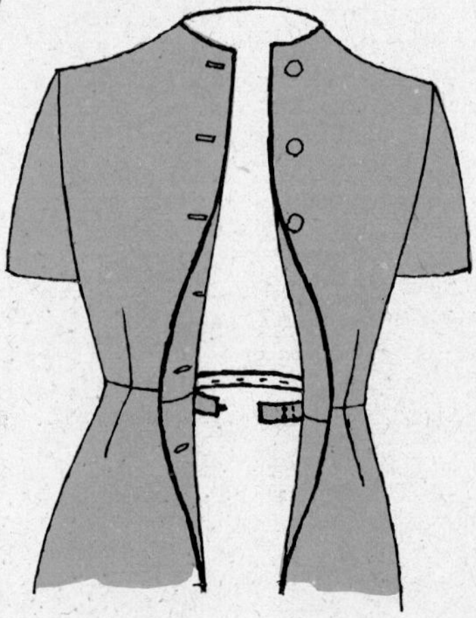

Plackets, loops

Dress placket

The left side of the dress has been left open for the zipper. It is easy to stretch this opening, since it is slightly bias. To prevent stretching, machine-baste placket seam closed, and sew the zipper in while the seam is temporarily basted.

The placket opening should be as long as the metal part of the zipper. Close the placket seam with a long stitch on the machine.

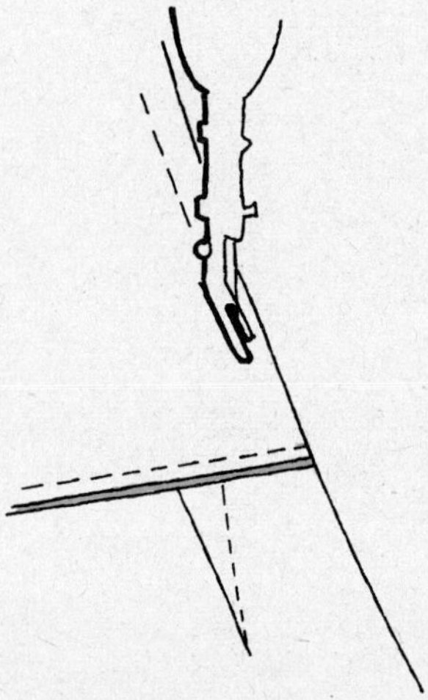

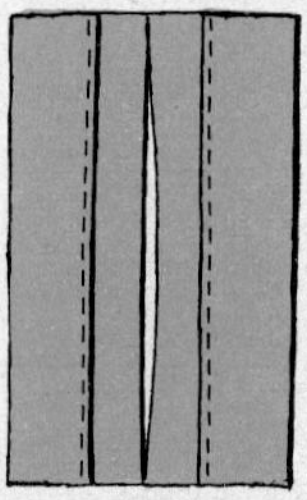

Check to make sure the waistline seams are together. Then press the seam open. If the seam allowance is less than ⅝ inch, add seam binding to extend it.

Use the zipper foot when sewing in the zipper. Set the adjustable foot to the right-hand side of the needle.

Turn the dress inside out, with the back of the dress under the front, right sides together. Open the zipper and place it face down on the back seam allowance, with the teeth edge of the zipper at the seamline, the bottom stop of the zipper at the lower edge of the basting. Stitch from the bottom of the tape to the top. A woven guideline on the zipper tape indicates how far in to sew.

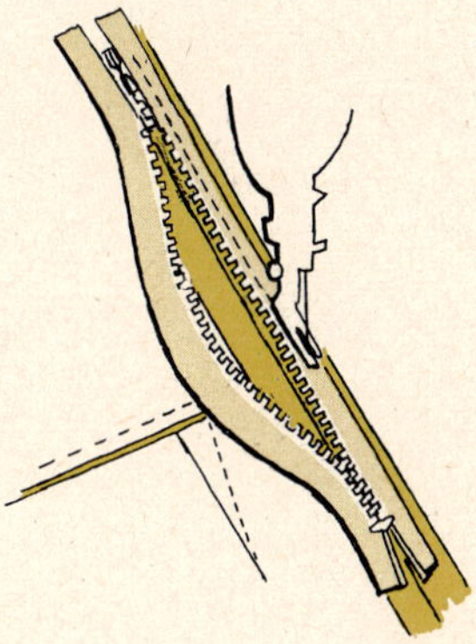

Close the zipper and turn it face up. The back seam allowance turns under, making a narrow fold along the zipper. Shift the zipper foot to the left-hand side and stitch on this fold from one end to the other. Sew only through the seam allowance fold and the zipper tape.

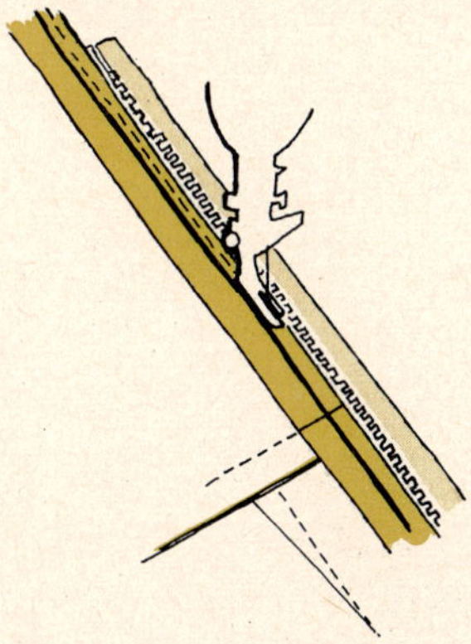

Next, turn the dress right side out. Press lightly along the seam.

Occasionally, if the waist is very small, there will be a little puckering at the waistline. To correct this, turn the dress and rip in on the waistline seam to the placket closing, so it shapes to the curve of the waist.

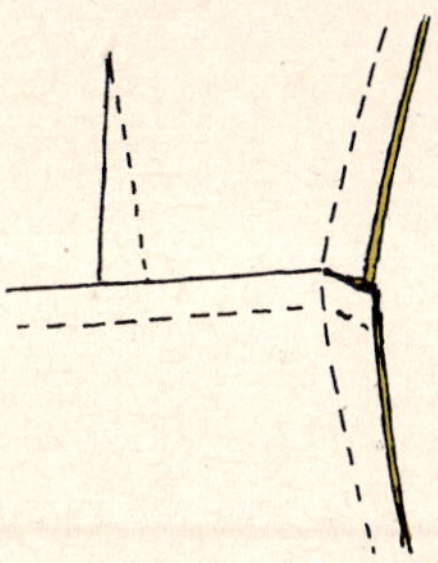

Turn the dress right side out and sew the zipper from the outside. The zipper automatically falls under the front of the dress. Stitch across the top, down the side, and across the bottom of the zipper. Although you can't see the zipper, you can feel it under the seam. Rip out the basting stitch and the zipper is completed, neatly in place.

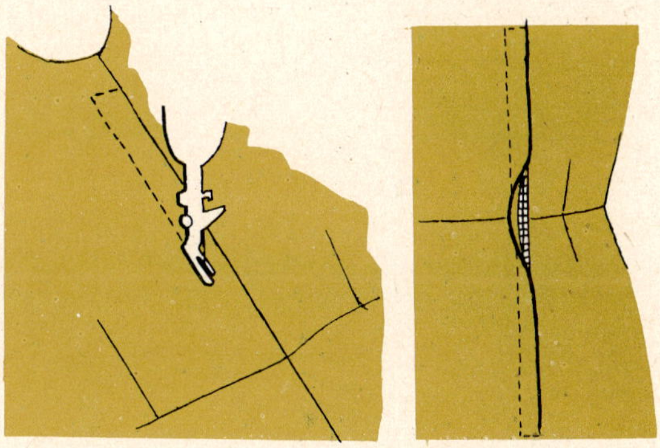

Sleeveless dress

This dress will be much easier to put on if you leave the left armhole seam open. Use a neckline-type zipper rather than a dress zipper. Allow ¾ inch clearance at the top.

Sew placket opening with a machine-basting thread as you did with the dress placket. Follow the same instructions for putting in this zipper as given for putting in the skirt zipper.

By hand, finish off the armhole facing to the inside of the zipper. Then sew a hook at the underarm seam at the top of the zipper.

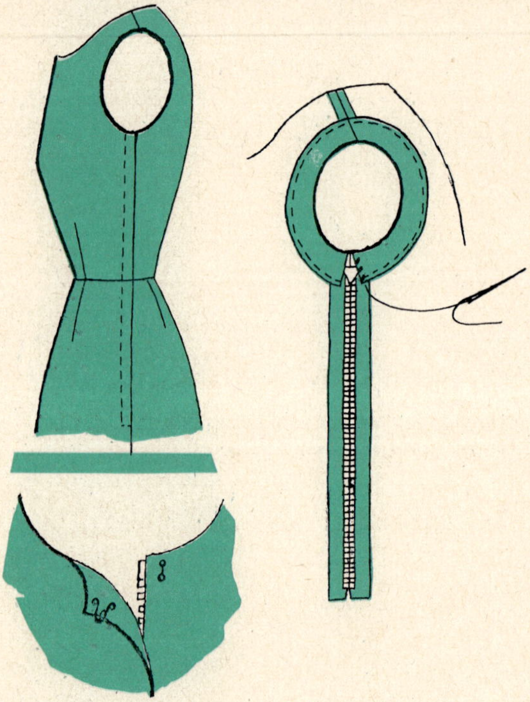

Front or back neckline opening

This type of zipper application is used at the neckline back and front, down the open-back dress, at sleeve openings or front dress openings.

It is inserted so it resembles a slot seam. When used only for a neck or sleeve opening, the zipper can be put in earlier before so much of the dress is assembled. When used at back and front necklines, it can be inserted before the shoulders of the dress have ever been joined.

When it is used down the back, however, the dress must be completely assembled so that the zipper can extend from the bodice and into the skirt.

Sew up the back opening with a machine-basting stitch, as you did for the side placket. If the seam allowance is less than ⅝ inch, extend the seams with seam binding. Be sure that the waistline seams match.

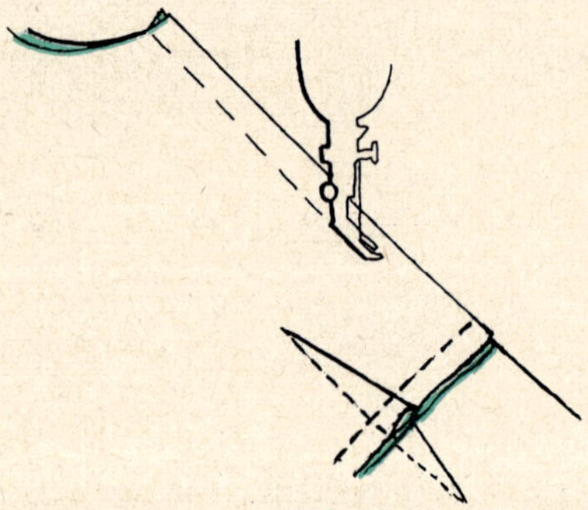

Press open the seam. Open the zipper and place it face down, on the extended seam allowance only. The teeth of the zipper should be along the seamline. Use the zipper foot and sew the tape only to the seam allowance.

Sew from the bottom to the top along the woven guideline on the zipper tape. The top of the zipper should be ¾ inch from the neck edge.

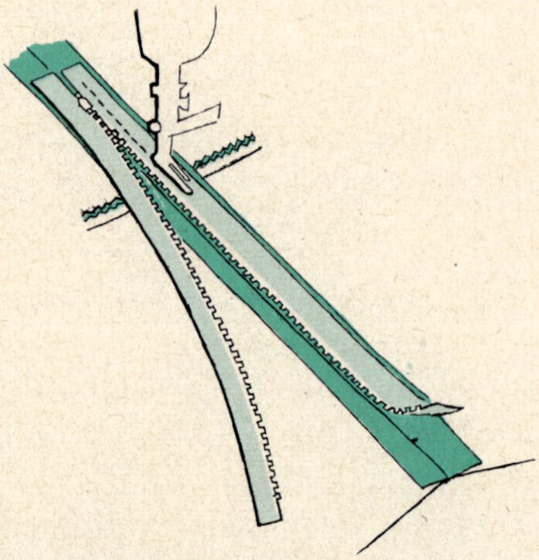

Close the zipper. Turn the dress to the right side. On the right side of the dress, the zipper will be in place under the center of the seamline.

Stitch down one side of the seamline, across the bottom, and up the other side about ¼ inch away from the seam. Remove the basting line, press, and the zipper is finished.

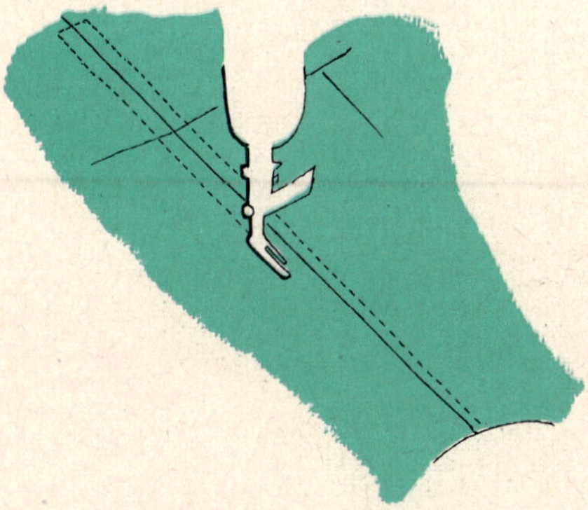

On the unfinished neck or sleeve opening, the zipper should be placed approximately ¾ inch from the open edge of the neck or cuff.

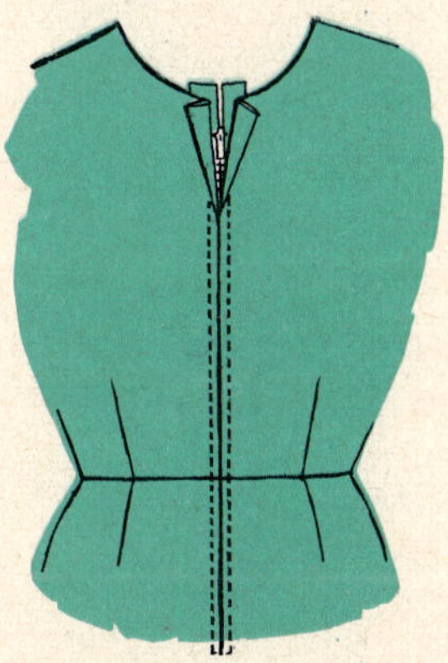

Skirt placket

This type of placket can be used in skirts, slacks, and shorts—whenever the opening is on the side. If the garment opens down the back, use the neck-type application with skirt zipper—slot-seam type of insertion.

The side seam placket should be the length of the metal part of the zipper, plus ⅝ inch seam allowance, and an extra ¼ inch for clearance of the zipper head. Sew up the placket opening with a machine-basting stitch. Press open the seam. If the seam allowance is less than ⅝ inch, extend it by stitching seam binding along the edge. Use the zipper foot, adjusted to the right-hand side for stitching. Turn the skirt inside out. Place it on the machine, with front skirt up, right sides of the front and back skirts together, back seam allowance extending.

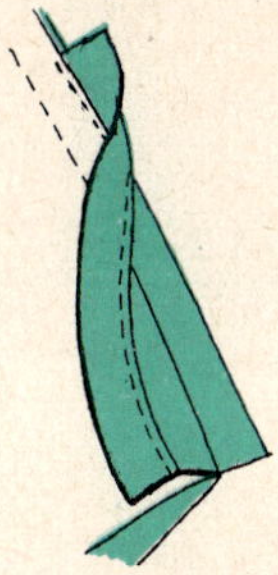

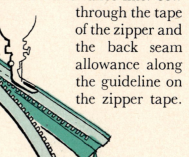

Open the zipper and place it face down on the seam allowance, teeth edge at the seam allowance line. Sew through the tape of the zipper and the back seam allowance along the guideline on the zipper tape.

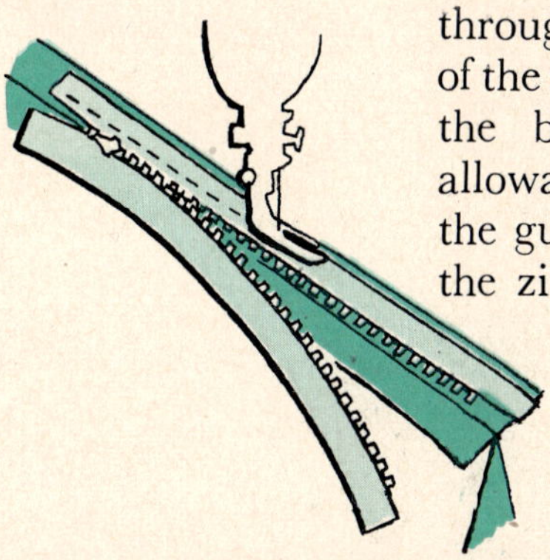

Close the zipper and turn right side up. The back seam allowance turns under, making a narrow fold along the zipper. Adjust the foot to the left side and sew along this fold from bottom to top of tape.

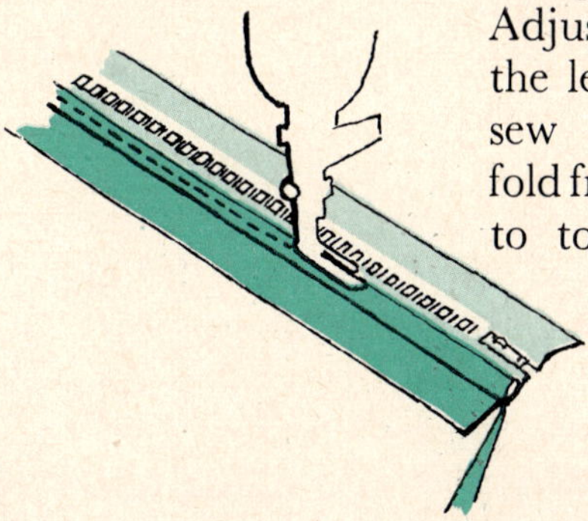

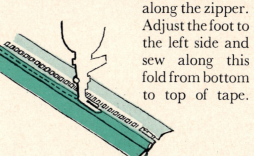

Turn the skirt right side out, and lightly press the seam. The zipper falls under the front skirt. Stitch from the top of the skirt along the zipper to the bottom, then across to the side seam. Sew back a few stitches to finish. Remove the basting thread and the zipper is finished.

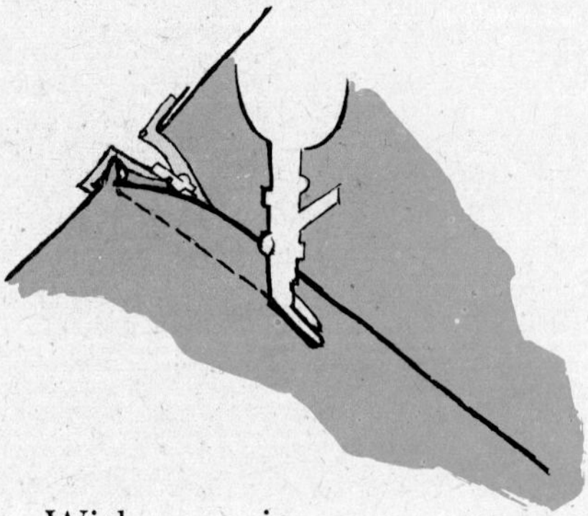

With experience, you can put zippers in without pinning. In the meantime, pins should be enough, with no need to baste the zipper.

On certain fabrics, it is better to put zippers in by hand. This is usually in more dressy fabrics, and will be illustrated in Chapter 10.

Belt loops

If you want to use belt loops, make them now. They're usually placed at the side seams, and can be crocheted or done with a blanket stitch.

The belt loop should be longer than the belt, so the belt will easily slide through the loop.

Hand-crocheted belt loops

Use a knotted double thread about two feet long. Fasten it securely with short back-stitches in the side seam at the point where the top of the belt will be. Pull the needle

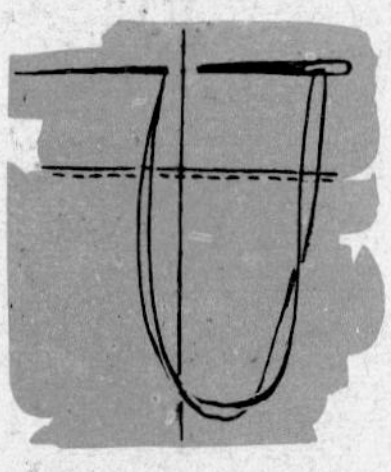

through the fabric to form the loop. Hold the thread with the needle in your left hand. Slip the loop over the thumb and first two fingers of your right hand.

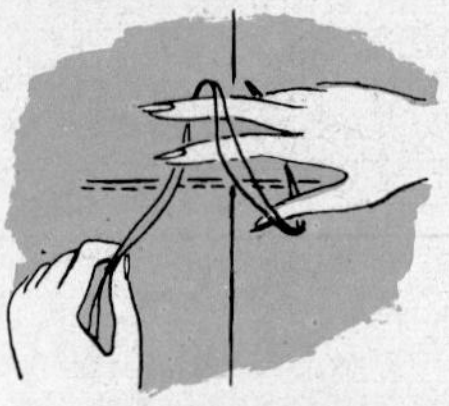

With thumb and forefingers, pick up the needle thread, pulling it through the first loop to form a new loop. Continue until you have a chain long enough for the belt to slip through.

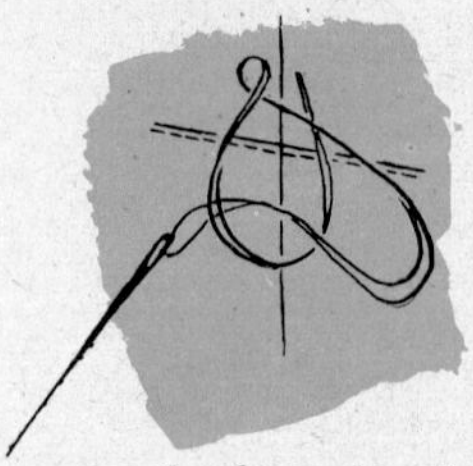

Finish the chain by slipping the needle through the last loop. Pull to form a knot. Sew to the side seam. Fasten securely on the wrong side of the garment.

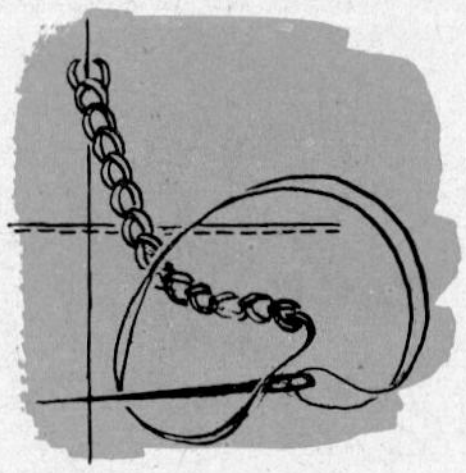

Hand-made belt loops

Bring the needle through from the wrong side above the belt line and take a stitch below the belt line.

Work back and forth two or three times. Then blanket stitch over strands of thread, drawing the stitches firm. Fasten the last stitch securely.

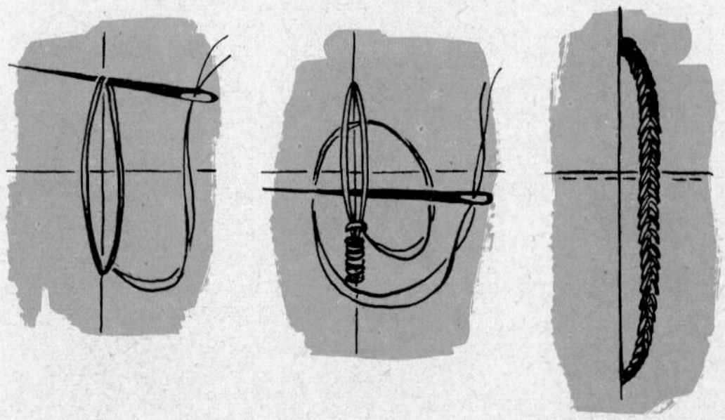

Chapter 8

Handling special types of fabrics

Some fabrics require special handling. In this chapter you'll learn how to cut, stitch, press, and care for such fabrics as jersey, chiffon, lace, velvet and many of the man-made fabrics.

The need for special handling does not mean that these fabrics are difficult to work on and sew. Lace, for instance, is easy to sew, and its texture makes it very simple to hide mistakes.

For all these fabrics, however, there are special ways of cutting and sewing that enhance their beauty. Don't "shy away" from these special types. Rather, learn how to sew beautifully on them all for more diversified and enjoyable sewing. They will add glamour to your wardrobe.

Jersey

Jersey was originally made of wool or worsted in a tubular form. Now you can buy it in cotton, rayon, silk, nylon, and blended fibers. Wool and cotton jerseys, and some blends are in tubular form; rayon, silk, and nylon jerseys are available open and one-ply like other fabrics. These jerseys can also be cut like other fabrics. Any of the tubular jerseys, however, require special cutting.

Cutting jersey

Review the brief section on cutting wool jersey in Chapter 4. Wool and cotton jerseys come in tubular form, and are more economical to cut because they have two fold lines. However, do not lay your pattern pieces on this original fold line. It is usually stretched off-grain by the fabric finishing process, and it is impossible to remove the crease. Instead, refold the jersey, making fresh folds where the fabric is to be cut. When refolding, be sure to follow a rib to keep it straight on the length-grain. You can gauge the cross-grain only by measuring across the end of the fabric for the straight of the goods and by cutting along this line.

Many novelty weaves are now available in jerseys. These sometimes have a nap. To be safe, cut all the pieces in one direction. When the pattern has wide pieces such as a flared skirt that cannot be cut on the width of folded goods, the jersey will have to be cut and opened. Cut the jersey along one fold line but also be sure to cut it along a rib. Cut the skirt so the crease is inconspicuous.

Sewing jersey

Jerseys are treated so they won't stretch on the length, but since they are knitted fabrics, they will stretch on the width. Take this into consideration when you sew jersey.

When you sew the length seams of jersey, use an easy tension on the machine and stretch the material a little as you sew. The jersey will snap back into shape. You have sewed more stitches to the inch and created elasticity in the seam so you need have no fear of the length seams popping whenever there is any strain put on them.

It is important to stay the cross seams on jersey fabric so they will not stretch. On the shoulders, sew a piece of seam binding in the seam to keep the shoulder from stretching out of shape.

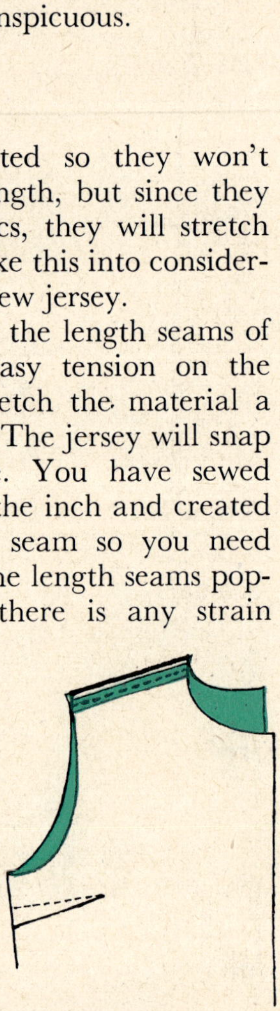

Staying the shoulder seams.

Always stay the waistline of a jersey dress with a seam binding sewed into the seam after the skirt and waist are joined. Or, you can use a grosgrain ribbon as a stay. Tack it by hand into the waistline after the dress is finished.

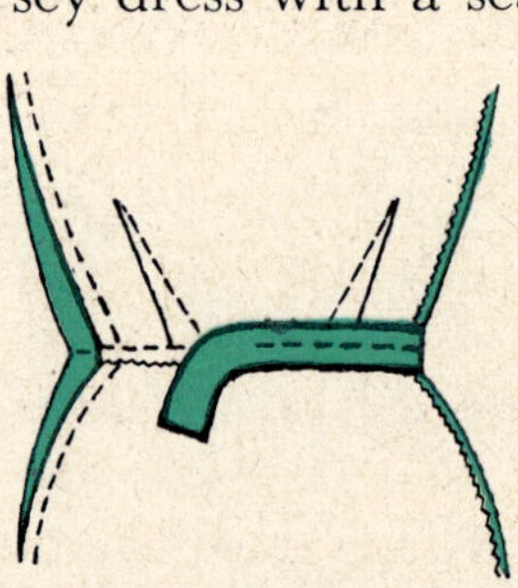

Staying the waistline.

If there is a yoke treatment in the design of the skirt or bodice, this should be lined before the yoke is sewed to the dress. China silk or any soft fabric makes a suitable lining. Cut the yoke lining from the same pattern and sew the right side of the lining to the wrong side of the dress. Stitch just outside the seam allowance line. There is one exception to the rule of staying the cross seams of jersey. When the bodice and sleeves are all in one piece, the shoulder seam runs down the top of the sleeve from the neckline. This shoulder seam must be stretched rather than stayed. Or, the top sleeve seam will look puckered and uneven, and the sleeve will not shape to the arm.

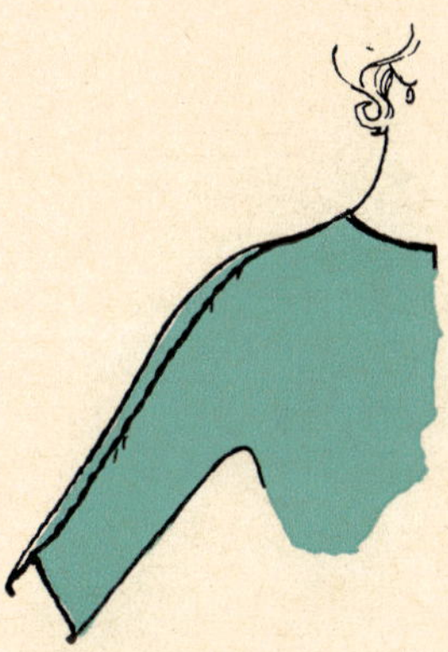

Lining the jersey sheath or skirt

Always line a jersey skirt with a soft lining like China silk. Simply hang the lining from the waist. (For details, see "Linings," Chapter 5.)

Completely interline jersey sheath dresses, again using a soft silk. (See "Interlining the Sheath.")

Allow a jersey dress to hang 24-48 hours before marking the usual 2-inch hem and sew seam binding on the edge. Slip-stitch the hem.

Chiffon

Chiffon is a very thin, sheer fabric. The finest, softest chiffon is made of silk, but it's also made of rayon, synthetics, wool, and long staple cotton. Because it is so light and sheer, there is a tendency for the fabric to shift as you cut it. A few easy professional tricks will prevent this.

Cutting chiffon

If the dress can be cut on the fold of the goods, tear off the ends to be sure the grain is straight. Then fold on the length, matching the selvages and the ends. Either pin these together or stitch with a machine-basting or hand-basting stitch all around.

When you lay out the fabric, be sure the cutting surface is not too slick, since chiffon has a tendency to slide. If you use the dining room table, an old tablecloth under the chiffon will help. If the floor is your cutting board, spread an old sheet and pin it firmly to the rug. Lay the chiffon out on this.

Because chiffon is so sheer, it is easy for it to slide off-grain as you cut. When you use the floor, you will have enough room to lay out the entire piece of fabric and all the pattern pieces at once. You can square up the ends and pin them to the sheet or the rug, if necessary, to hold them in place.

If you work on a small table where you have to fold the fabric and shift it as you lay out the pieces, it is a good idea to put a piece of tissue paper under the end of the chiffon, square up the corners of the fabric with the paper, and pin it firmly in place. This will hold it on grain until you begin to pin the pattern pieces into place. Lay out, and pin all the pattern pieces before you cut.

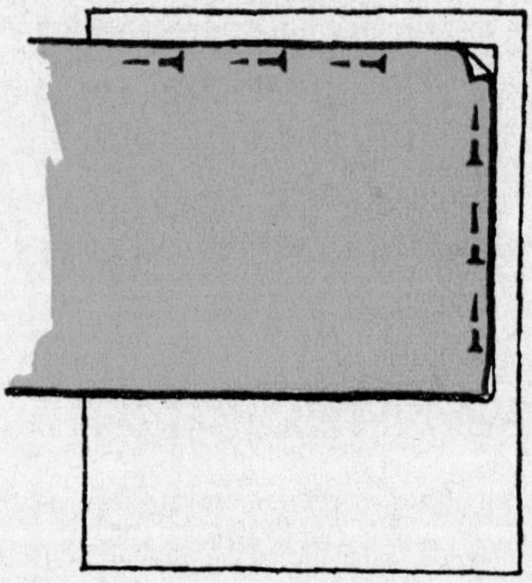

When cutting, be sure your shears are sharp. As you pin the pattern, use more pins than usual, and place them closer together. A printed pattern with a margin that falls away as you cut is another asset. By cutting through the paper, there is less chance of the chiffon shifting.

Cutting tips for special styles

Chiffon can be used for dressy evening styles and is also used successfully for shirtwaist styles, shirts and skirts. When chiffon is used, the type of dress you are making will affect the handling of certain points in these styles, and will call for special cutting techniques.

Chiffon skirts

No matter what the style, the skirt is usually made with at least two layers of fabric, sometimes more. This gives the chiffon a sheer, wispy look, with no taffeta or silk slip showing underneath. On a dirndl skirt, the outside skirt hem should be from 6 to 12 inches deep. Keep the underskirt sheer with only a hand-rolled hem or fine machine-edge.

Be sure to allow extra material for the double skirt and the deeper hem. When cutting this type of skirt, the pieces are usually just straight lengths. It is better to tear the lengths, rather than to try to cut them. If any shaping is needed at the top of the chiffon skirt, such as for unpressed pleats, pin the paired lengths of fabric together at the selvage and ends, and then cut the pieces from the pattern.

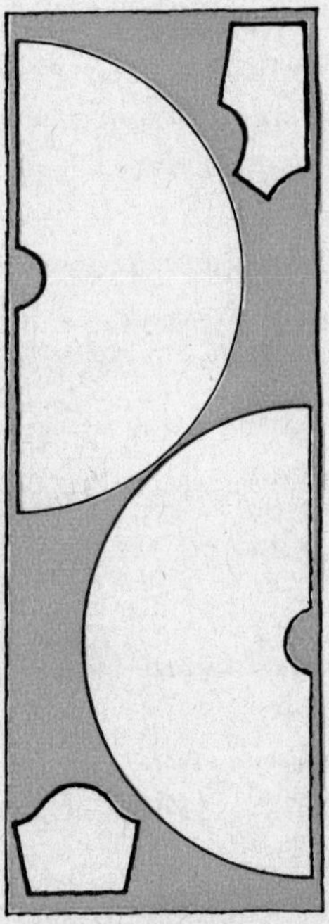

For a full, circular skirt, which is often made from chiffon, it is also easier to tear the chiffon into the lengths needed for the pattern pieces. Pin the chiffon together and cut from the pattern. Corners of chiffon will be left where the skirt is cut away to form the half circle. Cut other pieces of the pattern from these fabric ends.

Cut the circle skirt the finished length, plus about ½ inch for a narrow hem. All layers of this skirt are the same length. The outside skirt as well as underskirt should have a fine rolled hem. Let the skirts hang for a considerable time before the hems are marked and finished. Chiffon is so soft that it has a great deal of stretch, and since most of the circular skirt is on the bias, this means additional stretching.

A trick the professional uses on this type of skirt is to make the underskirt of two half circles of chiffon, which are softly shirred into the waistline. It takes about 4 extra yards of fabric for the additional panels, but the finished garment is well worth the additional cost of fabric. A circular skirt in chiffon is beautifully soft and graceful. If the remaining pattern pieces can be laid out in even lengths, use the following method which is

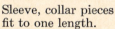

Bodice pieces fit to one length.

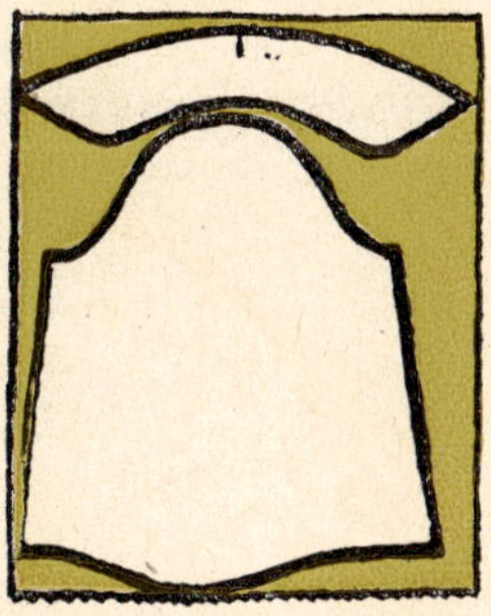

Sleeve, collar pieces fit to one length.

a favorite with the professional sewer. Tear the amount of chiffon, match the selvages and ends, and cut small sections at a time. This guarantees the true grain of the material.

Cutting the bodice

The trick in working on chiffon is to make it look as sheer as possible. When you start to cut the shirt-type bodice, keep in mind how it will be finished. If the pattern has separate facing pieces, avoid the facing seam by cutting the facing all in one with the front. Pin the pattern facing piece to the pattern front on the seam allowance line. Also, cut the facing

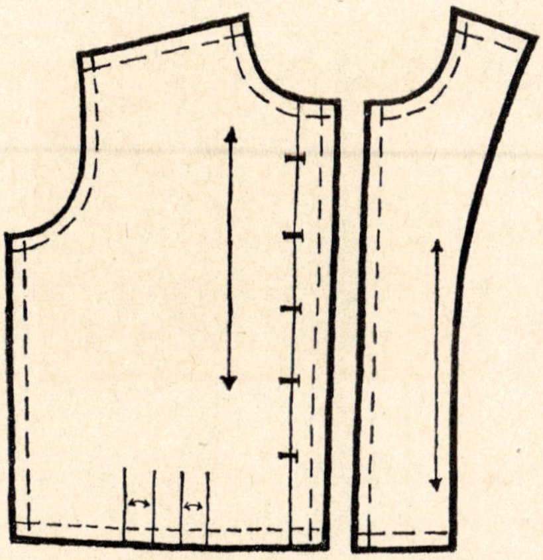

away to give just a narrow band down the front, rather than shaping up to the shoulder. The width of the facing should be the same from either side of the center front line, so that the band down the front looks centered. The loose edge of the facing can be turned back ¼ inch and stitched. Be sure to allow for this seam allowance when cutting the facing.

Another way to keep the front as

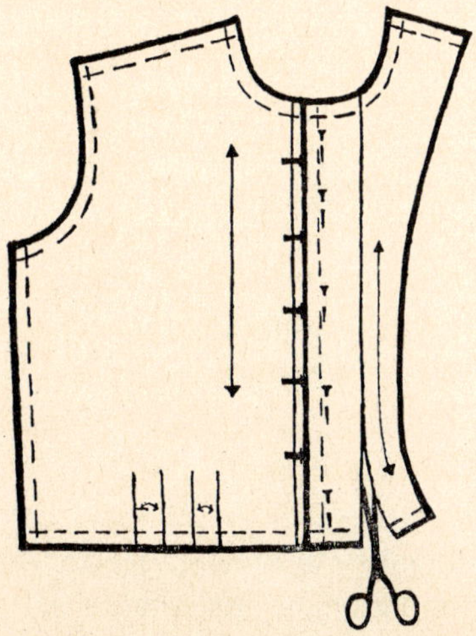

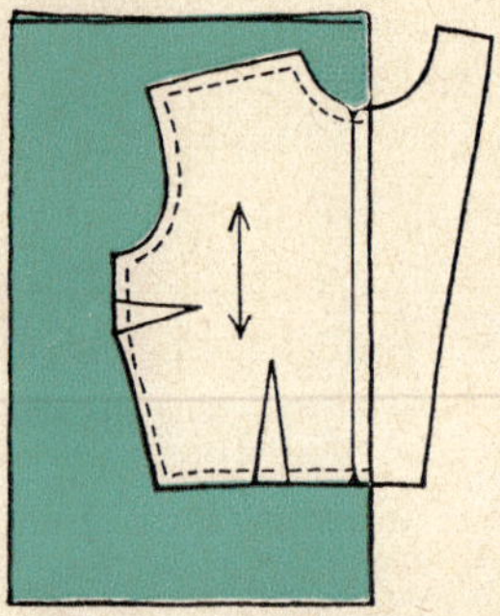

sheer-looking as possible is to cut the whole front of the chiffon garment double.

Lay the bodice pattern on a double thickness of the chiffon, with the fold edge of the facing on the fold line of the chiffon.

When you make the dress front double, the back can be either double or single. The sleeves, however, are almost always made from only a single thickness of material.

Never interface the front collar or cuffs of the chiffon shirt-dress. Usually, small buttons and small, hand-made buttonholes are preferred on lightweight fabric. The buttonholes are often made up and down, rather than across the fabric. Otherwise, they have a tendency to sag.

For very dressy chiffon fashions, the bodice is usually made double, but the way this is done depends on the style of dress and whether it is to be mounted. (See Chapter 10 on cocktail and evening clothes.)

The neck and sleeve edges of chiffon are usually finished with a hand-rolled edge or fine roll binding. The binding is made as in Chapter 6.

Sewing chiffon

Keep your equipment in good order. Start with a new needle on the machine. A blunt one will pull fabric threads, and cause puckering along the stitching line.

The pressure of the presser foot should be heavy enough to prevent the chiffon slipping to the side, light enough so it will not mark the fabric.

Stitch bias seams over tissue paper to prevent stretching. This is not necessary on other seams.

You'll find a slightly smaller stitch—about a 15-18—is better for chiffon. There is no need to buy special thread; use mercerized cotton thread No. 50.

Seams used on chiffon

If the chiffon skirt is very full, or is worn over matching slips, you can use a regular pinked seam. This makes the skirt hang more softly. The seam is almost invisible on the right side, especially on dark colors.

On circular skirts, you can leave the selvage on as the seam finish if it has shown no signs of shrinking when pressed with light steam.

French seams are preferred at underarm and shoulder seams of bodice. If the skirt's slim, and the slip is not a perfect match, it's better to use a fine French seam as a finish.

If you're uncertain about which type of seam to use, sew a regular seam in the upper skirt piece. Hold it over the chiffon and slip fabric as it will be used. If the seam shows through, use a French seam.

Never use French seams at the armholes, however. Instead, sew the sleeve on the regular seamline. Then run a second stitch about ¼ inch outside of this line. (If you made the French

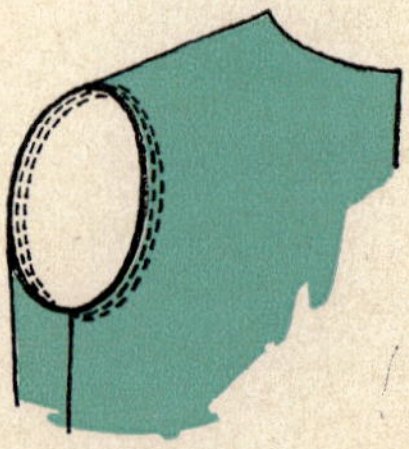

seams narrower than ¼ inch at other parts of the dress, then use the same width for this stitching so the seams will look uniform.) Trim away the armhole seam at the second stitching. Overcast this edge by hand, or by machine if you have a zigzag machine or a zigzag attachment for your regular machine.

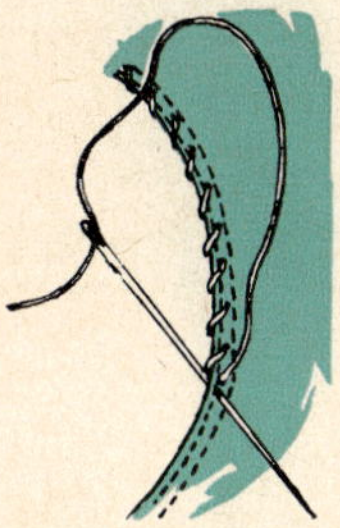

French seams

A self-finished seam is recommended for chiffon. Pin or baste the wrong sides together on the seam allowance line. Stitch ¼ inch from this line for the first stitching. Remove original pins or basting. Trim the seam very close to this stitching and press to one side. Then turn the seam wrong

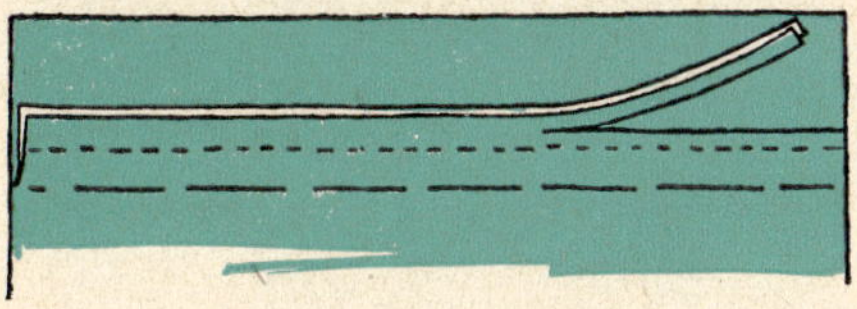

side out and pin or baste on the original seamline, and stitch.

No raw edges should show on the

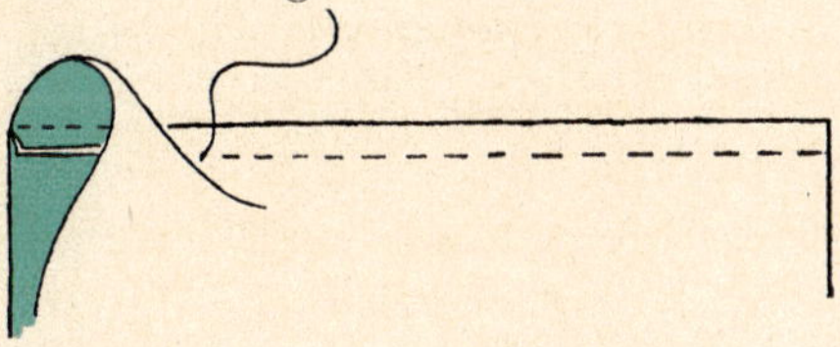

right or wrong sides. If you find fuzz showing along the right side, the under seam was not trimmed close enough, or it started to ravel after it was trimmed. To prevent this, press the first seam to one side before you trim it. It means less handling of the seam after trimming, and less chance of the seam raveling.

For a finer seam, which is both possible and desirable on sheer fabrics, sew the first stitching slightly closer to the seam allowance line.

Be sure however, to allow enough width to cover the trimmed seam after it is turned to the wrong side for stitching. You can, with care, make a French seam as fine as ⅛ inch when it's finished.

Rolled hems

This hand-finished edge is used on sheer fabrics. You can use it to hem an entire circular skirt, or just to finish a neck edge. It gives a quality look to clothes, as well as eliminating the need for facings or other heavy finishings that spoil the sheer effect of the chiffon fabric.

Run a row of machine-stitching ¼ inch from the edge. Trim the edge close to this stitching line. You'll find it much easier to roll over this machine-stitch and the roll will be smoother and more even.

Roll the edge a few inches at a time between thumb and forefinger.

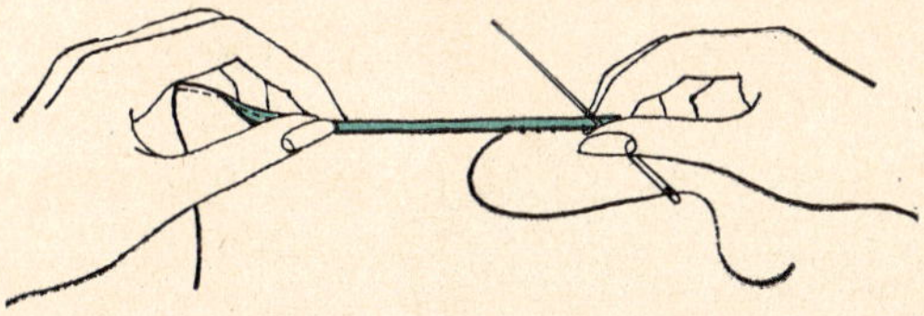

Then, use a slip-stitch to catch the roll in place. Take just a single thread of the fabric for each stitch. Continue rolling the material a few

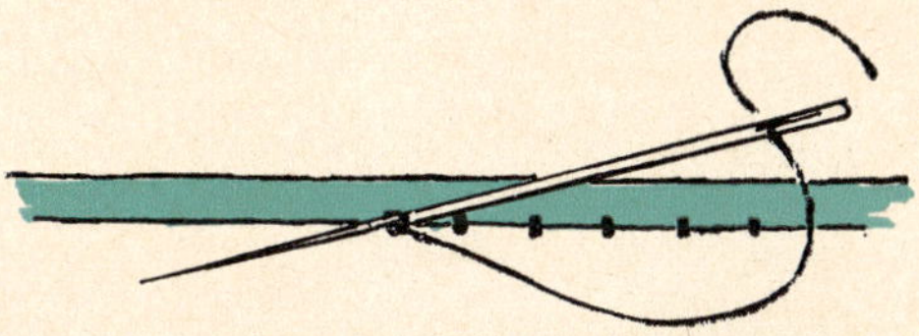

inches at a time. If you find a point that seems to resist smooth rolling, the machine-stitch is too tight. Clip the stitch and the material will smooth out and roll correctly. (Additional information is in Chapter 10.)

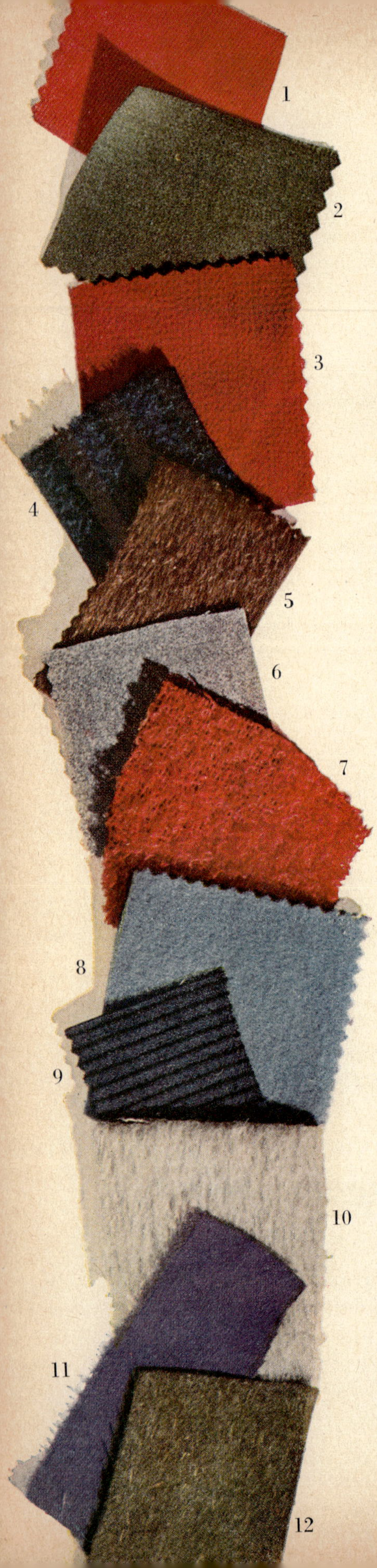

Fabric Dictionary

1, 2 Gabardine

(1) Cotton gabardine, and (2) wool gabardine. Gabardine is a tightly woven twill material. The cotton is a much coarser twill than the wool. This material is usually finished with a high sheen. It is made in many different fibers and blends.

3 Wool crepe

This is a lightweight fabric made of many fibers. It has a crinkled surface obtained either by use of (1) weave, (2) embossing, (3) hard-twist yarns, or (4) chemical treatment.

4 Chinchilla

Chinchilla is a heavy, twill weave coating. It has a napped surface that is rolled into little tufts or nubs.

5 Fleece

This is the name of a fabric that has a deep fleece-like, napped surface. It may be a pile fabric, or the fleece effect may be obtained by a napping process.

6 Flannel

Flannel is a fabric of medium weight, in plain or twill weave, that has a slightly napped surface.

7 Boucle

A fabric woven or knitted with looped or knotted surface. It usually has a spongy effect and feel.

8 Duvetyn type coating

Duvetyn is a twill weave fabric with a fine, velvety, napped surface that is raised to hide the weave.

9 Wool ottoman

The rib of ottoman is widely spaced and in a contrasting color.

10 Zibeline

Wool fabric made in coating and suiting weights. The nap is long and lustrous, running in one direction. Often camel's hair or mohair shows in the nap of zibeline.

11 Wool broadcloth

This is a very different fabric from cotton or silk broadcloth. It has a glossy finish with a nap running in one direction. It can be made either of wool or worsted.

12 Cashmere

This fabric is made from the extremely soft hair of the Kashmir goat from India. Similar goats are now raised in this country. Cashmere is most often used in combination with sheep's wool

13 Terry cloth
Terry cloth is cotton toweling fabric with loops on one or both sides. It is water absorbent, and comes in many colors and designs. You can buy it by the yard.

14 Chambray
A plain cotton fabric woven with a colored warp and a white filler. It also comes in stripes, checks, and dobby design.

15 Dotted swiss
A sheer, crisp, cotton fabric with a woven clipped dot. It comes with a contrasting dot or in the same color.

16 Organdy
This is a sheer, light, wiry fabric. It must be treated so that it will keep a crisp finish permanently.

17 Surah
A soft lustrous fabric with a twill weave. It is usually silk, but also comes in other fibers. May be plain, stripes, or prints.

18 Dobby
A small geometric design is woven into the cloth. It is similar to, but more simple than a jacquard weave.

19 Bedford cord
Bedford cord is a heavy cotton or woolen fabric with a cord or ridge running lengthwise through it.

20 Striped cotton
This fabric is a novelty bedford in a striped cotton.

21 Batiste
The fabric is named for Jean Batiste, a linen weaver. It is a sheer, very fine, lightweight fabric.

22 Gingham
Plain weave cotton fabric. Gingham is woven in checks, stripes, and plaids of two or more colors.

23 Gingham
Gingham is also made in companion checks of different sizes. They can be used together or separately.

24 Sateen
This is cotton cloth made in a satin weave. It is often treated for high luster and crease-resistance.

25 Broadcloth
Closely woven fabric with a fine cross rib and a lustrous finish. This is a sheer in cotton and blends.

26 Birdseye pique
It is a fabric with a diamond-shaped motif. It also comes with a lengthwise wale or a waffle weave, honeycomb, and a large diamond pattern called bullseye. Birdseye pique is usually a cotton, but it can also be made from other fibers.

27 Cotton broadcloth
This is an all cotton fabric in a heavier texture than sheer broadcloth (25). It has a soft hand and good luster.

28 Seersucker
A cloth with a woven stripe created by weaving some of the warp threads slack and others tight. Seersucker comes in stripes, plaids, checks, and in many colors.

29 Voile
A lightweight sheer in a plain weave, with a crisp feel. It comes in beautiful colors and prints.

30 Plain plisse
Fine cotton fabric, soft or crisp hand, with a striped or all-over blister effect, created by weaving or chemical process.

31 Printed plisse
Printed plisse is used for sleepwear. Made in colors and prints.

32 Embroidered linen
Linen is made from flax fibers. It is used particularly for embroidery, and is a very beautiful fabric.

33 Linen
Linen is a strong, lustrous fabric made of smooth-surfaced flax fibers. It is available in plain weaves, from handkerchief linen which is sheer, to heavy suiting.

34 Linen damask
This fabric is often used in tablecloths. It is also now being made in beautiful textures for dresses.

35 Silk linen
It is actually a silk, woven to resemble the linen weave.

36 Percale
Printed or a plain cotton sheeting fabric. A good construction is 80x80 (eighty-square). It usually has a smooth, dull finish.

37 Cotton crepe
Cotton crepe is a fabric with a crinkly or pebbly surface. It comes in many weights and fibers.

38 Pongee
Plain woven fabric from raw silk, comes in light and medium weight. Its natural color is a light tan, but it is now printed and dyed in many lovely colors.

39 Lawn
Lightweight cotton cloth, often given a crease-resistant finish. It can be dyed or printed, and novelty types made with a sateen stripe or crinkled to look like plisse.

40 Printed georgette crepe
A sheer, that is heavier than chiffon, made of a twisted yarn both ways of the weave to give a pebbly, crepe effect.

41 Velveteen
This is a cotton pile fabric that looks like velvet but, unlike velvet, is woven singly. It comes in twill back or plain weave. Twill back is better and holds the pile more firmly.

42 Sailcloth
A very strong, firmly woven cotton canvas. Originally, a heavier fabric used for sails. Now made in a weight suitable for apparel.

43 Corduroy
A cut pile fabric that comes in a wide or narrow wale. It has a plain weave or twill back. Twill back is better quality. It is usually all cotton, though new types are made with a spun rayon pile and cotton back.

44 Novelty corduroy
This corduroy is made to look like a birdseye weave.

45 Pinwale corduroy
Pinwale corduroy has an extremely fine wale, with a soft hand. Now made in some types that are washable, require little ironing.

46 Madras
Fine cotton shirting with a woven design. Fabrics can be dobbies, jacquard stripes, fine cord or checks, or coarse, homespun cotton plaids in colorful patterns. Made in India.

47 Denim
Washable, strong-twilled cotton cloth, either dyed in the piece or woven with a colored warp and white filler.

48 Striped denim
Denim is made in plaids, dobbies, stripes, can be printed, or given an iridescence by weaving two colors.

49 Poplin
Poplin is often waterproofed and treated for wind resistance.

50 Duck
A tightly woven cotton or linen fabric. It is similar to canvas and can have a plain or ribbed weave. Made in various weights.

51 Twill
Heavy cotton cloth with a diagonal weave is usually called twill. Actually, twill is a weave with a diagonal rib, or lines. Twills are made from many fibers and combinations. The best known types are flannels, serges, gabardines, and surahs.

52 Challis
A soft, supple, very light, plain woven fabric made from worsted, wool, rayon staple, cotton, and blends. Printed in small floral, Persian, or cravat prints that are identified with challis.

53 Wool jersey
Wool jersey comes in tubular form, and is very economical to cut.

54 Cotton jersey
This is a heavier knit, and is made up in heavier designs.

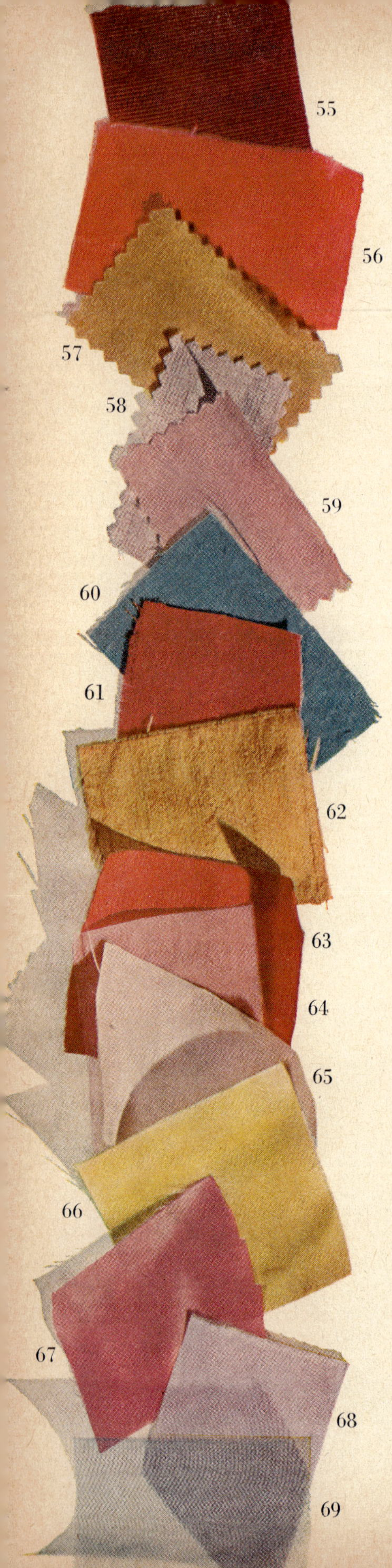

55 Bengaline
A fabric similar to faille, only much heavier, with a definite crosswise rib. Used for dresses, coats, trimmings and draperies.

56 Rayon taffeta
A fine, plain weave fabric, smooth on both sides, usually with a sheen to the surface. Made originally of silk, now it is made of rayon and from blends of several fabrics.

57 Silk broadcloth
Silk broadcloth is a light, thin fabric with a lustrous surface. It is very closely woven, with fine embedded ribs.

58 Tussah
This is a term for uncultivated silk. The filaments are coarser, stronger and more irregular. Fabrics can be made wholly or partly of wild silk.

59 Honan
Wild silk of the finest quality. It comes from Honan, China, and is made in a pongee type fabric. It's now imitated elsewhere.

60 Shantung
Plain woven fabric originally made on hand looms from wild silk. It has a rough, nubby surface due to imperfections in the yarn.

61 Crepe
Name applied to fabrics with a crinkled or puckered surface, obtained by various combinations of twisted yarn.

62 Antique taffeta
Crisp taffeta made of a slubbed yarn, simulating types made in ancient times before silk was finely cultivated.

63 Peau de peche
This is a soft, closely woven dress silk with a slightly roughened surface, similar to the skin of the peach.

64 Organza
Organza is a wiry, sheer fabric, which is softer than organdy but of the same plain weave.

65 Peau de soie
Very soft dress silk, with a satiny surface and a mellow luster.

66 Faille taffeta
It is a fabric with flat horizontal ribs, finer than bengaline.

67 China silk
Very lightweight, soft fine silk, used especially for lining dresses, skirts, and suits. It is also used in scarfs.

68 Tissue taffeta
Tissue taffeta is a very sheer type of silk taffeta.

69 Net
This is a mesh fabric, ranging from tulle to fishing net.

70 Brocade with gold thread
This is an unusual fabric, since the background is an ottoman weave. It is woven with a tarnishproof gold thread.

71 Barathea
Closely-woven fabric with a characteristic pebbly weave. It is used for dresses, neckties, and lightweight suits.

72 Brocade
This is a rich jacquard fabric with an allover interwoven design. The pattern is emphasized by contrasting surfaces and colors. The background may be satin or twill.

73 Velvet
This fabric has a short-cut pile to give it a smooth, rich, luxurious surface, soft to the touch.

74 Ottoman
Heavier fabric with a definite rib. The rib extends from selvage to selvage. Similar to bengaline but with a heavier rib.

75 Boucle brocade
This is a new fabric with the design worked in a boucle weave.

76 Slipper satin
Strong, compact, durable satin of heavy quality. Made of silk, rayon, acetate, synthetics or a mixture of fibers. On slipper satin the back is sometimes of cotton.

77 Lame
Fabric woven of metal thread made of nontarnishable yarns.

78 Moire
Moire is a finish giving a waved or watered effect to a fabric, usually a corded silk, rayon, or blend.

79 Reversible brocade
Brocade woven in metal thread and colors that can be used on either side. It can emphasize the colored or metallic side.

80 Chiffon
A very light, soft, sheer fabric in a plain weave. Chiffon is made of silk, rayon, wool, cotton, and blends.

81 Jacquard
A type of loom which makes intricate patterns, such as brocades and damasks. Smaller, intricate patterns are called jacquards.

82 Silk satin
A type of weave with yarns floated to the surface to give a lustrous face. It is made of silk and other fibers, and fiber blends. It is made in many varieties, and is also elasticized for use in making bathing suits.

83 Silk damask
A glossy, patterned satiny jacquard weave. Silk damask is similar to brocade but is more flat.

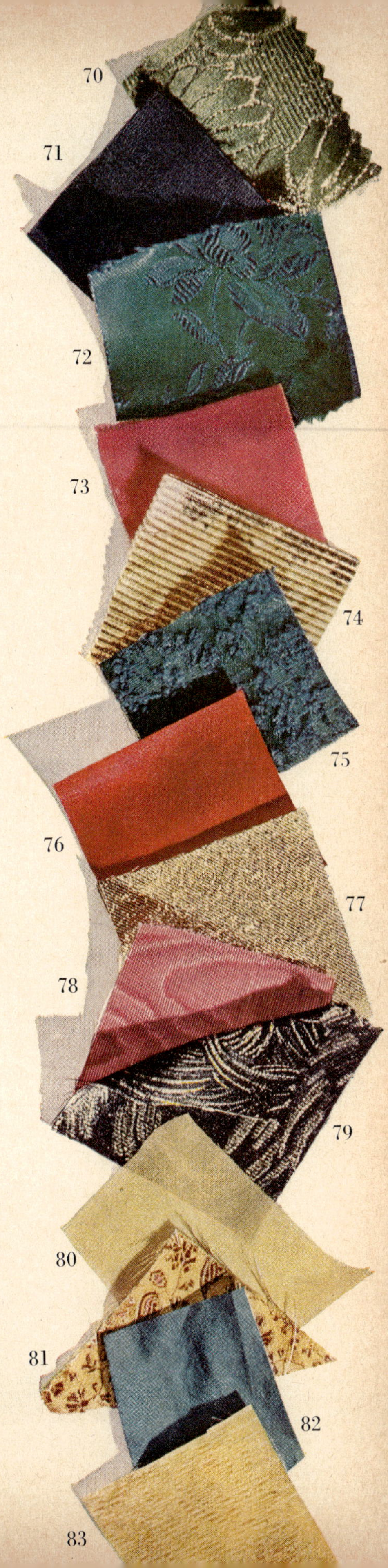

Lace

Lace is made of a network of threads that form a decorative design. It is made by hand or machine, from silk, rayon, cotton, nylon, or a combination of yarns. It looks delicate, but it's actually quite sturdy.

It's easy to handle, even for the beginner. Since there's so much design in the lace itself, it's better to make it up in very simple styles.

This versatile fabric can be made into any type of garment from slacks to wedding dresses, even coats and suits. It is both flattering and beautiful to wear, as well as practical. It doesn't show soil. Wrinkles fall out quickly when you hang lace up.

Best of all, lace is easy to sew! A little applique conceals mistakes. It's important to understand the many types of lace, and to learn how to cut them by taking advantage of all the pattern possibilities.

First, consider allover patterned lace. The weight of the lace determines the type of garment you make.

Every type of allover lace has a pattern. In some, the pattern is connected, resembling an indefinite print. Cut it as if it were a print fabric. There's no need to match the pattern. It can also be cut in any direction.

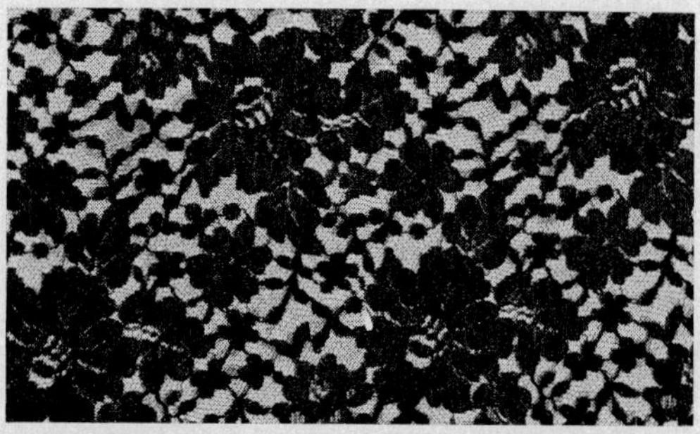

In some allover patterns, the design is very definite and is connected, sometimes running the width or length of the lace. With careful planning, a dress can be cut so the design finishes the neckline, sleeve edges or hemline. These touches can add a distinctive look to your lace fashion.

Usually, no finish is necessary on this edge. Just cut around the design and leave it. Study your pattern to

make certain where it should be cut to give this exquisite finish. Remember lace does not have to be cut on grain, so you have considerable freedom in cutting this type of lace.

The lace below is an unusual one. It is called a cross-dye lace. The design is on a contrasting color net. The motif stands out as if it were appliqued. This lace is made up over a lining the color of the net so the design stands out against the dark background. Each motif stands alone

and can be cut out and used as delicate applique touches on other garments. For instance, you can put each motif on a blouse or chiffon dress. If your dress is one of the popular combinations of lace and net, the applique of lace to the net will not only be decorative but will integrate the design and fabrics.

Another allover lace has a finished edge, called a flounce. This is a lace that can be used in many ways. The design can be cut away to make an edging that can be applied to other parts of the dress. Medallions can also be cut from the design and applied

to a garment for a beautiful trim.

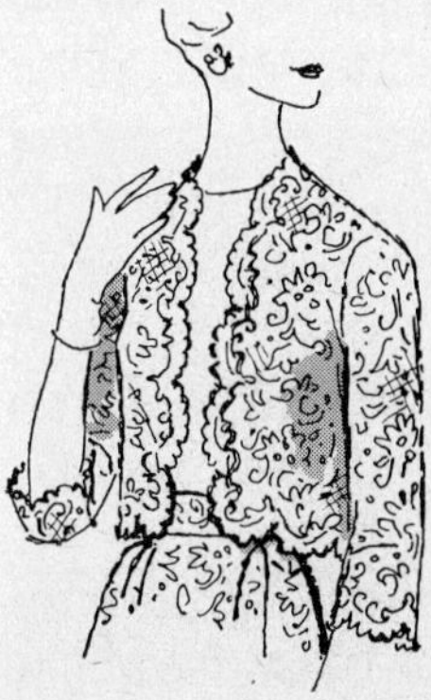

This flounce is a re-embroidered lace. It is quite expensive because the design is outlined in cording and applied after the lace is finished. Another lace you might want to buy is the allover lace with the matching edging. The dress can be cut from the allover lace

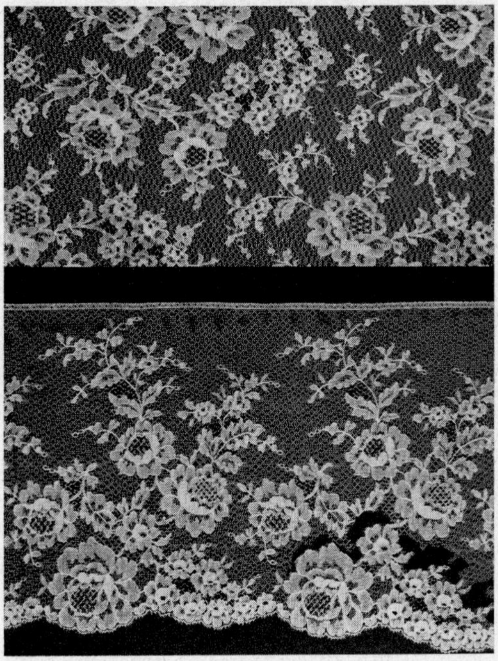

and the finishes at the neck, armhole, and hem line put on by appliqueing the separate edging. When this separate edging is used on a scoop neck, it is almost impossible to tell that the finished edge is an applique.

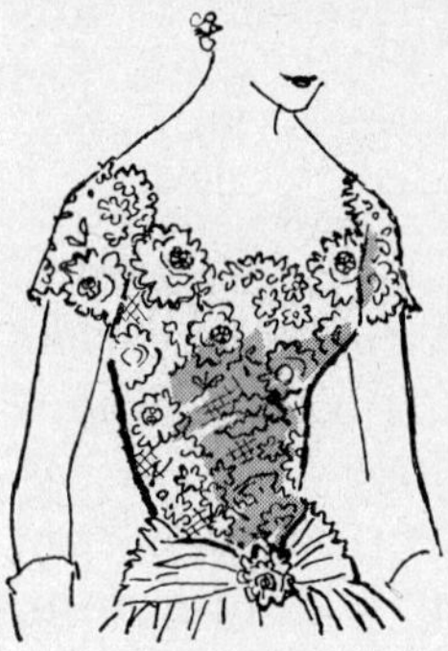

Sewing lace

At one time, all pieces of the lace dress were appliqued together to look sheer and show no seams. Laces are now used in so many unique ways that this type of seam is seldom necessary. Now laces are mounted to give a different texture suitable for the styles in which they are made. In mounting, the seams are very inconspicuous.

The applique method of joining laces so the seams are invisible can be used for piecing and mending. To applique, overlap the pieces of lace to be joined and match the design.

If it's impossible to match exactly, make the design match as closely as possible. Baste the lace together. The edges of the design are whipped by hand or by a zigzag machine stitch. Trim the raw edges close to the stitching. Press lightly over a soft towel. If

you prefer, you can also join the seams of your dress by applique, as the custom dressmaker does.

French whipped seam

Sleeves can never be set in with applique. To keep them sheer-looking, sew the seam on the regular seamline. About ⅛ inch away sew another stitching line. Trim the seam to this second row of stitching. By hand, do a fine whipping stitch, catching both lines of stitching at once. It forms a fine cord seam. This is the way to join seams on all sheers where the seams should be inconspicuous.

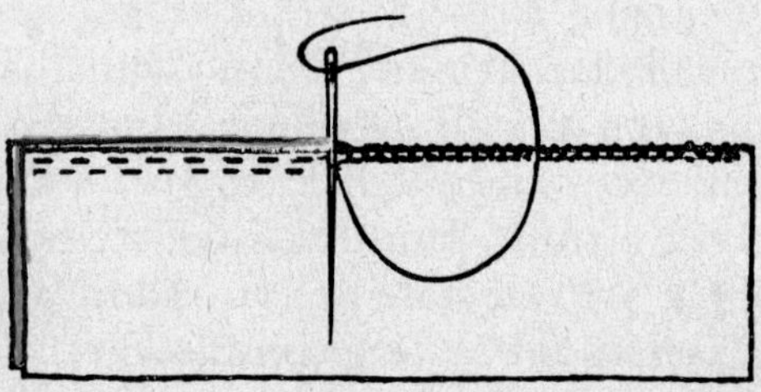

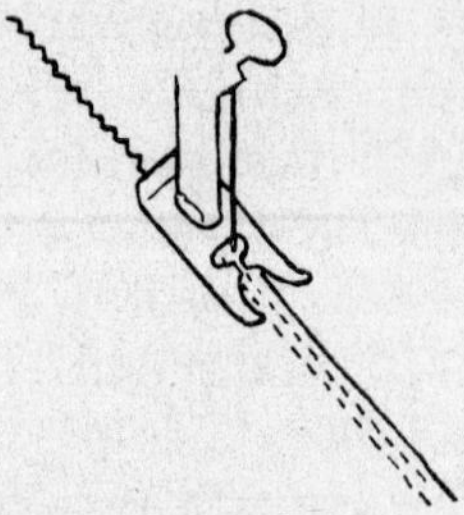

You can also do this cord seam on a zigzag machine. Bight of the stitch must be set deep enough to catch both the stitching lines. The tension of the stitch brings them together to form this fine cord-like seam.

Mounting lace

This sewing technique is used on lace as well as other sheer fabrics.

The style of garment you are making as well as the effect you want to achieve will determine the lining fabric you'll use with lace.

If you're making a full flared coat, mount the lace over taffeta, or a similar fabric that has a crisp hand. Or, mount the coat on a layer of thin silk and a layer of interfacing to give the lace the right texture.

Lace is mounted as an interfacing is built into a garment. The pattern pieces are cut of the lace, then re-cut of the lining and the interlining.

Lay each piece of the garment, right side up, over the lining and interlining. Stitch around each piece, holding all thicknesses together. Sew through the center of the dart before sewing in the darts through all thicknesses of fabric. Then assemble the garment as if you were working with just one layer of fabric.

Another trick to use in mounting lace is to mute it when necessary. For instance, if you plan to mount the lace over shiny taffeta, the sheen may show through and cheapen the effect of the garment. A layer of matching net between the lace and the taffeta will tone down, or mute, the high lights of the lining fabric.

This can also be done when lace is used over a contrasting color. On an open design lace, the under color may look too bright or harsh, spoiling the luxurious look of the fabric. Match the net to the lace, muting the brightness of the lining. A contrasting net between a matching lace and lining produces a slight iridescence.

Many laces are finished with a crisp hand. A lace that is too soft can be given the desired texture by lining it with a crisp net. As you can see, sewing on lace gives you an opportunity to try many effects.

When lace is lined, simply use regular seams as you sew it up. The seams hardly show when the fabric is mounted, and there is no double thickness at seamlines to show through. The lining makes the seam invisible.

If the dress is to be sheer and lacy over the arms and shoulders, do not line it all the way to the top. Instead, build a slip or bodice into the top of the dress. Since this technique is used for many evening and dressy clothes, it is described in detail in Chapter 10.

When you mount the lace, turn the hems in the same manner as for any similar garment. The weight and the type of the under-fabric which you select, and the flare of the skirt will be the determining factors.

Many other types of hems are also used on lace, since not all lace fashions are mounted. Chapter 10 shows other techniques for making lace garments or using it as a trim.

Beautiful lace fashions are becoming to women of all ages.

Velvet

Velvet is a nap-fabric—with a short, soft, thick warp, pile surface. Originally, it was made of silk, but now is available in cotton, rayon, nylon, and combinations of fibers.

Velvet has great versatility, because of the many types and weights in which it is made. It is used for suits, coats, dresses, sportswear, and negligees. Velvet is now given a crush-resistant finish that not only makes it resistant to crushing, but also to wrinkling, spotting, and sagging.

It can also be given a crisp finish, making it suitable for many more styles of clothing, and making it easier to cut and sew. These new wear and easy-care features have increased the popularity of velvet fashions.

Cutting velvet

All velvet has a nap, and must be cut with the pieces going in one direction. Usually the pattern gives the amount of extra yardage needed when a nap fabric is used. If this information is not listed on the pattern, add ½ to ¾ yard to the yardage requirement for 39-inch fabric.

Cut all pieces with the nap running up toward the top of the garment. Then, as you "look into the nap," as it is called, the color is richer and deeper in tone. If pieces were cut in either direction, the garment would look as if it were two shades.

If you can lay out all the pattern pieces on the fabric when folded on the length, then fold the velvet with the naps together. Pin pattern pieces to the wrong side of the fabric.

If the pattern pieces must be laid out on the open fabric, place one layer of velvet face down on a table and put one-half of the pattern pieces in place to estimate how much length is needed. Then tear across the velvet at this point.

Roll back the velvet with the pinned-on pattern pieces. Slide the length of velvet onto the table, nap side up. Place the first piece of velvet over this, naps together, and repin the pattern. Check to be sure the nap is running in the same direction on both pieces to prevent a variation in color.

Use sharp pins to pin your pattern pieces to the fabric and sharp shears when you cut it. A good quality pin will not mark the fabric. Velvet is now much sturdier; it is treated to eliminate many of the old hazards which made it difficult to sew.

Pick a simple pattern for your velvet fashion. One that's not too complicated in cut, and with few seams is best. Avoid any top-stitching on velvet. Cut the facings of taffeta or some other lining fabric. If buttonholes are used on velvet, be sure to use an interfacing under the fronts to reinforce the buttonholes, and to support the buttons.

Sewing velvet

Use silk or mercerized thread for machine-stitching, but loosen the tensions just enough to prevent puckering. Make the stitch a little larger than for ordinary sewing, and use a new, sharp needle. Be sure the presser foot has the minimum pressure to prevent marking the fabric.

You can baste the seams together, although pinned seams are easier to manipulate. Pin on the seam allowance line with the pins placed parallel to the seamline.

The top ply of the velvet has a tendency to shift ahead of the foot as you sew. The trick is to hold the under layer taut as you work on the top layer. An awl or a pin will help to ease along the top layer as you sew. If the material shifts a great deal, check to see if the pressure is still too high on the machine, and release the presser foot a little more so you can sew the velvet more easily.

Another trick is to raise the presser foot at regular intervals to be sure the top layer is sewing correctly, and to ease the fabric along.

On a zigzag machine, there is a foolproof trick for sewing any type of velvet. Set the machine to give the longest stitch and the widest bight on the zigzag adjustment. It will sew the velvet easily and smoothly.

Pin the velvet seams together, then stitch the seams with this zigzag stitch. The pressure should be very light on the presser foot. This stitch serves as a basting, but is more secure. The upper fabric may shift slightly as you sew, but the following step allows for this.

Next, adjust the stitch on the machine to the regular sewing stitch and reverse the velvet so the bottom layer is now on top. Now sew the permanent seam. The upper layer of fabric is now held so securely that the amount of shift will be about the same. This method of sewing velvet will give you a beautiful unpuckered seam.

Seams

Velvet seams may be overcast, or pinked and overcast for a neater look.

They can also be bound with chiffon or net. (See sketches, below.) Finish the hem with a seam binding as on the other types of hems.

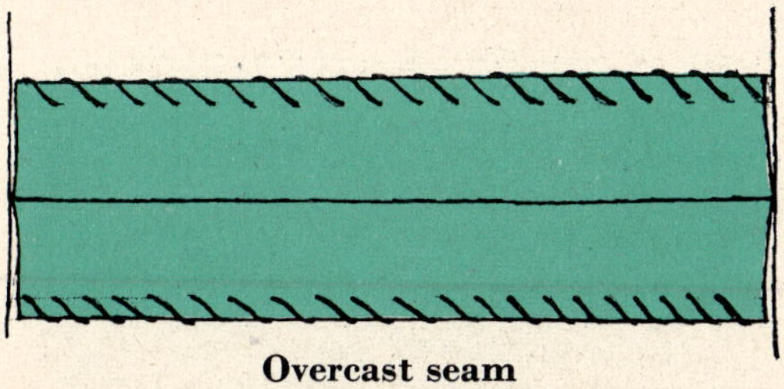

Overcast seam

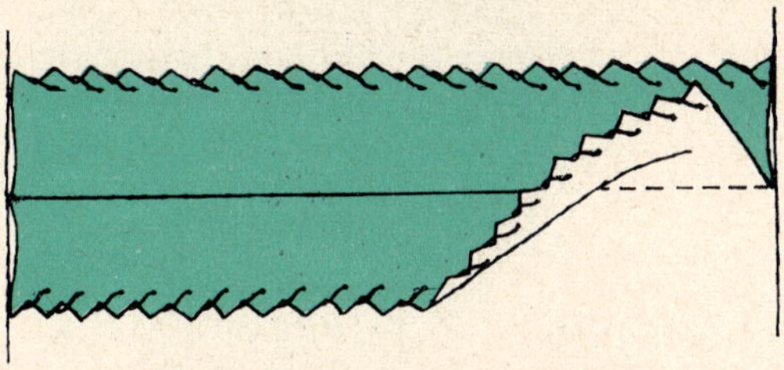

Pinked and overcast seam

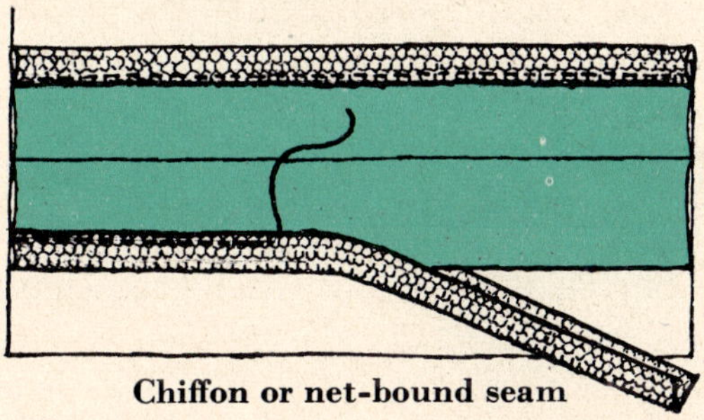

Chiffon or net-bound seam

Pressing

Velvet cannot be pressed as you press any other fabric because of the pile. Equipment available, however, makes pressing velvet very simple. If you sew much, consider buying a needle board. Use it for all other nap fabrics as well as for velvet. The board is pictured in Chapter 1.

The steam iron is another aid, and should be a part of every home sewer's equipment. You can also use a regular iron and sleeve board.

The needle board is a heavy canvas with fine wires projecting upright. The velvet is placed face down on this board, and pressed on the wrong side with a steam or warm iron. Press lightly, a small section at a time.

Even with a needle board, it is a

little difficult to get sharp edges at facings and hems. Remember that when the hem is turned back, the pile will be on the inside of the hem. Although you put the right side of the hem on the needle board, and even though you only press lightly, the inside of the hem will still be crushed. Here's a trick that will help.

Hold the steam iron just over the inside hem, steaming it heavily, without letting the iron plate actually touch the fabric. Now take a stiff brush, and while the velvet is still

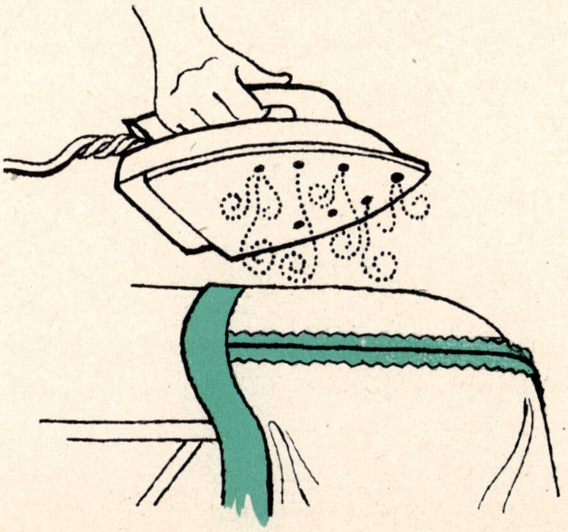

damp from the steam, pat it briskly with the bristle side of the brush. You'll get a sharp, beautiful hem with no press marks on either side.

If you have a steam iron but no needle board, use a leftover piece of velvet, pile side up, on the ironing board. Lay the piece to be pressed

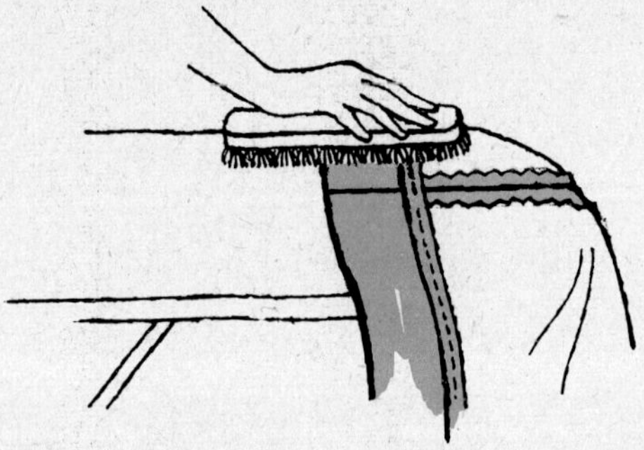

face down on top of it. The nap will interlock with the pile underneath, and you can press, but use a very light pressure. Let the steam from the iron do most of the work.

This method is still practical, although it is more difficult. Turn the regular iron upside down and slide it over the arm of the sleeve board so the plate is facing up. Let the iron heat, and then put a wet cloth over the face plate of the iron.

Place the wrong side of the velvet against the steaming cloth and draw it slowly across the face plate.

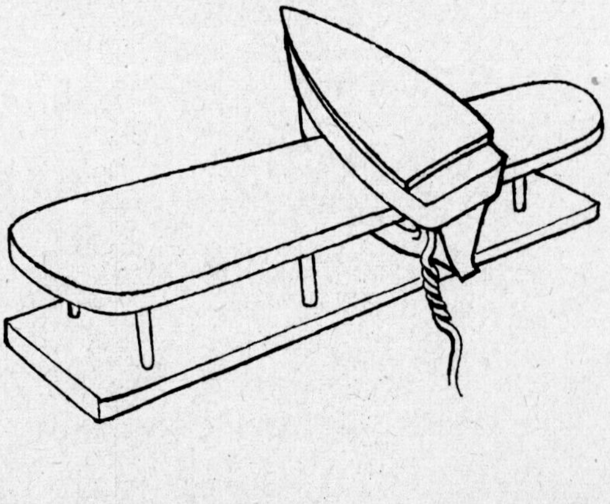

As you move the velvet, move the wet cloth so you're creating constant steam. Keep your fingers away from the velvet as touching the velvet will create fingermarks. Short seams can be pressed over a stiff brush. Turn the bristles up. The nap of the velvet interlocks with the bristles, and it can be pressed without marking.

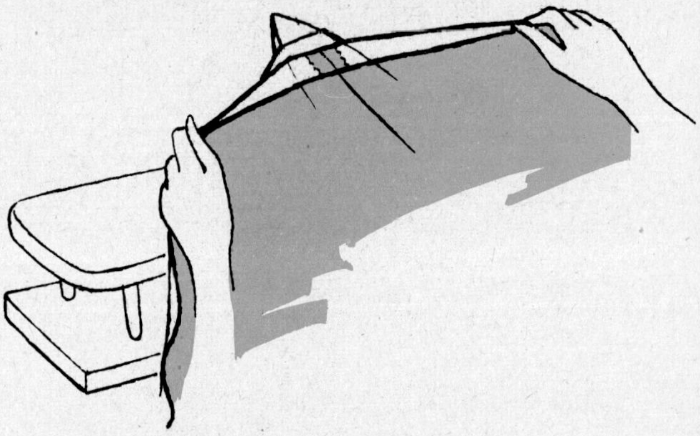

Steaming velvet

It's a good idea to steam velvet occasionally to keep the nap crisp and the color fresh and bright.

Years ago steaming was done by holding the crushed parts of the velvet over the spout of a steaming kettle. Only small parts of the dress could be steamed at a time.

Now you can hang your velvet dress in the bathroom while you take your shower. The steam will help freshen the color. Allow the garment to dry thoroughly before you wear it. You can also use a steam iron. Hold it as close to the pile as possible without actually touching the velvet. Or, of course, press the velvet over a needle board. Your dry cleaner can also steam velvet professionally.

Care for velvet fashions regularly and they'll remain fresh and crisp.

Facts about fabrics

It is a good idea to become familiar with the texture and hand of basic fabrics. Although each pattern gives suggestions as to the type of fabric suitable to the style you have chosen, the same pattern also shows a variety of views. All the fabrics suggested are not necessarily suitable for all the views shown. If you are familiar with the general characteristics of the fabrics suggested, you will be much more discriminating in your choice.

Although the texture remains the same, many fabrics are a combination of man-made fibers and natural fibers. Some are made up of a combination of several man-made fibers.

A fiber, to put it simply, is the fine thread from cotton, silk, wool, and flax, or the filament used to manufacture man-made fibers. These fibers are spun, woven, or knitted into a fabric.

When man-made fibers are used with natural fibers, it is to improve the properties of both. For instance, when a cotton that has a tendency to wrinkle easily is combined with a wrinkle-resistant man-made fiber, the cotton takes on the wrinkle-resisting property of the man-made. The cotton, however, which has a high moisture absorbency, will make the fabric cooler and more comfortable to wear.

All garments, as well as piece goods, are required to be tagged with the content of the fabric.

Man-made fibers are making sweeping advances in variety and versatility. It is a good idea to become familiar with the properties and care requirements of some of the major groups of man-mades, since they definitely affect any fabrics in which they are used, and are now used extensively.

Also remember that a blended fiber must make up a large percentage of the fabric to give its properties to the fabric. If there are several fibers blended in the fabric, the one making up the largest percentage of the fabric will dictate the characteristics of the manufactured material.

New blends will continue to come on the market. Information about these fabrics—their fiber content, and how to sew, wash and iron them—will be published as they are introduced to the public. Pattern and fashion magazines usually print this information. Be sure to keep abreast of new developments so you can take full advantage of these "miracle" fabrics being created for you.

Rayon

Rayon was the first of the man-made fibers. It is fairly strong, except when wet. It is the only man-made fiber that can be made into crepes. It has great versatility, since it can have a bright or dull, straight or crimped finish. Rayon is absorbent and dyes well, and can be blended with almost all other fibers.

You'll find it used in dresses, lingerie, drapery and upholstery fabrics, linings, suitings, and in many industrial uses. Be sure to check the hang tag for washability. Rayon is usually hand-washable, as well as dry-cleanable. Use a steam iron on this fabric, or, if a regular iron is used, be sure to adjust the temperature setting to low heat for rayons.

Acetate

Acetate is associated with luxury fabrics, although it is also used in volume fabrics. Acetate fabrics have a soft, lustrous appearance and drape well. They have good shrink- and stretch-resistance, and are resistant to moths and mildew. Acetate blends with silk, cotton, rayon, nylon, and other man-made fibers. It can be hand or machine washed or dry cleaned, depending on the fabric. Check the label and follow directions. Always press at low heat temperature.

Nylon

Nylon was the first commercially successful, true synthetic. It has strength, durability, resists abrasions, mildew and moths. It is sheer, making it a wonderful fiber for hosiery, lingerie, dresses, blouses, uniforms, sport clothes, and is, in fact, used in many industries. It wrinkles little, has excellent shape-retention, is washable, and dries quickly. Nylon needs little ironing and very little heat should be used.

Triacetate

This fiber won't shrink or stretch. It takes a permanent pleat well, resists wrinkles and has medium strength. It has a soft hand and drapes well. Triacetate blends with wool, cotton, rayon, nylon, and most other fibers. It is washable, quick-drying, and requires minimum pressing.

Acrylic fibers

Acrylics can be used alone or blended with other fibers. They have a natural, luxurious feel, have warmth and bulk, but are lightweight. The acrylics have good crease recovery and retain pleats. They are non-allergenic and resist damage from mildew, moths, sunlight, soot, and smoke.

Most blends are washable and require little ironing at a very low heat setting. They're particularly good for knits, can be washed with no fear of the garment losing its shape.

Polyester fibers

Originally, the polyesters were made for suit fabrics, but now have been blended to make soft, lovely dress fabrics. Polyester fiber has great strength, holds its shape, is wrinkle-resistant, and retains pleats well. It's lightweight, doesn't shrink or stretch, absorbs very little moisture. It washes easily, is quick-drying. These fibers need little or no ironing, but are sensitive to heat, so the polyesters must be pressed at low temperature.

Finishes

The natural fibers have also joined the march toward easier-to-care-for clothes. Special finishes on natural fibers give them many of the easy-care properties of the man-made fibers and blends. These finishes are too numerous to list in full, but they include such features as wrinkle-resistance, soil-repellents, crispness, shrink- and sag-resistance, and color-fastness. These new finishes and fibers mean better fabrics and easier care.

Chapter **9**

Play clothes and sportswear

Most sportswear and play clothes today are actually "separates"—a group of skirts, blouses, shirts, slacks, and shorts co-ordinated into a casual wardrobe for active living.

Although these clothes must be sturdy, they are easy to sew. They make an especially good starting point for the beginning sewer. Somehow, making a skirt seems an easy project. Next, you need a blouse to wear with the skirt. Before you know it, an entire dress doesn't seem too complicated to make, and another home sewer joins the ranks!

It's fun to make separates. The fabrics are firm and easy to work on, and are available in many wonderful colors. This chapter will show you how to use the short, simple techniques of the professional dressmaker in making smart, attractive play clothes.

Slacks

Let's start with slacks since they have become so much a part of the modern woman's casual wardrobe. They can be made of many kinds of fabrics, from denim for daytime wear to velvet or satin for evening.

Slacks can be very becoming if they are properly fitted. Most of the adjustments made in fitting a skirt can also be used for slacks. (See Chapter 3 for adjustments.) Hip and waist sizes are the same, and the adjustments do not vary. Special care is required in the fitting at the crotch and the tapering of the legs. Here are some pointers that will help give your slacks a sleek, slim, custom-made look.

How to measure for slacks

Buy the slacks pattern according to hip measurement. It is important for slacks to fit as closely to size as possible at the hip because of the shaping of the crotch. The closer to size, the fewer adjustments will be needed at this vital point on the slacks.

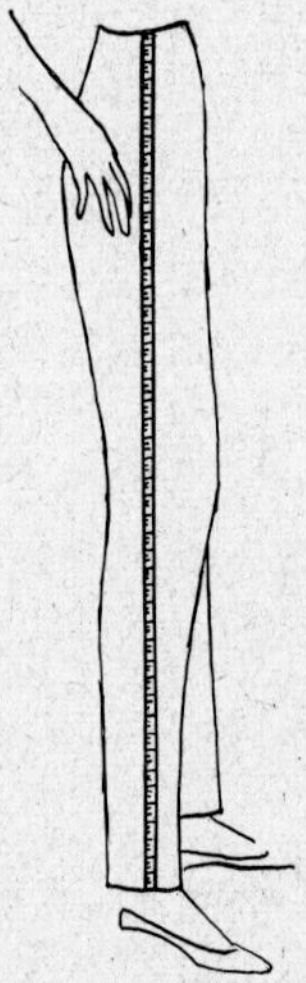

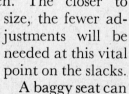

A baggy seat can ruin the trim, tailored appearance of your slacks.

Measure length of slacks from the side of the waistline to the desired length. To measure for the depth of the crotch, sit on a straight chair and measure from the side waistline down to the seat of the chair.

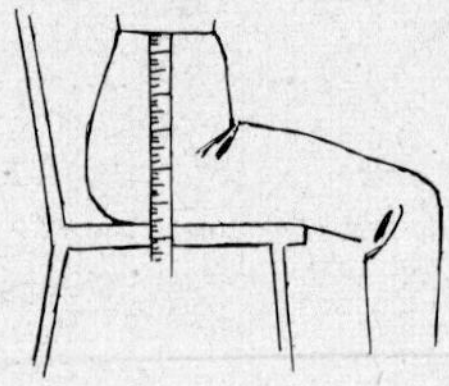

How to adjust for crotch measurement

On the front pattern piece, draw a line from the deepest point of the front crotch across to the side seam. The length from the waist to this line should be the same as the measurement from the waist to the seat of the chair. If the crotch is too long, fold a tuck across the pattern to shorten between waist and crotch. If too short, lengthen by slashing the pattern at same point and spreading.

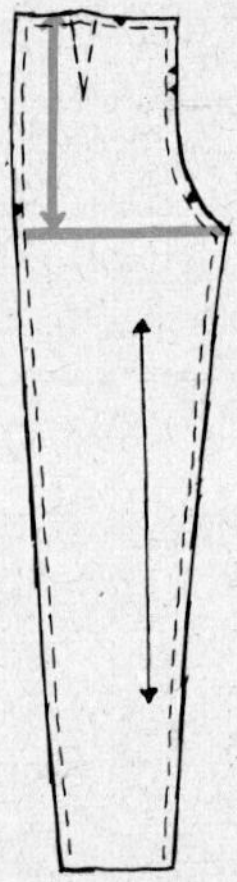

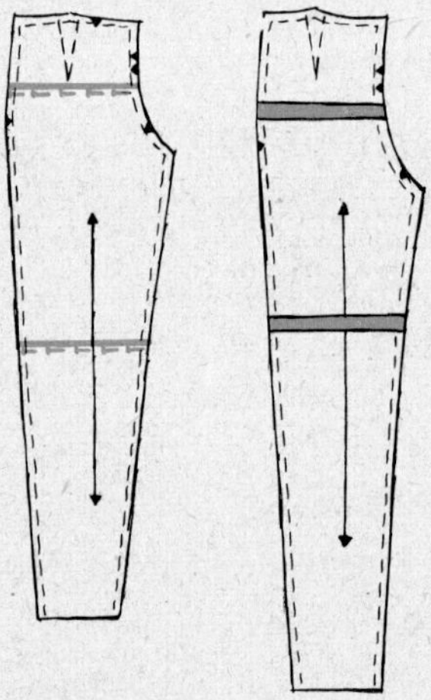

If the leg needs to be shortened or lengthened, make the adjustment in the leg below the crotch.

How to fit for the flat derriere

With this type of figure, the seat of the slacks will droop and be too large. First, adjust as you do for the same fault on a skirt. Take a fold across the back under the waistline, tapering out to nothing on either side.

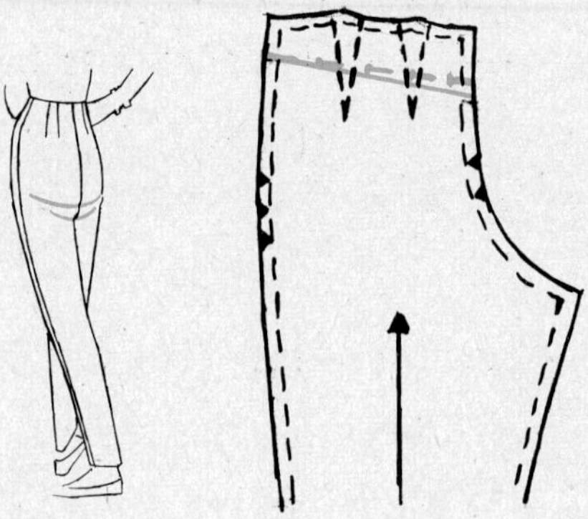

If the seat still looks too full, the darts are giving more cupping than is needed for the flat derriere. Rip out the darts and make each one a little more shallow.

Fit out the extra fullness at the side. Take a deeper seam from waistline to hipline, tapering the seam to nothing below the hip.

Make the adjustment in the pattern by taking in the same amount with a fold from waist to hip, tapering to nothing, on one side of the pattern.

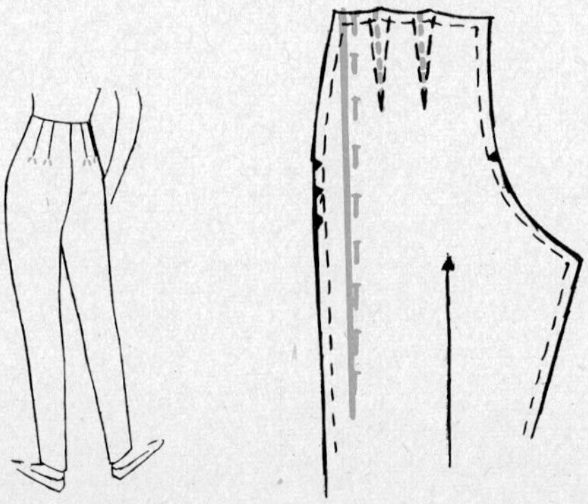

If the slacks are too round below the fullest part of the hip, make the back crotch smaller by pinning a tuck just back of the crotch seam on the back only. This eliminates the extra fullness. Pin this same tuck in the pattern. Rip, and recut the back crotch seam from adjusted pattern.

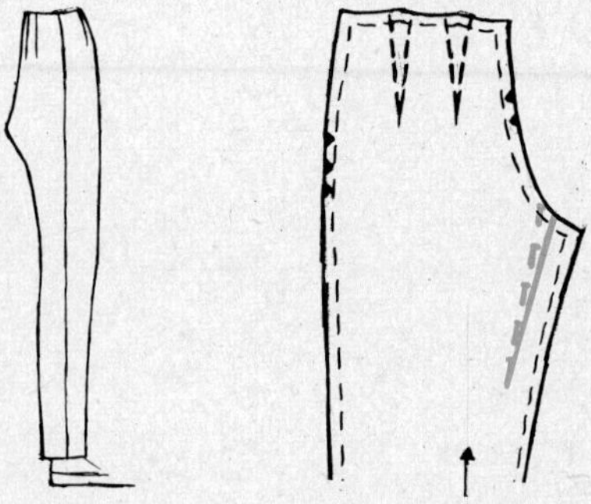

If you use a pattern from another company the next time you make slacks, it may be necessary to refit the crotch. The slope of the back crotch seam may vary with the patternmaker. The degree of the slope is all you will need to check. The basic adjustments will be the same.

How to fit the full derriere

The front of the slacks fits this figure fairly well, but the full back needs extra fitting. The seat needs more cupping than the pattern allows, to fit the very round hips. Take the back darts in deeper to give the

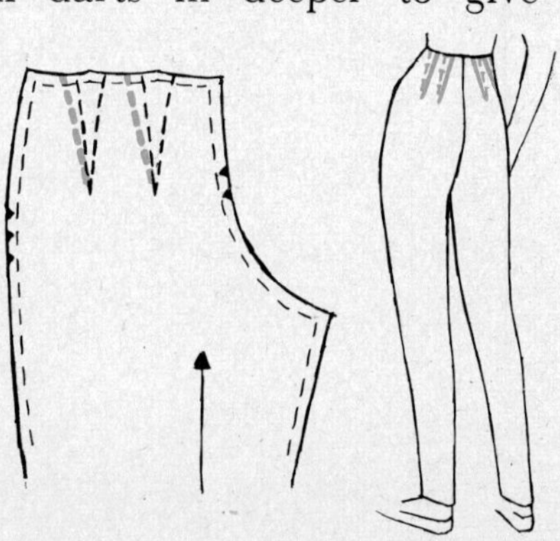

slacks more cupping, a smoother fit.

Usually the waistline is smaller in proportion on this figure, so adjusting the darts also reduces the back waistline size. If the waistline is already correct, an extra amount can be added at the side seams to compensate for the deeper darts.

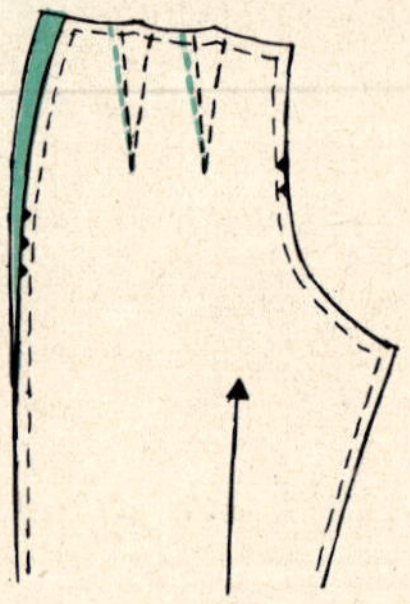

Determine how your own waist size compares with the waist measurement on the pattern. If the size is the same, allow a little extra on the waistline as you cut, in case you must make this back alteration.

If the pattern measurement of the slacks is larger than your waist size, cut your slacks the same size as the paper pattern size, which will allow sufficient material to take larger darts in the back waist.

If necessary, the front waist size can be made smaller by fitting a dart from the waistline toward the hip at the side of the pattern.

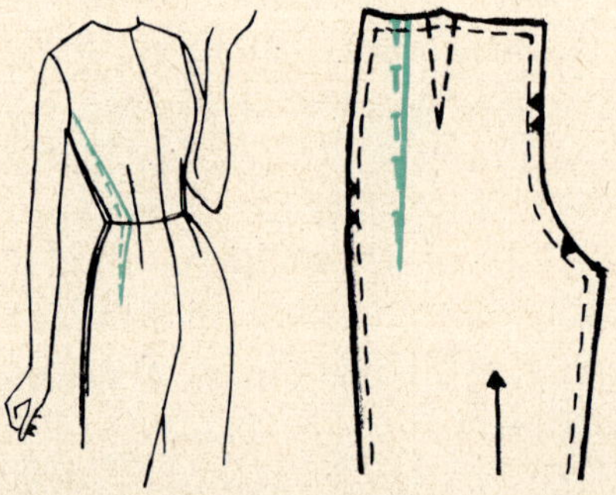

If the slacks are already cut, make the waistline smaller by fitting out the extra fullness at the side seam. Be sure to make the same adjustment in future patterns.

Pattern companies are now making proportioned slacks which fit as far as height is concerned. The depth of the crotch, however, is an individual problem that does not necessarily depend on height. So even the proportioned slacks pattern will require some additional adjustments.

Cutting slacks

Adjust the pattern very carefully to your correct size before you cut. Check the type of fabric you are using to see if it has a nap or other surface that indicates it must be cut with all the pieces running one way.

Check the grain line carefully to be sure it is straight as you lay out the pattern. Measure from the grain line to the selvage as you pin the pattern in place. This is important to the correct hang of the slacks.

Cut the waistband on the length or cross-grain. It will be interlined to prevent stretching. Lay out all the pieces before cutting. Cut, following the adjusted pattern. You will not need to make any allowance when the pattern has been adjusted.

Sewing slacks

Mark darts, pocket placement, and other detail before removing the pattern. Some patterns indicate a mark for the crease line. Put pins along this line to mark as you do for darts. After the marking is done, remove the pattern. The darts can be sewed in the front and back pieces as described in Chapter 5.

Before sewing the seam, it is important to press the crease in the front and back of the leg. Place the front of the slacks on the ironing board, right side down. Fold one side back along the crease mark so the right side of half the leg is facing up. Press carefully along this line.

Usually, this crease runs into the waistline dart which becomes a continuation of the crease. The back sections of the slacks are pressed in the same way, except that the crease is made 8 inches from the waistline, regardless of the back fitting darts.

If no crease line is given on the pattern, fold the leg wrong sides together, with the inside and outside seam edges even. Press along the fold and this will give the correct crease line on the leg.

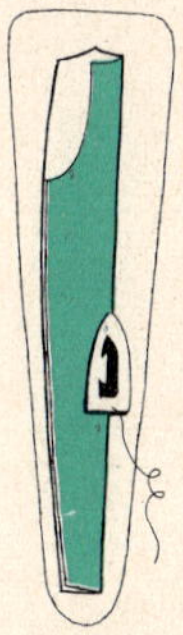

Join the back and front pieces at the side seams. The side pocket can be put in as you join the seams, as shown in Chapter 6. If the slacks have a ranch-type pocket, you'll learn how to apply it later in this chapter.

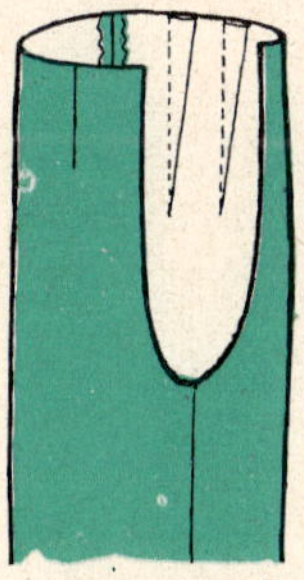

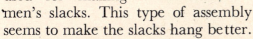

Next, join the inside leg seams. This is the method used for making men's slacks. This type of assembly seems to make the slacks hang better.

If the slacks have a side seam zipper closure, sew the zipper in on the left side as shown in Chapter 7.

Many women prefer the zipper down the back, which gives a smoother fit at the sides and doesn't interfere with the side pocket. If you want a back zipper, sew up the center front and continue it toward the back.

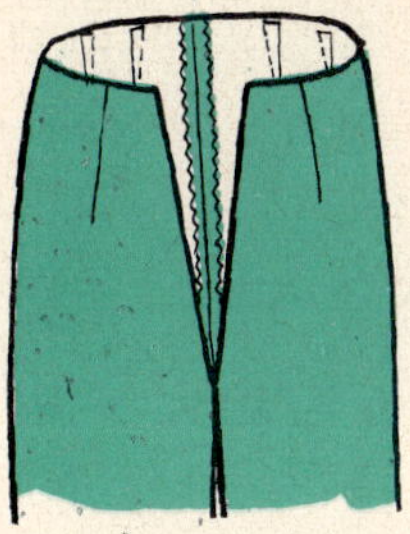

Leave the back seam open for a 7- or 9-inch zipper, whichever is the best. Apply the zipper in the same way as shown for the neckline zipper in Chapter 7. Use a slot-seam type of application. If you prefer the fly-front type of slacks for a slimmer and generally more flattering appearance, it is not difficult to convert a pattern to the fly-front type. The placket or fly starts about 2 inches up from the crotch seam. Stitch about 2 inches from the back crotch seam to 2 inches toward the front. Clip the seam at this point. Only this much seam is sewed at the back so that it is easier to insert the zipper. If you like, you can sew all the back seam, just leaving the front open from the 2-inch mark. Use the special trouser zipper for the fly-front opening to give a neat closure.

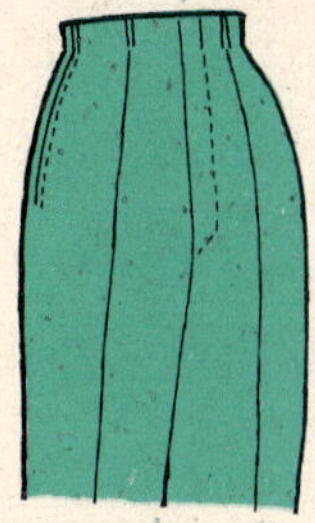

Your pattern gives two right fly facings and one left fly facing. If the fabric is lightweight, these can be cut from the same fabric. If your slacks are of a heavy fabric, face the right fly piece with a lining fabric. Put the right sides of the two right fly pieces together and stitch all around. Leave just the top edge open. Turn right side out. Press.

Turn back and stitch $\frac{1}{4}$ inch on the outside edge of the left fly facing. Sew the

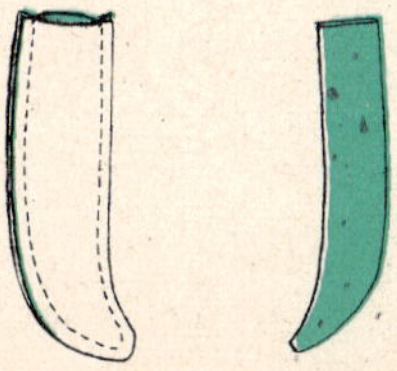

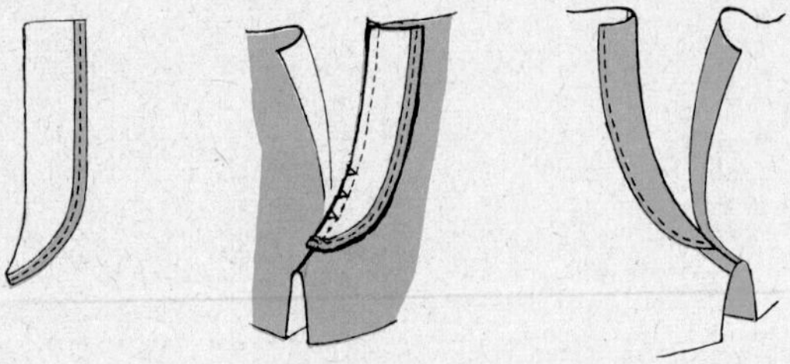

left facing to the left front opening of the slacks, right sides together.

Clip and trim the seam and press the seam to the inside.

Place the zipper right side down at the right front opening, with the tape of the zipper along the seam edge. Sew close as possible to teeth of the zipper with the zipper foot.

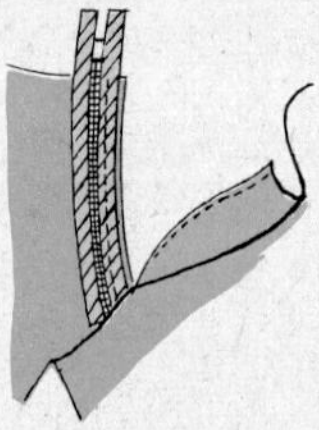

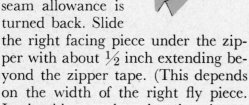

Turn the zipper right side up. The seam allowance is turned back. Slide the right facing piece under the zipper with about ½ inch extending beyond the zipper tape. (This depends on the width of the right fly piece. It should extend under the zipper, the width of the seam allowance.)

Stitch along the fold edge of the seam, close to the zipper. Catch the fly piece in stitching as you sew.

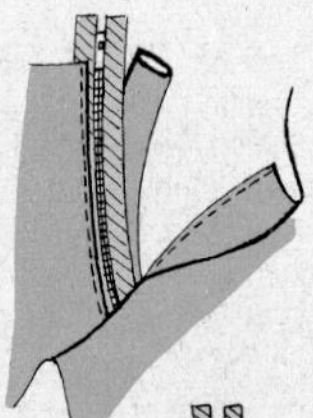

Now, lap the left front to the seam allowance line and pin or baste.

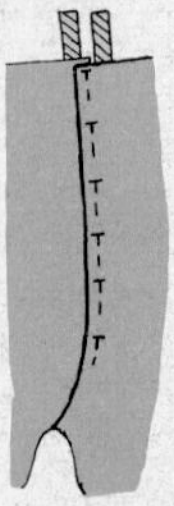

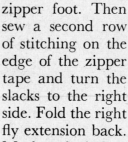

Turn the slacks to the wrong side. The tape of the zipper will now be against the left facing only. Pin the tape just to the facing. Sew the tape close to the zipper teeth, using the zipper foot. Then sew a second row of stitching on the edge of the zipper tape and turn the slacks to the right side. Fold the right fly extension back.

Mark and stitch on the outside of the slacks, catching back the left facing. The extension will now fall in place under the zipper. Reinforce the lower end of the fly on the right side with a bar tack, catching all thicknesses of material with the tack. If the zipper is longer than the placket, unzip it and cut it off at the top when the waistband is sewed on to the slacks.

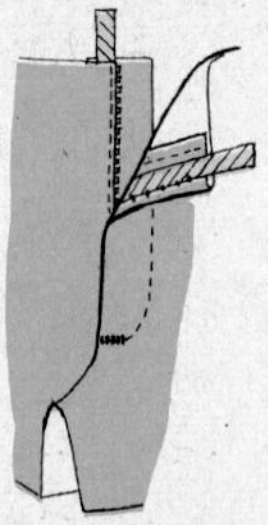

The next step is to sew up the back crotch seam. Nylon thread is your best choice for this seam on women's slacks. It is strong, and has a lot of elasticity that will stretch enough when you're bending or sitting.

Men's slacks can also be sewed at the seat with nylon thread for additional strength and elasticity. (See the section on "Men's Slacks" in this chapter for another sewing method.)

Making the waistband

There are three ways to put the waistband on women's slacks and skirts. All three methods can be done by machine. The choice of method, however, depends on the fabric used.

Lightweight fabric

Press the waistband in half on the

length. Cut a strip of medium-weight, non-woven interfacing the width of half the band, less the seam allowance. Trim off the seam allowance at either end. Lay the interfacing along the fold line on one side of the band. Stitch into position all around.

Fold the right sides of the waistband together and stitch across the ends. Then turn right side out and

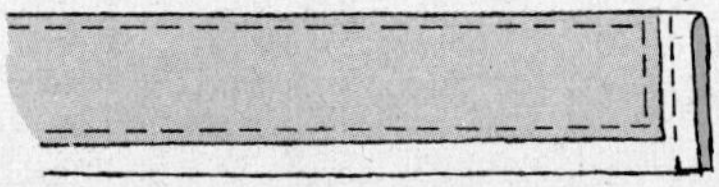

press. Turn back the seam allowances on the length of the belt and press.

Pin the interfaced side of the band

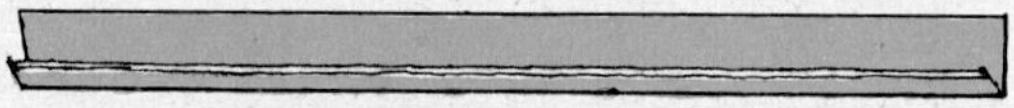

to the inside of the slacks. The front edge of the band should be lined up even with the edge of the placket opening. On the fly front, the edge will

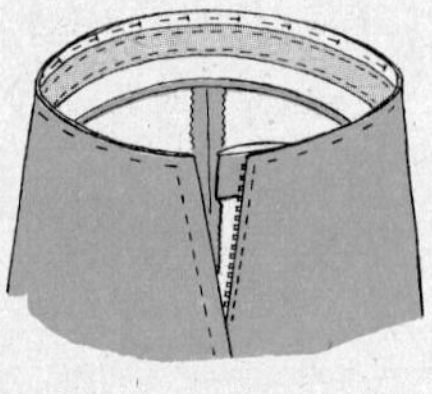

be even with the left side of the front opening. Stitch the waistband to the slacks, along the crease line.

Press the waistline seam into the waistband and turn under the seam allowance on the loose edge of the waistband. Pin to the right side of the slacks and stitch. It is not necessary to trim the seam at the waistline.

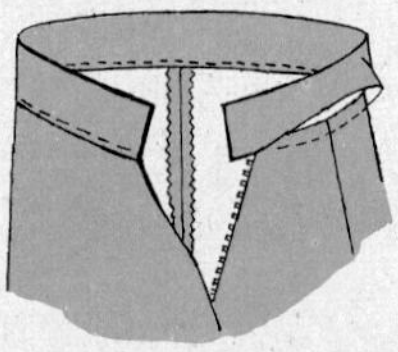

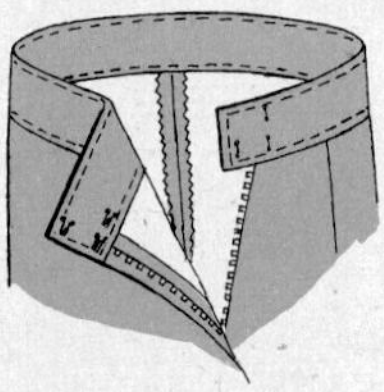

Medium-weight fabric

Cut the waistband on the length of fabric along the selvage. If no selvage edge is available, bind one edge of the fabric with seam binding.

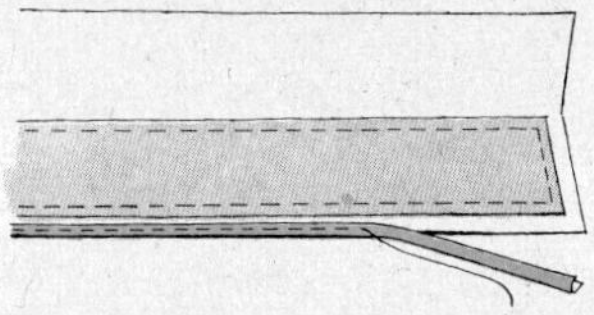

Press in half on the length. Cut an interfacing of the non-woven fabric, the width of the band, minus seam allowances. Stitch to the inside of the band on the selvage or bound side. Sew the ends, turn to the right side and press the ends. Turn back the seam allowance on the length of the band and press. Pin the right side of the waistband to the right side of the slacks (the unlined side) and stitch. Drop the selvage or the bound side of the belt to the inside. Pin into place on the right side and stitch.

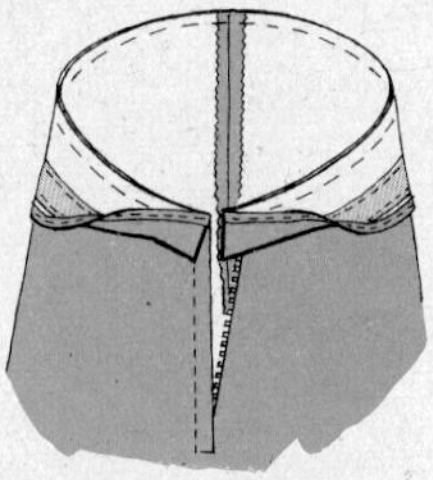

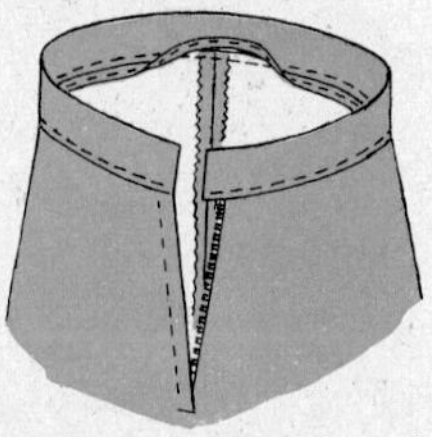

No seam allowance is turned back on the inside band. It lies flat against the slacks which makes the waistline look and feel less bulky.

Heavy-weight fabric

Cut the belt on the lengthwise or crosswise of the fabric. Fold in half on the length and press. Trim off one side of the band ½ inch from the fold. Buy grosgrain ribbon or belting half the width of the waistband.

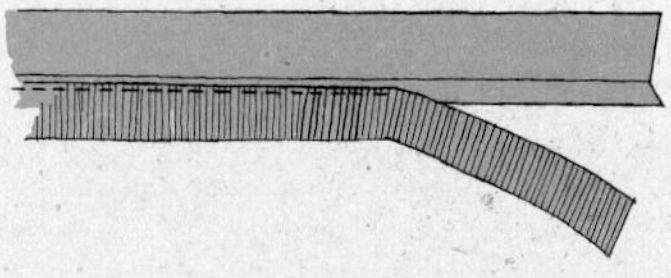

Use this ribbon or belting as a facing. Sew it to the cut-away side of the band along the fold line.

Sew the ends of the belt. Then sew together the right side of the waistband and the right side of the slacks.

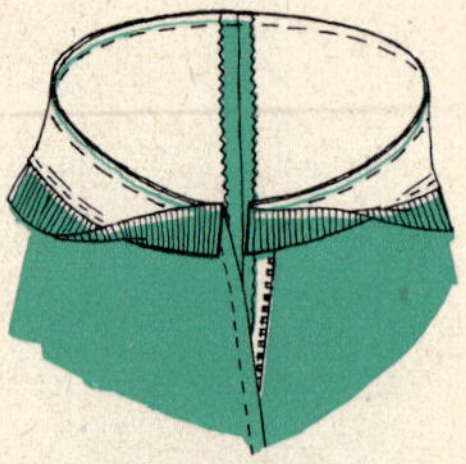

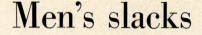

Press the seam up into the waistband. Drop the ribbon or the belting facing to the inside of the slacks.

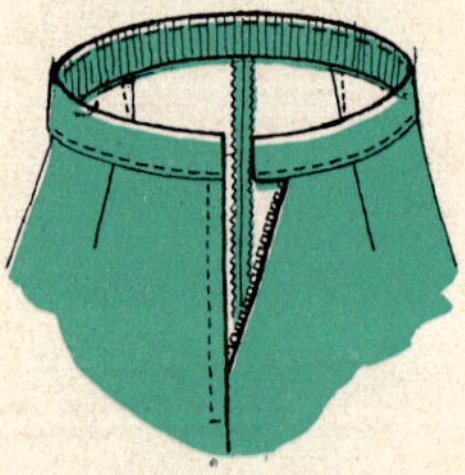

Stitch along the seamline on right side to hold band in position.

These methods can be used on skirts and women's slacks. Use the one most suitable for the weight of your fabric.

If the trouser zipper is too long for the front opening of the slacks, zip the head down and cut off the extra length of zipper at the waistline.

Sew the waistband to the slacks, catching the tape of the zipper in the waistline seam. This acts as the stop for the top of the zipper. The zipper head locks into place at any point when the tab is depressed.

On men's slacks the waistband is made in two pieces, a left side and a right side band. The zipper is put into them in the same way.

Men's slacks

Patterns for men's slacks do not come in proportioned sizes. Instead, the pattern gives a waist and inseam size. Buy the slacks pattern according to the correct size of the waist.

Measure the man for the inseam and outside seam for correct length. Compare his inseam measurement to that given on the pattern. If the pattern has to be made longer or shorter, check the outside seam measurement of the pattern before making the alteration. On the front slack pattern piece, measure from the waistline to the finished length on the outside seamline. If this has to be lengthened or shortened the same amount as for the inseam, make the necessary adjustment across the leg below the crotch. The pattern will indicate where alteration should be made.

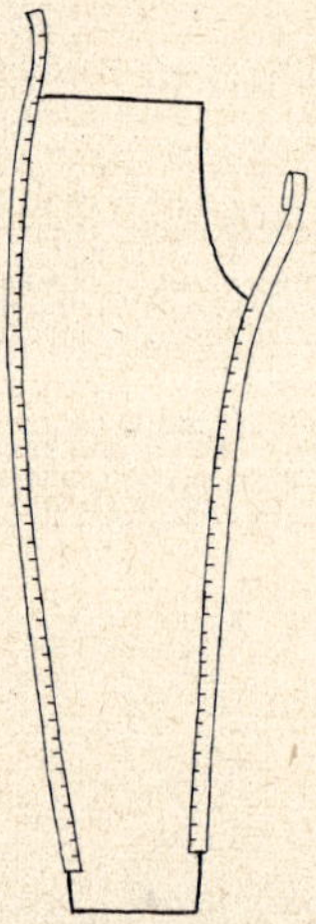

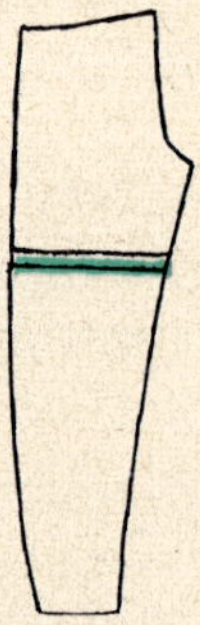

If the outside seam measures longer or shorter in proportion to the inseam measurement, an adjustment has to be made between the waist and the crotch to insure a proper fit.

For example, the inseam measurement is 32 inches, and the outseam measures 43½ inches; when you compare it to the pattern, you find the inseam of the pattern is 32 inches, but the outseam measures only 42½ inches. Add the extra 1 inch of length to the length of the crotch (right).

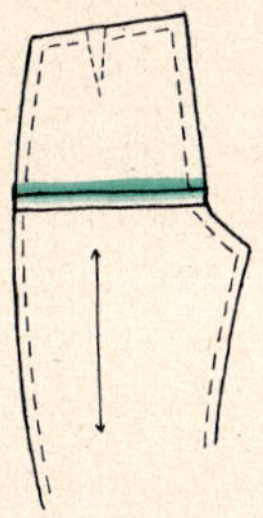

Follow the pattern guide as you lay out the pattern for cutting. Before cutting the back add extra fabric on the center back for a let-out seam. Add by tapering from nothing at the seat to 1½ inches at back waistline. Add same amount to waistband length.

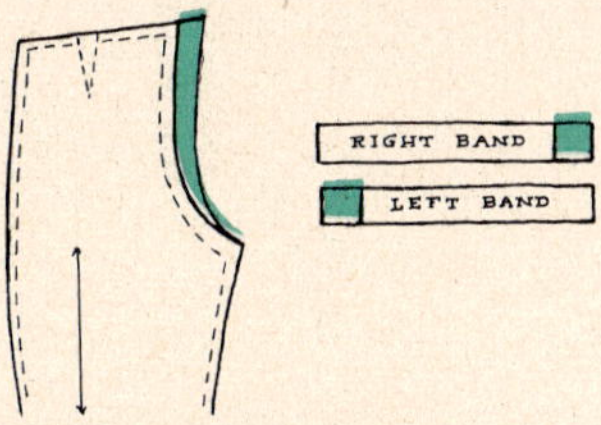

Mark the fabric carefully for darts, pockets, and any other detail. Also be sure to mark original back seam.

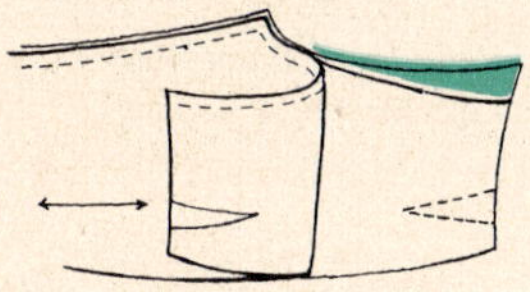

Sew in the back darts first. Press carefully. Put in the back pockets next. In lightweight fabric, the back pockets can be made of the same fabric as the slacks. In heavier fabric, make the pockets from a lining fabric, but face with self-fabric.

Each pattern company has its own shaped pocket piece. Some show the pocket made from two pieces, others show the pocket in one. The principle in making them is the same. Cut facing strips 2½ inches wide for the pockets. Then sew the strips to the pocket on the pattern piece markings (A).

A
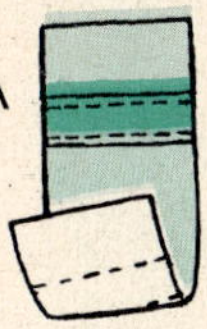

Mark the correct position of the back pocket on the slacks with basting stitches (B).

B
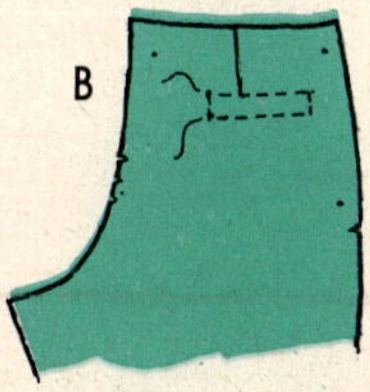

Pin the pocket piece to the right side of the slacks, matching marks, but sew around the basting mark from wrong side, forming a rectangle (C).

C
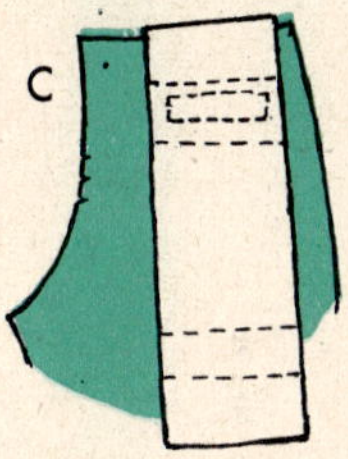

Slash the fabric through the center of the stitching to ½ inch of either corner. Then clip to the corners (D).

D
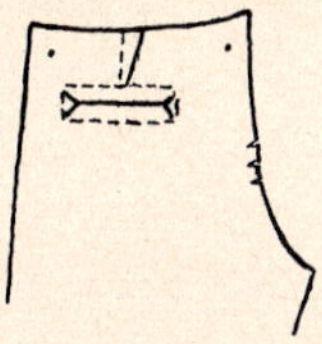

Turn the pocket piece to the inside of the garment through the slash. Fold lower pocket to form a welt. Stitch the welt by machine on the right side (E). Sew ends of pocket on inside as for a buttonhole.

E
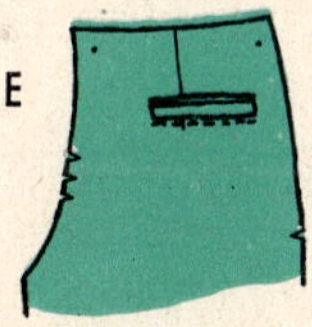

F
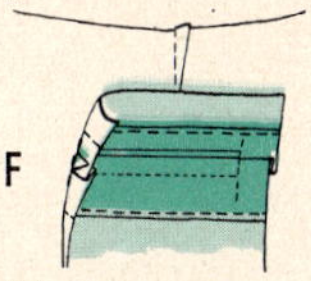

Trim off the top of this pocket piece 1 inch above the pocket slash (F).

Fold the pocket, with the outsides together, along the fold line. (For a two-piece pocket, pin the two pieces with the outsides together.) Stitch the pocket pieces together close to the edge (G).

G
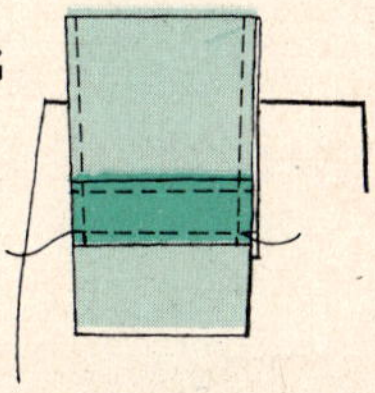

H

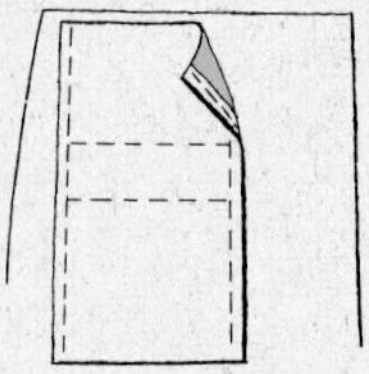

Turn the pocket right side out and stitch again, turning under edges of upper pocket (H).

I

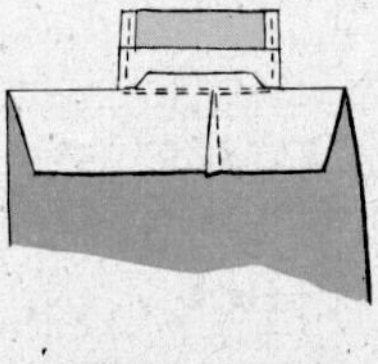

From the outside, turn slacks down from waist, stitch across top pocket seam (I).

J

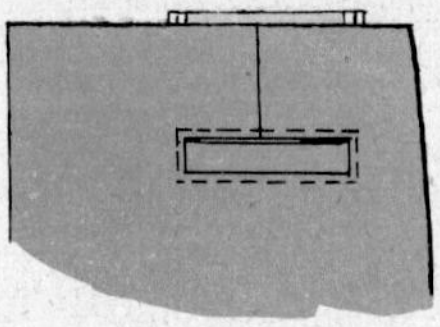

Press it from the right side, and then top-stitch the upper seam through all thicknesses of the pocket (J).

Next, stitch the top of the pocket to the waistline of the slacks.

Before joining the side seams, press the crease line in on both back and front slacks as you did for women's slacks. Follow the same procedure for joining the seam, sewing the side pockets and finishing the fly.

The back seam of men's slacks is finished in a different way. Put the waistband on first before you sew the back. Belt carriers must be made before the waistband is sewed. Cut a strip of fabric long enough for eight belt carriers, 1½ inches wide. Turn the edges in ¼ inch. Press. Fold in half and edge-stitch each side.

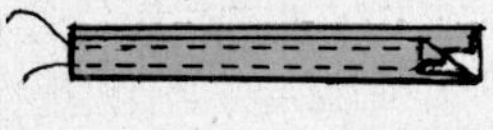

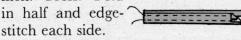

Cut the fabric strip into lengths and sew one edge of each strip to the waistline of trousers where marked.

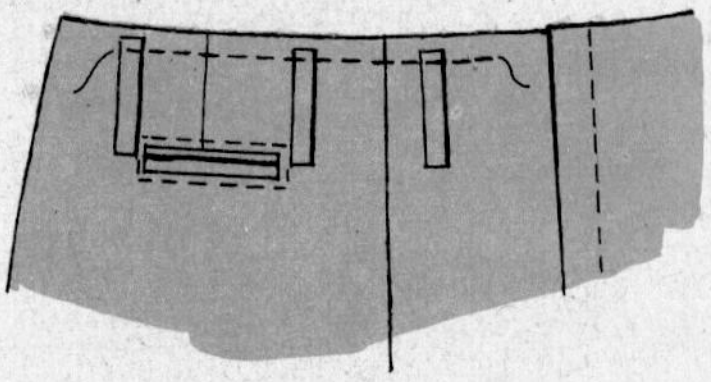

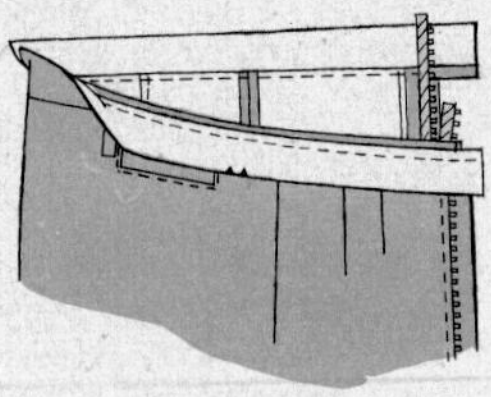

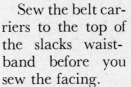

Unzip the zipper and sew the right and left waistband to the right side of the slacks. After sewing in place, cut off the ends of the extended zipper.

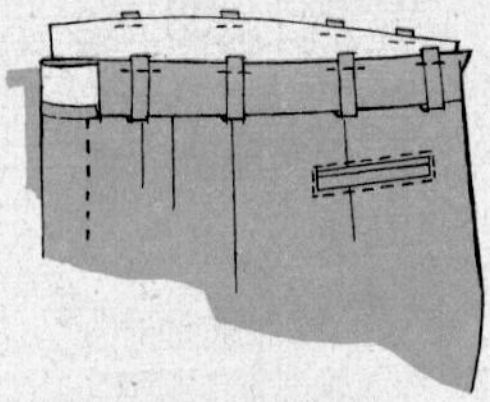

Sew the belt carriers to the top of the slacks waistband before you sew the facing.

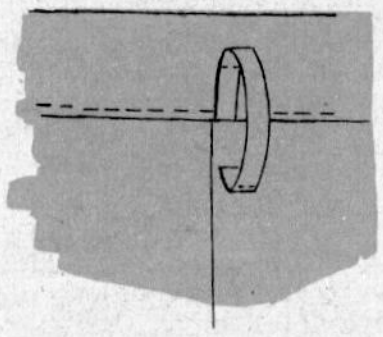

If you prefer the belt lower on the waistband, sew the belt carriers lower. Press them so they extend over the waistband for about ¾ inch. Turn under the edge ¼ inch and sew the carriers to the trousers about ¾ inch below seamline of the waistband.

The left front waistband will extend beyond the edge of the slacks. Turn the waistband to the outside.

Cut the waistband lining on the bias. Press back on the fold line and cut a strip of non-woven interfacing the width of the finished facing piece.

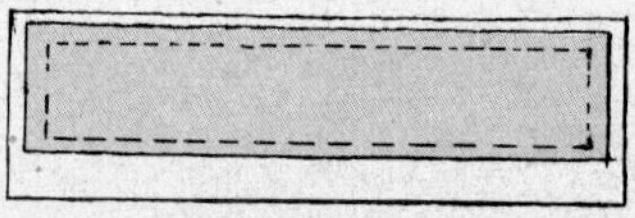

Stitch this strip to the inside of the facing, just under the seamline and inside the fold edge.

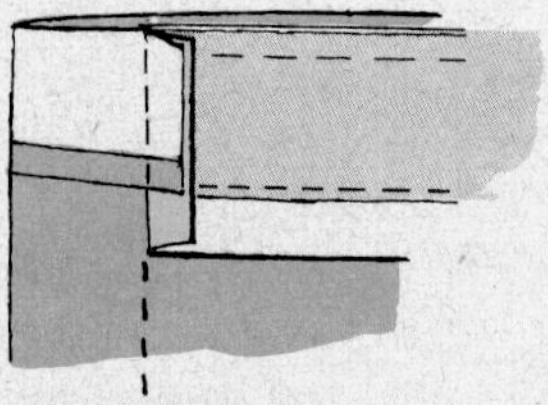

Stitch the end of the left waistband to the facing, with the right sides together, and then press the seam toward the facing.

Stitch the upper edge of the waistband and facing together around the waistline. Then trim the seam close.

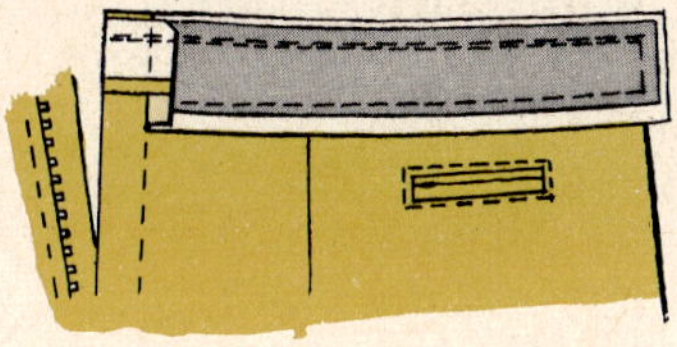

Turn the facing and left front waistband to the inside and press. Baste through the seam from the right side, catching the facing.

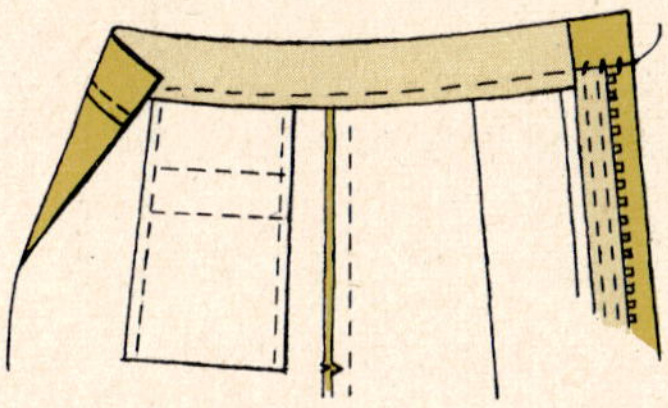

Stitch on the waistband side close to the edge of the fabric.

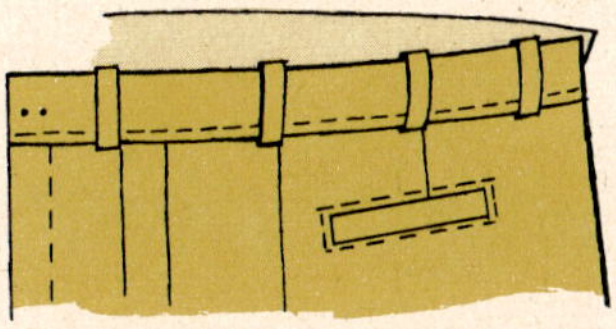

Pin and stitch the right side of the facing to the right side of the waistband. Sew across the front end that extends beyond the fly.

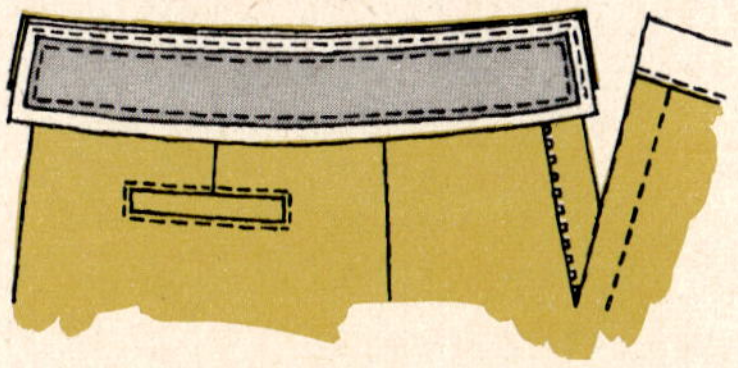

Trim the seam, turn the facing to the inside and press. Baste from the right side, holding facing in place. Edge-stitch along the waistband seam.

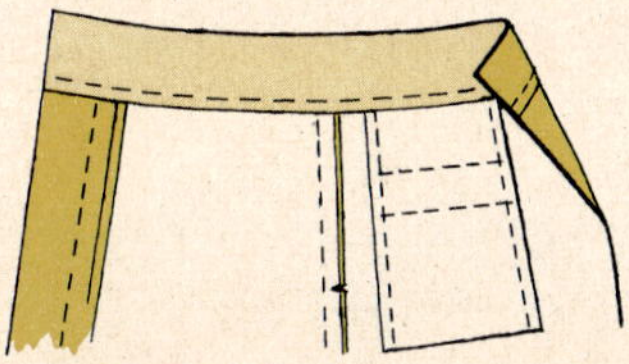

On the lightweight fabrics, the back seam can be sewed with nylon thread as shown for women's slacks. Sew to the middle of the waistband on the original stitching line.

Press the back seam open, turn under the seam edges and tack the let-out seam to the inside facing.

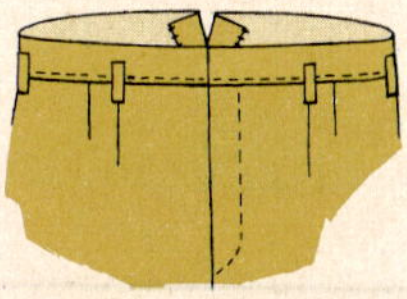

In heavier fabric, sew the back for about 3 inches from the crotch seam. Leave the seat open for about 9 inches. Sew up the upper back and waistband as for the lighter fabrics.

Sew up the back seat by hand, using buttonhole twist and a back-stitch

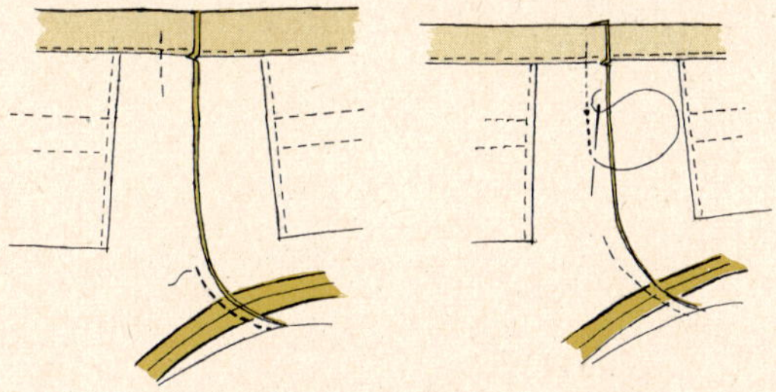

for a sturdy seam. This will give elasticity to the seat. Make a buttonhole on the left side of the waistband and on the pocket in the back.

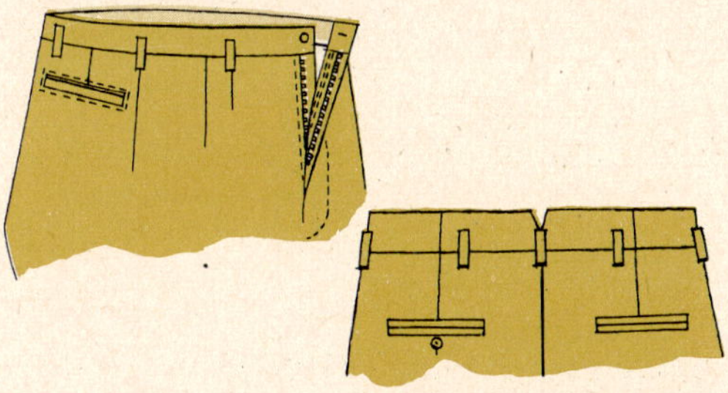

Tailor supply shops sell a large hook that can be used at the waistline instead of the usual buttonhole and button.

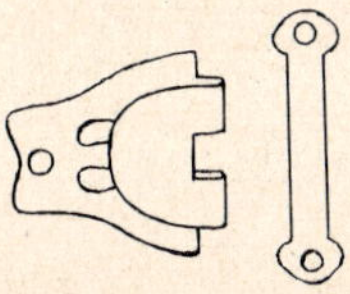

Making cuffs on slacks

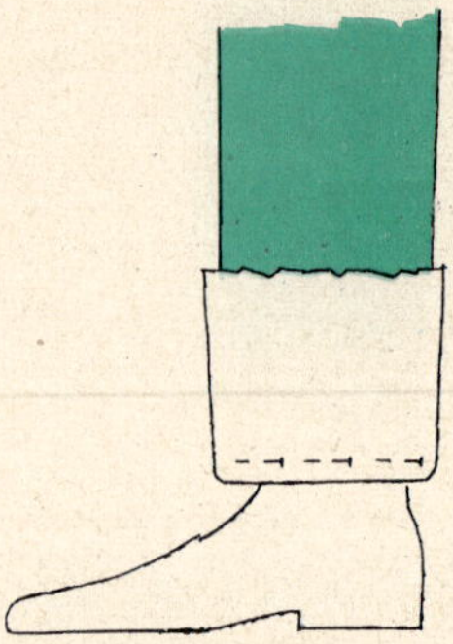

Turn the bottom of the slacks to the right side at the length you want. The finished length of the slacks varies with fashion and with the man's taste. Measure and baste the length all around. Measure up 1½ inches from this line and fold down.

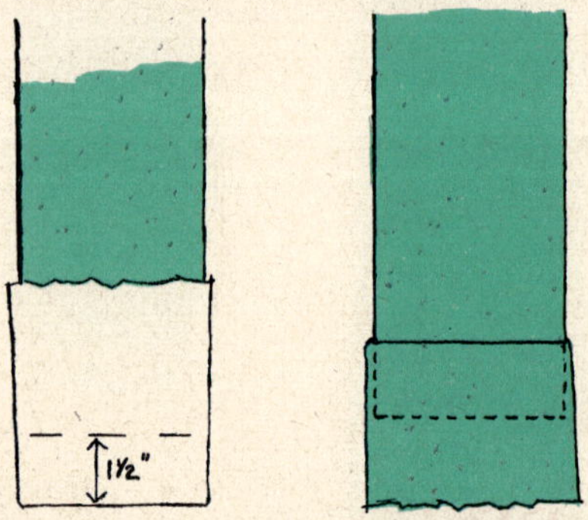

This line is the edge of the cuff. Press this fold. Turn under the remaining length to the inside and catch-stitch to the inside of the leg.

Press again, and the cuff is finished. Turn down the cuff at the side and inseam and loosely tack the seams together about ½ inch from the top edge of the slack cuff. This method can also be used in altering the length of all men's slacks.

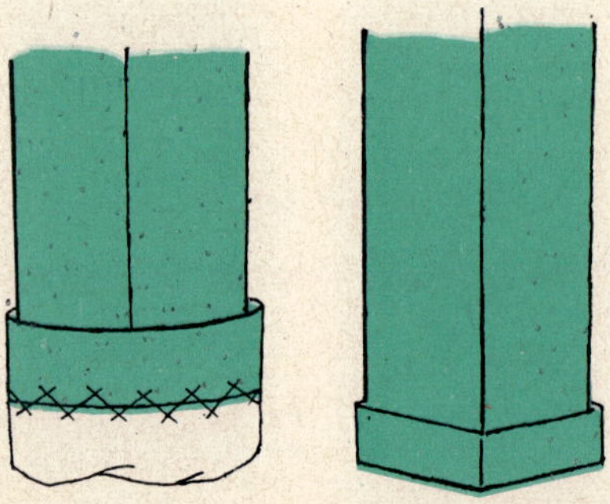

Sport shirts

Men's and women's sport shirts are made exactly alike, with one exception. The man's shirt buttons left over right, the woman's buttons right over left. Both shirts can be sewed completely by machine and require very little fitting. There are many styles of sport shirts, but the basic way of making them remains the same.

Men's measurements

Buy a man's shirt pattern according to chest measurement. Although the neck size is also given on the pattern, it makes little difference in cutting, since the sport collar does not fit the neck tightly as the dress shirt does.

If the man's neck is much larger than the pattern size, increase neck size by cutting the neckline slightly larger and increasing the collar size.

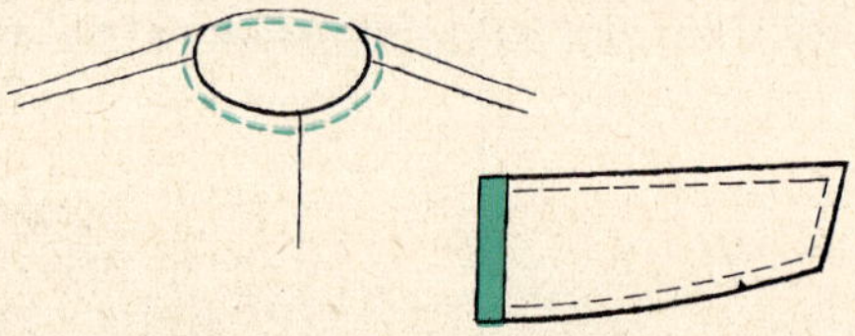

In rare cases, the shoulder width may have to be adjusted. If the pattern shoulder is too wide, it can be made narrower by a fold through the yoke and into the front shoulder.

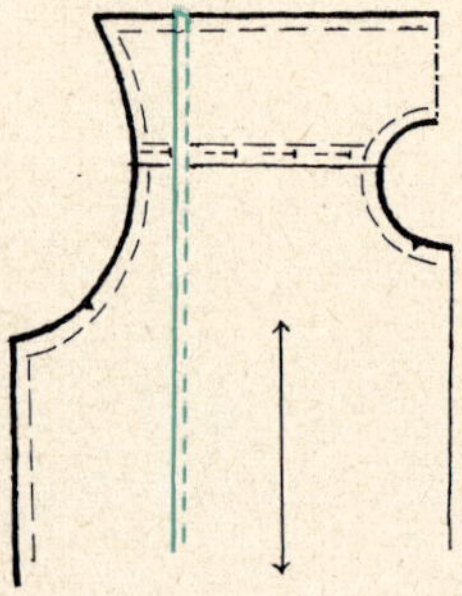

The back of the shirt can be made smaller simply by shirring in or pleating the excess, according to the back style of the shirt.

The length of sleeve is important in all types of shirts. If the sleeve is too long, it is in the way; and if it is too short, it binds uncomfortably as the cuff slides up the arm.

Measure the man's sleeve from the center back of the neck to the wrist for the sleeve length. If the shoulders need to be narrowed, make this adjustment before you measure for the length of the pattern sleeve.

The pattern for a man's shirt gives the chest measurement and sleeve length for the size. For example, a pattern with a size 38-inch chest has a 33-inch sleeve length. If the shirt you plan to make requires a 35-inch sleeve, you'll have to cut through the sleeve and add the two extra inches in length. If you narrowed the shoulder ½ inch, you will have to lengthen the shirt sleeve 2½ inches.

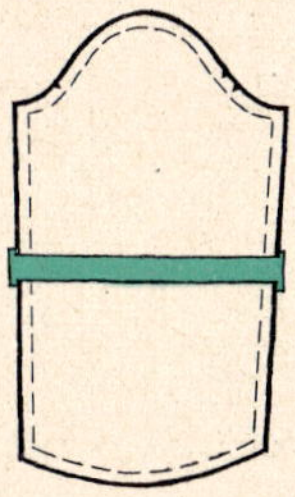

Also check the length of the shirt before it is cut. Measure from the back of the neck to the length shirt he wants. Pin the yoke to the back of the shirt pattern and measure this length. If it has to be made longer, add length to the shirt bottom, unless there is detail there, such as vents on the side. In that case, cut across the shirt between the waist and the hip and lengthen the shirt there.

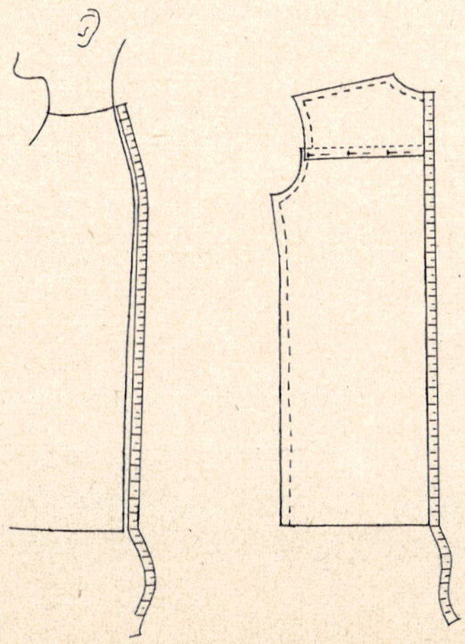

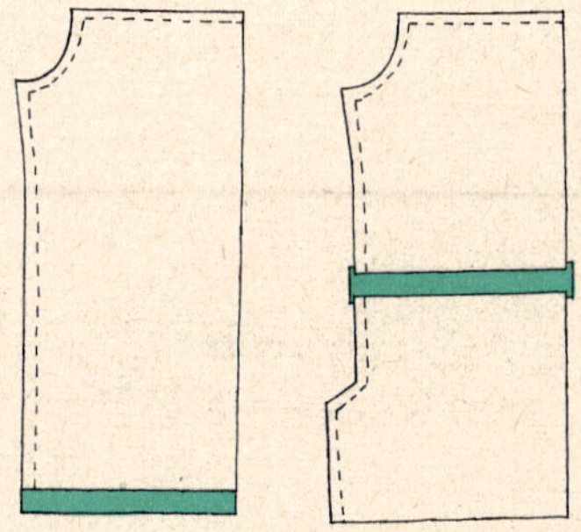

Women's measurements

The shoulder width on a woman's shirt can be altered according to her basic muslin. If the shoulder has to be narrowed ½ inch in a regular dress, narrow it the same amount in a shirt. If the waistline was lengthened or shortened in the dress, adjust it in the shirt pattern the same amount.

Lengthen or shorten the sleeve the amount adjusted on a regular pattern sleeve. Always take a woman's arm length from the top of the shoulder to the wrist, so the shoulder adjustment will not affect the sleeve length.

The woman's shirt, in some cases, will have a small bust dart to give a little shaping over the bust, but the shirt does not follow the contour of the figure as a dress does.

If the bust is extremely full and needed a deeper dart fitted on the basic muslin, it's a good idea to fit a similar dart in the shirt.

The front of the shirt will have to be made longer to allow for the dart, but this extra fitting will make the shirt more becoming to the full figure. As you see, both men's and women's sport shirts require a minimum amount of fitting.

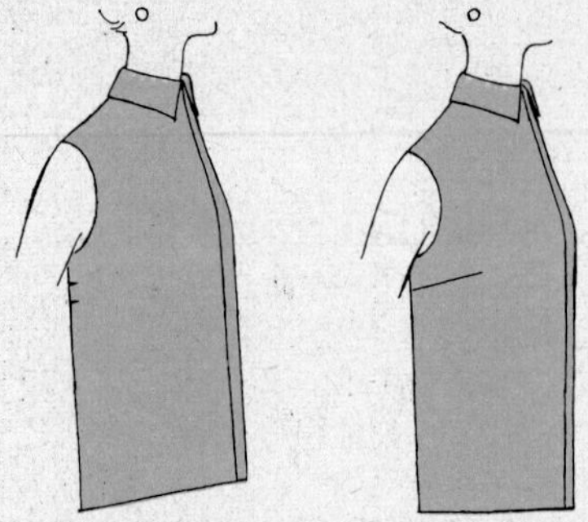

WRONG RIGHT

Cutting the shirt

In cutting the shirt, be sure to follow the grain lines of the pattern. If the shirt is plaid, match the plaid at the back and front armholes. Yokes, collars, and cuffs are always cut on the length grain, except when fabric

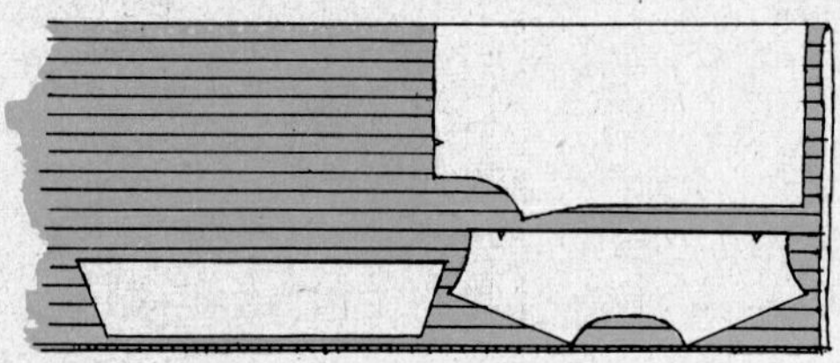

has a pattern or nap that makes it one-directional.

Then it is cut with all pieces one way. The shirt yoke is always cut with a facing. On lightweight fabrics, cut the yoke of self-fabric. If the shirt is made in a wool fabric, line the yoke in thin silk, rayon twill, or soft taffeta.

Sewing the shirt

Make the pockets, cuffs, and collar first. Interface the collar and cuffs, using any fine, crisp cotton such as lawn or cambric, a fine linen, organdy, or a commercial woven interfacing to give them body.

Sew your interfacing choice to the inside of the under collar at the seam allowance line. Put the right side of the under collar to the right side of the upper collar and then stitch the two all around the edge.

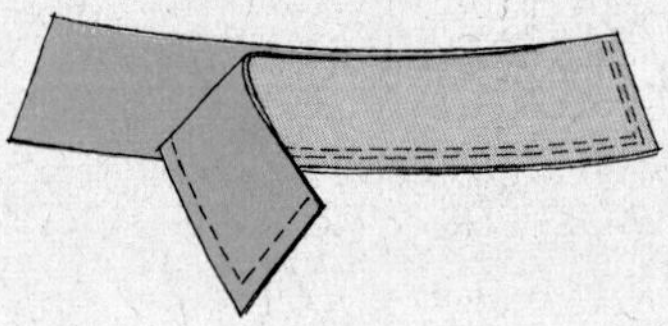

If non-woven interfacing is used, cut off the seam allowance around the outside edge before sewing it to the collar. Never catch the interfacing seam allowance in with the seam. This also applies to the cuff.

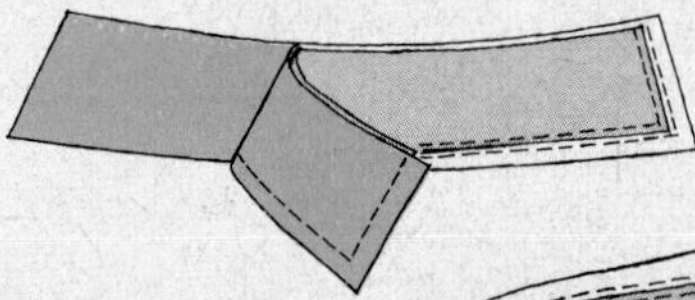

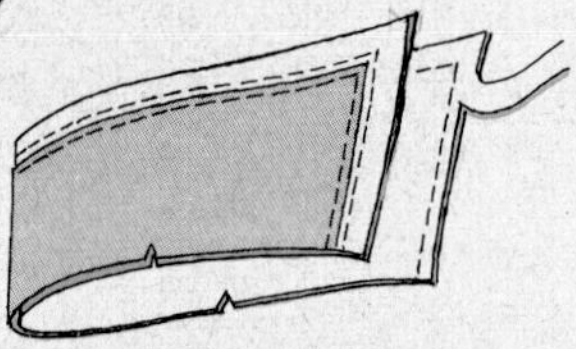

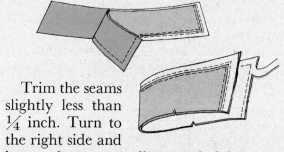

Trim the seams slightly less than $\frac{1}{4}$ inch. Turn to the right side and baste, then press all around. Make the cuff the same way. If the collar

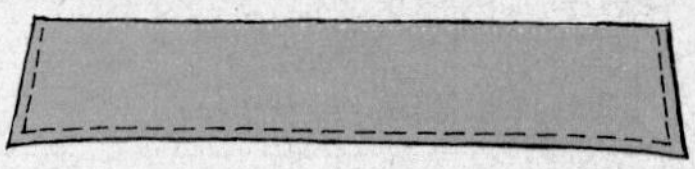

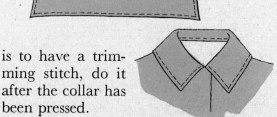

is to have a trimming stitch, do it after the collar has been pressed.

Sew the trimming stitch on the cuff after the cuff is sewed to the sleeve. Make the shirt pocket as shown under "Patch Pocket" in Chapter 6.

Mark the shirt for the placement of the pocket, the center front, and the fold line of the facing, on the front shirt piece. Remove the pattern and press the facing back on the fold line.

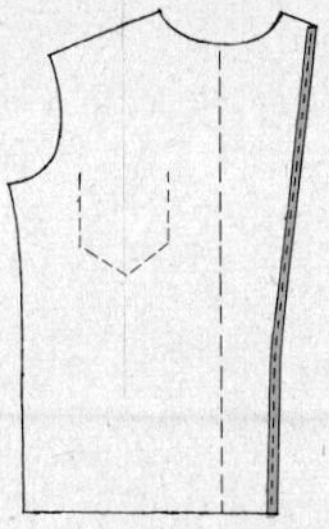

Turn under 1/4 inch seam allowance at the outside edge of the facing and stitch.

Pin pocket into place and stitch to the shirt. It can be edge-stitched or sewed in 1/4 inch, whichever you prefer to do.

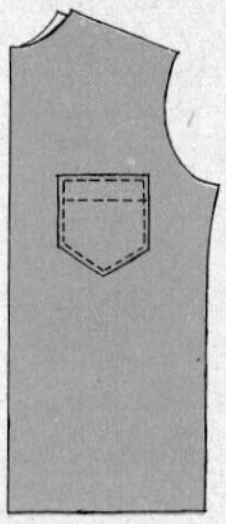

Put a clip mark at the top of the center back shirt. Mark for the back shirt fullness. If it is unpressed pleats, clip at the pleat marks. If it is shirred, clip at the marks for the shirring. Mark all notches on all pieces as you go. Remove the pattern.

If the shirt back has pleats, fold them into place and stitch them at the seam allowance line.

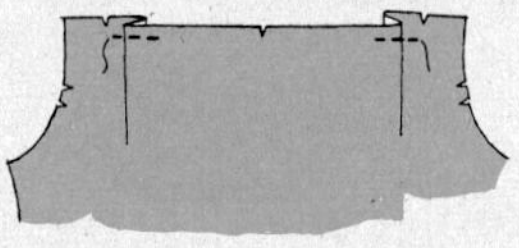

Sew the shirring in with a large stitch on the machine. Sew one row of stitching from one shirring mark to another on the seam allowance line. Then do a second line of stitching 1/4 inch from the edge.

Mark the notches on the yoke pieces. Mark the center back at the neck and lower edge. Remove pattern.

Pin the right side of the yoke facing to the inside of the shirt, matching the center clip marks and the side notches.

If it has shirring, ease into place by shirring it on the bobbin thread.

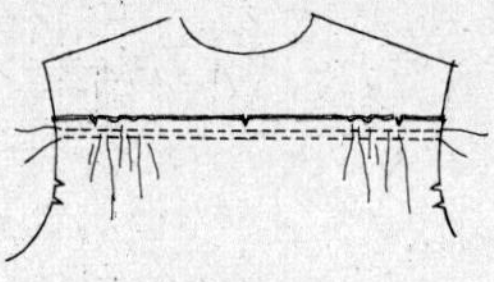

Pin the rest of the yoke to the back shirt on the shirring line. Sew on this line. Pin the right side of the yoke to the right side of the shirt on the original stitching line. Stitch along this line. If the yoke is striped or plaid. be sure you do

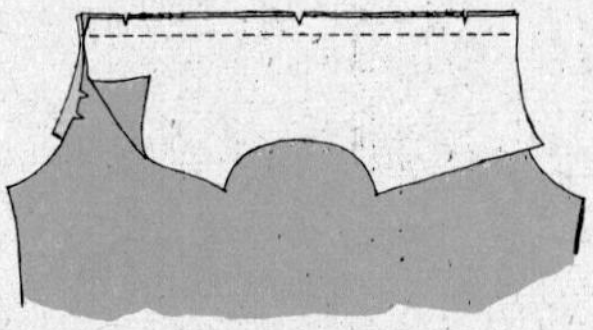

the stitching along a straight line of the shirt stripe. Press this seam carefully. If the yoke is to be edge-stitched, you can do it now. Sew it on the right side.

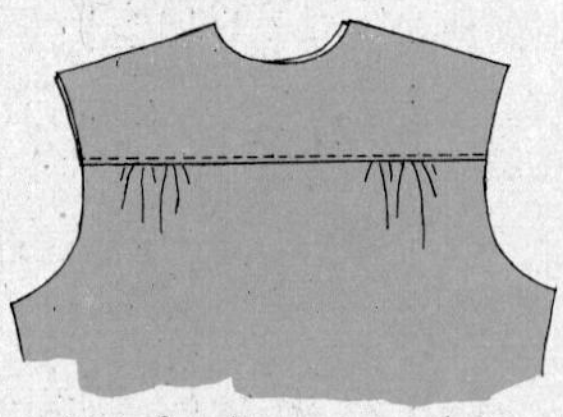

Pin and sew the right side of the yoke facing to the wrong side of the shirt front. Press the seam toward the yoke.

Turn under the seam allowance on the yoke and pin it to the shirt front, so that it just laps the original stitching line.

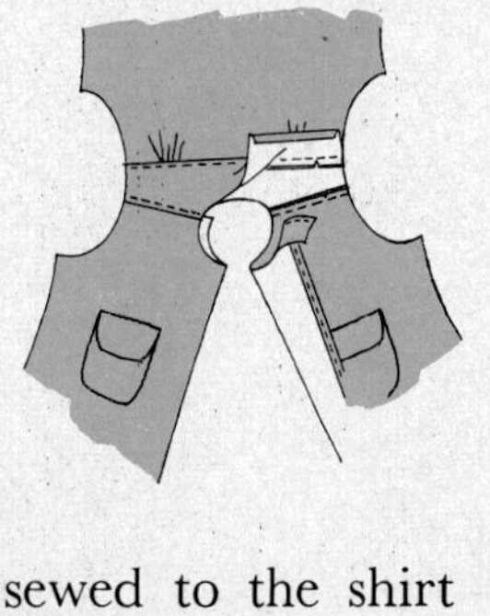

Edge-stitch it along the fold edge. The front yoke can also be sewed to the shirt with an inside seam. Turn under the front edge of the yoke and pin it to the front shoulder seam so the seam is between the yokes. Pin for the

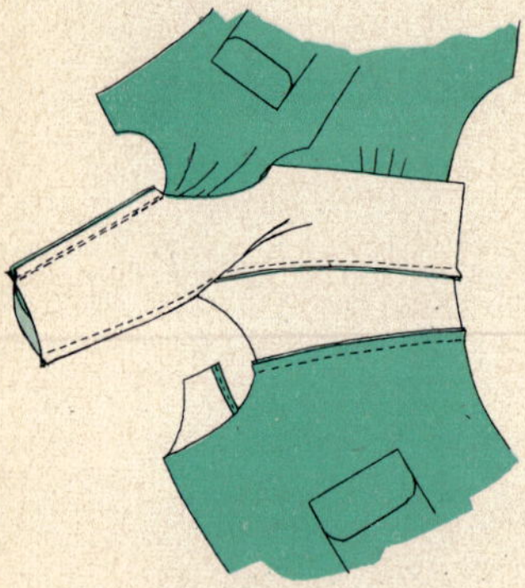

whole length of the seam on the inside. As you do, the yoke at the shoulder will be turned inside out for that short length. Sew it this way. Pull the yoke back in place and the seam will be between the two yoke pieces. This is the preferred way of sewing it. Press the seam and then do the edge-stitching on the yoke.

At this point, sew on the collar. While the shirt is open, the collar is easy to apply. Since this is a convertible collar, you will need a loop for the neck closing.

Make a handmade loop of thread. Or, use a self-fabric, which is the most desirable method for quality and convenience. Cut a short piece of bias 1 inch wide and 1 inch longer than the finished loop. Fold the bias lengthwise, right sides together, and stitch about ¼ inch from the fold.

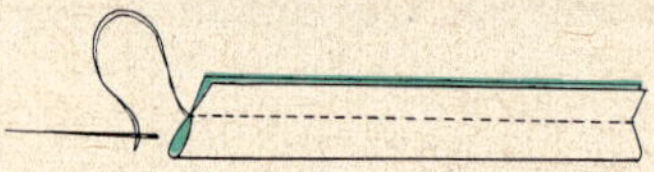

Stretch the bias as you sew. Trim the seam ⅛ inch. Turn the bias and form the loop by sewing ends together.

Tailored collar

Mark the center back of the collar with a clip mark. Match the back of the under collar to the center back of the neck and pin around the back from shoulder seam to shoulder seam. Pin the front of the collar from the center front line of the shirt to the shoulder line, but in front, pin the upper and under collars together. Now sew the loop to the shirt neck.

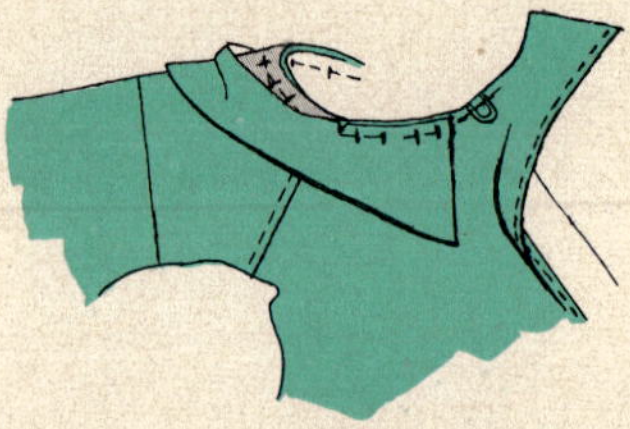

Slash to the seam allowance line on the upper collar where it is loose at the shoulder seam.

Fold the front facing back over the front neck so that the collar edges are between the facing and the neck. Turn under a seam allowance at the top of the facing.

Stitch around the neck, catching the facing, double collar, and neck in the front. As you stitch, fold the upper collar back at the shoulder line so just the under collar is stitched to the back neck. Continue around, catching the facings and the front collar edges to the front neck.

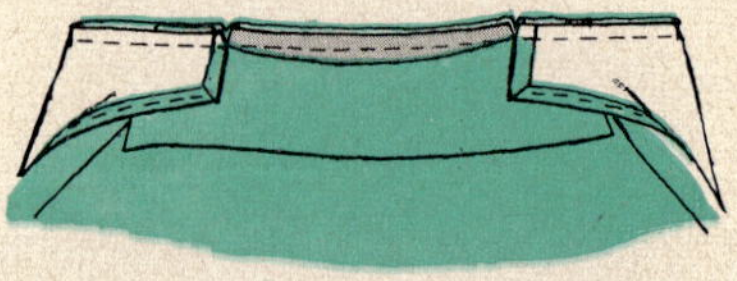

Trim the seam at the front neck. Clip into the seam allowance at intervals around the neck curve, to keep the neck from drawing.

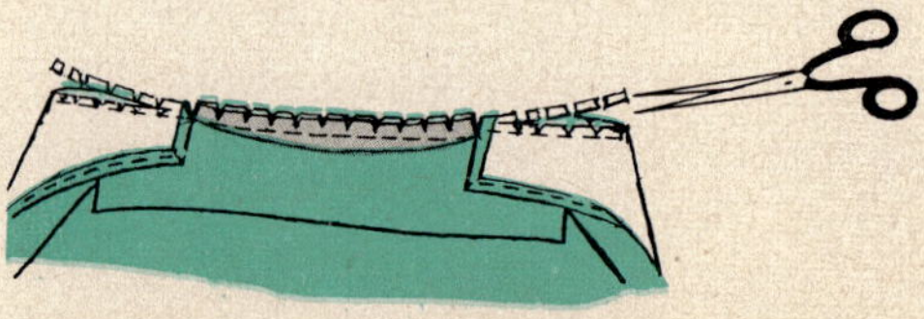

At the shoulder seam, clip the neck and under collar to the stitching.

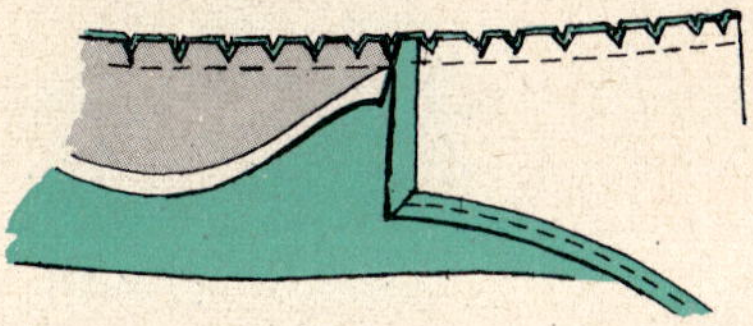

Turn the facings to the inside. Turn the back neck seam into the collar. Fold under the loose edge of the upper collar and pin it over the neck seam to cover the raw neck edge.

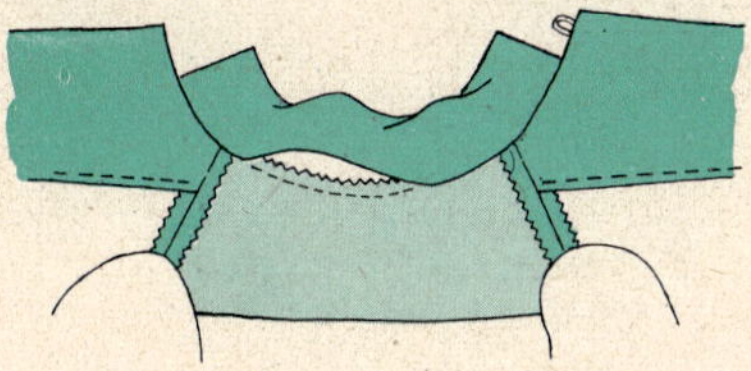

The top edge of the neck facing and the edge of the back collar can be machine-stitched in place.

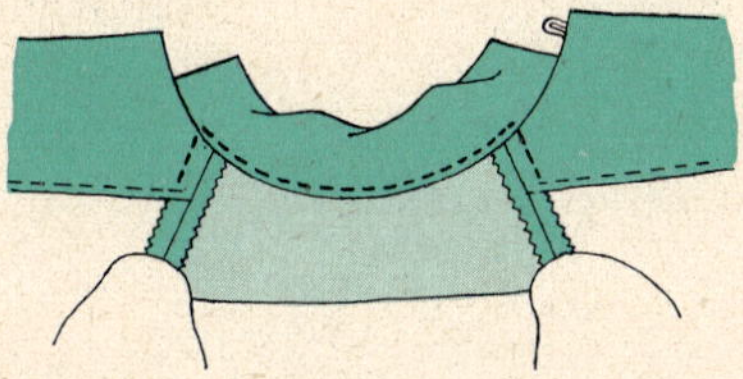

Sleeve placket

From the pattern, mark the sleeve for the placket. Then stitch the point at the end where it is to be slashed. The placket is made up of the underlap and overlap. Cut the underlap from the pattern piece so that one edge is on the selvage. Fold over $\frac{1}{4}$ inch on the other edge and press. Fold again, so the first fold edge comes just inside the selvage edge, and press.

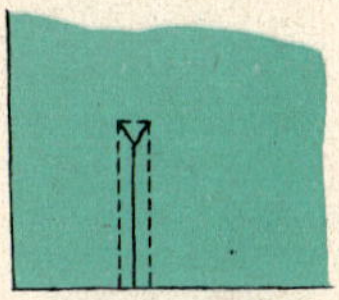

Slide the folded piece over the back edge of the slash. The selvage edge will then be to the wrong side of the sleeve. Next, pin and stitch along the fold edge. The underlap is sewed in one stitching.

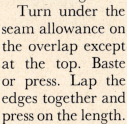

Turn under the seam allowance on the overlap except at the top. Baste or press. Lap the edges together and press on the length.

Stitch the right side of the overlap to the wrong side of the front slash edge and press the seam toward the overlap.

Fold the overlap to position along the seamline and pin. Then pin the overlap to the sleeve, with the point in the center. Pin across the overlap, catching the underlap at the end of placket opening.

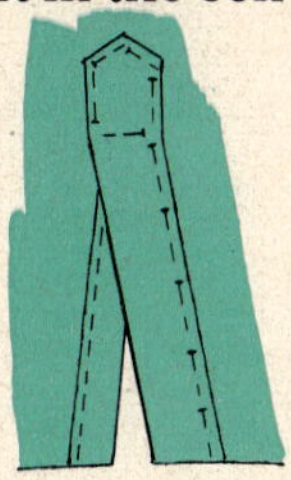

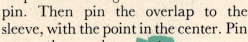

Then stitch the overlap, starting across the band to hold the underlap secure, around the point, and down the side. This completes the placket.

Assembling a shirt

The sleeves can now be sewed in the

shirt. Pin the right side of the sleeve to the right side of the armhole and stitch. Trim the shirt seam to about ¼ inch. Press the sleeve seam toward the shirt. Turn under ¼ inch of the sleeve seam and baste or pin to the shirt. Stitch along the edge

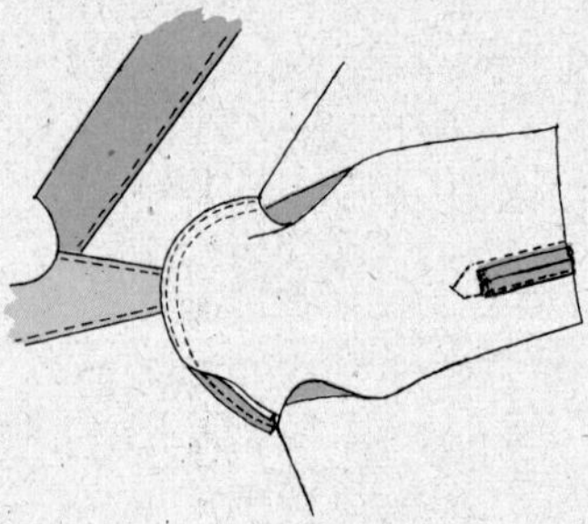

an even distance from the original stitching line. If you can stitch it more evenly from the right side, the seam should be basted instead of pinned. Press this seam, called a flat feld seam.

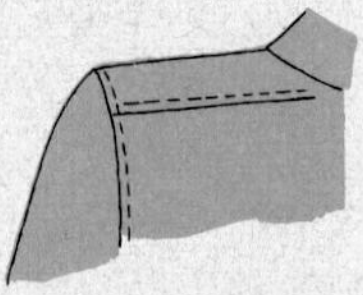

With the right sides together, pin and stitch the underarm seam and sleeve for the entire length. Trim the back seam allowance to ¼ inch. Press the seam toward the back of the shirt. Turn under the edge of the front seam and pin or baste to the back. Stitch the entire seam allowance as you did for the armhole seam. It's easier to stitch this seam from the inside.

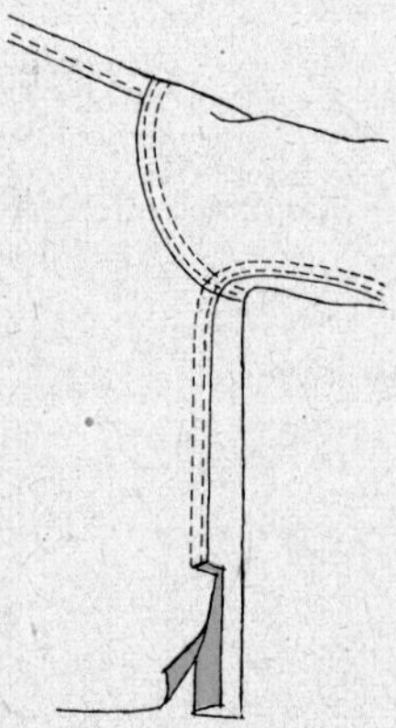

Regular cuff

You are now ready to attach the cuff. Gather or pleat the lower edge of the shirt sleeve, whichever way the pattern shows. Pin the right side of the under cuff to the wrong side of the sleeve and stitch.

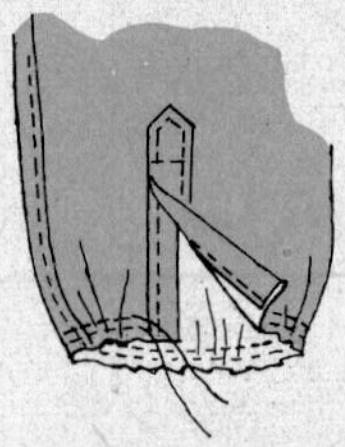

Turn under the loose edge of the upper cuff and pin to the right side of the sleeve, just covering the stitching. Next, edgestitch this across the top of the cuff.

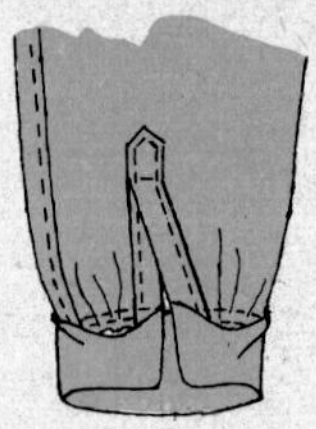

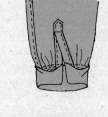

Now stitch the cuff all around as you did on the edge of the collar. The stitching should be the same width from the edge.

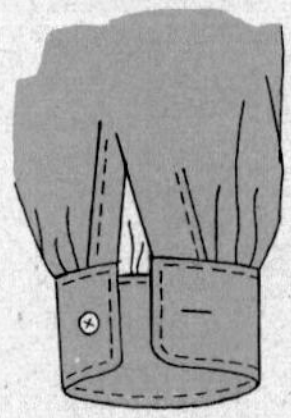

French cuff

On the French cuff, the underlap of the placket is turned under the wrong side of the sleeve. It does not extend into the cuff. The right side of the cuff is sewed to the inside of the sleeve at the first stitching. This is because the cuff folds back on itself, and the under cuff becomes the outer cuff.

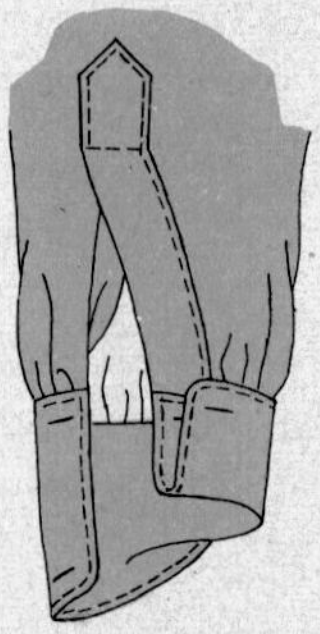

Roll-up sleeve

This is the straight shirt-sleeve made with no cuff so that it can be rolled up. On the sport shirt, the underarm seam is a flat feld seam which is finished on either side so that the sleeve need only be hemmed.

When this sleeve is used on blouses where flat feld seams are not used, here is one way to finish it.

Cut the sleeve long enough to make a very deep hem, about 8 inches. Fold under the sleeve edge and stitch. Turn the deep hem to the inside and slip-stitch. The sleeve can be rolled up with a clean seam at cuff.

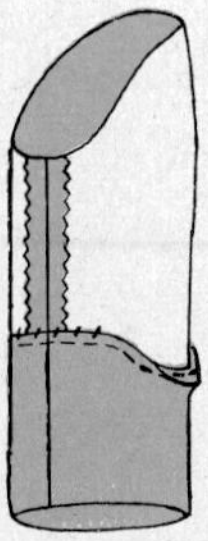

Hemming a shirt

The sport shirt is finished either with a straight hem all around, or with side vents. The pattern usually shows both shirt finishes.

Turn the lower edge of the shirt under 1/4 inch and press. Fold the right side of the facing to the right side of the front shirt. Stitch the facing and front together along the hemline. Turn the facing under and press. Fold back the hem at hemline, stitch, press.

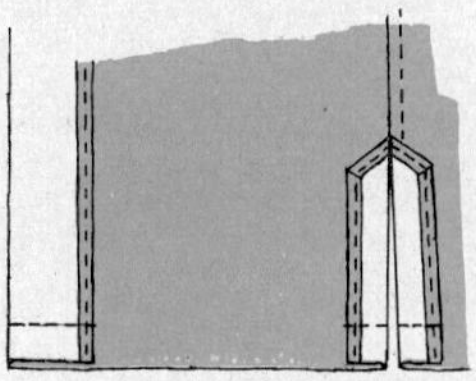

When there are side vents, turn under the outside edge and press. Fold the right side of the vent to the right side of the shirt, as you did for the facing, and stitch along the hemline. Turn the vent to the inside, pin, and stitch.

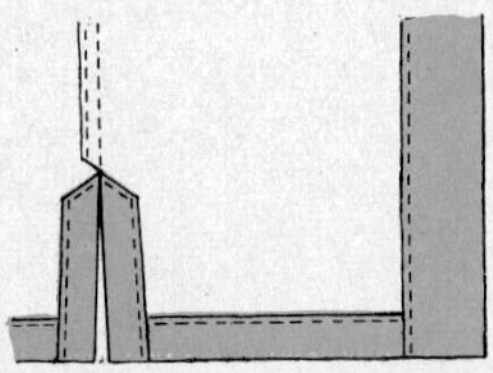

If possible, make the buttonholes by machine on the buttonholer. The woman's sport shirt is made exactly the same way, except the buttonholes are made on the right instead of left.

Blouses

You can sew most of your blouse with regular seams, and in the same way that you assembled the top of the dress shown in the preceding chapters.

There are, however, many types of necklines used on blouses and play clothes. Some are a little complicated to make. You'll find instructions for making these on the following pages.

All the other types of collars you'll want to make for sportswear are some variation of the collars described in this and other chapters.

Tie collar

Any neckline can be made with a tie collar, which is easy to make. For the narrow tie collar with the short bow, cut a strip of fabric about 20 inches long and about 3 1/2 inches wide. If you want a more impressive bow, measure the length and width and cut it to allow for a larger size.

If the blouse opens down the front, turn the facing to the right side and stitch the neck edge to the point where the blouse will lap. Then clip the neck seam where the stitching ends.

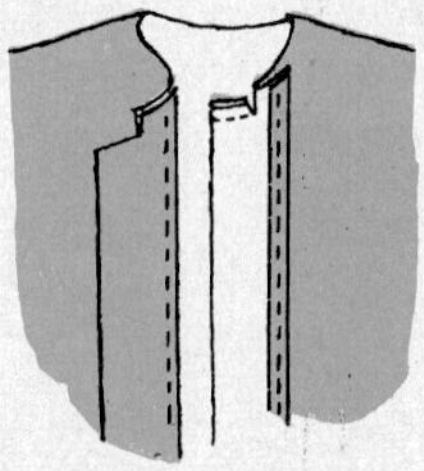

Trim the seam and turn the facing to the inside. With right sides together, pin and stitch the tie collar to the neck, as far as the clip marks.

Be sure to start the center of the tie at the center back neck. Fold the ends, right sides together, and stitch along the edges and across the ends. Trim the seam allowance and turn to

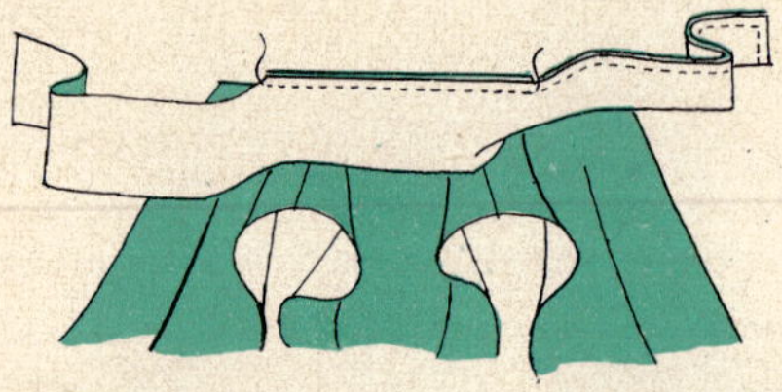

the right side. Now turn under the loose edge on the inside of the tie and slip-stitch it securely to the blouse neck.

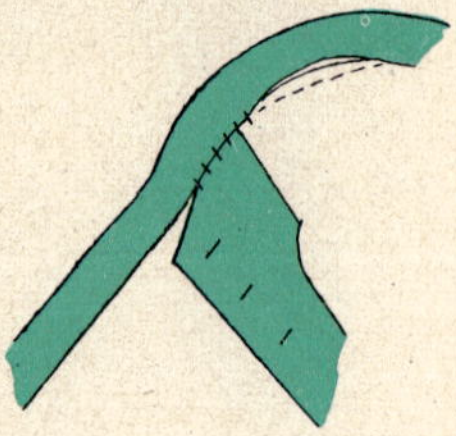

Turtle-neck collar

This collar is cut on the true bias. On the low neck, it is made a continuous piece. The higher neck has a back or front opening.

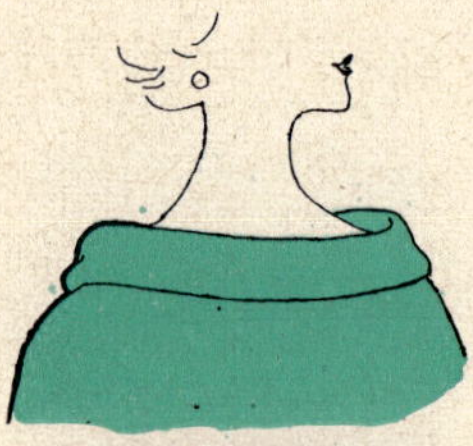

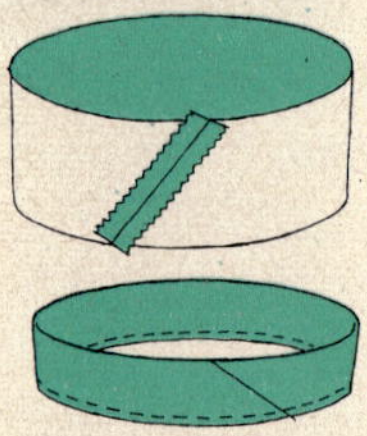

Join the bias on the straight grain. Fold in half on the length and baste the edges together. Then pin the collar to the neck of the blouse and try it on. The collar should roll and stand away from the neck slightly. If it rolls too flat, the collar may have to be made smaller.

Some fabrics, when cut on the bias, stretch more than others, so it is important to test the collar before you make it. The bias can be eased in, but too much ease will spoil the collar. Adjust and sew the collar to the desired size. Fold in half on the length and press lightly on the fold edge.

Do not make a sharp crease. Pin and stitch the right side of the collar to the right side of the neck. Trim and clip the neck seam.

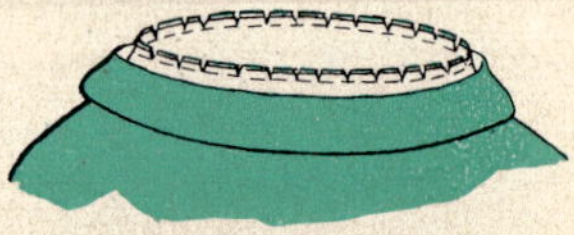

Press the seam into the collar and then turn under loose edge of the collar and pin over the seam. Hold the collar taut in your hands, stretching it slightly to see whether it twists.

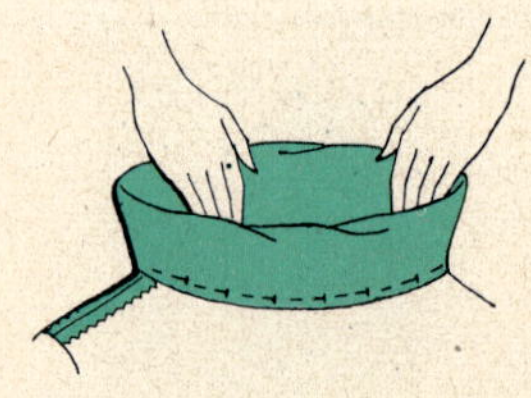

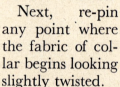

Next, re-pin any point where the fabric of collar begins looking slightly twisted.

The bias will stretch unevenly so that the collar can be spoiled if this is not checked. When the collar is smooth, slip-stitch the inside seam.

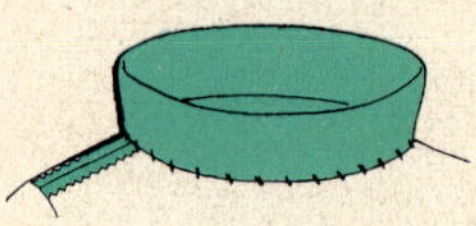

Tab neck opening

This neck, or versions of it, is used for many types of clothes, from sport shirts to pajamas. Many blouses also

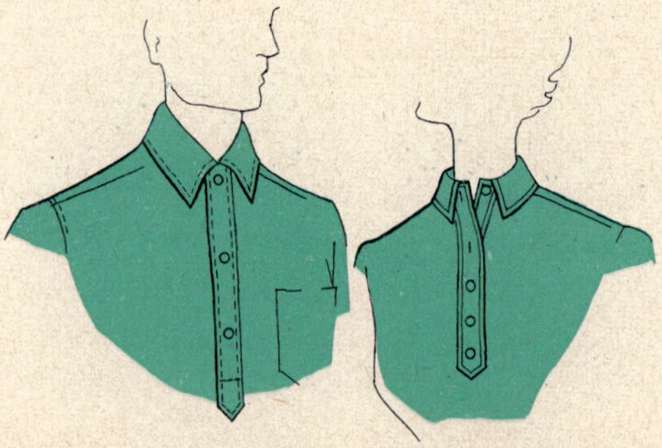

have this opening. It is a trim, neat neck closing, when properly made.

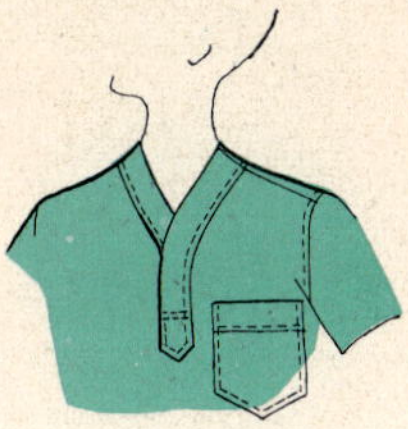

On the front, reinforce the end of the neck opening by stitching on the seam allowance line on either side and across the end. Slash into the corners. Cut the neck bands from pattern pieces. Trim off the ends of three pieces 1½ inches above the point, or on the pattern mark. Two of the bands will be used as facings. Sew these to the sides of the front opening on the inside of the shirt, the seams to the right side. The end will extend below the slash. Trim and press the seam toward the facing.

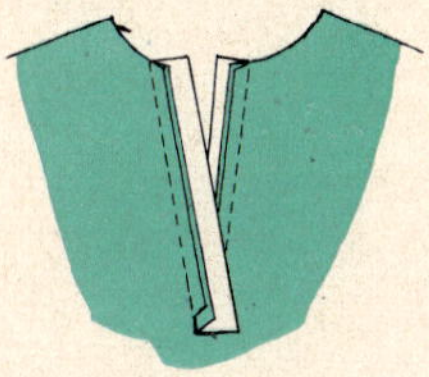

Pin and stitch the outer band to the facings, right sides together, at the neck edge.

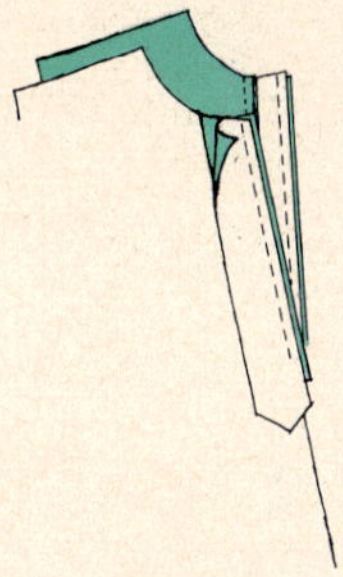

The left band has the point on the man's shirt, the right band has it on the woman's. Trim the seam.

Turn the band to the outside. Then turn under the seam allowance on the loose edge and around the point.

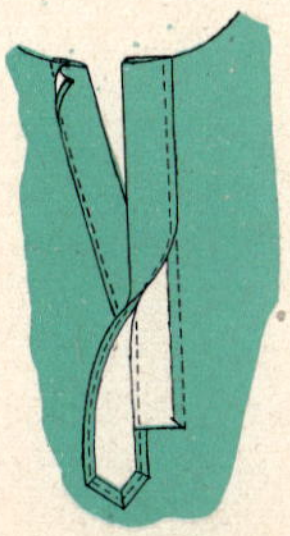

On the underlapping band, top-stitch the band to the front. Stitch the end of this band to the front between the slash marks, with seam to the right side.

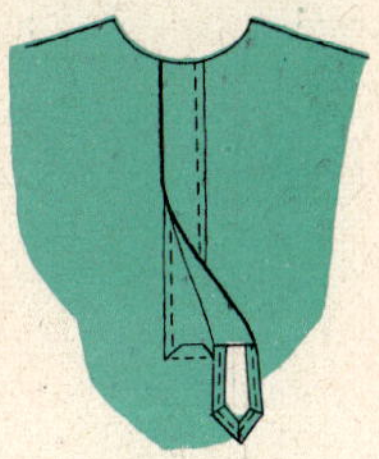

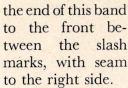

Lap the upper band over the under band, centers even. Top-stitch around top band, continuing around point and across band above point.

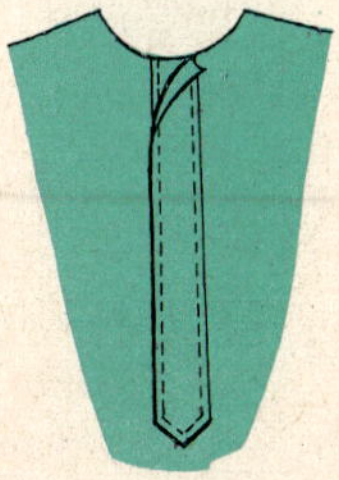

Blouse hems

If the blouse is to be worn outside, it can be finished with a regular hem or facing. When the blouse tucks in, the weight of the fabric must be considered before you decide on the hem.

If the fabric is soft and fine, you can sew a seam binding to the edge, turn and slip-stitch it to the blouse.

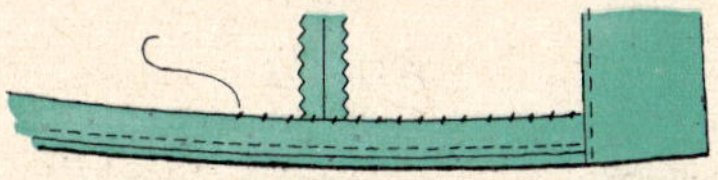

In a heavier fabric that might show a ridge under a tightly-fitting skirt, sew a row of stitching ¼ inch from the lower edge of the blouse. Pink this

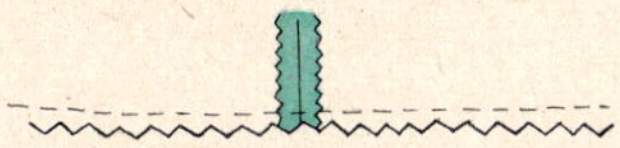

edge. If the fabric has a tendency to ravel, turn under the edge. Stitch two rows of stitching about ¼ inch apart.

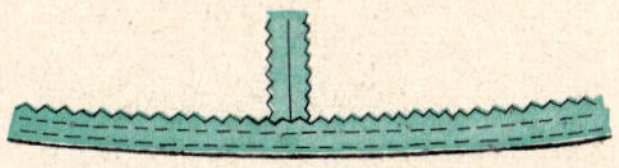

Shirred sleeve

When the full sleeve has an opening

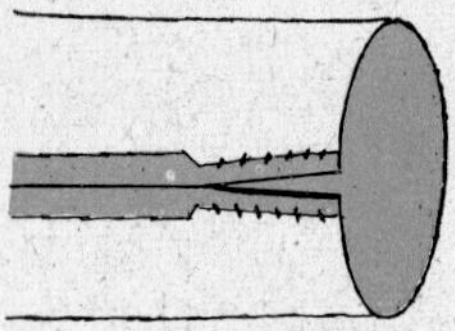

at the seam, just turn under the edge of the seam and hem to the sleeve.

If the opening is made with a slash, it must be faced. Then turn and stitch the outer edges of the facing piece. Pin the right side of the facing to the right side of the sleeve along the slash mark. Stitch from 1/4 inch on either side of the slash mark, tapering to a point. Take one stitch across the point. Double stitch around the point to reinforce it.

Slash between the stitching lines to the point. Turn to the wrong side and press. Sew up the underarm seam and press. Sew two rows of stitching around the lower end of the sleeve for gathering.

Gather the lower edge of the sleeve. Pin the right side of the wristband to the wrong side of the sleeve. Adjust the gathers to fit, pin and stitch.

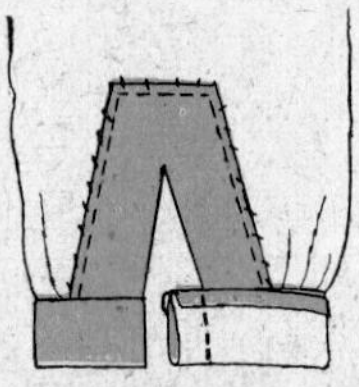

Fold the wristband with right sides together and stitch the ends. Turn to the right side. Turn under free edge of cuff band. Pin to right side of sleeve covering the seamline. Top-stitch.

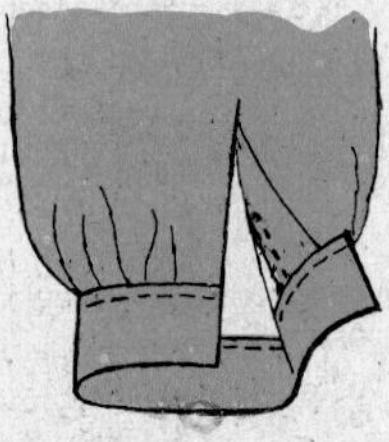

Skirts

The directions for making a slim, straight skirt have been given in other chapters. The following directions are for other types of skirts.

Gathered skirt

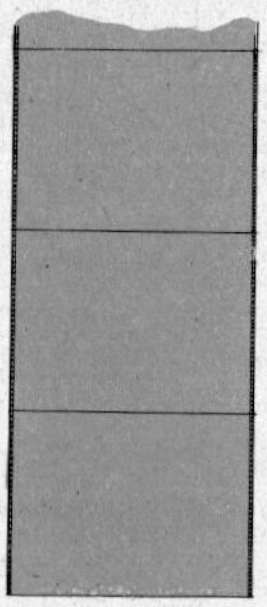

This is the easiest skirt of all to make. No fitting is necessary, and there are only straight seams to sew on it.

Cut out the skirt pieces in lengths unless the pattern shows it cut on the cross-grain as for a border print

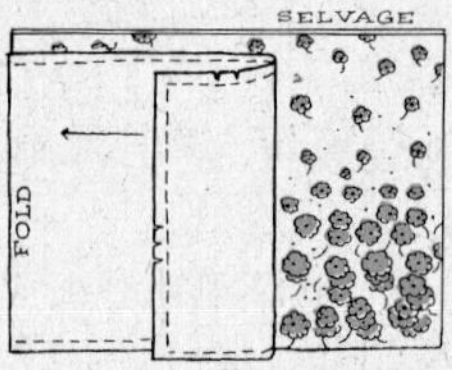

skirt. When cut on lengths, the shirring is done on the cross-grain which gives much softer folds.

Sew up the seams, leaving part of one seam open for the placket. Then, sew the zipper into the placket.

When doing the gathering stitches, sew from seamline to seamline, a section at a time. This is the easiest way to shirr in the fullness, and there is much less chance of breaking the shirring thread and having to start over. Use nylon thread in the bobbin for shirring. It is much stronger and not likely to break. Sew two rows for shirring along the top edge of the skirt on the right side. The first row should be on the seam allowance line, the second nearer the skirt edge.

Make the waistband as described at the beginning of this chapter. Mark

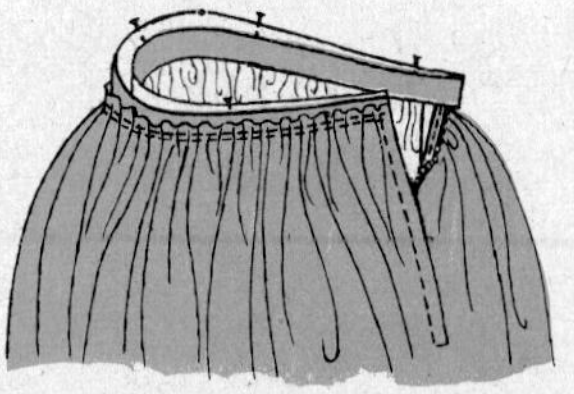

the band for center back, front, and side seams. Pin to the wrong side of the skirt at the same points.

Gather the fullness to fit the band. Pin and sew the band to the skirt. Press the seam toward the band.

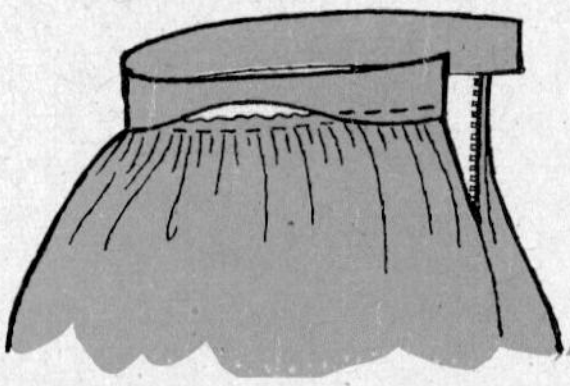

Turn under the raw edge of the band and lap it over the seamline. Then edge-stitch the band to skirt.

Turn the hem, give it a final pressing, and the skirt is finished.

Any adjustments made at the waistline on your basic muslin must also be made in this skirt, even though there is no fitting needed. If a dart had to be taken across the top of the skirt under the belt to make it hang right, correct this in the skirt.

Measure down on the back skirt the depth of alteration dart. Trim this off the skirt top before shirring. The skirt will hang correctly, won't dip in back.

Pleated skirt

The professional dressmaker has skirts pleated by a pleater. This is a good idea if you can have it done conveniently, since professional pleating is permanent and more accurate.

When making pleats, you usually allow three times the hip measurement for the regular side pleat.

If you have a more elaborate skirt in mind, check with the pleater for the amount of fabric you will need.

When you send a skirt to a pleater, it must be specially prepared. Decide how wide a piece you will need and cut enough lengths to give the amount.

Fabric is never pleated with the pleats running across the grain. The fabric would be too wiry, and the pleats would not stay in place.

Sew the lengths together along the selvage so you have a long strip. Press and turn the hem. Sew on the seam binding and slip-stitch. The hem must

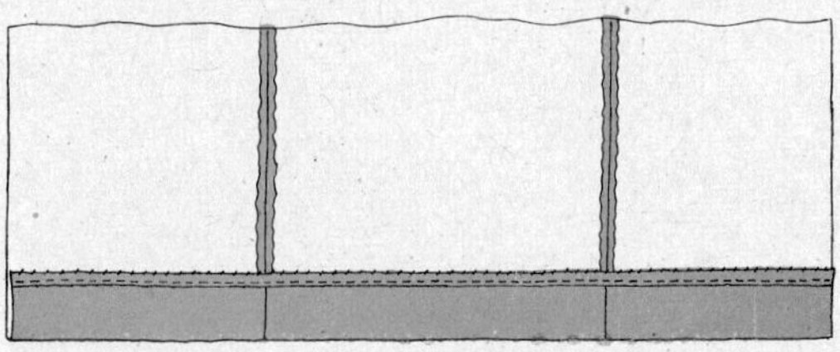

also be put in before pleating. Fabric is now ready for the pleater.

There are two ways to make this type of skirt. You can ease it onto the waistband and allow it to hang soft from the waist, or you can fit the skirt to the hip, and stitch the pleats to fit the hipline.

When it hangs from the waist, the skirt should have an easy look over the hip, so allow as much as can be eased in. Sew two rows of shirring around the waistline. Use a nylon

bobbin thread so the shirring won't break. Ease in the waistline on the shirring thread as much as possible. Pin the waistband to the top. Put the skirt on and pin around the waist

to check the fullness and hang of it.

If it hangs correctly over the hip, the waist ease is right and you can press to smooth this out. As you press, keep the pleats even at the hip, but press the fullness as it fans toward the waist.

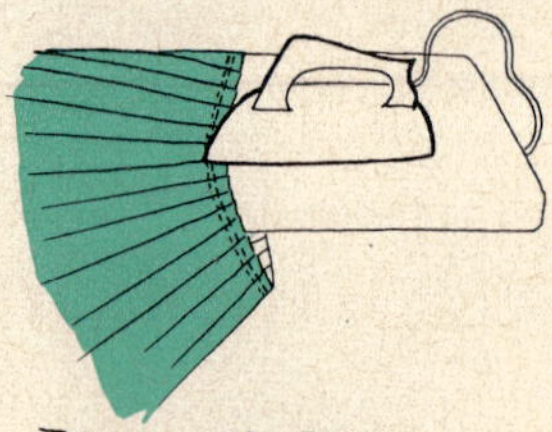

Sew up the side so the front pleat just laps over the back, forming another pleat. Sew it up to 7 inches from the top to form the placket opening.

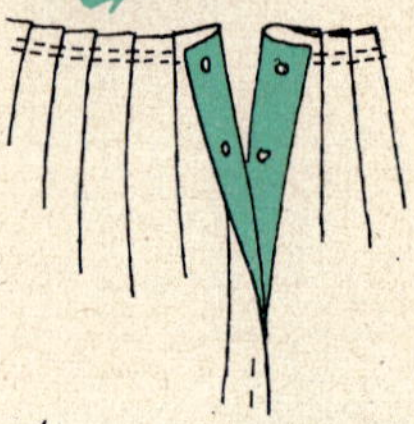

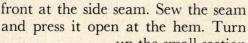

You will only need to sew a few snaps here. Apply waistband. Rip hem on back and front at the side seam. Sew the seam and press it open at the hem. Turn up the small section of the hem and then restitch it in place. Press the pleat at this point to get a sharp line, and the skirt is finished. If, on your basic muslin, your skirt has a back adjustment under the belt, trim off this same amount of material at the back of the pleated skirt before you ease the waistline. Otherwise, the skirt will dip in the back, and the pleats will hang open.

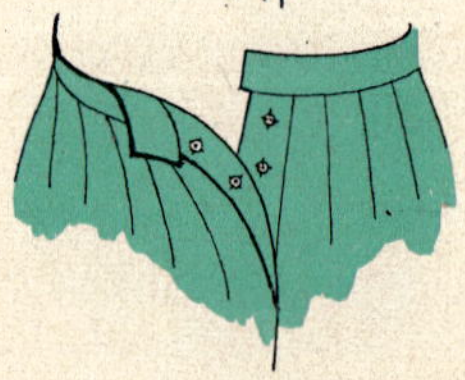

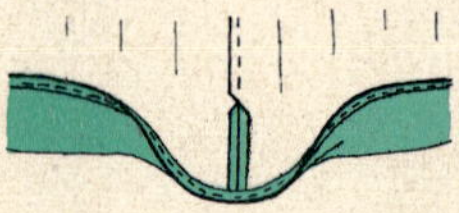

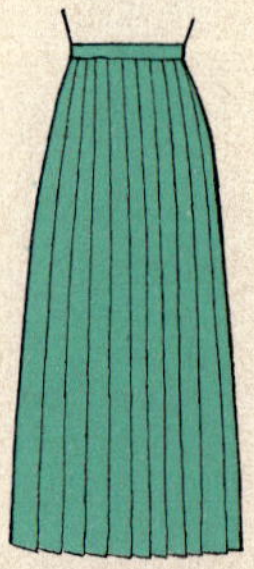

Fitted pleats

Before you fit the skirt, baste the pleats in position at hipline point, or about 9 inches down. Make up the waistband and pin it around the waist. Lap the top of the skirt over the band at several points and pin right side out around the figure.

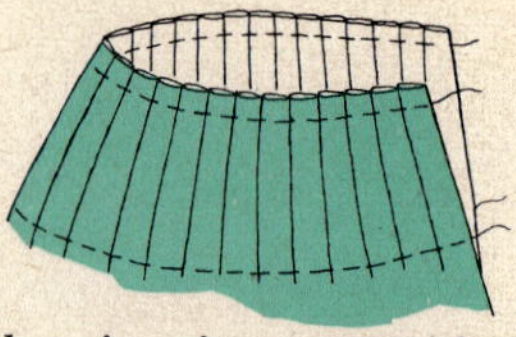

Starting at the front of the skirt, pin the edge of the pleat to the skirt and toward the waistline. Do this all around the figure, fitting as you go. There will be more fitting at the back and hips than in front. The pleat is tapered in at the top to shape in to the waistline.

Here is the trick. Don't just move the fold line of the pleat to the left. If you do this, the pleats will pull toward the left all around the skirt. Instead, refold on the pleat edge and then lap a little to the left, so that the amount you are taking in is the same on the pleat and on the lap. Then unpin the waistband and the side seam after carefully marking the fitting line. Remove the skirt. Measure and mark the depth the pleats are to be stitched. While the skirt is open and spread flat, edge-stitch each pleat. Carefully follow the fitting line. Sew from the bottom of the pleat to the waistline,

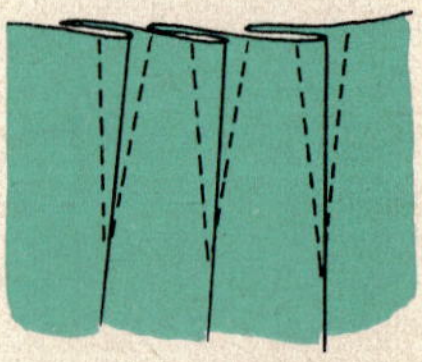

so the pleat will not pucker at the end. When the skirt is all stitched,

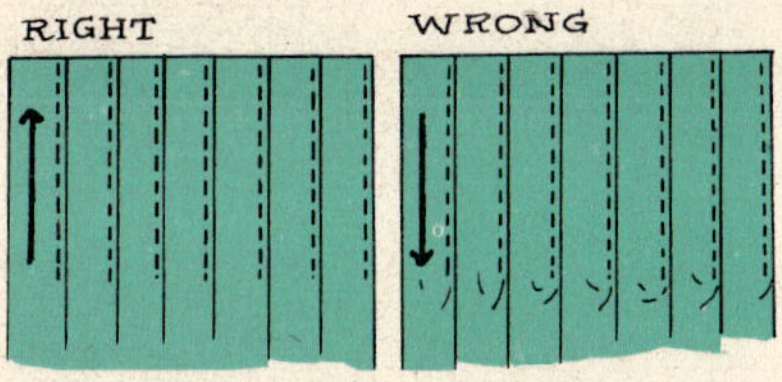

finish as you did for the pleated skirt. At the side opening, stitch the pleat up to the opening, then stitch only on the pleat edge. If your basic muslin was adjusted at the waistband, lift and fit the same amount out of the back of your pleated skirt.

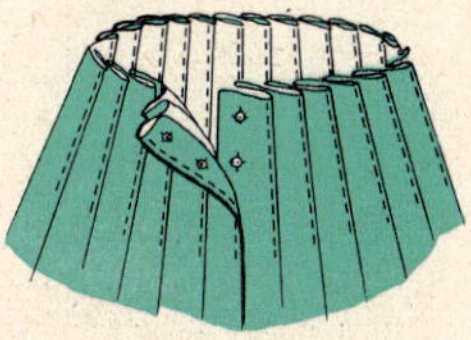

Self-pleating

On plaids, it is advisable to pleat the fabric yourself and work out the depth and size of the pleat according to the plaid.

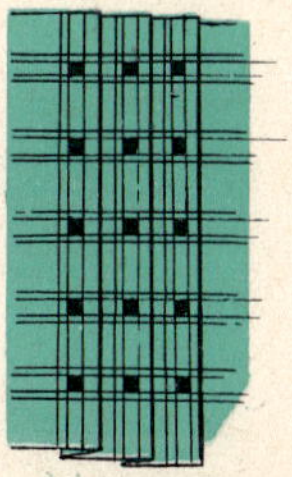

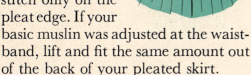

Lay the fabric on the ironing board. Fold the pleat on the plaid line. Stretch it slightly on the board and carefully pin at either end of the pleat in the padding of the board to hold it in place. Press with the steam iron. Pleat a section at a time until the whole skirt is pleated.

On plain fabric, you can mark the pleats from the pattern with tailor's chalk. Clip in at pleat line at either end of skirt.

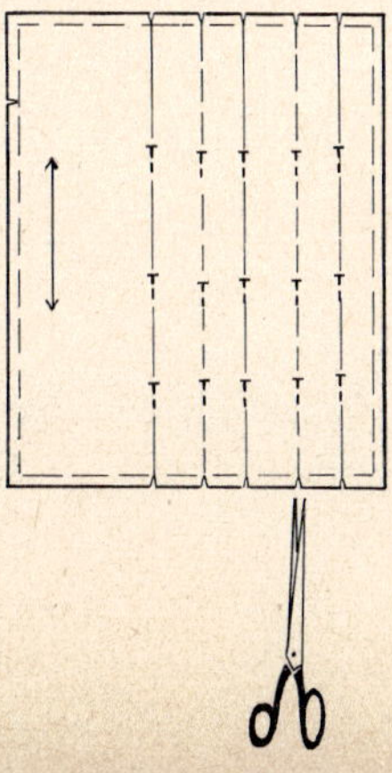

Place the fabric on the board and pin and stretch the same way, matching the clip marks at either end and the chalk marks on the length.

Press the pleats in the same way. After the skirt is pleated, it can be treated as you did for the commercially-pleated skirt, easing or fitting it the same way. The hem on this type of skirt is put in last.

Types of pleating

There are three types of flat pleats: box pleats, inverted pleats, and side pleats. All other fancy pleatings are a combination of these types. The side pleat is always folded right to left. This is the pleating professionals will use unless you choose one of the others. When you pleat a skirt yourself, be sure the side pleats go this same way.

You can fit the box-pleated skirt another way, but it's time-consuming. Take a small dart in the center of each pleat to fit the waistline size.

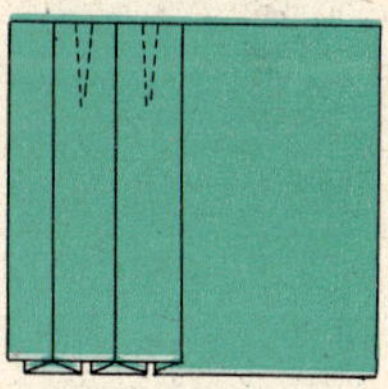

Two other types of pleating—accordion and sunburst—will be described in Chapter 10. On fabrics that do not hold a pleat well, or that may have to be washed often, edge-stitch the pleats. After hemming, stitch from the hem toward the top along pleat edge. The inside fold of pleat can also be stitched like this, but one stitching is enough.

Halters

Here are two different types of halters you can make. Also included are the instructions for lining each. Any other halter you make will be a variation of these two types. Two suggested variations are the tie-back halter and the closed-back halter.

Drawstring halter

Pin the lining to the halter, right sides together, and stitch all around. Leave a small section of the underarm seam of the lining open. When stitching across the neck and down the sides, leave ½ inch open at the side seam close to the neck opening.

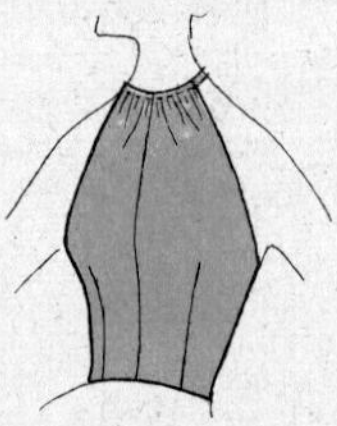

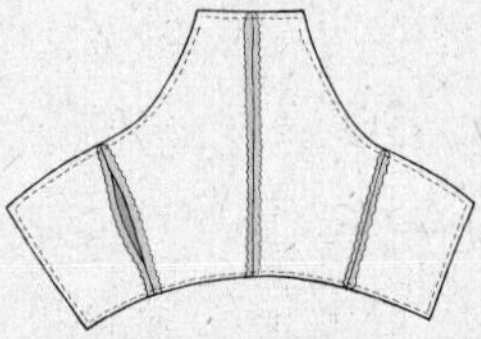

Turn the halter right side out through the opening in the lining. Baste around the edges and press.

Measure down from the neck and stitch the two thicknesses together to form the casing. Make a soft tubing ½ inch thick, about 20 inches long. Draw through the casing to form the ties. (Chapter 6—directions for making tubing.) Make buttonholes by machine at waist. Sew on buttons.

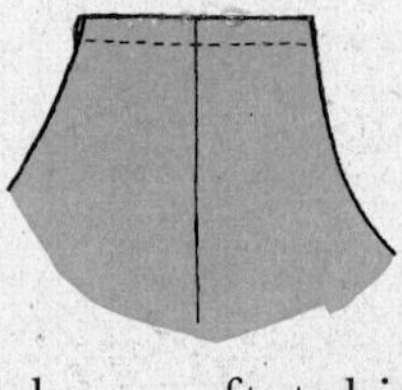

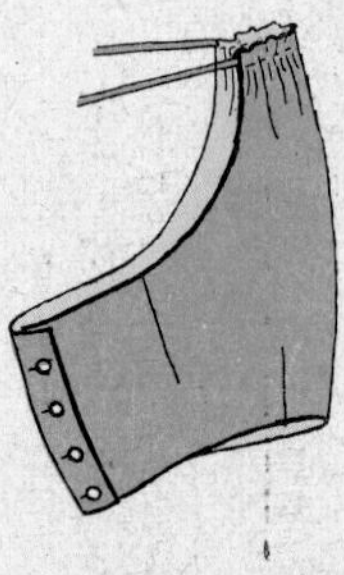

Closed-back halter

The back of the neck is joined and sometimes pleated to give a soft drape to this halter. Cut the lining and halter from the same pattern. Sew them up separately. Pin the right side of the lining to the right side of the halter. Leave a small opening at the underarm seam of the lining. Stitch all around the two pieces, except at the back neck seam.

Leave 2 inches open on each strap. Trim and clip the seam all around except where the ends have been left open. Turn to the right side through the lining opening. Baste and press all around. Take one back strap and push it into the end of the other strap. Pull both straps out through the lining.

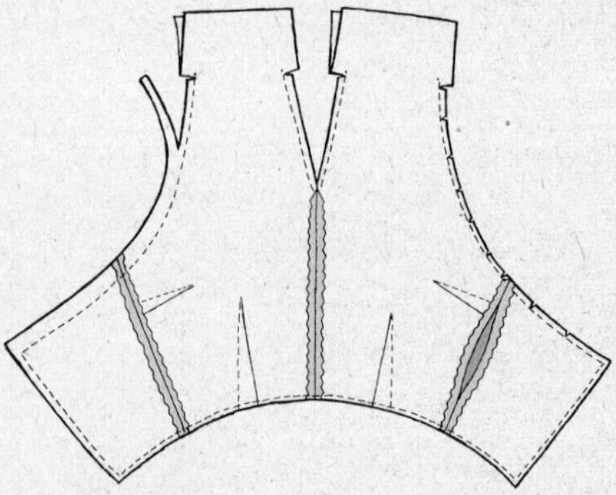

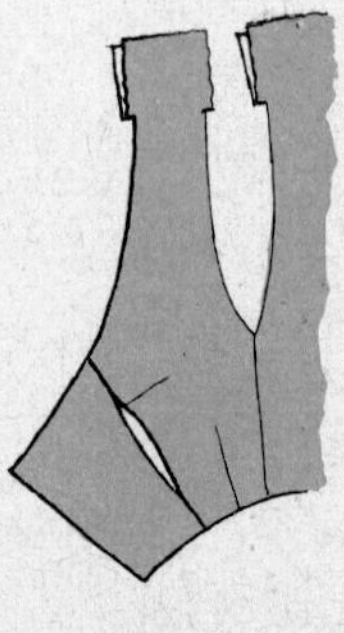

The seam allowances of the straps will be together. Pin and stitch the lining ends together and the halter ends together. Press the seams open. Pull the straps farther out so that the side seam stitching shows. Then pin and stitch the sides of the straps.

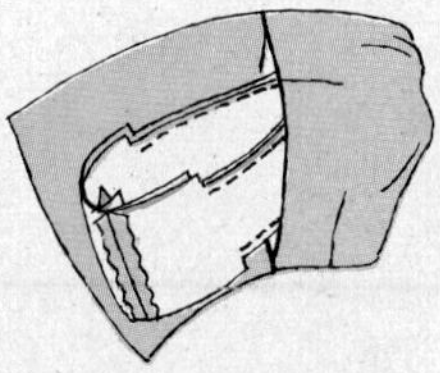

Pull the straps back to the right side and the back neck is finished. Then press it.

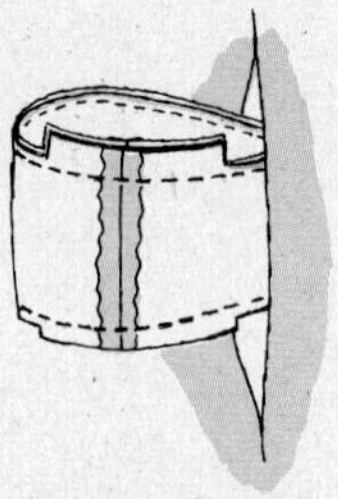

If the back halter is pleated, sew the pleats after it is finished.

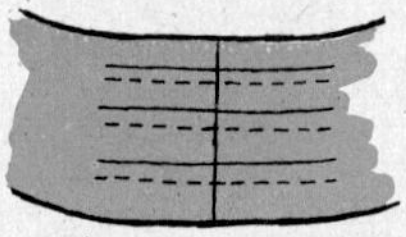

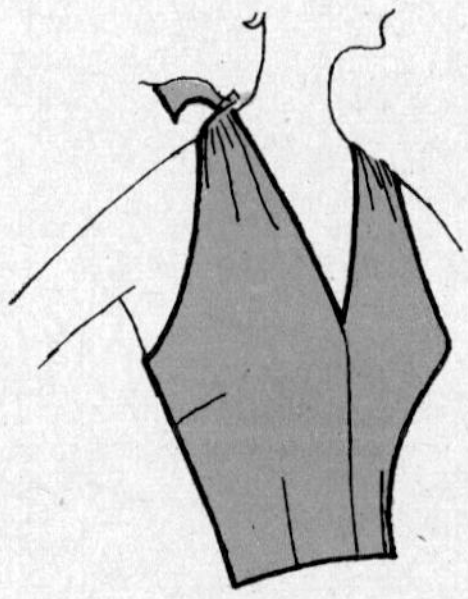

This same method is used to make the tie-back halter, except for the ends which are finished separately and not joined at back neck.

Machine buttonholes are best for play clothes and bathing suits, because they are fast and easy to do. If you prefer bound buttonholes, they can be made before the halter is lined.

Types of seams

There are only four types of seams that you should know how to use for making sportswear.

Flat feld seam

This seam is used on shirts, pajamas, shorts, and other tailored garments. Sew a plain seam. At the side seam, press the seam toward the back. Press the armhole seam toward the neck. After pressing, trim the under seam allowance. Then turn under and pin or baste the upper seam edge over the trimmed seam edge. Top-stitch close to this upper seam edge so the two rows of stitching look even. Press, and the seam is finished.

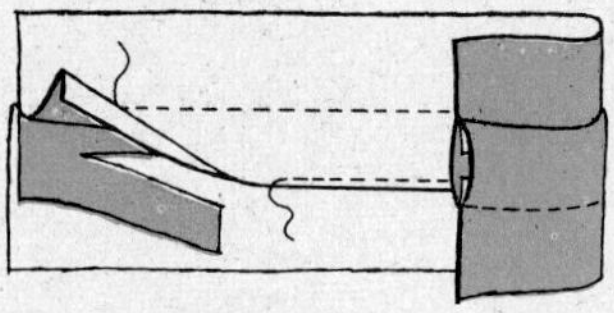

Edge- or top-stitching

Make a plain seam. Press both edges of the seam to one side. Stitch through all thicknesses of fabric on the right side along the seamline.

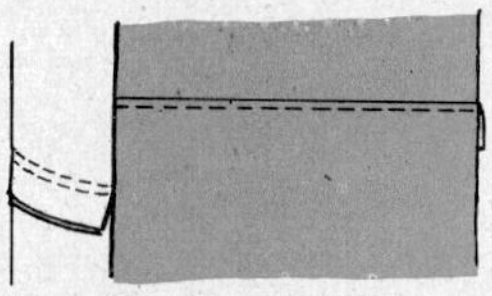

Hand-stitched feld seam

This seam is used on bulky fabrics where both sides of the seam must be finished, but the fabric is too thick to top-stitch. This seam is always made on the wrong side of the fabric.

Sew the right sides of the fabric together in a plain seam. Press to one side. Trim away the under seam. Turn under the raw edge of the upper seam and hem it in place by hand. Use it on bulky reversible fabrics.

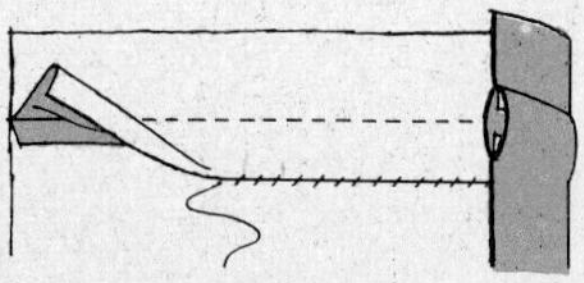

Double-top-stitched seam

Although this seam was not used in this chapter, it is often used for a decorative effect on many types of play clothes. Stitch the seam and press it open. Then, on the outside, stitch on both sides of the seam, close to the seamline. Press.

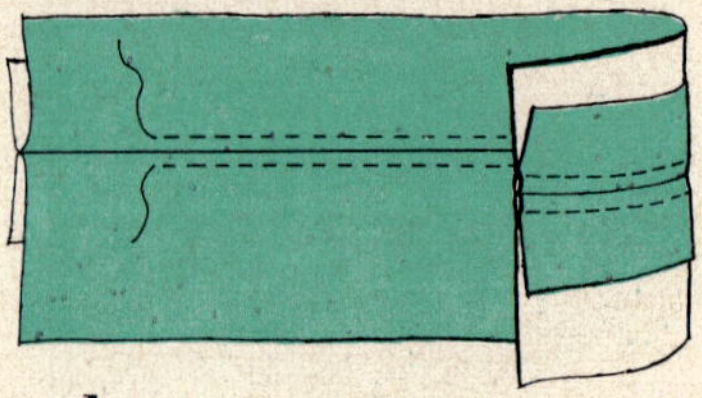

Bar tack

This tack is used at the end of the pocket, or to reinforce the end of the fly. Take a few vertical stitches to form a padding. Do a satin stitch as you work over padding and through fabric. A bar tack can be made on the zigzag machine with close satin stitch.

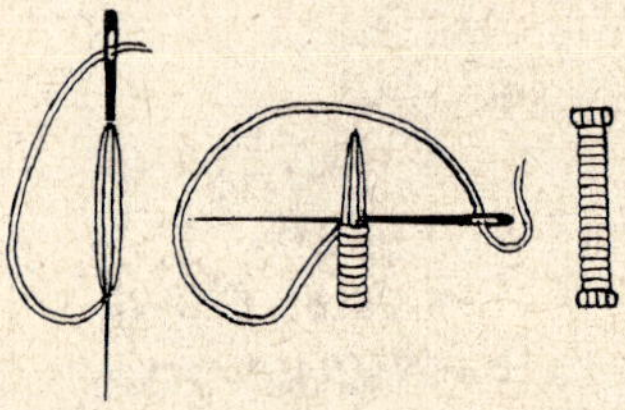

Hip pockets

This pocket is used on skirts, slacks, shorts. A version of it is also used on men's slacks. The ranch-type pocket is made on the same principle, only shaped a little differently.

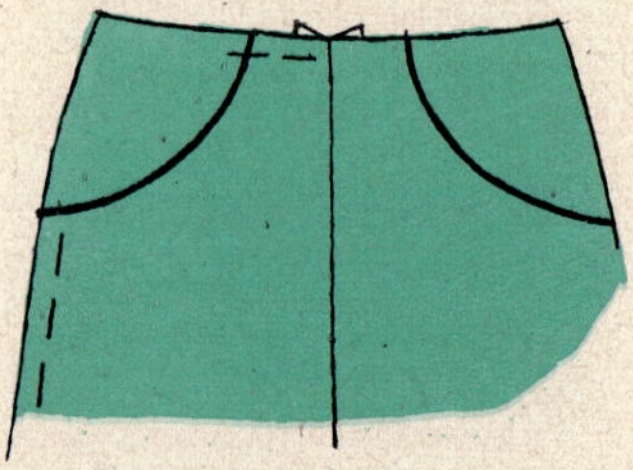

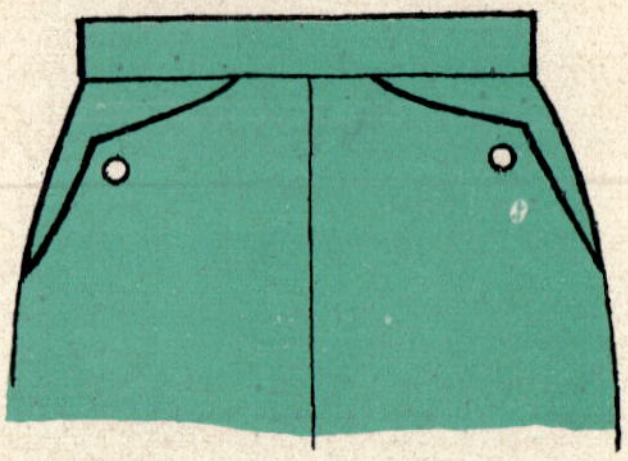

Pin the right side of the pocket facing to the right side of the garment front and stitch. Trim the seam

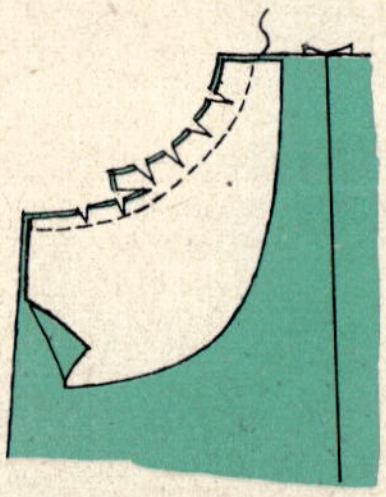

and clip the curve. Turn the pocket facing to the inside of the garment. Baste and press the edge. Pin the right side of the pocket to the right side of the facing and stitch all around the pocket. Stitch the top edge of

the pocket to the garment. Join the side seam of the garment, and the pocket is finished.

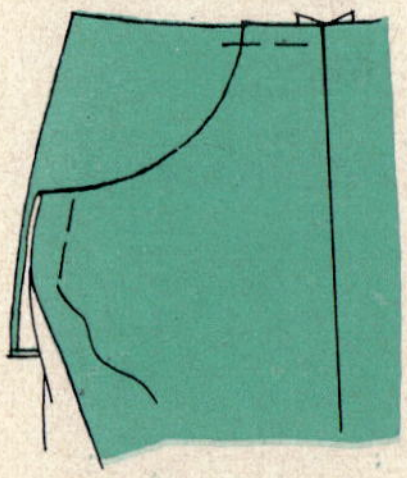

the top edge and down the placket opening (as shown below).

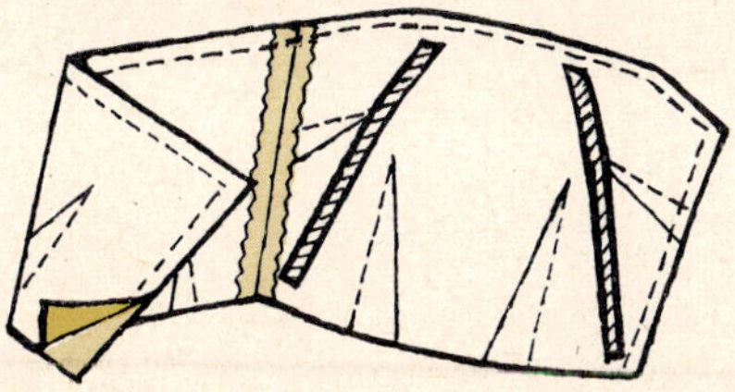

Trim the seam and turn it to the right side. Baste around this edge and press. Stitch the edges together at the waistline seam.

The slip will be joined to the dress only at the waistline. Since the bodice is loose-fitting and the slip is form-fitting, they cannot be sewed together at the zipper.

A zipper will be inserted in the slip for a smooth-fitting placket. The slip will be left free close to the side seam so the zipper can be applied.

After you sew the waistline edges together, clip into the seamline about 1½ inches in from the placket.

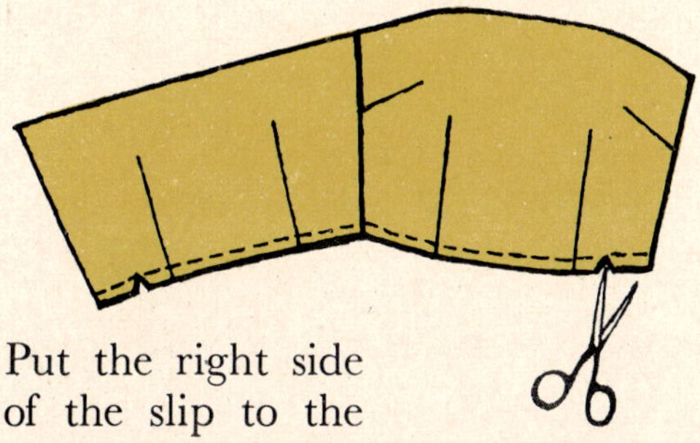

Put the right side of the slip to the wrong side of the dress top and pin them together. Turn back the lining at the clip marks so it's not caught to the bodice near the placket.

Stitch the pieces together all around.

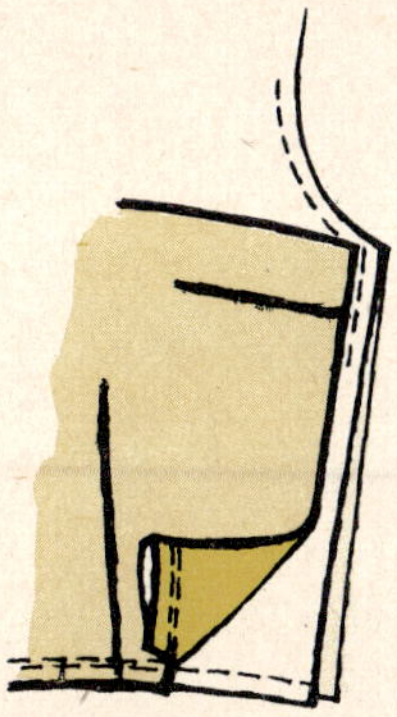

Now, sew the slip skirt together, leaving a placket opening on the left side.

Sew up the seams of the dress skirt. Shirr or pleat (whichever the pattern shows) the waistline fullness of the dress skirt to fit the slip skirt.

Clip the waistline seam of the slip skirt, as you did on the slip top. Clip 1½ inches from the placket. Sew skirt and slip together as far as the clip marks. Pin and stitch the skirt and waist together.

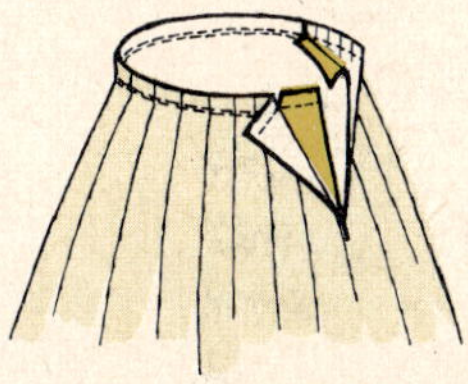

Catch all the four thicknesses of the waistline to clip mark. The dress seam is also clipped at this point, and dress and slip seams are sewed separately.

Then, sew a zipper in the dress and slip. The slip will fit snugly to the figure, while the bodice will have a softly, bloused look.

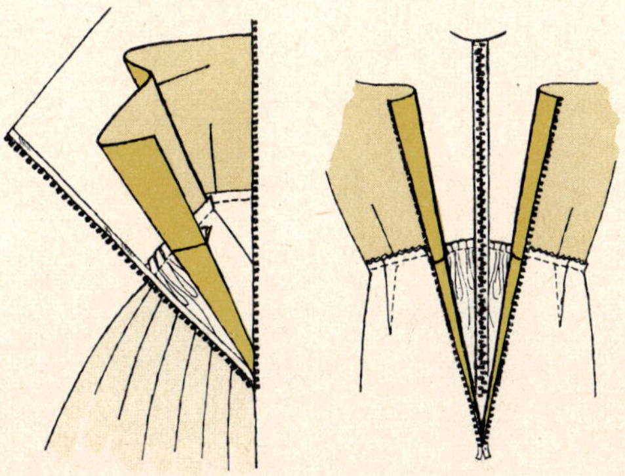

Style 2

This style (shown below) has a loose dolman sleeve that does not fit close to the body, so the under-bodice of the dress must be made separately.

The full skirt and slip can be cut from the same pattern. Cut the slip in taffeta or crepe, depending on how much flare you want in the skirt. Sew skirt and slip separately, leaving the left side open for a placket. Pin the right side of the slip to the inside of the skirt and stitch around the waistline and the placket opening.

Make the slip top double. Sew up the slip top and lining separately, leaving the placket side open. If you're not going to use shoulder straps (the dress will look prettier without straps), bone the lining as you did for Style 1. Pin the edges of the top and placket opening together.

At the waistline, clip in on the seam 1½ inches from the placket opening. Stitch around the top of the bodice, down the side placket opening, and to clip marks at the waistline of the bodice.

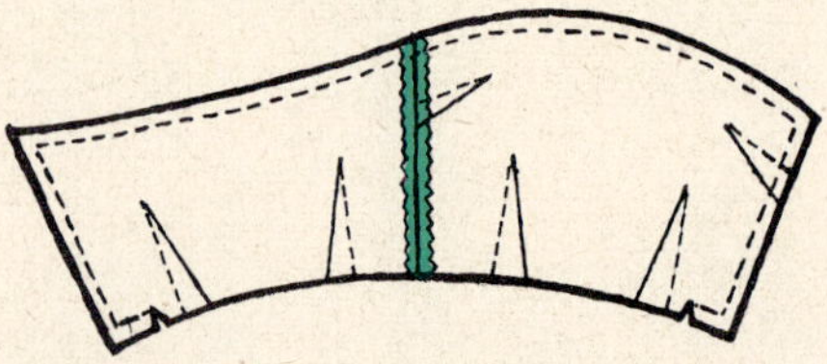

Trim the seam. Turn the slip top right side out, baste, and press all around. Stitch the waistline seams together at the seam allowance. Then you can sew hooks and eyes down the side placket opening of the slip top.

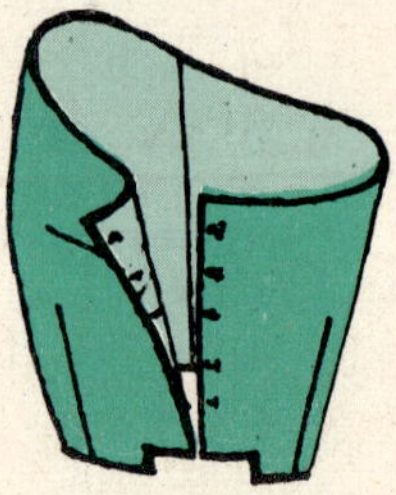

Next, make up the top of the dress. Remember to use fine French seams to keep the sheer look. Finish the neck and the sleeves with a fine bias binding. Leave the placket open on the left side of the top.

Pin the right side of the waist to the right side of the skirt at the waistline seam and stitch all around.

Now pin and stitch the right side of the slip top to the inside of the dress at the same waistline seam.

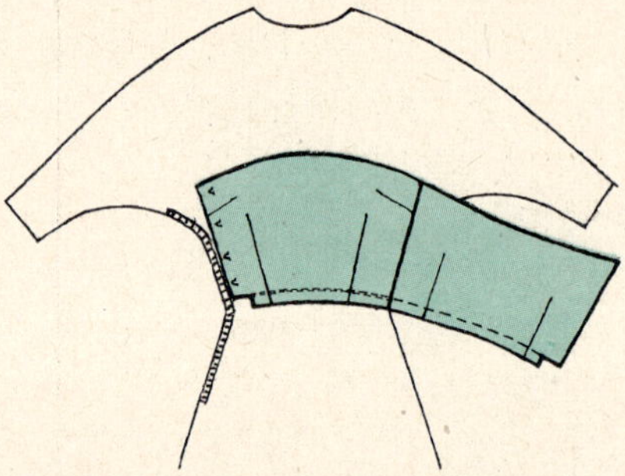

In this style the zipper is inserted in the skirt and blouse top only. The skirt slip is caught in as the zipper is sewed. The under-bodice is hooked together, and is left separate from the bodice.

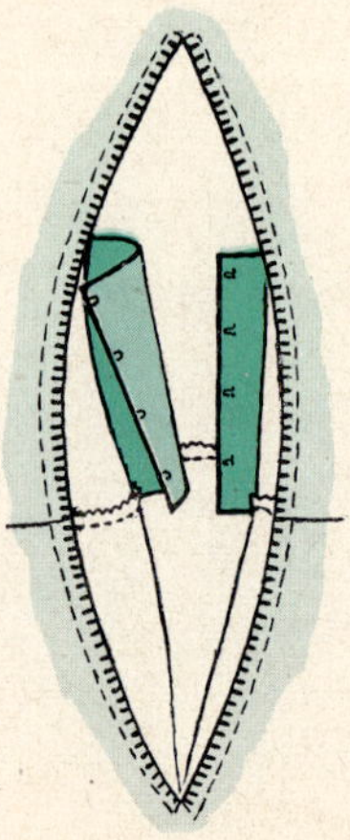

All dressy clothes should be finished with an inside gros-grain-ribbon belt. It holds the waistline firmly in place and it also prevents stretching.

Cut the grosgrain 3 inches longer than the waistline. Turn under a ½-

inch hem on one end and a 1-inch hem on the other. Sew the eye in the middle of the 1-inch hem and the

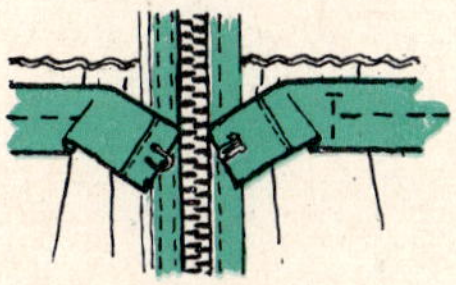

hook on the end of the other hem. Tack in the waistline so the hooked ends fall under the waistline opening.

Style 3

This style, with a fitted top and slip, is used most often and is made in all types of fabrics. Here, the slip is built into the bodice by sewing dart to dart and seam to seam, so the slip is a part of the actual construction of the dress. Until you have worn a dress made this way, you will have no idea how comfortable it is to put on, and zip up; you can be confident that it looks and feels just right. And, with this style, there are no hard-to-conceal shoulder straps and underpinnings for you to worry about.

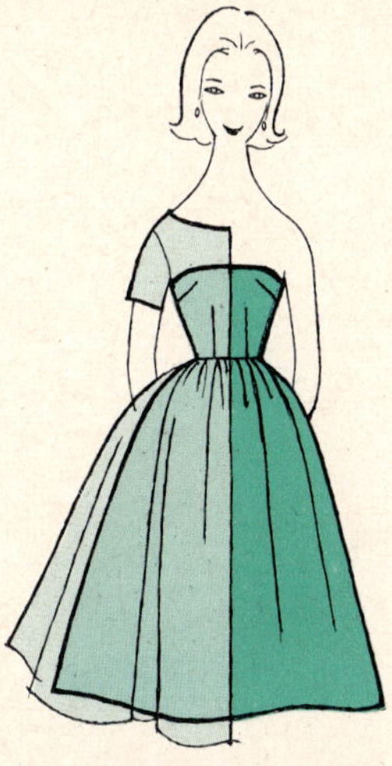

Slip

Since the slip will be sewed to the bodice, it should be cut from the bodice pattern. Pin the darts in the back and front bodice pattern, and hold it against a dress form or your own figure. Mark the shape of the slip on the pattern piece. Make a tissue tracing of this so you have a pattern

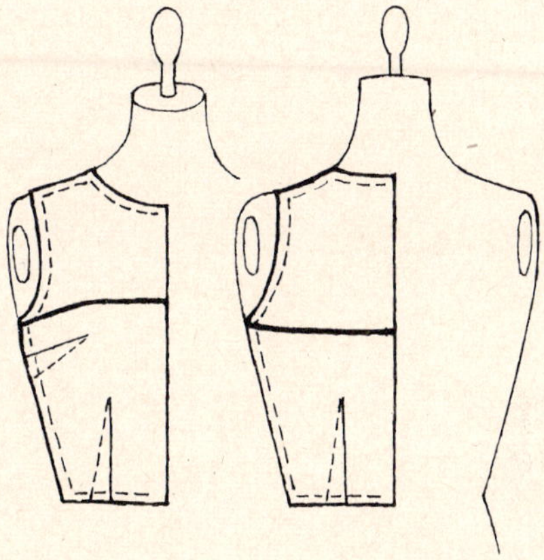

to work from. The fabric of your dress will influence the way you make

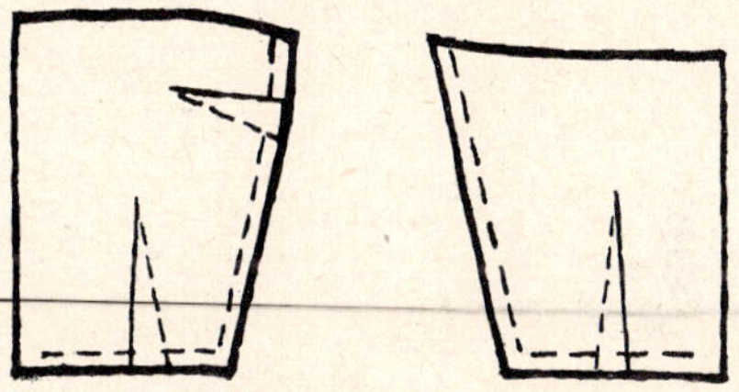

the slip. If the dress is a sheer, crisp fabric, such as organdy or organza, taffeta or a firm cotton will be best for the slip, since these materials have the crispness best suited for this type of upper fabric.

If you use a shiny taffeta, it should be muted, so that it will not show through the sheer fabric. When you cut the slip top, cut two layers of taffeta and one of organdy. Use the layer of organdy over the taffeta to mute the sheen; use the second layer of taffeta as a lining.

Place the organdy over one piece of the front and back slip top and sew together all around the edge.

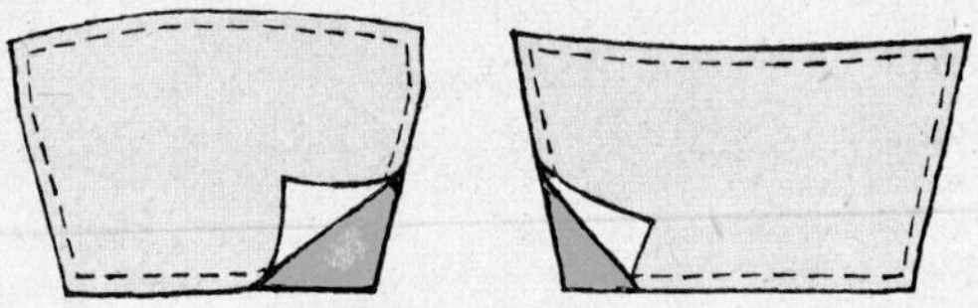

Pin the taffeta lining to the slip pieces along the top edges, with the layer of organdy between the two.

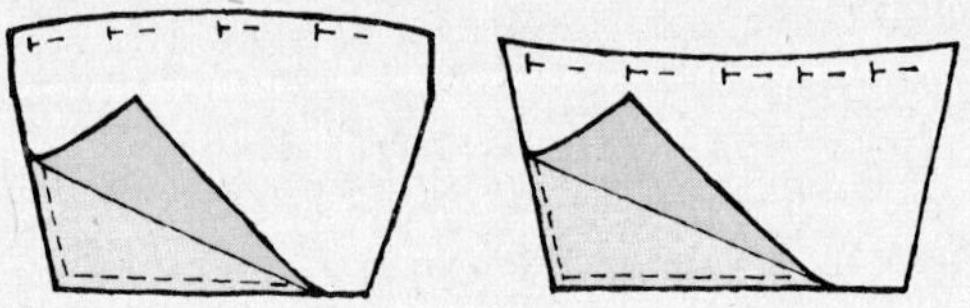

Sew this edge, trim the seam, turn right side out, baste, and press the edges. Holding all thicknesses together, sew all around the open edges.

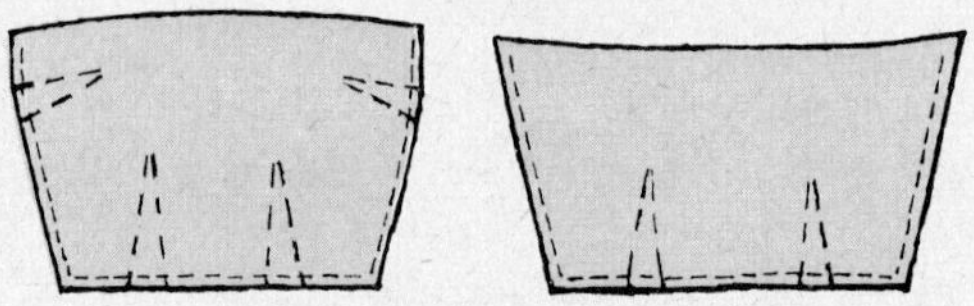

Your finished front and back slip bodice is made of three thicknesses of your fabric choice. Take the pattern piece and mark the darts on the taffeta side of each bodice piece. This final step completes the slip which is now ready to be sewed into the bodice.

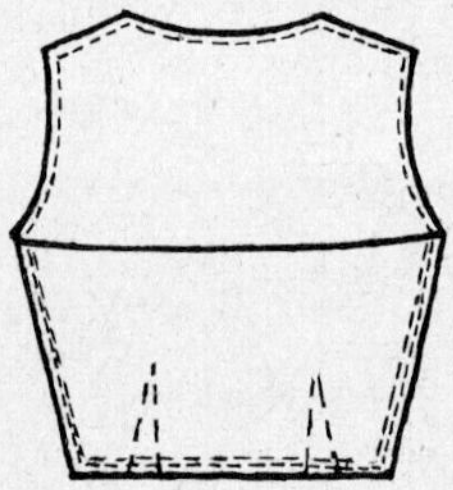

Bodice

Remove the pattern from the bodice pieces. It is not necessary to mark the darts, since the slip is already marked. Fit and pin the edges of the slip to this inside bodice and sew all around. To hold all thicknesses together, run a row of stitches through the center of each dart before you permanently sew in all the darts.

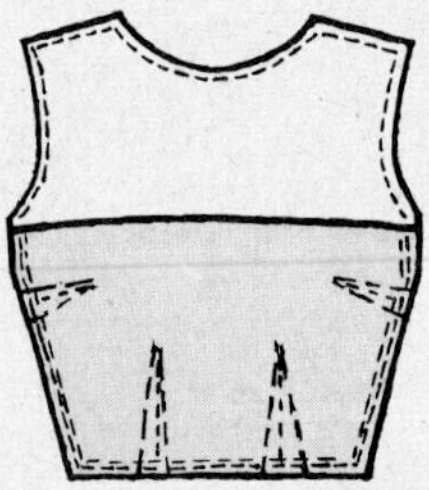

The waist darts are pressed toward the center of the bodice, the side darts pressed down. The bodice is made up as if it were a single thickness of fabric.

The slip top is sewed in and is then completely finished. No dart or seam will show through to the right side, which gives the dress a more expensive, custom-made look.

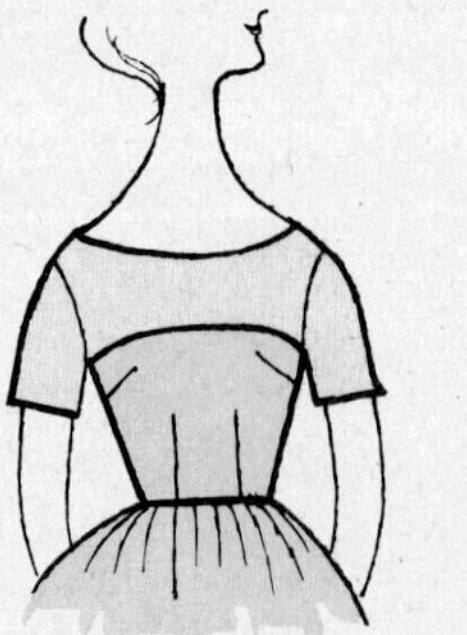

Skirt

The slip and skirt are cut from the same pattern but sewed separately. They can then be handled in one of two ways. Both layers can be sewed together and then shirred at the waist; or they can be shirred separately and joined together at the waist.

Check the appearance of the bodice and skirt together to decide which method you want to use. Usually, if just the skirt and slip are put together, the sheen so carefully muted on the bodice, will show in the skirt. Two layers of organdy over the taffeta will eliminate this problem.

Or, shirr a small part of the skirt and hold it over the slip to see if the color matches the bodice. If it does, then shirr the slip and skirt separately and sew them together before joining to the waist. This will make the skirt look beautifully bouffant.

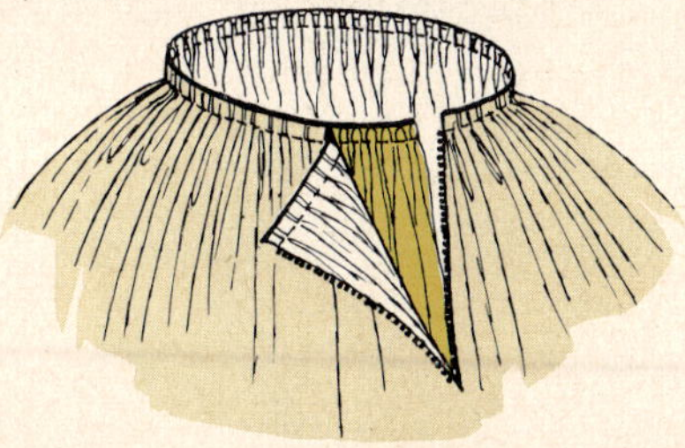

If this treatment would make the skirt too full to be becoming to you, then make the slip with a fitted top, but flared at the hem. Shirr only the upper skirt and join it to a slip that fits smoothly at the waistline.

In any case, there is no problem in putting in the zipper. The layers of the skirt and lining and also the lining and bodice are sewed together, so the zipper placket is applied just as it is in a regular style dress.

Style 4

This is a variation of Style 3. The bodice is in contrast with the rest of the dress. It can be a sheer dress with a lace camisole, or a lace dress with a contrasting underbodice. Make the lace bodice like the slip top in Style 3, with this exception. Make it with a layer of flesh-colored taffeta.

Over this place a layer of chiffon or organza in the same color as the lace, and then put the lace over the chiffon or organza.

The skirt presents no problems since it is the same color as the lace and is lined in a matching slip fabric. Make up the skirt and slip separately whether the dress has a full or slim skirt. For a full skirt, sew the slip to the waistline—then shirr or pleat it. Join bodice and skirt as if you have only one layer of fabric. Put in the zipper as on any other type of dress.

Style 5

This dress style has a neck and shoulder line that are very flattering, but hard to keep in place. It requires a bit of engineering, but the final results are well worth the trouble.

Regardless of the fabric, the lining or slip top is usually made to fit up to the top of the dress, rather than cut like a low slip top. An exception is the lace dress with a finished edge of lace outlining the neck and shoulders. If the upper fabric is as soft as crepe, the slip should be cut in an equally soft lining fabric.

Taffeta would be better for the slip facing. However, when a heavier dress fabric is used, both slip and lining can be cut from taffeta.

Use the bodice pattern to cut the slip and its lining. Carefully pin the wrong side of the back and front bodice pieces to the right side of the slip top and stitch all around close to the seam edge. Mark the darts on the

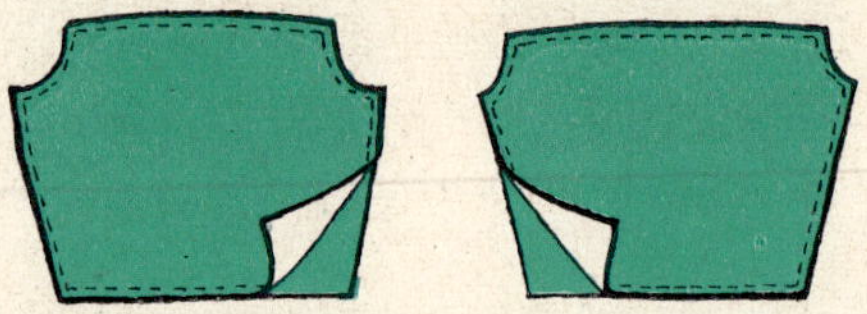

wrong side of the slip. Run a stitch through the center of the dart, holding both thicknesses of fabric together. Pin and sew in all the darts.

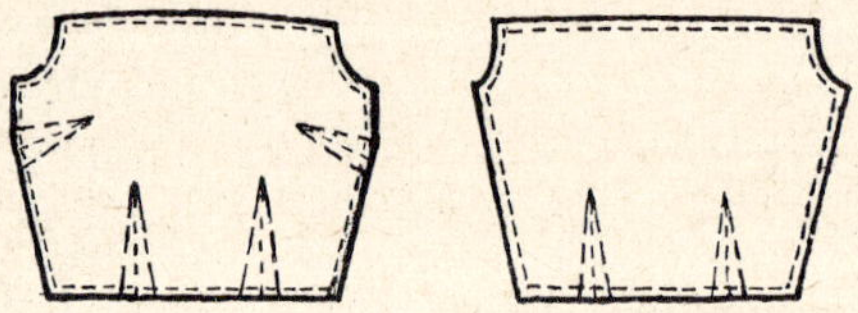

Sew up all the seams, except those on the left side, where you will leave a placket opening. Press carefully.

Now sew up the lining for the slip top. Sew in all darts and seams, leaving a placket opening. Press all darts and seams, and you are ready to put the boning in the slip.

More boning is needed in this style to hold up the top of the dress. In the front, sew the boning from the top point of the armhole down the side of the bust to the waistline. The darts just under the bust are also boned.

In the back, the boning is sewed to the darts, and is also stitched from the top of the bodice to the waistline just in slightly from the side seam.

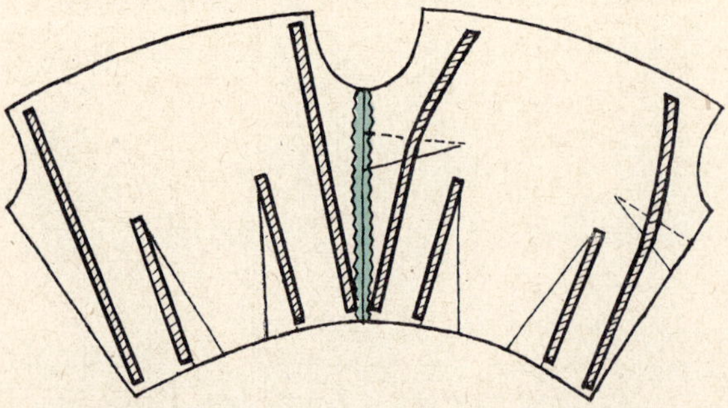

Pin the boned side of the slip lining to

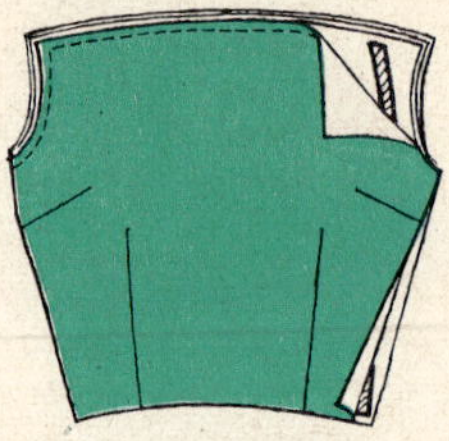

the wrong side of the bodice and stitch the top edges of the neck and armholes together. Tack the waistlines together by hand. If the dress has sleeves, finish the tops of them, except where they sew into the armholes. Next, carefully pin and sew the sleeves at the underarm.

To finish the neck edge, cut facings about 3 inches wide from the dress fabric or taffeta. If there is no pattern piece for the facings, cut them from the top of the bodice pattern.

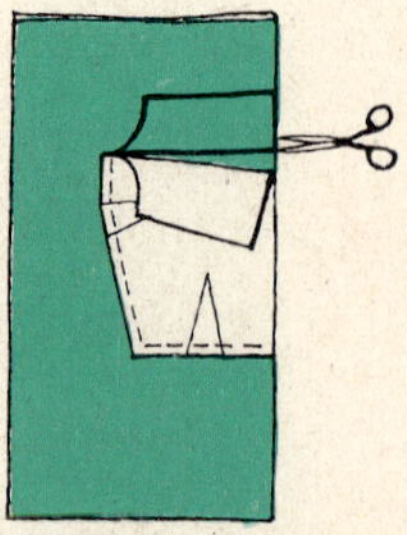

Turn back the seam on the outside edge of the back and front facing. Pin the right side of the facing to the right side of the neck. Also pin along the inside seam of the armhole. Then stitch the facings in place.

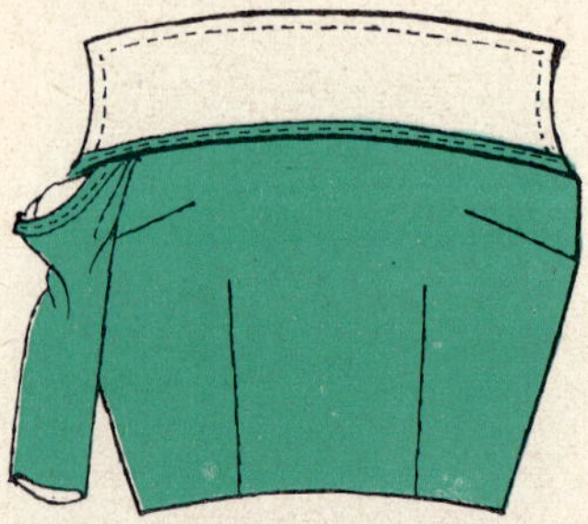

Trim the seam and turn to the inside. Baste and press the neck edge. Tack the facing to the inside. To keep this type of sleeve in position, the only solution, barring adhesive tape, is strong, narrow elastic. Pin a piece of elastic to the bodice at the point where each sleeve is joined and stretch it along the edge of the sleeve to the back bodice. Pin the elastic so that it feels comfortably snug and hugs the arm or shoulder.

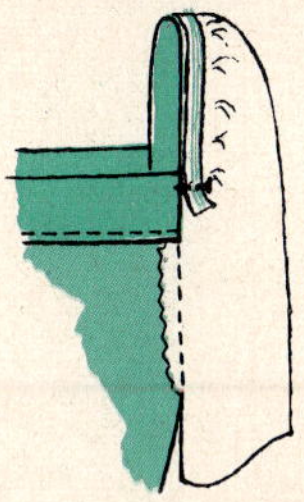

Measure the length of the elastic and cut another piece the same length for the other arm. Sew the ends of the elastic to the inside of the back and front bodice. Use a catch-stitch along the inside of each sleeve; the thread will make a casing through which the elastic can slide. Don't catch the elastic in the stitching.

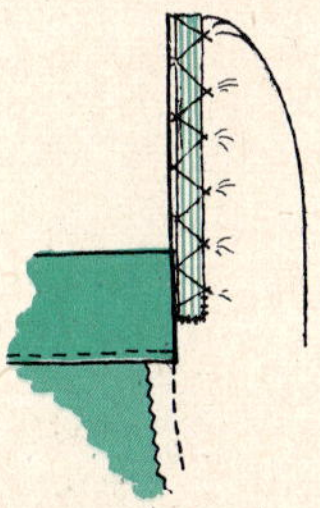

When the dress is off, the elastic will pucker because it has intentionally been made tighter than the sleeve. When you put the dress on, however, the elastic stretches inside the sleeve and holds it in place.

There are always many variations of every style. Here are two variations that are almost as popular as Style 5. And they differ from it just enough to be confusing to the average home sewer.

Lace top

The first variation is the lace type mentioned previously. This style is made with a finished edge of lace used at the neck and shoulders. The top line of the slip follows the neckline of the dress but is about 1 inch lower. This is so that the edging will show to

the best advantage against the skin. It follows Style 5 to the point where the slip top is ready to be faced.

Then pin the right side of the facing to the right side of the slip along the top edge and stitch. Trim the seam, turn to the inside, baste, and press. Then pin the two thicknesses together at the armhole and stitch. Fit the lining into the lace bodice and stitch at the armhole. Stitch the unlined sleeves into the armhole. Tack the armhole seam to the facing by hand. Apply the elastic to the sleeve top as you do for Style 5, but this time use flesh-colored elastic so it won't show through the lace. The inside lining is turned under and sewed by hand over the waistline seam.

Draped collar top

The second variation of this style is the same basic dress, with a softly draped collar that covers the shoulders much like a sleeve.

This collar is draped over the arm rather than set into the armhole. The armhole, therefore, must be finished in a different manner than the other.

Follow the original instructions and sew the bodice to the slip top. Before sewing the lining, finish the

drape collar piece where it fits over the arm and along the lower edge. Pin to the bodice. Try it on to be sure it hasn't stretched. It should comfortably hug the shoulder, should stay in place, at least reasonably well. Clip the neck seam at the points where drape collar piece sews to the dress.

The wrong side of the collar is pinned to the right side of the top edge of the dress and stitched in place.

Let the collar drop down over the bodice and out of the way. Put the right side of the lining to the right side of the dress. Pin the top edge and also around the armhole. Stitch all around. Trim the seam, clip all around the armhole seam, turn to inside, baste, and press. Use elastic in the shoulder drape as in the sleeves.

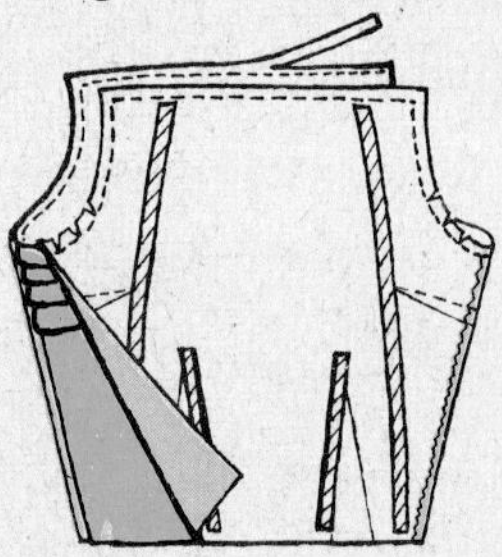

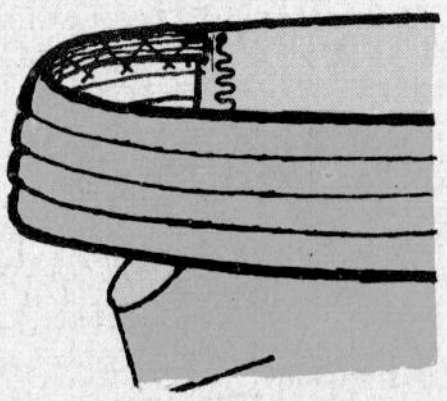

You will need to add one special bit of boning to this top. Use a small zigzag stay for the side of the armhole. It is a fine wire, bent so that it looks like a zigzag line. Whip the stay firmly into place along the seam allowance line of the armhole.

Sew all the thicknesses of the bodice together at the waistline and then join whatever style skirt you choose to make to the completed top.

Lace-top dresses

Often the bodice of a dress is cut from an allover lace that has no particular design or pattern.

In this case, it is better to use the lace as if it were a regular fabric. In other words, finish off both neck and sleeve edges with a regular facing. Don't use the edge of this type of allover lace as a finish.

Lace can be used over a matching or contrasting color. If a contrasting color is used, try the lace over it to test the effect. If it looks too bright and harsh, you can mute the lace slightly by placing a piece of matching net between the lace and the slip. It will reduce the sheen.

When you cut the dress, cut a layer of lace, a layer of net, and the lining, all from the bodice pattern. Sew the three layers together, and make the dress as if you were working with just one layer of fabric.

The facings can be cut from either the lining or the net to keep the finishes smooth and flat. Make up the dress as you would any other fabric.

Strapless tops

The strapless top is used with many styles of clothes, even for sports clothes, but it is especially popular for formal dress.

The strapless top can be simple or elegant in style, but the construction is the same.

This style top must be especially well-supported so it is comfortable to wear. The trick in keeping the strapless dress in place is to make a corselet and fit it into the bodice. The dress pattern usually includes a pattern, from which you can make the corselet.

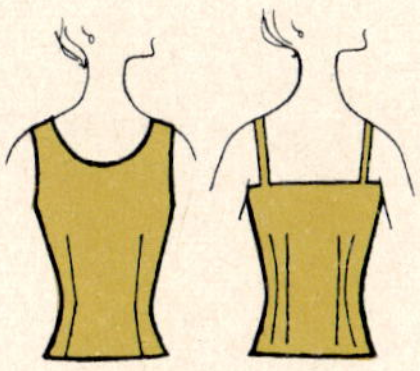

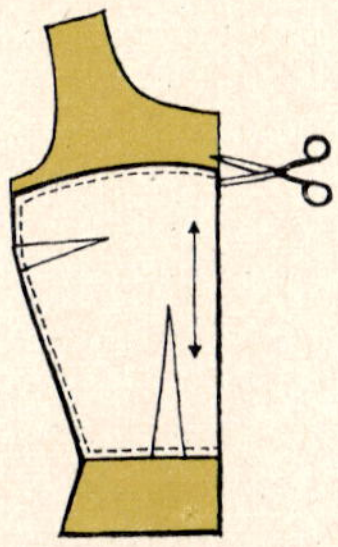

If the pattern has no lining, however, you can use any pattern that has a fitted top.

If the top of the bodice pattern is not the same shape as the top of your strapless dress, reshape it from the original dress pattern. Cut the bodice top double so it can be lined. Also cut it to extend about 4 inches below the waist. Assemble the top, sewing in all the darts. Baste the side seams together for a fitting. If the fabric that you are using marks easily, it is a good idea to baste in the darts.

Even though you make adjustments on the top from your alteration muslin, it will usually need another fitting. The pattern may allow more ease than you need, so check carefully.

The top must be very tight and closely fitted to your body if it is to stay in place. When the bodice is fitted, mark adjustments carefully in the lining and corselet. Finish sewing the dress top and the lining.

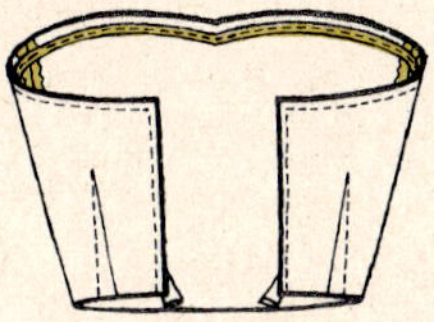

Next, pin the right side of the lining to the right side of the bodice and sew it around the top and down the back opening. Use a tape in the top seam to ease it in a little. This gives a softer and more rounded look to the bustline. Trim all around, turn to the inside, baste, and press.

If your skirt's completed, join it to the top. Pin the right side of the waist to right side of skirt and sew them together at the waistline. Turn the seam up into the waist. Press. Pin the loose edge of the lining over the waistline seam and slip-stitch.

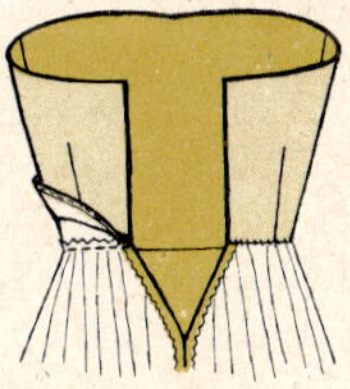

For details on various types of skirts you can make, see the "Skirts" section later in this chapter.

Make the alterations on the corselet that were made on the dress. Sew up the corselet, and it's ready to be boned. On the front, sew boning from the side of the bustline to the side waistline seam. It is also boned under the bustline. Back waist darts are boned, with additional boning used just back of the side seams.

Sew the right side of the facing to the right side of the corselet. Trim the seam, turn the facing to the inside, press and tack in place.

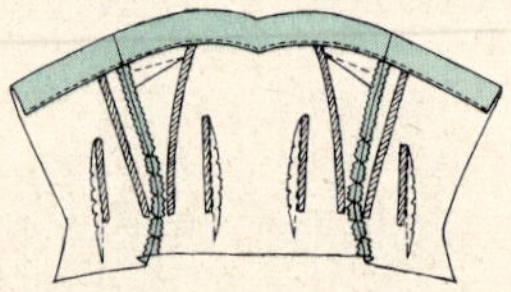

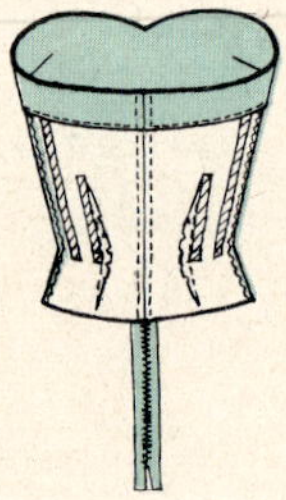

Sew the zipper in the back of the corselet before the corselet is sewed to the dress. The zipper will be longer than the corselet, since the same zipper will finish the back dress opening. Sew the zipper in just as you do for the neck application. Pin the top edge of the corselet ¼ inch in from the top of the dress, boned side against the inside of the dress. Tack in place all around. Pin the corselet to the dress waistline. Be careful to get it correctly placed. Then tack it by hand.

Inserting zippers by hand

Follow the same technique as used in sewing the zipper by machine. Use a back-stitch, as shown in Chapter 7.

Take a small stitch and bring the needle slightly ahead of that first stitch. Take a back-stitch, putting the needle in at the end of the preceding stitch. Continue this way until zipper is in place.

Next, carefully pin the back dress opening in place along the back opening of the zipper in the corselet. Sew the back of the dress by hand along the original stitching line of the zipper. This puts the strain of the opening on the corselet so the back of the dress stays smoothly and firmly together without wrinkling. Also sew by hand the lower part of the dress opening to the extended zipper.

Next, make a grosgrain ribbon belt to sew on the inside waistline of the dress. The belt will hook together at the back under the zipper.

Your dress will fit correctly, stay in place, and will be both beautiful and comfortable to wear.

The dress with a slight sleeve can also be made with a corselet top for a good fit. Treat the sleeves as you do on the less formal top.

It is always a problem to hang this dress because the top is likely to be crushed out of shape if it is hung just from the waistline. To solve the problem, cut 2 pieces of seam binding 1½ yards long. Fold the pieces in half on the length and press. Then stitch the edges of the seam binding, and make two long loops. Stitch the ends of each loop on the inside of the dress at the waistline side seam. Tack the tape to the inside facing at the top of the bodice, about 4 inches in from the underarm seam. The loops can be hung over a hanger, and the dress will hang top side up and will retain its shape.

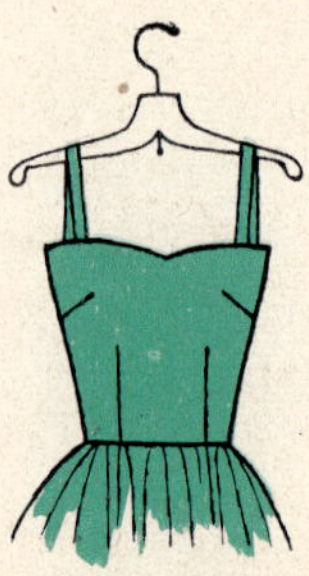

Skirts

The fun of sewing dressy clothes is that you can make them so individual and original. First, there are many beautiful fabrics to choose from, with a wide selection of colors and color combinations, and there's the creative fun of combining different types of fabrics and textures.

Most exciting of all, you can combine different styles of tops and skirts that are becoming to you. Make them up as separates, which are wonderful for at-home and evening wear, or make a one-piece dress, combining the features you like.

The skirts described here will show you how to achieve certain special effects. You can pick your favorite to combine with a lovely top, or simply to make as a skirt.

Heavy, full, shirred skirt

This skirt is usually made from heavy, rich fabrics that need no trimming or detail to make them beautiful. Fabrics like moire, slipper satin, brocades, taffetas, bengalines, ottomans, or Lyons velvet that have body, weight, and a wonderful texture are ideal for this skirt. It is made of straight lengths sewed together and shirred to give fullness.

These skirts look wonderful in bright colors, and can be worn with beautiful chiffon shirts, jersey tops or even with cashmere sweaters for a stylish, high-fashion look.

These skirts are too bulky to shirr on the machine, because the stitch is not long enough to ease this amount of bulk into a normal waistline size.

There is a professional trick to shirring these skirts. Shirr by hand. Measure the waistline size and divide it by the number of panels in the skirt. For example, if the skirt has four panels, and the waistline size is 26 inches, you would shirr each skirt panel to 6¼ inches.

Sew up the panels of the skirt, but leave a seam opening for the placket. This can be either on the left side or down the back of the skirt.

You'll want to line the skirt in soft China silk, taffeta, or some other fine, thin fabric for added quality.

As a rule, the hems of these skirts are left soft and only lightly pressed. Turn the amount of hem desired in the skirt. Turn the edge under ¼ inch and press. Then cut the lining the finished length of the skirt. Bring the wrong side of the lining to the wrong side of the skirt and stitch around the top edge of the skirt.

Fold the skirt hem over the lower edge of the lining and slip-stitch the hem to just the lining. Press the hem so lightly that the edge is softly rolled rather than sharply creased. Now you're ready to do the shirring by hand on this dressy skirt.

Gathering by hand

Knot the thread. Use a running stitch and take stitches that are the same length on both sides of the fabric. Be sure to catch the lining in this stitching. Stitch at least two rows.

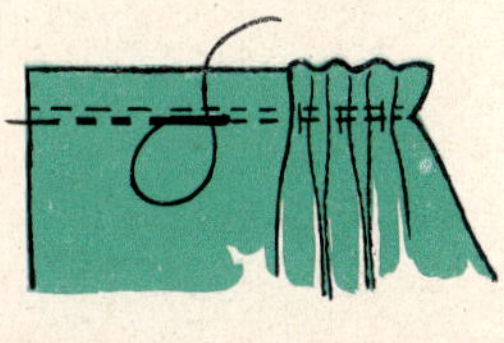

Draw the fabric together to form even

gathers. Shirr to the amount figured for each panel. Finish the end of a panel with a back-stitch. Then shirr the next panel in the same way. Shirr one panel at a time since this is easier to handle and to size. When it is finished, the skirt can be sewed to a bodice, or a waistband can be applied. If you use a waist-band, put the zipper in the skirt be-fore attaching the waistband.

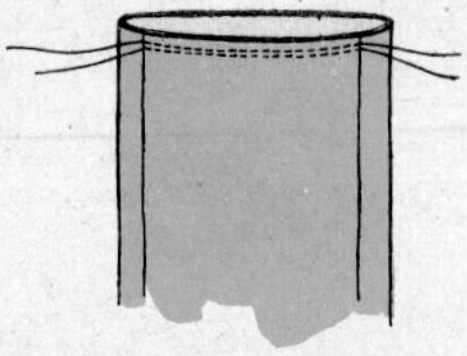

Gauging

Gauging is another form of shirring which has two distinct advantages.

It is a method of shirring a great amount of fabric into a small space, which is good on very bulky fabrics.

It also gives a decorative effect. Take long stitches on the right side of the fabric and short ones on the wrong side. Make at least three rows, and be sure the stitches in each row are identical—a long stitch under a long stitch, a short stitch under a short one. The fullness will lie in narrow folds, and the top of the skirt will have a flat and smooth appearance.

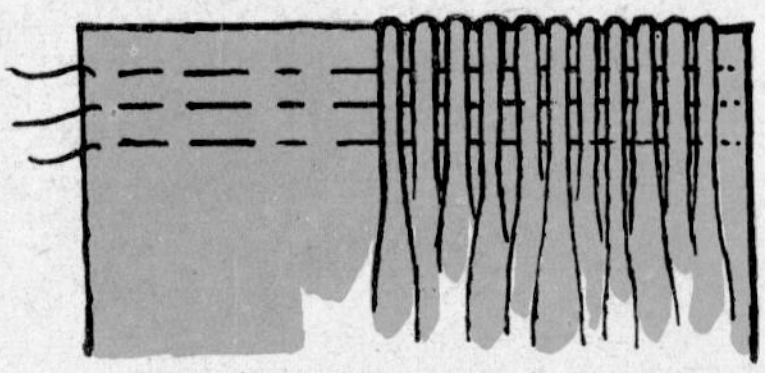

Mounted skirts

This skirt has a distinctive shape, achieved by mounting it over an interlining. It can be a full skirt, bell skirt, barrel skirt—or who knows what new shape still to be designed.

Bell skirt

This skirt is small at the waist and actually bells out toward the hem so it doesn't fit close to the hip.

To retain this shape, the fabric must be very stiff or be mounted on another fabric that has the proper texture. Best lining to use for this skirt is non-woven interfacing which won't lose its crispness, won't collapse after wearing or dry cleaning.

This skirt is either gored or darted to achieve the bell shape. Cut the skirt pieces from the pattern. Cut them again from a firm, non-woven interfacing. Lay the wrong side of each piece over the interfacing and pin together just outside the seam allowance line. Stitch all around the pieces except at the hem.

Now sew up the skirt as if it were just one fabric. Leave the interfacing in the hem. Turn up the hem the desired amount, and press lightly. The interfacing is crease-resistant so the hem will not be too sharply defined. Sew a seam binding to the edge of the hem and slip-stitch to the interfacing.

No mark shows on the right side. Again, join the skirt to a bodice, or make it as a separate skirt.

Barrel skirt

This style is sometimes called a "lantern" skirt. This skirt fits the waist, bells out from the waist to a lot of fullness at the hip, and then shapes in toward the hem.

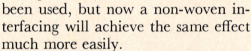

Obviously, this skirt requires support to keep its shape. In the past, a hoop would have been used, but now a non-woven interfacing will achieve the same effect much more easily.

Cut and mount the skirt pieces individually as you do for the bell skirt. The barrel skirt, however, has a facing instead of a hem, so the non-woven interfacing can also be stitched across the bottom of the skirt.

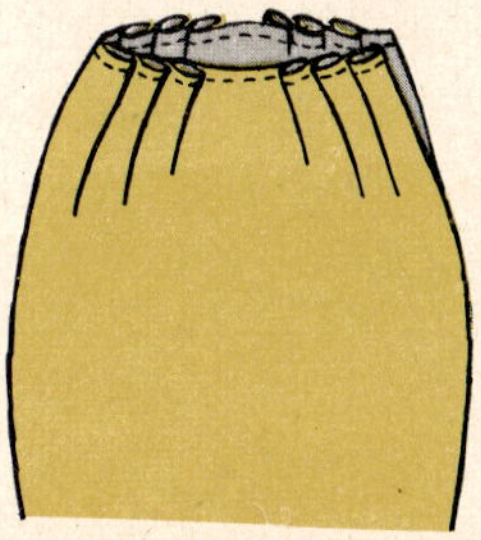

Sew all the skirt pieces together. At the waistline, fold the interfacing into the pleats with the upper fabric.

Run a machine-stitch around the waist to hold the pleats in place.

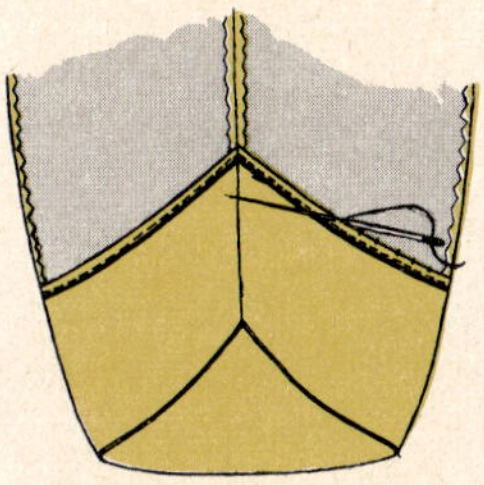

Sew right side of facing to right side of skirt. Turn to the inside, bringing the facing in slightly beyond the seamline. Baste and press the facing this way. Sew a seam binding to the inside edge of the facing. Then slipstitch it to the interfacing.

Mounting sheers and laces

Skirts of such soft fabrics can be made into styles usually reserved for heavier fabrics if an interfacing is used to give a new texture to the upper fabric. Since the upper fabric is sheer, it must be lined in an opaque fabric so the non-woven interfacing underneath will not show through.

The lining can be of taffeta or any firm fabric in the same color as the upper material. If the lining has a sheen, you may decide to use a second layer of the sheer to mute it.

Cut all four layers of the skirt from the same pattern. Sew each of the four skirts up separately. Join all the layers of the skirt at the waistline and stitch them together.

Now pleat or shirr the top of the skirt, depending on the style. Because each layer hangs separately, the skirt retains the soft texture of the upper fabric and still has the bouffant look of a heavier fabric.

If the skirts are in straight lengths, make the hems as follows: Since the top layer is sheer, turn a deep hem, from 8 to 12 inches on chiffon; the second layer needs only a fine rolled hem which can be made by hand or

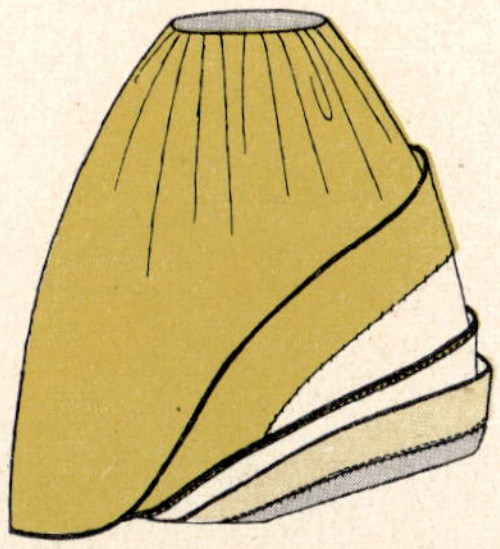

machine; turn up a deep hem in the lining and catch it to the interfacing which has been cut off at the finished length. The skirt will hang nicely, have a free and graceful sweep.

If the skirt is made of a lace flounce, let the edge of the lace serve as the finish on the upper skirt.

Soft, full, shirred skirt

Whether it is shirred or shaped, the effect of this skirt should be light and airy. Although this skirt is often more full than a mounted one, and as a rule, has much more fabric in it, there is no feeling of bulk.

Let's take the shaped skirt first. Here are some of the many fabrics from which it can be made.

Net and organza

The texture of these two fabrics reacts in the same way, and handling techniques are similar. In the shaped skirt, the fullness flares from the fitted waist, so there is no worry about color shading at the waistline as there is with the full, shirred skirt.

In making these skirts, it's important to be lavish with fabric. Always use at least two layers of the upper fabric in the skirt—three or four layers of net or organza are even better.

Organza and net are so transparent that it takes several layers to make a skirt sheer and wafty, with no suggestion of a slip showing through.

You can make the slip of a fine, crisp fabric like taffeta. It should always be faced with horsehair so it billows at the hem without being stiff. (See the section in this chapter on "Horsehair facing.")

Cut all the skirt layers and slip from the same pattern. Sew each layer of the skirt individually. They are joined only at the waistline and along the zipper. Pin all the layers of the skirt together and stitch. Next, baste the skirt to the bodice or waistband.

Try on the skirt so the hem can be marked. If the dress is to be full-length, stand on something to raise you at least a foot from the floor so you can mark the hem with a skirt-marker. Mark all long skirts this way.

You will find the chalk-squirting marker is much faster. Hold the marker against the top layer of fabric. As you squirt the chalk, it penetrates all the layers of the sheer fabric, easily marking all of the lengths at once.

On net, simply cut off the skirt at the finished length. It needs no other finish. For organza, however, cut the hems about ½ inch longer than the finished length. You can hand-roll all the layers, if you like, but this is a lot of work, so usually only the top layer of fabric is hand-rolled. The under layers of the skirt can be machine-rolled.

Machine-rolling

This is a good finish for all sheers. Turn under the edge of the skirt a little below the finished line, and sew along the edge by machine. Trim

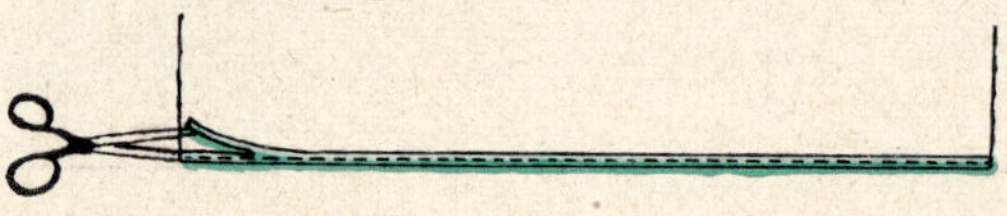

away the raw edge as close to the stitching as you can. (Use small embroidery scissors.) Turn the fine edge of stitching to the wrong side and stitch again on the original stitching very close to the edge. When completed, the finished machine-rolled edge looks like a fine thread line.

Horsehair facing

Horsehair comes in many different widths, is transparent and on the bias. It can be eased and shaped readily. If it is not available in the color of your dress, dye it to match.

One side of the horsehair has a heavy thread woven along the edge. This thread can be used as a shirring thread if the horsehair is to be

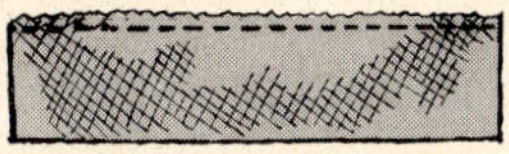

shaped. If the skirt is cut in straight lengths, sew this edge to the hem, with the thread concealed in the fold, or pull out the thread.

Pin horsehair to the right side of the dress with both of the edges even. Sew the two together 1/4 inch in from the edge. Turn the horsehair

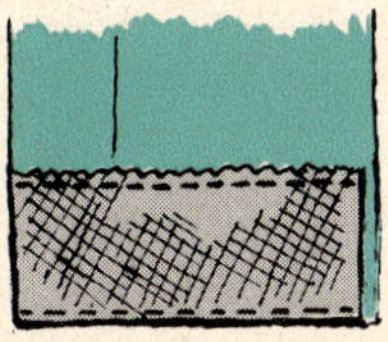

to the inside. The fabric rolls over the edge of the horsehair so 1/4 inch of the fabric shows along the inside edge of the hem. Ease the horsehair to shape it to the inside of the skirt.

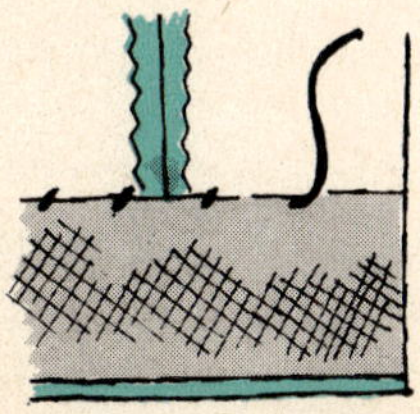

Then slip-stitch the horsehair in place.

Chiffon skirt

If you want your skirt to flare at the bottom, put the chiffon over a crisp fabric, and face the fabric in horsehair. If the skirt is to hang softly with the fullness clinging to the body, cut the slip of a soft fabric, from the same pattern as the upper skirt. Make a narrow self-hem in the slip. Although the skirt hangs close to the body, it will still have a lovely, flowing movement as you walk.

If you use a straight, slim slip under the chiffon, even though the top skirts are full, they will hang close at the hem, with just a suggestion of fullness when you walk.

Lace skirt

The shaped skirt of lace can have several net layers over an under layer of crepe or of taffeta. Face the lace with horsehair so the skirt hem stands away, and the net skirts underneath look fuller, and frothier.

Finishing the shirred skirt

The hems are finished like those on other soft, full skirts. The differences are in the pleating or shirring at the waistline of the skirt.

If it is to be joined to a bodice made from the same sheer, it is important that the skirt look the same color where it joins. If the bodice has been mounted over a layer of sheer and a lining, the skirt should be mounted over the same number of layers before it is shirred or pleated. Any other treatment could make the skirt look darker than the bodice.

Sheath skirt

This skirt should be lined with a soft, thin fabric, just as the daytime sheath dress is lined with similar fabric.

All skirts are a variation of those described. Learn how and why certain linings and interlinings are used, so you will always know how to achieve exactly the effect you want.

Sunburst pleating

This pleating must be done commercially. You'll need the same amount of fabric as for a circular skirt.

Cut it into two lengths. The fabric should be 39- to 44-inch width for a daytime-length skirt. Be sure that the fabric is on the straight grain.

When the fabric is returned from the pleater, spread it out flat to mark for the waistline. The waistline can be eased in so that the skirt will look a little fuller and softer.

Lay the skirt pattern over the pleating and mark for the waistline. Measure from this mark to the edge of the skirt at the selvage, and at the center front. If there is enough length

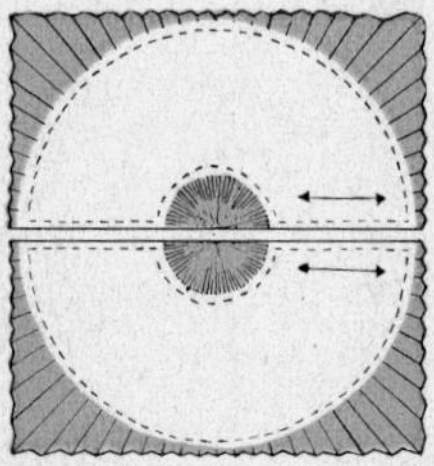

to the skirt, cut a bigger waistline circle, allow for a hem and for a seam allowance at the waistline. Run two rows of shirring to ease in the waistline. Sew up the side seams, leaving the left side open for the zipper. Try to sew along the crease line of the pleat so the

sides will hang straight down.

Sew on waistband and let the skirt hang for at least 24 hours. Then try skirt, and mark for the hem. Finish the skirt with a hand-rolled hem, or sew a seam binding to the edge, press back, and slip-stitch.

Accordion pleating

These pleats are made on the straight of the goods, and stand out like an accordion. In other words, they are not flat side pleats. This type of pleating can only be done commercially. Check with the pleater to be sure he makes this type of pleating, and to find out how much fabric you will need to make this type of skirt.

Sleeves

Sleeves in dressy clothes are much the same as in other types of dresses. Two sleeve finishes—the full sleeve with the elastic casing, and the long sleeve with the loop closing at the wrist—are often used for these fashions. The loop closing at the wrist is often used on wedding dresses.

Sleeve with elastic

Finish the lower edge of this sleeve with a hem or facing wide enough to take the elastic. Turn under ¼ inch on the edge of the sleeve and press.

Fabrics for evening wear

Use appliques to trim special dresses

Glamour trims add beauty

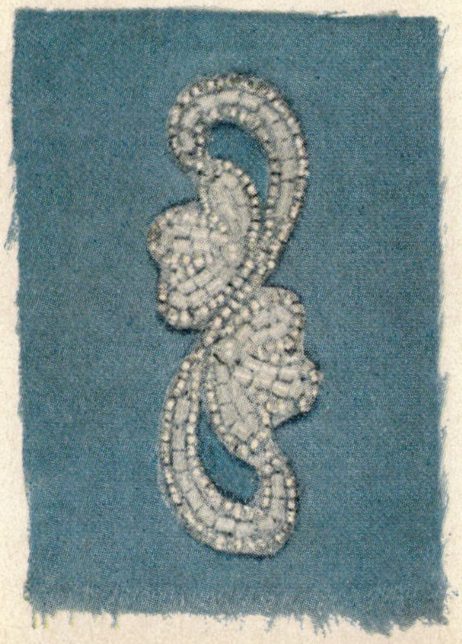

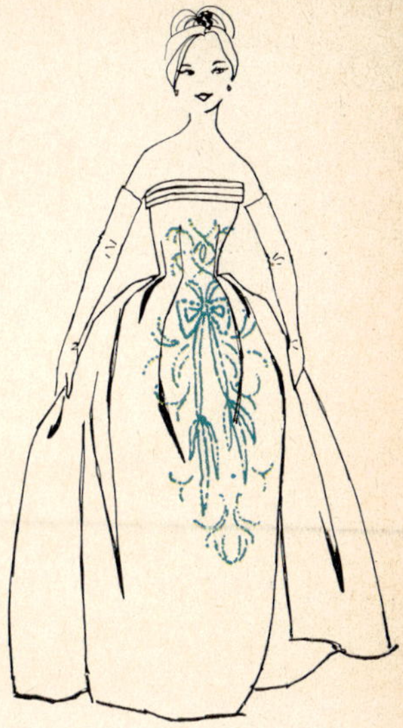

to evening fashions

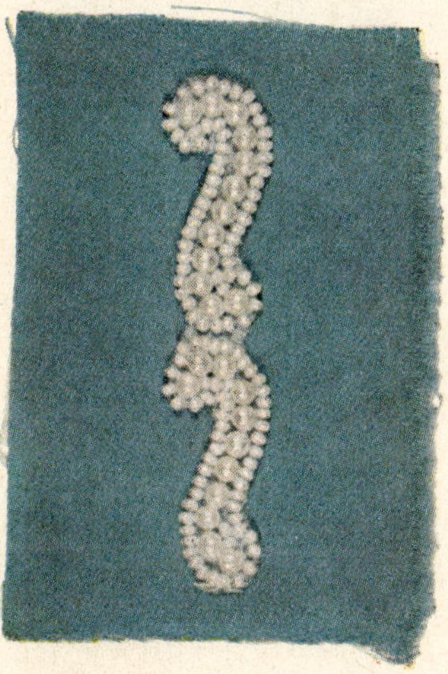

Measure the width of the hem. It should be ¼ inch wider than the elastic. Turn the hem under, press. Stitch around the edge of the sleeve. Stitch the hem in place, but leave a small opening at seam. Insert the elastic, making it a little smaller than the point on the arm where it is to fit.

Lap and sew the ends of the elastic. Slip-stitch opening for the elastic. When a facing is applied, stitch by machine close to the edge of the sleeve. Turn and press to the inside. Cut the facing a little wider than the elastic plus seam allowance. Turn under the seam and stitch by machine.

Looped sleeve opening

See Chapter 6 for instructions on how to make the cording. In making this sleeve, it's important to get all the loops exactly the same size.

Here's an easy professional trick to guarantee perfect loops. Take a piece of tissue paper and fold it double. Pin the ends of the cording to a piece of fabric to test how big a loop you will need for the button. Make the loop as shallow as possible so that the closure will look neat.

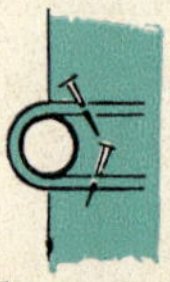

Mark on the tissue two parallel lines showing the depth of the loop. Across these, mark lines that indicate exact width of the loop, much as you mark for a cord-bound buttonhole. Shape the loops inside these markings, sewing along one parallel line and catching the ends of loops that have been shaped toward the other parallel line. Each loop is fitted inside its own little square.

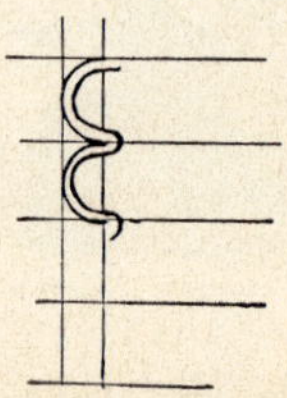

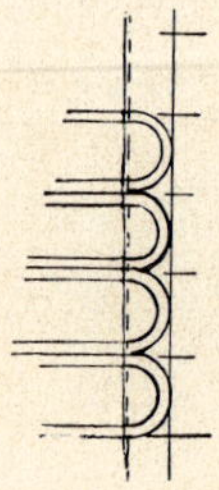

When you have made enough loops for the two sleeve openings, remove them from the paper. Pin each string of loops to the right side of the sleeve opening and stitch string to the seam allowance line of sleeve along the thread line of the completed loops. Then, sew either facing or seam binding to the right side along this same stitching line. Turn the facing or binding to wrong side.

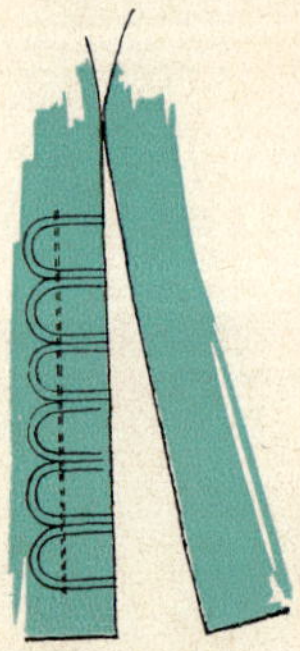

The loops will extend from the edge of the sleeve opening to lap over the edge where the sleeve buttons will be sewed on.

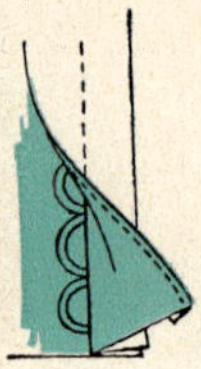

Trimmings

In the trimming departments of local stores you'll find beautifully-made motifs in beading, embroidery, laces, sequins, rhinestones, and lovely embroidered ribbons. You don't have to be an expert seamstress to use them. Simply tack them in place. Let your imagination run riot. Discover trims that make sewing fun, and give your clothes a professionally-made look.

Chapter 11

Tailoring the dressmaker suit

This is the fashion era of the dressmaker suit. Perhaps you, like many other women, have several of these suits in your wardrobe. No matter what the current fashion may be, somehow your favorite always seems to be in style. Each season new designs are introduced, but styles from previous seasons are still fashionable. In fact, many of them are becoming classics. It seems that any style of dressmaker suit is fashionable, as long as it is a flattering style on you.

Once you start doing tailoring, this type of suit may become your favorite project. It gives you a feeling of accomplishment that no other type of sewing can. And, surprisingly enough, many styles of the dressmaker suit are often very easy to make.

Adjustments

Adjustments from basic muslin

Buy your suit pattern in the same size as you do a dress pattern. Extra size is allowed in suits for the lining and also for wearing over blouses.

The suit is made for the same size figure as the dress, but, because of the extra ease, it will appear larger.

Make any necessary adjustments in the suit pattern in the same places and in the same amount as you did on your basic muslin pattern.

It is important that the suit fit the width and slope of the shoulders correctly, so if your basic muslin has shoulder adjustments, be sure to make them on the suit.

The following sketches show how basic muslin shoulder adjustments are applied to a suit. Refer to Chapter 3 for detailed information on adjustments.

Adjusting shoulders

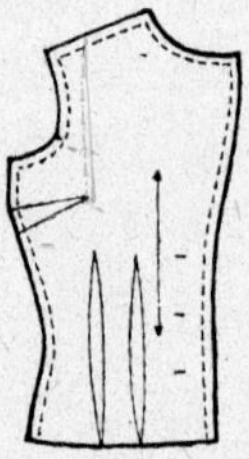

Narrow the suit shoulder with a tuck at the same point and for the same amount as on the basic dress muslin. If the lower front of your suit jacket hangs open, correct it with a dart under the front neck.

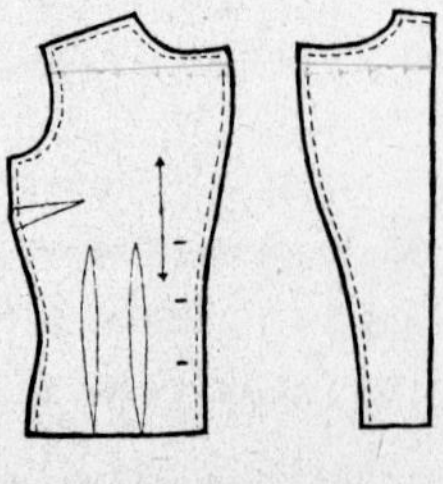

Pin the dart under the neck of the suit and the facing. Make the dart in the same amount and at the same point as on the basic muslin pattern, except extend it into the lapel.

Dolman sleeve

This sleeve is confusing to many women. Because it is a loose-fitting shoulder, they believe there's no need to adjust the pattern first. Or, they are uncertain about where and how to adjust it, because there is no armhole seam. Lay muslin over the dolman pattern. Mark where armhole would naturally be.

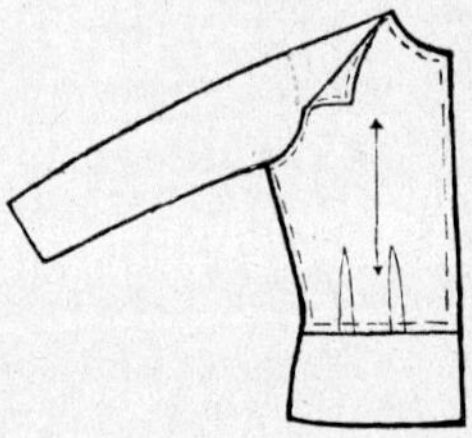

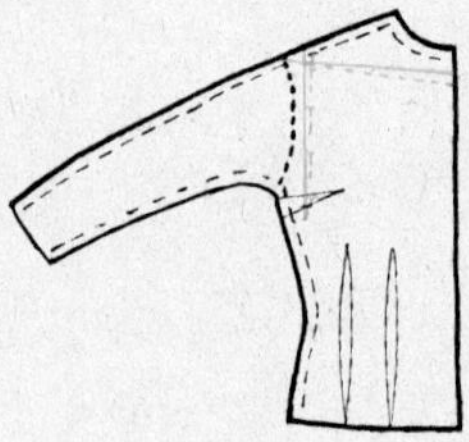

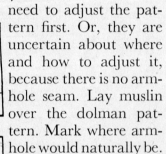

On the dolman sleeve, pin tuck to narrow the shoulder inside armhole mark. Dart taken under the neck slopes out toward this same mark.

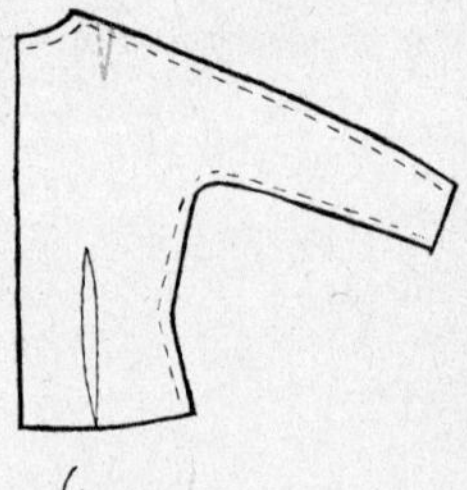

When only the front shoulders have been narrowed, sew a dart in the back shoulder. This gives a better fit and the back and front shoulder seams will be the same width. (See "Round Back" in Chapter 3 for further adjustments.)

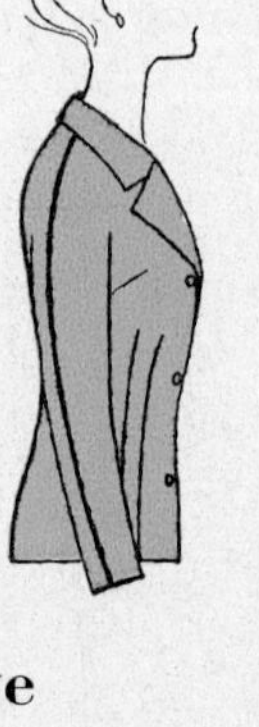

If needed adjustments are not made in the shoulder of the dolman sleeve, shoulder seam will twist toward back.

Modified dolman sleeve

In this style, there is no armhole seam

at the shoulder, but the side gore forms an underarm seam. It is vital that you adjust this shoulder before cutting the suit. Because of its shaping, it can't be corrected later.

Pin the side gore to the front before making adjustments. Draw a line to indicate the shoulder width. If needed, pin a dart under the neck.

Narrow the shoulder with a tuck. Do this while the pieces are pinned together, so the adjustments will be in the right place. Then unpin the pattern pieces, leaving the adjustments in place and ready to cut.

Make a deeper back dart, or add one if there is none, for a better fit.

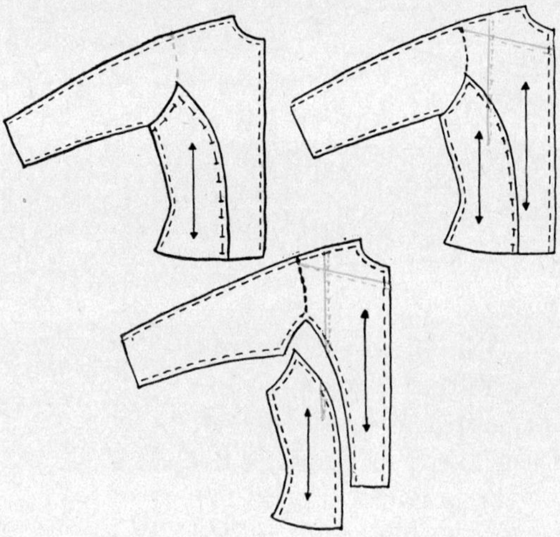

Bust adjustment

When the bust needs more fullness than the pattern allows, it is necessary to give more cupping. (See Chapter 3, section on the "Full busted figure" for adjustments.) Lengthen the front suit pattern by the same amount as you did on your basic mus-

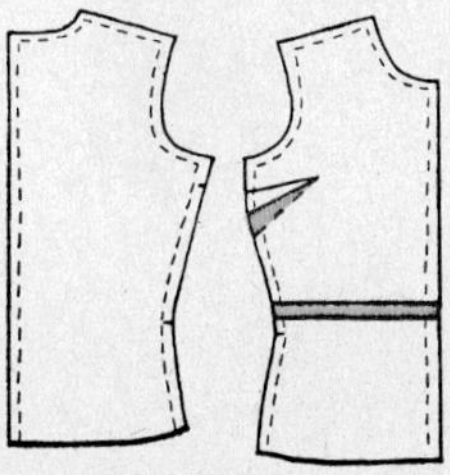

lin. This extra length is taken up in the deeper dart. The deeper dart gives more cupping, and the back and front side seams will be the same length.

Chapter 3 shows how to increase for the fuller bust in the princess line. The same adjustment applies to the modified dolman sleeve.

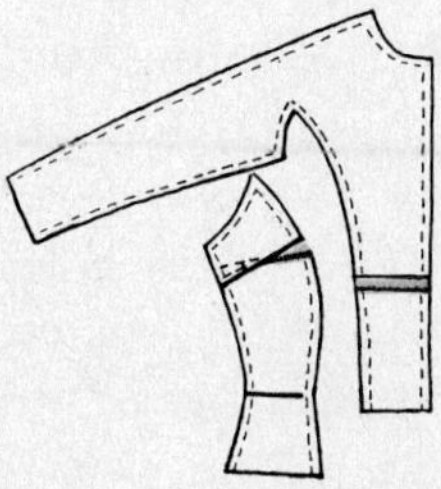

Slash the front piece and spread the same amount you lengthened the waist on your basic muslin. Slash the side gore across through the dart. The dart lines are lapped and the front edge of the gore spread. This gives greater fullness to the bust, eliminates the dart.

Adjusting for the waistline size

If the waistline of the suit needs to be made smaller, it is easy to do a little extra fitting on the front darts, and take in the side seams slightly. Fitting-in on the front darts will actually give a better fit to the bustline of the jacket.

The waistline can be increased by adding a small amount at the side seam. To increase a larger amount,

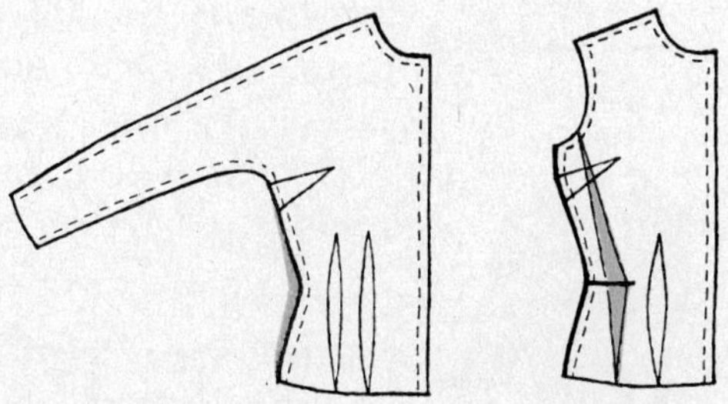

slash in on the waistline. Slash toward both the armhole and the hipline and spread the necessary amount.

Style details with braid

Broadening the back

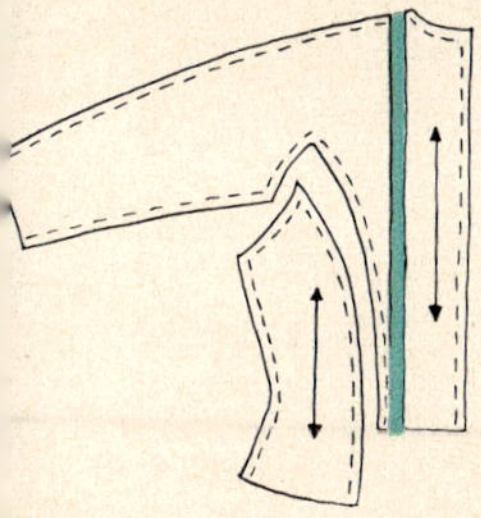

Slash the pattern for the entire length to broaden the back. The sketches show how to broaden the shoulders only on the three types of patterns. Slash the

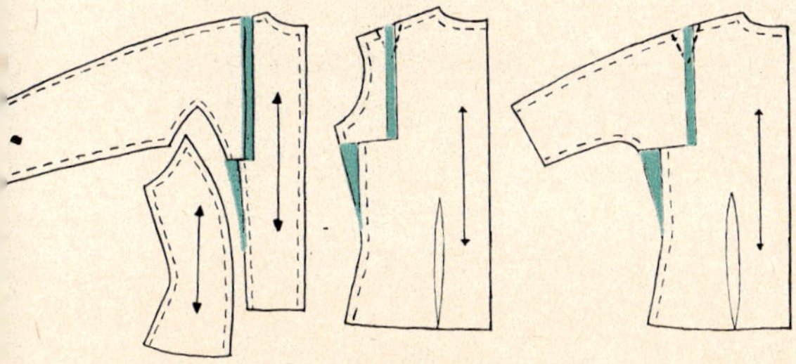

pattern under the arm and up to the shoulder. Spread it the amount indicated on your basic dress muslin. At the underarm, taper the seam to nothing at the waist. When the back only has been broadened, take up the extra

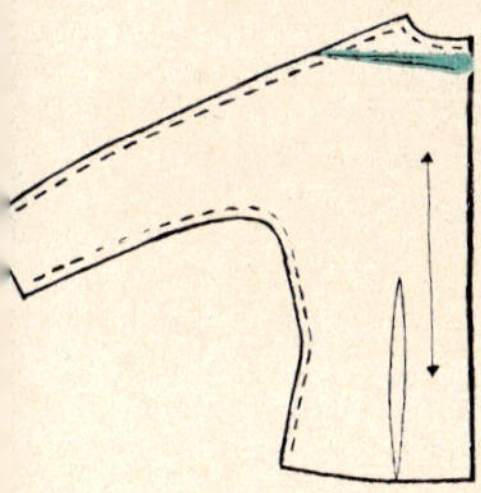

width in a dart at the back shoulder. If your basic pattern needs a dart or slash under the back neck, make the same adjustment in the suit. Slash or fold toward the approximate armhole seam. Shorten the waistline with a tuck across the pattern. Or, lengthen by slashing at the same point on all three styles. Adjust according to the alteration on the basic muslin.

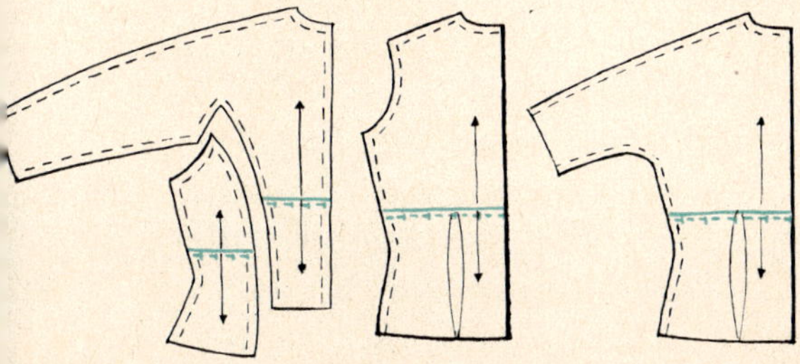

Cutting and assembling

Although dressmaker suits are made of all types of fabrics, they are most often made from woolens. Check for a nap fabric, especially with woolens, since many of them have a surface detail that must be handled carefully.

Fleece, cashmere, broadcloth, alpaca, and camel's hair, have a nap and must be cut with the nap running down. If cut with the pieces in either direction, the garment will look as though it is two different shades.

Other fabrics, although they do not have an actual nap, may have a surface texture that will look shaded unless the pattern is cut all one way.

Flannels, crepes, and most tweeds, are usually safe to cut in either direction. Try to cut *all* woolens one way, whenever possible. Since these fabrics are very wide, they can usually be cut one way without waste.

Many suits have dolman-type sleeves. When the sleeve and body are all in one, the pieces can seldom be cut in pairs from fabric on the lengthwise fold. They must be laid out on the open fabric. Lay out all the pattern pieces on the wrong side of one layer of fabric. This is the layout for one half of the suit.

Tear or cut across the fabric. Turn this remaining piece over so the

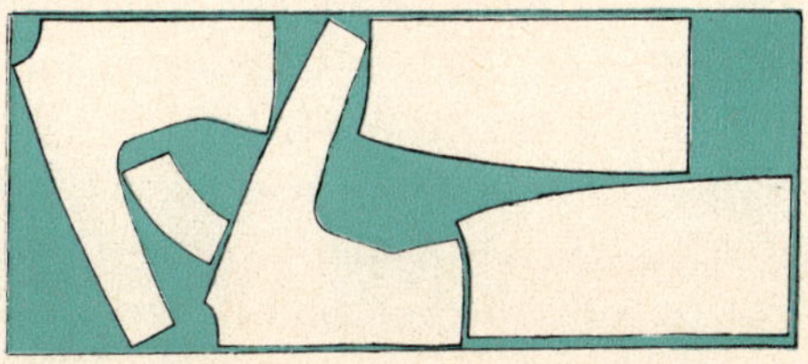

right side is face up. The fabric on which the pattern pieces are pinned is laid on the second length of fabric right sides together. Be sure the nap, if any, is running in the same direction. When the suit is cut, all pattern pieces will be in pairs.

If you cut one layer at a time, it is easy to cut two right fronts or two left backs quite by accident.

Unpin the pattern and shake out each piece. Place them together again and repin the pattern. You may find that the under piece of the fabric is a little larger, even though both have been cut from the same pattern.

This is because the surfaces of wool sometimes stick together, forming little bubbles on the underside. Smooth out and re-cut the fabric, so that both pieces are the same size.

Next, check to see if the wool is very soft or stretchy. If so, it would be better to mount the fabric on a thin cotton interlining to give it firmness and body. This interlining is usually done with almost all fabrics, except the very bulky ones.

Use thin lawn, cambric, muslin, or a commercial interlining, which is excellent. Be sure all are pre-shrunk before you cut. Cut jacket pattern pieces again from interlining fabric.

Before removing the pattern, mark on the interlining for any inside detail such as darts or tucks. Mark them with tailor's chalk or tracing wheel. Pockets, trimmings, or outside detail can be marked on the right side of the suit fabric with tailor's chalk and then basted, since these marks must remain on the fabric for a while.

Slash at the front neck mark where the collar joins the jacket. Lay the wrong side of the jacket pieces to the unmarked side of the interlining. Then press the two pieces together and pin all around just outside of the seam allowance line. Stitch together with a large stitch on the machine. This is called "mounting the fabric." Your suit jacket will have a much firmer texture, be easier to handle, and stay pressed longer. Wherever there are darts, stitch the two layers of fabric together by machine through the center of the dart. Then stitch the darts.

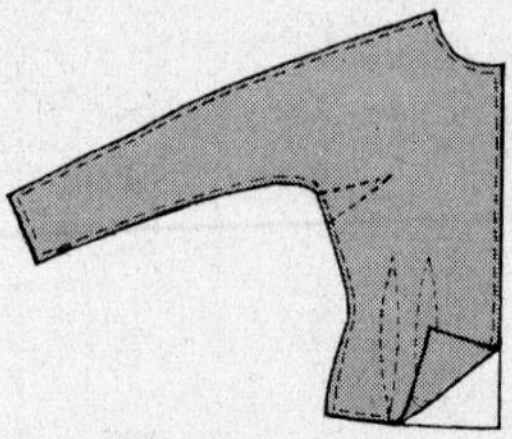

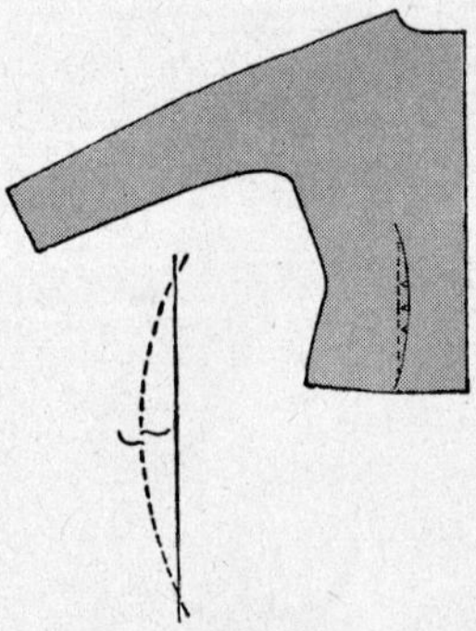

When sewing the darts, in a suit, start from the center of the dart. Sew first to one end, then the other, leaving about 1 inch of thread hanging. Since the suit will be lined, the threads won't show and the dart will taper to a sharper point.

Make up any trimming details such as pockets, bands, or bows, so they are ready to try when you fit the suit. If you plan to use braid or other trimmings such as a belt, contrasting collars, or unusual buttons, have them all handy so you can try them and decide on the final trim.

Sew the underarm and shoulder seams, but do not press them. Sew the sleeve seams so the sleeves are ready to try. Don't press any part of the suit at this point. The first pressing is the most important, since this is when the molding and shaping are done. This permanently affects the fit and appearance of the suit.

Instead of pressing the seams and

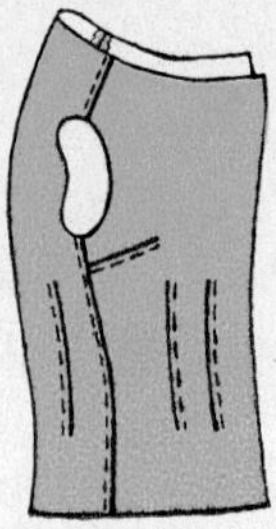

darts, baste them to one side so they will be flat while you are trying on the suit. Sew the easing stitches in the sleeve cap.

Using a large stitch, sew two rows—one on the seam allowance line, the second 1/4 inch from the sleeve edge. Now sew from underarm notch completely around the sleeve back to the underarm notch.

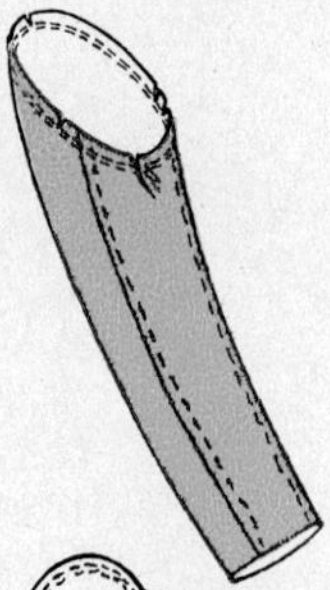

Baste the seams on the sleeves to one side. Press a crease very lightly into the sleeves for the fitting. Lay a two-piece sleeve on the ironing board with the under sleeve up. At the lower end of the sleeve the crease should be at the back seamline.

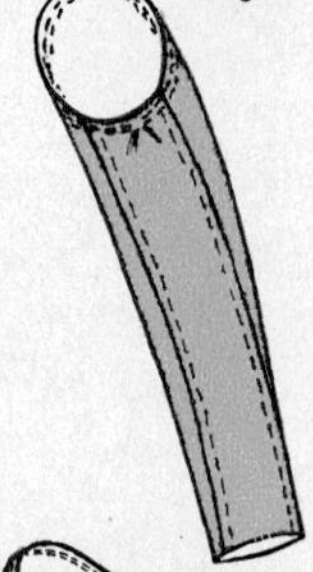

As you press, the front crease at the top of the sleeve should be 1 1/4 inches from the front underarm seam.

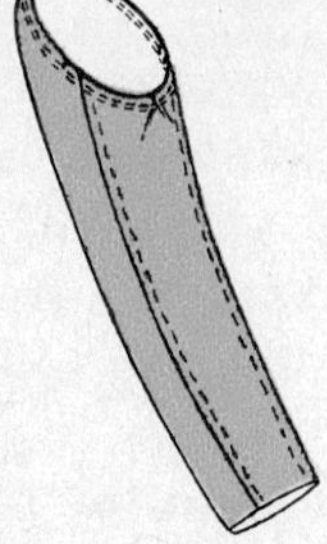

Ease in the fullness around the sleeve. The top of the sleeve should be flat for about 1 inch. The fullness at the back of the sleeve should come on either side of the back sleeve seam, and, the cap of the sleeve should be eased on either side of the top. Also ease in the sleeve a little under the arm so it fits high and snug to the armhole.

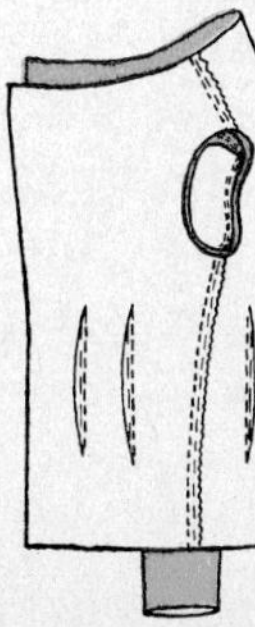

Now baste the sleeve into the jacket for fitting. If you adjusted the skirt to your basic muslin, it can be sewed and pressed before the fitting. Make up the waistband for the skirt and baste it to the waistline. Be sure to fit the jacket over the skirt, and over a blouse or sweater if you intend to wear one with the suit. You'll be surprised at how much ease a sweater can take up inside a suit jacket.

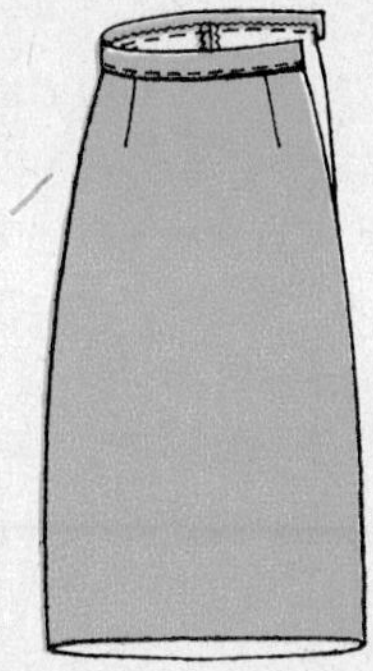

Be sure the center front of the suit is marked with a basting thread so it is correctly lapped for fitting.

Check the fitting points adjusted from the muslin to be sure the skirt hangs as it should. If there are any minor adjustments to be made, like making the waist or hip a little tighter, pin them in now.

If a fold forms under the waistband, pin it for correcting later. Generally, if you have worked from your fitted basic muslin, the skirt should be a perfect fit. Slip the jacket on and pin it carefully down the front. Check it at all points where the basic muslin was adjusted to make sure the same adjustments have been correctly made in the suit. Remember, too, that the suit will have a lining, so the jacket should be a little easy. (See lining section in Chapter 12.) Check and mark the most becoming jacket length.

If any additional fitting is needed, check the alterations listed in Chapter 3. If the shoulders are too wide, for instance, pin a tuck from the shoulder down toward the bust, bringing the sleeve to the correct shoulder point. After you have finished fitting the suit jacket, rip out the sleeves and re-cut the shoulder width from the corrected jacket pattern.

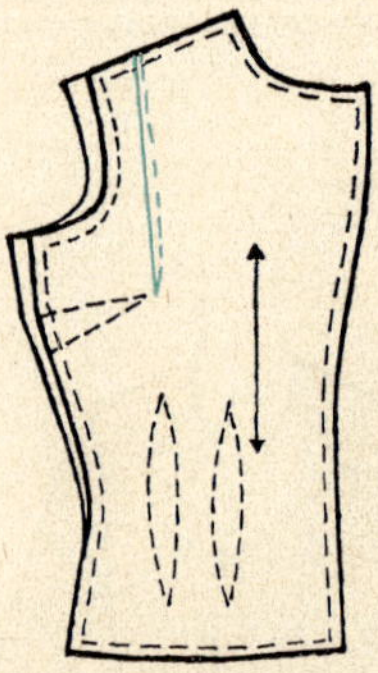

Make any other adjustments the same way. Pin them in as you did on the basic muslin and re-cut the piece from the adjusted pattern.

Check the hang of the sleeve. It should hang so the up-and-down grain and cross-grain are both straight. The slight crease you pressed in the sleeve helps in the fitting.

If any of the seams or darts need to be changed, you can rip and re-sew them and no mark will show, since they have not yet been pressed.

Make all the corrections on the suit. Remove the basting from the seams, and the suit is ready for pressing. Remove the sleeves until the jacket is finished, and put them in last.

Pressing

You'll need a tailor's ham to press your suit properly. (See instructions on how to make the ham in Chapter 1.)

Use the wide part of the ham for shaping and molding both the hip and bustline. The narrow end of the ham is always placed toward the waistline as you press your garment.

It is more convenient to press with the ham on a sleeve board which makes it a little higher. If you are short, this may not be comfortable, so place the ham on the ironing board.

First, place the shoulder seam of the suit so it shapes along the edge of the wide end of the ham. Mold and press the shoulder so the back curves around the edge of the cushion as it will fit the curve of the back shoulder.

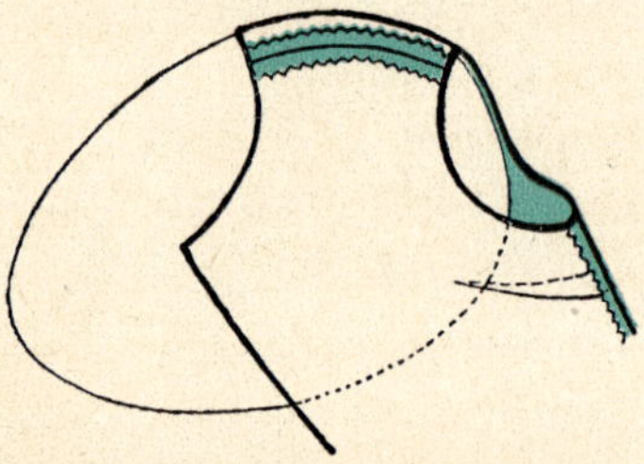

This actually stretches the back a little along the shoulder seam.

After it is pressed, the front shoulder will be concave as you hold it over your hand. The back shoulder will follow the curve of the back of your hand, as the suit jacket will fit the back shoulder.

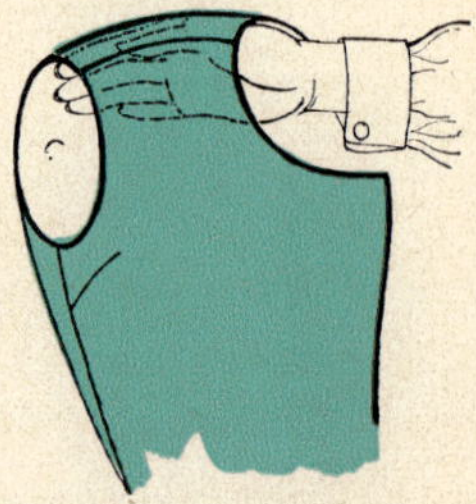

If the shoulder is sewed correctly, then molded as described, the suit back will never look too narrow.

Next, press the underarm seam open, with the wide part of the ham toward the bustline. Press the darts on the ham, molding and shaping the roundness of the bustline. Press the hipline next, molding it over the wide part of the ham. The hip rounds out, following the shaping of the side seam and the jacket darts.

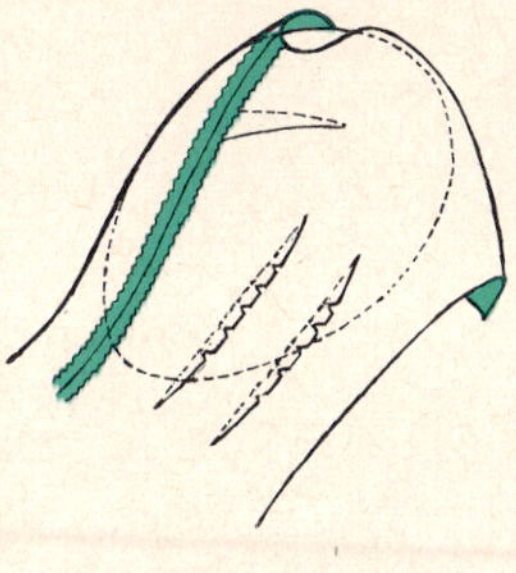

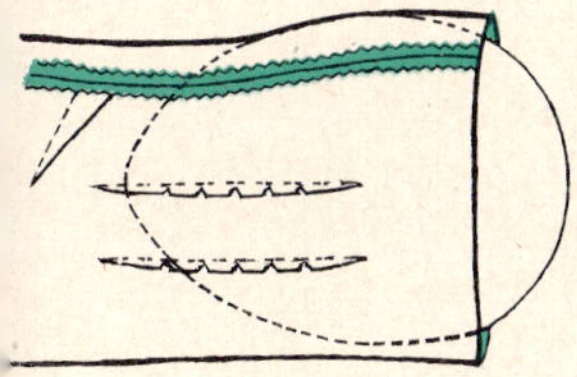

On the back, press the same way, with the wide part of the ham first toward the top to shape the upper back and shoulders; then press toward the hip, rounding and molding the hipline.

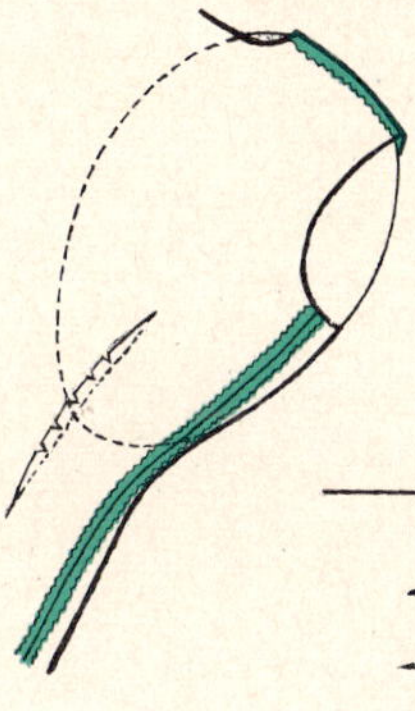

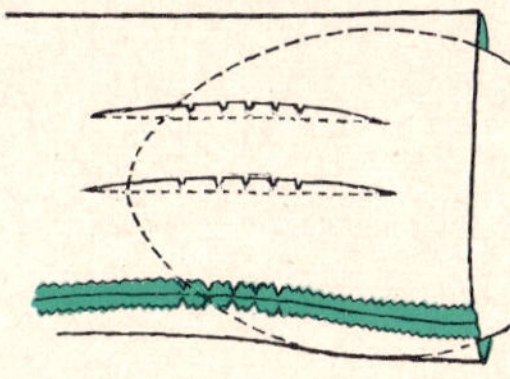

When pressing the suit at the waistline, it is necessary to clip in on the waistline darts and seams if the suit is a fitted style.

On the box-type jacket, you will only have to mold the shoulders, bustline, and upper back of the suit jacket over the tailor's ham. The rest of the suit jacket can then be pressed flat on a regular ironing board.

Interfacing

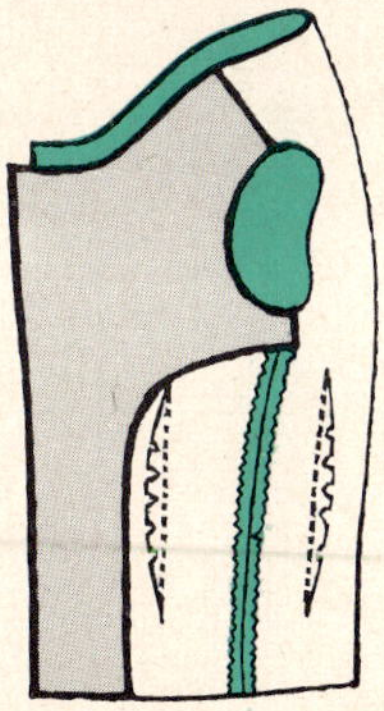

The front of the jacket is now ready to be interfaced.

For a suit with a set-in sleeve, cut the interfacing to extend out to the shoulder. Usually, the pattern includes a separate pattern piece for the interfacing. If the facing pattern piece is used, with an extension added for cutting the interfacing, a slight change must be made. Cut the extension for the shoulder the same as the pattern, but add an extra inch on the inside edge of the facing. The interfacing should always be at least 1 inch wider than the facing. If no interfacing pattern is included, use the jacket pattern front. Cut along the front, the shoulders, and armholes of the jacket pattern. As you cut the inside edge of the interfacing, extend it 1 inch beyond where facing would finish.

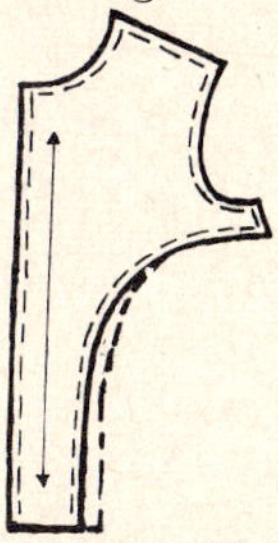

Curve the interfacing just over the bust and to the side seams about 3 inches below the armhole.

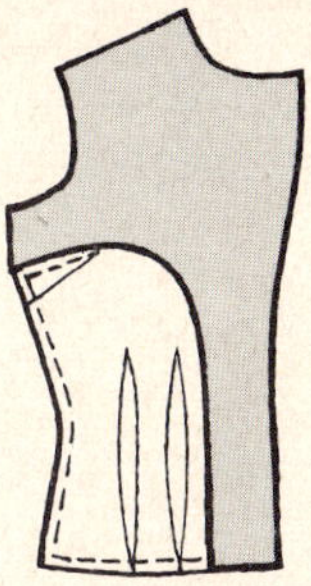

(On a suit with a dolman sleeve, cut the interfacing only 1 inch wider than

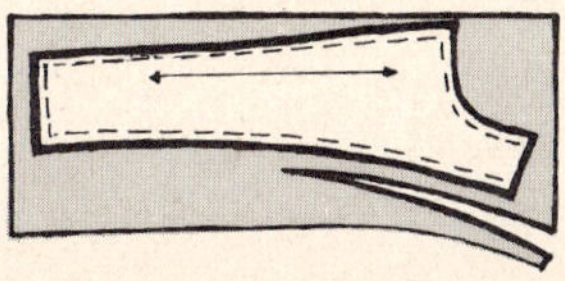

the facing. Interfacing doesn't extend into the shoulder, since the shoulder is soft and molded to the figure.)

Cut the interfacing from hair canvas. Then fit it into the suit jacket around the armhole, the neck edge, and along the inside edge.

Place the suit over a tailor's ham with the right side out. Mold and shape it over the tailor's ham to be sure the interfacing fits smoothly to the inside. From the right side, baste the interfacing into the suit along the shoulder seam, around the armhole seam, and down the inside edge of the suit jacket interfacing.

Run another basting stitch from the center of the neckline straight down the front of the jacket to the hem, catching the interfacing.

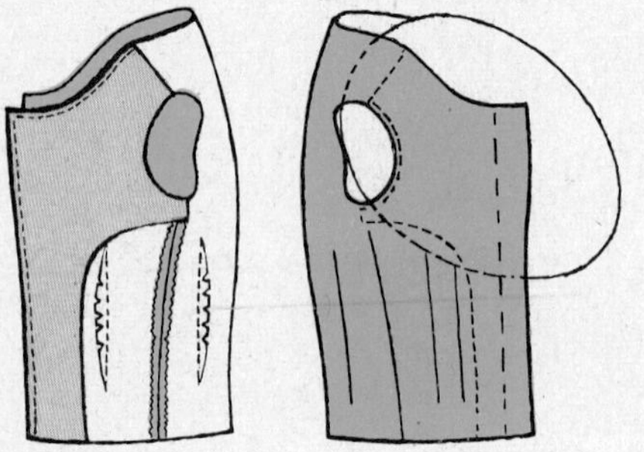

Take the front pattern piece and mark on the right jacket front where the top buttonhole is to be placed.

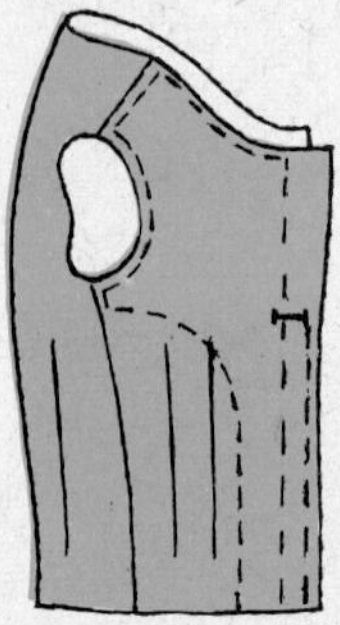

Mark it exactly where the pattern indicates, because it will serve as a guide for the roll line. Mark it with a short basting thread. Mark the left side of the jacket the same way. Baste the lower part of the interfacing to the jacket along the front edge to buttonhole mark.

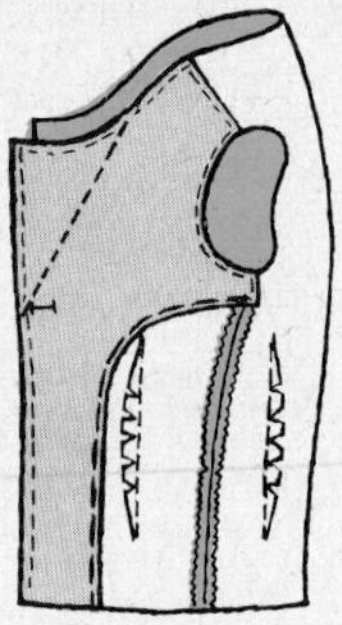

Now you are ready for a crucial point in making any suit—the rolling of the lapel. The roll line runs from the outside edge of the buttonhole mark toward neckline between the shoulder and the center front.

Roll the lapel over your hand with the interfacing on top. Start a padding stitch about 1 inch inside of the roll line. Work the padding stitch up and down the lapel, inside the seam allowance line of the front edge and the neck edge. The stitches can be as fine and close together as you like.

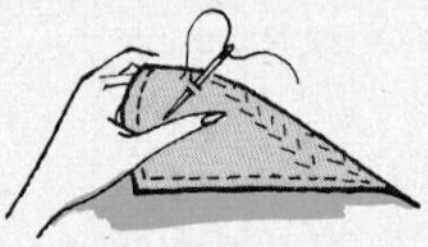

The lapel rolls over your hand as you work, so the roll will be sewed in permanently. Finish rolling the lapel on both of the jacket fronts.

Trim away the seam allowance on

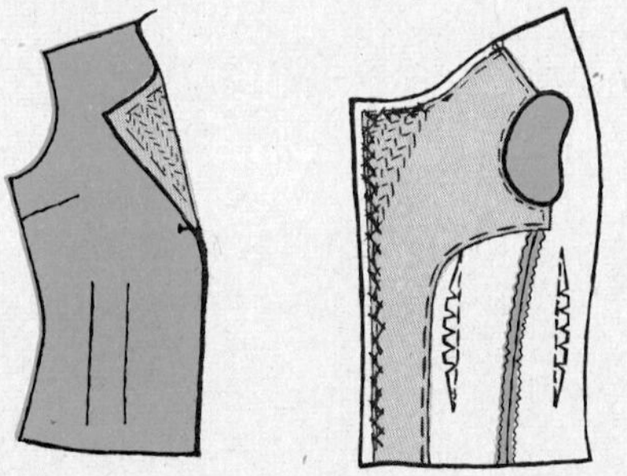

the front edge of the jacket and around the neck. The amount of fabric cut away should be slightly more than $\frac{5}{8}$ inch seam allowance.

Now you are ready to sew the interfacing to the inside of the suit. Sew this by hand, using a catch-stitch around the front edge of the jacket and neck edge. Sew it to the shoulders and around the armhole with a run-

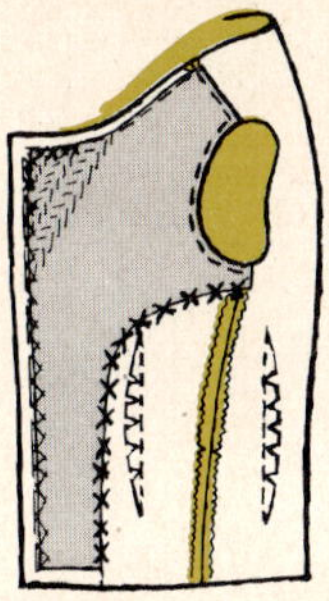

ning stitch. On inside edge of the interfacing, use a long catch-stitch, picking up only a few threads of the surface, so the stitching won't show on the right side. Make this stitch rather loose. If part of the interfacing can be sewed to inside darts, so much the better. The back of the suit can be interfaced. Cut this interfacing on the bias from the back jacket pattern.

The interfacing can be lightweight muslin or a commercial interfacing in a crisper finish. When cutting, follow the pattern at the neck edge, armhole, and to about 3 inches below the armhole at the side seam.

Then curve across the back to about 5 inches below the neck. Sew the back interfacing by hand around the outside jacket edges. Interfacing is not tacked to the suit body. The inside edge hangs free.

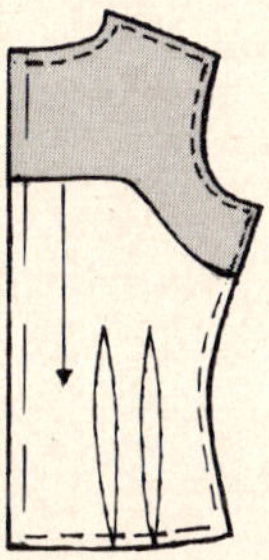

Taping

Always tape the front edge of the suit to keep it firm and to prevent stretching. A ¼ inch linen tape is best. You can also use a ¼ inch twill tape, but be sure it is preshrunk.

Baste the tape to the front edge of the suit along the seam allowance line and across the neck edge to the center front line. Also tape the width of the facing across the lower front edge on the hemline.

Baste the edges of the tape with a zigzag stitch. Keep it smooth and even along the seam edge. Ease it in if it has to be shaped to any curve. Sew

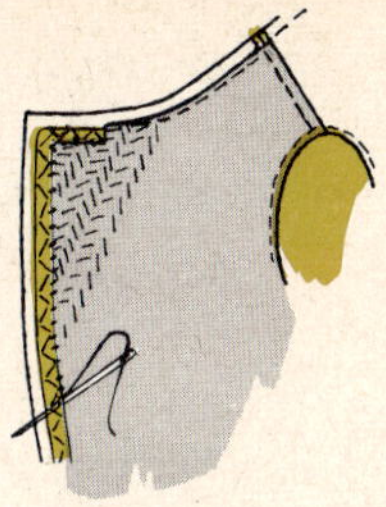

the tape permanently with a fine hemming stitch along seam edges. On outside edge, pick up a few threads of fabric. Sew inside edge to the interfacing only.

Buttonholes

Slip the jacket on and pin it together down the front. The top buttonhole has already been marked. Carefully indicate the front waistline. Put a pin ½ inch below it for placement of the waistline buttonhole.

Remove the jacket. Check the front jacket with the pattern piece to see if the placement of the waistline buttonhole is the same as the one marked on the actual pattern. If not, remark waistline buttonhole on the pattern.

Measure and remark all the buttonholes on the jacket pattern front so they are evenly spaced between the top and waistline buttonholes.

From this corrected pattern, make the tracing from which you will make all the buttonholes. (See the instructions for making the cord buttonhole that are given in Chapter 6.)

Interfacing hipline and hem

The hemline of the jacket is generally interfaced to give a firm, smooth edge. However, the style of suit must be considered in deciding how deep

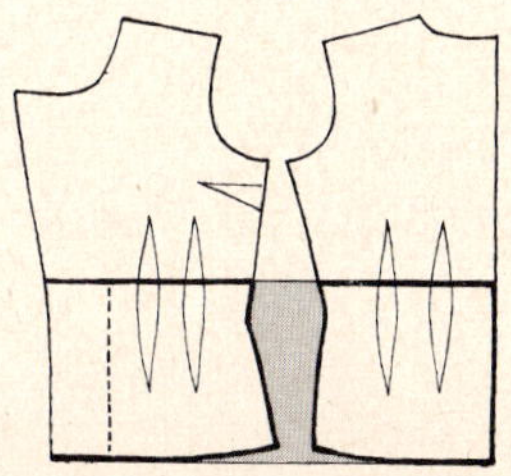

the interfacing should be. Sometimes the hipline of the suit is arched to give a rounded look at the hip. This must be interfaced to hold the shape —one of the non-woven interfacings would be best. Cut the interfacing from the back and front suit pattern, following the lower edge of the jacket and cutting a little above the waistline mark shown on the pattern.

Sew up the side seams, press them open, then stitch about 1/4 inch on either side of the seamline.

Cut out the center of the darts. Lap the edges together, put a strip of interfacing underneath. Stitch on each side of the cut edges to shape.

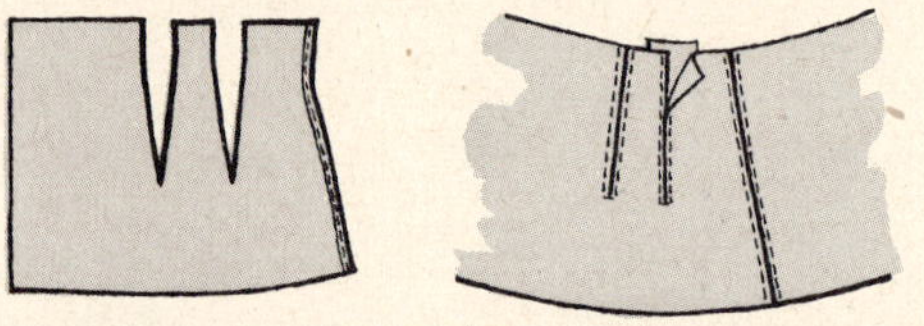

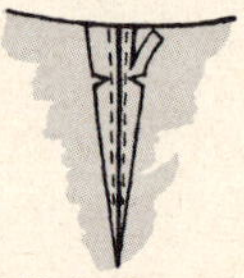

Or mark and sew the dart, slash it open and stitch it on either side of the seamline.

This keeps the interfacing flat and smooth under the suit fabric, but gives the correct arch to the hip.

Press back the hem of the jacket. At the lower edge, cut away the interfacing the width of the hem and fit it to the inside of the jacket on the fold line of the hem. Pin the interfacing along the back and front darts and the side seams. Cut off the front of the hip interfacing so it just laps over the front interfacing.

Catch-stitch the interfacing along the hem crease and at the top edge. On the seams and darts, do a running stitch through the interfacing, to the matching dart or seam. Be sure none of the tacking shows on the right

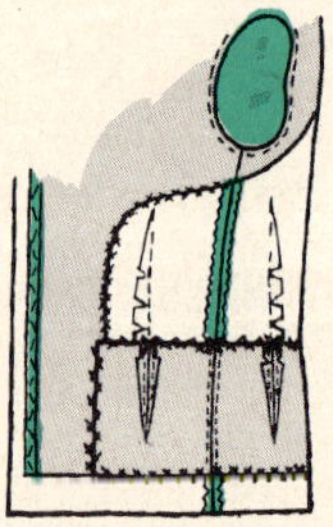

side. If the whole hipline doesn't need interfacing, do only the hem.

Cut the interfacing of hair canvas or non-woven interfacing. The hair canvas interfacing is cut on the bias, 1 inch wider than the depth of the hem. The non-woven interfacing is cut 1 inch wider than the hem and to the shape of the edge of the jacket. Both interfacings are sewed in the same way.

Pin lower edge of interfacing just inside crease for hem. Don't stretch the lower edge of the suit. Catch-stitch both edges of the interfacing to the suit. Be sure no stitching shows on the right side of the jacket.

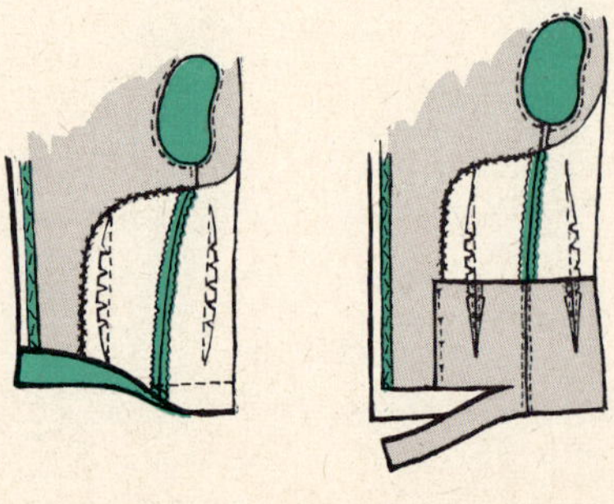

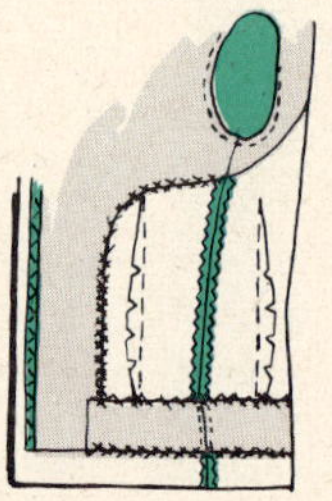

Collars

Notched collars

This collar has a notch where it joins the neck seam. The under collar is always cut in two pieces on the bias and with a center seam, so it will roll softly and uniformly, be easier to mold under the upper collar.

Cut the interfacing from hair canvas on the bias, using the same pattern as for the under collar.

Sew up the center seam of the under collar and press the seam open. On

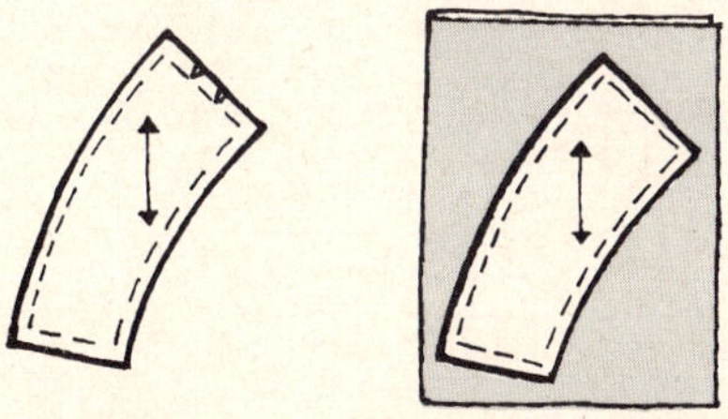

the interfacing, press open the seam, and then stitch on either side of it to hold the seam allowances flat. Cut off the seams close to the stitching.

Place the interfacing against the inside of the under collar and pin

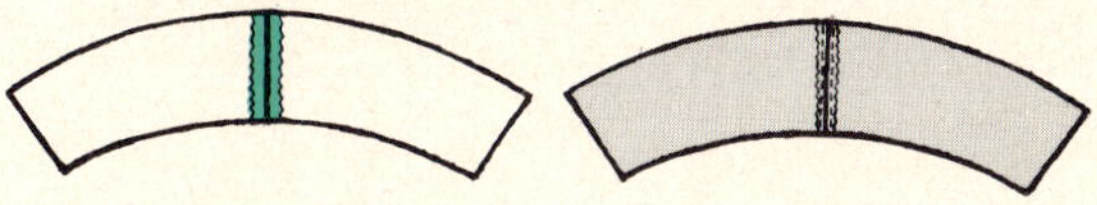

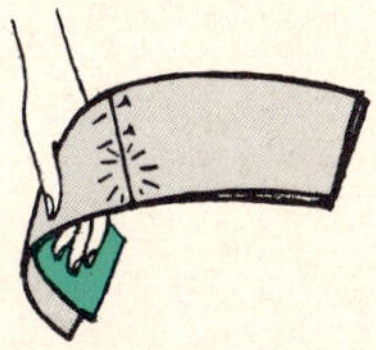

to hold the center seams together.

This collar must have the roll line sewed in. This is done by hand, using thread the color of the suit.

Start at the neck seam allowance line, ½ inch to the side of the center seam. Use the same padding stitch used for the lapel. Roll the collar over your index finger and start the padding stitch, forming a small circle in the center of the collar.

As you do the padding, ease the interfacing in slightly, while rolling the collar over your finger. Work from one side of the collar to the other, making an ever-widening circle. Do the padding stitch only to the seam allowance line all around.

Finish center of collar. Then continue the padding stitch on either side of the collar from the outside edge to the neck edge, until you've completely padded the jacket collar.

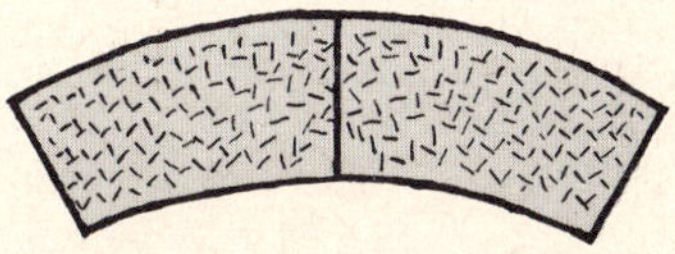

If the interfacing has been eased in enough, you may find that there is very little seam allowance left on the interfacing. In any case, trim away the interfacing to the seam allowance line all around the collar. When rolled correctly, the ends curl toward the under collar.

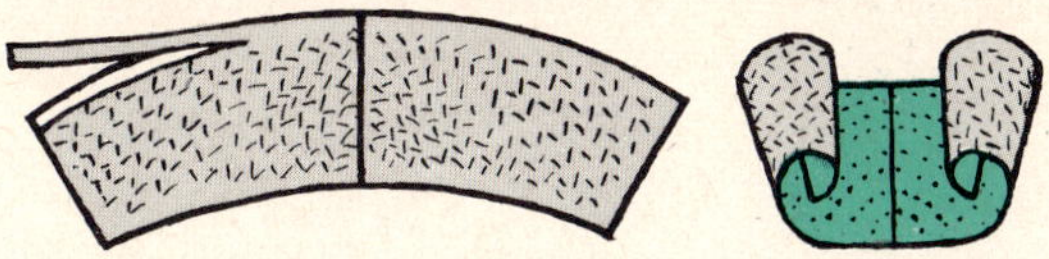

The collar is now ready to be applied to the suit. First, put a stay-stitch in the neckline to keep it from stretching and to permanently hold the neck size. Tape is never used as a stay in necklines and armholes of fine custom suits. Always stay-stitch necklines and armholes by hand.

Stay-stitching the neck

Use a single strand of silk buttonhole twist for this stitching. Start at the center front of the neck, or where the collar will be sewed.

Bring the needle through from the inside of the neck, just outside the seam allowance line. Then take a back-stitch ½ inch long, and bring the needle forward ¼ inch, next to the original stitch. The needle should always come out at the top of the stitching line. Draw in on the thread a little before you take the next ½ inch back-stitch. Do this stitch all around the neckline. Measure to be sure the neck is same size as pattern. See detailed sketch of stitch on page 230.

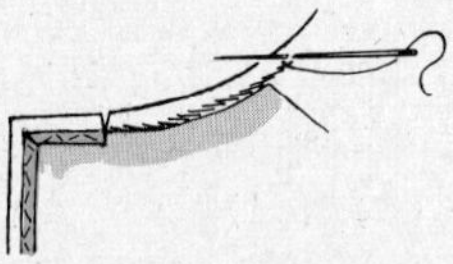

This stitching can be done in the same color thread as the suit or in a contrasting color. You may find contrasting thread is easier to see when sewing the collar.

Now you will see how important it is to notch the front of the neck where the collar joins the jacket.

Pin the front of the collar to the jacket so the seam allowance line is at this notch at both sides of the neckline. Match the center back of the under collar to the center back of the neck. Pin the rest of the collar to the neckline all around on the seam allowance line. The stay-stitching at the neck can serve as a guide on the jacket, and the trimmed-off interfacing indicates the seamline on the collar.

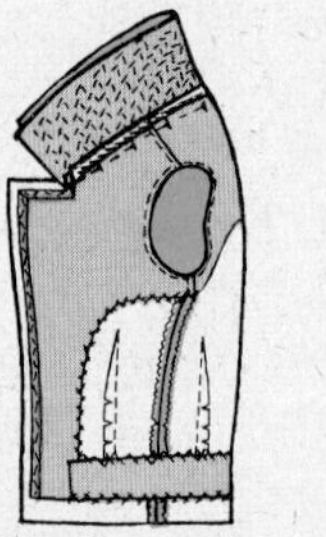

Stitch the collar to the neck. Remember to sew back a few stitches to lock the stitching where the collar finishes at either end.

Clip in to the neckline stitching at this point. Clip in on the neck seam and press it open all around. Press the neckline over a tailor's ham so that the neckline will not be stretched.

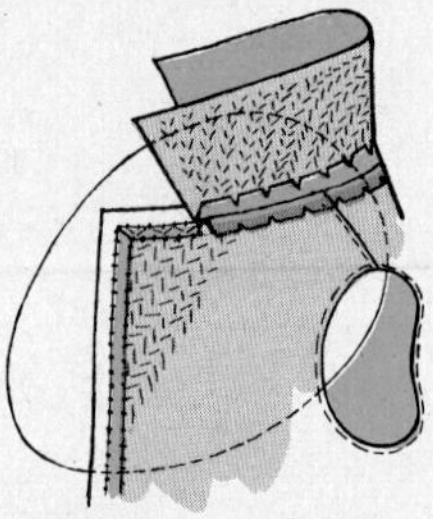

Facing and upper collar

Join the upper collar to the facing. The collar and facings can be sewed to the suit in one stitching.

Mark the notches very carefully on both pieces before removing the pattern. Also mark by clipping the point where the collar joins the facing to form the notch. If the collar has a mark indicating where it matches the shoulder seam, also clip this.

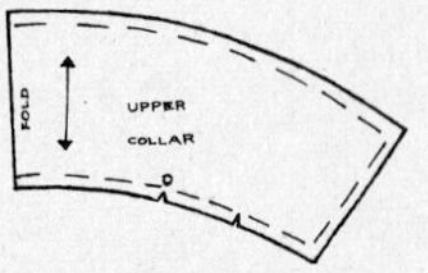

Pin the collar to the facing, matching the seam allowance line of the collar to the clip mark on the facing.

If the collar is marked for the shoulder seam, pin at the seam allowance line at the top of the facing. Be sure to match the neckline notches of facing and collar. Sew the two pieces together along the seamline.

Ease the collar in a little around the curve of the front neck. Sew back a few stitches at the front edge of the collar to lock it. Clip in to the stitching line at this point. Clip in to the curve seam of the neck and press the seam open.

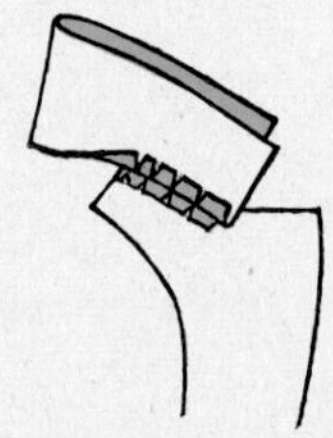

Bring the right side of the collar and the facing to the right side of the suit, with the edges

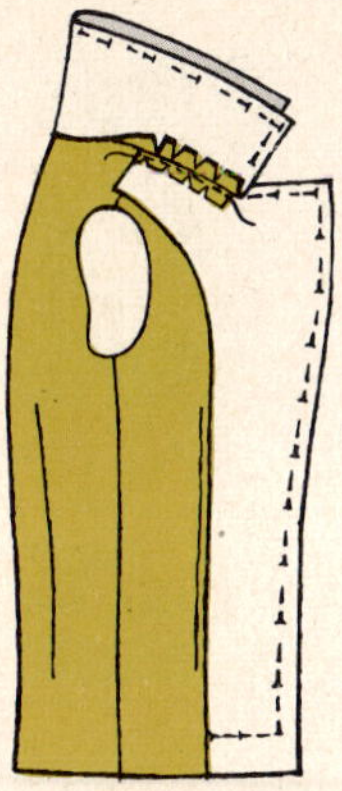

of the collars and the facing together, and the neckline seams directly over each other. Baste neckline seams together, easing in facing side slightly.

Pin the facing and collar to the suit and under collar along the interfacing or at the seam allowance line.

Ease the facing in a little along the top of the lapel. As you pin the front edges of the suit together, ease the facing slightly along the lapel line. Also ease the upper collar at the front edges and for the entire length.

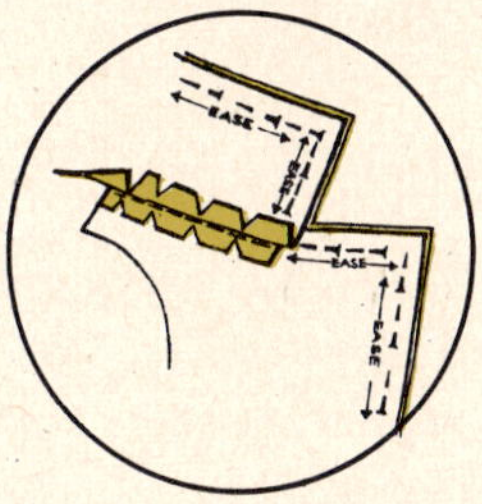

Start to sew from the right-hand side of the suit on the inside, and from the bottom of the jacket to the back of the collar. Do the same thing from the left-hand side of the jacket.

This keeps the ease from shifting as it might if you sewed all around the jacket. It also assures that the lapels will roll the same way.

When you sew into the notch, be sure to sew just to the base of the clip mark, and then up the side of the collar on the seam allowance line.

This part of the notch can often be spread open, so the collar and top lapel seam are in a straight line. Stitching it this way sometimes helps to insure that the notch is sewed correctly.

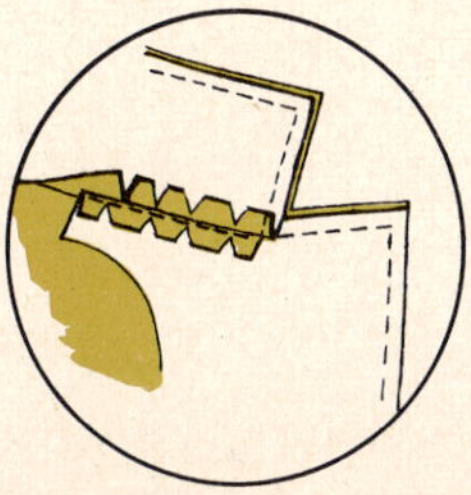

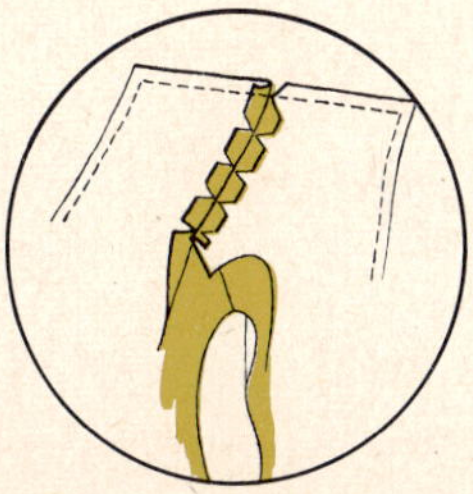

When the facings are turned to the inside, the top edge of the lapel should look as if it is a continuous part of the neck seam. The collar should be at a direct angle to this seam. Turn the facing, and check this point to make sure that it is correctly sewed.

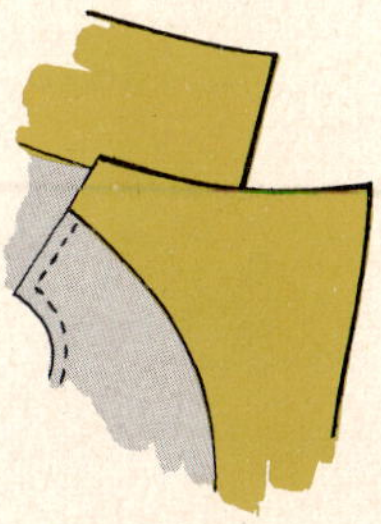

If the notch is correct, trim the seam to graduated widths. Make the suit seam quite narrow, the facing slightly wider. Trimming the seams this way, makes the front edge of the jacket flat and smooth. Turn the facing to the inside, and baste around the edge

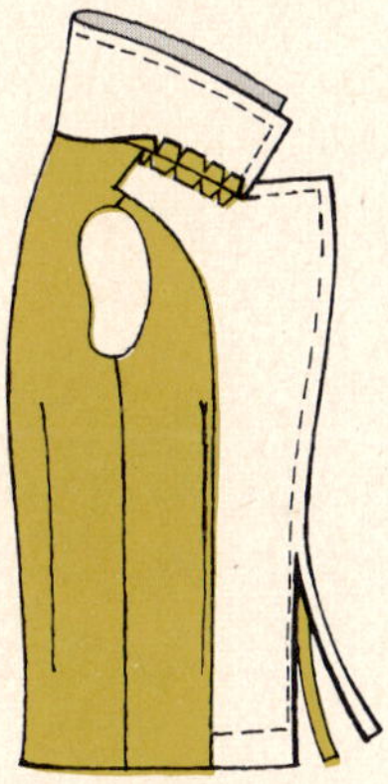

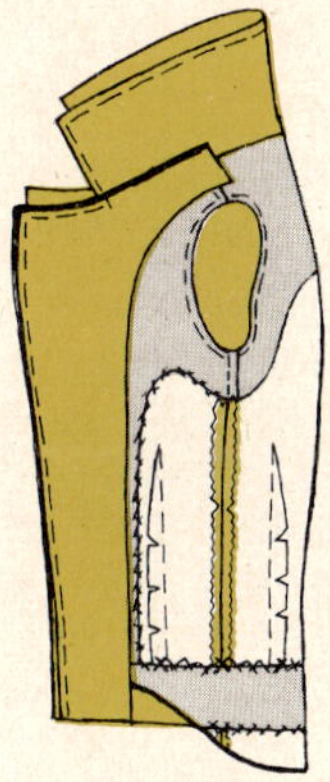

of the suit. At the lower front edge of the suit, bring the facing in just slightly from the seamline edge.

As you baste around the lapel, bring the suit back a little from the seam edge. Baste the under collar so its edge is also in just a little from the seamline. This is done so you are not pressing the collar on seamline,

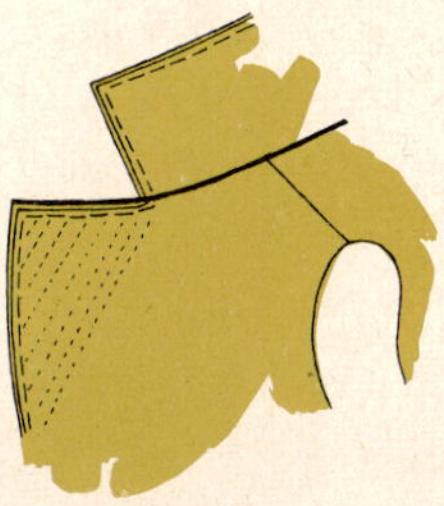

but on a fold of fabric along the front edge of the suit. This gives a sharper line, and an invisible seam.

On lightweight fabrics, as the facing is sewed around the collar and lapel, it can also be sewed across the hemline. Then when it is turned, the lower edge of the suit jacket is finished at the same time. With a heavier fabric, turn up the hem and turn under the facing,

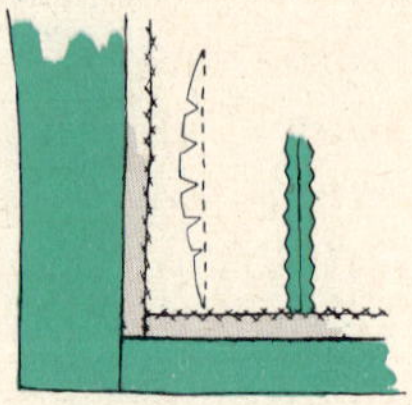

and finish by hand as the facing is tacked to the jacket. Press the facings back on the inside at the lower part of

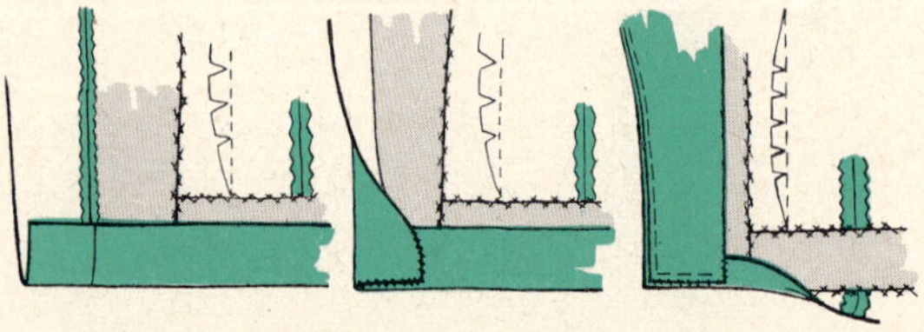

the suit jacket, as it was basted. Then press the lapel on the suit side. Press the collar on the under collar side. Do all pressing over the tailor's ham.

Roll the collar and lapel over your hand and do a diagonal basting all

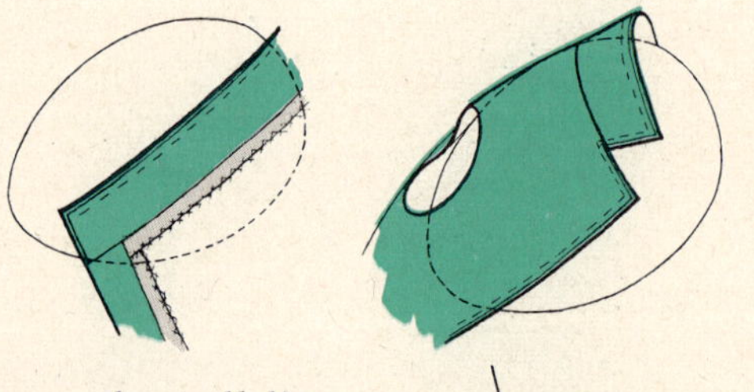

along the roll line, holding the two thicknesses in place as they will roll. Put the right side of the jacket down on the ham, smooth back the lower facings and pin into place. Roll back

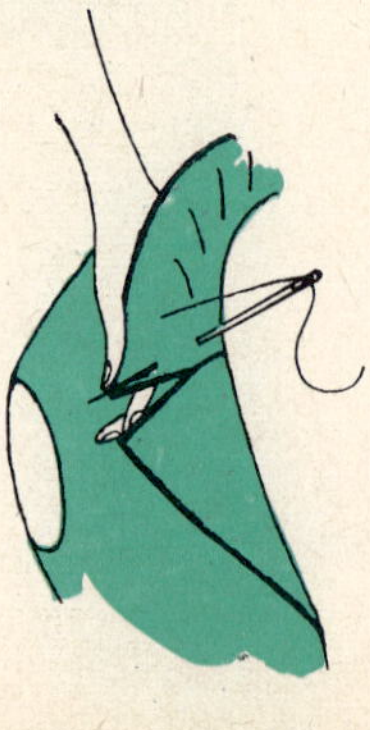

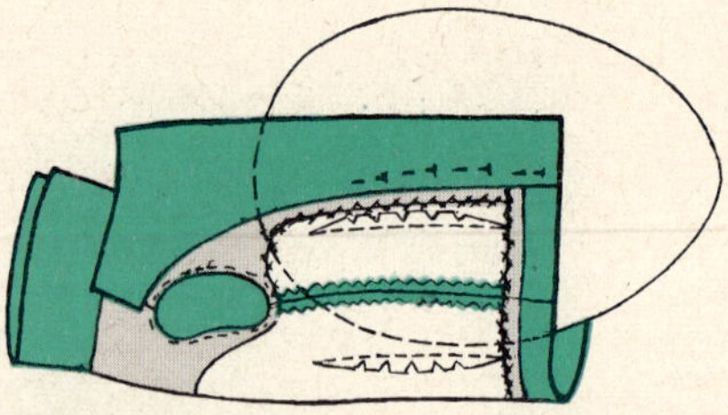

the lapel and place it face down on the table. Then smooth back the upper part of the facing and pin to the inside of the suit. The lapel is rolled under first, so the ease in the collar and facings will not be pulled to the inside of the suit when the collar and facings are finished.

If smoothed back too much, the ease would be eliminated, spoiling the roll of the collar and the lapel.

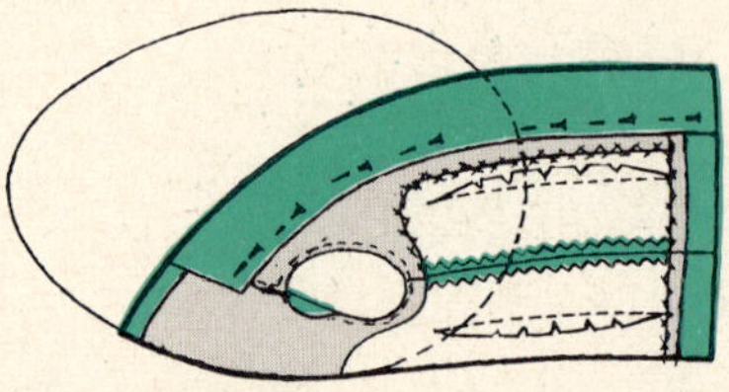

Roll the upper collar back and pin the loose edge to the back neckline. Be sure that the upper collar has enough ease so it will roll over the under collar and set correctly.

The reasons for a collar "dog earring" are (1) not enough easing done when upper collar and facings are sewed to the suit, and (2) facings and collar finished to the inside without allowing ease where the collar and lapel roll over the under collar and lapel.

Do a running stitch around the collar and shoulder to hold in place.

On the facings and hem, catch-stitch the edges to the interfacing.

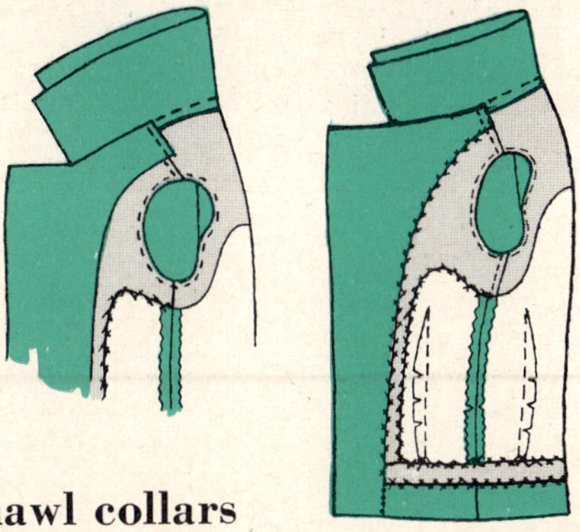

Shawl collars

There are two ways the shawl collar can be constructed. It is a good idea to know how to make both, since different patterns show both ways.

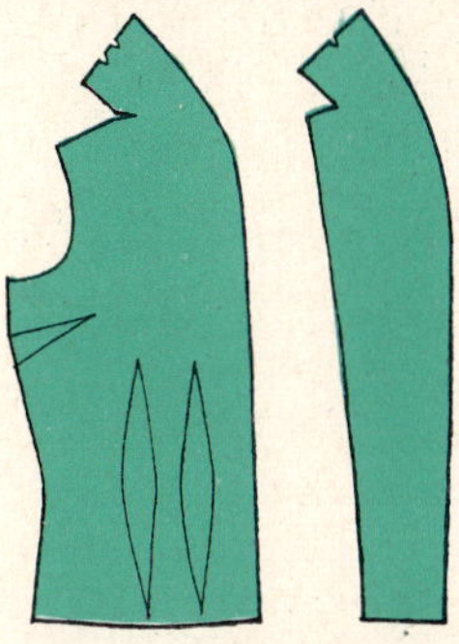

The first way is to cut the under collar in one piece with the front of the suit jacket, cutting the upper collar in one piece with the facing.

The interfacing will also be cut with collar and facing in one piece. Cut the interfacing from hair canvas,

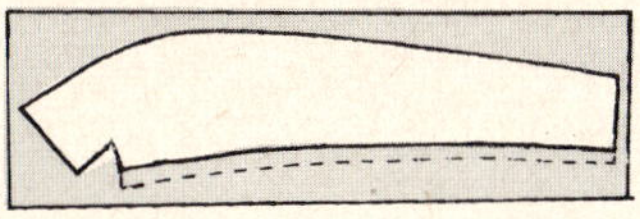

one inch wider than the facing. Sew up the back neck seam. Trim away the seam allowance at the back of the neck and top shoulder of the interfacing. Then carefully pin this edge to the seamline of the neck and shoulder of the suit. Roll the collar back from the mark of the first buttonhole, to the back of the neck, as you do when making the notched collar. Put pins along the roll line to hold it. Smooth the interfacing into the inside of suit

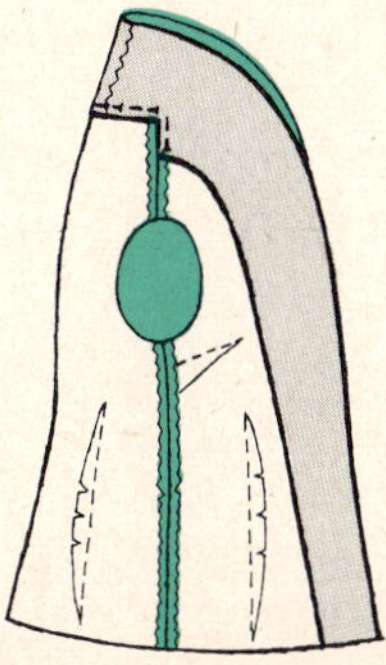

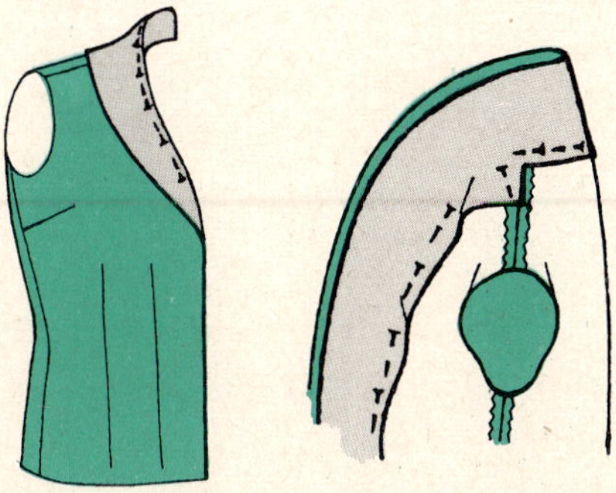

and pin the inside edges to the jacket.

Start at the left side of the lapel, about 1 inch deeper into the jacket than the roll line, and begin a padding stitch.

Work back and forth around the collar and lapel until the whole collar is padded to the seam allowance line at the collar edge.

Trim the interfacing at the seam allowance line. Catch the interfacing to the neck with a running-stitch across the back neck and shoulder seam. Catch-stitch the rest of the interfacing to the inside of the jacket as

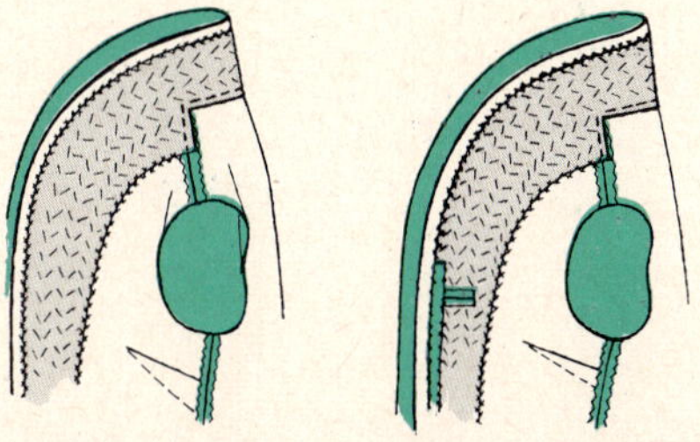

you do for the notched collar. Use tape as for the notched collar on the front suit edge to the top buttonhole mark. Never tape around the collar.

Facings

Join the back collar seam of the facings and press. Pin the right side of the facing to the right side of the suit.

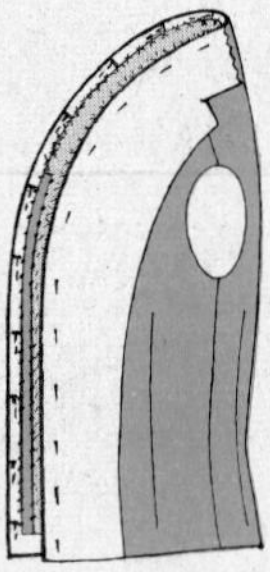

Ease the facing around the collar and lapel. Pin on the suit side along the edge of the interfacing.

Stitch the facing to one side of the suit from the hem to the back neck. Then stitch the other side of the suit from the hem to the back neck. This keeps the facing ease from shifting as it is stitched. The roll of the collar will be the same on both sides. Trim the front seam allowances to graduated widths. Turn the facing to the inside. Baste the edge of the collar and facings for pressing. On the lower front of the jacket, bring facing in slightly from the seam edge and baste. Press the front edge carefully. Press the lower edge of the jacket on the facing side. Press around the collar on the suit side. Before tacking the facing to the inside of the jacket, roll the collar over your hand and do a diagonal basting stitch around the collar to hold it at the roll line. At the lower front of the jacket, smooth the facing to the inside and pin the edges to the jacket. Roll the collar and lapel back, and smooth the facing to the inside. When the collars are rolled back before the facings are tacked, the roll line won't be spoiled. Catch-stitch the facings to the inside as you do for the notched collar.

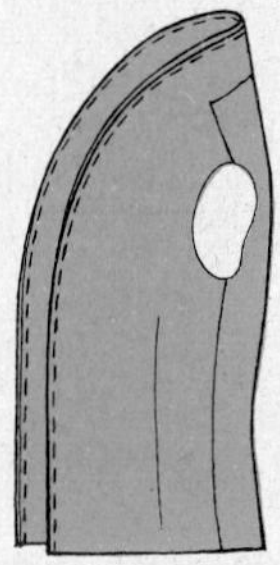

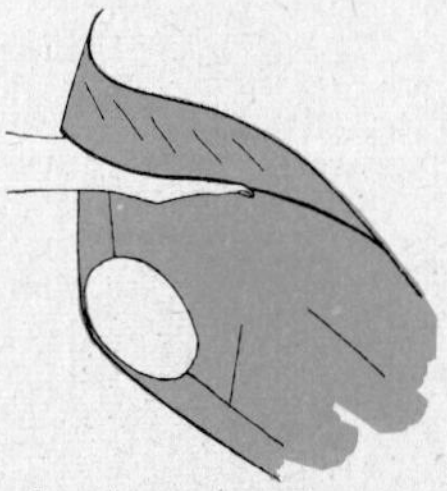

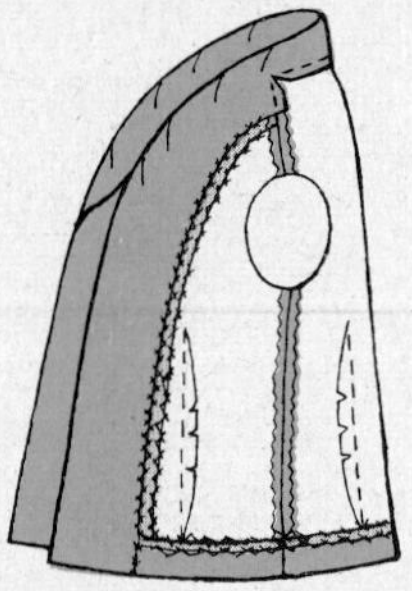

The second way the shawl collar can be constructed is by making the under collar as a separate piece and sewing it to jacket, forming the shape of the shawl collar. The facing and upper collar are cut in one piece as in the other construction. On this second style, interface the collar and suit front separately, as you do on the notched-collar suit. After the collar is sewed to the suit, apply the facing as you do for the regular shawl collar.

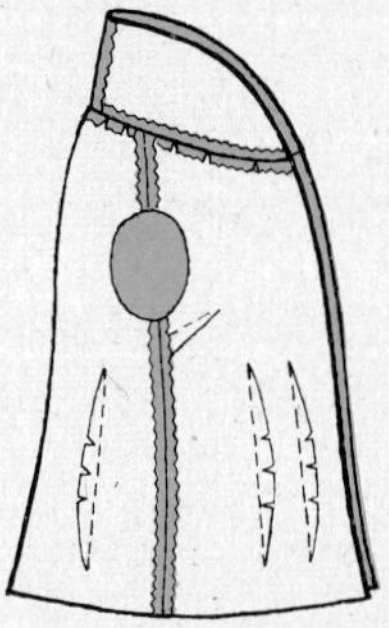

Shawl collar with a notch

This collar can be constructed like either of the shawl collars. Along the lapel on the pattern, you will find a notch marked to simulate a regular notched collar, or to provide a trim.

Carefully mark the exact placement of the notches on both lapels of the suit. You can do this with a basting

stitch. Follow the same procedure in making either of the shawl collars. The only difference is that you must carefully cut away the interfacing around the notch mark.

When the edge of the suit is taped, be sure to run the tape around the edges of this notch, so it will remain firm. Miter the tape at the points, but at the inside corner, fold it to the reverse side, forming a perfect corner. Sew the tape to the suit just as you do for all other styles.

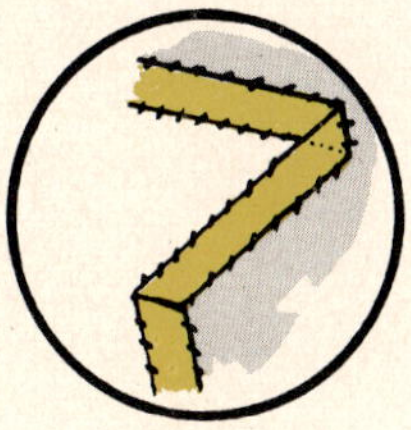

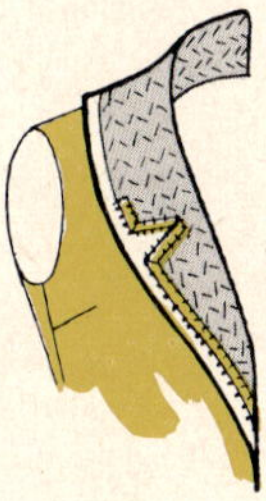

Cardigan-type jacket

This jacket is simple to make, since it has no collar to be applied and rolled. After the suit is assembled and fitted, cut interfacings of hair canvas or non-woven interfacing. The interfacing extends into the shoulder, as in the suit with the set-in sleeve.

Cut off the seam allowance at the front edge and neck of the cardigan.

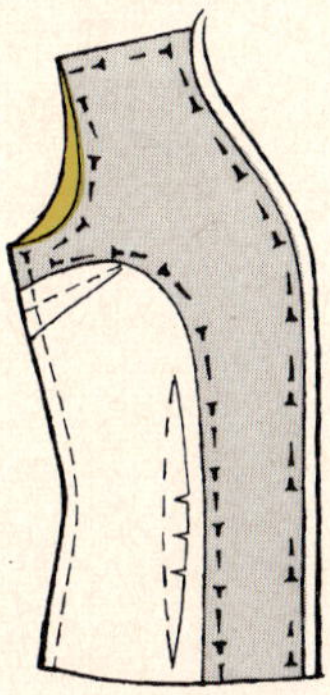

Fit it to the inside of the suit jacket, with the edge of the interfacing at the seam allowance line of the front edge of the suit.

Pin it all around the edges and into the suit jacket.

To interface the back neck, cut the interfacing piece one inch wider than the back facing piece. Cut off the seam allowance at the neck. Fit the interfacing into the back of the jacket. Lap interfacing at the shoulder line. Then, catch-stitch the edges of the interfacings to the jacket. Pin the facing to the suit and sew along the interfacing on the suit side. Trim the seam allowances to graduated widths. Turn the facing to the inside and baste all around the edge of the suit jacket.

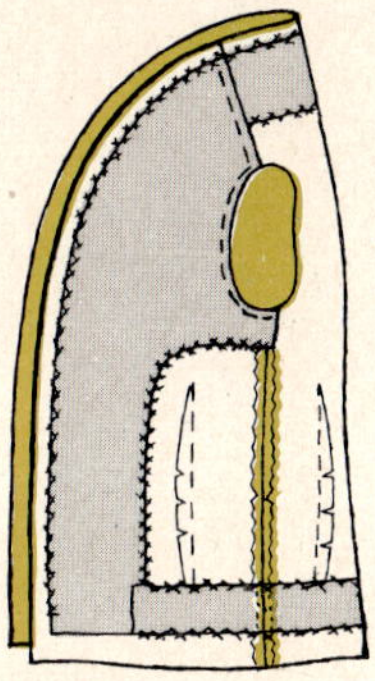

Be sure that you bring the facing back just a little from the seamline on the inside of the suit jacket. Then press the jacket.

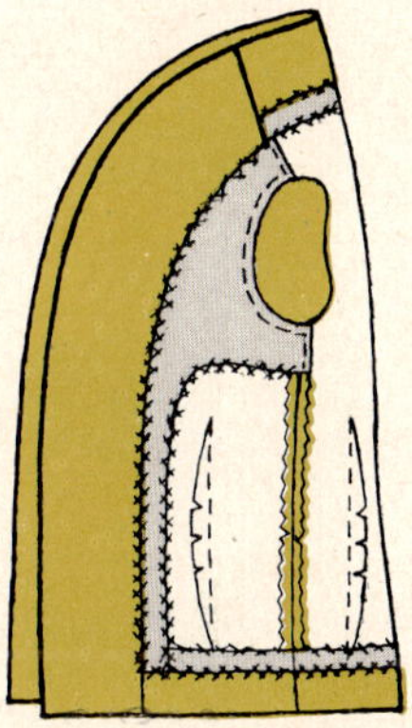

After you have pressed the facings, carefully pin them to the inside of the suit jacket. Then use a catch-stitch to fasten them to the interfacing.

Peter Pan collar

Instructions for making this collar for a dress are given in Chapter 6. The same basic method is used in making it for a suit, with only a slight difference. On the suit, the pattern provides an under and upper collar. Cut the under collar on the bias with a seam at the center. Join the center seam and press open.

Cut the interfacing of hair canvas from the same pattern. Sew, then press the seam open and stitch back the seam allowances on both sides. Trim the seams close to the stitching.

Pin the interfacing to the wrong side of the under collar, along the center seam. Roll the collar over your index finger. Start the padding stitch from the center of the collar.

Work in a circle, but inside the seam allowance lines. Work back and forth in an ever-widening circle through the center of the collar. Fill in either side with a padding stitch.

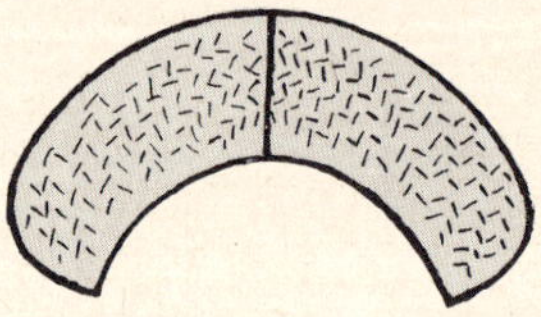

As you work, roll the collar over your finger, easing the collar as you sew. The collar edges should curl back toward the center of the collar, if you have correctly rolled it.

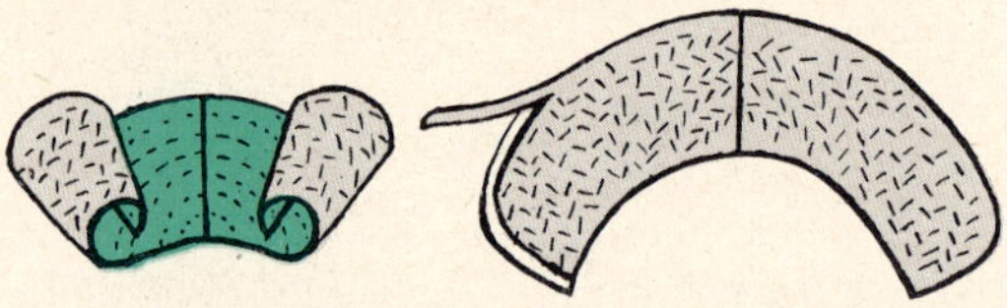

Trim off the seam allowances all around. Pin the under collar to the upper collar, right sides together. Pin on the interfacing side. Sew all around the edge of the interfacing, easing in the upper collar a little as you pin and sew. Trim off the seam allowance to graduated widths.

Turn the collar right side out. Baste all around, bringing the under collar in just slightly from the edge.

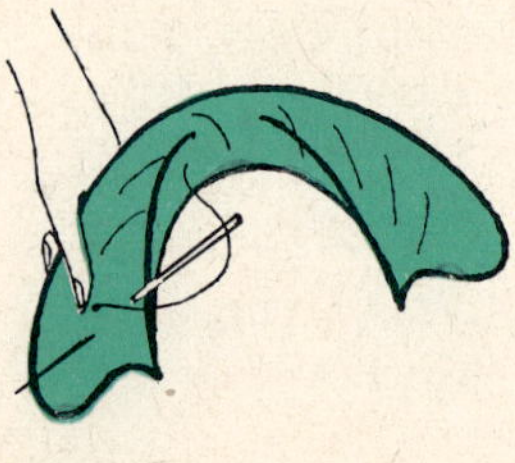

Press the collar this way. Roll it over your hand with the right side up. Do a diagonal basting on the roll line.

Sleeves

The sleeves can be finished just before sewing them in the jacket.

Turn the sleeve inside out. Press open the back seam allowance, using a sleeve board. Next, press the front sleeve seam. As you press the seam open, clip it for the entire length. Stretch it on the length.

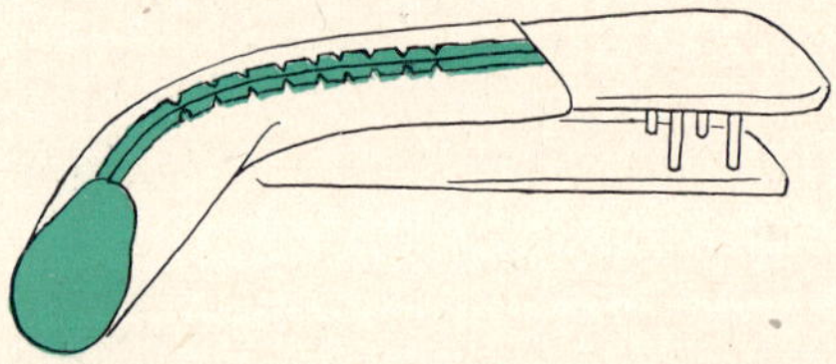

Now turn up the sleeve on the hem mark and press along this line.

Cut a strip of interfacing on the bias 1½ inches wider than the sleeve hem. Pin one edge of the interfacing just inside the hem crease. Pin it all around the sleeve, lapping the interfacing edges at the back seamline.

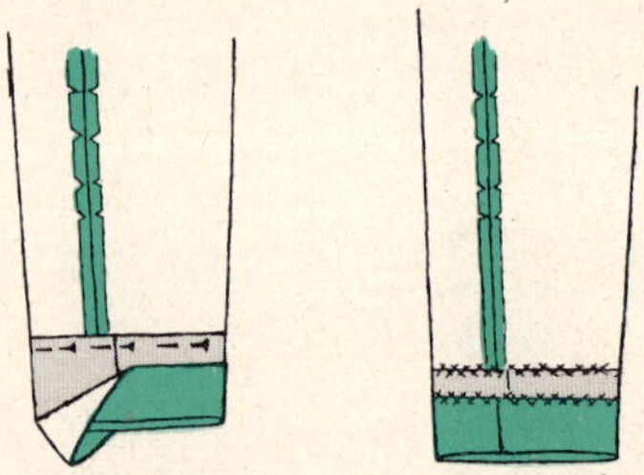

Pin the upper edges to the sleeve. Catch-stitch both edges to the sleeve. Turn the hem and catch-stitch the edge to the interfacing.

Turn the sleeve right side out. The top has been eased in to the size of the armhole. Place the sleeve top over the tailor's mitt or ham and press, steaming out the fullness from the seam allowance, and shaping the cap in the top of the sleeve.

The armholes of the suit should be stay-stitched the same as the neck was before the collar was applied.

Use one strand of silk buttonhole twist. Start at the underarm of the jacket and do the same back-stitch all around the armhole on the seam allowance line. Ease in the fullness

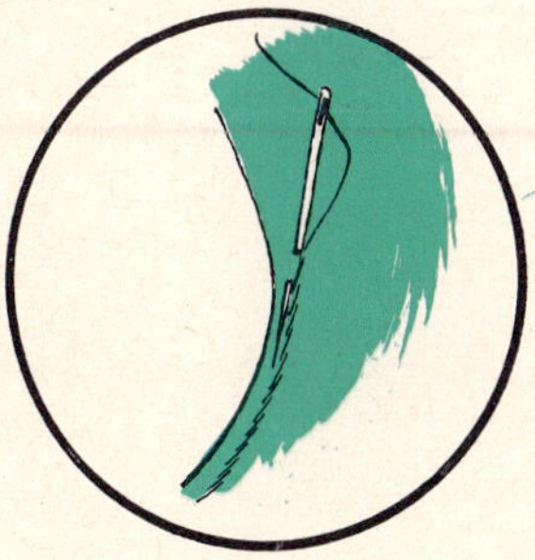

at the front armhole of the jacket, which gives a better fit to the bustline.

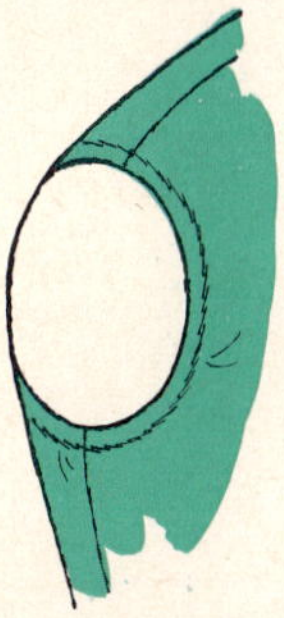

At the back of the jacket, the fullness is eased in the armhole to help shape the back to the roundness of the shoulders. Pin the sleeve into the suit. Be sure to match the slash marks to the top and the underarm seams as well as to all notches. Pin on the sleeve side with the pins placed along the seam allowance line and parallel to the seam.

When you sew, start at the underarm and sew along the pin line, removing each pin as you come to it. The sleeve will go in with no trouble. The ease won't shift when the sleeve is pinned, as it can do when it's basted.

Lining

The method for lining a suit is similar to the method used for coats. See the section on lining in Chapter 12 for directions on lining your suit.

Stitches

Here are the instructions for making the various types of stitching mentioned in this chapter.

Diagonal basting

This type of basting is used for holding several layers of fabric together. Take short stitches across the fabric, forming long vertical stitches on the top side. It is easier to do diagonal basting if you work backward.

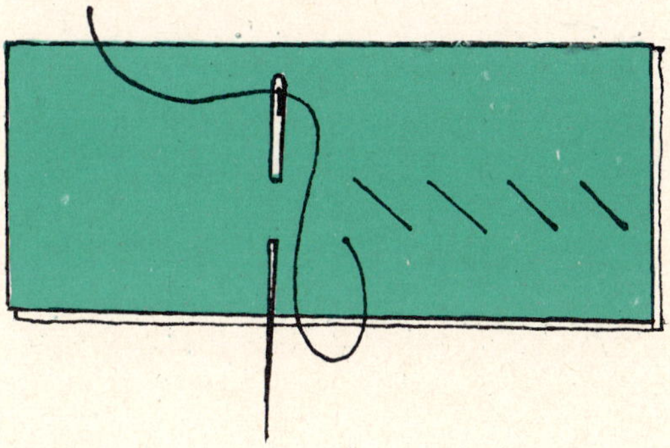

Padding stitch

This stitch is similar to diagonal basting. It is used on lapels and collars to keep the interlining in place and to securely hold the roll line.

Work up and down the roll line, taking short stitches toward you. As you work back and forth, the stitch forms a herringbone design.

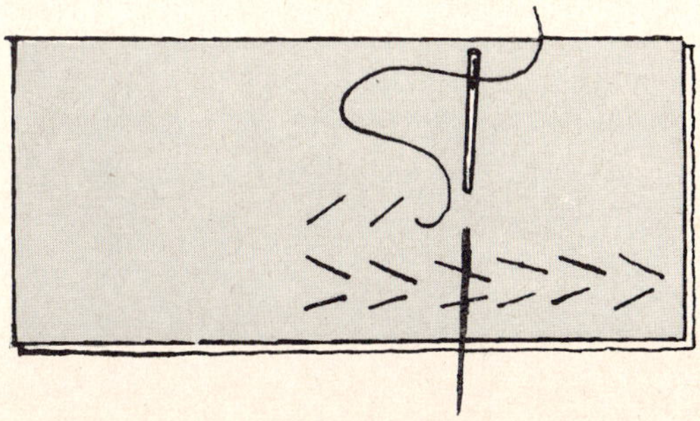

Catch-stitch

This stitch is shown in Chapter 7.

Hemming stitch for tape

Working from right to left, catch a thread or two of the suit fabric. Then pass the needle through the edge of the tape. Make small stitches to hold the tape firmly in place.

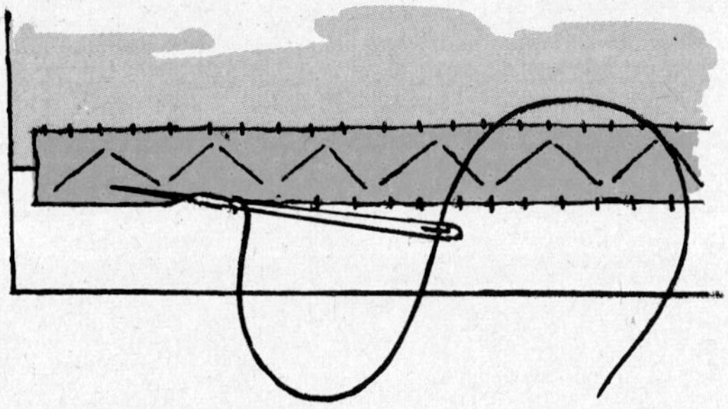

Running stitch

This stitch is shown in Chapter 7.

Design detail

Most suits are basically simple. The body of the suit is finished, and then the design detail is applied.

Usually, this detail is in the form of pockets, banding, braid, bows, and innumerable other trimmings that can be purchased in the trimming department of a store or made at home from self or contrasting fabric.

Use your ingenuity and make clothes that are really individual by choosing tasteful trimmings. You'll find inspiration everywhere.

Most women who sew like to adapt ideas they see used in ready-to-wear. Look through fashion magazines, department stores, display windows—wherever clothes are displayed. Make a note of the things that interest you, or cut photos of designs you like from magazines. Then when you make a suit, instead of an ordinary patch pocket as the pattern shows, you might substitute one of your design ideas.

Here are a few ideas for easy-to-make, but different, types of pockets.

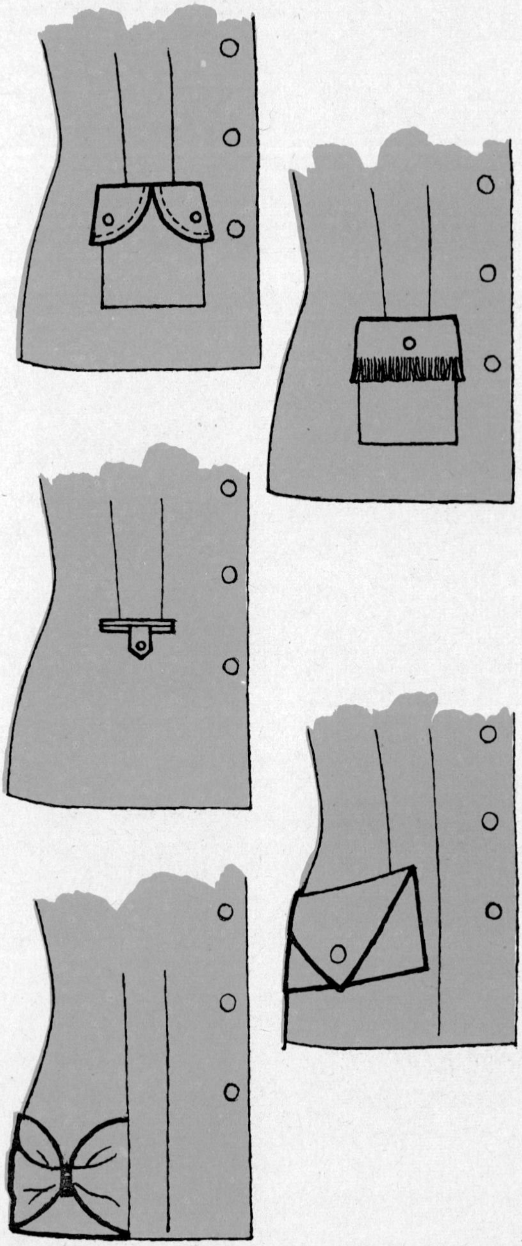

Chapter 12

Tailoring tricks on coats

Statistics show that women make fewer coats than any other type of garment. This is rather surprising because coats are relatively easy to make. Actually, when you stop to analyze it, very few pattern pieces are needed to make the average coat.

Of course, there are some extremely complicated styles, but this is true of any type of clothes you make. Many home dressmakers always visualize a coat in a heavy tweed or woolen fabric, and that stops many of them before they've even begun. Actually, coats are made of all kinds of fabrics—from chiffon to heaviest fleece. Admittedly, the notched-collar coat is a little difficult to handle when it is made in a heavy fabric, but why start with this type of coat? Instead, consider making a straight box coat or flared coat with a cardigan neck. There's no collar to make and very little fitting to do. Make it in a medium-weight tweed. This fabric doesn't show mistakes and is easy to handle.

Next, you might try a glamorous evening coat in satin or brocade, with a deep Peter Pan collar, or a big scarf collar. From there you can go on to make a basic black coat, perhaps a little more fitted, and with a big notched collar. It's amazing how well you can do, when you build up to it gradually. Tailoring can be satisfying as well as economical.

Alterations

When you buy a coat pattern, always get the same size you wear in a dress or suit. The pattern allows enough ease to fit over other garments and for the coat lining.

The fitting alterations made in your other clothes also apply to the coat. Review Chapter 3 on fitting and altering the basic pattern before you cut any garment. Chapter 11 also shows additional alterations on suits.

If you haven't yet made a basic muslin for yourself, do it before you cut your coat. There are two important fitting points to check on a coat —the hang in the front and back.

Very full bust

Even though the coat fits around the figure, the very full bust will affect the way the coat hangs.

With this figure problem, the coat appears to ride up in the front and hang low in the back. A simple alteration shown on the basic muslin will solve the problem.

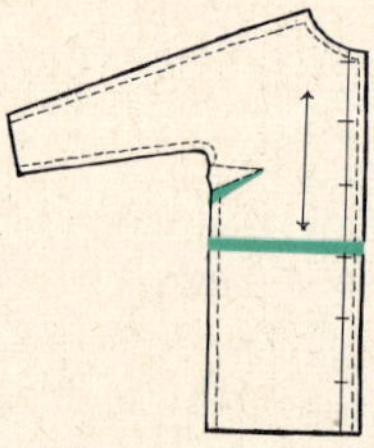

Slash through the coat pattern across the front, add to the length. If you don't need to lengthen the front, you'll definitely have to shorten the back. Whichever you do, add either the amount you lengthened the front, or the amount you shortened the back, to the front dart. Take up the side bust dart this extra amount, and the coat will hang correctly. This adjustment works for the loose-hanging coat. On the fitted coat, make adjustments in the same amount, at same points as on muslin.

Round-shouldered figure

The figure curves forward, causing the coat to droop in the front and hang open. Round shoulders cause coat to ride up in the back, protrude at the center.

The alteration for this fault will also show on your muslin, so correct the pattern before you cut the coat.

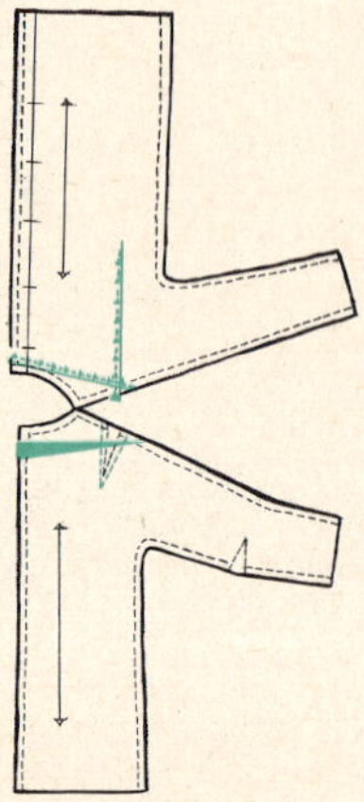

With this figure problem, the chest is hollow and the front shoulders are narrow. Shorten the front with a dart under the neck and narrow the front shoulders as shown on the muslin.

At the back, open the pattern under the neck to give more length for the rounded back. Make a deeper back dart which shapes coat to rounded back and narrows top back shoulders so front and back shoulder seams are same length.

Types of fabrics

You can make a coat of almost any fabric. With the many interlinings and interfacings available, you can create any line you wish, regardless of the weight of the fabric. Choose the interlining best suited to the fabric, weight, texture, and coat style.

Coat fabrics from animals

Wool — Camel's hair — Cashmere

Vicuna — Mohair — Alpaca

Assembling

Unlined coat

If possible, cut the seams a little wider on lighter-weight fabrics. Cut out, mark, and sew up the coat as you do for all dresses and suits. Baste in the sleeves and try the coat. Then mark any additional fitting that's needed.

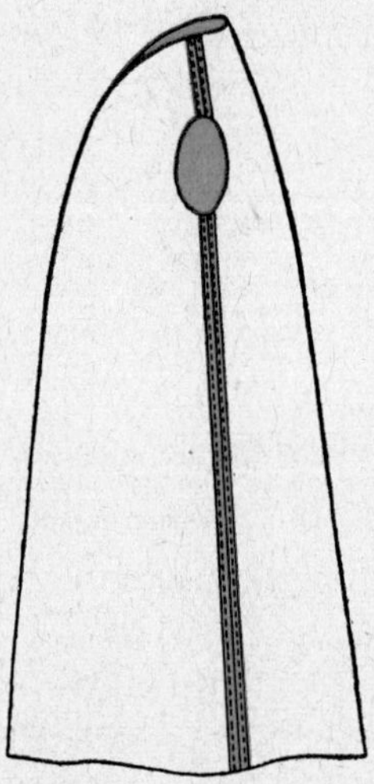

Finish all seams before the sleeves or facings are sewed to the coat. Do this as you sew up the coat. Simply turn back seams on each edge by machine. Never sew one seam across another unless the first seam is completely finished. If the seams are not wide enough to turn back, bind the edges with seam binding. Either bind the armhole seams, or turn in and whip the seam edges by hand.

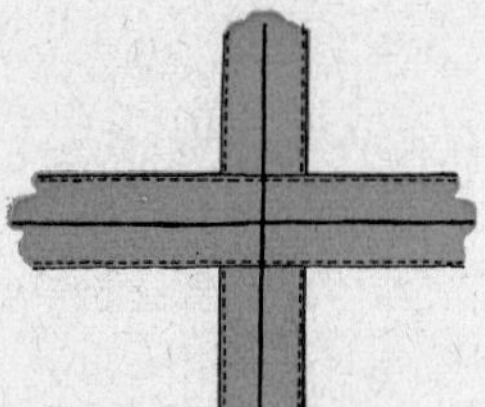

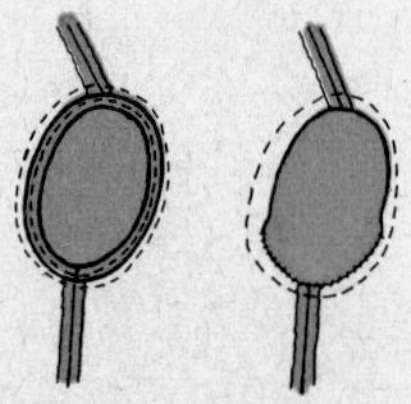

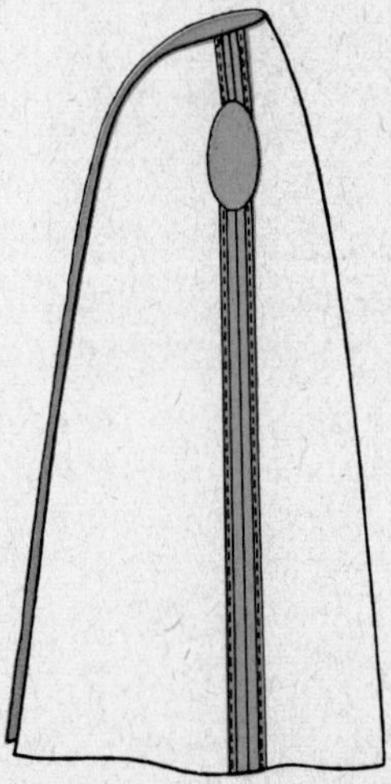

Coats that are washable can be interfaced with non-woven interfacing or a commercial woven interfacing. Or, you may prefer to use an organdy or lawn that has been preshrunk. In any case, sew the interfacing to the facing before applying it to the coat.

If there are buttonholes in the coat, make them first. Be sure to use a piece of non-woven interfacing under each one so it won't ravel.

If the coat has a collar, make it as you would for a dress. (See sections on collars in Chapters 6 and 9.)

Cut the interfacing from the same pattern as the facing. Be sure the interfacing is preshrunk. Pin and stitch it carefully all around the facing close to the seam edge. Bind the inside edge of the facing as you did the seams, or cut away the interfacing on the inside edge for 1/4 inch. Turn this edge back and stitch it.

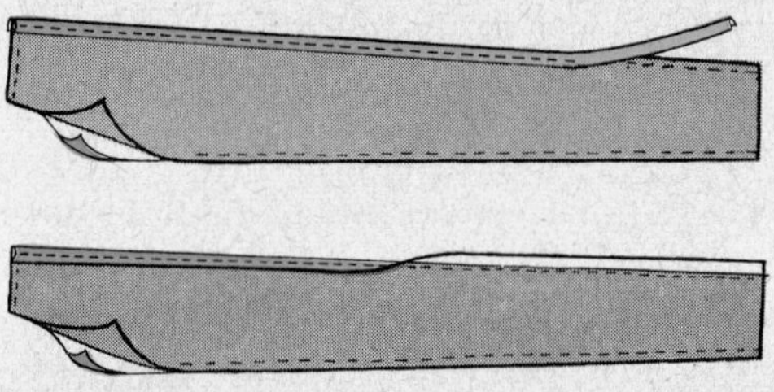

Apply the coat facing as you would for a dress. Then turn the hem of the coat, trim, and press. Sew a seam binding to the hem edge. (See Chapter 7 for information on hems.)

Evening coats

These coats are cut in fabrics that should be made to look crisp and perky. Cut out the coat and then cut the interlining from the same pattern. Make sure the interlining is preshrunk.

Remove the pattern from the cut-out pieces, after marking darts, tucks, and any other details on the interlining. Then put the wrong side of the coat against the unmarked side of the interlining. Press the two layers together; then pin all around the edges and sew the two layers just outside the seam allowance line.

After it is mounted, sew up the coat and try it on for a fitting. If there are any alterations needed, correct the pattern and recut from it.

The evening coat will not have the interfacing of hair canvas, generally used for suits and coats. If the coat has a cardigan neck or a set-on collar, like the Peter Pan collar, it can be interfaced with non-woven interfacing, or a commercial woven one. These are lightweight but have good body.

Also, it is important that the color of the interfacing doesn't show through the upper fabric. Hair canvas, which is available in beige or gray, sometimes shows a shadow when used with lighter-colored silks.

When the coat has a rolled lapel, use a woven interfacing. When the roll is on the bias grain, it gives a softer line than if a non-woven interfacing is used.

Facings, buttonholes, and collars can all be finished the same way as on the dressmaker suit. Lining a coat will be illustrated later in this chapter.

Wool coats

If you use a heavy, firm fabric, the coat does not need to be mounted. Otherwise, use the same type of interlining as for an evening coat. Again, make collars, facings, and buttonholes as for the dressmaker suit.

Pockets

There are many different types of pockets. They serve as design details as well as being functional.

The inside patch pocket with the flap, or the regular patch pocket with a flap are usually found on the more casual type of coat. Welt pockets or flap pockets are more dressy. There are interesting variations of each.

Patch pocket

The patch pocket on a coat or suit must be lined. Cut the pocket from the coat fabric, and the lining piece from the coat lining. Make the lining ⅛ inch smaller than the pattern.

Sew the right side of the lining to the right side of the pocket at the top edge. Leave 2 inches open in the center. Fold back on the hemline, with right sides together. Stitch the edges on the seam allowance line. Trim seam, and clip on the curve.

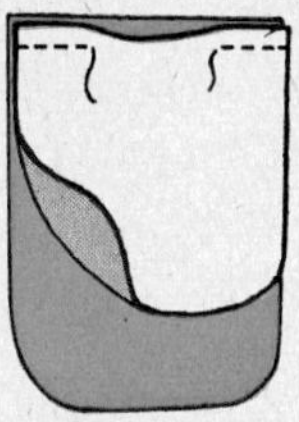
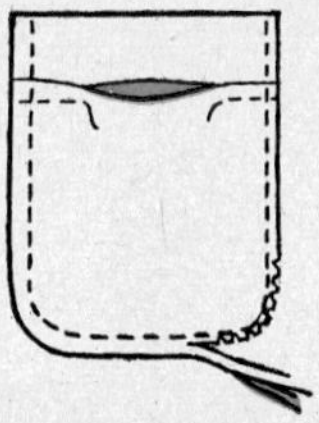

Turn the pocket right side out through the opening at the hem.

Slip-stitch the opening. Then baste around the pocket. The lining, which was cut smaller, will be ⅛ inch in from the pocket edge.

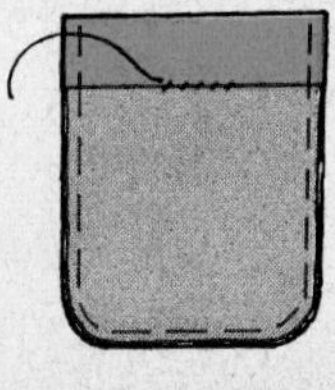

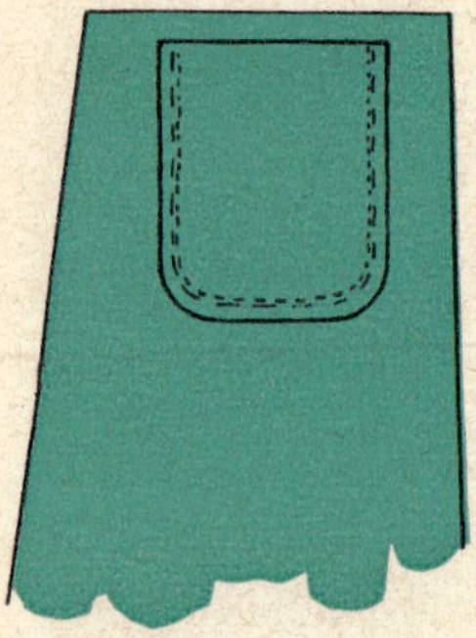

Sew the pocket to the coat by hand or by machine. Baste the pocket to the coat.

Top-stitch about 5/8 inch in from the pocket edge. Slip-stitch the edges by hand, or use a trim stitch all around the pocket before it's sewed to the coat by hand. Use a buttonhole twist.

Pocket with flap

A flap is often used with a patch pocket. Line the flap with coat lining. If the fabric needs body, interface it. Stitch the interfacing to the outside seamline of the flap.

Trim 1/8 inch off the lining. Sew it to the flap, with right sides together and edges even. Trim the seam and clip all around the curved edge.

Turn right side out, baste, and press the edge. Top-stitch 5/8 inch in from the finished edge.

Stitch the pocket flap 3/4 inch above the pocket, right side of flap to the coat. Trim the seam to 1/4 inch.

Turn the flap down over pocket and top-stitch 5/8 inch down from seam.

Inside flap pocket

Mark the position of the flap pocket on the coat with a basting thread.

Make the flap as for a patch pocket. Pin the raw edge of the flap to the top of the basting line, right side of flap to right side of coat. Stitch on the seam allowance line.

Cut pocket pieces from coat fabric. Make them 2 1/2 inches deep, 2 inches wider than the flap. Stitch one piece with the edge along the stitching line of the flap. Stitch on the seam allowance line, with the stitches just clearing the flap edge underneath.

Turn to the wrong side. Slash between stitching lines to 1/2 inch of the ends. Clip diagonally to the corners.

Turn the pocket piece to the wrong side. Fold a pleat at either end, forming a welt at the lower pocket opening. Then stitch into position from the right side.

Turn the coat back. The small point at the end of the pocket is visible over the end of the welt. Stitch the point across this end. The flap turns down on the outside; the flap seam turns up on the

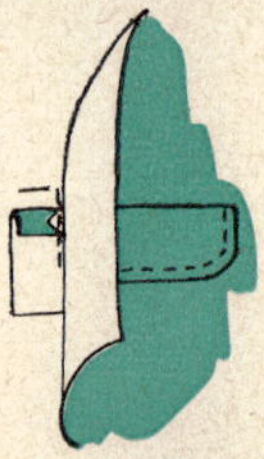

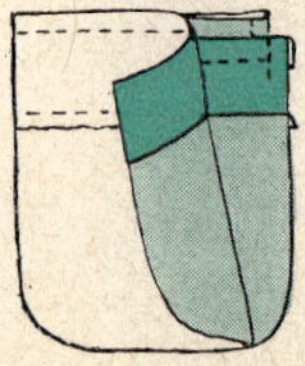

inside. Sew the pocket piece (with lower lining added) along the welt seam. Sew around the pocket pieces on the inside, and the pocket is finished.

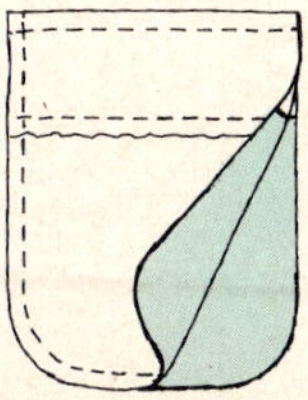

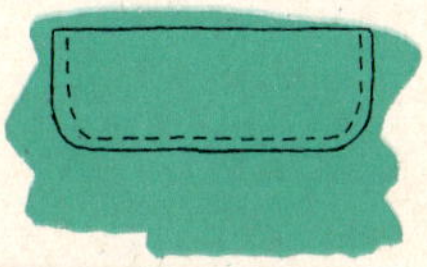

Simulated patch pocket

After finishing the pocket, turn the coat to right side. Run a basting stitch, outlining the pocket and catching all thicknesses together. Stitch along this line by machine. Mark a second row ⅝ inch from the first one and stitch by machine. This looks like a patch pocket, but gives a more tailored appearance to coat.

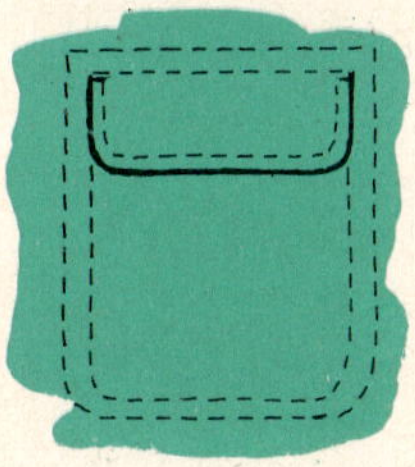

Diagonal welt pocket

Mark the position for a welt pocket with a basting line on the right side of the coat.

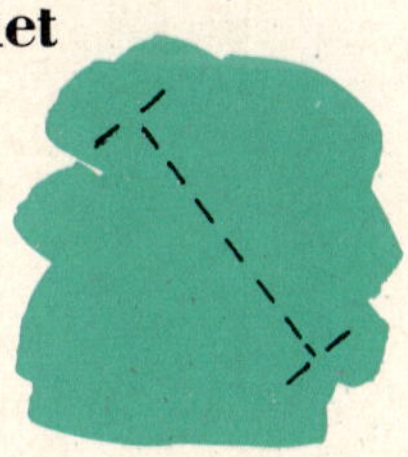

Cut 2 shaped welt pieces from the coat fabric, and one piece from the interfacing. Sew the interfacing to the welt facing. Pin the welt and facing, right sides together, and stitch. Trim the seam and clip to the stitching line

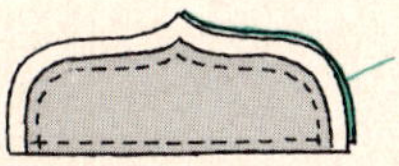

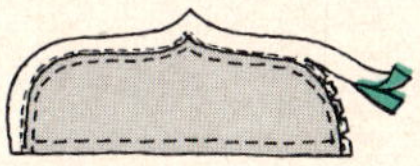

on the curved edges. Turn to the right side and baste in place. Press, and then stitch all around.

Place the welt on the lower side of the pocket line of the coat and stitch on the seam allowance line. Pin the upper pocket piece on the upper side of the pocket line, with the raw edge lapped to the stitching line of the welt. Stitch on the seam allowance line, which should just clear the edges of the welt underneath. Turn to the inside. Slash between the two rows of stitching to ½ inch of either end. Slash diagonally into the corners. Turn the pocket piece to the wrong side. The welt turns up on the outside; the seam allowance turns down on the inside.

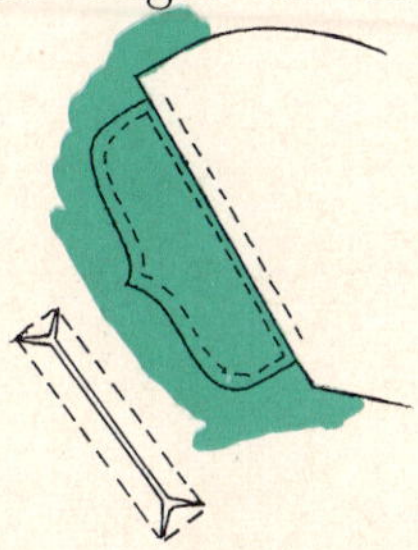

Stitch the under pocket to the seam of the welt on the inside and sew the pocket pieces together around the edges, catching the points at the corners of the pocket. In heavy fabrics, pockets are half-lined as for the flap pocket. Turn to the right side. Press the welt up. Stitch around sides with an invisible slip-stitch, or on the machine along trim stitching.

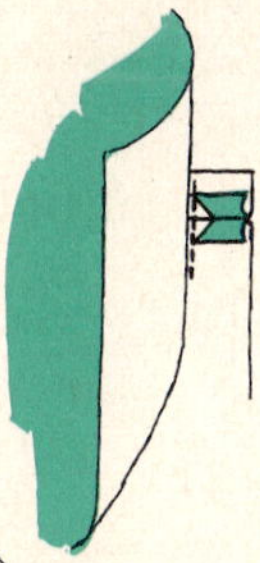

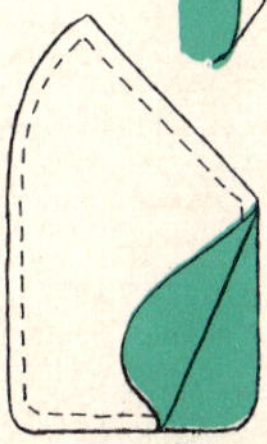

Use the same method if the welt is on the straight of the goods.

Seams

For general sewing, a plain inside seam is used for coats. However, many interesting trimming ideas can be worked out with different types of seams. The garment doesn't have to be cut in any special way to take advantage of these seams.

If you decide your coat would look better with a little detail, you can work it out on the original seamlines.

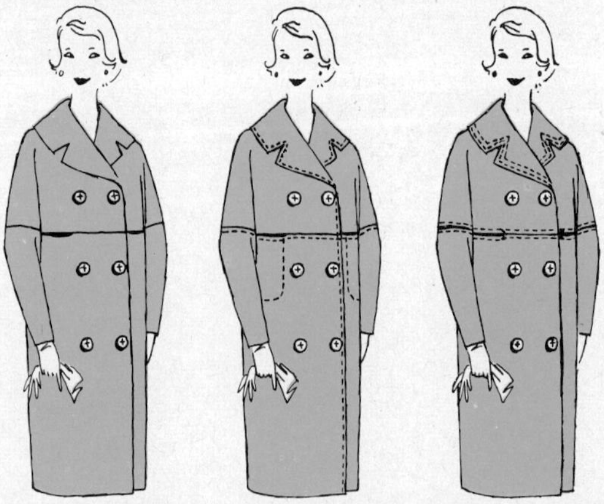

Plain seam — Welt seam — Slot seam

Slot seam

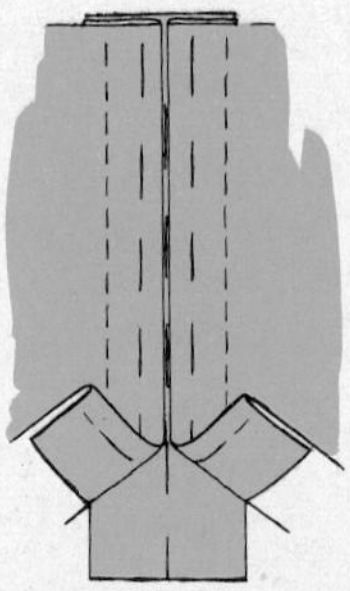

Hand-baste or machine-baste the regular seam, and press it open. On the wrong side of the seam, place a strip of fabric the length of the seam, but slightly wider than the seam allowances. Baste the center of it down the middle of the seam. On the right side, run two rows of basting an equal distance on either side of the center seam. Stitch along these lines. Remove the original basting stitch. The seam will spread, showing a little of the underlay.

Welt seam

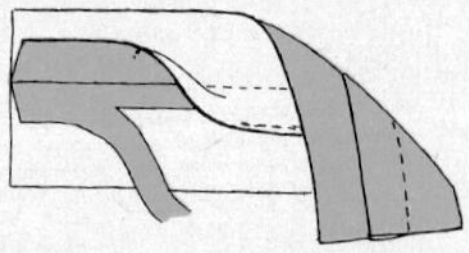

This type is suitable for very heavy fabrics. Sew up the seams, right sides together. Decide which side of the seamline should have the welt. Cut the seam to $\frac{1}{4}$ inch on this side. Press the other seam over this trimmed edge and stitch. The distance you stitch from the seam will be the width of the welt. This seam gives a more tailored look to a coat. Use it around armholes, yokes, and along sleeve seams.

When stitching, be sure tensions on your machine are not too tight, and that pressure of the presser foot is not too heavy for the fabric.

Tucked seam

The seam allowances are generally made wider where this seam is to be used. On a heavy coat, the tuck should have a little width to be effective.

Turn under the seam allowance on one edge and baste; lap this over the other edge so the raw edges meet at the inside. Stitch as far from folded edge as the depth of tuck desired.

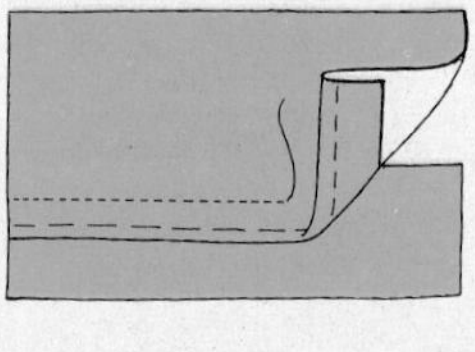

Double-welt seam

Make a welt seam. Turn to the right side and add another row of stitching close to the fold edge of the seam.

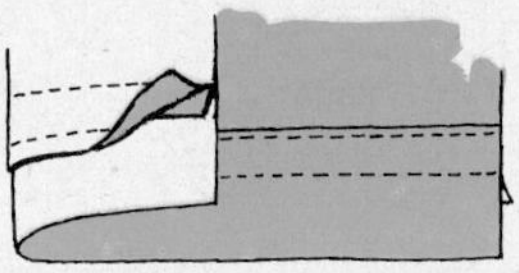

This seam is frequently used on active sportswear, and is often stitched in a contrasting color.

Bound-edge seam

Fold and press the seam binding so the under edge is just a trifle wider than the upper edge. Press the seam open. If it has started to ravel, trim the edges. Slide the tape over the edge, with the narrow fold on top.

Stitch along the edge of the binding through three thicknesses of fabric. This seam is used on fabrics that ravel easily, as well as unlined jackets and coats. (See illustration on page 74.)

Stitched-edge seam

On lightweight fabrics, finish the edges by turning under ¼ inch on each edge and stitching by machine. Stitch with loose tension close to the seam edge so the seam won't pucker on the inside. (See illustration on page 74.)

Hand picking

This is done in a matching buttonhole twist. Hold the garment with the right side toward you, and do a back-stitch. Take a very small back-stitch, slide the needle between the layers of fabric, and pick up a tiny stitch on the wrong side. Bring the needle to the right side again and take another back-stitch. When you come to the roll of the lapel, the underside is actually the right side, so bring the needle all the way through the fabric. Do same back-stitch on lapel side.

Interlining

You can sew the interlining to the lining, and then sew it into the coat. Or, it can be applied to the coat separately before the lining is put in.

When it is sewed in with the lining, the interlining will have to be redone if the coat is ever relined. On the other hand, some people believe that the interlining loses its warmth and should be replaced anyway. Both methods are shown, so you may choose whichever one you prefer.

Applying interlining directly to the coat

Cut the interlining from the lining pattern. Trim away the seam allowance down the front and around the back neckline. Cut the interlining away at the hem so it is 1 inch shorter than the finished length.

Mark for the darts at the back and front shoulders. Slash the darts, lap the amount the interlining is to be taken in, and top-stitch it so there is no bulk. This is the only machine-stitching you will have to do.

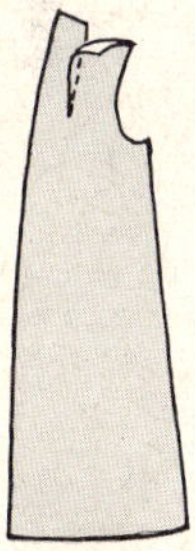

Turn the coat inside out. Take the back interlining first and lap it over the side seam, shoulder, and back neck. Sew it by hand along these seams. Next, apply

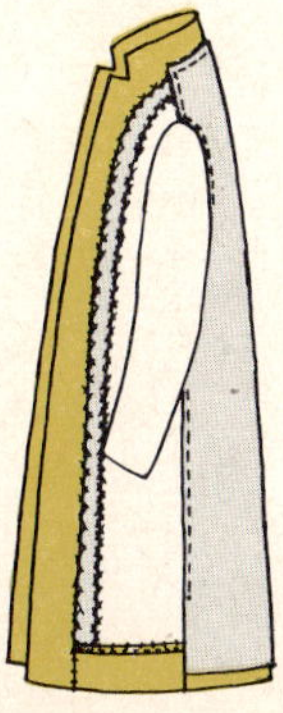

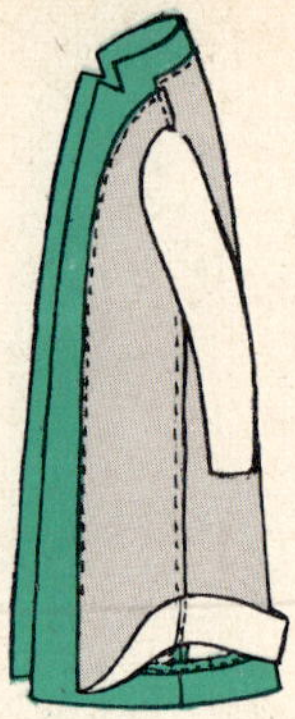

the fronts. Lap the front seams over the back at the sides of the coat. Sew these in place with a loose running stitch. Sew the interlining to the coat to within 6 inches of the hem. Below that, just the back and front interlining seams are joined. Lap the front shoulder seam over the back seam and tack.

The back interlining extends to the collar edge. In the front, it overlaps the facing edge for the entire length. If the coat has a back neck facing, the back interlining will just

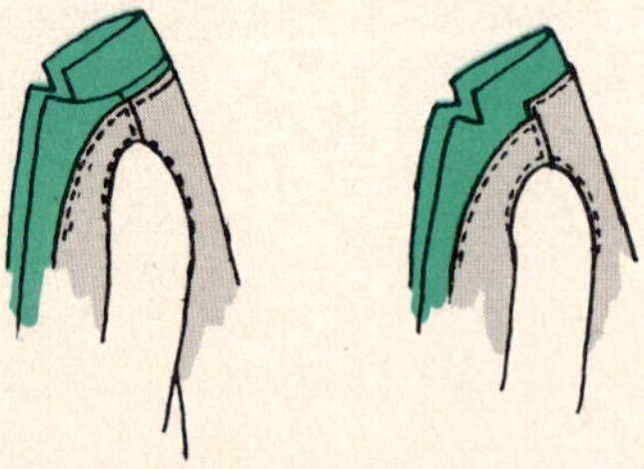

lap this facing edge. Usually, only the upper sleeve is interlined; however, if you need the added warmth, interline the under sleeve. It is sometimes advisable to interline the entire sleeve. Then you can also sew in an extra panel by hand along upper sleeve for warmth.

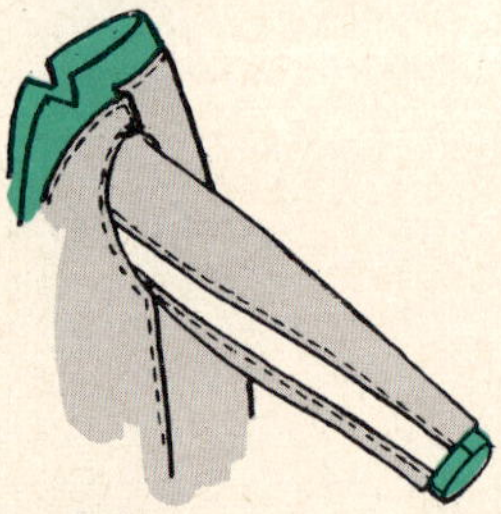

Cut the interlining a little shorter than the finished sleeve length of the coat, so it just laps the hem edge.

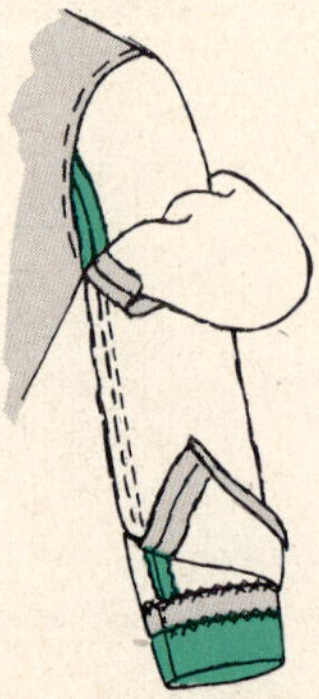

Next, carefully lap the interfacing along seam allowance line and tack.

Lining

Cut the lining from the lining pattern. Mark and sew any darts or tucks in the lining. The back of the lining has a pleat for ease. Press this pleat for the entire length. Sew by machine across the top close to the neck to hold the pleat in place.

Sew up the side seams and shoulders. If the back neck has no facing, the back shoulder seam will be longer than the front, which is cut off to finish at the front facing. When the shoulders are stitched, leave 5/8 inch of the seam allowance open at the front shoulder. Press open all the seams of the lining. Lap the shoulder seam of the lining over the shoulder seam of the coat. Tack the seams together.

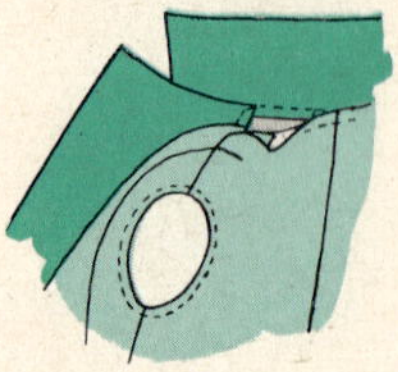

Lap the side seam of the lining over the side seam of the coat and pin to fit. Tack the seams together, to about 6 inches from the coat bottom.

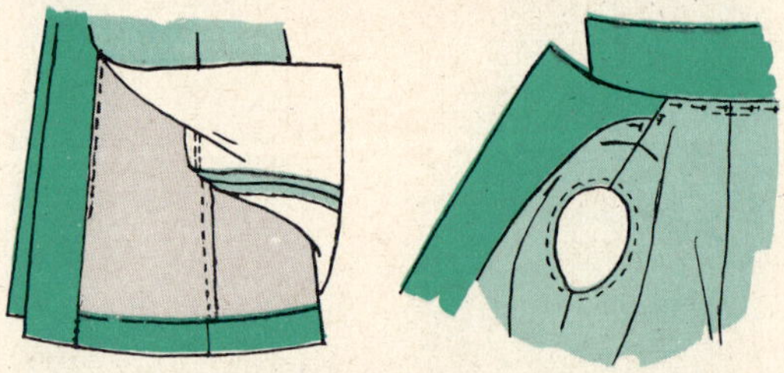

Clip to the seam allowance line all around the back neckline. Turn under a 5/8-inch seam, lap to the seam allowance at the back neckline and pin.

When pinning the front lining, start

at the bottom of the coat. Measure at the side the amount the lining hangs below the coat. Check to see that the same amount extends below the coat in front. The reason for this is that the front lining is cut slightly on the bias along the bustline.

By starting to pin the lining at the bottom and working up, the facing will be eased in over the bustline as it should be, and there will be no possibility of the fabric stretching here as so often happens.

Turn under the seam allowance at the front and lap it over the front facing. Pin along both fronts. Slip-stitch the lining to the facing and back neck. Leave about 6 inches of the lining free at the lower end of the facing. The hem turns up over the interlining where it is sewed.

The lower edges of the lining can now be sewed to the facings. Baste

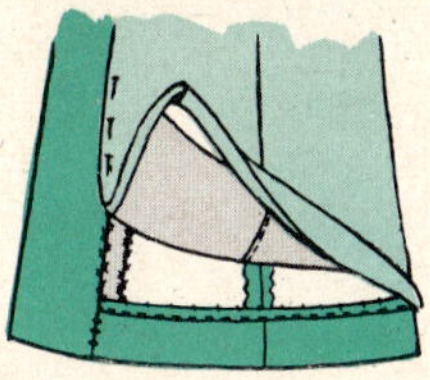

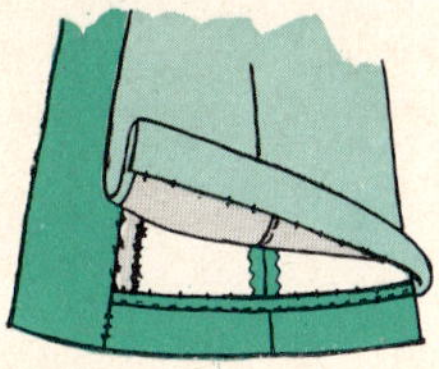

the lining to the armhole seam. Sew up the sleeve lining. Turn the coat sleeve and sleeve lining inside out.

Place the wrong side of the sleeve lining against the wrong side of the coat sleeve. Lap the lining seams over the coat seams. Tack the seams together by hand to about 3 inches above the sleeve hem and to 2 inches from the top. Turn the coat sleeve inside the sleeve lining.

To do this, put your hand in the lining and turn it over the sleeve. Turn under seam allowance at top of sleeve. Lap it to the armhole seam allowance and pin the sleeve to fit. Sew sleeve lining by hand. Pin the lining

to the sleeve about 5 inches above the hem. Turn under the lining at the lower edge of the sleeve and pin over the edge of the hem. Slip-stitch by hand. The lining folds down in the sleeve, making a shallow fold just below the stitching. This gives a little ease in the lining so the sleeve will hang smoothly and not draw or pucker.

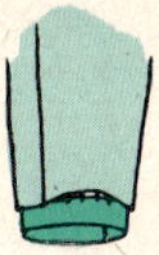

At the hemline, use long French tacks to hold the lining to the coat at the side seams. Stitch holds lining firmly, doesn't show.

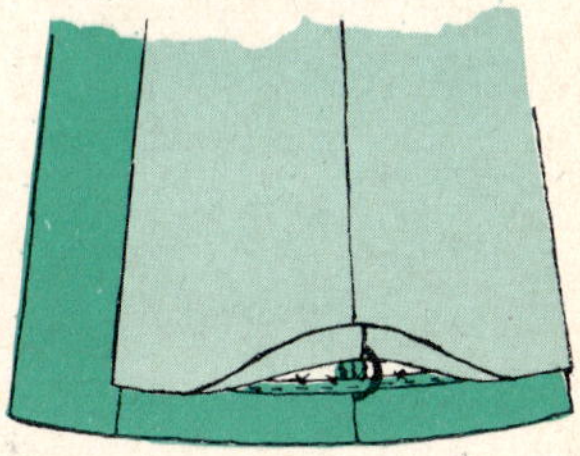

Sewing lining and interlining together

In this method of interlining the coat, the lining and interlining are cut from the same pattern, except for the back. The back lining is cut with a pleat; the interlining is not. Press

the back pleat in the lining. Place the wrong side of the back lining over the back interlining and sew all around. Sew the front lining pieces to the front interlining pieces. Sew the darts or tucks in the back and front pieces. Sew up the side seams and shoulder seams of the lining. Sew the lining into the coat as you do in the interfaced coat.

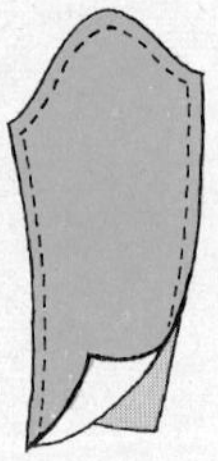

Lining the jacket

Line the jacket the same as the coat except at the lower edge. On the short jacket, the lining is attached at the hemline. Trim the lining even with the finished length of the jacket.

Baste the lining to the jacket about 5 inches above the hem. Turn under the seam allowance at the lower edge of the lining and lap over the raw edge of the hem. Pin and slip-stitch.

The extra length of the lining will form a fold above the hem of the jacket. Press. This extra fold will

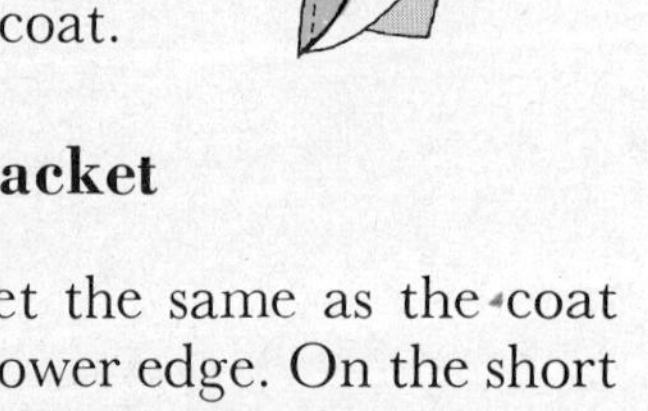

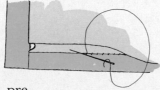

give ease and prevent drawing. The front lining which was left unfinished to about 5 inches above the hem can now be finished to the front facings.

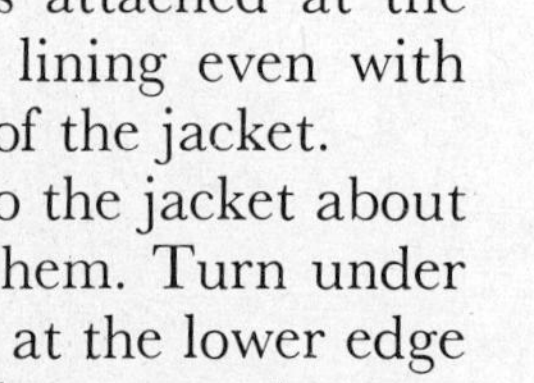

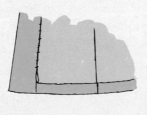

Linings can be made in contrasting colors or of a print to match a blouse or dress worn under the coat or jacket.

Binding

There are innumerable types of bindings available. They are made in wool, silk, rayon, and cotton. They are woven like military braids or cut, folded, and pressed of actual bias fabrics. There's a wide range of colors, with some even woven in two or three colors, so the binding is really a decorative trim. Most of these bindings come folded, ready to apply.

Commercial binding

This binding can be sewed entirely by machine, or partly by machine and finished by hand.

Slide the binding over the edge of the suit or coat to be bound. Start to baste along the edge, catching both edges of the binding at once.

When you come to a point around which the binding has to be mitered, there is a trick the professional uses that makes binding easy to apply.

If you are binding the front and neckline, sew the binding to the very end of the front edge before you turn the corner. Sew across the end, holding the two layers of binding together at the top edge of the coat. Slightly stretch the binding and start binding around the neck.

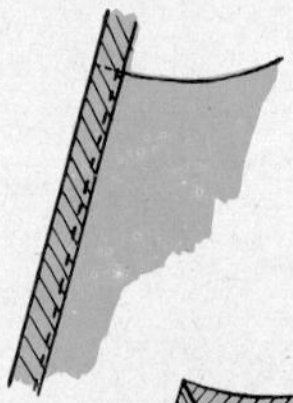

At the corner, fold the binding so the corners miter. Mold and shape the binding around the neck, basting it into place. Follow the same procedure on the other

side of the coat. Press the binding very lightly, then stitch by machine all along the binding edge.

In some cases, where there is a rolled lapel, it is better to sew one side by machine and finish the other by hand. In this case, baste just one side of the binding to the right side of the coat or jacket.

To be sure it is put on evenly, keep the fold along the edge of the garment. Baste one side all around. Follow the same procedure just described at corners. Do first stitching by machine, finish inside by hand.

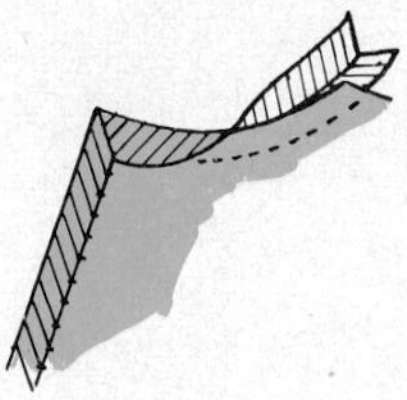

Self-fabric binding

These bindings are always beautiful and decorative. They are not hard to make if you press and shape the binding before it is applied.

Cut the bias twice the width of the finished binding, plus double seam allowances. Again, press it in half on the length. Now fold back the seam allowance on the double fold and press that. Stretch as you press. Open the pressed binding. The creased line of the seam allowance is stitched to the right side of the jacket. If the binding is 5/8 inch wide, it should be stitched about 1/2 inch from the jacket edge.

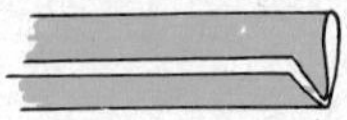

Fold over the edge of the jacket to the inside and tack the second fold edge to the inside. When the jacket has a pointed lapel or neck, the bias must be mitered. Lay the bias on the jacket as it will be sewed. Fold and press the miter at the outside corners, actually shaping it to the jacket as it will be applied.

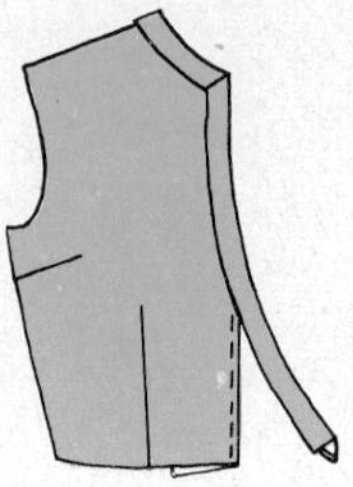

Open the bias to the wrong side. A crease line will appear where the miter was pressed.

Stitch on this crease line to the folded seam allowance line to finish the miter.

Trim away the excess seam before turning.

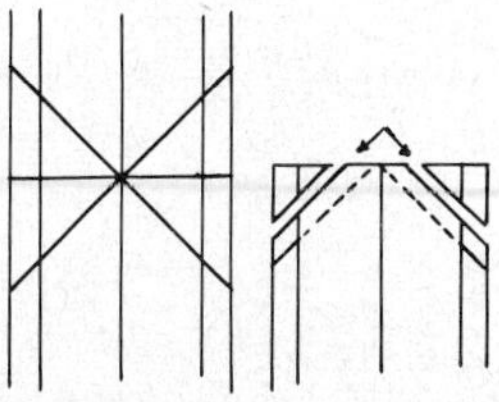

The jacket can be bound with the pressed and shaped binding and you'll have a perfect miter at the point. The miter is shaped to the inside corner and then pressed the same way.

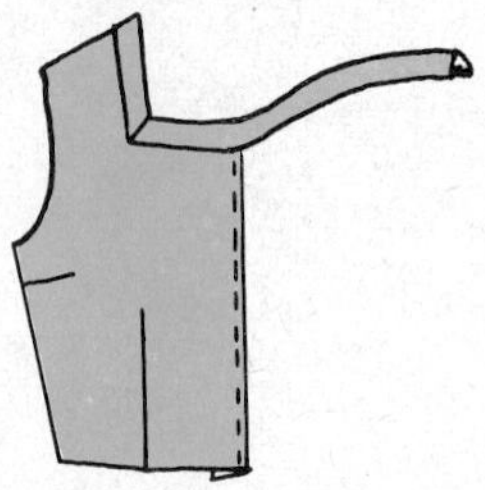

Open the bias. The crease lines will show on the inside. Stitch on these lines to the seam allowance fold line. Next, trim as shown. Turn, and you will have a perfect miter for the inside corner.

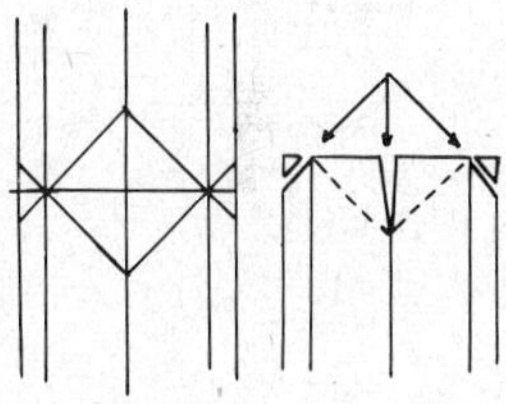

Finish the sleeve edges with the bias, too. It can be made either way, all by machine or first stitched by machine and then finished by hand stitching.

Binding as trimming

Bindings can also be used as design on your clothes as well as binding edges. See the color photographs in Chapter 11 for ideas on how bindings can be used to lend interesting effects or color to suits.

Reversible coat

The reversible coat that can be worn either side out is usually made in two contrasting fabrics. It may be two beautiful shades of satin used in an evening coat, or a plain and a plaid for a casual coat.

You actually make up two separate coats. They can have set-in sleeves or sleeves cut in one with the back and front. They can also have collars and cuffs or the cardigan-type neckline.

The cardigan-neckline type is the easiest to make. The interfacings are sewed by hand to the inside of one of the coats. Tape the edge of the coat along the interfacing line as you would for any coat. Pin the right sides of the coat together on the outside edge. Leave the hem edges free. Stitch all

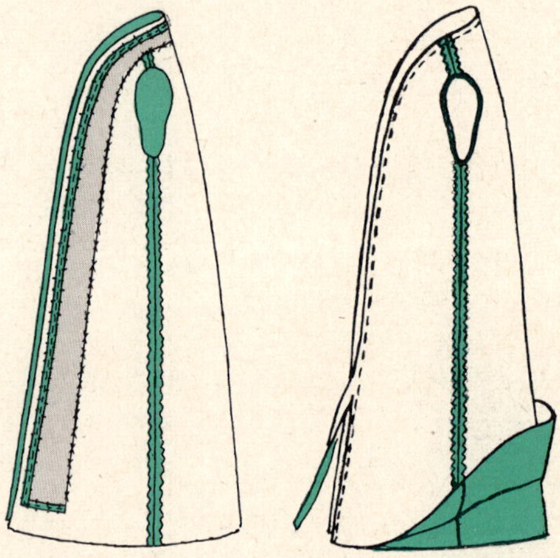

around on the interfacing side. Trim the seams to graduated widths. Turn to the right side, baste, and press.

Sleeves

To finish the ends of the sleeve, turn the edges of the upper and under sleeve under and pin together. Turn the sleeve to the inside between the two layers of coat. Pull the sleeve toward the hem of the coat so you can sew the sleeve edges. Bring the pinned edges together on the inside and stitch all around. Trim the seam to grad-

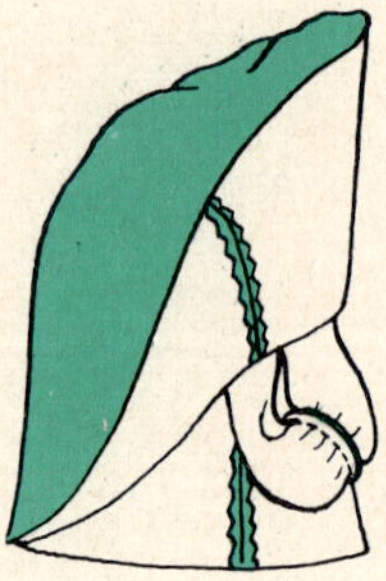

uated widths and turn back to the right side. Baste. Press around edge.

The inside seams of the coat must all be tacked together. The armhole seams were already pressed open before the coats were joined. Now pin them together very carefully along the seamline and do a blind-tacking stitch on the right side to hold them together.

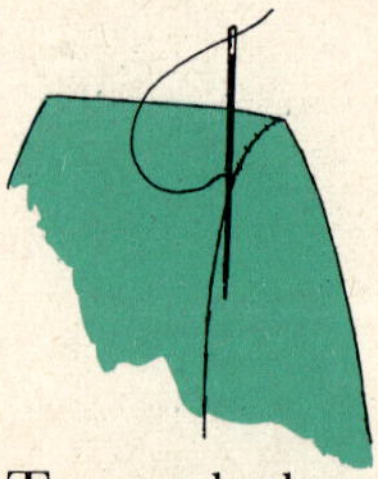

Lap the side seams of the two coats and pin together along the seam on the inside. To reach these seams, work from the hem where the edges have not been joined.

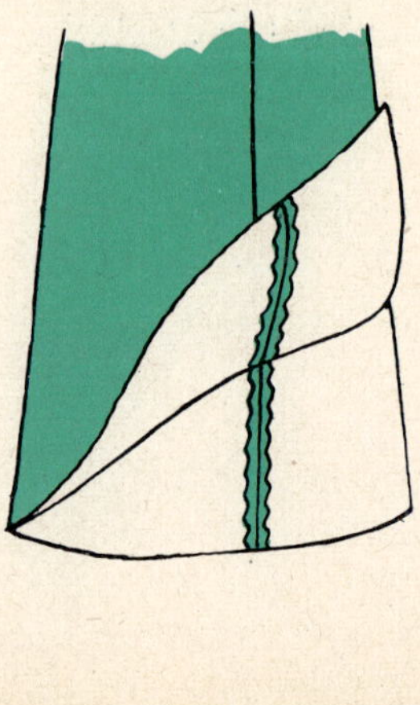

Sew the side seams together to 8 inches from the bottom of the coat. Turn up the hem all around the entire coat. Sew a seam binding to the hem edge, or just pink and stitch it. Sew the hem to the inside of the coat. Use a tailor's hem to hold it in place.

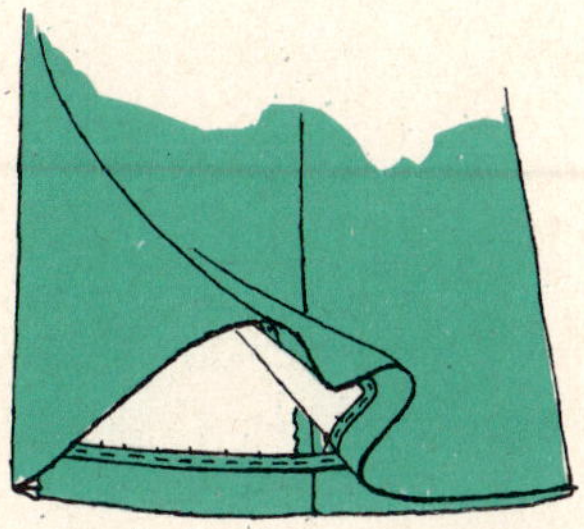

Then slip-stitch the lower edges of the coat fronts together for 4 inches. Hold them together at the seams with long French tacks.

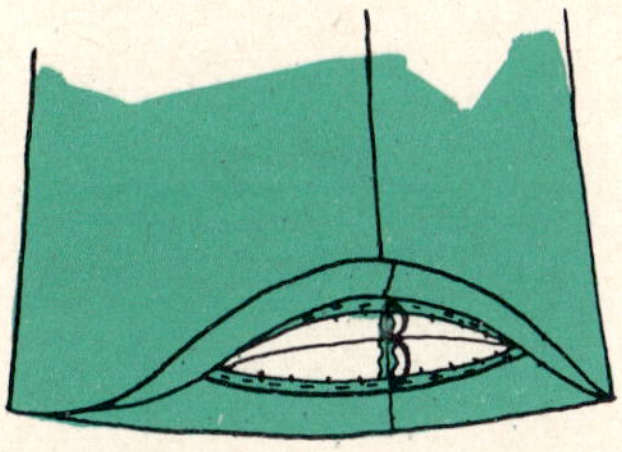

Reversible coat with collar

If the reversible coat has a collar, you must decide whether or not you want contrasting collar and cuffs on the coat when it is reversed.

If the coat has a shawl collar, you have no choice. The collars will be contrasting, because this collar is cut in one with the body of the coat. The under coat becomes the upper collar, as the coat is worn with the collar turned back.

The coat with the set-on collar and cuff can be made so the entire coat is one color, regardless of which side is worn on the outside.

Collar and cuffs

Cut collar and cuffs of the two fabrics and make them up. Interface them, but don't use a padding stitch.

Before you sew the two layers of coat together, sew the collar to the neckline of one side of the coat and the cuffs to the ends of the sleeves. The contrasting color of the collar and the cuffs should be against the coat side on which it is sewed.

Finish the coat as you do the reversible one. Each side of the coat will be all one color.

Finishing details

Patch pockets are generally sewed on both sides in matching shades.

Two sets of buttonholes will have to be made if the coat buttons. They can be bound buttonholes, or machine or hand-made buttonholes.

Regardless of which type of buttonhole you use, make a set on the right-hand side of each side of the reversible coat. In this way, the buttonholes that are on the right-hand side of the coat when it is worn on the outside will be on the left-hand side when the coat is reversed.

Sew the buttons in the corners of the reversed buttonholes, so, regardless of which side is turned out, the right-hand side will always button over the left-hand side of the coat.

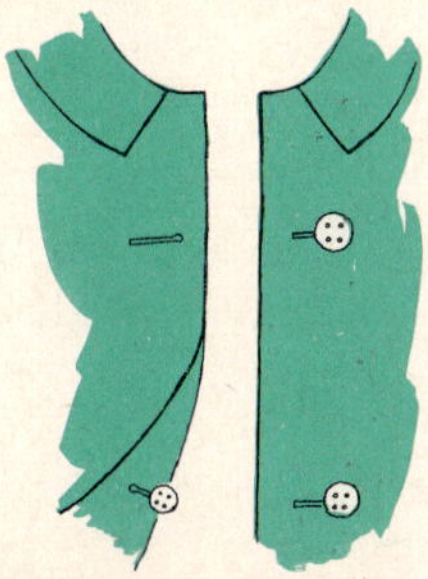

You will have two sets of buttons and buttonholes on one coat.

Bound reversible coat

This is still another way the reversible coat can be put together—by binding it with a contrasting or self-binding around all the outside edges. Actually, this is the easiest method to use in making the reversible coat.

Again, cut out and sew up the two layers of the coat. Press both carefully. Press open all the seams, including the armhole seams.

Turn one coat right side out and one inside out. Slide one coat inside the other, wrong sides together. Pin the armhole seams together and then tack by hand. Keep tacks close to the armhole seamline.

Tack the underarm seams and the shoulder seams together. Pin the edges of the coat together all around. If the hems are to be turned, leave the lower edges of the coat free.

Try on the coat and mark the hems. Turn under and finish the hems to the inside of each coat. Stitch the edges of the coat and sleeves together on

the right side along the seam allowance line. Cut off the seam allowance close to the stitching line, and the edges are ready to be bound.

Whenever a binding is used as a finish, it is customary to sew along the seam allowance line on the right side, and to trim it at this line so it will be less bulky under the binding.

If the reversible coat has a Peter Pan type of collar, it should be bound before it is sewed to the coat. It is sewed between the coats at the neckline with an inside seam. The coats are clipped to the seamline at the front where the collars end. These edges are turned to the right side, stitched and trimmed as for the cardigan coat. The binding is applied from the center front neckline down the front of the coat.

Notched collars are sewed to each coat with regular seams. Then the coats are sewed together around the collar and front on the right side at the seamline. Trim to the stitching as you do on the cardigan. The binding is sewed to the collar and fronts separately. The notch is never mitered.

Chapter **13**

Sewing for children

A mother of two or more children is usually eager to learn all the short-cut sewing methods she can. She's most interested in making a garment quickly and well—one that will stand up under hard wear.

A grandmother or doting aunt, on the other hand, is more inclined to make a stylish little dress with fine embroidery or applique and loving attention to detail.

Whether you do it the fast and easy way, or slowly and with meticulous care, sewing for children can be rewarding and lots of fun.

Selecting a pattern

Never use age as the deciding factor in selecting a pattern for a child. Children the same age differ widely in height, weight, and build. Choose the pattern according to the breast measurement for a girl and the chest measurement for a boy. A short, chubby girl of 6 may need a size 8 pattern, while a tall, thin six-year-old may only take a size 4 pattern. Both would probably need adjustments in length, but these changes are far easier to make than altering the whole pattern.

Measurements

After you have the right size of pattern, take the child's measurements and compare them with the chart on the back of the pattern envelope.

When taking a child's measurement, hold the tape measure snug with a finger between the tape and body. The pattern allows all the necessary ease. Here are measurements you need.

Chest: Measure around the fullest part of the chest.

Waist: Take a snug measurement at the natural waistline.

Hips: Only needed for pants. Take at the fullest part of the hips.

Back waist length: Take from the base of the neck to the waistline.

Garment length: Take in back from the waistline to the finished hemline of the skirt, or from the side waist to the finished length of the pants.

Most of these measurements can be compared with the measurements on the pattern envelope. These additional ones make altering the pattern easier.

Front waist length: Measure from the base of the throat to the waistline.

Back and front shoulder width: Measure from armhole seam to armhole seam, 2½ inches down.

Top of shoulder: Measure from the neckline to the point where the sleeve sets in the armhole.

The pattern can be adjusted from measurements alone. Adjustments on a child's pattern are easier than on an adult pattern. The child's pattern only needs adjusting for size, whereas the adult pattern must be adjusted for figure and posture faults.

Take out all the pattern pieces for the dress style you are making. If the pattern waist is smaller than the child's measurement, divide the amount you need by four. Add this amount to the side of the back and front patterns before you cut.

For instance, if the pattern has a 22 inch waist size, and your child has a 24 inch waist, the difference would be two inches. This amount divided by four is ½ inch. You would add this amount to the back and front

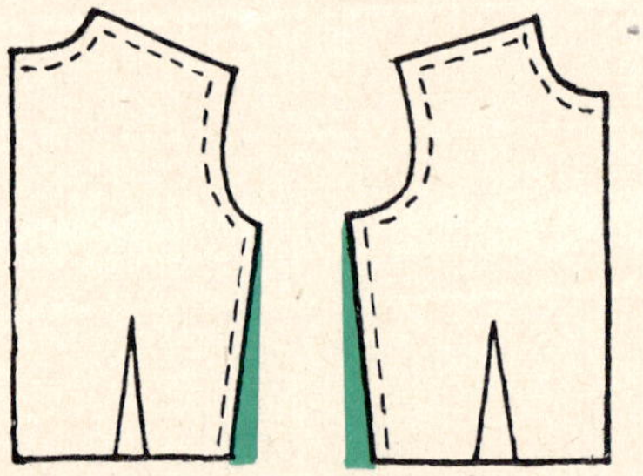

pattern pieces at the side seam to increase the waistline two inches.

Compare and adjust hip measurement the same way. It isn't necessary to measure the pattern at these points.

Compare all other measurements by measuring the actual pattern. The exception is the back waist length, which is given on the measurement chart. Compare the child's measurement to this. To lengthen, slash the pattern between the waist and breast and spread. Lengthen both front and back waist pieces the same amount.

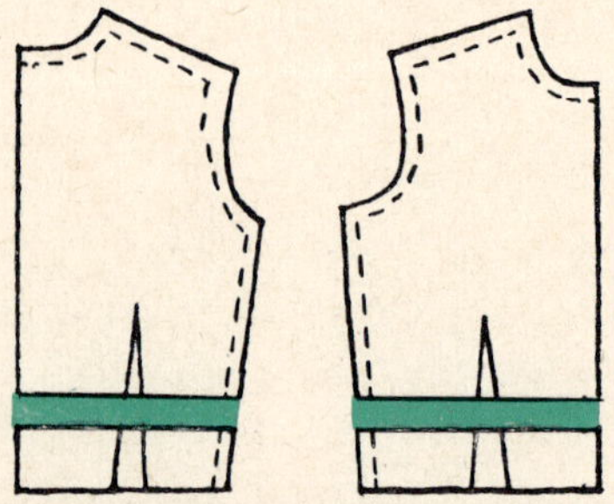

Shorten the pattern with a tuck at the same point. Compare the skirt length with the pattern. Lengthen or shorten the skirt length at the bottom of the skirt pattern piece.

Measure the back and front shoulder widths on the pattern pieces at the same points you measured on the child. Compare with child's measurements.

A slight difference is nothing to worry about. Remember the child's dress should not fit like a woman's. The child needs space for growth.

Check the top of the pattern shoulder measurement with the measurement taken on the child. If it has to be altered at the top of the shoulders as well as at the armhole seam, adjust the shoulders. Narrow the shoulders with a tuck from the top of the shoulder

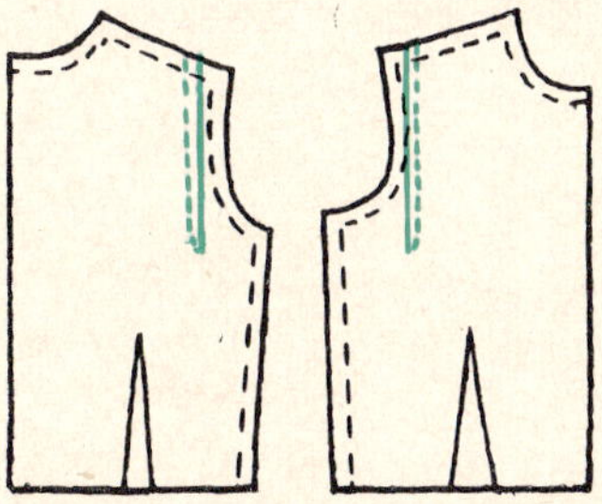

toward the chest as in a woman's dress.

To make the shoulder wider, slash the pattern across under the armhole

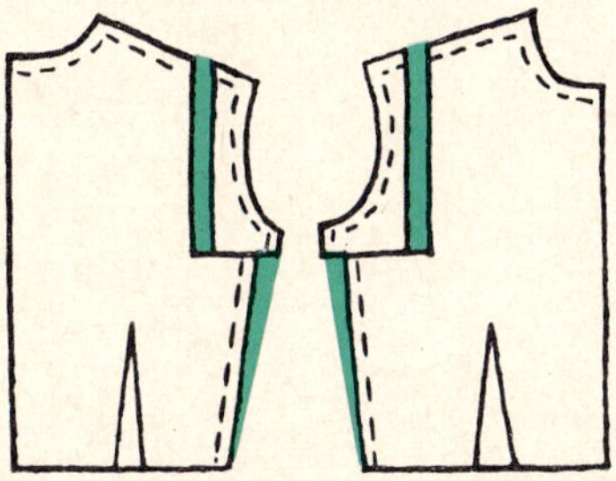

to the center of the shoulder. Spread the necessary amount. Make all the adjustments in the pattern before you cut. Lay out the pattern according to the instructions on the layout guide. Cut out all pieces.

Fitting the dress

Take the cut-out pattern, one piece at a time. Mark all darts, tucks, or gathers. Sew up all darts, tucks, or other detail by machine. There's little danger of having to rip anything out.

Join the back and front waist. Sew up the underarm of the sleeve. If it is a puffed sleeve, sew the gathers at either end. Shirr sleeve to fit armhole. Baste it into the dress.

The other end of the sleeve can be shirred to the approximate size but leave the shirring threads loose so the sleeve can be adjusted.

Sew up the seams of the skirt and gather the top of the skirt as for any shirred skirt. Gather it to fit the waist size. Then baste the skirt and the waist together.

The dress is now ready to be fitted. There are no pins in the dress to stick or scratch, so the child won't mind the fitting.

Pin the dress in place. Then check the fit of garment.

Check the width of the shoulders. Make a note of how much to add or take in. Just pinch in the amount the shoulders need to be narrowed and make a note of it. If the shoulder is too narrow, rip out the sleeve basting and check how much shoulder can be let out. Correct this when dress is off.

Tie a belt around the waist to check the waist length. If it drops below the belt, the waist needs to be shortened. If it rides up over the belt, it needs to be lengthened.

Make a note of the adjustment. Sometimes the whole bodice may be too large. Pinch a tuck the length of the waist to see how much it should be taken in. This can be altered after the dress is off. Measure the hem and turn it up for the correct length.

Now check the sleeve. If it is much too loose, shirr it to the right size with a gathering thread. Tie it to the correct size and the dress can be unpinned and removed. Make all the alterations on the pattern and recut the dress to the altered pattern.

If the waist was too large, fold a tuck the length of the pattern the amount measured. Recut the dress to the altered pattern.

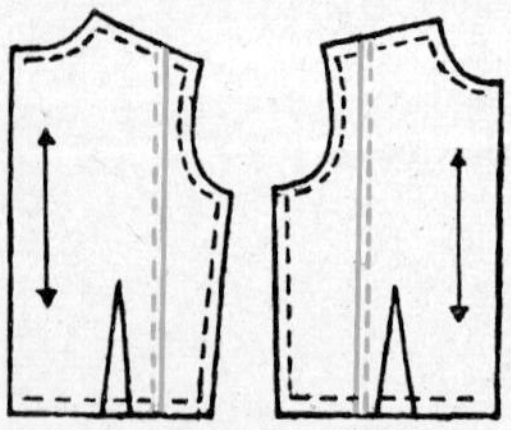

If the waist was too long, recut to the correct length. Or, leave the extra length for a let-out tuck in the waistline seam for future alterations.

Don't cut away the extra fabric in the skirt length. Leave a deep hem so the skirt can be lengthened for additional wear as the child grows taller.

As you can see, there is little fitting necessary if the pattern is altered to the child's measurements before it is cut. If you buy the pattern according to breast size, it will fit the child correctly whether she is chubby or thin.

Only the lengths of the garment will need any adjusting. Necklines and armholes will fit the child with no need for alteration.

Let-out seams

Most children seem to shoot up in height before they gain weight. Allowing for this sudden growth is no problem when you use let-out seams.

When you cut the bodice, allow from $1\frac{1}{2}$ to 2 inches on the length of the bodice for a let-out tuck. Add this extra length to the adjusted pattern.

For instance, if you had to add one inch to the waist length for your child, add an additional $1\frac{1}{2}$ inches for the let-out tuck. Join the skirt to the waistline, taking only a $\frac{5}{8}$-inch seam. Just above this, take a $\frac{3}{4}$-inch deep tuck on the inside of the bodice. Sew it on the machine with a large stitch that can be ripped easily.

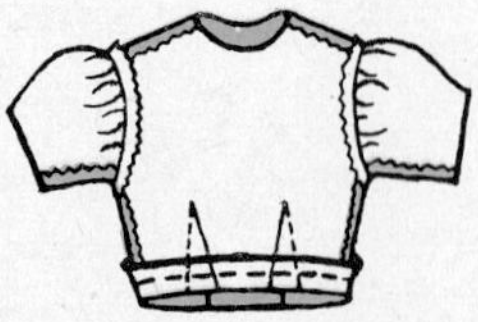

Press the tuck up. Make the top of the dress as you would if the tuck were not there. Be sure not to catch the tuck in any trimming or finishing detail, so when you rip it open to lengthen the waist, it's not sewed in with any finishing. The amount the waistline is lengthened depends on how deep you make the let-out tuck.

Let-out skirt tuck

When cutting the skirt, add several inches on the length in addition to the amount needed for a full hem or to give greater length for the taller child. Turn the hem at the correct length and press the hemline all around.

Before sewing the hem, make a deep tuck close to the edge of the hem, taking up the extra length added to

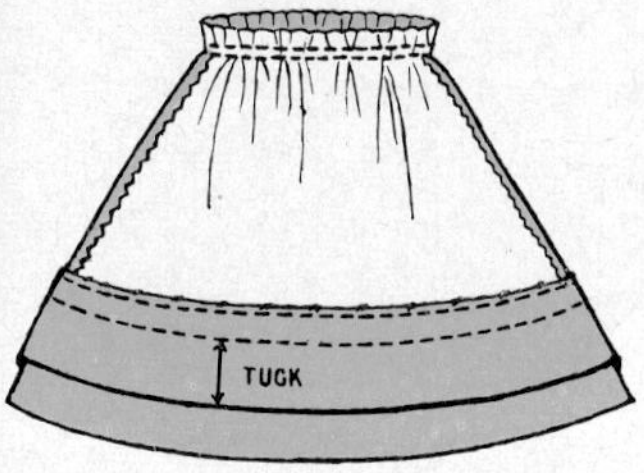

the skirt. Sew it with a large stitch by machine. Finish the hem by hand. Press the tuck toward the hemline. The tuck can be made as deep as you like, as long as it doesn't hang below the hem edge. If you want to let the hem down 2 inches for instance, it isn't necessary to rip out the hem. Sew tuck 2 inches in from original stitching line. Fold line of the hem will drop 2 inches without having to rip out the hem.

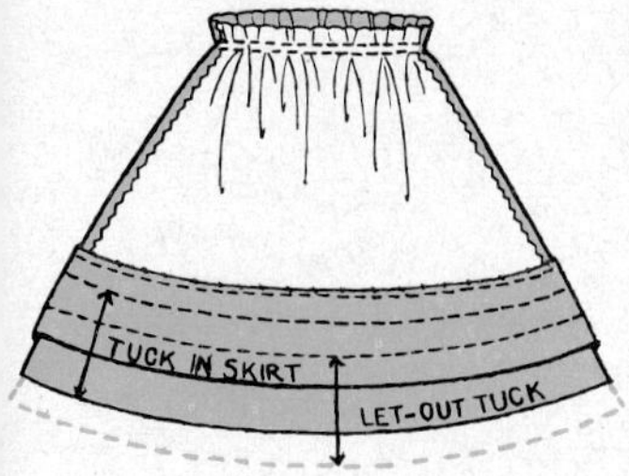

Shoulders

Shoulders seldom have to be made wider. If you want to allow a let-out seam at the shoulder, however, you can cut the shoulder of the dress 1 inch wider than the pattern.

Slash the pattern from the top of the shoulder toward the waist. Spread one inch. Sew up the bodice of the dress and set in the sleeve. Take a tuck on the inside of the dress along the armhole for about 2½ inches toward the back and the front.

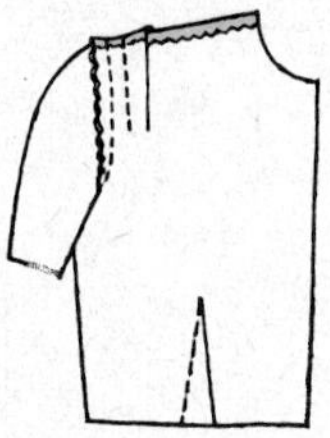

This tuck releases fullness toward the breast, but the stitching over the shoulder holds the fullness in place so the shoulders aren't too wide. This tuck also gives softness to the dress. When the shoulder has to be widened, the tuck, sewed with a large stitch on the machine, can easily be ripped. As the tuck is made narrower, the shoulders become wider. The ½-inch let-out tuck in each shoulder allows enough fabric to enlarge the shoulders 2 inches.

Let-out waistline

Many pattern companies make children's dresses with an elasticized waistline across the back. The waistline expands as the child grows.

If your pattern does not have this feature, it's easy to add it. When you cut the bodice pieces, add a little extra fabric on the side seam of the back bodice. Don't sew up the back darts. If a shirred skirt is used, shirr the back skirt to the size of the back bodice. If the skirt is fitted, cut the back skirt larger to match the back bodice. If it has darts, don't sew the back skirt darts. Join skirt and waist with a regular inside seam.

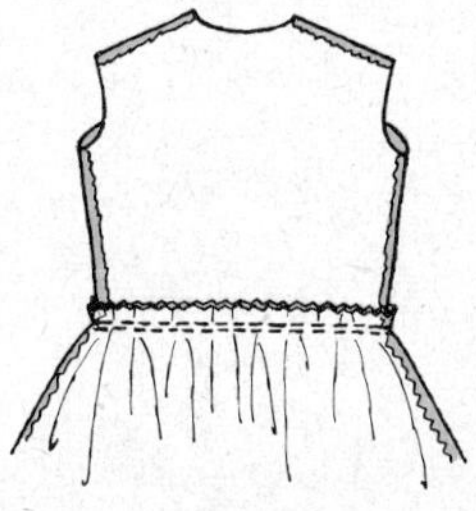

Use a 1-inch commercial bias binding. Unfold and sew one edge along the back waistline on the seam allowance line. Sew the other edge to the bodice to form a casing. Draw a ¾-inch elastic through the casing so the waistline fits snug. Tack the elastic at the side seams where the casing ends.

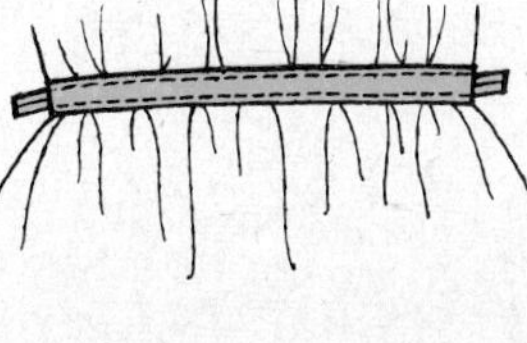

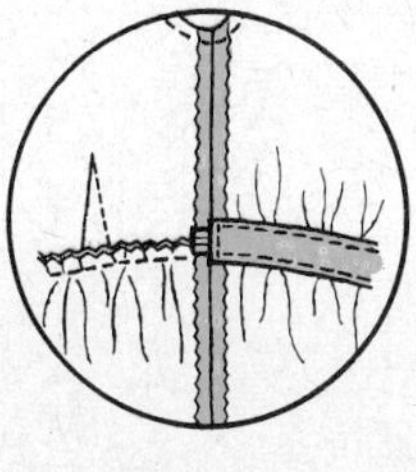

Trace these applique
designs, actual size,
for a sprightly trim.

Ready-to-sew applique accents

Party-pretty dress trims

Perky color touches

Trace, cut to actual size. Sew by hand in a contrasting pattern.

Seams

On most children's dresses you can use an inside seam. French seams are better for very lightweight or sheer fabrics, except at the armhole where French seams are never used. On a lightweight fabric, just stitch the armhole seam a second time, ¼ inch from the original armhole seamline and trim.

For a sheer fabric, stitch the armhole seam a second time. Trim and whip raw edge as on any sheer dress.

With fabrics like organdy, that are both sheer and crisp, the seams have a tendency to irritate a child's tender skin. To avoid this, spread the armhole seams. Turn the edge of each seam toward the inside. Overcast the folded edges together. This makes a hand-turned French seam.

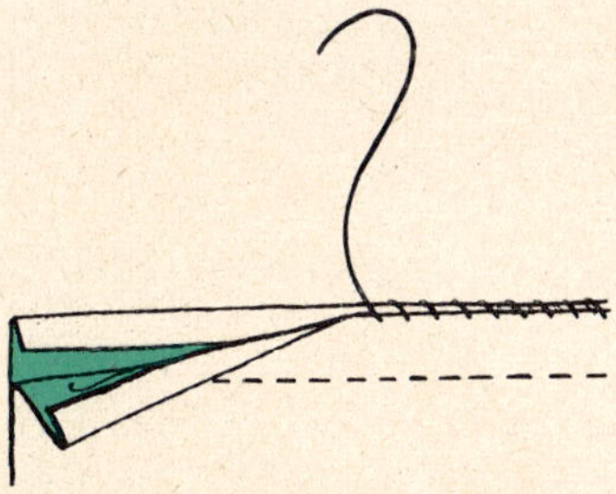

Another seam used for the same purpose is the hemmed-over seam. Trim away one side of the seam. Fold over the untrimmed seam and hem it over the other at seam allowance line.

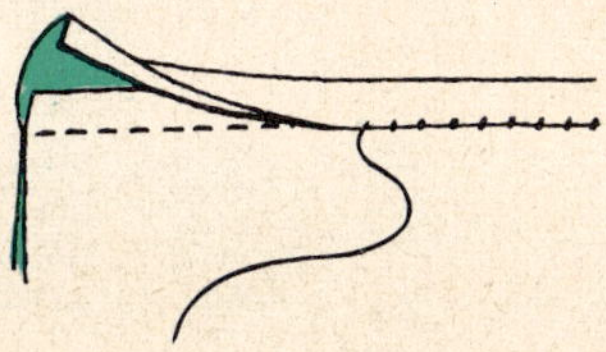

Neckline finishes

The necklines on children's clothes are either bound with bias or finished with a collar. It is important to keep the neckline from stretching, since this can cause the dress to set badly.

A too-large neck or too-wide sleeve makes a child look thin, and the dress look too big. When you buy a pattern by the child's chest measurement, armhole and neck size are usually correct.

Run a stay-stitch around the neckline to hold it in shape. Check it with the neck size of the pattern. If it has stretched, ease it in to the pattern size.

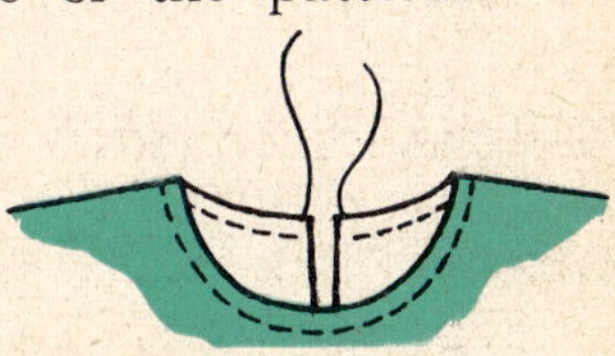

It is not necessary to interface the collar on a child's dress. It is better to keep it soft and pliable.

Collar

Cut the upper and under collar. Set any ruffling or trimming in the seam as you sew the collar together.

Lace or eyelet should be ruffled before it is applied to the collar so it will shape to the curve of the collar edge. Many of these trims come already ruffled, and are easy to apply.

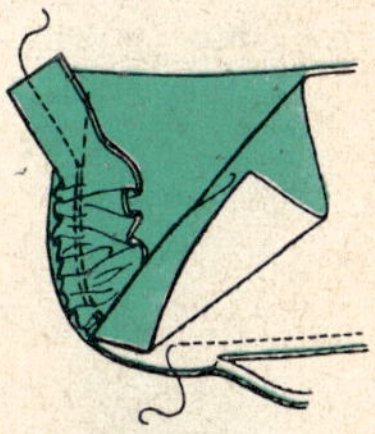

Sew the edge of the ruffling along the edge of the upper collar on the right side. Taper the ruffling to a point at the ends of the collar.

Contrasting cording in a collar edge is popular. (See Chapter 6.)

Gathered neck

The soft gathered neck is popular on children's dresses. It is always finished with a bias binding. Most patterns give a guide piece for the size to which the neck should be shirred.

On sheer fabrics the neck is shirred just to the size of the guide. Otherwise, the guide piece can be cut out of the fabric and used as a stay. Put the wrong side of the stay to the inside of the dress and shirr the neck to fit. Sew the stay into place. Cut and press the bias binding as shown in Chapter 6. Sew the binding to the neckline on the right side, stretching it a little as you sew.

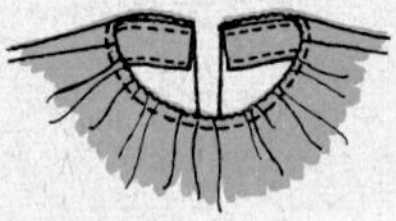

Start at the shoulder, where piecing is done. Leave a 2-inch end loose. Sew all around the neck to about 4 inches from where you began stitching.

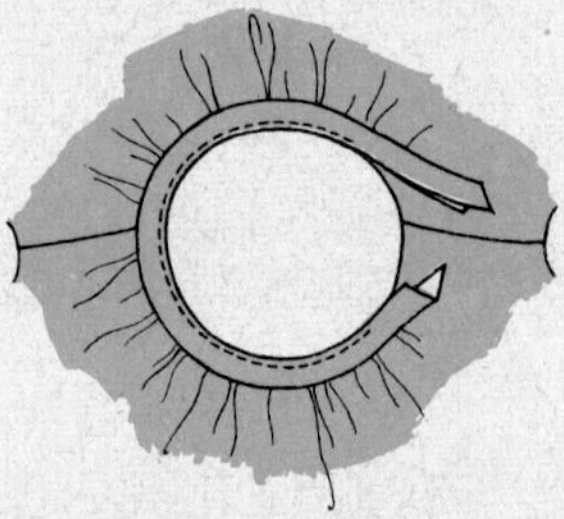

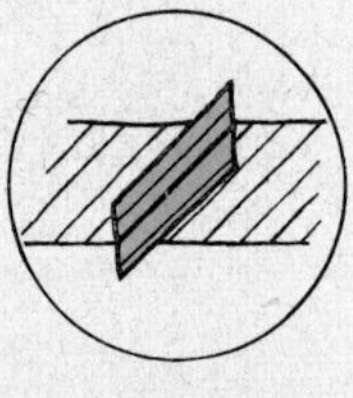

Carefully measure and match the bias on the straight grain. Sew the bias together so that it's continuous at this point. Press the seam open. Press again on the original fold. Stitch this small section to the neck edge. The bias should always be joined this way at the neckline, sleeves, and wherever a continuous binding is needed.

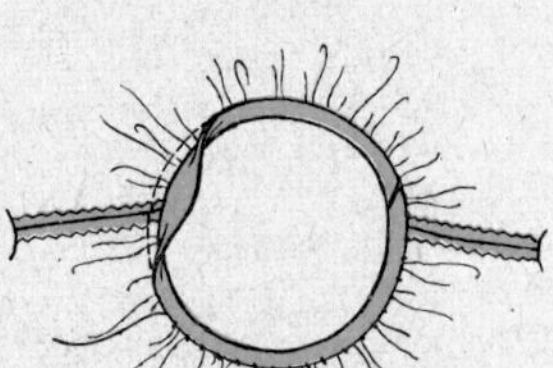

Never lap at a joining. This gives a bulky look. Fold bias over seam and sew fold edge by hand along the original seamline.

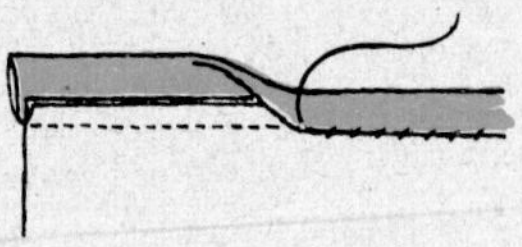

Making ruffling

The softest ruffling is made on the bias. It can be cut in strips and hemmed. Most professionals make the ruffling on a double fold.

Cut the bias twice the width, plus seam allowance. Press in half on the length. The trick is to sew the edges together first to prevent twisting when it is put through the ruffler. All sewing machines have this attachment.

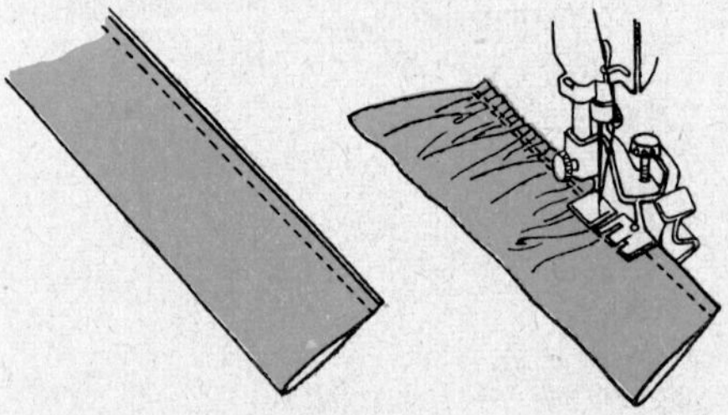

Scallops

Scallops are a favorite trim on children's clothes. They can be used at necklines, on collars, bandings, or at the hems. To get them even and well-shaped, make a tissue paper pattern.

Trace the part of the dress pattern where you want the scallops. You can use a scalloping ruler to mark the size of the scallops. Figure the number and size of scallops that will evenly fit the space. Mark the scal-

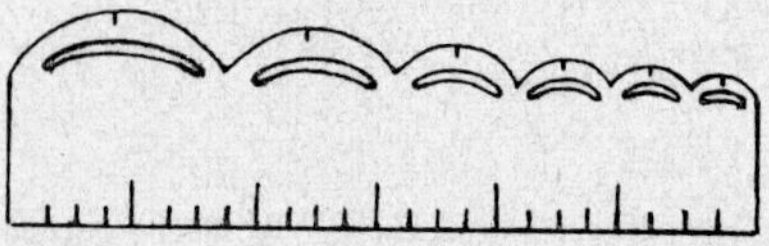

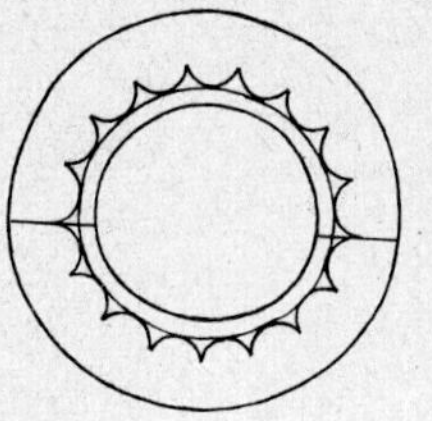

lop design on the tissue. Put the finished edge of the scallop along the seam allowance line. Pin the facing to the dress, right sides together. Pin the tissue tracing over this. Sew through the tracing as you sew around each scallop. Take a single stitch across the base of each scallop, so the corner can be clipped and turned better. Remove tissue. Trim around each scallop. Clip to the stitching on the curve, and well into each corner before turning it.

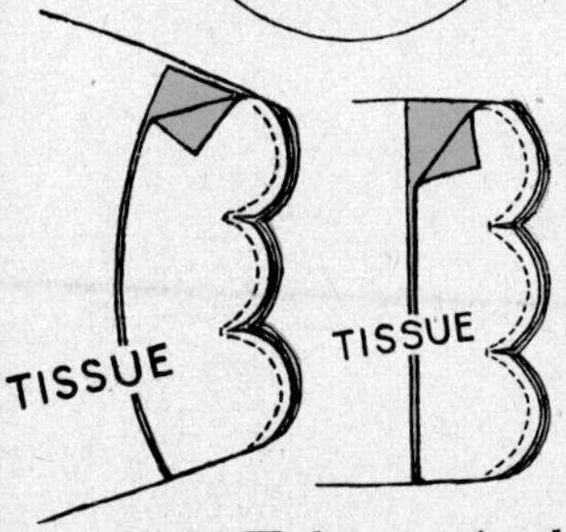

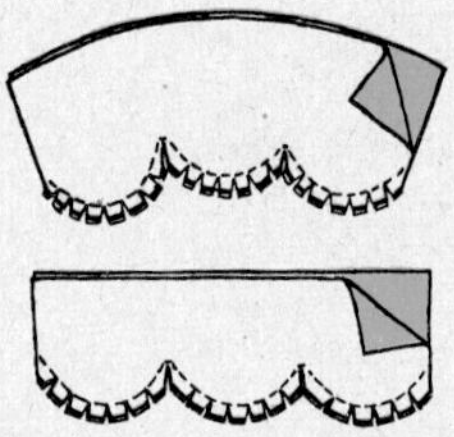

When the facing is turned to the inside, run your fingernail around the inside of each scallop so it turns completely, to give a full, round shape. Then press scallops carefully. Finish as for any facing. If an interfacing is needed, use the non-woven type and mark the scallops on it. Cut away the seam allowance all around each scallop. Sew along the edge of each scallop when sewing to facing.

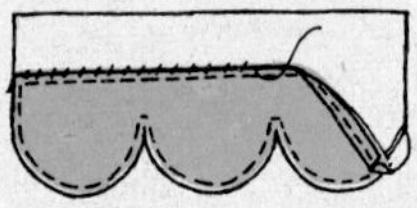

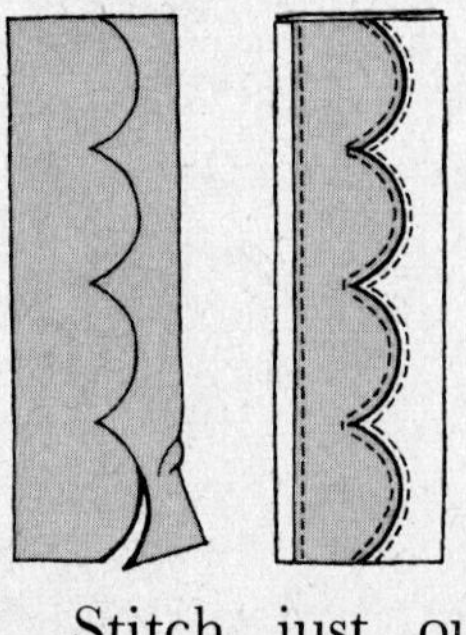

Stitch just outside each scallop when sewing the facing to the dress. Trim, turn, and press as described above to finish.

Hems

On a straight skirt, turn under the skirt edge ½ inch by machine. Turn up the hem on the hem mark and press. Slip-stitch by hand, taking a back-stitch every few stitches so the hem

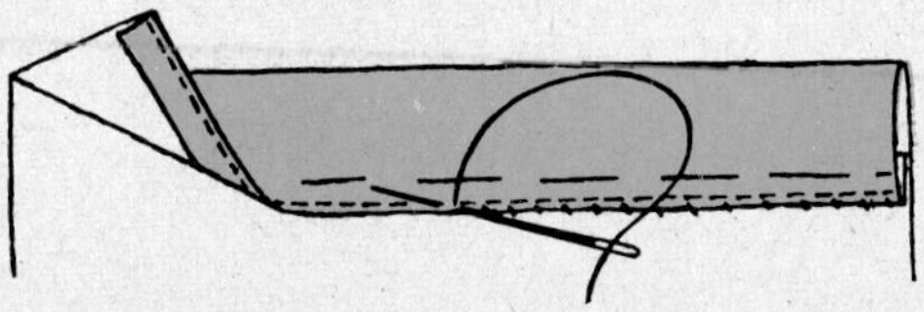

is strong. Use a commercial, flat-fold bias binding to hem the flared skirt. Unfold one edge and put it to the hem edge, right sides together. As you sew the bias binding, stretch it; the bias eases in the hem fullness.

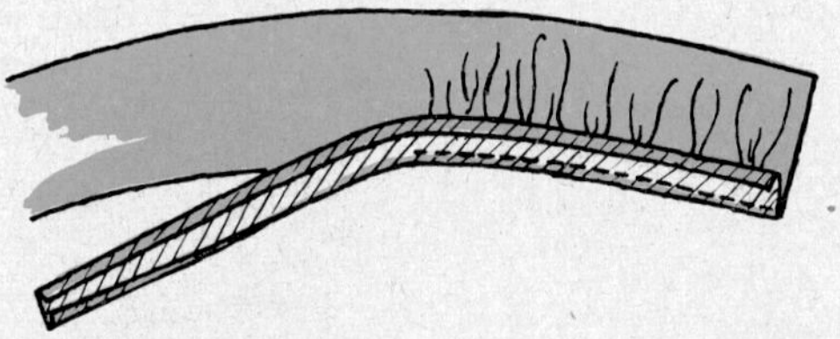

When the hem is turned to the inside and pressed, the fullness adjusts itself to the inside of the skirt. Slip-stitch the fold edge of the bias to the skirt and the hem is finished.

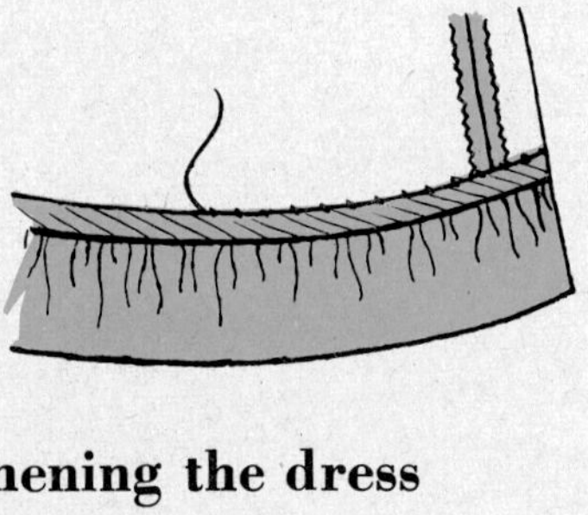

Lengthening the dress

Here are some easy and attractive ways to lengthen a dress, using self-fabric or trim of a contrasting color.

View 1

This style shows contrast used at the waistline of both skirt and bodice to lengthen them. Self-fabrics can be used the same way, with pretty trimmings concealing the seams.

View 2

Here the contrast is used at the hem to lengthen the skirt. A yoke is also cut from it to lengthen the bodice. White organdy and lawn are wonderful fabrics to use. Edged in lace or banding, they give a dainty touch.

View 3

The contrast is used in bands to add to the skirt length. Bands can also be used in the bodice to give length. This dress could also be made with a bodice that has a contrasting yoke.

Sleeves

Be sure the sleeve is fitted fairly close to arm size. If the sleeve is too big around, the child's arm looks thin. When making a puff sleeve, carefully shirr it to the arm size.

If the sleeve edge has a fitted band, make the band about two inches larger than the arm. A sleeve bound with bias should also be about two inches larger than the arm.

Sleeve band

Cut the sleeve band from the pattern piece. Measure and sew the band to the correct size for the arm. Press open the underarm seam of the band, then press in half. Pin the band to the underarm seam of the sleeve, one edge of the band to the inside of the sleeve. Shirr the sleeve to fit the band.

Smooth the shirring so it is even all around. Pin and sew the band to the sleeve. Sew on the shirred side of the sleeve. Press the seam into the sleeve band. Turn under the free edge of the sleeve band, pin over the seam. Edge-stitch it on the right side.

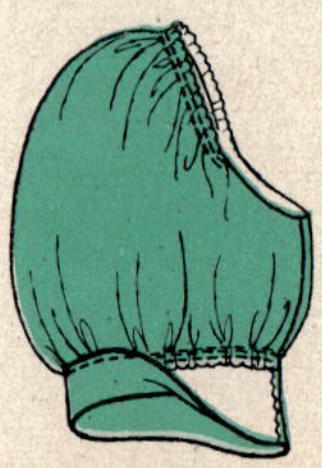

Bias binding

Press the bias on the length. Cut to the correct arm size, plus seam allowances. When you cut the bias to be joined, be sure to cut it on the straight grain. Join the bias, then press the seam open, and re-press the length fold. Pin both edges of the bias to

the right side of the sleeve. Shirr the sleeve to fit the bias. Then pin and sew the bias to the sleeve edge.

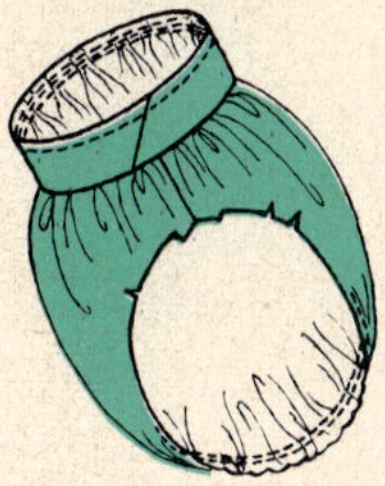

The sleeve can be finished by machine. Now trim the seam more than half the width of the bias. Fold the bias over the seam so the fold extends beyond original stitching line. Turn to the right side. Sew by machine just under the fold edge of bias. The neck can also be finished this way.

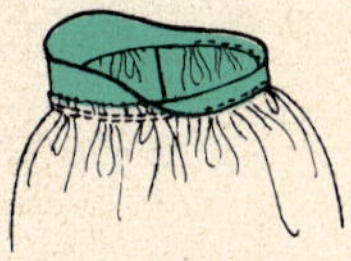

Ruffled sleeve with casing

The full shirred sleeve can easily be made with a ruffled edge. Cut the sleeve 3 inches longer than for a regular sleeve. Turn back a 2-inch hem. Turn under ¼ inch on the hem edge and pin and stitch to the inside of the sleeve. Measure down ⅝ inch from this stitching and stitch a second row to form the casing. Cut a piece of ½-inch elastic 1 inch smaller than the arm girth. Draw it through the casing, lap the ends, sew together. The sleeve will be puffed with a ruffled edge.

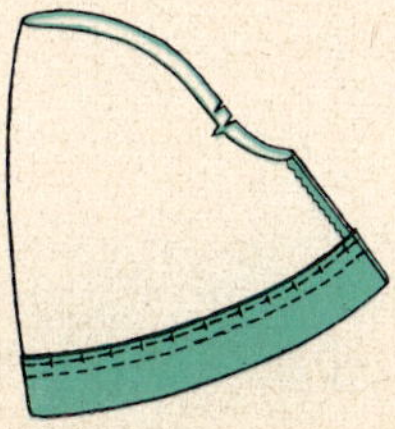

If you want a fuller ruffle to the sleeve, the ruffle can be sewed on separately. Sew a piece of ruffling along the edge of the regular puff sleeve, right side of the ruffling to the right side of the sleeve.

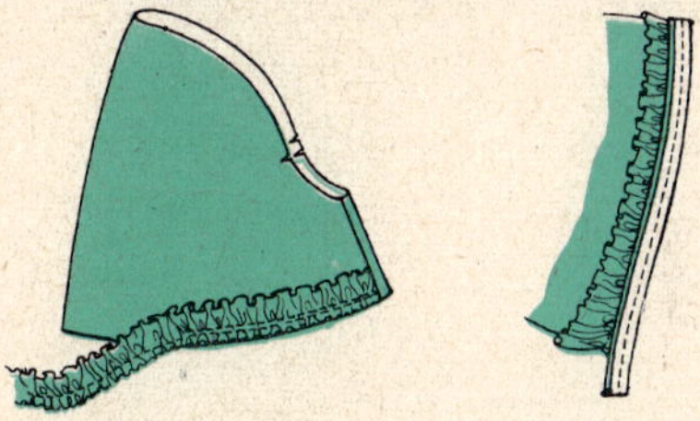

Sew the edge of a commercial bias binding along the same seam, with the right side of the binding along the ruffle. Turn the binding to the inside, stitch the loose edge of the binding to the sleeve for a casing. Draw the

elastic through the casing and sew the ends together by hand. There'll be a very full ruffle at the sleeve edge.

Cording

Cording is often used on children's clothes as a trim. It is available in a variety of colors and textures, ready to sew. Or, you can make cording yourself. See Chapter 6 for complete instructions on how to make it.

Skirt placket

Zippers are seldom used in children's dresses. A placket is used when a child's dress opens down the back.

The back skirt may have a seam or be slashed. In either case, the placket for children's clothes is easy to make.

Placket used with a seam

Sew up the back skirt seam to the point marked on the pattern for the placket opening. Clip into the seam at this mark. Sew for 1 inch on either side of the clipped seam as a stay-stitch. Then trim off part of the seam width.

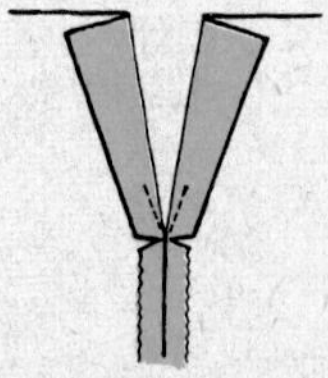

For the placket, cut a strip about 1½ inches wide and double the length of the placket opening. If possible, cut it along the selvage. Fold under the raw edge for ¼ inch and press. Then fold on the length so the fold edge is just inside of the selvage edge and press. Slide the placket piece over the seam, with the selvage edge on the under side. Pin in place. Then at the base of the placket opening, pin it so that the fold edge is along the stay-stitching. Stitch on the right side along fold edge of placket piece, and the placket is finished. Use this method wherever a placket is needed.

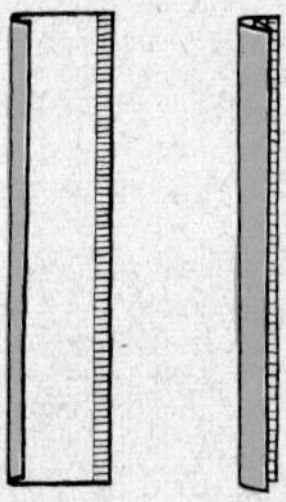

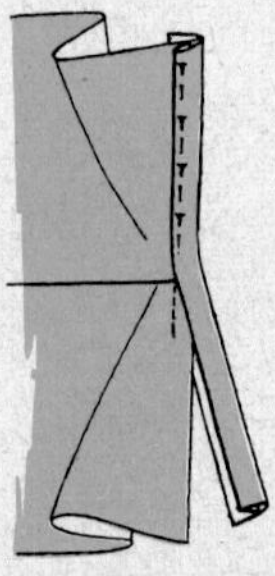

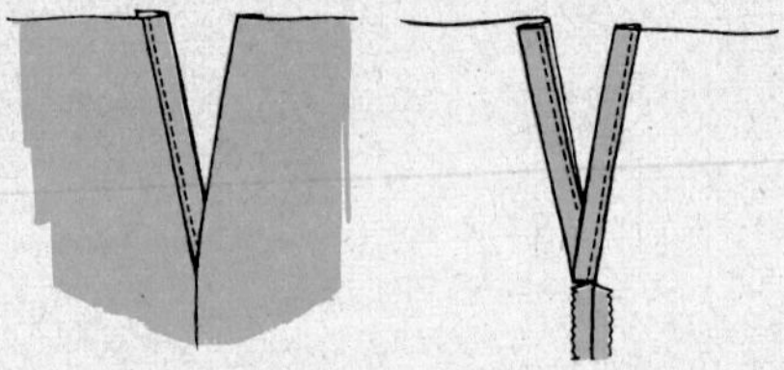

Slash placket opening

Mark where placket is to be sewed. Sew a stay-stitch along the placket marks. Slash to the point of the stay-stitch. Fold and press the placket piece as for the placket used with a seam. Slide the placket piece over the edges of the slash, making sure that you catch the placket piece along the stitching line at the lower point. Pin and stitch along the fold edge, and the placket is finished.

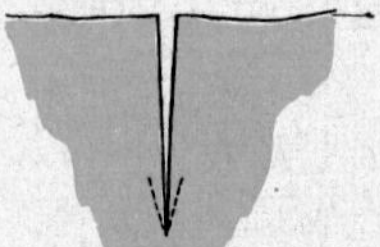

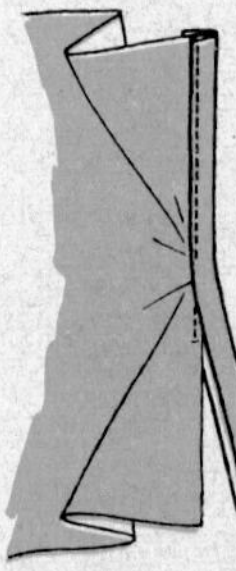

Types of fabrics

Use easy-care fabrics—blends of man-made fibers that shed soil and wrinkles, need little or no ironing, or natural fibers treated to give the same properties. Fabrics should also be soft, pliable, and have some absorbency. Colors should be colorfast, and patterns relatively small.

Making coats

Children's coats are easy and fun to make. They're also economical. One real economy factor—you can make a coat so it can be let out to grow with your child. And you can choose the fabrics and colors that are most becoming and long-wearing.

Coats can be made from many types of fabrics. If you want a coat to give good service for several years, choose a quality fabric equal to the workmanship you'll put into the coat.

Buy the same size pattern for a coat as for a dress. The pattern allows the necessary ease for linings and for wearing over other clothes. Don't buy too large a pattern. The neckline and coat top will look too large.

If any adjustments need to be made on the coat—like lengthening the waist or narrowing the shoulders—make them in the pattern before cutting. Leave extra length on the hem and sleeves so you can adjust the coat in length as the child grows.

If the fabric is soft or lighter in weight than is practical for a coat, mount the entire garment. See "Evening coats," Chapter 12. After the coat is cut out, cut the coat pieces again in a lightweight commercial interlining.

Remove the pattern from the coat and mounting fabric after marking any darts or tucks on the fabric. Markings for the placement of pockets or other trim should be made on the right side of the coat pieces.

Put the wrong side of the coat pieces to the unmarked side of the mounting fabric pieces and pin all around. Press the pieces together. Re-pin if either layer shrinks. Sew the pieces together all around just outside of the seam allowance line. Now you are ready to assemble the coat.

Pin and sew all the pieces of the coat body together. Also, sew up the sleeves and baste into the armholes.

Press the seams carefully and try on the coat for size. There should be no alteration needed if you followed the adjustments necessary for the dress.

Don't overfit the coat. If the shoulders seem a little wide, it is better to use a small pad rather than to recut them. (Use a small pad in any case to give a better look through the shoulders.) Remember that the coat must fit over other clothing, so be sure there is plenty of ease. A box-type coat can be easier through the shoulders than a fitted princess line.

Mark for the hemline and length of sleeve while the coat is being tried on. Remove the coat and finish it. Interface the coat with hair canvas or a non-woven interfacing. If the coat has a lapel, hair canvas is a better choice. Cut the interfacing so it is 1 inch wider than the facing and extends into the shoulder. This also helps give a better shoulder line.

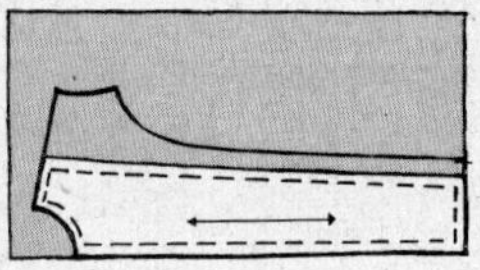

If the facings are attached to the coat, fold them back and press. Cut the front seam allowance off the interfacing and pin the cut edge along the fold edge of the facing. Catch-stitch the front edge along the fold line so no stitches show on the right side.

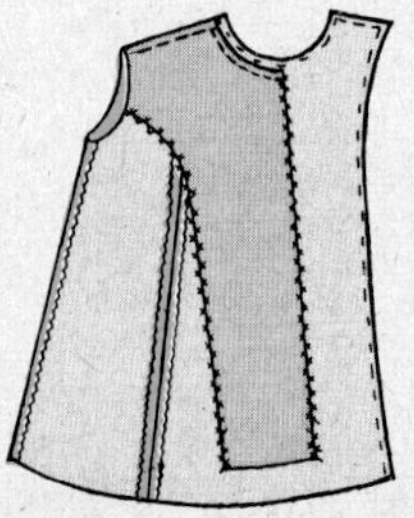

Trim away the seam allowance around the neck of the interfacing and sew along the neck and shoulder to about 2 inches from the armhole. Catch-stitch the inside edge of the interfacing to the coat.

Make the buttonholes as shown in Chapter 6. Make the collar and sew it to the coat as shown in Chapter 12.

Before the facings are finished to the inside, turn up the hem. If the coat has a deep hem that will be let down later, it is important that no marks of the hem show on the right side of the coat. To prevent this, cut a strip of interfacing about 2 inches deeper than the hem.

If the coat is a box-type, there will be no shaping at the hem, and so a straight piece of interfacing can be cut. If the coat is a princess line style, then the interfacing should be shaped to the flare of the coat.

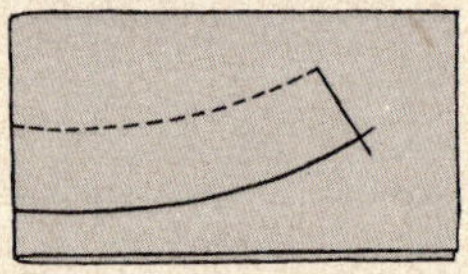

Press up the hem on the princess coat. Lay the bottom of the coat on the interfacing so it is smooth and mark around the lower edge with pencil or tailor's chalk. Also mark along front edges of the coat.

Measure up on the interfacing 2 inches more than the depth of the hem and cut the interfacing piece.

Pin the lower edge of the interfacing along the fold edge of the hem on the inside. Catch-stitch this edge to the coat. Smooth the interfacing into the rest of the coat. Pin and catch-stitch the upper edge to the inside of the coat. On the princess line coat, it need only be attached at seams. It is necessary to ease in the hem on this style of coat. Sew along the edge of the hem with a large machine stitch. Ease fullness in on this thread so the hem fits smooth to the inside of the coat.

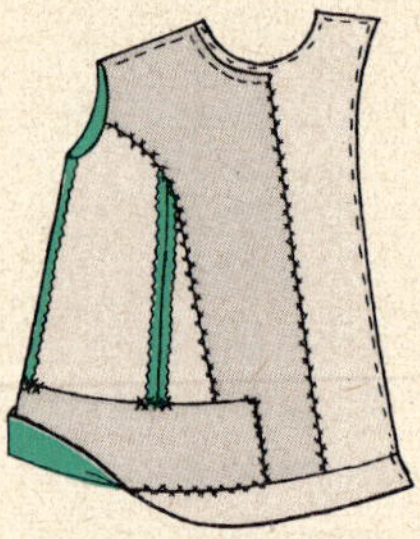

Sew a seam binding to the edge of the hem. Pin the hem to the inside of the coat and catch-stitch it only to the interfacing.

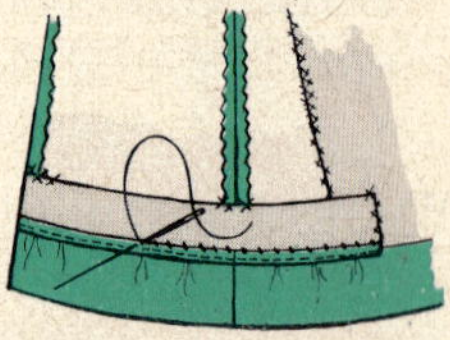

On the straight coat, the interfacing is sewed along the fold edge of the hem, but the upper edge must be catch-stitched to the coat for entire length. Be sure to pick up just a thread of the coat so that the stitches won't show on the right side of the garment.

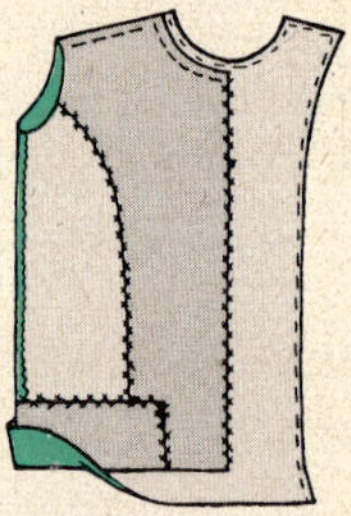

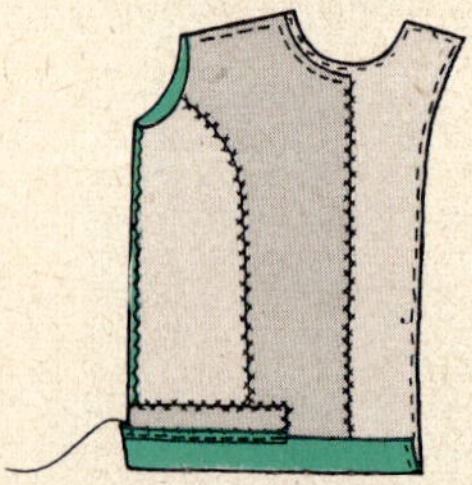

The straight hem can be pinked or finished with a seam binding depending on the weight of the coat. Turn the hem and catch-stitch it to the interfacing. For a coat with a lapel, follow the instructions in Chapter 11 on how to correctly roll the lapel and apply the collar and facings.

Sleeves

Turn the sleeve on the hem mark. If the sleeve will be let down later, the hem will be deeper than is generally allowed in coat sleeves. Press the hem back on the sleeve. Next cut a strip of interfacing on the bias 2 inches wider than the hem.

Catch-stitch one edge along the fold edge of the hem and on the inside of the sleeve. Lap the interfacing where it comes together at the underarm seam and catch-stitch.

The top edge of the interfacing is catch-stitched to the inside of the

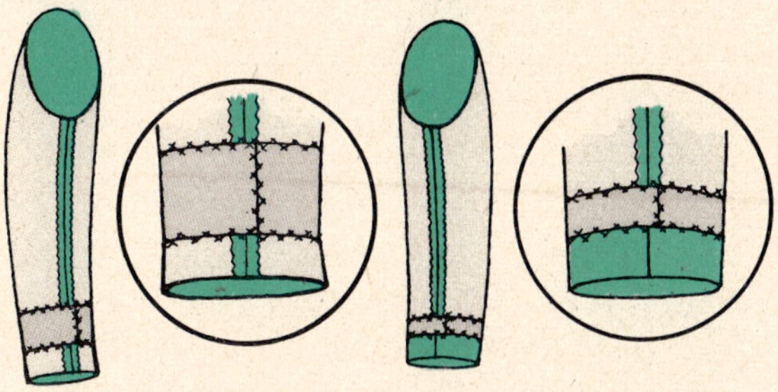

sleeve. Turn up the hem and catch-stitch it to the interfacing. (See Chapter 11 for setting in the sleeve.)

Lining a coat is shown in Chapter 12. The only difference is that the hem of the lining should be made as deep as that on the coat, so it can also be let down when the coat is lengthened. Also make the sleeve lining longer and turn up the extra length in the sleeve until the sleeve is ready to be lengthened.

Letting out the coat

It is always a good idea to buy a little extra fabric when you make children's clothes. It can be used later on for altering or letting out garments as the child grows.

On the princess or box coat, the hems of the sleeves and coat can be lengthened if the child has grown taller. This is usually the only alteration needed the first year. Later the shoulders of the coat may have to be made bigger on the princess style.

The straight box coat has an easy fit, so the shoulders may not need adjusting. On the princess style coat, the size can be increased by setting in a straight strip of fabric in the seam of the gores. This can also add a decorative touch to the coat.

Remove the lining since it will also have to be let out. Rip open the side gore in back and front.

Nothing else on the coat will need changing. Cut a strip of fabric the width the coat is to be increased, plus seam allowances. Here are some decorative details that can be added.

View 1

This style has a strip of fabric tucked across before it is sewed to the coat. It gives a pretty trimming detail.

View 2

On this coat, the strip was cut into

three lengths and faced to form little points. Then it was sewed together, buttons were sewed on the points and inserted into the coat. It adds a decorative trim in addition to providing extra size for added wear.

View 3

This view shows the strip cut to flare at the bottom, then pressed to form pleats. The addition of this strip of fabric allows enough ease for considerable growth. A pocket flap can be sewed on to give more detail.

Finishing details

Fastenings

Buttons used on children's clothes should be washable. Pearl, bone, and plastic buttons are washable and colorfast, so they don't have to be removed from the clothes before washing.

Zippers are also washable, and can be used in many places on children's clothes. Dot snap fasteners are practical, particularly for very young children's clothes. These fasteners come in kits, are hammered into cloth.

Another type of fastening is made of nylon. In tape form, it has fine hooks on one side, loops on the other that interlock when pressed together.

You'll find all of these fasteners available in the notions department of a department store.

Embroidery stitches

Embroidery and applique are attractive on children's clothes. They can be done by hand or with a zigzag sewing machine. It's possible to do a great variety of stitches on these machines. Sewing machine companies offer instructions on how to make many types.

Hand embroidery can be as simple or elaborate as you care to make it. Some women are expert at handwork and find great pleasure in doing exquisite work. If you're unfamiliar with embroidery, start a project using simple stitches. You'll get charming effects.

Outline stitch

Work from left to right. Bring the needle out on the line, and take a short back-stitch. Keep the thread under the needle, bringing the needle out where the last stitch went in. Continue this way to outline the design. Keep all stitches the same length.

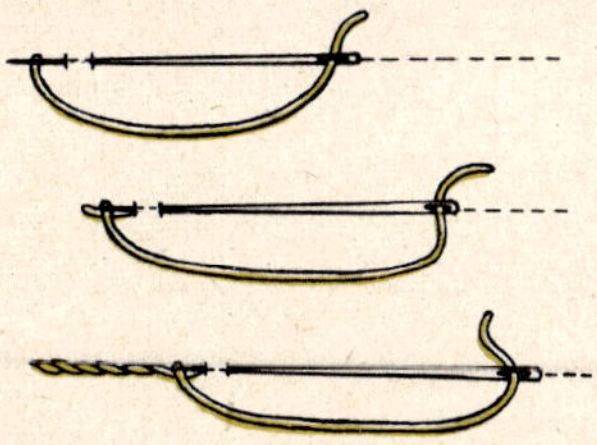

Satin-stitch

Pass the needle over, then underneath the fabric. Keep stitches close together so they fill in the design. To give a padded look, the design should first be filled in with tiny running stitches. Satin-stitch over these.

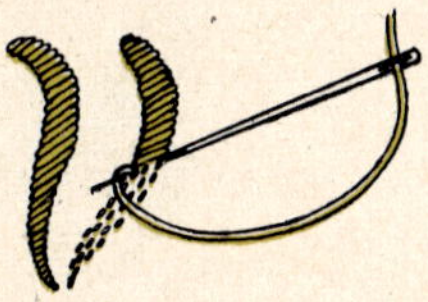

Chain-stitch

Bring the needle and thread to the right side of the fabric. Hold the thread to form a loop. Insert the needle at the same point where the thread was brought through. Bring it out a short distance ahead to form the loop. Keep loops the same size.

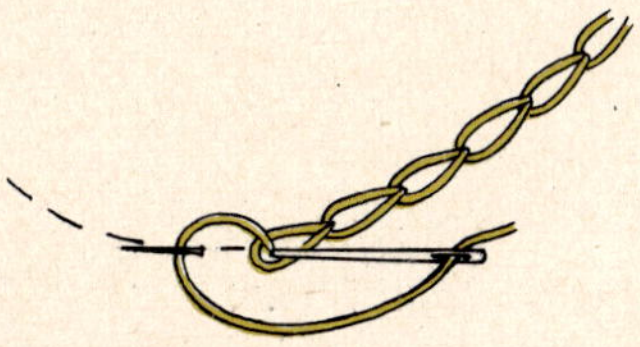

Feather-stitch

Bring needle up through the material on the design line. Take a short slanting stitch on the right side of the material, pointing needle to left or right. Hold the thread down with the thumb to form the loop. Take the next stitch on the opposite side of the line, pointing the needle the opposite direction. Continue this way, keeping all stitches the same length.

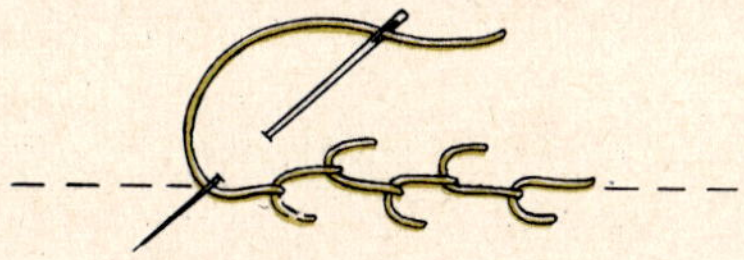

Blanket-stitch

Work from left to right with the edge to be blanket-stitched toward you. Mark a line for the depth of the blanket-stitch. Bring the thread to the right side of the fabric on this line.

Hold the thread with the thumb and bring the needle through the line on the right side of the fabric and out over the thread at the edge, forming a loop. The space between stitches can be any width you want. The length of the stitch can be varied to give an assortment of stitches.

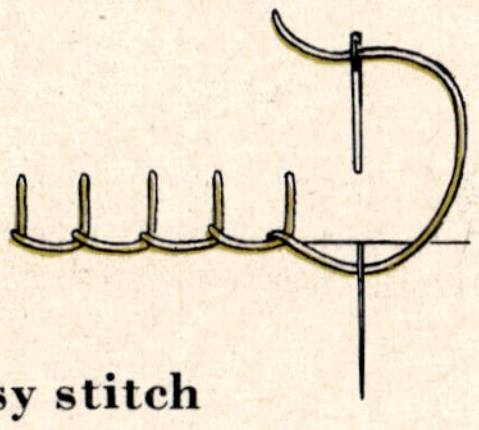

Lazy-daisy stitch

This basic stitch is the same as the chain stitch. Each individual loop is worked from a center point. After each loop is made, return the needle to the same point and continue to the next loop. Be sure to make the lazy-daisy stitches the same length.

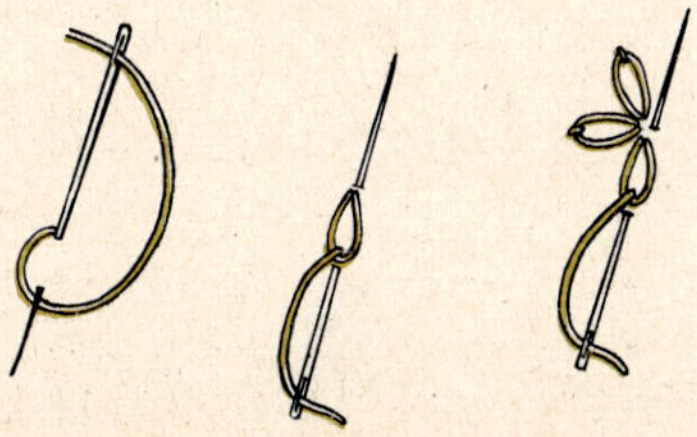

French knot

Bring the needle to the right side at the point where the knot is to be made. Point the needle in the same direction as the thread. Wind the thread around the needle two or three times. Push the needle back through the fabric at the point where the first stitch was taken. Pull the thread through to the wrong side, forming the knot.

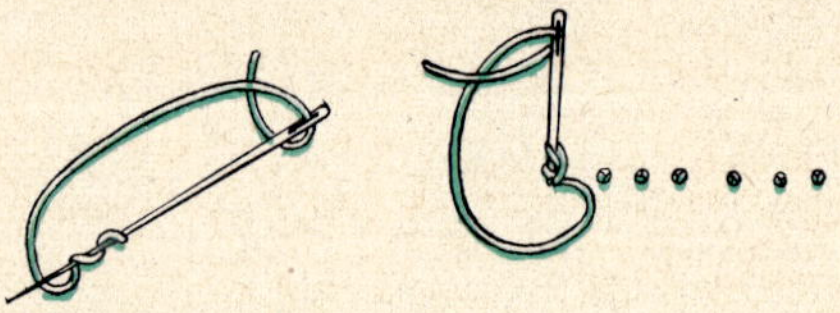

Cross-stitch

Work from the left to right. Bring the needle through the fabric at the lower left-hand corner. Insert the needle at the upper right-hand corner of the cross and bring it under the fabric and out at the lower left-hand corner of the next stitch.

Sew across the fabric, making all the stitches in one direction, crossing all the stitches. Keep the stitches together at both the top and the bottom of each cross-stitch.

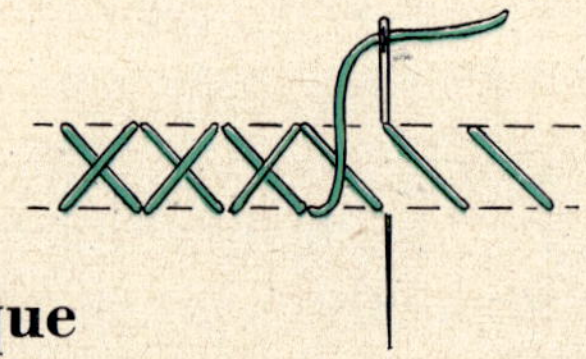

Applique

This is a method of applying one piece of fabric over the other with either a fine slip-stitch or a decorative stitch. Usually the decorative stitch used is a blanket-stitch or a feather-stitch. Sometimes the pattern contains a transfer pattern from which the applique design is cut.

See pages 252, 253, 256 for applique ideas. Also check children's coloring books or story books. Simply trace the designs. For hand applique, the design should be traced to the finished size and cut out, allowing ¼ inch seam allowance. A machine-stitch run just outside of this line makes it easy to work applique.

Turn the seam allowance of the applique piece just inside the machine line. Pin or baste the piece in place. Sew it on with a decorative stitch.

For machine stitching, the applique can be cut, allowing ¼ inch seam allowance. Stitch it in place with a fine zigzag stitch on the applique line. Trim close to the stitching line. Restitch the raw edge and stitching line with a satin-stitch.

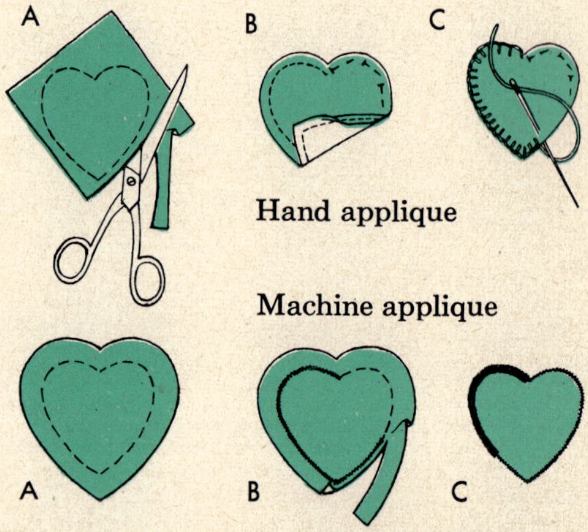

Rickrack

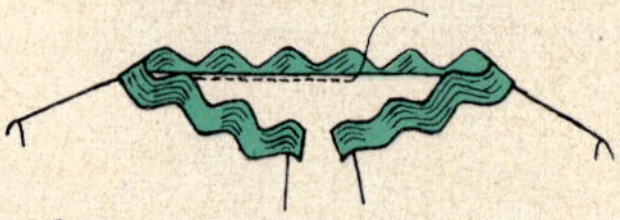

This trim can be sewed flat to the garment through the center so the full width of rickrack shows. It can be applied around edges so just one edge shows, with the rest of the rickrack to the underside of the garment.

Chapter 14

Be your own designer

Every woman has designing ability, although she often doesn't suspect it. This is true of all women, not only those who sew. Listen to a customer in the ready-to-wear department of a store as she describes in detail the style of dress she wants. Sometimes it may be a style worn by a friend, or a fashion pictured in a magazine that has influenced her.

Many times such definite ideas are based on long years of experimenting until, at last, she finds the lines best-suited to her figure.

All women are concerned about line and design, and strive for originality and individuality in their clothes.

Use patterns creatively

Unless a woman can make her own patterns, the only guide she has in creating new fashions is the commercial pattern. Ready-to-wear can easily be duplicated by the judicious use of these patterns. There is nothing to prevent the changing or interchanging of pattern pieces. Pattern companies advise against it only because they plan fabric and yardage charts for the views shown on the pattern envelope. If you depart from these views, you'll also have to figure yardage and other detail yourself, which you will learn later in this chapter.

Interchanging pattern pieces

All patterns are made to the same basic body line. The sleeves of one size 14 dress are the same size as the sleeves of another size 14, providing they both have the same type of armhole. In other words, the set-in sleeve fits the armhole of any other pattern the same size with a set-in sleeve. This illustrates only one of the many possibilities in creative sewing.

If a bodice you like is attached to a not-so-becoming skirt, find a suitable skirt pattern and switch.

There is one technical point to watch. On the patterns, you will notice that the waist and skirt darts line up to look like one continuous line in front. This makes the figure look taller, more slim and gives a neater look to the dress. Watch detail like this when you start to switch pattern pieces. It is easy to move the skirt dart so it lines up with the waist dart. Then measure from the center front of the bodice to the inside dart line, and measure the skirt from the same points. Move the skirt dart so the inside line of the dart is the same distance from the center front as on the waist. If there are two darts in the waist and the skirt, both should be lined up, using the same method. Often, the darts match with no need of adjusting.

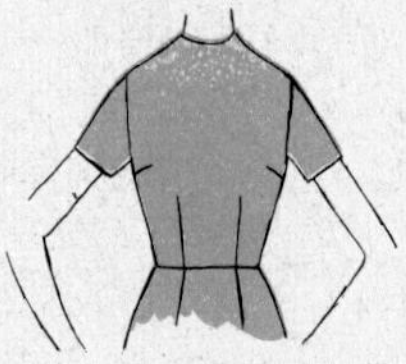

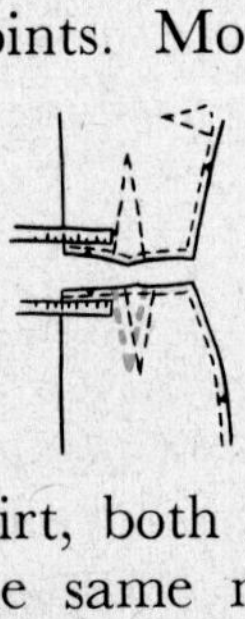

Pattern changes

The next step toward more creative sewing is learning to make minor pattern changes to achieve the style you want. These changes can be made with the use of two or more patterns and do not require pattern-making skill.

Necklines

The pattern may show exactly the dress you want to make except for the neckline. If it is merely a question of reshaping the neckline, the front and back pattern pieces can be pinned to a dress form and the new shape marked with tailor's chalk or pencil. When marking for any detail on a pattern, always indicate the finished line first. It is easier to visualize size and proportion before the seam allowances are marked. After you have decided on the finished shape or depth of the neck, the seam allowance can then be added or allowed for in cutting. Be sure to cut out the facings at the same time you are making the desired alterations on the neck.

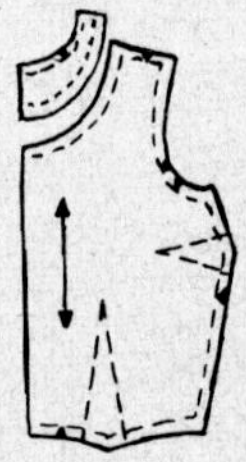

Mark the outline of the neck and the shoulder on tissue paper. Measure in 2½ inches from the outline of the neck and cut the facing here. Save the tissue facing with the pattern for future use.

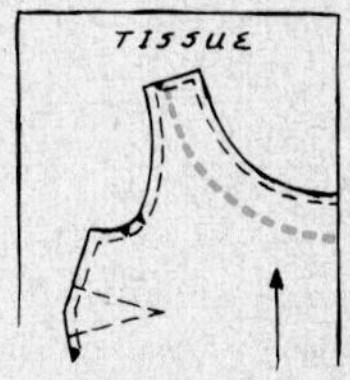

It is a tricky business to cut a collar. If you want to add a collar to a collarless neckline, the safest way is to find a pattern with a correctly shaped collar. Use the collar from this second pattern just as it is. Re-cut the neckline of the dress you are making to adjust it to the pattern from which the collar comes. Lay the front and back bodice of this pattern over the bodice pattern of the dress. Be sure to line up the center and shoulder line as you check

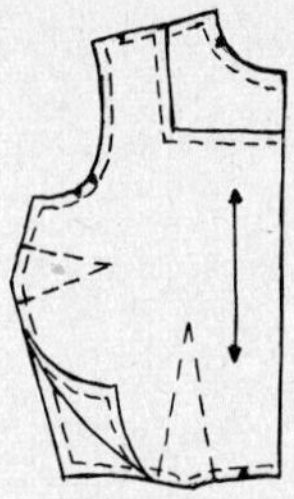

them. Remark the neckline of your dress to the second pattern so the collar will fit and roll correctly. It is always safer to re-cut a pattern change from the pattern you want to copy. By this method, you are certain the size and shape will not be distorted.

Sleeves

Short, long, or ¾ sleeves are all interchangeable in the same pattern size as long as the armhole style is the same. If you prefer a shirred sleeve to a straight one, find the sleeve pattern you want and substitute.

It is more complicated to duplicate a special style feature, such as a dress with a square-cut armhole.

Look for a pattern that has the special armhole and sleeve you want. This pattern may not be at all like the original dress you are copying except for the sleeve and armhole. Lay the bodice pattern with the new armhole over the one to be changed. Again, be sure the shoulders and center front and back lines are matched. Remark the armhole change on the pattern you are using. Cut along the new line as you cut out the bodice. Use the sleeve from the second pattern.

Figuring yardage

For any of the pattern changes just described, there would be little change in yardage. When a short skirt is made long—a long skirt made short, or a full skirt replaced with a slim one, there will be a definite change in yardage. You can quickly figure the difference in yardage by checking the pattern layout guide.

For example, the pattern guide for a full skirt shows four lengths of fabric. A slim skirt needs only two lengths at most, with space left along the side to lay in the extra pattern pieces. If the fabric is wide enough and has no nap, slim skirt pattern pieces can be interlocked so they only take 1½

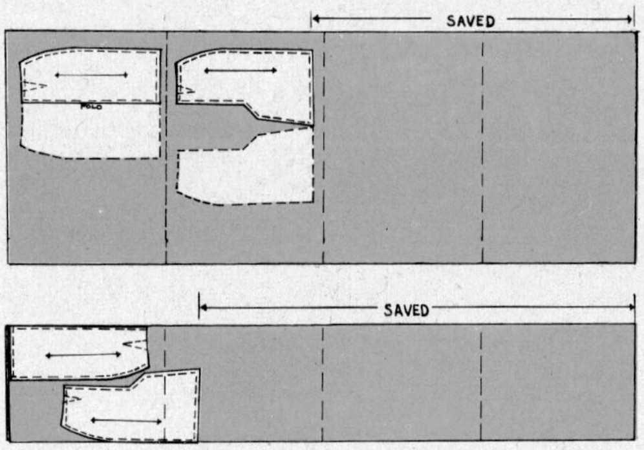

lengths. Next, check the skirt length and buy 2 or 2½ lengths less fabric, depending on the fabric and the pattern you are using.

When making a floor-length skirt short, check your pattern layout guide to see how the skirt pattern pieces are arranged. If the pieces take two complete lengths, then multiply by two the amount you shorten the skirt. Deduct this length from the total yardage.

If by shortening the skirt, the pieces can be interlocked when laid out, deduct the amount the skirt was shortened, plus an extra skirt length.

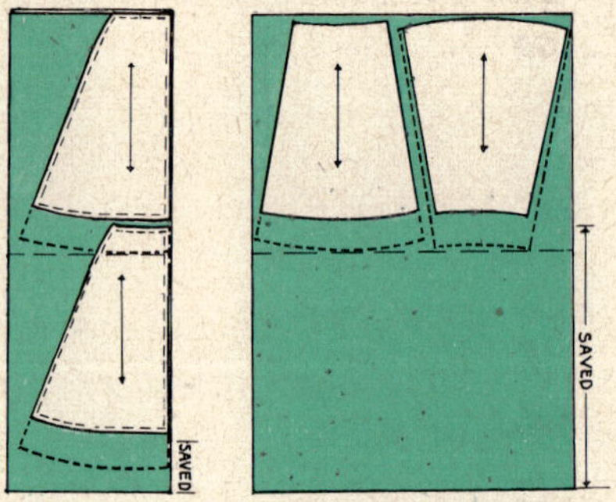

To lengthen skirt, do the opposite.

Where to find design ideas

The pattern changes so far are from designs found in pattern catalogues.

Most women who sew want to be able to duplicate styles they see in ready-to-wear. The combined talents of some of the world's finest designers go into creating these clothes. They are experts in the use of color, line, and trimming detail. The woman who sews can learn a great deal from studying these clothes and incorporating the ideas into her own dressmaking.

Where can you find style ideas? Read the fashion magazines. Latest trends and style lines are reported, and top ready-to-wear manufacturers advertise their newest creations in the fashion books. Local department stores, both in fashion shows and in window displays, also present a constantly changing fashion picture. Newspapers are also a good source of inspiration. Learn to make notes, even sketches, so you won't forget ideas that appeal to you. This is how a designer works.

Basic body line

Don't confuse this term with the *basic pattern*. The basic body line refers to a dress reduced to its simplest parts. It is a shell over which design detail can be applied. Patterns like this are usually labelled "easy-to-make." Over these simple, basic lines the most elaborate design ideas can be applied.

When you want to copy a dress, examine it carefully to decide whether it is a basic body line with trimming, or a specially designed and cut dress. The basic body line with trimming is not difficult; the other type is not quite so easy to duplicate.

Surface detail in designing

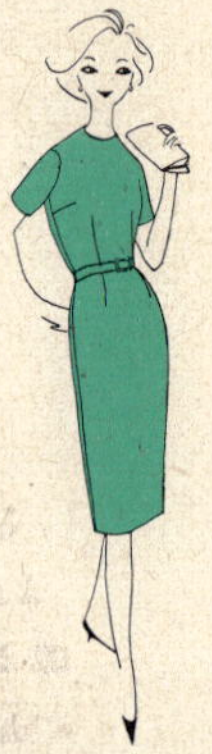

The basic body line to be trimmed is a simple sheath dress. Over this you can place a design detail of self-fabric or trimmings available ready to apply.

All trimmings, even those of self-fabric can be applied after the dress is finished. But be moderate. One design detail to a dress is enough.

View A

This style shows a 1½-inch self-band down the front. The band is completely finished, just tacked at neck, waistline and hem. Large buttons are sewed through the dress and band as trim.

View B

This trim can be a self or contrasting band. It is finished to fit across front shoulders and is tacked in place by hand. The band around hip is also completely finished to size and tacked by hand. To make it even around hip, measure from the finished hemline to the hipline and then baste in place.

View C

This trim can be self or contrast. It is cut on the bias and shaped and pressed as shown in Chapter 6. Start at the back of the neck opening and sew bias into place on the bodice. Pin and sew it around the sleeves. The bows are made separately and then tacked on.

View D

This trim is made from two or three lengths of fabric (depending on the width and weight of the fabric). It is shirred on a waistband and made into a peplum or tunic, depending on size of figure and length you want.

Color in design

The use of co-ordinated colors and contrasting fabric textures are popular techniques in designing ready-to-wear.

You can apply these same techniques to your own dress designing. For instance, you might make the bodice of one color, the midriff or belt of another, and the skirt of a third color. More and more patterns are showing

this treatment; fabric requirements are given for each color.

If you want to change a one-color dress into this style, it is easy to figure the yardage for the other colors. If the fabric is narrow, you will need two skirt lengths for the skirt—about $1\frac{3}{4}$ yards for the average height.

To figure the yardage for the bodice, indicate the fabric width on your cutting table and lay out the pieces. This is the amount of yardage you will need. Figure the yardage for the midriff or belt the same way. In fact, the correct yardage for any pattern changes can be worked out successfully by following this simple method of checking width and placing pieces.

Choose colorful trims for individuality

Lovely laces are easy

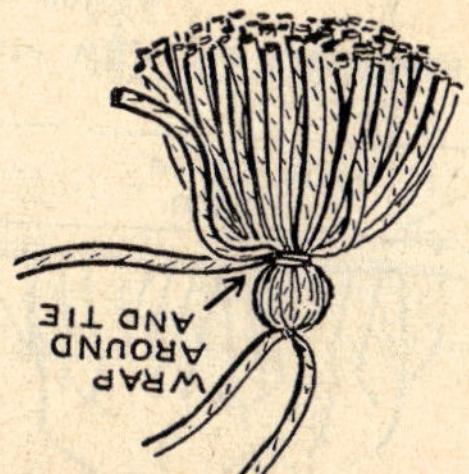

With a strand of yarn about 9" long wind twice around the tassel near the top. Pull tightly, tie firmly and let ends hang as part of tassel. Trim ends.

Make some of each color. Arrange tassels in long cone shape at each corner of tablecloth (see photograph, page 101) and pin on temporarily. Each corner uses approximately 34 tassels. Fewer tassels may be used if desired. Secure by pulling strand of yarn at top of tassel through to the wrong side of cloth, and sew.

After tassels are in place, run a thread through the metal hanger on the Christmas balls. Thread this into a needle and sew the balls to the cloth, arranging them between the tassels as shown in the photograph. About 10 to 12 balls are used on each corner.

White (and other colors) burlap available from bon bazar, 228 W. 4th St., New York 14, N. Y. Prices per yard for 38" width, 59¢, 52" width, 89¢. ◆

Consumers' Guaranty—page 6

PRINTED IN THE U. S. A. BY THE CUNEO PRESS, INC.

Vary patterns

All design ideas are not added to the surface of the dress. Sometimes the cut of the dress gives the style detail. If a pattern is not available with the exact line you want, select the one most similar and proceed to make the necessary changes.

View 1

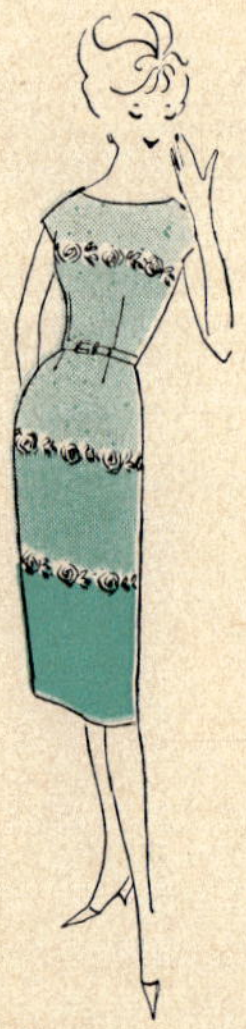

This is a straight sheath dress, but four colors are used in its design. It is simple to duplicate. First pin the waist and bust darts in the bodice pattern, then pin bodice on a dress form. Mark depth of yoke on the front and back pattern with pencil or chalk. You can only mark this correctly when all fitting darts are pinned, and it molds to the form. Remove pattern, unpin darts and cut along this mark—the finished line. Paste a strip of tissue

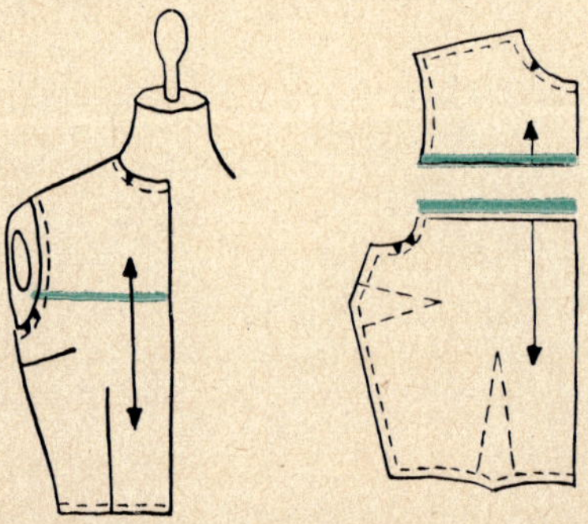

on the yoke and the lower bodice, adding a $\frac{5}{8}$ inch seam allowance.

On the skirt, first mark the finished length. Measure up from the hem for widths of skirt sections. Watch the proportion so the colors will be evenly balanced. Draw the lines across the skirt pattern. Pin to the dress form and stand back to check how the sections appear to the eye.

When the proportion seems good, cut the skirt pattern along these lines.

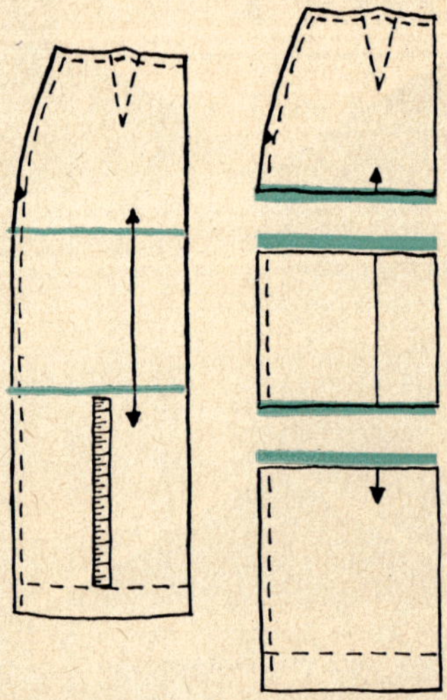

Label each piece to avoid misplacement. Add $\frac{5}{8}$ inch seam allowance on each cut seam. (It's best to add the seam to the pattern rather than trying to remember to add it as you cut.)

Indicate on the cutting table the width of fabric you will use. Lay out the pattern pieces for each color and measure the yardage needed for each. Your pattern is ready to cut.

View 2

The bodice is not changed. It is simply bound in the colors of the skirt. Measure the finished length of skirt and divide it into three sections, each one slightly wider than the one above.

Multiply the number of skirt lengths by depth of the top band, and add the amount needed for top color. For the center section, multiply the depth of the band by number of skirt lengths. For the lower section add depth and hem, multiply by the number of skirt lengths. This will give you an accurate estimate of yardage you will need.

View 3

This dress is styled as a straight sheath with contrast used at yoke and hem. Measure and cut the yoke as for the other views. Measure and cut the lower section of the skirt as for View 1. Again, lay out yoke and hem pieces to check the yardage needed. Subtract this from the yardage requirement on the pattern envelope to determine the amount of yardage needed for the contrasting fabric.

All these styles have braid, lace, or other trimming used at the seams where the colors join. This treatment is not necessary, but it does give a more finished look to the garment. Or, you can use a cording of one of the dress colors in the seams. See Chapter 6 for instructions on making cording.

Making patterns

Have you ever been unable to find a dress pattern with a midriff section? Usually the detail is so simple you could cut it faster than the time required to search for the pattern.

Midriff pattern

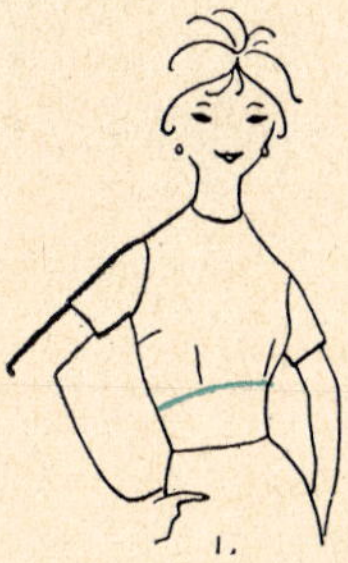

Pin in the darts on the front and back of bodice pattern pieces. Pin to dress form. Decide depth and shape of midriff pieces and mark with pencil.

Remove the pattern pieces from the

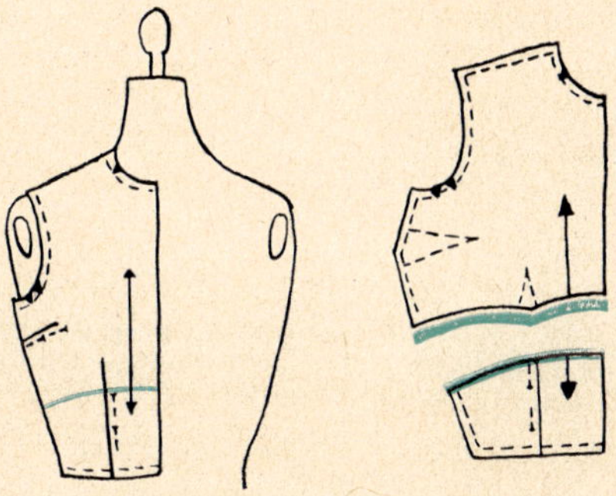

dress form and cut along the marked line. Unpin the darts on the top bodice pieces and add seam allowances at the cut line. Leave the darts pinned on the lower bodice pieces. Trace this piece on tissue, making the midriff pattern. Add the seam allowances before you cut the fabric.

Plastron front

Again, pin in the darts on the front bodice and pin the bodice to the dress form. Mark on the pattern the width

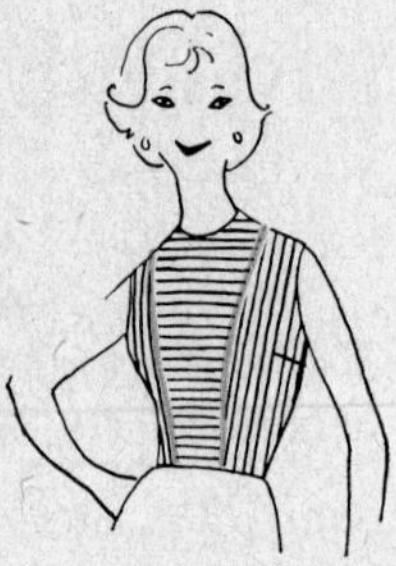

and shape of the plastron front. The width of the lower edge is often along the inside dart line. Remove the pattern and unpin the darts. Cut on the

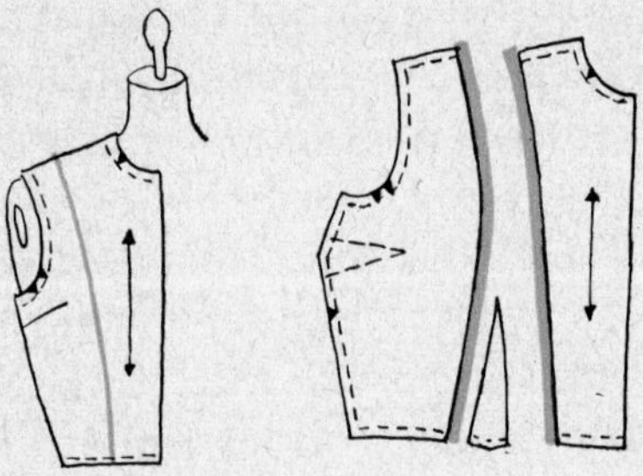

marked line. Add the seam allowance to the front or plastron piece. The side piece is shaped along the outside dart line. This eliminates the fitting dart but keeps the fit, much as a princess line is cut. Add the $5/8$ inch seam allowance to the outside piece.

Bib front

Again pin the dart into the front bodice pattern and pin the pattern to the dress form. (The bib can be made while the pattern is flat on the table, but shaping it on the form gives a better idea of the proportions for your figure.) Mark the shape and size of the bib on the pattern. Remove the pattern from the form and unpin the darts. Cut out bib along the marks. Add seam allowances around bib and to the bodice where the bib will be sewed.

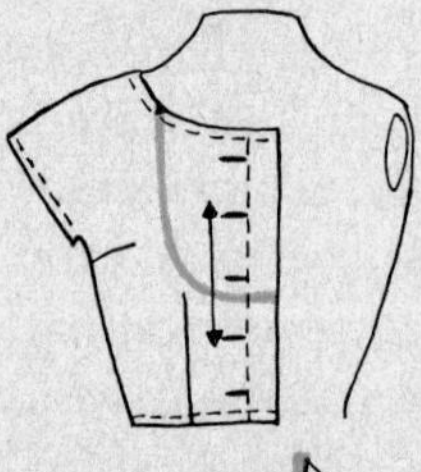

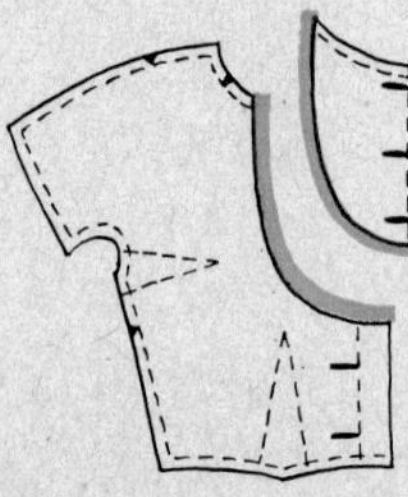

Fagoting

This trim is used between seams to give a decorative touch to a dress. You can buy it by the yard in tape form and insert it into the seam. Although it is more time-consuming to do, fagoting is attractive when done by hand (A). Or, make bias tubing and use it in the seam (B).

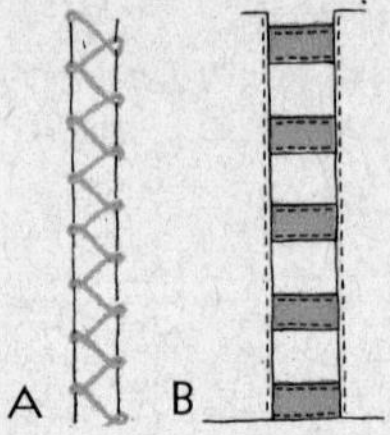

The pattern must be specially cut for fagoting. Use it to give line and detail to a dress. Pick a bodice pattern you like and decide where to use fagoting detail. Cut a duplicate of the bodice pattern in heavy paper. Pin the darts in the bodice pattern and pin the pattern to a dress form. Mark the placement of the fagoted seams on the pattern. Remove the pattern piece

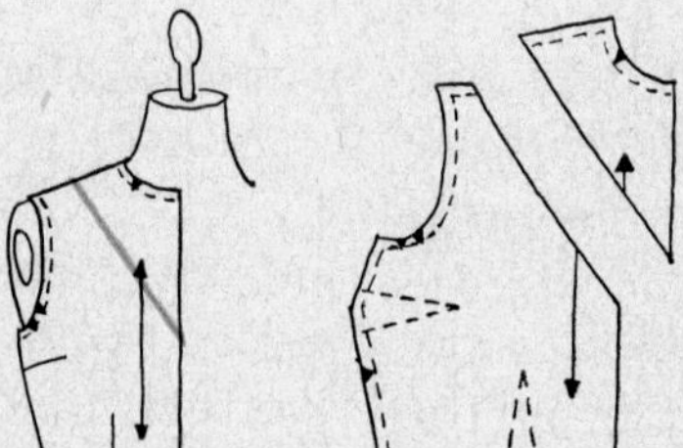

and then cut along the marked lines.

Before marking for seam allowances on the cut edges, decide which type fagoting you would like to use.

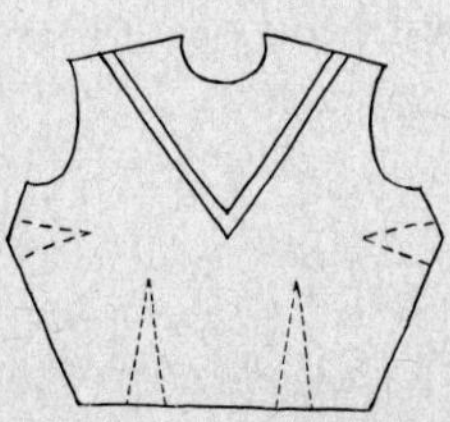

Fagoting tape

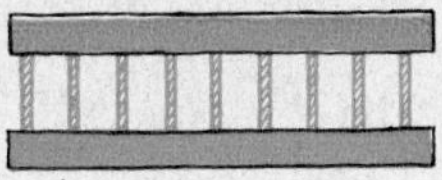

This tape comes in ¼-inch and ½-inch widths. If you use ½-inch tape, the seam allowance where the fagoting is applied will be ¼ inch. Mark the seamline with a basting thread. Pin the tape to the bodice, right sides together. On the bodice, stitch along the ¼-inch basting line to the base of the tape so only the fagoting shows on the right side. There is no need to miter the tape at the corners or points. Just cut the tape at the points. The thread of the fagoting finishes to the end of the seam and open triangles are left at the corners. The heavy paper pattern is only used when this trim is applied by hand. Follow the instructions on how to use the pattern in the section on hand fagoting.

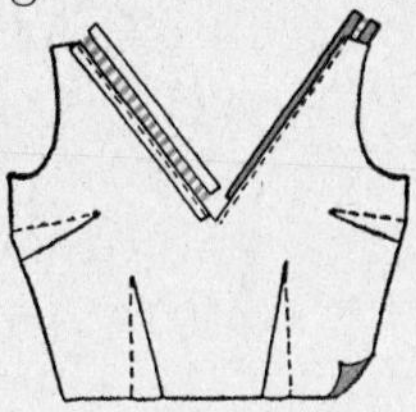

Hand fagoting

There are many types of stitches used in hand fagoting, and you can make them any width you like. If the stitch is ¼-inch wide, then add ¼-inch to the cut edges where the fagoting will be applied when you cut the bodice pieces. Turn back a ⅜-inch seam and baste. Mark on a heavy paper pattern the width and placement of the fagoting. Baste the bodice pieces carefully along these lines. Now proceed with the fagoting.

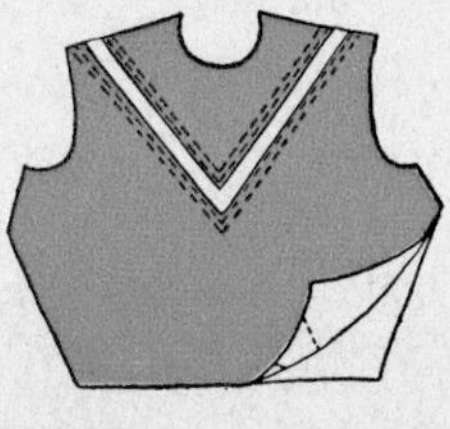

Bar or ladder fagoting

Use embroidery thread or buttonhole twist for this type of fagoting. Bring the needle out on one edge, take a stitch directly opposite in the other edge. Wind the needle around this thread three or four times and bring it back to starting point. Slide the needle through the fold for the next stitch. Space the bars any width you like.

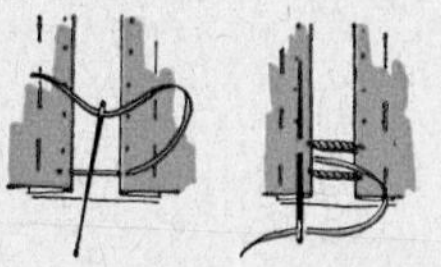

Criss-cross fagoting

This is done like a catch-stitch—work backward and from left to right. Bring the needle from underneath on the left edge. Slant the needle to the right edge and take a stitch under the right fold. As you work the stitch back and forth, the needle always passes under the thread of the preceding stitch. Use any width of fagoting you like, depending on the space you want.

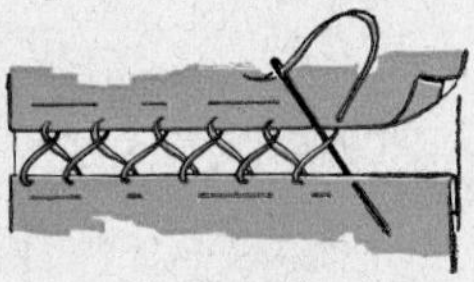

Self-fagoting

This can be made of tubing (see instructions for making tubing in Chapter 6) or of narrow grosgrain ribbon. When using tubing, stitch on each edge. Mark lines on a piece of tissue paper for the width of fagoting trim. Cut tubing in lengths ½-inch longer than the finished width. Mark the space between each strip. Stitch ends to each line. Remove the tissue and stitch tubing to either side of seam.

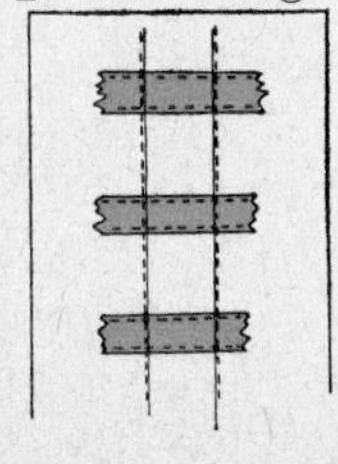

Designer tricks

An allover tucked or pleated dress may seem like a great deal of work; even a tucked yoke or shirt front may appear formidable. Ready-to-wear manufacturers are able to make dresses featuring partial or complete tucking at moderate prices because they send out the yardage to be tucked by machine and cut the dress from the tucked fabric. Many large cities have shops for this work, or you may tuck your own.

How to measure for tucking

Decide the size and spacing of the tucks you want. Make a sample of the tucking by basting four or five tucks in a strip of fabric. Measure the width of tucked fabric. Open the basted tucks and measure again. If the fabric is one inch in width with basted tucks and three inches after releasing the tucking, you will need fabric three times the width of the pattern piece.

If the fabric is not wide enough, tucking can be pieced at any point. Be sure to allow extra for piecing.

To figure the yardage for a simple bodice top, measure the length of the back and front waist patterns. On a size 14, for instance, it would be about 20 inches. Allow a few extra inches on the length. Next, measure the widths of the complete back and front waist patterns. On a size 14, they would each be about 20 inches wide.

If your fabric is 45 inches wide, and the tucking takes up three inches to one, your piece of fabric would be 15 inches wide when tucked. One more length of tucked fabric will give you an additional 15 inches. Split it and you'll have two 7-inch widths of tucking to make the front and back pieces wider. The amount of fabric you will need for a tucked top will be 20 inches multiplied by 2 for both bodice lengths, plus an additional 20 inches for piecing. To piece, turn back the edge of one piece along a tuck. Lap over the edge of the other tucked piece so the spacing between tucks is even. Stitch along original stitching of tuck. Tucks are pressed so the fold edges form a box or inverted center. Fold on the center of the piece and cut the back and front waist pieces.

The same method of figuring yardage can be applied to pleating. Figure

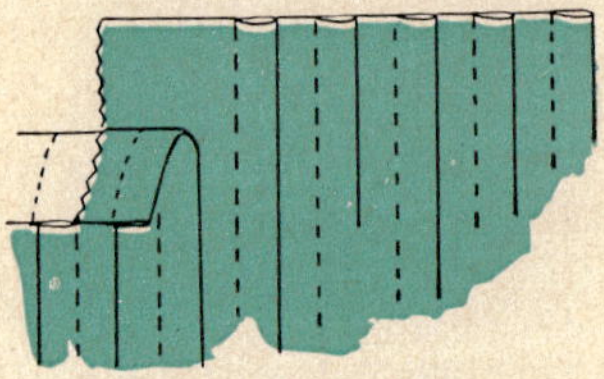

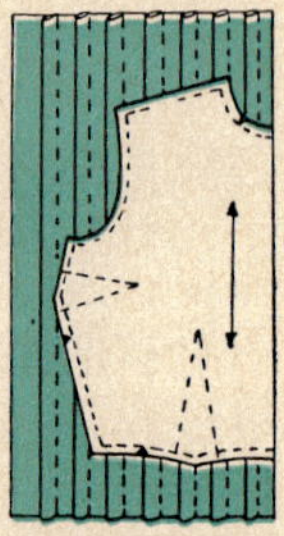

from the hip measurement plus a little extra for ease. Tucked or pleated skirts are generally cut straight to the hem with no flare. More shallow, or more widely spaced pleats and tucks take up less fabric. It is wise to plan tucking and pleating that will fit the width of your particular fabric. Weight also determines the number of tucks.

View 1

This dress is made of fine pleating and lace. The fabric is a soft sheer

pleated in ¼-inch side pleats. Figure amount you need from a strapless sheath pattern. Cut the pleating in lengths for the bodice and skirt. Space the lace evenly and baste it in place. The pleating can be cut out from under the lace for a more sheer look. Cut the sheath pattern from the pleating and mount over the lining pieces. The lining of China silk or another soft lining is cut from the sheath dress pattern.

View 2

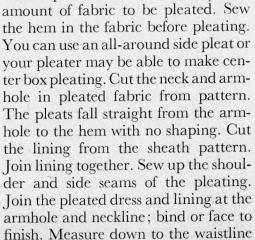

This dress is made entirely of pleating. Shirred at the waistline, the dress drapes into a softly pleated skirt. You can use a dress pattern with or without a waistline seam. The straight sheath without a waistline seam is less bulky at the waist. Measure from sheath pattern for the amount of fabric to be pleated. Sew the hem in the fabric before pleating. You can use an all-around side pleat or your pleater may be able to make center box pleating. Cut the neck and armhole in pleated fabric from pattern. The pleats fall straight from the armhole to the hem with no shaping. Cut the lining from the sheath pattern. Join lining together. Sew up the shoulder and side seams of the pleating. Join the pleated dress and lining at the armhole and neckline; bind or face to finish. Measure down to the waistline and mark with a basting thread all around. Sew a 1-inch casing around waistline. Cut elastic 1 inch smaller than the waist size and draw it through the casing and join ends. Hem the lining. Use a cummerbund or belt, preferably of the same fabric; a color may be used for a contrasting effect.

Contrasting detail

Detail such as cording, banding, piping, binding, and buttonholes can be done in a contrasting color to give a design touch to your clothes. Plan this detail ahead of time because it is sewed into the dress as it is made. Avoid the spotty use of contrasting detail. Notice how subtly designers use it.

Contrasts in texture and sheen can also give a spark to your sewing—satin used with linen, wool, dull crepe or tweeds, for example.

The sketches were taken from ready-to-wear designs and show the tasteful use of contrasting trim. Proper placement is as important as the trim.

Commercial trimmings

A designer has many sources for trimmings. If she wants a bodice embroidered, she has only to call in a specialist who not only will do the embroidery, but also create a new design for her. She has sources for braid, ribbon, laces, and trimmings of all kinds.

The home sewer also has a wide selection of trimmings available in the trimmings, notions, lace and ribbon departments of local stores.

These trimmings can be sewed to clothes without any pattern changes. Just look for a pattern similar to the basic body line of the dress you want to copy. Usually, a full-skirted dress is more elaborately trimmed.

Color photographs in this chapter show trimmings with sketches of ready-made clothes on which they are used.

Although no pattern changes are needed, it is sometimes easier to apply trimmings as you make the dress. For instance, banding can be sewed to a shirred skirt more easily before the skirt is shirred. First, assemble the skirt pieces and stitch them; apply the banding you have selected; and do the shirring. Turn the hem and your trimmed skirt will be finished.

On a straight skirt, leave the left side open while the banding is being sewed on. It is easier to stitch when the skirt is open and flat. Sew up the left side and then turn hem.

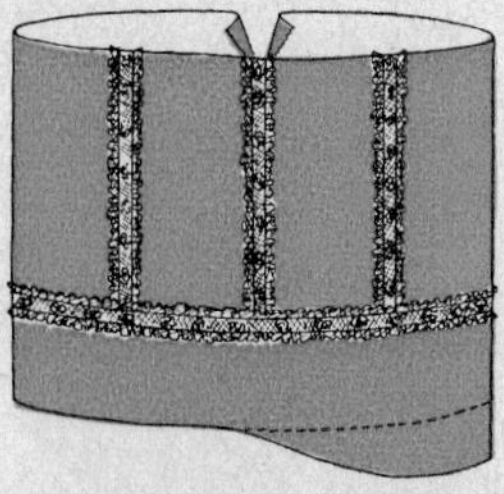

Gathered skirt

Straight skirt

The left side of the bodice should also be left open if banding is to be sewed around it for trim.

When banding is used vertically, sew the darts in front and back bodice pieces, leaving the seams open until the banding has been applied. Bandings should shape in toward waistline for a more flattering line. Have one band follow shape of waistline dart for a better over-all appearance. A few designer tricks can help you trim even more effectively. For example, black lace used with black fabric is always elegant, but can be made even more beautiful by using color under the lace to highlight it. A flesh color used under lace makes it look very sheer, and gives the effect of cutwork.

Lace banding

Sew lace over ribbon, with the latter slightly more narrow, for a beautiful effect. Sew the ribbon to the garment and add the lace last.

Lace motifs

These motifs are very effective when sewed over contrasting linings. Cut the outline of the motif in a contrasting lining. Baste the lining to the wrong side of the motif, and trim it slightly smaller around the edge. Place the lined motif on the dress and baste it in place. Applique by hand with a fine overcasting stitch, or with a fine satin stitch, using a zig-zag machine.

Beading

Beading is an insertion through which ribbon can be drawn. Strips of self-fabric cut on the bias can substitute for the ribbon for a lovely effect. Beading is also available with the ribbon already threaded through it.

Ribbon and embroidered braid

Use these trimmings with lace edgings or rickrack sewed along each edge for a more colorful effect.

Beads

This trim can be sewed by hand to spark a print or lace dress or as an allover design on dressy clothes.

Sew the beads on with a fine backstitch, using a very fine needle. Sew each bead, following a pattern. Different beads offer varying effects.

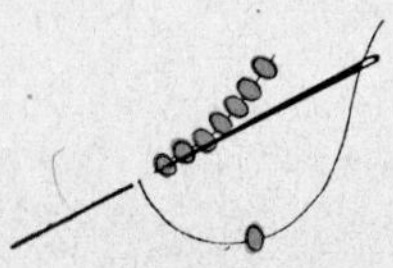

When you sew the beads on lace, match the thread carefully. If you are sewing beads in clusters, use a running stitch on the lace from cluster to cluster, instead of starting with a new thread as each design is repeated.

Sequins

Sequins should also be sewed on with a backstitch to follow a definite design. They are often spotted on lace to give it sparkle. Sew the sequins singly by using a bead in the center of each sequin, adding a dimensional effect.

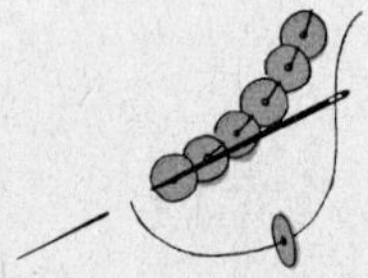

Again, use thread the same color as the lace and do a running stitch from point to point where sequins are used.

Passementerie

This is the application of soutache braid in a design on coats, suits, and dresses. The braid can be applied by hand or by a special braiding foot. Soutache comes in many colors, or white can be dyed to match fabric.

View 1

This sketch shows a design worked in soutache braid. It eliminates the need for jewelry.

View 2

This style shows soutache used to outline an applique around the edge of a bolero. When sewing by hand, use a running stitch through center of braid.

Designer blouses

Beautiful blouses can be made by combining strips of lace and tucking, or embroidered banding down the front.

View 1

This blouse combines embroidered organdy banding with cotton lace banding and edging. Use organdy banding as center. To either side of the organdy, add insertions of lace, organdy banding, lace again, and a ruffled lace edging. Sew a length of blouse fabric to either side of the insertion. Fold along the center of the center band and cut the pattern front for your blouse. Make the rest of the blouse of plain fabric. The neck can be finished with bias binding and a bow.

View 2

This blouse combines tucks and lace on the crossgrain. Measure the length of fabric needed for blouse. Measure for placement of first tuck and sew it across the fabric. Using 1½-inch lace, sew one edge of the lace below the first tuck. Trim the fabric under the lace close to this first stitching. Sew the lower edge of the lace to the cut edge of the fabric. Measure and sew two more tucks in the fabric. Sew another length of lace the same way. Continue until you have as many bands as you want across the front of the blouse. Fold in half and cut the two blouse fronts from the tucked piece. Sew a center band of plain fabric for the buttons and buttonholes. Cut the rest of the blouse and collar from untucked fabric. This blouse can be made in any fine, sheer fabric.

View 3

This style combines fine tucks and insertions of lace or eyelet in vertical fashion. This combination gives the blouse a dainty, feminine look. Cut the rest of blouse from plain fabric.

Chapter 15

Accessories and wardrobe planning

Making an attractive costume is only one part of being smartly dressed. Accessories—suitable belt, buttons, trimmings, a becoming hat, correct handbag and shoes, attractive jewelry—also contribute to the smart, fashionable look of an ensemble.

Just as with clothes, some accessories will not be particularly becoming to you. The smart woman chooses her accessories as carefully as she does her dress. She adapts the current fashions most suitable to her.

In choosing any accessories, good taste is the most important criterion. Some women can wear fashion extremes more easily than others. If you aren't comfortable wearing a certain accessory, don't wear it. Choose accessories that suit your personality.

Basic dress you can wear everywhere

Accessories for a casual suit

Key accessories to suit color

Buttons

There is a definite trend in buttons each season as in other fashions. Check the type of buttons used on new ready-to-wear for a fashion clue.

Button sizes

Big buttons may look fine on a tall, well-built figure, but they'll overpower a petite one. Pick a button that's smaller and in better proportion for the small figure, but that still follows the fashion trend.

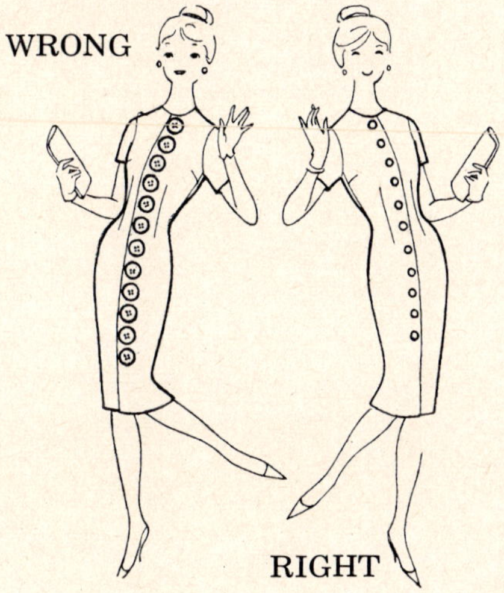

The reverse applies when a small button is fashionable. No matter how it's used, a ¼-inch button will look inappropriate on a size 40 dress. In this case, pick a larger button that would still be considered small for this size figure. Try different button sizes on the dress during the fitting before making buttonholes.

Colored buttons

If the buttons are to match the garment, be sure they really match. A shade or two difference in color can ruin the effect. Do your matching under a good light.

Use contrasting colored buttons with care so they don't look spotty. Usually, when used, these buttons are the style detail of the dress, so keep the dress simple in design and fairly neutral in color.

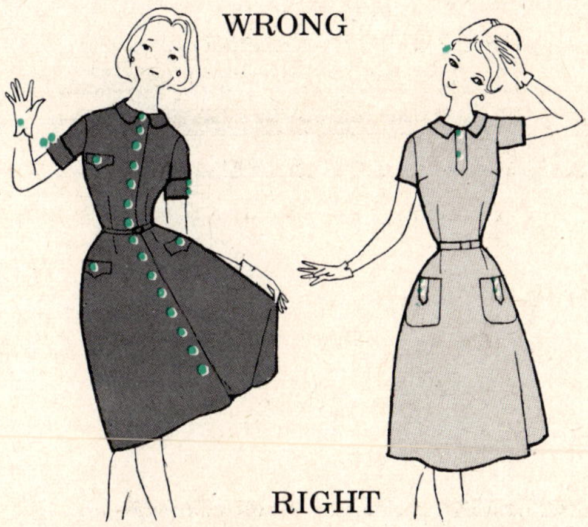

Black or white buttons are always a safe choice for a contrasting fabric.

Buttons for different fabrics

It used to be easy to select buttons for fabrics. The rule was "dressy buttons for dressy fabrics, and tailored buttons for tailored fabrics."

Now buttons are matched to fabrics in new combinations that lend interest and variety. Jeweled buttons are used on tweeds as well as on chiffons—pearl buttons on velvets and flannels as well as on cottons and linens.

The old standbys are always good. Bone buttons are smart on flannel or tweed suits, while silver and gold buttons are good on plaids and checks, tweed, fine worsteds, wools, velveteens, and corduroys. Pearl buttons can be used on practically any fabric.

The more simple the button you select, the better. Use a bone or plastic button on tailored dresses and coats. A plain two- or four-hole button with either a dull or shiny finish is always in good taste. Black jet buttons are also perennial favorites.

Self-covered buttons

Many women use these buttons for almost all of their clothes because they are unsure of the right type of commercial button to buy. Self-covered buttons have a place in dressmaking, but they can be used unwisely.

There is a definite style trend in self-covered buttons. The simple flat top button in 24 or 30 line is used most often in ready-to-wear. It is small and trim in appearance. Usually, the larger the self-covered button, the more homemade the garment looks. Many companies make molds for self-covered buttons you can make at home.

If the garment or its trimming is particularly elaborate, the addition of a fancy button would be too much. This is a natural place for small, inconspicuous self-covered buttons.

Often dressy fabrics like satin or brocade are so beautiful that to use a decorative button would be "gilding the lily," so again a self-covered button is better. They are also a better choice on fabric colors that are difficult to match.

Avoid using a self-covered button in a contrasting color. Contrasting texture, however, can be interesting. For instance, use a satin button on a dull-surface wool to match a satin blouse or trim, or use a jersey button on a wool flannel or tweed to match suit trim or blouse.

Belts

Belts come in many widths, fabrics, and colors. Style trends range from the extremely wide belt to the very narrow belt. Size and body structure influence your choice.

Be sure belts match the color of any commercial buttons on the dress, with these few exceptions. With pearl buttons, use patent leather, calf, or novelty-type summer belts; for jet buttons, use patent leather, polished calf, or suede. With metal buttons, use calf, suede or patent leather.

A self-belt is a good choice when you're in doubt. Most department stores will make one from your fabric, or buy a kit and make it yourself.

The belt width you choose depends on your size and figure. The more matronly figure looks best in a narrow or self-fabric belt. These are inconspicuous and more flattering to the fuller figure. If you have a small waistline and flat diaphragm, you can wear a wide belt. A full skirt nipped in at the waist by a wide belt also helps to de-emphasize full hips.

Belts in contrasting color can pick up a tone in a bright print or highlight a dark or neutral shade. However, color used around the waist emphasizes the waistline, so be sure yours is trim enough to stand this attention. Black belts in patent or other leathers are usually safe to wear on prints and soft colors. Contrasting texture is also interesting.

Cummerbunds of self-fabric flatter any figure if the rib cage is small, the diaphragm flat, and the bust high. They should fit smooth and flat.

Hats

Every woman knows what a lift a new hat can give. If the hat is wrong, however, it can ruin the whole outfit.

As for other accessories, choose a hat according to your figure. A very small hat on a large woman makes her look out of proportion—a too-small head on a large body.

A hat should also be suitable in size, color, and design to the garment with which you will wear it.

Suitable size

Try the hat with the garment to see if the entire ensemble is in balance. Check in a full-length mirror so you can be sure you are not accentuating a specific figure problem.

Suitable styles

Hats can be made of feathers, flowers, felt, or fur. The hat style determines the occasion and the outfit with which it should be worn.

A casual tweed suit looks best with a tailored cloche or a simple beret. A dressy suit or dress needs a more glamorous hat—perhaps a soft one of satin, feathers, velvet, or flowers, but simple in design.

A basic suit or dress offers a wide choice of all accessories. These styles can be dressed up or down according to the occasion. (See pages 286-287.)

A simple, basic suit looks stunning at a party when it's dressed up with a hat of feathers, flowers, or net and smart accessories. It becomes a daytime suit for shopping or luncheon when worn with more tailored accessories. (See page 288.)

WRONG

A short stocky figure with a short neck and a large bosom looks even shorter, becomes top heavy under a large, wide hat (A).

Hat size applies to costume as well as figure. This coat with a large, high collar has all of the weight at the top of the figure when a big hat is put over it (B).

A too-small hat used with a sleek, slim dress like this gives a bare, unfinished look to the outfit (C).

RIGHT

On Figure (D), the hat is scaled down in width and is much higher to give a taller, slimmer look. It sets higher on the head, which is more flattering to the short-necked figure.

The smaller hat, on Figure (E), gives a clean, more balanced look to the coat with the high collar.

The larger hat, worn with the scoop-necked sheath, takes away the bare look of the head and neck and gives a better balance to the figure (F).

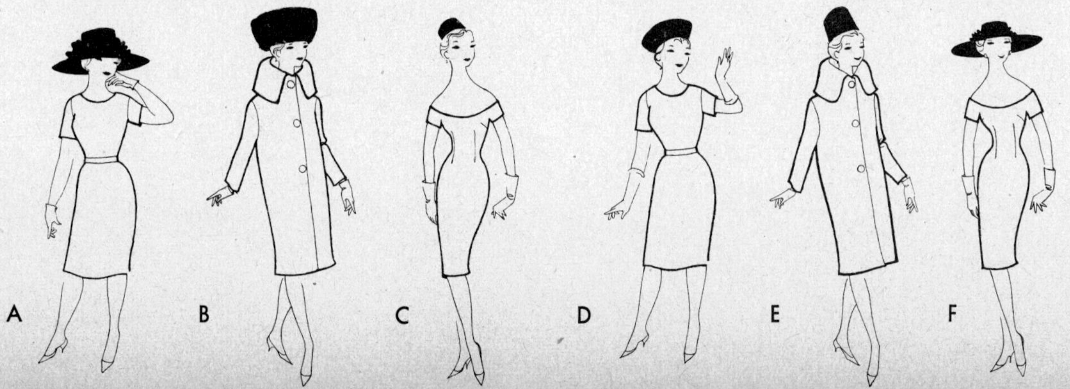

Handbags

Remember the rules about color, size, and suitability. A small person looks overburdened with a too-large bag; a large woman looks out of proportion with a very small one.

A bag doesn't have to be expensive to look smart. Many inexpensive handbags give excellent service. Choose one in a simple style, with a covered frame and as little trimming as possible. Metallic trims and frames tarnish and scratch and eventually make the bag look shabby.

Choose a bag suitable to the occasion. The over-the-shoulder bag belongs with a casual outfit; a dressy bag of suede or fabric is out of place with a sweater and skirt. Usually, a dressy bag is smaller than the one generally used for everyday.

Suitable colors

Accessory colors change from season to season. Sometimes, it is fashionable for all accessories to match an ensemble in a monochromatic scheme.

Many petite women choose matching accessories regardless of the style trend. The small figure looks taller when there is no contrasting color to break the height (A).

Often, different shades of the ensemble color are considered smart for accessories. This can also flatter the small figure, since there is no sharp contrast to cut the height (B).

Sharp contrasting accessories are also fashionable. They can be in subtle, grayed shades or in bright, sharp colors. Whatever the style, study your size and type carefully, and discreetly use the color you choose.

If you are short, save the strong color for a handbag, scarf, gloves, or jewelry. Don't use it where it will shorten your height. A tall figure can use a contrasting hat, belt, or shoes.

Black or neutral accessories can be used freely. Avoid a spotty look when using bright colors.

View 1

This sketch shows how accessories—hat, bag, gloves, jewelry, and shoes—of the same color can look spotty against a dress of another color.

WRONG

View 2

Here's a pleasing amount of color used in bright accessories. Hat and blouse

RIGHT

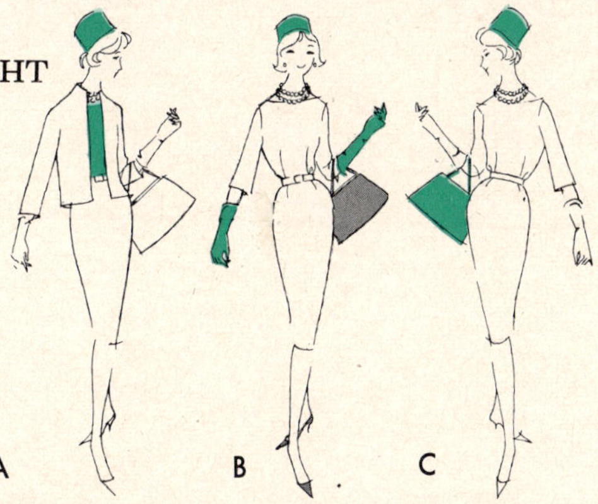

match (A). Hat and gloves are of the same shade, neutral shoes and bag (B). Hat and bag highlight the color (C).

View 3

Neutral black can safely be used for all accessories. Other neutral shades like gray, brown, taupe, and navy, can also be used more freely. Often, two neutrals can be used, with a third color to brighten the whole outfit. Grayed shades of a bright accessory color can also be used in the same ensemble without overdoing the color.

RIGHT

Wardrobe planning

A constant source of humor is the woman with a closet full of clothes and nothing to wear. Too often a woman has many clothes, but nothing suitable for some special occasion.

Many women are inclined to ignore common sense when planning their wardrobes. They find it hard to resist current fashions. No matter how fashionable a new color or design may be, don't buy it if it's unbecoming. You'll never feel comfortable wearing it.

Plan your wardrobe carefully. Consider both day-to-day business life and social activities in your planning. With a little thought, you can extend your wardrobe and eliminate the need for a great variety of accessories.

Extending your wardrobe

This doesn't mean mix-matching everything in your wardrobe; nor does it mean making a dozen accessories to change the "little basic dress."

Instead, it means careful planning to get greater use out of each item in your wardrobe, changing and replacing a few things at a time so your clothes always have interest.

Everyone has a skirt, jacket, or other clothing that they wear only once in a while. It is usually out of style before you get any real service from it. Often, you also have accessories for these stray garments. You can often integrate these little-worn articles into your wardrobe by simply adding a few new items.

BASIC DRESS AND JACKET. Start with a basic dress and jacket of the same fabric. You'll get more wear from the fitted jacket if you make a pleated skirt of the same fabric. Usually, a short jacket requires a blouse. A print blouse adds a touch of color. Add a matching print skirt, and you have a print dress. You can also wear the short jacket with the print dress.

SOFT SUIT. Get extra mileage from a soft suit by making a basic top from the leftover fabric. Wear the top with a slim skirt, and it makes a smart, basic dress. Add a tailored shirt in a colorful check to the skirt for casual wear. Make a checked skirt to wear with the shirt, and you have a soft, shirt dress. Or, combine the checked skirt with a sleeveless blouse. Careful planning with a few extra yards of fabric gives extra wear to the suit.

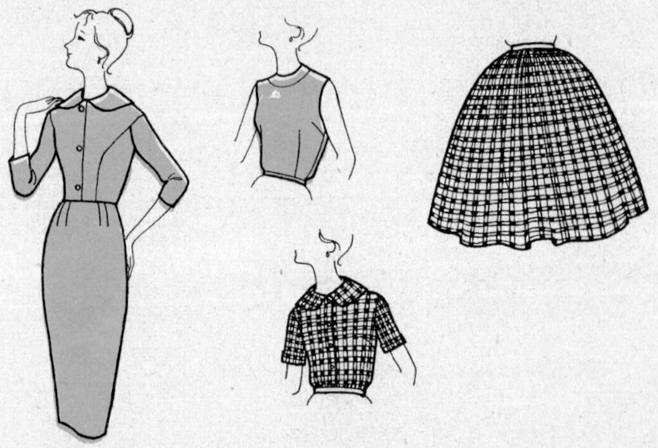

CASUAL SUIT. A plaid jacket and pleated skirt are wonderful for casual living, but will extend your wardrobe even more if you make slacks from an extra 1½ yards of the plaid. A soft jersey top can be worn with the pleated skirt or the slacks. Make a slim skirt to match the blouse for a more dressed-up look. Bermuda shorts in a contrasting color would be smart with the jersey top or the plaid jacket.

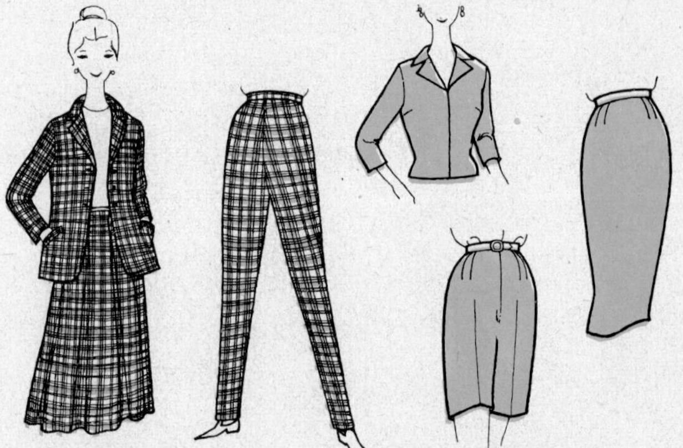

COCKTAIL SUIT. This suit will give you limited wear unless you put each piece to work. Make a basic blouse in a pastel satin to wear with the suit skirt for dress occasions. A full-length skirt in a darker pastel gives extra wear to either the blouse or the jacket. A long-sleeved blouse in soft chiffon is good for at-home wear with the long skirt. Add a chiffon skirt, and you have a daytime dress.

With this kind of wardrobe planning, your clothes will go on from year to year, always fresh and fashionable.

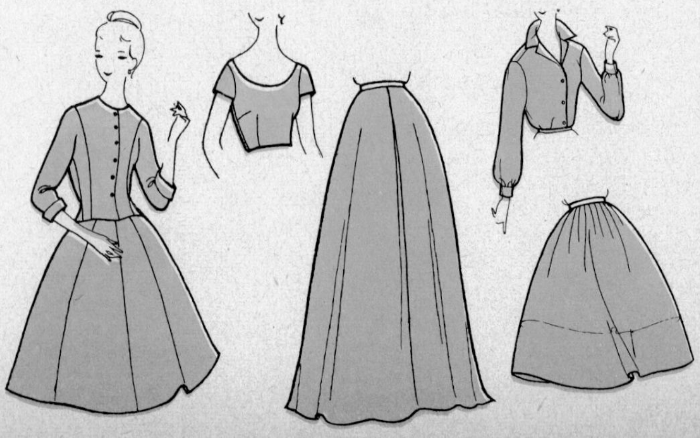

Chapter **16**

Improving ready-to-wear clothes

Most women, even those who sew a great deal, find it necessary to supplement their wardrobes with ready-made clothes. Ready-to-wear seldom gives as good a fit as clothes made at home. This often means expensive alterations. The solution lies in learning to make these alterations yourself—but as a professional does them.

When you shop for a dress, of course, try to find one that requires little altering. The ready-to-wear market has many sizes for different figure types. Find the one suited to you. Half-sizes, for instance, are for a more mature figure with a fuller, lower bust, narrower shoulders, shorter waist, and full hips. Try several sizes until you find the one that gives you the best fit.

Remember, each manufacturer has his own body line, so a dress from one manufacturer may fit better than another brand dress in the same size.

Never buy a dress that is too small. It may be possible to let it out, but the whole cut of the dress will look skimpy. Also avoid the dress that is many sizes too big. You'll have to remake the entire dress.

When you try the dress, analyze it carefully to see how much alteration will be necessary. To alter correctly, much of the dress must be taken apart. Pulling in or letting out a little here and there just won't do the job!

On the following pages are some actual photographs of fitting for ready-to-wear alterations.

View 1

View 2

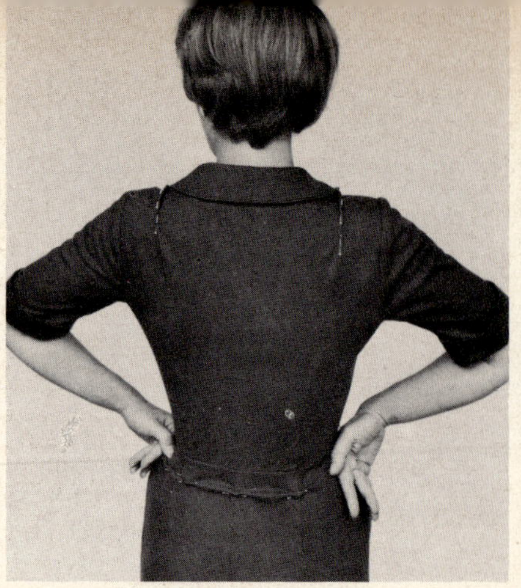

View 3

Adjusting ready-to-wear dresses

Set-in sleeve

View 1

This inexpensive dress was chosen in a junior size to get a better waist and skirt length. Neither needs altering. This is important since it's difficult to shorten the waist, and impossible to lengthen it on a fly-front dress like this. The shoulders need narrowing, and the droop under the bust needs additional adjusting to make the dress fit correctly.

View 2

Here, the shoulders have been fitted to the correct width by a tuck over the shoulder as in fitting a basic muslin (as shown in Chapter 3). The width of tuck is the amount the shoulders have to be narrowed.

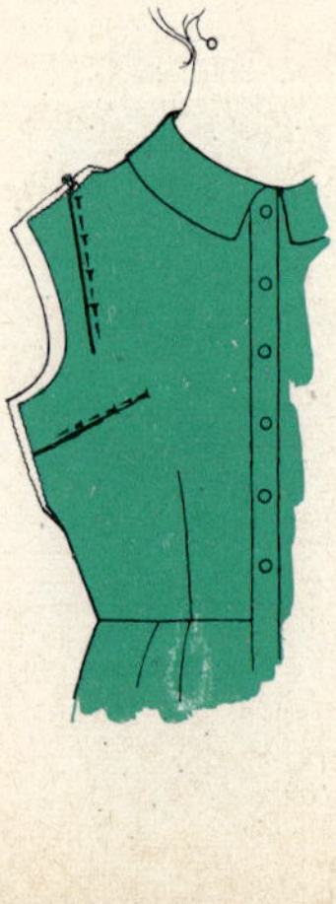

Remove sleeves. Rip open the underarm seam to 3 inches from the waist. Rip the shoulder seam to 2 inches from the neck. The droop under the bustline is fitted out by extending the bust dart.

Pin and sew this dart deeper on the inside. To re-mark the dart on the inside, use tailor's chalk along the inside pin line. Unpin the outside and repin on inside chalk line.

Fold the left front dress over the right. Cut amount of the tuck from the right shoulder, using the left armhole as a pattern. Reverse and cut the left side from right armhole. A slight amount comes off the underarm bodice seam as well.

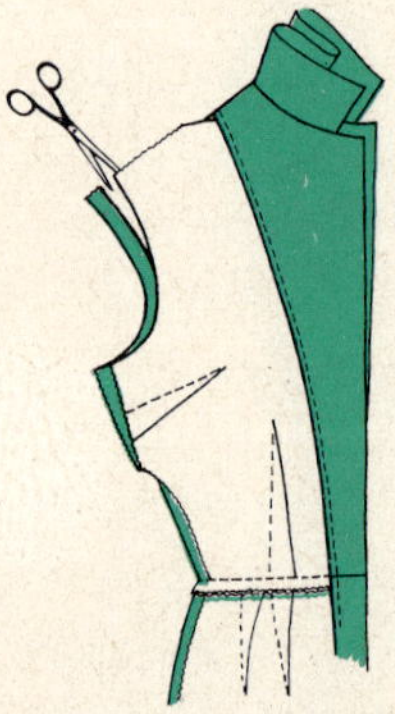

The back shoulders don't need narrowing, which indicates a round-shouldered figure. Sew the extra back shoulder width into a dart to give a better fit to the back shoulder, and

View 4

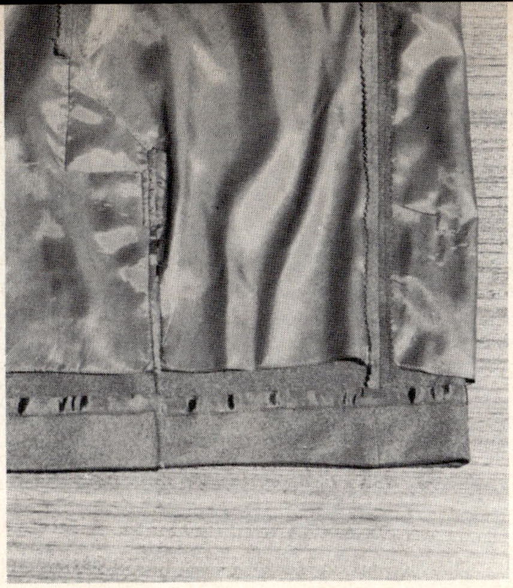

View 5

View 6

so the shoulder seams will be the same length when sewed. Sew the back dart in the same amount that the shoulders were narrowed.

Sew up the shoulder seams. The underarm seam can then be resewed, and the sleeve reset and sewed in to finish the bodice alterations.

View 3

Altering the back skirt of this dress is necessary, because a fold forms under the waistline, indicating a swayback posture. To alter, rip apart the skirt and waist. Trim the amount taken up in the back tuck off the center back skirt. Taper to nothing on either side. Reshape the darts, if necessary, and resew the waistline.

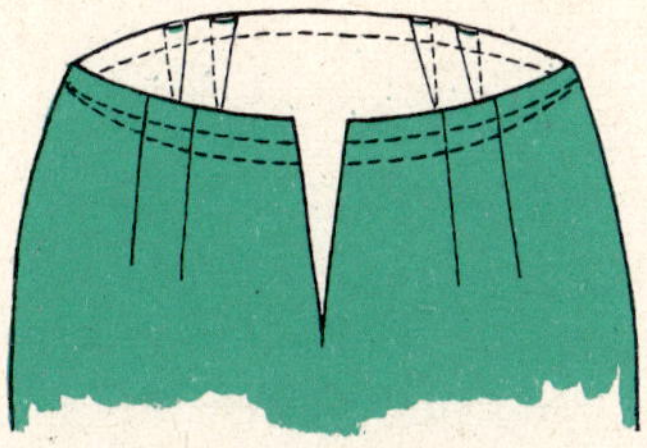

View 4

This dress is poorly finished on the inside. The hem is sewed by machine —the binding is cheap, and the seams aren't pinked. If the inside of a dress is neat, the outside will also be.

View 5

Replace the seam binding with a finer one, and pink the seams. Finish off the raveled lining. Even the hem and sew it in by hand.

The whole dress looks more expensive because of these improvements on the inside finishing. A few changes also improve the outside of the dress.

Often, an inexpensive dress is made of a fabric comparable to that used in a much better dress. The quality is cheapened, however, by the use of inexpensive buttons and trimmings—in too great profusion.

View 6

This dress shows much improvement when new buttons and a belt are added. The pearl buttons were removed and self-buttons substituted. Extra fabric for the covered buttons was obtained from a deep sleeve facing for the roll up sleeves.

The belt is leopard, but a smart leather one could be used. The fake handkerchief was removed from the pocket, and a smart pin substituted.

View 1

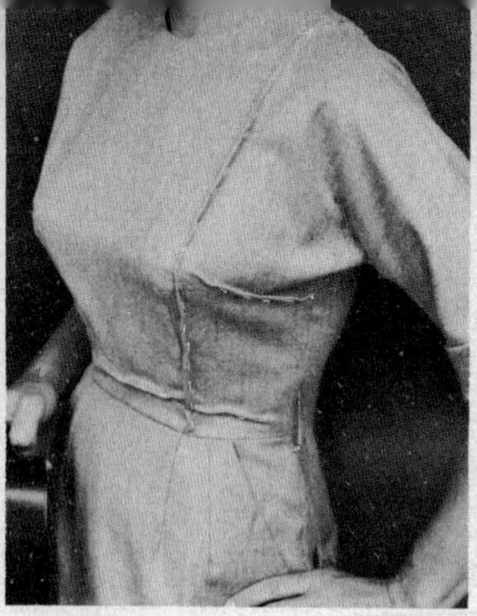

View 2

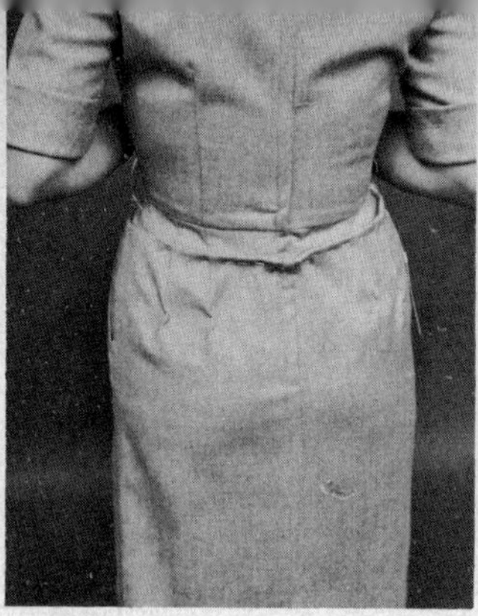

View 3

View 4

Dolman sleeve

View 1

This ready-to-wear dress has a dolman sleeve. It is a regular size 10, and some fitting is needed. The front shoulders are too wide, the skirt too tight, and the front waistline a little too long. There's also a slight droop under the bustline.

View 2

Fit the shoulder by folding a tuck down the dress front toward the bust. A dart shapes the back for a better fit for the slightly rounded shoulder. Take the bust dart in a little deeper to remove the droop under the bust toward the side seam.

The waistline needs shortening only in the front. Mark a tuck across the front just above the waistline. Try the belt to be sure the waistline is in the right place.

View 3

The back skirt droops toward the center back, which usually means the figure is slightly sway-back or is very flat at the back hip. To correct this, raise the skirt in the center back only. Pin a dart across the top skirt, tapering to nothing at each side, indicating the amount to raise the skirt.

The hip size of the skirt is too small, so more hip room is needed. There isn't enough seam to let out, so raise the skirt at the waist to give extra hip room. The skirt is long for this figure, since the dress is in a regular, rather than a junior, size.

Rip the waist and skirt apart. Cut off the top of the skirt the amount to be shortened, reshape the darts and seams to line up with those in the bodice since the waist size is correct. Open the

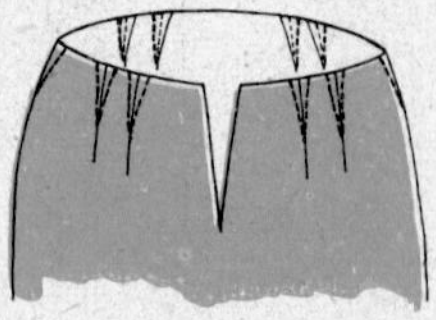

shoulder seam to about 1½ inches from the neck. Rip the entire underarm seam. Rip off the front cuff only. Measure the tuck and mark the amount the front shoulder has to be narrowed. Fold the left side over the right, with the seam edge at this mark. Recut the right side to the shape of the left side. Reverse and recut the left side from the right. Cut the front sleeve shorter, too. The shoulder width is really narrowed at underarm seam on this sleeve. Sew the back shoulder dart in as fitted.

Resew the shoulder seams. Then repin the bust darts and stitch to the fitting marks. Next, sew up the underarm seam. Resew the cuff to the front sleeve to complete this step.

When sewing bodice and skirt together, raise the skirt slightly on the front waist to correct the waist length (A). To correct a back skirt droop, trim the amount of excess fullness off the back skirt. When resewed to the bodice, it will hang correctly (B).

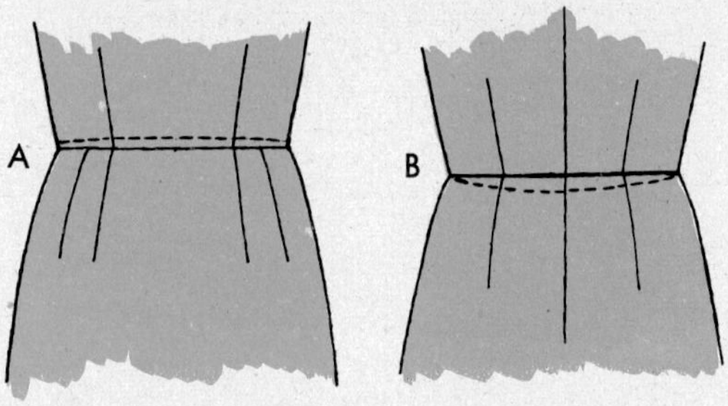

Resew the back zipper in the skirt. Make the back skirt opening deeper to compensate for the amount taken off the top of the skirt.

View 4

This dress is simply styled. When buying ready-to-wear, choose clothes that are almost classically simple in detail. They look more fashionable and minor alterations can improve them.

Also, the less trim the manufacturer puts on the dress, the more quality can go into the dress itself.

An alligator belt replaces the inexpensive one on the dress. Add a pin at the neckline, and the dress is smart enough to be worn anywhere.

General alterations

There are many more alterations that can easily be done to improve the fit of your ready-to-wear dress.

Shortening the skirt

Rip out the hem and press out the old crease mark. Re-mark for the new skirt length. Turn the hem and press. If the hem is too deep, cut it to about 3 inches, turn, sew on a fresh seam binding, and slip-stitch by hand.

Lengthening the skirt

Rip out the hem and press out the crease line. Measure to see if there is enough hem to let down. A 1½-inch hem, plus a ½-inch seam binding gives a 2-inch hem—quite adequate for a straight skirt. On a full skirt, the hem can be as narrow as 1 inch.

If there is enough to turn, fold back on the new hemline and press. Measure and trim the depth of hem all around. Sew seam binding to the edge of the hem and slip-stitch it in place.

To face the skirt, use a bias fabric—taffeta for a non-washable and cotton for a washable one. Cut the bias 3 inches wide. Sew the right side of the bias to the right side of the skirt just below the hem mark.

Turn the facing ¼ inch in from the skirt edge. Turn under loose edge of the bias, about ¼ inch and stitch. Slip-stitch to the inside of skirt.

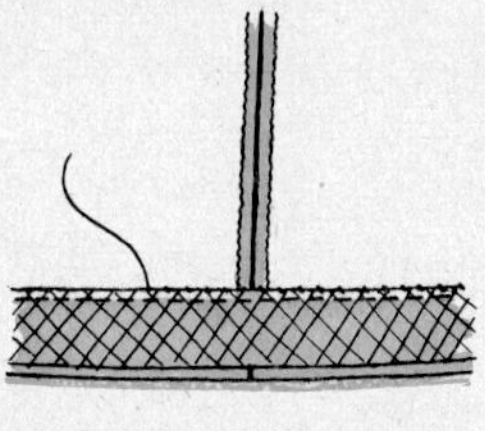

Increasing the waistline

Check the inside of the dress before you buy it to see how much seam allowance can be let out. Remember, if you let out each side ½ inch, it will give 2 extra inches in the waist.

If there is not this much seam to let out, you can still increase the waistline by letting out the back and front waist darts or back and front shirring. The same amount will have to be let out in the skirt waistline, so be sure you have the extra space in the skirt darts or side seams.

The skirt waistline can also be increased if there is enough length to the skirt to raise it as you did to increase hip size. When you cut the extra length off at the top, the waistline is automatically made larger. To do it correctly, the dress must be ripped apart at the waistline.

Increasing the hipline

See View 7, dress with dolman sleeve.

Making the hips smaller

The hipline of the skirt can be made smaller simply by taking in the side seams the amount to be decreased.

When the buttocks are flat, the seat of the skirt appears to bulge. This can't be fitted out. Instead, rip open entire back skirt and make back darts more shallow. Take out extra size at the back side seams of the skirt.

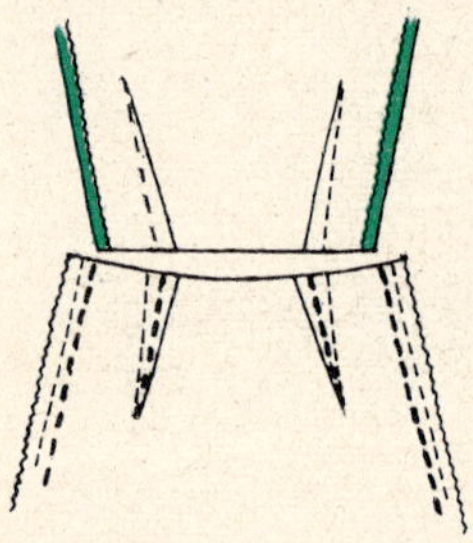

Making the top smaller

Sometimes the top of the figure is much smaller than the rest of the figure. It's necessary to buy a dress that fits the waist and hip, but is too large in the shoulders and bodice. Fit this dress by taking a fold down the front and back, narrowing top and shoulders. Rip out the sleeve. Open part of shoulder seam and the underarm seam. Mark how much is to be cut from armhole and underarm. Use a smaller size pattern to recut. Resew shoulders and underarm seam.

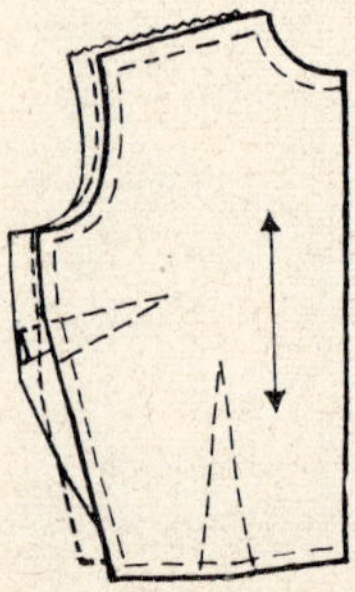

Rip open the underarm seam of the sleeve. Lay the pattern of the smaller sleeve over the ripped sleeve and recut the sleeve top to this smaller size. Use this method to shorten a sleeve if there is a complicated cuff treatment. Resew the underarm seam of the sleeve. Set sleeve into new armhole.

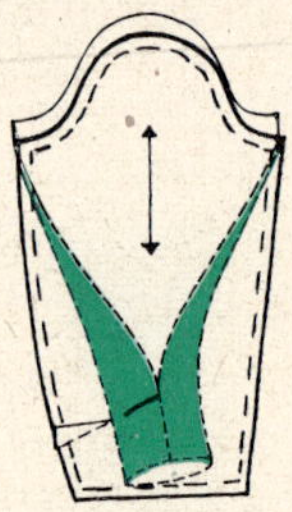

Sleeves

If the sleeve length needs adjusting, recut the top of the sleeve to shorten it while the sleeve is ripped out of the dress. The sleeve can also be shortened at the lower length. Just turn up the lower edge and re-hem.

If it has been faced, rip off the facing, and cut the sleeve the desired length plus seam allowance. After the sleeve has been cut off, it may be necessary to take it in a little. Refit and sew the facing back on. Check at the elbow to be sure the elbow darts fit at the point of your elbow. These can be ripped and moved up or down for a better fit.

Fitting out back neck fold

When a fold forms under the neck, pin the fold out with a dart. Rip the back collar or facing and open the shoulder seam. Make a tissue tracing of the back of dress. Pin dart in tissue. Recut the neck and slope of shoulder to tissue tracing.

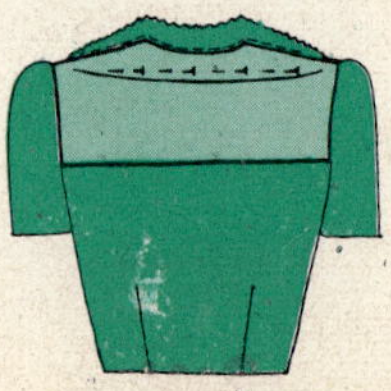

Chapter 17

Making curtains and draperies

Just as there are new products that make dressmaking easier, there are many innovations on the market to simplify sewing for the home. These include pleater tape for tailored headings, rings and loop tape for cafes.

Curtains

Cafe curtains

For your initial project, make some cafe curtains. Depending upon the style, they can be simple or elaborate.

Fixtures

Attach the cafe rod and bracket to the window frame, or mount a rod and socket inside the frame. There's a variety of rings you can use on both types of rods—ornamental clips, pinch clips, brass or plastic sew-on rings.

Measurements

Measure from the top of the rod down to either the sill or apron—whichever length you prefer. When planning tier curtains, allow a 3-inch overlap.

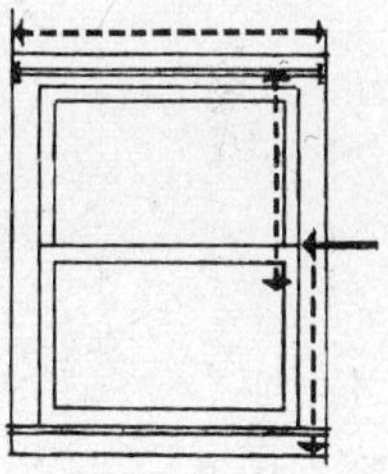

Headings

Scalloped tops. You have two choices. One type uses scalloped pleater tape which is sewed directly to the top of the curtains. The loops slip out when the curtains are laundered.

The other scalloped top is made without pleater tape. Add 3 inches plus seam allowance to the curtain length. Press back ¼ inch, then turn 1 inch at the sides of the curtain for hems. Pin and stitch. Press back

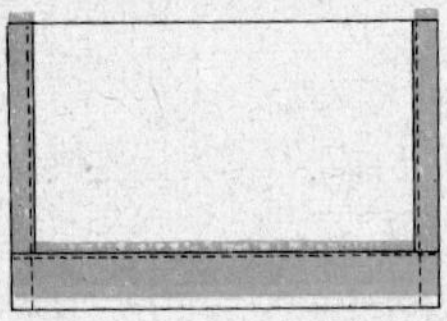

¼ inch on the lower edge. Turn up a 3-inch hem, pin and stitch in place.

Cut a facing strip 4 inches deep and the width of the curtain, plus seam allowances. Use a non-woven interfacing for stiffening. Mark for the scallops on the interfacing.

Divide the curtain width into fifths. There are usually six rings per curtain. Make a pattern of the scallop size. Mark each scallop with one inch between, or shape to a point. Cut out the scallop design to the finished size on the interfacing.

Sew it to the facing. Sew the facing

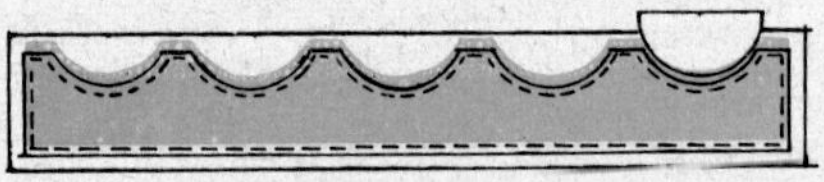

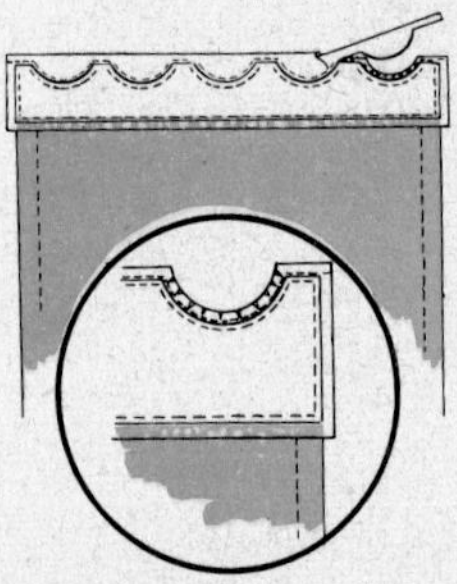

to the curtain top along the interfacing edge. Trim the seam to ¼ inch. Clip in on the seam along the curve.

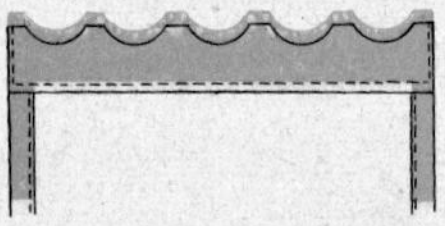

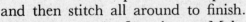

Turn the facing to the inside. Turn under seam allowances at the lower and side edges and press. Pin in place and then stitch all around to finish.

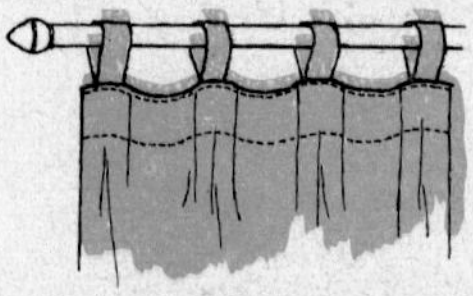

Looped tops. Make loops of self-fabric or contrasting tape and sew into seam as facings are applied or to top of the straight hem.

Decorative braids with a woven loop also eliminate the need for rings. Sew the braid to the curtain top.

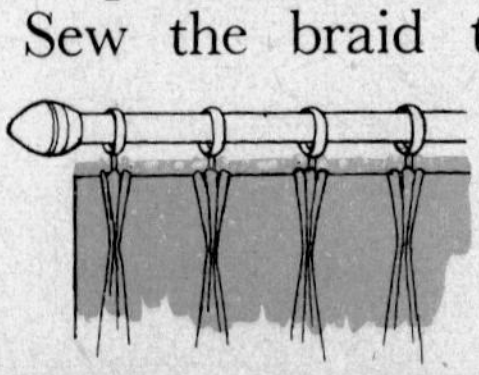

Pinch-pleated headings. Use pleater tape and hooks for top of this curtain. Hang on rings.

Sheer curtains

These curtains help soften the appearance of bare window glass, help insure privacy, and form a neutral background from outside the house.

Measurements

Measure from the top of the rod to the sill, the apron, or the floor for length. Measure the width from outer edges of fixture brackets or the window frame. Add enough fabric to the width for the return—the distance of the rod from the wall on each side.

To the length, add fabric for the hems. Lower hem should be at least 3 inches deep. Add 1¾ inches for upper hem, when a single hem is used. When heading and casing are used, add at least 3¼ inches. The curtain should be at least two to three times as wide as window, depending on sheerness of fabric. Use enough fabric so curtains hang full.

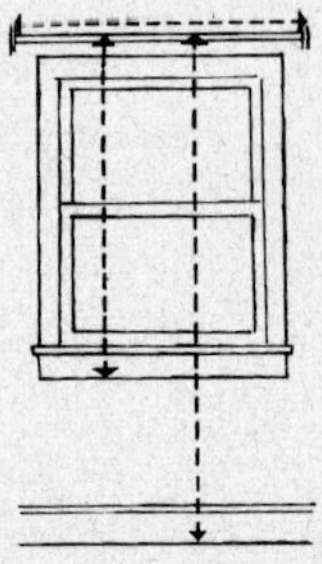

Stitching

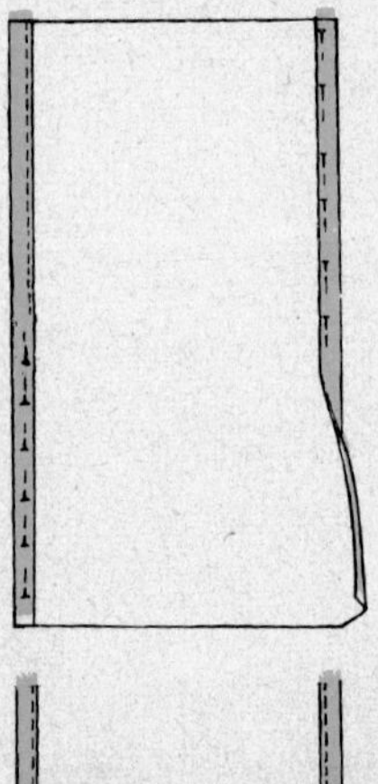

Trim off selvages. Join lengths with French seams. Press back ¼ inch, and make a 1-inch hem on each side. Pin and stitch. Turn under ¼-inch at the lower edge and press. Turn under a 3-inch hem, press, pin and stitch.

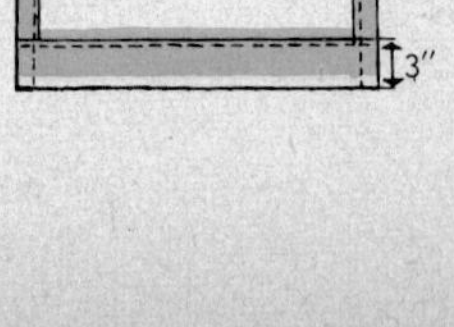

Follow same method at top edge (A). For casing, measure down 1½ inches from top, pin and stitch (B). When just a hem is used at top, turn under ¼ inch and press. Then turn under 1½-inch hem. Press, pin and stitch (C).

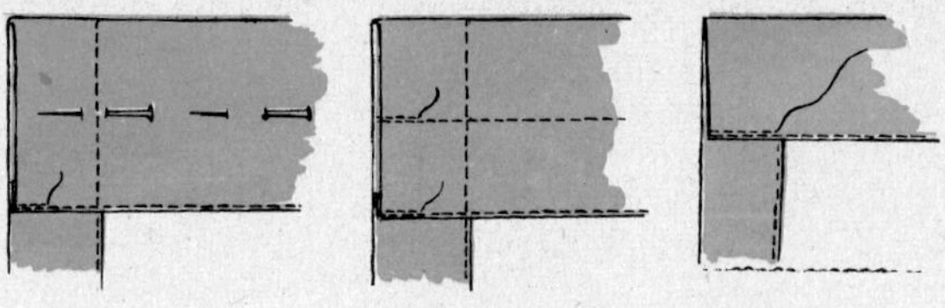

A B C

Draperies

Unlined draperies

Measure from the top of the rod to the window sill, apron, or floor. Add 6 inches for a double 3-inch hem. For a pleated heading, add 5½ inches for the turn-under and the heading. If you plan to use pleater tape, just add the amount of the seam allowance, plus the heading.

The drapery width should measure 2½ to 3 times the window width, plus 2 inches on each side for the hems. Measure from the outside edge of the fixture, plus the amount of return. (See sketch of window, opposite page.)

Turn under ½ inch at the side edges and press. Turn back 1½-inch hem, and baste. Then stitch by machine or blind-stitch by hand.

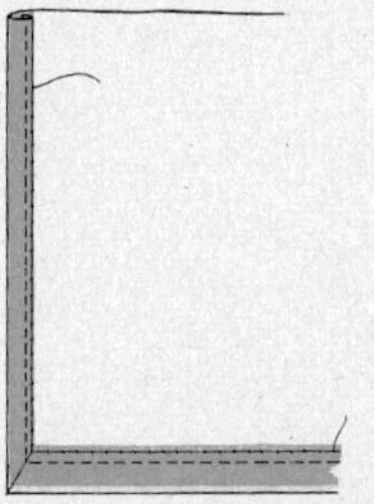

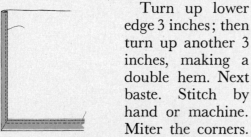

Turn up lower edge 3 inches; then turn up another 3 inches, making a double hem. Next baste. Stitch by hand or machine. Miter the corners.

Stiffen the drapery top with a non-woven interfacing or with buckram, available in 4-inch width, ready to use.

Pin one edge of the stiffening ½ inch from the top, and ¼ inch from each edge. Sew the bottom edge of the buckram to the drapery. Turn the top edge over the stiffening and baste. Then turn down the hem along stiffening edge and press. Pin and stitch.

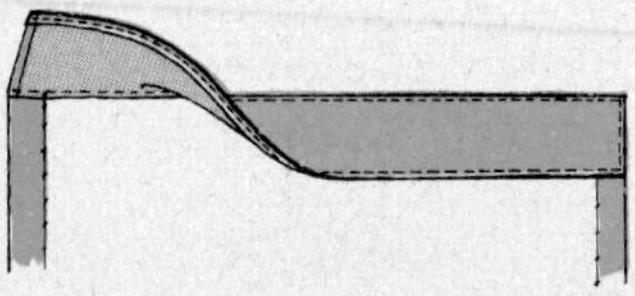

Headings

Several types of pleated headings can be used on draperies.

Measurements are about the same. *Pinch pleats.* Measure in about 3½ inches from each edge. Measure another 4 inches and fold and pin the first pleat. Bring end pleats together and fold to form a center pleat. Next, fold end pleats to center pleat to form another pleat. Continue this way until the top of the drapery is pleated. Sew from lower end of the pleat to the top for 4 inches. Divide this large pleat into three small pleats and stitch across the bottom. Hang pinch-pleated draperies on brass rings.

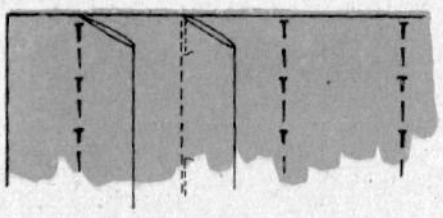

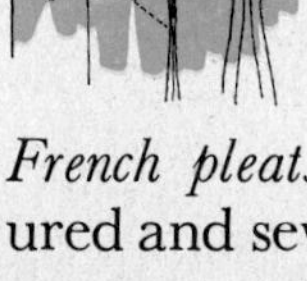

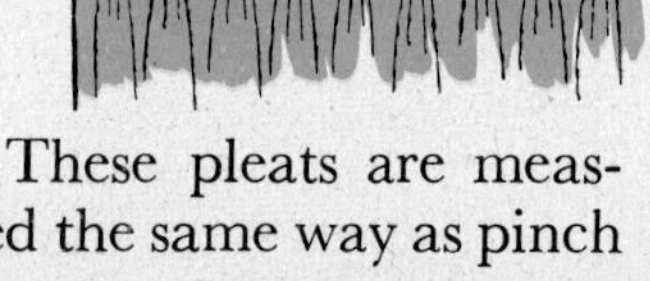

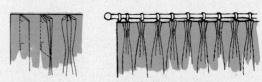

French pleats. These pleats are measured and sewed the same way as pinch pleats. Divide the large pleat into three small pleats and sew together by hand. Sew through the material several times, draw thread tight, finish on inside. Use a traverse rod.

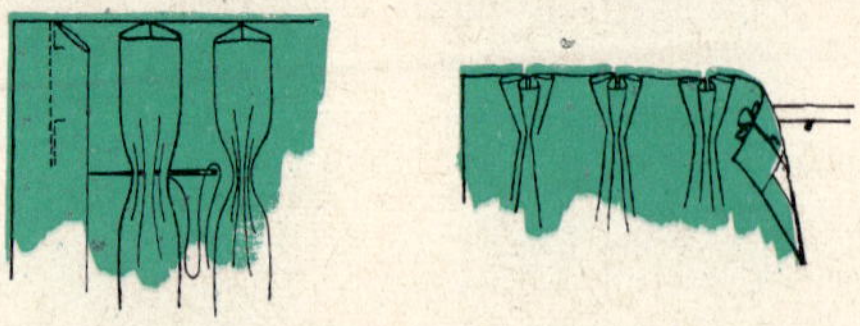

Box pleats. This pleat is generally made about 2 inches wide. The box is made by spreading the big pleats to fold the same distance to each side. Press and tack in place. The distance between each box should be about the same size as the pleat.

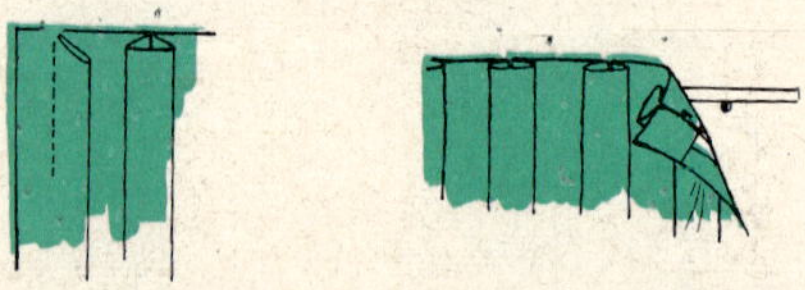

Special tips. Pin hooks can be used on the back of all headings and the draperies hung on brass rings and rods, or traverse rods. The top of the dra-

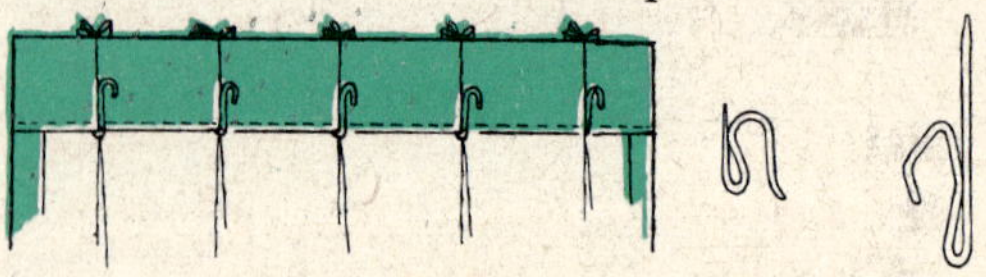

pery can also be stiffened and hemmed and the top edge sewed to brass or wooden rings and hung on a pole. This is effective in any style room.

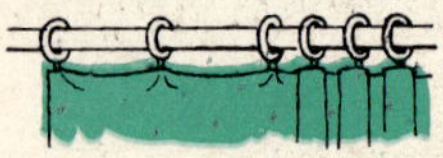

This type of drapery can also be hemmed and sewed to form a casing and a heading, as for a sheer curtain. The pole can be inserted in the casing and hung to form a heading.

Lined draperies

Measurements

Take the same measurements as for an unlined drapery. Add 6 inches on the length for double 3-inch hems. Add only a seam allowance, plus the amount of heading, to the top. Cut the lining 2½ inches shorter than the drapery, but add 5 inches for double hems. When you cut the lining, make it 6 inches narrower than drapery width.

Matching

If you're using patterned fabric, allow extra fabric to insure perfect match. To determine the amount of material you need, measure from the top of one design to the same place at the top of the next design. The number of inches in the pattern repeat must divide evenly into the length required for the entire drapery. If it does not divide evenly, increase allowance of total length until the figure is divisible by the pattern repeat.

Making the lined drapery

Turn up a double 3-inch hem. This can be sewed by machine or hand. Make

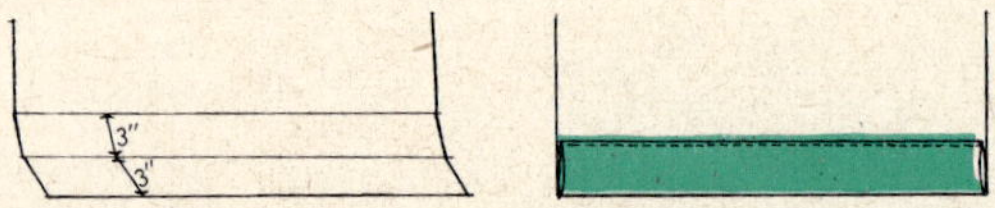

a double 2½-inch hem in the lining. Pin right side of the lining to right side of the drapery and sew down.

Easy-to-sew window ideas

Attractive new window treatments are an easy and economical way to change a color scheme or decor. Make your curtains and draperies from easy-to-sew fabrics in a wide selection of colors and patterns. Look for long-wear features. You'll find fabrics treated to shed soil, resist sunfading, retain crispness.

See pages 301-302 for instructions on how to make these trim cafe curtains with scalloped heading and valance shown. Sew-on rings hold curtains on cafe rod.

Filmy sheers filter sunlight and as-
ure privacy. The softly pleated val-
nce adds a touch of elegance, which
s suitable for a more formal room.

Floor-to-ceiling draperies form a background for this pleasant conversation group. Draperies have pinch-pleated heading. They hang on a special traverse rod, made to round the corner, and hold draperies snug to the ceiling. Drapery weights help make them hang correctly.

each side, with the top edges even.

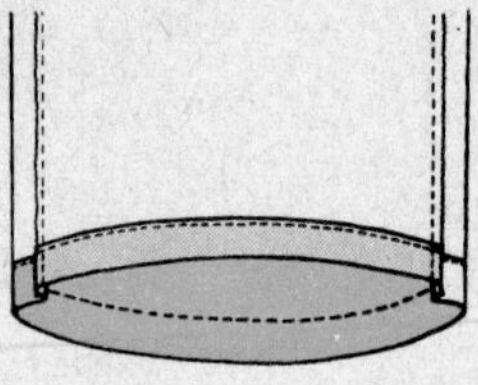

Press the seams toward the outside edge. Center lining so $1\frac{1}{2}$-inch hems turn back on either side of drapery.

If the heading is to be finished with self-pleating, then you can sew the stiffening in now. Lap a 4-inch strip of non-woven interfacing or buckram about $\frac{1}{2}$ inch from the top and stitch. Turn drapery to the right side. Press so the $1\frac{1}{2}$-inch hems are even all the way down (A). Corners of hem can be mitered (B), or sewed straight to drapery. Tack hems together with long French tack (C).

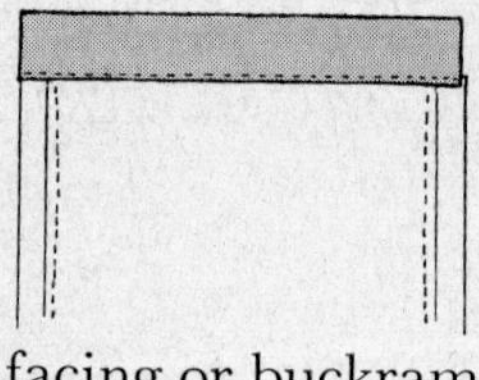

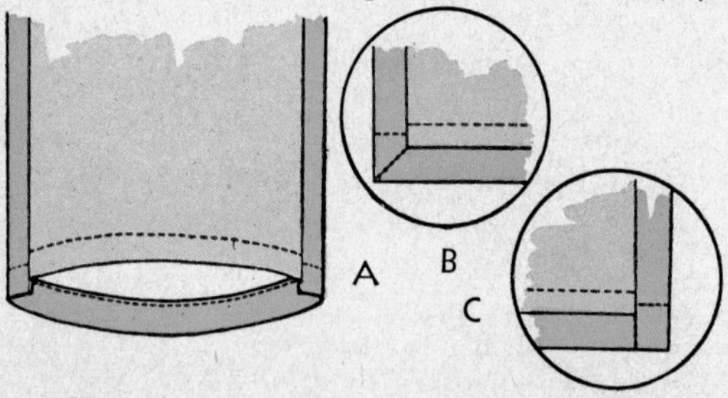

Finish the top of the drapery as shown for unlined draperies, with

the type of heading that you prefer.

When pleater tape is used, the width and fullness of the drapery can be figured very easily. Use the pleater hook in the tape and pleat the tape to find the spacing and number of pleats

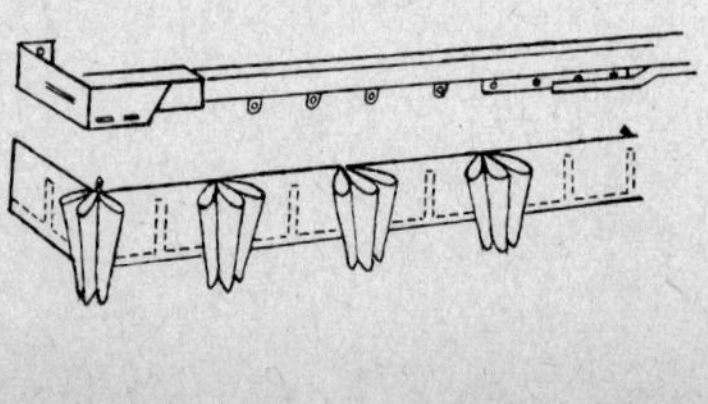

for your drapery. Remove hooks and measure the tape needed for drapery.

When the drapery has been lined, turn to the right side without adding any stiffening. Press so the lining is centered. Sew the top of the pleater tape over the top of the drapery, catching in the lining. Lap the edge of the tape to the seam allowance line. Leave a $\frac{1}{2}$-inch extension at either end of the drapery.

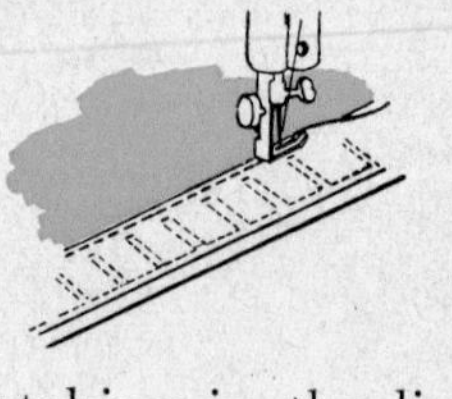

Turn the pleater tape to the inside and press. Turn under the $\frac{1}{2}$ inch at either end. Pin and stitch along the sides and along the edge of the tape under the pockets used for the hooks.

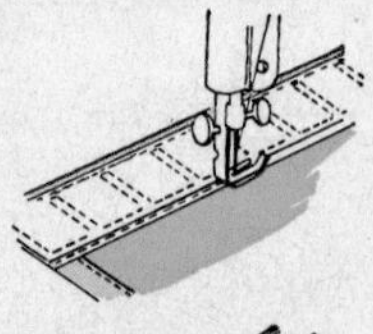

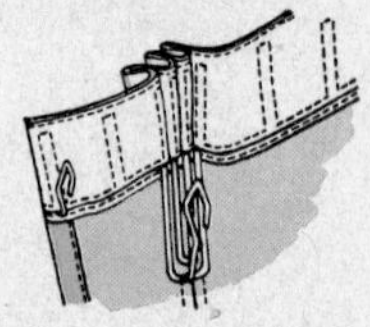

Insert the hooks in the pockets planned for in the original test pleating. The cluster of pleats can be placed where you prefer. A single end hook can be used at each end.

Draperies can be made in separate lengths and held together at the top with a double prong slip-on hook. Insert one prong in the edge of the drapery and the other prong next to the last pleat in the second panel. On the right side, sew a hook in the edge of the overlapping panel and a thread loop in the adjoining panel. Do this to the hem at intervals.

After hanging draperies run your hands up and down fabric creasing it in folds. Tie sections loosely with strips of cloth to "set" the folds.

Chapter **18**

Sew your own slip covers

Slip covers are inexpensive, easy to make. New slip covers stay fresh longer, give a wonderful lift to an old sofa or chair. Combined with new draperies, they give a welcome color change.

Preparing the furniture

Be sure the old upholstery is clean. Repair any sagging springs before you fit the slip covers. Mend rips or tears in the old covering. If some of the stuffing has flattened or hollowed out, fill in with new padding.

Cover the padded places with heavy muslin and sew to the original cover. The slip cover will hide any patches.

Fit the chair in muslin first. This is actually cheaper and faster. Mistakes made in the muslin pattern can be pieced and patched, which avoids wasting good upholstery material.

Using muslin also saves on fabric yardage because you now have a pattern, and it's easier to match the design. You can make a new slip cover whenever you choose without having to fit the chair each time. This cuts your work time in half.

When fitting the chair, follow the seams of the original upholstery. Watch the grain to be sure the piece is shaped correctly. If the chair has a spring seat, the corners of the upholstery will be boxed, so the fabric won't tear as the springs contract.

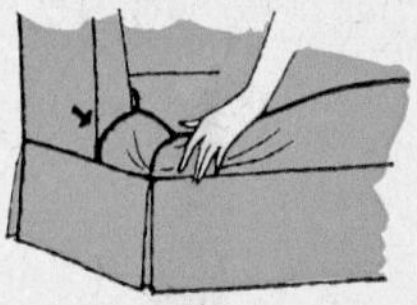

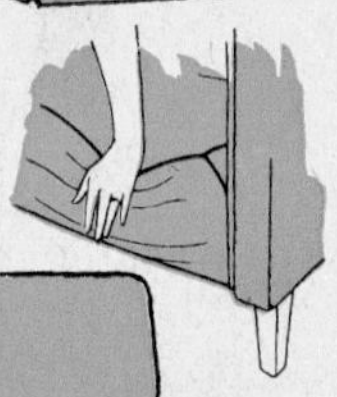

The same fitting is necessary in the slip cover. This will be shown as the chair is fitted.

As a rule, both the T-cushion and the square cushion have spring seats.

Fit the muslin

Measure the inside back from top to platform. Add 3 inches for the tuck-in. Measure the chair platform to 6 inches from the floor. Add 3 inches for the tuck-in. The inside back piece and platform can be made in one piece with 6 inches added for tuck-in at back seat crevice.

Cut muslin according to measurements plus extra width on each side. Allow ⅝-inch seam allowance. Pin, starting from the center at the top of the chair. Smooth down toward the seat of the chair. Shape around the arm, and clip in on seam allowance.

Allow a 3-inch tuck-in at (A), and a 3-inch tuck-in at the back crevice on both the inside back and seat (B). Fold back 3 inches for the tuck-in at the seat sides (C).

Measure the back length and width. Add ⅝-inch seam allowance and cut muslin. Pin the center of the muslin to the top of the chair at the center. Pin and shape down each side of chair to 6 inches from the floor.

Measure length of the top band from seam where the arm and band are joined. Measure width of the band. Cut muslin strips. Start at the center top of the chair and pin muslin to the inside back and back of chair. If necessary, shape with a seam at top corners of chair. Use ⅝-inch seams throughout.

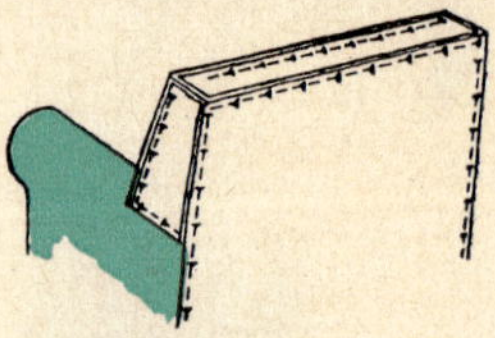

Measure the inside edge of the arm from the outside roll of the arm to the platform of the chair. Add 3 inches at the seat for tuck-in.

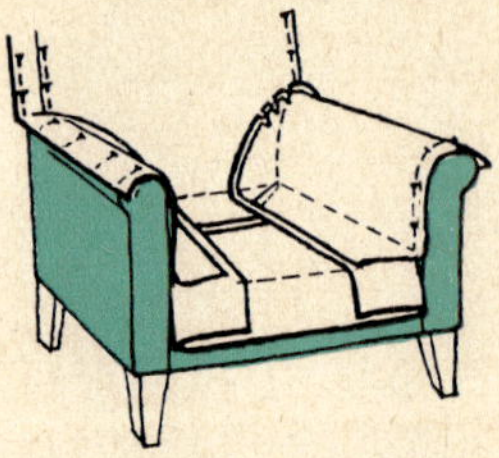

Shape the muslin to the back of the arm to follow shape of the tuck-in on the inside back where arm joins. Only one arm needs fitting in the muslin. Measure the depth and width of the outside arm (A). Then cut the muslin and fit it to the edge of the inside arm and top band. Pin to the back muslin piece.

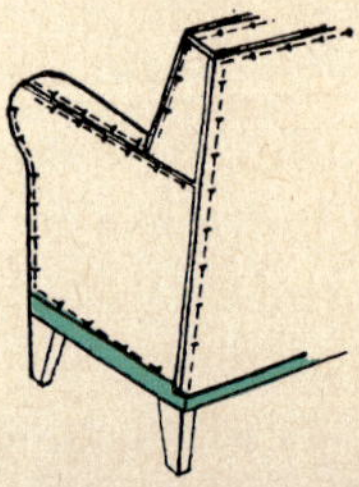

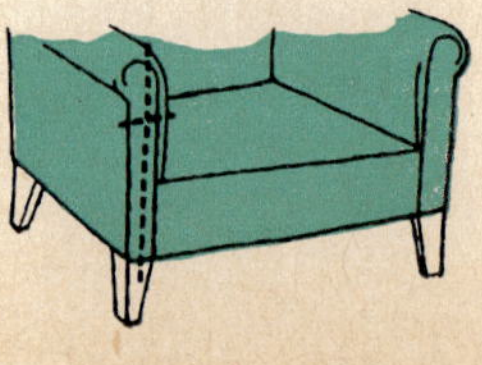

Measure length and width of the arm plate. Cut a

length of muslin and pin and shape it to fit the arm plate. Pin to the inside and outside arm pieces. Allow ⅝-inch seams. The arm plate is pinned to just the platform on the inside front, but to the full length on outer arm.

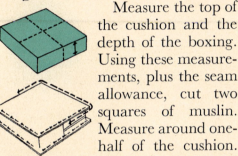

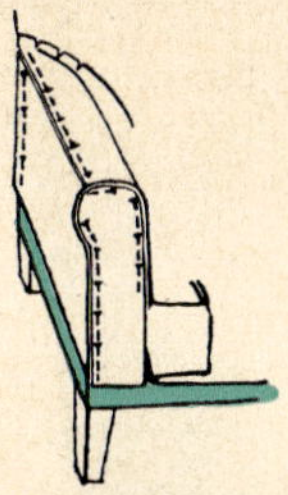

Measure the top of the cushion and the depth of the boxing. Using these measurements, plus the seam allowance, cut two squares of muslin. Measure around one-half of the cushion. Cut three bands this length plus 4 inches. Add the seam allowance to the depth measurement.

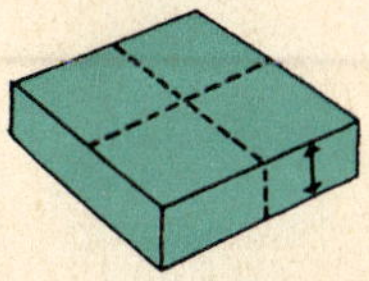

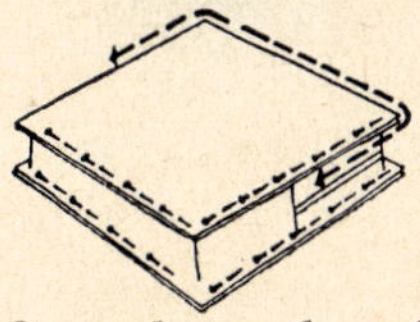

Mark all seam allowances in pencil before the muslin is unpinned from the chair. Fold the back, inside back, and seat pieces in half and make sure they're even. Cut duplicates of the arm pieces from the muslin.

Lay out the pieces and measure for the fabric needed. Mark fabric width on floor or table. Lay muslin pieces within width and measure. If you're using a print, center major motif at inside back above cushion, on arms and outside arm pieces, at front and center of cushion. Allow extra fabric for matching.

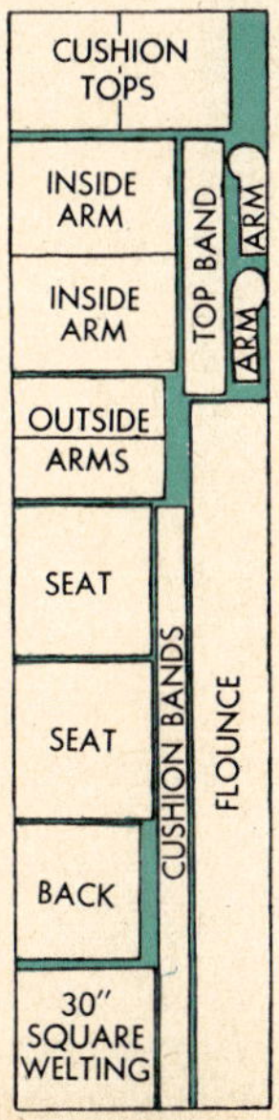

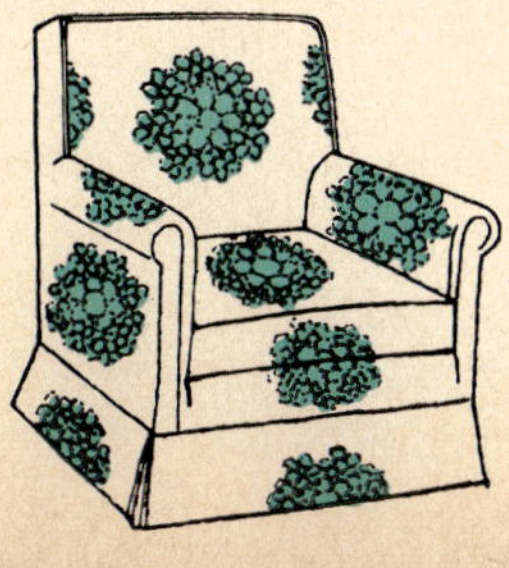

Sewing the slip cover

The easiest way to make a slip cover is in sections. Start with the cushion cover. Chapter 6 shows how to make cording for the cushion. If you want to use contrasting trim, ready-made cording is available in solid colors.

Sew cording to right side of top section of the cushion, with the seam allowance of the cording along the cushion edge. Clip seam allowance at the corners before turning. Leave several inches of the cording free at either end so it can be joined correctly.

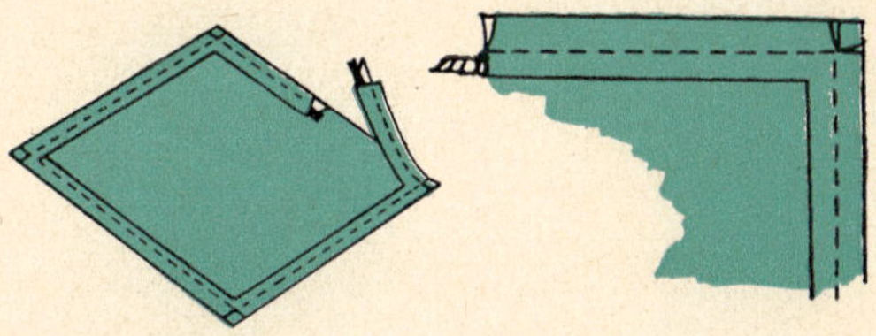

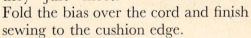

Join the bias on the straight grain. Cut the cords so they just meet. Fold the bias over the cord and finish sewing to the cushion edge.

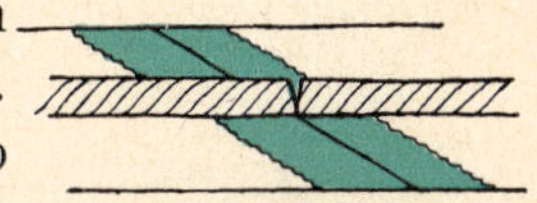

For cushion boxing, press two of the three bands in half on the length. Sew zipper between the two fold edges with a slot seam. Turn under 2 inches on the ends of the remaining band. Lap it over the ends of the zippered band and stitch 1½ inches in from the fold.

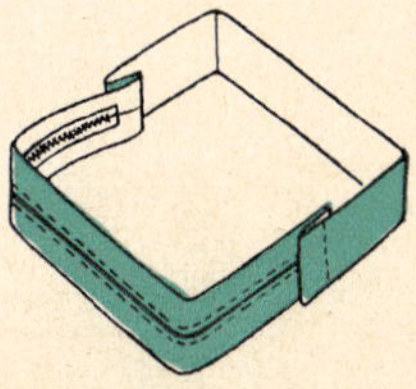

Sew the upper and the lower cushion pieces to the boxing with inside seams. Then turn to the right side through the zipper opening.

Gripper tape can be used as a closure instead of a zipper. Cut the two boxing bands $1\frac{1}{2}$ inches wider than those used with a zipper. This allows a $\frac{3}{4}$-inch overlap needed for closure.

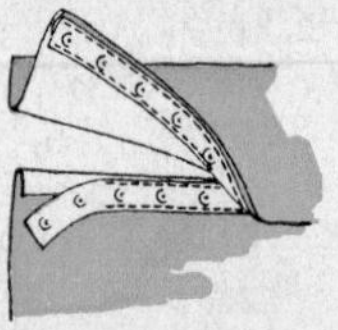

Next, make back section of chair.

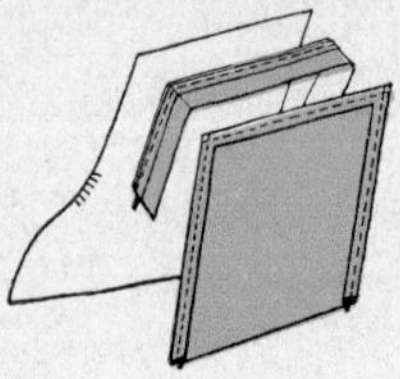

Sew cording around three sides of the back piece. Join the top band and sew cording around the front edge only.

Sew the back to the top band, leaving the seam allowance free at the lower band where it joins the arm.

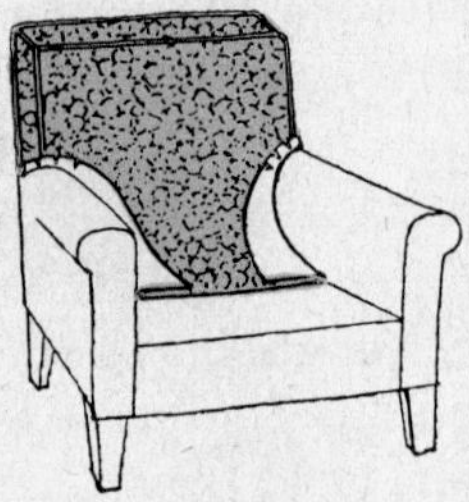

Sew the inside back piece to the top band, leaving the same seam allowance free. Fit to the back of the chair.

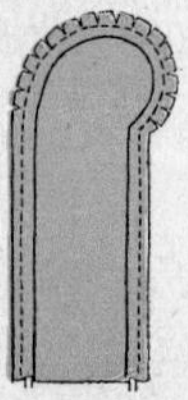

Next, sew cording around the armplate. Clip the cording seam allowance so it follows curve of arm.

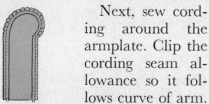

Join inside and outside arm piece. If you cord this seam, sew the cord to the right side of one piece first. Pin the pieces to be joined together.

Stitch it just inside of original stitching line on the wrong side of the corded piece. Then mark depth of the chair seat on the front armplate. Sew armplate to the arm sections from this point to the end of the outside arm piece. Fit to chair. Sew back section of outside arm to lower edge of top band. Sew around seam where the arm joins inside back piece. This seam continues to the end of (A).

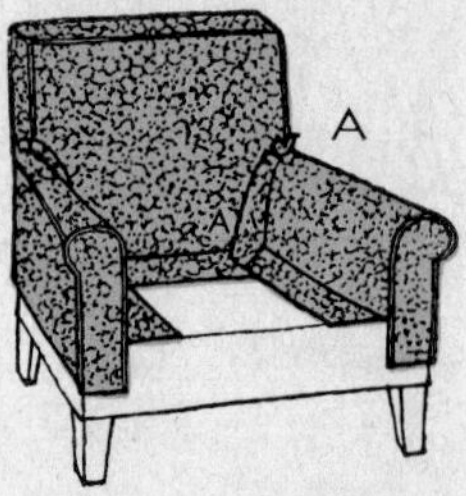

Fit the seat of platform piece in the chair. Here, boxing allows for the spring action at the front of the chair. Sew back and side edges to the inside back and inside arm pieces forming the tuck-in. Fold the front piece down over the apron of the chair and pin the corner, forming a boxing. Clip the seam allowance at the base of this. Turn the pinned corner to the inside and sew with an inside seam. Turn to the right side. Sew the seam allowance below the clip mark to the armplate.

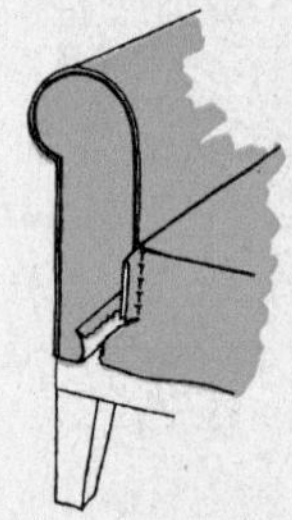

On the T-cushion, the spring action is at point (A). The seat is cut with the 3-inch tuck-in at the sides but is shaped to the front of the chair with just seam allowances added.

The apron band is cut separately. At section (A), the boxing is made by inserting a square gusset piece that sews to the front armplate, inside of the T, and the seat side tuck-in.

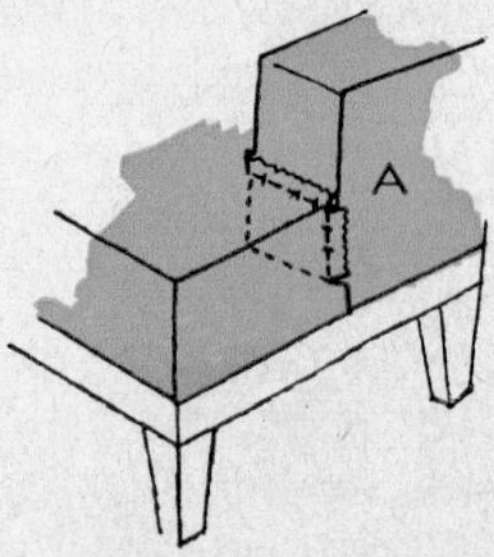

Flounces

General length of the flounce is 7 to 8 inches, although the length may

Fresh, new slip covers add sparkling color and longer life to your furniture.

vary. Measure from the floor to the point where the flounce will be attached

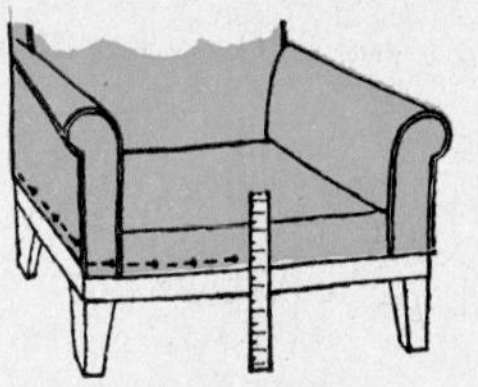

to the slip cover. Cut flounce the desired length plus $1\frac{1}{2}$ inches for hem and $\frac{5}{8}$ inch for the seam allowance.

Cut the flounce pieces across the fabric on the same grain as the slip cover. The number of lengths necessary depends on the style. Cut strips on the length only when a fabric such as a stripe is used around as a trim.

Straight flounce

Cut 4 strips the length of the chair sides plus seam allowances at either end. Sew corded or moss fringe to the bottom of the slip cover on line where flounce joins.

Inverted pleats

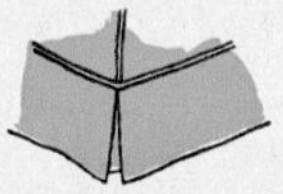

Measure depth of pleat at each corner. Add 4 times this amount to the distance around the chair. Cut strips to this length. Joining seams should come inside, under pleat.

Box pleats

Pleat fabric strip to determine the size and depth of the pleats. Arrange pleats so they are evenly spaced with the center of a pleat in center front. Multiply number of pleats by number of inches in each pleat. Cut necessary number of strips. Do any piecing under pleats.

Gathered flounce

Cut fabric 2 to 3 times the distance around the chair. Fabric weight and desired fullness determines the number of strips.

Circular flounce

Use heavy paper to make a circular pattern. As an example, measure two 16-inch lines at right angles. Draw a circle from one line to the other, forming a pie-shaped piece. Measure 8 inches up from the curve. Draw a second circle. Cut on this line for the circular flounce pattern.

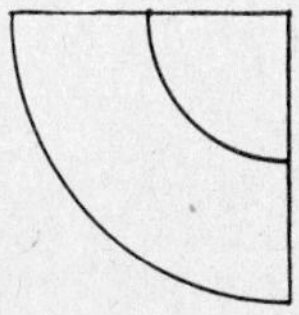

When measuring for a circular flounce, allow for a $\frac{5}{8}$-inch seam allowance, a $1\frac{1}{2}$-inch hem.

Cut a test piece of muslin from the pattern. Stitch along the top curve seam allowance line and clip in to the stitching. Stretch and measure the top. Divide the distance around the chair by this figure to get the number of circles needed to make a circular flounce. If it should show $5\frac{1}{2}$ circles, cut 6, and take a little deeper seam when joining them.

Design repeat

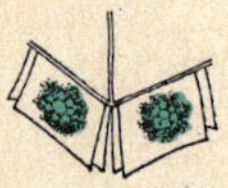

If your print has a definite design, pleat the flounce so the design is evenly spaced.

Flounces can be made double rather than hemmed. For the yardage, figure twice the flounce length plus seam allowances. For a lined flounce, the lining is cut 2 inches shorter than the flounce. Sew the lower edge of the lining and flounce together. Press back the hem. Sew the lining and flounce together at the top.

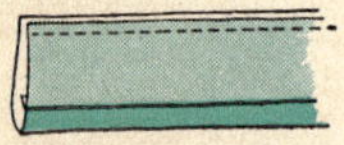

Slip-cover closure

Use either a zipper or gripper tape for the back opening. The closing can go on either side of the chair. Sew one side of the zipper to the arm side of the back opening.

Lap the corded edge of the back piece over the zipper and top-stitch. This can usually be done close to the cording so the stitching hardly shows. The zipper can be sewed right into the skirt on lightweight fabric.

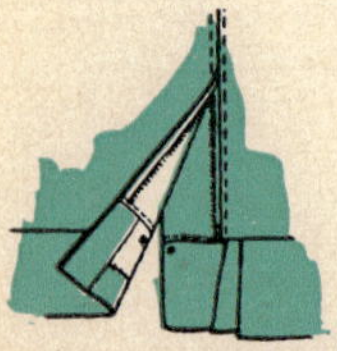

On heavier fabric, cut the skirt with an extension on the underside.

Sew the zipper just to the skirt. Snap extension to the underside of the skirt piece.

Gripper tape is sewed same way.

Sew tapes to the slip cover at each corner over the leg to keep the slip cover from riding up. Tie tapes under the leg of the chair.

Make the arm guards to protect areas that get the most wear and soil. Cut them from the arm pattern of the same fabric. Tuck in at the seat and snap or pin them under the arm.

If you want your slip cover to fit like upholstery, leave off the flounce.

Make slip cover to point of putting on the flounce. Put slip cover on chair. Chalk a line around bottom of chair apron. Trim three inches below line.

Trim cover around chair leg, leaving a $\frac{5}{8}$-inch seam allowance. Sew cording to this edge. Clip in on seam, turn to inside, and whip seam allowance back. Cut a piece of heavy muslin to fit over the bottom of the chair—inside the three inches turned back on the cover. Sew separating zippers on four sides of muslin and turn back of the cover.

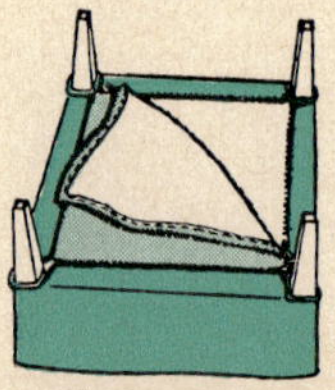

Fit the cover over the chair, zip lower muslin on underside of chair. This holds slip cover firmly in place. It is easily removed for washing. A sofa is slip-covered the same way as a chair.

Chapter **19**

Sewing for the bedroom

Sewing for the bedroom is easy and fun. Fitting is unnecessary when making bedspreads and covers; measurements and imagination start you out.

Figuring yardage

Make up the bed before measuring so the spread will be large enough to cover the sheets and blankets.

Measure the length and width of the top of the bed (A).

Measure the side overhang from the top of the bed to the floor (B). Add twice this figure to the top width measurement for the total width of the spread. Add two inches for seam allowances and hem on each side.

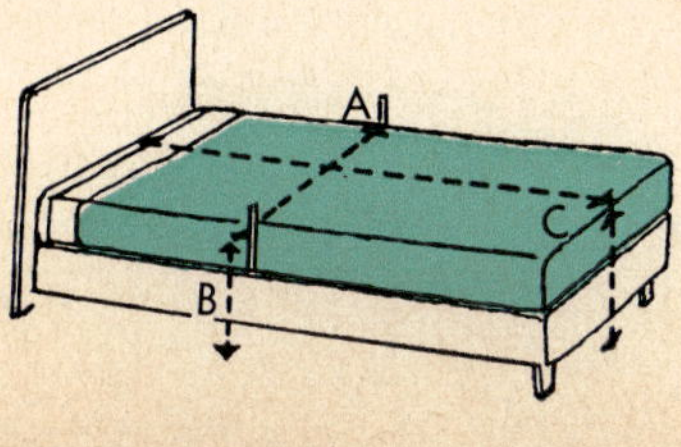

Measure the foot drop (C) and add to total length, plus two inches for the hem and seam allowances. Add 26 inches at top if spread covers pillow.

The yardage depends on the type of spread to be made, the height and width of the bed, and the width of the fabric. For example: a ¾ bed is 4 feet wide by 6 feet, 3 inches long, and about 20 inches high. Let's assume you are making a spread with plain sides and extra length to cover pillows from fabric 36 inches wide.

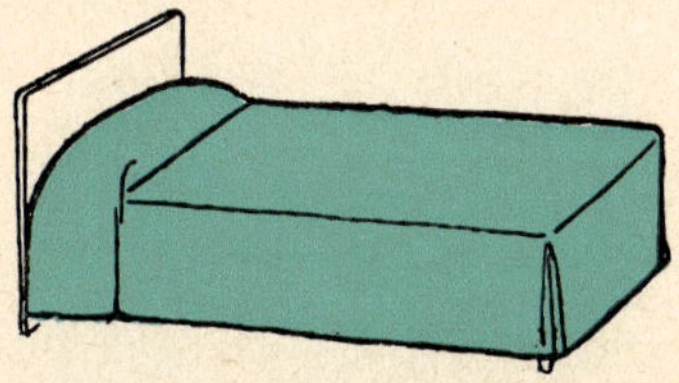

The width of the fabric is always used for the center top of the bed. If any piecing for width is necessary, do it on either side of the center.

The top of the bed is 6 feet, 3 inches. Add 26 inches for the pillow cover, 2 inches for the hem, 22 inches for foot drop, and 2 inches for seam allowances and hem. These items require a total of about 3½ yards.

Top width of bed is 48 inches; fabric is 36 inches. Piecings will be 6 inches, plus a 1½-inch seam allowance, or 7½ inches per side.

The side panels will be 26 inches long for the pillow cover, plus 6 feet, 3 inches for the length of the bed, and 2 inches for the hem. These measurements total 2 yards, 31 inches. Since the fabric is only 36 inches, it will take two lengths for either side. The pieces that come off these lengths will give you enough for the 7½-inch strips for piecing the top. The total yardage for this spread will be 9¼ yards; 3 yards, 18 inches, plus 2 yards, 31 inches, plus 2 yards, 31 inches.

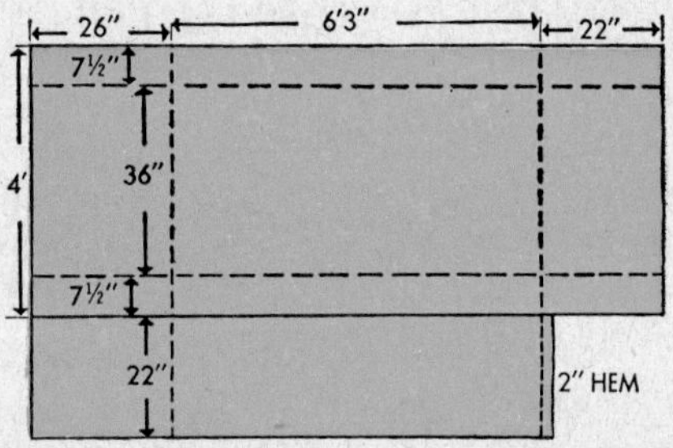

If you're making a special type spread, measure yardage accurately. The chart below is a safe guide.

Average bedspread yardage	**36-inch fabric**	**50-inch fabric**
Full-size bed—4'6"x6'3"—and three-quarter-size bed—4'x6'3"		
Plain sides	7½ yds.	6 yds.
Shirred sides	9 yds.	7½ yds.
Pleated sides	11 yds.	9 yds.
Twin or single bed—3'3"x6'3"		
Plain sides	5½ yds.	5½ yds.
Shirred sides	6½ yds.	6 yds.
Pleated sides	8½ yds.	7½ yds.

Types of spreads

There are several basic types of bedspreads. You can make any of them with variations of your own.

Bedspread with attached pillow cover

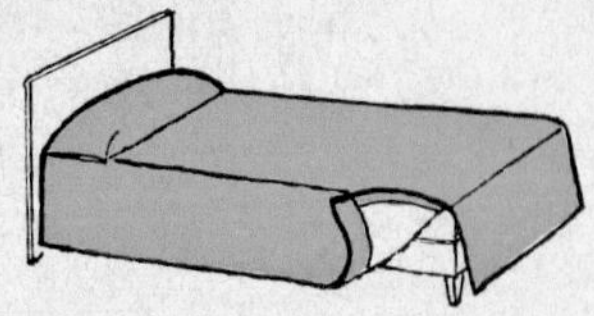

This spread is made with a piece for the bed top, two side panels and a foot panel. The pillow cover is attached separately.

If the fabric is wide enough, the whole top can be made in one piece with no side pieces needed. In this case, the fabric will probably be wide enough so the side panels can be made by splitting one length of fabric for both side pieces. This saves at least two yards from the estimate. The right side of the pillow cover is sewed to the wrong side of the bedspread. It turns back over the pillow and then tucks under front edge so that the right side of the pillowcase is on top.

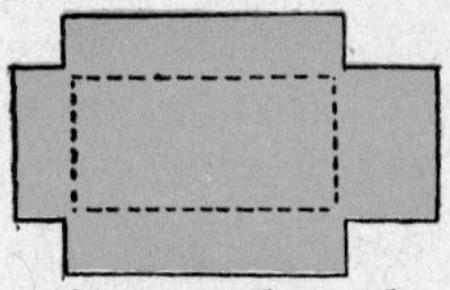

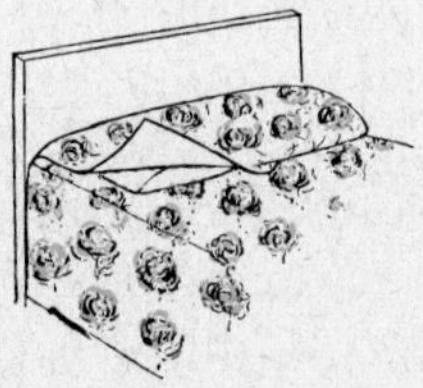

One-piece bedspread with shirred top

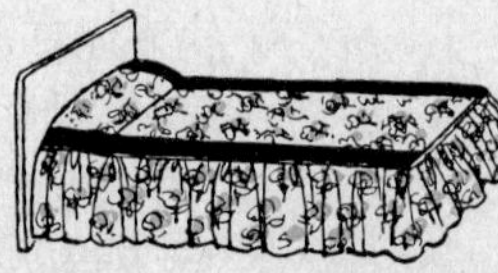

The top of this bedspread is made like the one just described, except that the pillow cover and spread are all in one. Side pieces can be in a contrasting fabric, either two colors or a solid color with a print. The full-

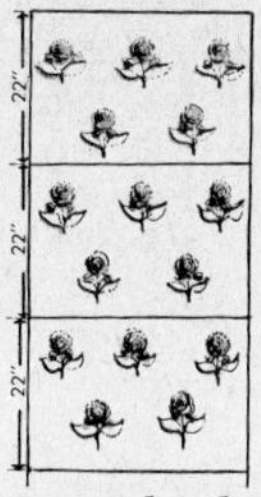

ness of the skirt should be at least three to one. The fabric should be cut in lengths and joined to make a full, shirred skirt. To find the correct yardage, measure around the three sides of the bed. Divide this measurement by the width of the fabric. This gives the number of panels. Multiply this by three, which gives the extra fullness needed for the skirt. Then multiply this figure by the length of the skirt, and divide by 36 inches to give the number of yards needed for a shirred skirt. For example: a $\frac{3}{4}$ bed measures 190 inches, or slightly less than 4 lengths of 50-inch fabric. Multiply by 3, which shows 12 lengths needed for shirring. The skirt is 22 inches long, including hems and seam. This figure, multiplied by 12, totals 4 yards, 20 inches needed. Always cut a shirred skirt this way. You save yardage and shirring is better on cross-grain.

Boxed coverlet with separate dust ruffle

The dust ruffle is made and figured as for the spread with a full, shirred skirt. Usually the top of the dust ruffle is made of muslin to fit over the boxed spring.

The boxing of the coverlet is made long enough to come down at least 2 inches over the top of the dust ruffle.

The coverlet can be made of quilted or non-quilted fabric, in a contrasting color or print. The top of the bed is cut of one panel that is centered. If it must be wider than the fabric, add the piecings at the sides. The side pieces are cut 6 inches longer and sewed to the back of the spread top so the coverlet will fit more securely. The corners can be sewed to form a boxing that fits the corner snugly. The side edges can be straight, scalloped, or finished with any detail you prefer.

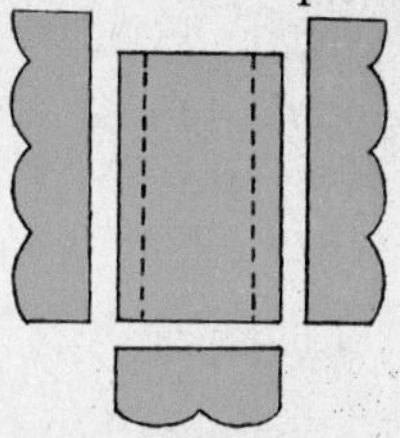

The top coverlet can be finished with deep points. (See color photograph, bottom of next page.) To make this spread, cut a pattern of this shape from heavy paper. Use it as a stencil to mark the design on non-woven interfacing. Cut out the design on the finished line. Sew the non-woven interfacing to the lining pieces of the side bands. These pieces can be of a special sateen also used in draperies. Pin the right side of the band to the right side of the lining and sew together around the edge of the interfacing. Trim all the seams to $\frac{1}{2}$ inch and clip in on the corners. Then turn right side out and baste all around. Press carefully and it is ready to sew to the top of the spread.

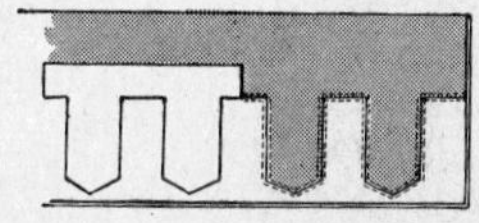

Corners can be finished with the edges separate and an underpiece at each corner. This is the method by which the corners are usually finished on the more decorative types of bedspreads.

This spread can also be made with a quilted top, and a pleated dust

In this handsome bedroom, a tailored, quilted spread tops a trim, pleated dust ruffle. When making the dust ruffle, measure and space the pleating to fit the sides of the bed.

Deep points detail this fitted coverlet. Use a pattern made from heavy paper as a guide in cutting the points. The corners are finished with separate edges and a corner underpiece.

ruffle. If you are using a print as shown in the sketch, center design on

each pleat. Measure length of skirt piece needed. Decide best placement of design for most economical fabric cut. Pleat one strip of fabric to determine amount needed for size to which fabric pleats. Then measure and space pleating to fit sides of bed. For better fit, plan an inverted pleat at corners. For yardage, figure number of pleats needed for circumference of bed, and number of lengths for pleating. See photo at left for another variation.

Boxed spread with attached ruffle

This spread is a combination of the ones just described. The top of the spread is cut. Then the side boxing is cut about the depth of the mattress. Add ruffling which is sewed to boxing rather than to a separate top as on dust ruffle.

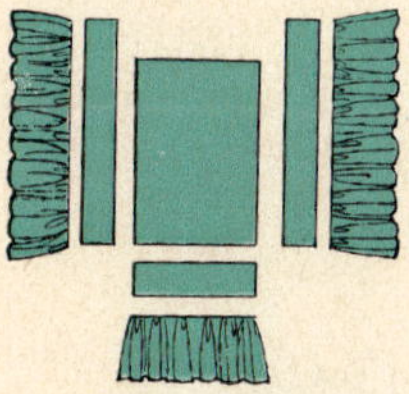

Draped spread

This bed covering is easy to make and is often combined with other styles. The dust ruffle is often used with a draped coverlet top instead of a boxed one. To make the throw, measure the

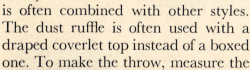

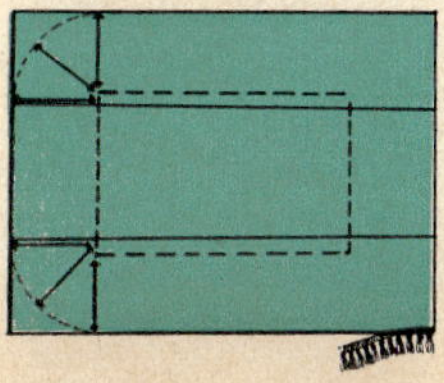

top of the bed plus the drop at sides and ends. Corners can hang in points or be rounded.

Tuck-in coverlet

This spread can combine a dust ruffle or tailored lower cover with an upper bedspread that is boxed or open at the corners, but made to tuck in under the mattress at the edges.

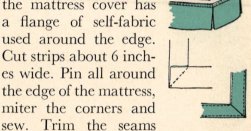

With the tuck-in top, the mattress cover has a flange of self-fabric used around the edge. Cut strips about 6 inches wide. Pin all around the edge of the mattress, miter the corners and sew. Trim the seams and press open. Sew muslin to inside edge of the flange. By doing this, only self-fabric shows where top tucks in.

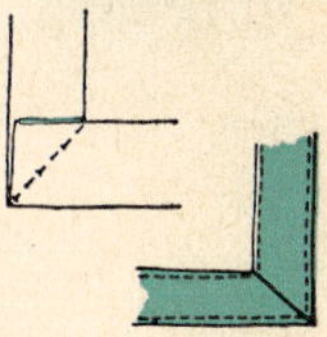

Trimmings

Trimmings are an important part in sewing for the bedroom. Braids can be used to join piecings on the top of the spread, and to lend a decorative trim. Many types of fringe are also available to finish the edges of coverlets and ruffles. Monograms are also smart and are a particularly good trimming for a masculine room.

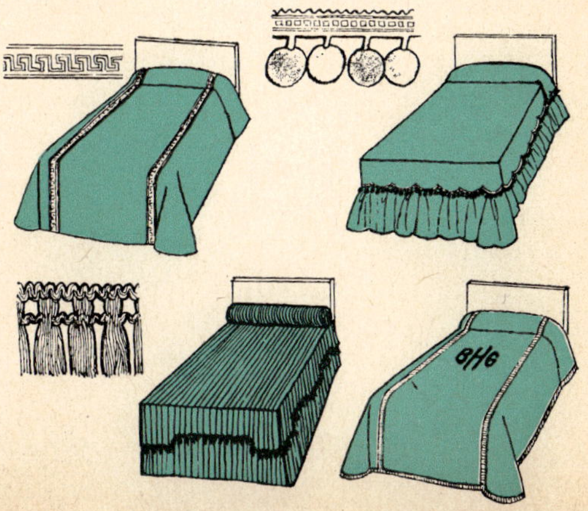

Bed canopies

Both the partial and the full canopy bed have become popular additions to the bedroom. They're easy to make and hang. Partial canopies are made like the drapery headings described in Chapter 17. Choose the heading you prefer and simply make it in the desired length. The partial canopy is usually hung from the ceiling to extend out

over part of the head of the bed. To hang it, attach a 1-inch wood strip to ceiling to form size of the canopy. Snap tape is applied to the sides of the wood strip while the other side of the snap tape is sewed to the top edge of the canopy.

The full canopy-top bed has a frame extending from the posters. The ruffled canopy can be made the same as the ruffles used for the dust ruffle. The snap tape is snapped to the sides of the canopy frame and can be sewed to the top edge of the ruffle. When the sides of the canopy are shaped, a pattern must be made so the sides will hang correctly. Use heavy paper and make a tracing of the top shape of the canopy side. Measure depth of sides and mark design on lower edge. Cut canopy from pattern. Line sides for greater body. Fringe or trimming can be sewed on lower edge. Sew snap tape along top and side canopy pieces.

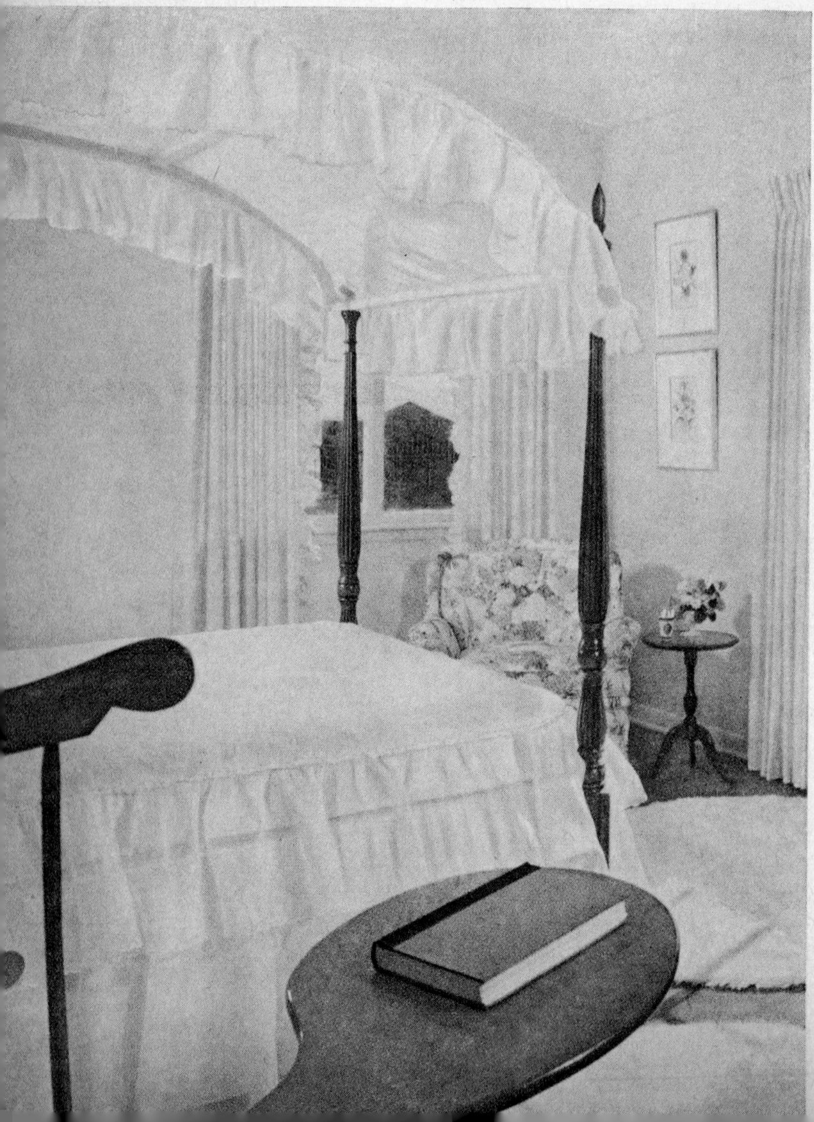

PARTIAL CANOPY

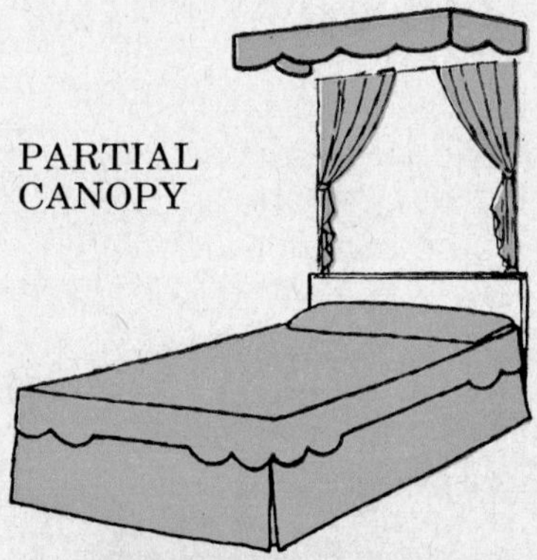

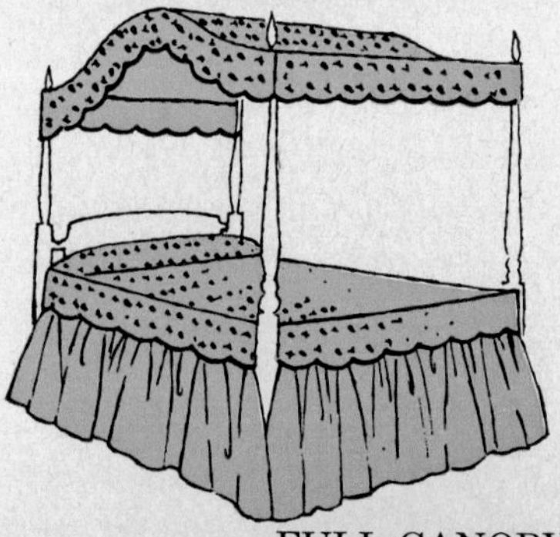

FULL CANOPY

Snowy organdy is used for this full canopy and ruffled spread—a good choice in feminine room.

Index

A

B

C

D

E

F

G-H

I-J-K

L-M-N-O

P-Q-R

S

T

U-V

W-X-Y-Z